The Port

The Port (present-day Hà Tiên), situated in the Mekong Delta and Gulf of Siam littoral, was founded and governed by the Chinese creole Mo clan during the eighteenth century and prospered as a free-trade emporium in maritime East Asia. Mo Jiu and his son Mo Tianci maintained an independent polity through ambiguous and simultaneous allegiances to the Cochinchinese regime of southern Vietnam, Cambodia, Siam, and the Dutch East India Company. A shared value system was forged among their multiethnic and multi-confessional residents via elite Chinese culture, facilitating closer business ties to Qing China. The story of this remarkable settlement sheds light on a transitional period in East Asian history, when the dominance of the Chinese state, merchants, and immigrants gave way to firmer state boundaries in mainland Southeast Asia and Western dominance on the seas.

Xing Hang is Associate Professor at the Department of Chinese History and Culture at the Hong Kong Polytechnic University.

The Port
Hà Tiên and the Mo Clan in Early Modern Asia

Xing Hang
Hong Kong Polytechnic University

Shaftesbury Road, Cambridge CB2 8EA, United Kingdom

One Liberty Plaza, 20th Floor, New York, NY 10006, USA

477 Williamstown Road, Port Melbourne, VIC 3207, Australia

314–321, 3rd Floor, Plot 3, Splendor Forum, Jasola District Centre, New Delhi – 110025, India

103 Penang Road, #05-06/07, Visioncrest Commercial, Singapore 238467

Cambridge University Press is part of Cambridge University Press & Assessment, a department of the University of Cambridge.

We share the University's mission to contribute to society through the pursuit of education, learning and research at the highest international levels of excellence.

www.cambridge.org
Information on this title: www.cambridge.org/9781009426985

DOI: 10.1017/9781009427005

© Xing Hang 2025

This publication is in copyright. Subject to statutory exception and to the provisions
of relevant collective licensing agreements, no reproduction of any part may take place without the written permission of Cambridge University Press & Assessment.

When citing this work, please include a reference to the DOI 10.1017/9781009427005

First published 2025

A catalogue record for this publication is available from the British Library.

Library of Congress Cataloging-in-Publication Data
Names: Hang, Xing, 1982- author.
Title: The Port : Hà Tiên and the Mo Clan in early modern Asia / Xing Hang, Hong Kong Polytechnic University.
Other titles: Hà Tiên and the Mo Clan in early modern Asia
Description: Cambridge, United Kingdom ; New York, NY : Cambridge University Press, 2025. | Includes bibliographical references and index.
Identifiers: LCCN 2024020577 | ISBN 9781009426985 (hardback) | ISBN 9781009426961 (paperback) | ISBN 9781009427005 (ebook)
Subjects: LCSH: Hà Tiên Port (Vietnam)–History–18th century. | Hà Tiên (Vietnam)–History–18th century. | Chinese–Vietnam–History–18th century. | Mạc, Thiên Tích, 1706-1780. | Mo family. | Southeast Asia–History–18th century. | Mạc, Thiên Tích, 1706-1780–Family. | Hà Tiên (Vietnam)–Biography.
Classification: LCC DS559.93.H385 2025 | DDC 959.79–dc23/eng/20240502

LC record available at https://lccn.loc.gov/2024020577

ISBN 978-1-009-42698-5 Hardback
ISBN 978-1-009-42696-1 Paperback

Cambridge University Press & Assessment has no responsibility for the persistence or accuracy of URLs for external or third-party internet websites referred to in this publication and does not guarantee that any content on such websites is, or will remain, accurate or appropriate.

Contents

List of Figures		*page* vi
List of Maps		viii
Acknowledgments		ix
	Introduction	1
1	The Port before "The Port"	26
2	Managing Hybridity	66
3	Situating Space through Verse	93
4	Ambiguous Associations	122
5	A Port with Many Faces	163
6	The Business of Business	204
7	Clash of the Titans	237
	Conclusion	276
Glossary		291
Bibliography		308
Index		329

Figures

1.1	The Mo clan shrine in Dongling Village, in present-day Leizhou, Guangdong	page 47
1.2	Statue of Mo Jiu, situated at the current Hà Tiên city limits	60
2.1	The spirit tablet of Mo Jiu's mother, housed at the Temple of Three Treasures	69
2.2	Inscription at the Temple of Three Treasures explaining Yellow Dragon's background and how he came to know Mo Jiu's mother	73
2.3	A bronze bell from the Temple of Three Treasures, now on the grounds of Thonburi Palace, Bangkok, and its inscription	74
2.4	The Chen clan shrine at Tiantou Village, Wuchuan County, Guangdong	76
2.5	A surviving section of Seashore Fortress on the grounds of the Temple of Three Treasures	81
3.1	Statue of the Jade Emperor and his attendants at the Daoist shrine that overlooks the site where Mo Tianci's literary society held its gatherings	98
3.2	The Stone Grotto, about three kilometers from the present Cambodian border	99
3.3	Fragments from "Idle Fishing at Sea Perch Creek" on a wall of the Mo clan shrine in Hà Tiên	101
3.4	The East Lake lagoon	106
3.5	The Big Golden Islet, once standing isolated in the middle of the Fortress River mouth, has now integrated with the mainland	107
4.1	Touk Meas Mountain, viewed from the center of Banteay Meas, around where Mo Tianci's forces successfully counterattacked and defeated Ang Mei Bhen's invasion in 1739	130
4.2	Mo Tianci's memorial to the Qianlong Emperor, c. 1770	157

4.3 A map of the maritime route from Guangdong to Siam, presented to the Qianlong Emperor by Mo Tianci, 1769	159
4.4 Tomb of Mo Jiu on Screen Mountain. The epitaph contains the *longfei* dating system	160
5.1 The epitaph on the tomb of Lady Nguyễn, Tianci's principal wife	172
5.2 Joint tomb of Mo Bang, who identified as a subject of the Qing, and his wife, a self-identified Viet	175
5.3 One of the two Lotus Pond reservoirs, built during the days of Mo Jiu	177
5.4 A statue of the Shakyamuni Buddha purchased by Mo Tianci from China in 1758	199
6.1 Portrait of Taksin and his spirit tablet	227
6.2 Mural of Chinese creoles dressed in Ming garb together with merchant-sojourners in Manchu outfits on the walls of Wat Buppharam in Trat	233
7.1 A roundabout in the Cambodian seaside city of White Horse, known in Khmer as Kep	249
7.2 The area around this creek in central Cần Thơ contained the citadel and garrison office of Mo Tianci, who relocated from The Port after 1771	262

Maps

1 Maritime East Asia　　　　　　　　　　　　*page* xv
2 Mainland Southeast Asia　　　　　　　　　　xvi
3 Water World　　　　　　　　　　　　　　　xvii
4 The Port's core area　　　　　　　　　　　　xviii

Acknowledgments

Similar to The Port, the creation of this volume would not have been possible without the support and encouragement of a large, transnational network of scholars, organizations, friends, and loved ones. First and foremost, I express my heartfelt gratitude to Choeurn Kim Heng, deputy director of the Office of Labor and Vocational Training at the Council of Ministers in Phnom Penh, and Pisut Phonglaohaphan, an independent researcher based in Bangkok. They possess vast knowledge of the histories of their respective countries, including an impressive command of primary texts written in older scripts and different grammatical formats. They have been able to pinpoint, describe, and interpret in English the relevant sections of the sources that relate to my project and provide translations of key passages where necessary. They have also proactively suggested leads to fresh sources and checked for the accuracy of the Khmer and Thai terms presented in this book.

The initiation of this project would not have been possible without the generous assistance of the ACLS Henry Luce Early Career Fellowship in China Studies and the Chiang Ching-kuo Foundation's Junior Scholar Grant. Their joint support allowed me to take a year's leave of absence from my regular pedagogical and administrative duties. I am also indebted to my former institution, Brandeis University, for extending this period by another half-year. As a result, I had the time and space to collect materials and embark on several extensive fieldwork trips to southern China and Southeast Asia.

Over the course of this project, I met, reconnected, and engaged with many interesting people who gave me ideas, insights, encouragement, assistance, and friendship. During my years at Brandeis, David Engerman, Greg Freeze, Paul Jankowski, Fangchao Ji ("JJ"), David Katz, Matt Linton, Joey Low, Hannah Muller, Steven Pieragastini, Amy Singer, Naghmeh Sohrabi, Govind Sreenivasan, Pu Wang, Michael Willrich, and Aida Wong provided advice and support. History 185a, a seminar that I devised, treats the histories of Hong Kong, Taiwan, and the overseas Chinese as an integrated unit. I taught it for the first time in the fall of 2012, when I was about to embark on my project. I acquired so much inspiration from the discussions and written contributions of the undergraduates enrolled in the course that I promised I would mention each and every one of them by name in this book. So here goes: Ava Blustein, Suwei Chi, Douglas Chin, Katlin Freschi, Wei Zhong Goh, Rachel Harrison, Bella Hu, Justin Kim, Hanjun Li, Dexter Lin, Félix Liu Ku, Johnny Loughrin, Katherine Lu, Zhuoxin Miao, Wendy Moy, Kyungwon Park, Tyler Roberts, Kenshiro Wakabayashi, and Xiaoyu Xia. They have, of course, graduated and moved on with their lives, and I hope they are doing well.

Outside of the classroom setting, Max Iascone and Michael Rock helped devise preliminary ideas for my project by obtaining materials from the Brandeis Library and through periodic discussions. Esther Cho exposed me for the first time to Vietnamese-language journal articles about the Mo clan that she had collected during her study abroad in Vietnam. Yulanda Huang took time out of her summer holiday to transcribe handwritten documents from the Qing archives into a digital format on a word processor. It was a hugely difficult undertaking, since much of the original consists of grassy script that is often illegible to an untrained eye. She did a superb job in deciphering most of the handwriting, greatly helping me understand the content of the documents.

Elsewhere Stateside, I am indebted to Hue Tam Ho Tai and Min-ho Kim for introducing me to the small but vibrant community of specialists in Vietnam studies. The Harvard-Yenching Institute provided generous support for conferences and workshops, both in Cambridge and Vietnam. In addition, I appreciate the assistance, advice, collaborations, and company of Tonio Andrade, Kate Baldanza, Adam Clulow, Arunabh Ghosh, Valerie Hansen, Kwangmin Kim, Miriam Kingsberg, Ari Levine, Eugenio Menegon, Grant Rhode, Michael Szonyi, Eric Tagliacozzo, Philip Thai, Robert Weller, Kären Wigen, Shao-yun Yang, and Guolin Yi. I remain perpetually indebted to my graduate advisers, Wen-hsin Yeh and Kenneth Pomeranz, for training me in the tools, methods, and ways of thinking in tackling historical questions and challenging me to constantly sharpen my analysis and broaden my horizons.

In Hanoi, I am incredibly grateful to Wei Hongping ("Daisy") and Nguyễn Tô Lan, who went out of their way to assist me, especially in the early stages of my project. They served as the foundation and well-spring for nearly all of my subsequent contacts and leads to repositories and sources in Vietnam. Nguyễn Tuấn Cường connected me to the library and resources of the Institute of Hán-Nôm Studies. His student, Trương Văn Thương, assisted with locating specific titles in the institute's collections and securing permissions from the leadership for photocopying. Jacky Son welcomed me in friendship and helped me blend into the daily lives of commoners in Hanoi. I fondly recall the evenings when we and several other friends would sit on plastic stools and enjoy the cool breeze in the narrow alleyways of the old quarter or next to the shores of West Lake and Red River alongside thousands of other residents. We would engage in idle chatter while chewing sunflower seeds or eating coconut ice cream. One early morning, we even witnessed a bust-up of street vendors by the Public Security Bureau!

In Biên Hòa, I am grateful to Lâm Văn Lang, head of the Tân Lân shrine dedicated to Chen Shangchuan, and his friend, Phan Quang Sơn, and Mr. Sơn's daughter, Văn Hạnh, for their generosity and hospitality. In Ho Chi Minh City, Pascal Bourdeaux introduced me to the European scholarly sources and specialists related to my topic. Trần Hồng Liên pointed me to epigraphic evidence at shrines and temples and important contacts across the water world. Võ Văn Sen, Lê Thị Ngọc Diệp, and other faculty at the University of Social Sciences and Humanities-Ho Chi Minh City, kindly invited me to campus, where I had a chance to share my ideas with its vibrant community. Nguyễn Ngọc Thơ answered many of my questions and helped with requests, especially during the pandemic, when it was impossible to travel to Vietnam. His students, Nguyễn Tuấn Nghĩa and Huỳnh Hoàng Ba, provided me access to repositories and helped obtain important scholarship on the local history of the water world.

This project has also allowed me to reconnect with Diệu Quang Tánh, my dear friend from undergraduate years and a Saigon native whom I met again for the first time since graduation. Despite his busy schedule, he went out of his way to share with me his local knowledge, bringing me to shrines and temples and other fieldwork sites and introducing me to private libraries and collections. He also took me deep into the world of the ethnic Chinese in Districts 5, 11, and 12. I especially enjoyed the wild motorcycle rides through the city, being constantly harassed by petty vendors selling lottery tickets, and our stimulating intellectual conversations at coffee shops and over street food.

In Hà Tiên, Thích Vân Phong, head abbot of Hibiscus Temple, enthusiastically gave me a tour of the grounds and the nearby Daoist shrine to the Jade Emperor and showed me their relics. During my stay in town, he invited me over to his temple to drink tea with him every day. I donated money to fund the complex's renovation and was given the honor of signing my name on one of the new tiles that would be placed on the roof! During a daylong boat excursion to the Pirate Islands (Đảo Hải Tặc), lying about twenty-eight kilometers southwest of Hà Tiên,

I had the fortune of meeting Huỳnh Lập and his future spouse, Trần Tư Bé, who were, at the time, students at An Giang University. I thank them for their wonderful company and conversations. My appreciation also goes out to Andy, the English owner of the Oasis Bar in Hà Tiên, who offered a wealth of local knowledge and travel tips, along with decent food. I must also acknowledge his motorcycle driver, Mr. Tay, who transported me to Stone Grotto and the Cambodian border.

Tam Sokrey, deputy chief of the Office of the Ministry of Rural Development, and his friend, Kim You (Li Jinyu), a sales manager, welcomed me to Cambodia and took care of me during the times when I stayed in Phnom Penh. Ret Saron, an award-winning local writer and expert in the Khmer language, voluntarily helped to translate key passages from a hugely difficult palm-leaf manuscript version of the Cambodian Royal Chronicles. What is more, he wanted no reward for his efforts. I remain deeply moved by his public spirit and passion for sharing the history and culture of his country with me.

I am further indebted to Dr. Loh Kai Kwong of Kuala Lumpur, cofounder of the World Association of Luo Clans. He kindly invited me to a conference organized by his clan association in Bangkok, where I had the fortune of meeting Buncha Rattanasrisomboon (Luo Qian), who is passionate about Chinese culture in Thailand. He took me on a tour of Chinese temples and shrines, Thai wats, and other historical sites in Bangkok related to King Taksin. Most memorably, we visited the ruler's Thonburi palace, which is on the site of a naval base and only open to the public on the occasion of his birthday from mid- to late December. In Singapore, I thank Claudine Ang, Bruce Lockhart, Yang Bin, and Seng Guo Quan for the meaningful conversations and conference collaborations both in the city and abroad.

I am grateful to Robert Antony and Chang Lanshin for their kindness and care. During our friendship of almost two decades, we shared wonderful moments together in Hong Kong, Macao, Shanghai, and the Boston area. Leonard Blussé has been a long-term mentor, advocate, and critic. I have benefited from his vast knowledge and insights both remotely and when our paths crossed in Asia and North America. It was likewise a pleasure to meet and catch up with Ronald Po in Hong Kong, Denver, and Shanghai. I want to thank the staff of the China Maritime Museum in Shanghai, in particular Shan Li and Zhao Li. My appreciation goes to Chen Kuo-tung, Lee Chi-lin, Lin Man-houng, Liu Shiuh-feng, and Li Yu-chung in Taipei and Cheung Wing Sheung and Lee Kuei-min in Tainan. In Guangzhou, I thank Li Qingxin, Zhou Xin, and the staff of the Guangdong Academy of Social Sciences. Liu Wennan, Wang Yi, and the Institute of Modern History at the Chinese

Academy of Social Sciences in Beijing have been incredibly helpful and supportive. Collectively, these wonderful people pointed me to archival sources and contacts, especially in China, offered their critiques and insights in conferences, talks, and workshops, and helped publish some of my work-in-progress.

At Nanning, I am deeply indebted to the late Professor Fan Honggui of the Guangxi University for Nationalities and his colleague Professor Wang Bozhong for organizing a fieldtrip with me to the Guangxi coastline. One highlight of the tour was the Dragon Gate Garrison and its relics related to Yang Yandi. I want to thank Gao Shan and the crew of Fangchenggang Television for interviewing me about the site despite the little knowledge I had at the time. Wu Xiaoling and He Liangjun of Qinzhou College (now Beibu Gulf University) accompanied us and offered their insights and expertise. I also want to express my appreciation to Professor Fan's wife, Liang Cimei, and his students Huang Ying and Chen Qiang for arranging the logistics, lodging, and entertainment associated with the visit. I can never forget that one midnight in Qinzhou when Chen Qiang literally broke into my hotel room, yanked me out of bed, and took me to sample the famous local night snack, known as "sour stuff" (*suan ye*): tropical fruits dipped into vinegar, chili, and other spices!

Chen Zhijian, the retired head of the Zhanjiang City Museum, and Ding Riping, director of the Leizhou Museum, provided invaluable guidance and expertise during my fieldwork journey to western Guangdong. Accompanied by them, I was able to visit the native places of Mo Jiu and Chen Shangchuan and enter their clan shrines. I am deeply indebted to the Village Committee of Dongling, Leizhou, for generously sharing with me the Mo clan genealogy. The same for the Village Committee of Tiantou, Zhanjiang, for making available the genealogies and other materials about the Chen that are incredibly difficult to locate elsewhere.

The onset of the pandemic severely affected my plans for onward travel to Europe. Fortunately, many repositories have already digitized large parts of their collection beforehand or during the pandemic, when their physical premises were closed. In addition to being grateful to these institutions for making their holdings public, I must specially thank the helpful staff of the France-Asia Research Institute (IRFA) in Paris. The director, Marie-Alpais Dumoulin, and Brigitte Appavou arranged for the scanning of documents for me on demand. They contain missionary letters and journals that formed a crucial part of my research.

At the height of the pandemic, from 2020 to 2022, I found myself stuck in Hong Kong, unable to return from my sabbatical. And as fate would have it, it has become my new permanent home. Throughout this difficult phase, I received much-needed local support for my research and writing. John Wong sponsored my access to the Hong Kong University Library, Ghassan Moazzin invited me physically to the Hong Kong University campus to present my work, and Gary Luk met me in-person to share ideas. I kept in touch remotely with Zhang Zhaoyang and Wang Yuanfei, who helped me uncover the meaning and historical allusions in poems related to The Port and decode some of the grassiest Chinese scripts from the archival documents that I had collected. Han Xiaorong, a friend and mentor for over a decade, gave me a new academic home, and I am thrilled to be his colleague.

I am grateful to the team at Cambridge University Press for bringing this project to fruition. Lucy Rhymer provided support and encouragement for my project ever since its inception and maintained her optimism and belief in its value throughout the process. The two anonymous reviewers offered thoughtful and constructive critiques that helped me highlight the relevance and significance of my work. Rosa Martin, Natasha Whelan, Jasintha Srinivasan, and Dhanujha Harikrishna saw the book through the production and marketing stages. Cheryl Hutty meticulously scrutinized and double-checked every page and every line during copy-editing. In addition, I thank Cynthia Col for her work on the indexing and for spending extra time to highlight remaining typos and other stylistic issues. Pei Qing, my esteemed colleague at the Hong Kong Polytechnic University, and his student, Lai Zhongyu, helped with the design and labeling of the maps. The Department of Chinese History and Culture at PolyU funded the costs related to production.

The pandemic made me realize the fragility of life and taught me to treasure all relationships, especially with family. I am grateful that my parents, Henry and Nancy Hang, and my in-laws, Nelson and Scarlette Miu, live in Asia, close enough for us to enjoy many moments of bonding. Finally, my wife, Kwun Suen, and my two children, Sheng and Qing, kept me sane and actively grounded in the human world throughout my research and writing. Their presence enriches my life and makes it meaningful and gives me the motivation to press on even during the most difficult times.

Map 1 Maritime East Asia.
Special thanks to Pei Qing and Lai Zhongyu

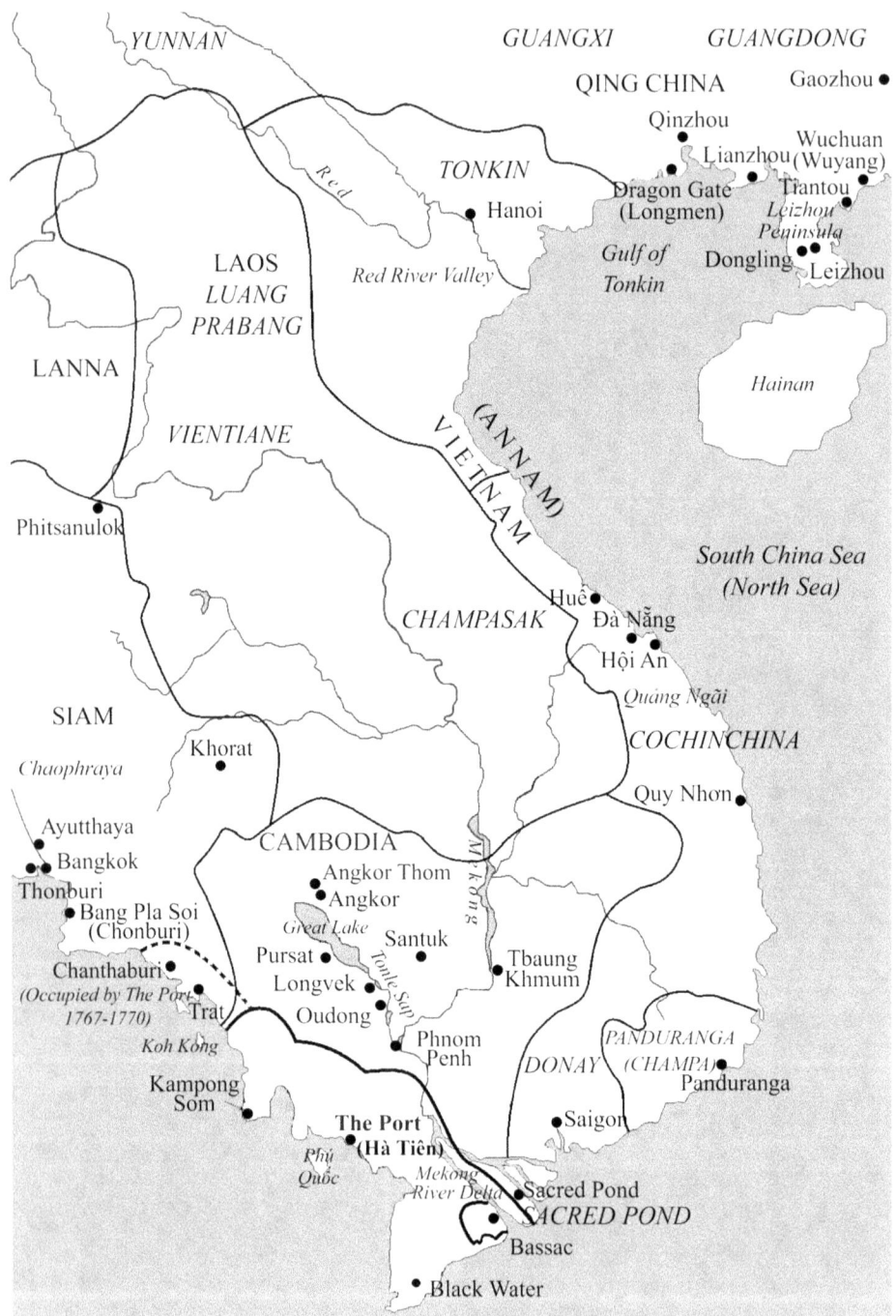

Map 2 Mainland Southeast Asia.
Special thanks to Pei Qing and Lai Zhongyu

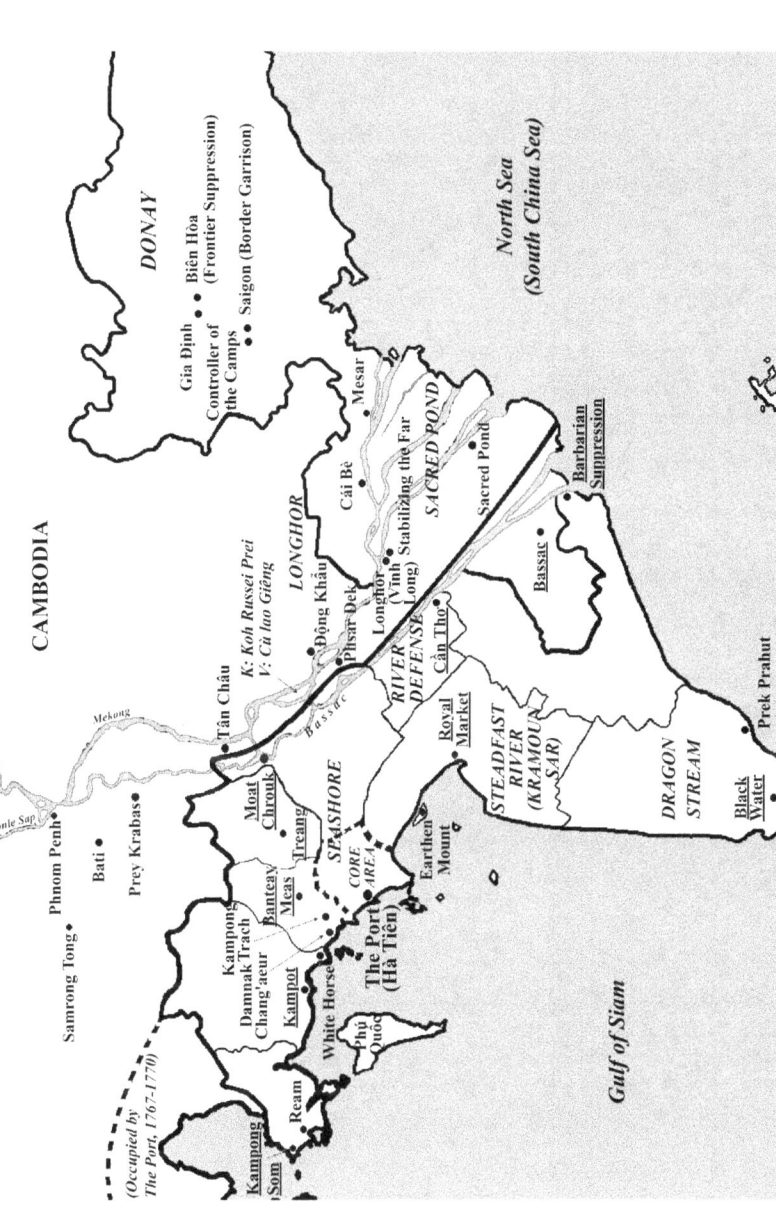

Map 3 Water World. Administrative seats of circuits and provinces under The Port's direct control or influence are underlined. If an administrative seat shares the same name as the province or circuit, then only the administrative seat is provided.

Special thanks to Pei Qing and Lai Zhongyu

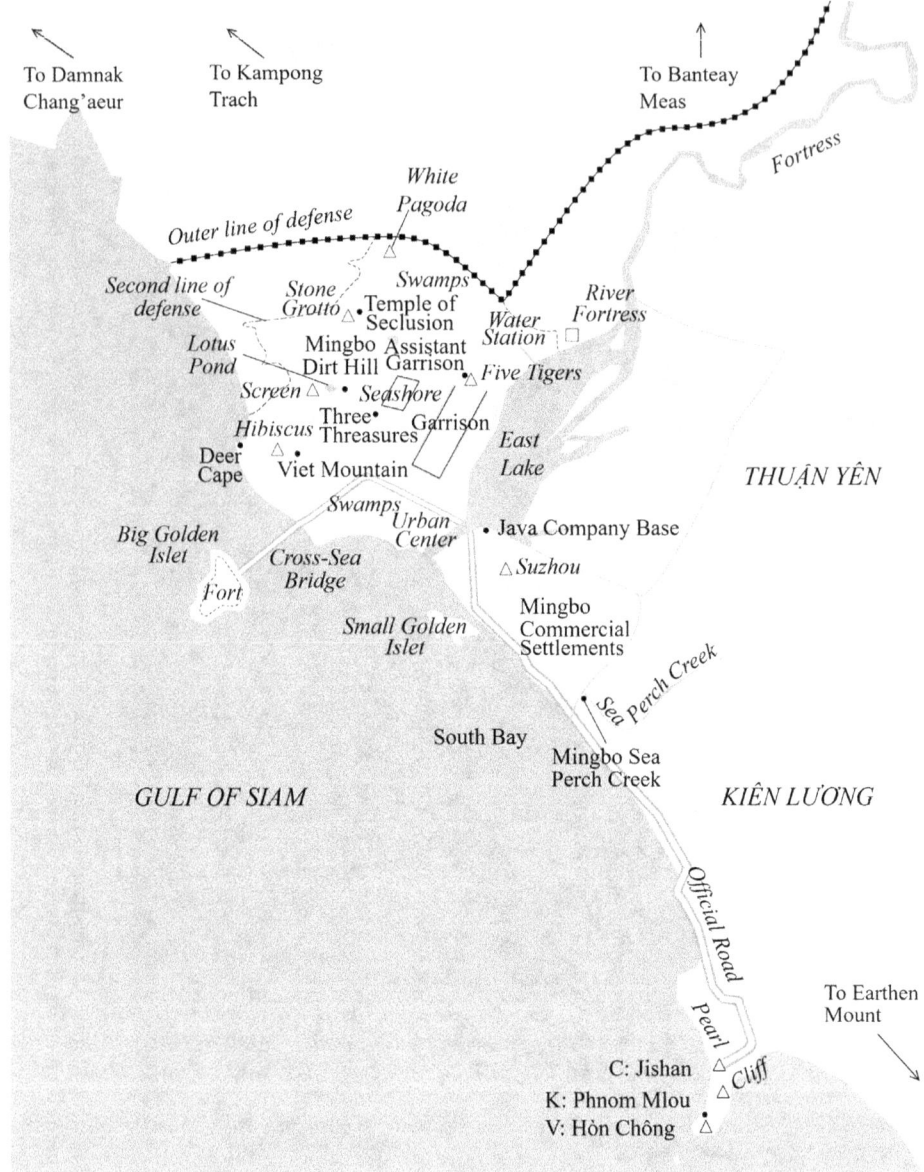

Map 4 The Port's core area.
Special thanks to Pei Qing and Lai Zhongyu

Introduction

The notion of free trade is commonly associated with European, particularly British, overseas expansion during the nineteenth century. Scholars consider the establishment of Singapore and Hong Kong as free ports to have facilitated the penetration of Western capital and Indian opium into the markets of East Asia. The vast quantities of coins, bullion, and drugs that flowed through these nodes contributed to the triumph of a global economic system centered upon an industrialized core in Western Europe and, later, North America.[1] What is less known is that just a century earlier, a port operating along similar principles already flourished in maritime East Asia, that vast region encompassing the East and South China Seas and extending southward to the Strait of Melaka. This port, situated on the Gulf of Siam coast, along the present-day boundary of Vietnam and Cambodia, benefited from its location at the intersection of the sea-lanes between China, Japan, and Southeast Asia, and mainland and island Southeast Asia. It was an ideal transshipment point for vessels from all these places and an exporter of natural resources from its own hinterlands. It also became a thriving financial center, minting coinage and concentrating capital in the form of bullion.

True to its position as a cosmopolitan maritime crossroads, the settlement went by a dizzying variety of names and orthographic variations. It originally belonged to Cambodia, which called it Peam, or "seashore." At times, it constituted its own province (*khaet*), or belonged to another province: Banteay Meas, the "golden citadel." Accordingly, the settlement also came to be known as Ponteamas or Ponthiamas to the Europeans; Phutthaimat to the Siamese; and Yindaima, Jundaima, or Bendi to the Chinese. The Austronesians, including Malay and Cham, would refer to it as Pantai Emas. Although a transcription of Banteay Meas, the term has its unique meaning of "golden seashore," a more

---

[1] Trocki, *Opium*, pp. 50–63, 220–221.

accurate geographic description of the place.² Alternatively, the Austronesians might refer to it as Kuala, or "river mouth." The Portuguese picked up on this term and spelled it Coal or Coalha. They also gave it their own name of Palmeiro or Palmerinha, perhaps a reference to a distinct variety of palm trees concentrated in the area whose fruit formed an essential ingredient in locally made cakes and sweetmeats.³ The Lao viewed the place as their "city of gold," or Muang Kham. It could also be Muang Kram, a hybrid Tai-Lao and Cham term meaning either "city of bamboo" or "city in a place submerged by water or next to the sea."⁴

The settlement's heyday occurred from the late seventeenth to the eighteenth centuries, when it came under the control of the **C: Mo** V: Mạc, a Chinese creole clan. The leaders probably borrowed from European – most likely Portuguese – corruptions of Peam, including Atiam or Athien, in giving it the Sinicized name of Hexian, or "fairy river." After **C: Mo Jiu** V: Mạc Cửu (1655–1735), the clan patriarch, submitted as a vassal to the south-central Vietnamese regime of Cochinchina in the early eighteenth century, its Nguyễn rulers accorded the settlement, transcribed in Vietnamese as Hà Tiên, the status of a frontier garrison (*trấn*). Chinese sojourners and merchants, whose ships frequently paid call at its shores, simply gave it the name of Gangkou. Rendered in various European sources as Cancao, Kankao, or Kangkhauw, it literally means "The Port."⁵ It is descriptive as it is succinct, so I will mainly use this term to describe the place.

Mo Jiu, the entrepreneurial genius behind The Port's rise and emergence as a prominent trading hub in maritime East Asia, was an immigrant from the Leizhou Peninsula in southern China's Guangdong Province. During the late seventeenth century, amid the collapse of the ethnically Han Ming dynasty (1368–1644) and its replacement by the Manchu Qing (1644–1912), he left his native place to seek his fortunes abroad. He ended

---

² Sellers, *Princes of Hà-Tiên*, p. 9; Ibn Ahmad, *Precious Gift*, p. 126; Li Qingxin, 'Mao shi,' pp. 121–130. In using the term "Austronesian," I refer more precisely to speakers of Austronesian languages residing on the present-day Malay Peninsula and in Indonesia, The Philippines, Cambodia, and Vietnam. I do not mean to imply that all of these people belong to the same ethnic group. In fact, speakers of Austronesian languages are often characterized by striking differences in culture and lifestyles, ranging from forest-dwellers to sea nomads to urban-based merchants. Nonetheless, there is linguistic, archaeological, and biological evidence of some level of shared ancestry in prehistoric times. See Bellwood, Fox, and Tryon, "Austronesians in History, " pp. 1–6. Moreover, as Bruckmayr, *Cambodia's Muslims*, pp. 10–13 argues, a great degree of mobility and fluidity of identities characterize certain Austronesian-speaking groups, such as Malay, Minangkabau, and Cham. Therefore, the use of the term "Austronesian" also aims at avoiding confusion. I adopt more specific ethnic labels, such as Malay and Cham, in accordance with their mention in primary sources and scholarly studies in particular contexts.
³ Malleret, *Delta du Mékong*, vol. 1, p. 14.
⁴ Trương, *Nghiên cứu*, vol. 2, pp. 14–15; Thurgood, *Ancient Cham*, pp. 339, 358.
⁵ Malleret, *Delta du Mékong*, vol. 1, p. 14; Mak, *Histoire du Cambodge*, pp. 365–366.

up in Cambodia, where he gained the trust of the king, and became head of the country's foreign mercantile community. He acquired from the ruler the territory of The Port as his personal fiefdom. Although he never formally renounced his ties to Cambodia, he simultaneously rendered tribute to Cochinchina in the early eighteenth century. This double allegiance guaranteed his autonomous power over The Port, which he proclaimed to be open and welcome to merchants from all lands.

C: **Mo Tianci** V: Mạc Thiên Tứ (d. 1780), Jiu's eldest son with a daughter of Viet pioneers, succeeded him after his death in 1735. Under Tianci, The Port's fortunes reached their height. He stood at the apex of a personal and militarized chain of command that oversaw tens of thousands of troops and hundreds of warships. At the same time, he embraced Chinese elite culture by promoting Confucian values and education and sponsoring literary exchanges with Qing and Viet literati, conducted both remotely by long-distance junks and in-person as his guests of honor. He also espoused a policy of tolerance, welcoming everyone to settle in his realm regardless of ethnicity or religious belief. Chinese, Viet, Khmer, Austronesians, and Europeans could reside and move about freely. Buddhist temples and monks received his support and patronage. Christian missionaries could establish parishes openly amid ongoing restrictions and persecution across most of East Asia. Not far away from their grand church in the center of town stood a mosque.

Tianci took advantage of the fierce geopolitical conflict between Siam and Cochinchina for influence over Cambodia to dominate the Cambodian throne in 1757. He moved up the Cambodian hierarchy until he became viceroy (*oupareach*), ranked third after the main ruler. He expanded The Port's territory to comprise the entire western Mekong Delta and Cambodian coastline, stretching from the South China Sea to the border with Siam. In subsequent years, he set out to exercise similar influence in Siam and Cochinchina after invasions, rebellions, and disorder plagued both kingdoms.

Although they were fully capable of doing so, the Mo avoided transforming The Port into a fully fledged state like its neighbors in mainland Southeast Asia. Instead, they exercised a deliberate ambiguity in representing their status to the outside world, while utilizing political and military resources in the service of economic expansion and profits. Apparently, their true aim was to establish an integrated civic space across East Asia where goods, people, ideas, and information could freely circulate. In this manner, the Mo could, like the head of a modern multinational company, better control and manipulate governments and the flow of money and resources.

The Port's period of prosperity overlapped with what scholars such as Carl Trocki and Leonard Blussé have termed a "Chinese century." The period witnessed a remarkable expansion of junk trade between China and Southeast Asia, driven by China's demand for Southeast Asian tropical products and the need for outlets for its products and labor. Qing merchants and sojourners forged an informal empire through the construction of durable networks that connected different ports across the China seas. They also opened new land in the sparsely populated Southeast Asian interior.[6]

Much of the scholarship has treated the explosion of Chinese commercial activity as somehow independent of the Chinese state, which exhibited indifference, at best, and often outright hostility toward this development. Yet, the rejuvenation of Chinese naval power in maritime East Asia, first achieved under the quasi-governmental Zheng organization based in Taiwan during the 1660s and later inherited by the Qing, also played a significant role. In fact, the innovative revisionist studies of Zhao Gang, Zheng Yangwen, and Ronald Po reveal that the Qing court recognized the value of overseas commerce and actively encouraged and protected the maritime activities of its subjects.[7] The Qing further reformed the China-centered tributary system of its Ming predecessor and adapted it better to the realities of trade and the presence of Europeans in the region.[8] The informal and indirect cooperation between state and merchant successfully marginalized the Dutch East India Company (VOC) and other European trading monopolies and colonial powers. As a result, Blussé shows, they were relegated to a few outposts and could only operate on limited routes.[9]

The Mo capitalized upon this larger economic and geopolitical climate to transform The Port into a center for Chinese junk shipping and capital. They became the biggest beneficiaries and intermediaries for the offshoring of the Chinese economy to Southeast Asia. Mo Tianci, in particular, also came to view the Qing as a protector of last resort. When the Myanmar invasion of Siam and the tragic death of the Siamese king in the 1760s threatened to upset the balance of power in mainland Southeast Asia, Tianci frequently exchanged envoys with the Qing court and Guangdong officials. He provided them with the latest news and intelligence regarding The Port's neighbors. He further attempted to enlist the Qing's assistance in backing his candidate for the vacant throne of Siam. Although the contingency for an alliance existed, given the Qing's own border conflict with Myanmar, it ultimately failed to materialize.

Tianci's disastrous unilateral invasion of Siam in the late 1760s led to a severe reversal of his fortunes. The campaign brought him into direct conflict with merchants and settlers from Chaozhou, in eastern

---

[6] Blussé, 'Chinese Century'; Trocki, 'Chinese Pioneering.'
[7] Zheng Yangwen, *China on the Sea*, pp. 321–326; Zhao Gang, *Qing Opening*, pp. 41–56; Po, *Blue Frontier*, pp. 143–180.
[8] Chia, 'Lifanyuan,' pp. 158–168. [9] Blussé, 'Chinese Century,' pp. 113, 121.

Guangdong. These newcomers spoke a different dialect from Tianci's compatriots from Leizhou and neighboring Hainan Island and were much less acclimated to the cosmopolitan local culture. They came in large numbers to the eastern Siamese frontier and soon infiltrated into the territory of The Port. With their support, Taksin (1734–1782, r. 1767–1782), a half-Chaozhou Siamese nobleman, successfully expelled Tianci and proclaimed himself king of Siam. In 1771, Taksin invaded and briefly occupied The Port before returning it to Tianci as part of a deal with Cochinchina to become the joint overlords of Cambodia. As a result, Tianci lost his dominant influence over the Cambodian court.

Six years later, Tianci's home territory was again conquered, this time permanently, by the Tây Sơn rebels and their Cambodian allies, fighting against the Nguyễn rulers of Cochinchina. In an ironic twist of fate, he sought asylum in Siam and placed himself at the mercy of his former rival, King Taksin, now a common enemy of the rebels. Tianci and his exiled followers were given a plot of land on the northeastern bank of the Chaophraya River in the heart of modern Bangkok. They made a tremendous yet overlooked contribution to the development of the city. But soon, Taksin suspected Tianci of plotting to seize the throne. He ordered the massacre of Tianci's family members and exiled the rest of his retinue across Siam. Witnessing with despair the bloodbath around him, Mo Tianci committed suicide. Two years later, Taksin received his own comeuppance when native Siamese nobles toppled him and put him to death.

The tragic demise of both men resulted from, and contributed to, the formation of consolidated states in mainland Southeast Asia. It also coincided with the decline of the Qing and the penetration of European maritime power into the South China Sea. As a result, overseas Chinese gradually became coopted into the service of European economic expansion and imperialism. The Port lost influence as a commercial hub until it became the sleepy, backwater Vietnamese border town of Hà Tiên. At the most basic level, this study provides a comprehensive narrative of The Port, from the rise and fall of the Mo clan and the vast scale of its trade and cultural exchanges to the everyday lives of the multiethnic and multi-confessional men and women residing in its territory.

Escaping the Relentless Southern Advance

Mainstream studies of The Port still rely heavily or exclusively upon a corpus of Vietnamese primary records. Although detailed and informative, these sources, including geographic gazetteers and travelogues, a genealogical biography of the clan, and official histories, mostly date from the nineteenth century. By then, Hà Tiên had become, at least partially, integrated into a unified Vietnam under the Nguyễn dynasty

(1801–1945). As Brian Zottoli points out, nearly all of the documents underwent editing by official hands, subjecting them to censorship and reinterpretation of historical events for the glorification of the ruling dynasty and Confucian ideological correctness.[10]

The publication and mass distribution of these and other classical texts during the late nineteenth century and beyond have resulted in further rounds of standardization. Large-scale translations were undertaken of the original Classical Chinese and demotic *nôm* scripts into Romanized Vietnamese (*Quốc ngữ*), making them widely available and accessible to the public. These efforts both reflected and stimulated the emergence of modern Vietnamese nationalism.[11] However, since multiple versions of the original texts exist that differ slightly to substantially in content from one another, publications often privilege one particular manuscript at the expense of omitting important content found in the others.[12] In addition, many printed works only provide the Romanized translation without the Classical Chinese text base, making it difficult to check for accuracy and meanings lost in the conversion.

Because these highly edited, published primary sources provide the most convenient narrative of The Port, later studies tend to position the polity and the Mo clan mainly within the Vietnamese historical experience. They focus on the Mo's contribution to the shaping of the country's present-day boundaries. This scholarship is strongly influenced by the narrative of the Southern Advance (*Nam tiến*), which sees the current Vietnamese state as the product of a centuries-long expansion of its territory and majority Viet ethnic group from the Red River valley around Hanoi to the south. A conscious vision of state-sponsored migration in this direction had taken shape as early as the eighteenth century. However, under the influence of early twentieth-century nationalism, the Southern Advance came to be redefined as the main driver of Vietnamese historical development. It was presented as a continuous process in which the Viet protagonists, under the sponsorship of successive dynasties from antiquity to the nineteenth century, expanded all the way down to the Mekong Delta and Gulf of Siam littoral. In the process, they overpowered, displaced, or assimilated the Cham of the south-central coast and the Khmer of the Mekong Delta and Gulf of Siam littoral.[13]

---

[10] Zottoli, 'Reconceptualizing Southern Vietnamese History,' pp. 16, 290.
[11] For more on the connections and contradictions between mass publication, the use of Romanized script, translation, and the emergence of modern Vietnamese nationalism, see Pelley, *Postcolonial Vietnam*, pp. 125–131.
[12] See Zottoli, 'Reconceptualizing Southern Vietnamese History,' pp. 33–51, for an analysis of how multiple versions of the same primary source differed in their contents.
[13] Ang, 'Regionalism,' pp. 3–7.

The terminus of this migration was a vast, fertile floodplain that mostly lies below sea level. It forms the core of what the Vietnamese call their "Southern Area" (*Nam Bộ*). Since it once belonged to Cambodia, the Khmer know it as Kampuchea Krom (Lower Cambodia), in contrast to the country proper, which was situated on a higher floodplain. Scholars have followed the key geographic feature of the Mekong Delta and Gulf of Siam littoral in labeling the area the water world or water frontier.[14]

During the Cold War, historians in the southern Vietnamese regime celebrated the Southern Advance as a historical inevitability.[15] In contrast to the Cham and Khmer, who appeared mostly as passive subjects, scholarly attitudes toward Chinese creoles such as the Mo proved more ambivalent. Nguyễn Nhã, for instance, welcomes them as important players in their own right. For him, The Port marked the terminus of the Southern Advance, and the Mo were transitional figures whose submission to Cochinchina set the stage for the territory's eventual absorption into the Vietnamese nation. Sơn Nam, on the other hand, credits the Viet migrants as the first ones to open new land in and around The Port and therefore the primary agents of the Southern Advance. The Mo simply established the infrastructure for their continued settlement and expansion.[16]

Until the 1970s, the communist north avoided mention of the Southern Advance, whose celebration of the majority Viet and territorial expansion contradicted official efforts to forge an identity that could encapsulate all the ethnic groups living within the boundaries of Vietnam. At the same time, it went against the state-sanctioned narrative of victimization and resistance of the masses against oppression from domestic elites and foreign invaders and colonizers.[17] The northern historian Phan Huy Lê attempts to forge a more ethnically inclusive narrative about The Port. Phan Huy Lê claims that as soon as Mo Jiu paid tribute to Cochinchina, he had voluntarily "become a naturalized Vietnamese citizen" (*nhập quốc tịch Việt Nam*). He and his son were, from then on, "Vietnamese of Chinese descent" (*người Việt gốc Hoa*).[18] Phan Huy Lê thus celebrated cultural diversity and the agency of non-Viet actors but subsumed them within Vietnam's overall history and identity.

After the country's unification in 1975, followed by the onset of liberal economic reforms in 1986, the Marxist narrative of the north gradually merged with the ethnocentric discourse of the south. Scholarly works of this period follow the framework of the Southern Advance but make

---

[14] Sakurai, 'Chinese Pioneers,' pp. 36–39; P. Taylor, *Khmer Lands*, p. 7.
[15] Ang, 'Regionalism,' pp. 11–13.
[16] Ang, 'Regionalism,' pp. 14–15; P. Taylor, *Khmer Lands*, pp. 20–22.
[17] Pelley, *Postcolonial Vietnam*, pp. 69–112.   [18] Phan, 'Đánh giá,' p. 42.

significant modifications to it. They describe the process of Viet expansion into the water frontier as natural and primarily peaceful. The land was empty, except for some sparse Khmer settlements. These scholars cite international law in asserting that Cambodia lacked the capacity, institutions, and population to exercise sovereignty. The Cochinchinese state, on the other hand, possessed the political, military, and legal mechanisms to fill the vacuum, allowing Viet and Khmer, together with later Chinese arrivals, to jointly open new land. The Southern Advance thus became a multiethnic project. Through cultural exchange and borrowing, a fraternal bond formed between the three groups. With the Viet leading the way as the elder brother, they would integrate the frontier and themselves into a unified Vietnam. Within this context, the Mo served as agents of the Nguyễn rulers in overseeing and sustaining migration to The Port and its surroundings, where Vietnamese expansion reached its natural limits.[19]

Strangely enough, this portrayal of the Mo fits well into the prevalent historiography of Cambodia, which embraced an anti-Vietnamese stance. This perspective took shape in the early 1970s amid the emergence of a Khmer-based nationalism cultivated by Lon Nol (1913–1985) and his Khmer Rouge successors. It takes pride in the ancient civilization of Angkor, which flourished from the ninth to fourteenth centuries. Although Angkor, at its height, enjoyed a sphere of influence over most of mainland Southeast Asia, historians took special interest in what was viewed as the lost Cambodian territory of Kampuchea Krom. There was simultaneously an attitude of hostility toward the ethnic Chinese and, especially, Vietnamese minorities in the country. This ethnocentrism was bolstered by a narrative of victimization of the Khmer in the face of relentless expansion from Vietnam, which flooded the water world with settlers and resorted to various stratagems and tricks to take away their land.[20] Despite the bitter moral castigation, the Cambodian historiography ironically validates the Southern Advance hypothesis. The Mo, perhaps on account of their Chinese background, receive little mention other than being portrayed as collaborators and facilitators of the Vietnamese land grab.[21]

---

[19] P. Taylor, *Khmer Lands*, p. 21; *Vùng đất Nam Bộ*: Nguyễn, vol. 4, pp. 166–174; *Vùng đất Nam Bộ*: Vũ, vol. 8, pp. 29–58; Đỗ Quỳnh Nga, *Tây Nam Bộ*, pp. 19–29, 324–338; Trần, *Nam Bộ*, pp. 8, 45–46, 79–154.

[20] Edwards, *Cambodge*, pp. 21–22, 250–253; P. Taylor, *Khmer Lands*, pp. 21–22.

[21] Some examples include Nuon, *Damnaer chhpaohtow tisakheanglich*, pp. 13–19; So, *Bravottesastr preah reachea nachakr Kampouchea*, pp. 27–28, 49, 90–91; Tea, *Rueng reav nei tukdei Kampouchea kraom*, pp. 58–59, 156–157.

Scholars based in the West have questioned the linear progression of the Southern Advance. In her pathbreaking work, Li Tana points to many examples of how the southward thrust of the Viet was reversed several times and for prolonged periods because of setbacks at the hands of the Cham. She argues that the outcome occurred more because of contingencies and accidental circumstances than because of any long-term design.[22] However, when it comes to the Mekong Delta and The Port, many studies continue to defer to the Southern Advance explanation. Confining the Mo to the role of facilitators of the final round of southward expansion proves limiting even if we are to only assess their significance for Vietnamese history.

Li has highlighted how Cochinchina represented a "new way of being Vietnamese" distinct from Tonkin, its northern rival based in Hanoi. Tonkin, under the Trịnh lords, looked toward the Chinese state in fashioning a Confucian bureaucracy and agrarian-centered economy. The Nguyễn, on the other hand, oversaw a militarized but decentralized order in a newly opened frontier that primarily relied on maritime trade for revenues. According to Li, the Viet in Cochinchina lived in a cosmopolitan and multipolar environment. They were heavily influenced through their interactions with Cham and other indigenous highlander groups and merchants, travelers, immigrants, and religious figures from China, Japan, Southeast Asia, and Europe.[23]

It is true that Cochinchina was subject to multipolar influences, but over time China increasingly became the dominant external and domestic factor. The Nguyễn rulers were highly pro-Qing and pro-ethnic Chinese in their outlook and policies. For instance, Qing subjects, even if they committed the most egregious crimes, such as sedition and outright rebellion, could not be executed. They could only be repatriated to China for capital punishment.[24] Knowledge of spoken Chinese became a requirement in examinations to qualify for a central government post. In 1702, one Nguyễn lord went as far as to seek investiture from the Qing as a tributary vassal separate from the north. Although Tonkin and Cochinchina were already de facto independent of one another, both continued to pay allegiance to a powerless Lê (1428–1788) court in Hanoi, because it was the only political authority recognized by the Qing. The Trịnh, too, had to exercise their power through Lê puppets. The Qing predictably refused the Nguyễn request.[25]

---

[22] Li Tana, *Nguyễn Cochinchina*, pp. 18–33.
[23] Li Tana, *Nguyễn Cochinchina*, pp. 59–116.
[24] Nguyễn Dynasty, *Thực lục*, vol. 1, pp. 140, 148.
[25] K. W. Taylor, *History of the Vietnamese*, pp. 326–327; Goscha, *Vietnam*, p. 41.

Nonetheless, because of Cochinchina's decentralized character, its people were exposed directly to all levels of Chinese, particularly southern Chinese, society and culture. The degree and depth of this influence certainly exceeded Tonkin, with the possible exception of interactions among the uppermost elites. Merchants, sojourners, and settlers from the Ming and, later, the Qing became the preeminent foreign presence from the mid-seventeenth century. Buddhist monks from China were treated as guests of honor at the court in Huế, which utilized the religion to enhance the prestige and bolster the legitimacy of the Nguyễn rulers.[26]

Large numbers of Chinese refugees flooded into Cochinchina amid the Ming-Qing transition. The Nguyễn assigned them to a special category: Minh Hương (Ming Incense; the last character was changed to mean Village after 1827). As Charles Wheeler notes, they formed their own communities and enjoyed exemption from taxes. At the same time, they could participate fully in Cochinchinese society. Over several generations, the Minh Hương and their descendants became creolized through intermarriage. They came to constitute a unique intermediary class able to bridge the Chinese and Vietnamese worlds. Although most retained their identification with their native places in China, their interests and careers were firmly tied to Vietnam, and they adopted its language and dress. This double affiliation allowed them to enjoy a position of privilege that exceeded the purely Chinese and Viet. They became diplomats, officials, and supervisors of foreign merchants in the Cochinchinese and, later, early Nguyễn dynasty bureaucracies.[27] Just as with the Viet, Cochinchina offered its Chinese residents a new way of being Chinese.

The Chinese character of Cochinchina, a much more creolized and eclectic version of the original through exposure to a multipolar and multiethnic environment, certainly held appeal for the Mo and explains, in part, why they were willing to render vassalage. Indeed, Mo Jiu himself took a Cochinchinese wife, who conceived his son and successor Tianci. Although the Mo and the Chinese creole elites and subjects of The Port enjoyed close ties with the Minh Hương, they were distinct in that they did not depend solely upon Vietnamese hierarchies. Nicholas Sellers sees Mo Jiu's act of submission to the Nguyễn as "less a genuine dependency … than … an assertion of independence from Cambodian rule."[28] He and his son hoped to leverage the formidable political and military resources of Cochinchina in preserving a balance of power in their

---

[26] K. W. Taylor, *History of the Vietnamese*, p. 326; Goscha, *Vietnam*, pp. 12, 39.
[27] Choi, *Southern Vietnam*, pp. 39–41; Wheeler, 'Placing,' pp. 40–41.
[28] Sellers, *Princes of Hà-Tiên*, p. 24.

neighborhood. They continued to participate in Cambodian affairs and, at times, paid tribute to Siam, Cochinchina's geopolitical rival, whether directly or indirectly through the Cambodian court in Oudong.

One could argue that The Port's dependence upon the Nguyễn, in fact, decreased over time, and a greater parity came to characterize the relationship. The Port built up a large military force in its own right that helped Cochinchina defend the crucial maritime approaches from the Gulf of Siam and South China Sea. The Nguyễn also relied upon the mediation of the Mo to ensure a friendly regime in Cambodia and peaceful ties with Siam. Moreover, The Port functioned as an alternative and much closer conduit of Chinese culture into Cochinchina. The Hà Tiên-based poet and journalist Đông Hồ points out that the emergence of southern Vietnamese literature owed directly to the influence of poetic exchanges sponsored by Mo Tianci's literary society.[29] Moreover, as Cao Tự Thanh and, later, Nguyễn Ngọc Thơ and Nguyễn Thanh Phong argue, Tianci's promotion of Confucian values outside of state-imposed orthodoxies and tolerance for diversity in their interpretation played an important role in Cochinchina's gradual shift away from a Buddhist worldview toward Confucianism.[30] It often appeared that the Nguyễn needed the Mo more than the other way around.

Indeed, Đông Hồ and other scholars native to Hà Tiên tout it as a special land with its unique features and historical trajectory. In addition to his studies, his former student and wife, Mộng Tuyết, wrote poetry and fictional stories about The Port and the Mo, adapted from local legend or stories that she had heard while growing up or conceived from her imaginative mind but based on the local environment.[31] Trương Minh Đạt, a former teacher at the Hà Tiên Public Secondary School (presently the Đông Hồ Number 2 Secondary School), published two large volumes that pieced together the main events and analyzed key questions in Hà Tiên's historical past.[32] He, along with his wife and son, regularly contributes to a blog maintained by Trần Văn Mãnh, an alum of the secondary school residing in France. Although the website primarily provides a platform for former teachers and classmates to reconnect and share their memories of growing up and living in Hà Tiên during the 1950s to 1970s, a growing number of posts focus on the Mo and their legacy for the town.[33] Despite the affinity for their native place, these

---

[29] Đông, *Văn Học*, pp. 15–34.
[30] Cao, *Nho giáo*, pp. 28–40; Nguyễn Ngọc Thơ and Nguyễn, 'Philosophical Transmission,' pp. 88–92.
[31] Mộng, *Chậu úp*, pp. 177–186.
[32] Trương, *Nghiên cứu*, vol. 1, pp. 9–10; vol. 2, pp. 5–6.
[33] Trần, *Trung Học*, https://trunghochatienxua.wordpress.com/

intellectuals are emphatic about it being an integral part of Vietnam. Their research aims to reconcile their local identity with their broader nationalist sentiments.

Đông Hồ has nonetheless taken the lead in overturning the notion of the Mo as generally compliant instruments of the Southern Advance. He argues that they had the full intention of forging a "small, independent kingdom."[34] Scholarship outside of Vietnam has built upon his assertions. Like Đông Hồ, Keith Taylor, through an examination of Mo Tianci's poetry, believes that Tianci, at the very least, had the ambition to become a ruler in his own right.[35] Chen Ching-ho, a pioneering specialist in the history of overseas Chinese in Vietnam, goes further, asserting that The Port "was a state of indisputable sovereignty."[36] Ryan Holroyd emphasizes that the final outcome of The Port's incorporation into the Vietnamese state came about because of a highly contingent process. It was the sum product of conscious and sometimes unwise decisions made by the Mo leaders rather than any inevitable force.[37] John Wong, Liam Kelley, and Claudine Ang avoid speaking in terms of clear boundaries. They argue that the Mo had to constantly negotiate their identity and allegiances in front of different state and non-state actors to maximize their interests and legitimacy at any given time in a complex and volatile environment.[38]

The Port as Translocal Hub

The pathbreaking findings, primarily from specialists of Vietnam and Chinese diaspora, have been a tremendous source of inspiration. I seek to build upon their efforts to expand our understanding of The Port's significance and contributions beyond the confines of national discourse. Accordingly, this study situates The Port and the Mo clan at the intersection of the histories and historiographies of Vietnam, the rest of mainland and island Southeast Asia, China, and the overseas Chinese. It engages with archival and published materials in multiple languages. They include underutilized Vietnamese sources, Qing official documents and private elite writings, Khmer and Siamese chronicles, Japanese trade records, journals and letters of the VOC, and European missionary accounts. Visits to fieldwork sites in China and Vietnam, whether by

---

[34] Đông, *Văn Học*, p. 36.   [35] K. W. Taylor, 'Surface Orientations,' pp. 967–969.
[36] Chen Ching-ho (Chen Jinghe), 'Mac Thien Tu and Phrayataksin,' p. 1537.
[37] Holroyd, 'No Man's Borderland.'
[38] J. D. Wong, 'Improvising Protocols,' pp. 246–247, 253; Kelley, 'Chinese Diaspora,' pp. 92–93; Ang, *Poetic Transformations*, p. 183.

me personally or other scholars, have yielded essential information from oral testimonies and epigraphic materials, such as steles, temple objects, tourist signs, and tombstone inscriptions.

Based on my findings from these sources, I argue that the Mo, while enjoying de facto independence, never intended to forge a formal state. Instead, they aimed to create what Melissa Macauley calls "non-statist forms of territoriality ... focused on territorial access, commodity production, and commerce." Their strategies for the administration of The Port and how they dealt with its neighbors was more about appropriating "local resources and [maximizing] personal and group benefits," while working through the governing authority and mechanism of others.[39] Strictly speaking, The Port was a non-state territorial space that existed to profit its main stakeholders. In many ways, its operations resembled a European long-distance trading firm, such as the VOC. The primary purpose of the VOC, and of its British and other counterparts for that matter, was to increase its value for its investors in the trade with Asia. To achieve this aim, the Dutch maintained a farflung network of trading posts and colonies stretching from the Cape of Good Hope to Japan.

Compared to the VOC, the Mo operated on a more informal level and with less supervision from any state. The core of The Port's administration was centered upon Jiu and his son and a group of militarized Chinese creole elites. They connected to each other through their native place affiliation of Leizhou and neighboring Hainan Island, marriage alliances, and personalized chains of command. In a sense, they represented a cross-section of Chinese local society transplanted onto a foreign setting. The Mo functioned like the gentry elite during the late Ming and Qing periods. The territory of The Port was their private landed property. They acted as models of Confucian propriety for their community and mediated between their locality and various state authorities. They resolved legal disputes, operated charities and schools, built roads and bridges, and maintained clan shrines. The only thing that they lacked was certification through the civil service examinations. Nonetheless, they made up for it through ties of vassalage to neighboring states and the promotion of Confucian values.[40]

This arrangement allowed the Mo to thrive within a maritime East Asian world characterized by multiple translocal connections. Matt Matsuda provides a workable definition of translocalism as "the specific linked places where direct engagements took place and were tied to histories dependent on the ocean."[41] These connections depended on

---

[39] Macauley, *Distant Shores*, p. 12.   [40] Brook, 'Family Continuity.'
[41] Matsuda, *Pacific Worlds*, p. 5.

boundary-crossing relationships between people of various locations that often occupy different physical, cultural, or political spaces. As Macauley puts it, they involve "the migration of people as well as … the circulation of capital, ideas, commodities, and disease."[42] These interactions do not necessarily involve official diplomatic interactions between the states to which they belonged. The Port functioned as a crossroads where multiple ethnic groups congregated to trade, sojourn, and settle down permanently. They enjoyed close ties to their native places but not primarily with the representatives of state power in the political centers.

The Port's survival and prosperity depended not upon the establishment of vertical hierarchies of control but rather on its role as a hub for the various horizontal networks of maritime East Asia. One of these horizontal associations consisted of primarily lower-level elites from the Qing and both halves of Vietnam. Mo Tianci established the Pavilion for Summoning Worthies (C: *Zhaoying ge* V: *Chiêu Anh Các*), a literary society that facilitated and institutionalized the long-distance, often anonymous exchange of poetry and prose between them and him and his leadership. It formed part of a broader effort by Tianci to overlay a unified ideological vision for The Port.

His father had promoted a synthesis of Buddhism and Daoism as a means of tapping into the Ming loyalist network and adherence to the prevailing Cochinchinese worldview. After coming to power, Tianci prioritized Confucianism but built upon this eclectic foundation. He did not adopt the neo-Confucian orthodoxy sanctioned by the late imperial Chinese and Vietnamese states. Based upon the teachings of the Southern Song (1127–1279) philosopher Zhu Xi (1130–1200), this orthodoxy advocated a structured hierarchy centered upon the imperial court. Instead, Tianci embraced the teachings of the mid-Ming statesman Wang Yangming (1472–1529), whose Heart-Mind school viewed subjectivity and emotions as the basis for social action and behavior. Although highly popular during the late Ming, it was marginalized during the early Qing since many elites blamed it for encouraging the moral relativism and individualism that brought about the former dynasty's collapse.[43] However, this decentralized variant of neo-Confucianism perfectly suited Mo Tianci's objectives for The Port. Its emphasis on human feeling served as the inspiration behind his sponsorship of long-distance literary exchange.

---

[42] Macauley, *Distant Shores*, p. 4.
[43] Rowe, *Saving the World*, pp. 124–126; Nguyễn Ngọc Thơ and Nguyễn, 'Philosophical Transmission,' pp. 89–90.

The Heart-Mind school justified a significant degree of pragmatism and even opportunism in the Mo's dealings with state actors. The Mo exploited the subtle differences in the conventions of the Sinosphere; defined as comprising China, Korea, Japan, and the fragmented space of present-day Vietnam; and the mandala model prevalent in Southeast Asia. Although both worldviews prioritized submission and the payment of tribute from lesser polities to a universal ruler, the mandala model was less institutionalized and more flexible toward subordination to multiple overlords and emphasized the personal charisma and authority of the monarch.[44] The Mo would submit to Cochinchina as a vassal in the Sinosphere sense but concurrently render tribute to the Cambodian and Siamese kings according to Southeast Asian conventions. Eventually, Tianci sought to place his own candidates onto the throne of these neighboring states. This fluid, multipronged strategy allowed the Mo to enjoy the full benefits of being rulers of an independent state without any formal recognition as such.

A similar flexibility characterized domestic governance. Like the late imperial Chinese gentry, the Mo integrated themselves into established state structures and utilized them to administer the daily affairs of their multiethnic subjects. For instance, they left the Cambodian hierarchy from before their occupation of The Port unchanged in regard to the Khmer, while adopting and adapting Sino-Viet offices for managing the Chinese creoles and Qing and Viet immigrants. The Mo also patronized and worked with different religions, including Mahayana and Theravada Buddhist sects, popular cults, Catholicism, and Islam. These were in themselves horizontal networks that possessed capabilities in recruiting settlers to open new land, exercising grassroots administrative control, and enforcing moral self-regulation. Local society in late imperial China shared similar characteristics. The gentry supervised a wide range of semiformal grassroots organizations, ranging from clan and native-place associations to merchant guilds and the management boards of shrines and temples. These bodies provided much-needed services to local societies in China at a time when population growth and commercialization severely strained the resources of the regular bureaucracy.[45]

Despite the Mo's pragmatism and tolerance for diversity, they hoped to ultimately "civilize" the "barbarian" frontier of the water world according to the standards of Chinese culture. Moreover, among the

---

[44] For an overview of the Sinocentric tributary system, see Kang, *East Asia*, pp. 25–81. More on the Southeast Asian mandala can be found in Wolters's *History, Culture, and Region*, pp. 27–40; Tambiah, *World Conqueror*, pp. 46–72.
[45] Kuhn, *Chinese among Others*, pp. 43–52.

Sinosphere states and the far-flung Chinese settlements across East Asia, they hoped to remove or at least temper down their political and ideological differences. In fact, Tianci intensified his literary project in the 1750s, forging ties with increasingly higher-profile Qing and Cochinchinese elites. Through their mediation, he was able to achieve direct contact with the Guangdong authorities and the Qing court, and frequently exchanged letters and envoys with them. Tianci or his officials were also most likely the ones who rendered his poetry into the Vietnamese vernacular as a means of popularizing Confucian values and Chinese culture among the Viet community. For the Mo, a greater ideological uniformity proved good for business, removing barriers to trade and ensuring the freer flow of goods and capital.

As Nguyễn Ngọc Thơ and Nguyễn Thanh Phong convincingly point out, Mo Tianci, in particular, found the Heart-Mind school to be well-suited for The Port's primary business of business, since it reconciled the conflict between personal profit and the greater social good.[46] The Mo took full advantage of The Port's ideal location at the crossroads of the junk routes. The Chinese, mostly from the southeastern provinces of Fujian and Guangdong, and Austronesian maritime networks that plied the waters of maritime East Asia, viewed The Port as a major hub. Li Tana and Paul Van Dyke show that the urban center of The Port and several subsidiary ports handled the export of natural resources from their hinterlands and transshipment of goods across the region. During this period, around half of the total trade between Guangzhou and Southeast Asia passed through its sphere of influence, allowing it to obtain a hefty surplus of silver. Meanwhile, The Port served as a center for the minting and circulation of metal coinage.[47]

In many ways, The Port exhibited surprising parallels with the Dutch East India Company. With each of the political actors of maritime East Asia where the VOC maintained a presence, it engaged in a unique relationship that was based upon the existing political structure and whether it enjoyed a favorable balance of power. Toward weaker parties, Adam Clulow shows, the VOC often resorted to violence, using its powerful ships and weapons to force open markets and obtain better conditions for trade. However, where the VOC stood at a comparative disadvantage, the Dutch proved willing to cooperate as equals or, in the case of Tokugawa Japan, even become subordinate vassals.[48] In colonies under direct VOC control, including its Asian center of operations at

---

[46] Nguyễn Ngọc Thơ and Nguyễn, 'Philosophical Transmission,' p. 90.
[47] Li Tana and Van Dyke, 'Canton'; Li, 'Mekong Delta,' pp. 150–152.
[48] Clulow, *Company and the Shogun*, pp. 96–147.

Batavia (present-day Jakarta), on the island of Java, it adopted a strategy that Tonio Andrade calls "co-colonization." The VOC recruited Chinese immigrants to open up the land and tapped into their trading networks. In exchange, the newcomers were guaranteed a safe environment for their business, bolstered by legal and military protections.[49] The Port likewise engaged in flexible foreign relations and relied upon Chinese as settlers and merchants.

These similarities are not entirely coincidental. New evidence uncovered from the VOC archives in Jakarta reveals that the Mo worked to integrate The Port into the company's monopolistic trading system in island Southeast Asia. They made ample use of Malay and other Austronesian networks that were active in the trade between the water world and the straits zone, comprising the Malay Peninsula and Sumatra. Mo Tianci, in particular, presented The Port to the Dutch as an Austronesian port principality. At the same time, he forged close ties with the Chinese mercantile community at Batavia. He borrowed from the city's institutions in managing the Qing merchants and sojourners at The Port, and appointed the grandson of the Kapitan, the head of the Batavia Chinese, to lead them. During Tianci's campaign against Siam in 1770, he upgraded the relationship with the VOC by initiating direct communications with the Dutch governor-general to secure weapons and military assistance.

According to the scholarly consensus, the VOC had largely ended its involvement in Vietnam and Cambodia during the second half of the seventeenth century, when it closed down all of its trading posts in the two countries.[50] Afterward, the company maintained a tenuous linkage to mainland Southeast Asia through its factory at the Siamese capital of Ayutthaya until the city's permanent destruction during the Myanmar invasion of the 1760s.[51] However, my research has uncovered the continuation of these ties in a robust, unofficial capacity. The VOC's reliance upon Chinese and Austronesian traders to access the water world, just as it had with many other ports in the China Seas, yielded much greater benefits and incurred fewer costs than a formal presence.

The pro-mercantile outlook of the Mo leaders, along with their flexible governance and promotion of Chinese culture, gave them a unique

---

[49] Andrade, *Taiwan Became Chinese*, ch. 6, ch. 8.
[50] For more on the fate of the VOC factory in Cochinchina, see Kleinen, 'Towards a Maritime History,' pp. 291–292. The closure of the factory in Tonkin, northern Vietnam, is documented in Hoàng, *Silk for Silver*, pp. 96–125. W. J. M. Buch speaks about the tragic end of the VOC trading post in Cambodia in 'La Compagnie des Indes néerlandaises' 2, pp. 233–237.
[51] Smith, *Dutch in Seventeenth Century Thailand*, p. 45.

advantage in a broader maritime world that was centered upon the China trade. As commercialization and demographic growth in China proceeded steadily apace over the eighteenth century, many areas, especially coastal provinces such as Fujian and Guangdong, faced mounting ecological pressure and shortages. Whether driven to desperation, enticed by new opportunities, or a combination of both, people from these two places went abroad in large numbers to Southeast Asia. In contrast to previous times, when diverse ethnic groups handled trade in maritime East Asia, the Chinese emerged as the dominant mercantile group and the largest source of outside settlers. Their expansion, Macauley shows, resembled an informal version of European colonialism in the investment of capital abroad to extract raw materials, recruit labor, and open new markets.[52]

Fundamentally, China was becoming more dependent than ever before on external sources to resolve its mounting demographic and ecological pressures. The intra-Asian trade, once centered upon the exchange of Japanese silver and copper with Chinese manufactured goods such as silk, became reoriented toward deepened bilateral exchange between China and Southeast Asia.[53] Much of the economy of southern China became offshored to Southeast Asia, which provided ghost acreages worked by Southeast Asian slaves and Chinese miners and planters sustained by locally produced rice and textiles. Southeast Asia, in turn, formed a market for goods from China, such as tea and porcelain. While Macauley views the offshoring as a development of the late nineteenth century, this study argues that it was, in fact, well under way over a hundred years earlier.[54] The Port and its hinterlands played a crucial role as an intermediary for the products and services necessary to supply and maintain an offshore Chinese economy.

The story of the Mo conforms to the assertions of Andrade and Macauley of an early modern convergence on both ends of Eurasia, whether in terms of economic growth, territorial expansion, or military technology.[55] Certainly, East Asia did not hit an ecological cul-de-sac in the manner described by Kenneth Pomeranz, at least not until well into the nineteenth century.[56] Yet, there was, at the same time, a divergence occurring within the larger framework of convergence. R. Bin Wong and

---

[52] Macauley, *Distant Shores*, p. 12.
[53] Myers and Wang, 'Economic Developments,' p. 564; Holroyd, 'Rebirth,' p. 11.
[54] Blussé, 'Chinese Century'; Trocki, 'Chinese Pioneering'; Macauley, *Distant Shores*, p. 74.
[55] Macauley, *Distant Shores*, pp. 6–12; Andrade, *Gunpowder Age*, pp. 297–306.
[56] Pomeranz, *Great Divergence*, pp. 22, 192.

Jean Laurent Rosenthal correctly highlight the crucial role played by the difference in political economies between the two ends of Eurasia.[57]

Unlike the VOC, the Mo never managed to acquire the full protection of either Cochinchina or the Qing, which were their greatest sources of political and economic support. Although Cochinchina sent troops to aid them on several occasions, these efforts were half-hearted at best. The Port was beneficial to Cochinchina precisely because its defensive capabilities covered the Vietnamese polity's porous and highly vulnerable southern frontier. The Mo could therefore deter geopolitical rivals such as Siam with their own resources and at minimal cost to the Nguyễn.

The Qing political economy, which was heavily invested in perpetuating the status quo of maintaining a domestic economy of primarily agrarian smallholders, went against bold, expansionary measures on its maritime frontier. The Qing admittedly demonstrated a great degree of pragmatism in its dealings with the Mo. In fact, a contingent moment occurred in the late 1760s, when the two almost joined forces in a campaign against a common enemy: Myanmar. In exchange for Tianci's cooperation, the Qing was ready to recognize The Port's dominance over the Siamese throne. Although the alliance ultimately failed to materialize, it shows that the Qing court could work together with an overseas Chinese creole group, even one that espoused a potentially subversive ideology, if doing so fulfilled its interests and ensured the security of its borders. However, the Qing did not provide any institutionalized or consistent mechanisms of support as part of a long-term vision of how to best exploit the Southeast Asian hinterlands. There certainly was no equivalent to the growing level of interest and attention that emerging Western European states paid to maritime East Asia despite its tremendous distance from their own shores[58]

Without sustained external backing, the fluid, cosmopolitan horizontal network forged by the Mo lost out to more committed state-builders determined to set firmer boundaries and hierarchies in their neighborhood. At the same time, ascendant European powers, particularly Great Britain, asserted their technological and financial advantages, based upon their growing military superiority over the sea-lanes. These developments facilitated not only the downfall of the Mo but also the gradual decline of autonomous Chinese power. The political and military aspects were marginalized or criminalized, while the economic role came under more vigorous supervision and regulation. Gradually and reluctantly, the

---

[57] Rosenthal and Wong, *Before and Beyond Divergence*, pp. 67–98.
[58] Schottenhammer, 'Qing China's Maritime Trade Policies,' p. 137; Zhuang, *Zhongguo fengjian zhengfu de huaqiao zhengce*, pp. 61–125.

Chinese diaspora became integrated as a vital part of the global European colonial framework during the nineteenth century.

Toward an Objective and Accessible Narrative

One of the most vexing problems that I have encountered while preparing this study has been choosing the appropriate orthography for identifying people, places, events, and concepts. The most straightforward way would be to name them according to their origins or primary area of activity according to current national boundaries. However, this approach ignores the tremendous degree of fluidity in eighteenth-century maritime East Asia and the water world, in particular. As an emporium located at multiple crossroads, The Port was a cosmopolitan place whose residents were multiethnic and polyglot, and many could assume several identities at the same time. Although we should be aware of this complexity, the narrative should also let readers understand and follow along with the storyline without getting overly confused with labels. I therefore seek to establish a balance between historical accuracy, objectivity, and accessibility.

For the transcription of Chinese terms, this work primarily utilizes the pinyin system. Exceptions to this rule include instances of a more popularly accepted spelling in English, so Taipei instead of Taibei, or a Chinese name appearing in a non-Chinese source whose original characters cannot be located, so, for example, Oeij Tshing (characters unknown). Vietnamese words are presented in the modern Romanized letters, complete with diacritics, unless an alternative spelling has gained wide currency in English. These include Hanoi rather than Hà Nội and Saigon in place of Sài Gòn. There is no standard transcription for Khmer, so I largely follow the spellings provided by translations of primary texts and secondary scholarship, with the consultation and advice of Choeurn Kim Heng. The Romanization of Thai is roughly based on the Royal Thai General System (RTGS), with the assistance and input of Pisut Phonglaohaphan.

I provide at the end of the book a glossary that pairs each term that does not use a Latin-based script with its original text. Chinese and demotic *nôm* characters are given for historical Vietnamese words dating from before the twentieth century. Khmer and Thai terms are matched with the modern versions of their scripts. Sometimes, the original text is included in the body chapters, mostly to validate the English translations. These do not appear in the glossary.

In places where political authority was ill-defined, contested, or fluid, such as The Port and much of the water world, and a person, place, event, or concept can be transcribed in multiple languages, all the variations are listed upon the first mention of the term. Each term is preceded by an abbreviation indicating the transcribed language: C (Chinese), K (Khmer), T (Thai), and V (Vietnamese). The variant spellings are then listed in the alphabetical order of the initial. If a term appears again later in the study, the one that is consistently utilized for the rest of the narrative is highlighted in bold: **C: Yang Yandi** V: Dương Ngạn Địch.

The prioritization of one spelling or Romanization inevitably touches upon disputed historical legacies and present-day political sensitivities. Some issues include overseas Chinese identity and its relationship to Chinese nationalism, the continued ambivalence of Vietnam toward its ethnic Chinese minority, and Cambodian irredentism toward the water world or Kampuchea Krom.[59] Knowing that any choice I make is somewhat arbitrary and potentially controversial, I try to ensure neutrality and fairness by basing the preferred spelling or Romanization according to one or more of four criteria:

1. It follows the standards of the political authority that controlled a particular place or conferred the ranks and titles, the biggest and most representative resident population, or the chief identity of an individual, whether self-identified or labeled as such by others, during the period of this study. For instance, Saigon is used instead of the Khmer Prey Nokor, and Mo Jiu instead of Mạc Cửu.
2. If the etymology of a word comes from a particular language, and it is retained in an adapted variation from another political authority, the original spelling or Romanization is still used. For instance, the Khmer Moat Chrouk is used for the settlement on the Bassac branch of the Mekong River rather than the Vietnamese adaptation of Châu Đốc.
3. If a term in a certain language is at least fairly well-known to English speakers, then it supersedes the others, regardless of historical precedent. The Vietnamese Cần Thơ refers to this major urban center of the Mekong Delta, and not the Chinese Qinju or Khmer Kampoul Meas, despite the Chinese and Vietnamese versions being derived from pronunciations of the Khmer original.
4. If the spelling or Romanization of a name or concept varies across different languages but translates into a similar or the same meaning in English, the translated term will be used. Accordingly, Deer Cape

---

[59] Tong, *Identity and Ethnic Relations*, pp. 175–200, 241–248; P. Taylor, *Khmer Lands*, pp. 252–254.

substitutes for C: Luqi K: Phnom Nay V: Mũi Nai, the Khmer village west of The Port center. The terms in the local languages are provided upon their first use in parentheses: Deer Cape (C: Luqi K: Phnom Nay V: Mũi Nai).

One controversial choice in terminology relates to the Mo and their identity. Some scholars have made the argument that the Mo and the Chinese of The Port came to primarily see themselves as subjects of Vietnam because of intermarriage with Viet women and vassalage to Cochinchina.[60] Mo Tianci, in particular, had a Viet mother and spoke the language. However, he and other elites presented themselves and The Port to the outside world in many other ways than just being Minh Hương from Cochinchina. For instance, Mo Tianci was comfortable in a Cambodian environment and had the Khmer name of Preah Sotoat. Moreover, Choi Byung Wook, Charles Wheeler, and Philip Kuhn convincingly point out that even Chinese creoles of mixed parentage who integrated well into other cultural settings retained patriarchal ties and corridors of communication with their native places in China.[61] During the eighteenth century, when the Mo enjoyed autonomous rule, sentiments toward the ancestral land were stronger.

Accordingly, I opt to transcribe the terms related to the Mo and The Port in pinyin. One exception would be if they appear in a source from a different language and the equivalent characters cannot be located. For people, places, or concepts with non-Chinese origins, the original spellings and Romanization are retained. For instance, the names, ranks, and titles specifically conferred upon the Mo and The Port by the Cochinchinese court, including Hà Tiên, and Cochinchinese officials and residents are provided in Vietnamese.

Admittedly, defaulting to pinyin is somewhat anachronistic, since it transcribes the terms into Mandarin, based upon northern Chinese dialects, while the overseas Chinese came primarily from southern China, which has much greater linguistic and cultural diversity. The Mo and their core leadership spoke Hainanese and Cantonese, while southern Fujianese (Minnanese), Hakka, and Chaozhouese sojourners and settlers were active in The Port and across maritime East Asia. Some scholars have questioned whether a uniform Chinese identity existed among members of the diaspora, and argue that they prioritized particularistic kinship, dialect, and native place connections above any broader

---

[60] Phạm Đức Mạnh, 'Cổ mộ,' pp. 1311–1312.
[61] Kuhn, *Chinese among Others*, pp. 70–71; Choi, *Southern Vietnam*, pp. 39–40; Wheeler, 'Placing,' p. 39.

community.⁶² A justification can be made for transcribing the terms related to the Mo and The Port and other Chinese groups according to the pronunciation of their dialects.

However, I find that particularistic loyalties, at least in the eighteenth century, coexisted with more encompassing frameworks of belonging. Despite the significant differences in customs and language, the Chinese diaspora shared an affiliation in varying degrees with a world order centered upon the Chinese imperial system. They subscribed to what Wang Yuanfei calls an "imagined empire." Unlike the "imagined communities" held together by modern nationalism, it assumes a status hierarchy in which various distinct groups conceived of their relationship to the empire in their own manner.⁶³ The imperial identity could manifest itself in clan and native place, class, political allegiances, or a combination of them all.

The Mo, despite their roots in Leizhou and reliance upon connections among their compatriots, rarely mentioned their native place. Instead, in their words and deeds, they chose to associate with the classical culture of the gentry elite rooted in the northern Chinese heartland, or Central Plain. They also expressed a subdued nostalgia for the Ming, but that was primarily about preserving the purity and continuity of Chinese identity abroad rather than an active political program. These non-parochial orientations remained consistent throughout their lives, and it also allowed The Port to become a major source of cultural influence for Cochinchina. My choice of pinyin, then, does have some historical basis. There was a common, albeit highly fragmented, early modern Chinese identity that spilled out of the confines of the imperial state.

I use "Chinese" in this study as an all-encompassing term for several related and interconnected subcategories. They include particularistic native place or dialect groups. There were Ming loyalists and Chinese creoles, the two often the same. They might be Qing subjects, including merchants who traded between China and other parts of maritime East Asia. They could be sojourners who resided abroad for a prolonged period with the expectation of eventually returning to their native places. They could also be permanent immigrants, but because of their later arrival compared to the Chinese creoles, they were less integrated into their host societies.⁶⁴ I opt for these more detailed terms, or some variation of them depending on the context, when referring to specific groups of Chinese.

---

⁶² Kuhn, *Chinese among Others*, p. 103; Pan, *Sons of the Yellow Emperor*, pp. 20–22.
⁶³ Wang Yuanfei, *Writing Pirates*, pp. 140–141.
⁶⁴ Kuhn, *Chinese among Others*, pp. 153–196; Pan, *Sons of the Yellow Emperor*, p. 35.

The second issue that has been widely discussed and debated relates to the name of Vietnam (Việt Nam) in referring to the country. The problem is that it was a neologism resulting from a compromise between the Qing court and Nguyễn Ánh (1762–1820, r. 1801–1820), the founding monarch of the Nguyễn dynasty, in the nineteenth century, after the events recounted in this narrative. Moreover, the use of Vietnam was rare after Ánh's death, only catching on again during the twentieth century. During our period of study, the country went by other names. Đại (Great) Việt was often used domestically, while Annam (C: Annan V: An Nam) referred to its role as a vassal state within the China-centered world order. However, a unified regime under either name never ruled over the entire area within the country's present-day boundaries, including much of the south. Annam, in particular, implies a more exclusive focus on its connection to China's historical experience. It can also create confusion, along with associations with the French colonial legacy, since Annam formed the central part of the three political units that constitute present-day Vietnam in French Indochina (1887–1954).[65]

The use of Vietnam is, admittedly, anachronistic and not historically accurate, as Liam Kelley reminds us. However, I agree with Charles Keith that it provides the most comprehensive and neutral way to describe the entire fragmented political space, its multiethnic peoples, and languages.[66] The alternatives fall short of doing so or get too confusing for the reader to follow along. For the sake of simplicity and convenience, I acquiesce to the use of Vietnam. Viet refers to the dominant ethnic group. Exceptions are made for specific historic contexts and quotations from primary texts.

An additional complication arises in the de facto and increasingly de jure separation of Vietnam into north and south during our period of study. Cochinchina refers to the realm of the Nguyễn. The term comes from Portuguese, but there are several theories about its meaning. It could have been a corruption of the Arab pronunciation for C: Jiaozhi V: Giao Chỉ, an archaic Chinese name for Vietnam. Or it may have referred to the intermediate position between Kochi (Cochin), in southern India, and China. Tonkin, under the domination of the Trịnh, also has Portuguese origins. It was a corruption of Đông Kinh, or Eastern Capital, which referred to Hanoi. These terms present tricky ambiguities. Tonkin shares the same name as the French protectorate over northern Vietnam, while Cochinchina was a direct French colony lying to the south

---

[65] Baldanza, *Ming China and Vietnam*, pp. 1–5; Keith, *Catholic Vietnam*, p. 17.
[66] Kelley, *Beyond the Bronze Pillars*, pp. 25–28; Keith, *Catholic Vietnam*, p. 17.

of Annam and encompassing the water world. Along with Annam, all three units made up the Vietnamese portion of French Indochina.[67]

Some scholars have tried to use the Vietnamese terminology contemporary to the sixteenth to eighteenth centuries in referring to the country's northern and southern halves. The Nguyễn realm was known as Đàng Trong (Inner Area), and the Trịnh ruled over Đàng Ngoài (Outer Area). However, Keith Taylor points out, these terms solely reflected the perspective of the south at the time. Their use was later inherited in an anachronistic manner throughout Vietnam during the Nguyễn dynasty, which was founded by a descendant of the Nguyễn rulers of Cochinchina. During our period of study, however, the Trịnh did not recognize the separation of inner and outer. There was only a single Lê dynasty whose southern frontier was in a state of perpetual rebellion.[68] Although Tonkin and Cochinchina certainly have their share of troubling connotations, they are a relatively neutral set of labels given to both sides and contemporary to their times. Moreover, readers without a Vietnamese background can more readily recognize and remember them.

The multiplicity of names and orthographic variations for places, people, and concepts is another testament to the fluidity and ambiguity of the world that the Mo lived and operated in. In fact, the Mo thrived within this decentralized framework, which allowed them to expand their territory and achieve greater profits while decreasing transaction costs. Through the skillful manipulation of both horizontal and vertical ties, they forged a unique space that was integrated into multiple states yet existed outside of them all. Their remarkable story forms the heart of the following chapters.

---

[67] K. W. Taylor, *History of the Vietnamese*, pp. 272, 484–485.
[68] K. W. Taylor, *History of the Vietnamese*, pp. 272–273.

1 The Port before "The Port"

> Hà Tiên of Annam used to be a remote wilderness. It has been over 30 years since my father opened it up. The people are starting to live in peace and have learned a bit about how to plant and cultivate.
> —Mo Tianci, 1736[1]

When did the Chinese first settle down in the water frontier of mainland Southeast Asia? How did their arrival lay the foundations for Mo Jiu's establishment of The Port? The official Nguyễn Veritable Records (*Thực lục*) and biographies, compiled during the mid-nineteenth century, provide a precise sequence of events. In the summer of 1679, a fleet of around fifty ships and over 3,000 soldiers and their families appeared off the coast of present-day Đà Nẵng, in central Vietnam. They were commanded by **C: Yang Yandi** V: Dương Ngạn Địch (d. 1688), head of the Dragon Gate (Longmen) Garrison, located in Qinzhou prefecture of extreme western Guangdong, bordering Vietnam. Joining him was his assistant, **C: Huang Jin** V: Hoàng Tiến, and **C: Chen Shangchuan** V: Trần Thượng Xuyên (1626–1715), military commander (*zongbing*) of Gaozhou, Leizhou, and Lianzhou (Gao-Lei-Lian), the three adjacent prefectures east of Qinzhou. They forwarded a petition to the lord (*chúa*), Nguyễn Phúc Tần (Lord Hiền, 1620–1687, r. 1648–1687), claiming to be subjects of the fallen Ming dynasty. Out of righteousness, they refused to submit to the new Manchu dynasty and requested refuge in Cochinchina.[2]

Lord Hiền deeply pitied the destitute crew and admired their steadfast loyalty. But the presence of so many armed men intimidated him and, unable to understand their language, he suspected their true intentions. Did they want to undertake a violent seizure of power and form a new base overseas after their defeat in the homeland? To be safe, the lord sent them far away from his capital in Huế to the fertile water world then under Cambodian control. Earlier in the seventeenth century, the Nguyễn had obtained from the Cambodian king an enclave at Saigon

---

[1] Hán-Nôm A. 441: Mao, *Hexian shiyong*, n. p.
[2] Nguyễn Dynasty, *Thực lục*, vol. 1, p. 82.

(K: Prey Nokor V: Sài Gòn). Lord Hiền was looking to expand the Cochinchinese presence into the sparsely populated hinterlands. These military units would allow him to readily achieve his aim without having to expend his personal resources. Accordingly, Lord Hiền ordered his vassal, the Cambodian king, to accept the refugees. They settled down in **K: Donay** V: Đồng Nai, the province surrounding Saigon. Chen Shangchuan and his soldiers ended up north of the enclave, in present-day Biên Hòa, while Yang Yandi and Huang Jin formed a base at **K: Mesar** V: Mỹ Tho to the south, on the banks of the main Mekong branch.[3]

This version of how the Chinese came to the water world has been the most widely referenced. It is largely lifted from an early nineteenth-century gazetteer on the water world. Its author, C: Zheng Huaide **V: Trịnh Hoài Đức** (1765–1825), was a Minh Hương who served as a Nguyễn dynasty official.[4] He, in turn, heavily based his writing upon a historical fiction entitled the *Việt Nam khai quốc chí truyện* (Chronicle of the founding of Vietnam), which dated, at the latest, back to the early eighteenth century.[5] The novel only mentions Yang Yandi, claiming that he fled with his men in defeat after the Qing occupied their base. His original destination was Nanjing.[6] However, Yang's fleet, consisting of 200 ships, blew off course during a storm and was decimated, with only fifty remaining. When he finally saw land, he ordered his troops to attack and conquer the place. A subordinate stopped him, telling him that it was Cochinchina and went on to describe how powerful and prosperous it was. Yang quivered in fear and decided that he had no other choice than to submit to the Nguyễn lord. The rest of the narrative is similar in content to the nineteenth-century sources except at the end. The lord ordered the Cambodian king to grant Yang and Huang Jin a base at Mesar. Yang then became sworn brothers with the Cambodian ruler and paid tribute to the Nguyễn lord every year.[7]

After this dramatic story, drawn and adapted from the historical fiction, Đức's gazetteer and the official compilations go on to document the arrival of Mo Jiu in the water world, treating it as a completely unrelated event. Jiu had migrated to Cambodia to escape the Qing and stayed at the river port of Phnom Penh. After obtaining territory at The Port and achieving phenomenal success, his new settlement immediately came

---

[3] Nguyễn Dynasty, *Thực lục*, vol. 1, p. 82.   [4] Trịnh, *Thông chí*, pp. 200–201.
[5] Zottoli, 'Reconceptualizing Southern Vietnamese History,' p. 3; Wheeler, '1683,' pp. 142–143.
[6] From the perspective of historical accuracy, Nanjing was an unlikely destination since it had already fallen to the Qing decades before Yang's base.
[7] Nguyễn, *Việt Nam khai quốc*, pp. 251–252.

under threat from the Siamese, who took him hostage. He eventually managed to escape and, soon after his return, sought protection by becoming a Nguyễn vassal.[8]

The primary narratives of the Dragon Gate and The Port's establishment blend nicely into nationalist-inspired Vietnamese historical studies written in the twentieth century and beyond. They argue that the water world before the seventeenth century was an empty space with no true master. Although there were some Khmer and Austronesians, they formed scattered, atomized communities, and the Cambodian state exercised little to no oversight over them. The Viet settlers were the first to arrive on a sufficiently large scale to fully possess the land. The Cochinchinese state followed suit, establishing institutions for effective governance not just for the Viet but also for the Khmer and other ethnic groups. Vietnamese scholars use the phrase: "the people come first, and the country follows after" (*dân đi trước, nhà nước theo sau*) to characterize this symbiotic process of expansion.[9] The story of the hopeless and lost Ming loyalists reinforces the notion of the Chinese as complete strangers whose arrival in the water world occurred entirely under the guidance of the Viet and the patronage of their Nguyễn hosts.

But a careful examination of multiple historical records shows that the Ming loyalist refugees were not stepping onto terra incognita. During the sixteenth century, well before the arrival of the first Viet, Chinese merchants and settlers, along with Japanese, Austronesians, and Europeans, already had an established presence in the water world, especially the Gulf of Siam littoral. They benefited from the emergence of an intra-Asian trade centered upon Ming China's voracious demand for silver from Japan and the New World. Moreover, the Cambodian court, dependent on this lively commercial exchange, paid special attention to the maritime zone. It actively welcomed different foreign groups to its shores. Besides their business, it also enlisted them as mercenaries to strengthen its control over the coast and support its struggle against Siam, its preeminent rival before the intervention of Cochinchina. As Cochinchinese involvement intensified over the seventeenth century, the Chinese acquired an increasingly prominent position as a third force able to balance out the two formidable neighbors.

The Ming loyalists themselves were no strangers to the water world. They had extensive commercial ties throughout the South China Sea. From at least the mid-1660s, they established bases in precisely the areas

---

[8] Nguyễn Dynasty, *Thực lục*, vol. 1, p. 273; Trịnh, *Thông chí*, pp. 303–305.
[9] *Vùng đất Nam Bộ*: Nguyễn, vol. 3, pp. 548–562; Trần, *Nam Bộ*, p. 8, pp. 79–157; Đỗ, *Tây Nam Bộ*, pp. 198–231.

of the water world where the Nguyễn lord purportedly authorized them to settle down. As the latest group of Chinese arrivals in Cambodia, they were also the largest and most organized. They owed much of their strength to their association with the Zheng family, the leading anti-Qing resistance force in southeastern China, based in Fujian and Taiwan. The Zheng revived Chinese maritime power in East Asia, a preeminence that the Qing inherited after eliminating them in 1683. By stepping out of an exclusively Vietnamese historical context, and factoring in Cambodian, maritime East Asian, and global perspectives, we can also discover significant connections between the Dragon Gate and Mo Jiu. Although not entirely conclusive, much evidence points to both being originally part of the same group of Ming loyalist arrivals in the water world. It certainly challenges the Vietnamese narrative, which treat the two as largely separate from one another. Whether directly or indirectly, the enterprising Mo Jiu exploited this relationship in forging his own polity at The Port.

Multipolar Confluences

Since ancient times, The Port, together with the northern littoral of the Gulf of Siam, stood at the crossroads of the shipping and trade routes encompassing the China Seas, Strait of Melaka, and Indian Ocean. From approximately the first to the fifth centuries CE, the area had experienced a lengthy period of power and prosperity as the core part of the thalassocracy of Funan. At its height, Funan dominated coastal Southeast Asia and controlled the flow of goods between China and India. Although multiethnic in its composition, the population appears to have consisted mostly of Austronesians. After the fifth century, Funan experienced decline and marginalization from Asian maritime trade and gradually disappeared from the historical records.[10]

The subsequent situation in the water frontier remains unclear. There is evidence of scattered Austronesian-speaking communities inhabiting small villages along the river mouths and coastline of the Gulf of Siam. Some of them resided entirely on their boats. They were probably closely related to and often communicated with the Orang Laut, the sea peoples active in the waters farther south, around the Strait of Melaka and the island of Sumatra. They would fish, conduct small-time trade, or engage in piracy upon passing ships.[11]

---

[10] Hall, *Early Southeast Asia*, pp. 49–59.
[11] Trịnh, *Thông chí*, pp. 168, 176–184; Trocki, 'Chinese Revenue Farms,' p. 332.

The rest of the water world entered the orbit of the Angkor Kingdom, as Khmer descended into the Kampuchea Krom floodplain from the heartland of the Great Lake. They followed the Tonle Sap River to Phnom Penh, where the river integrates into the main eastern Mekong branch and the western Bassac tributary, both flowing in a southeastward direction. The most fertile areas of the water world lie along these two channels. The waterways leave behind fine soils suitable for the wet-rice agriculture that the Khmer primarily practiced. They also feed into a dense network of canals that crisscross the delta, providing a source of irrigation and an efficient means of local transportation by boat. The Khmer settled down in large numbers between the two rivers, mostly on higher elevated levees to avoid flooding. Some continued farther down to the coastal areas. Where the main Mekong branch and the Bassac fan out into many river mouths before emptying into the South China Sea, the Khmer took up residence on top of sand dunes parallel to the sea. They hovered above a landscape characterized by frequently submerged swampland.[12]

Eventually, upon reaching the Gulf of Siam littoral, the swamps on the north and east give way to a chain of low-lying forested hills. Along the present-day Vietnam-Cambodia border, the elevation starts to climb. What the Vietnamese call the Seven Mountains (*Thất Sơn* or *Bảy Núi*) and known in Khmer by various names for the individual peaks, begin southwest of the Bassac river port of **K: Moat Chrouk** V: Châu Đốc. Although not higher than 700 meters, they mark the beginning of the Cardamom and Elephant Ranges, which extend all the way westward to the Thai border. Between the mountains and the Gulf of Siam lies a long strip of beach ridge that starts at Royal Market (K: Phsar Reachea V: Rạch Giá) and stretches across the Cambodian coastline to Kampong Som (present-day Sihanoukville). The Port's harbor and urban center lies at the heart of this seaside plain. Unlike the Austronesians, who typically lived on the ridge, the Khmer preferred to settle in the interior, on the elevated bases of the hills. Both groups also ventured into the gulf itself, where they would find hundreds of forested islands, large and small, perfect sites for fishing. The biggest of them is Phú Quốc (C: Fuguo K: Koh Tral), with an area of 574 square kilometers.[13]

Philip Taylor, based upon his extensive interviews and visits to Theravada Buddhist temples (*wat*) during his fieldwork in Kampuchea Krom and an analysis of the etymology of names, has provided tentative evidence of some form of royal oversight during the Angkor period.

---

[12] P. Taylor, *Khmer Lands*, pp. 70–88, 102–104.
[13] P. Taylor, *Khmer Lands*, pp. 128–218; Kitagawa, '*Kampot*,' pp. 395–396.

A few kings may have undertaken tours to the water world during the fourteenth century. A customs administration may have been established in certain ports that handled overseas trade. The temples may have acted as vehicles of local governance and forwarded revenues to the center.[14] Overall, however, the water world constituted a marginal frontier within Angkor's sphere of influence.

This area once again acquired a position of prominence after the fourteenth century amid Angkor's decline, which occurred in tandem with the growing power of its former vassals, especially Siam under the Ayutthaya Kingdom (1351–1767) and Laos. In 1431, after Siamese forces sacked Angkor, the royal court fled eastward. A more downsized kingdom was reestablished and centered upon the vicinity of Phnom Penh. The city's access to the sea-lanes through the branches of the Mekong made Cambodia ever more dependent upon the maritime Asian trading networks.[15]

This development coincided with China's increased reliance upon silver from overseas to sustain the monetization of its commercialized economy. The Ming partially relaxed its long-standing ban on private trade and travel abroad in 1567. However, it continued to forbid direct ties with Japan, the largest supplier of silver, because of the refusal of the Japanese warlords to abide by the tributary system and their encouragement of illicit smuggling and piracy, which wreaked havoc on the mainland coastline. As a result, Southeast Asia, including Cambodia, became a meeting ground for Chinese and Japanese traders. By the early seventeenth century, the Chinese, most of them from southern Fujian (Minnan), constituted the largest group of foreigners in Cambodia, numbering 4,000–5,000 people. The Japanese population was tiny in comparison, at around 80–100 families, but exercised a disproportionate influence. They handled the exchange of silver for Chinese silk and other luxury products and procured, for the Japanese market, deer and other animal skins that served as decoration in samurai armor. The Japanese also controlled the production sources and crucial links in the domestic supply chain.[16]

Around this time, the Europeans appeared in the sea-lanes of East Asia. They competed fiercely with each other and with local merchants to control the flow of spices, essential for preserving and flavoring food, and

---

[14] P. Taylor, *Khmer Lands*, pp. 134–137, 153–161; Hall, *Early Southeast Asia*, pp. 161–200.
[15] Hall, *Early Southeast Asia*, pp. 161, 326.
[16] Reid, 'Flows and Seepages,' pp. 37–38; Gipouloux, *Asian Mediterranean*, p. 91; Cheng (Zheng), *War, Trade and Piracy*, pp. 132–133; Iwao, *Nanyō Nihonmachi*, pp. 90–91; van der Kraan, *Murder and Mayhem*, pp. 8, 12–13.

other natural resources from island Southeast Asia to India and Europe.[17] Eventually, they, too, entered the intra-Asian silk-for-silver exchange. After seizing Melaka in 1511, the Portuguese successfully connected the Ming to Japan through the establishment of outposts at Macao, off the tip of Guangdong Province, and Nagasaki in Kyushu.[18] In 1571, the Spanish acquired a base at Manila after their conquest of the Philippine Islands and made it a transit point for silver from the New World.[19] Since at least the middle of the sixteenth century, an Iberian colony flourished near Phnom Penh, together with missionaries of the Dominican and Franciscan orders dispatched from Melaka and Manila.[20] These "Iberians" were highly diverse, consisting of Europeans, Africans, South Asians, and mixed creole offspring.[21]

The expansion of Portuguese influence in island Southeast Asia prompted a dispersal of large numbers of its Austronesian population to ports across maritime East Asia, where they mixed and forged a pan-Malay trading diaspora. Destinations included Phnom Penh and the water world of Cambodia and Ayutthaya, the capital of Siam. These communities were founded upon a shared belief in Islam and the acceptance of Arab and Persian cultural influences. Other groups, such as the Cham, Javanese, the Minangkabau of Sumatra, and the Bugis from Sulawesi, retained their ethnic affiliation but could simultaneously affiliate with the broader Malay identity. They, too, circulated among the different ports in the region, forming their own networks.[22]

Over the course of the seventeenth century, the Dutch East India Company (VOC) expelled the Portuguese from the Malay Peninsula and Indonesian archipelago, largely achieving domination over the spice trade to Europe. In 1619, it established an Asian headquarters for operations at Batavia, on the island of Java. From there, the company oversaw a burgeoning network of trading posts, or factories, that eventually stretched from the Cape of Good Hope to Japan. As it sought to control the intra-Asian trade, the VOC engaged in territorial acquisition. To compete with Macao and Manila in the supply of silver to China, and to establish a base for the export of deerskins to Japan, it occupied the island of Taiwan in 1624.[23] The motivation to overpower its rivals in the trade in deer and other animal skins prompted the Dutch to also open up factories at Phnom Penh and Ayutthaya in 1636. In 1641, the Dutch

---

[17] Bulbeck et al., *Southeast Asian Exports*, pp. 5–6.
[18] Gipouloux, *Asian Mediterranean*, pp. 113–119.
[19] Brook, *Vermeer's Hat*, pp. 64, 152–184.   [20] Hall, 'Coming of the West,' pp. 13–15.
[21] van der Kraan, *Murder and Mayhem*, p. 13.
[22] Bruckmayr, *Cambodia's Muslims*, pp. 9–24.
[23] Nara, 'Zeelandia,' pp. 161–167; Cheng (Zheng), *War, Trade and Piracy*, pp. 131–132.

seized Melaka from the Portuguese, followed by Makassar in 1667. As a result, Portuguese took refuge in Cambodia in much larger numbers than before.[24]

Besides Phnom Penh, many foreigners established a presence in the water world. The Gulf of Siam, in particular, served as an important waterway for trade and access to the South China Sea. For this reason, it was hotly contested between Cambodia and Siam. From the mid-fourteenth century, political and economic competition between the two kingdoms intensified, often erupting into full-scale warfare. Contrary to the Vietnamese scholarly consensus that the Cambodian court exercised no effective management over the water world, it, in fact, paid careful attention to the consolidation over at least the strategic coastal area. It divided the maritime zone into two sets of provinces. Sacred Pond (K: Preah Trapeang V: Trà Vinh), Bassac, and Black Water (K: Tuk Khmau V: Cà Mau) guarded the mouths of the Mekong from the South China Sea. Situated along the Gulf of Siam were Kampong Som, Kampot, Kramoun Sar, Banteay Meas, and Seashore, or The Port's core area.[25] Collectively, these provinces became the first line of defense for Phnom Penh from Siamese naval invasions and, when Cambodia was strong, the staging ground for campaigns against Siam.

There is much confusion about the relationship between Banteay Meas and The Port. As Sakurai Yumio and Kitagawa Takako show, European sources contemporary to the eighteenth century, and often even the same record, give conflicting narratives about the place they called Ponteamas.[26] Sometimes they consider Banteay Meas and Seashore to be the same place, and on other occasions, to be separate. In similar fashion, the various versions of the Cambodian Royal Chronicles either speak of a single Banteay Meas or list Seashore as a distinct province.[27]

Perhaps the answer lies in the fact that Seashore originally constituted an integral part of Banteay Meas, being, literally, its seashore. Some Cambodian sources also call it the "river promontory of Banteay Meas."[28] They are referring to The Port's main waterway, known as Fortress River (C: Jiangcheng V: Giang Thành). It has two sources, both from mountains about forty to fifty kilometers away from the city center. After the branches join about two kilometers from the current Vietnam

---

[24] Cheng (Zheng), *War, Trade and Piracy*, p. 123; van der Kraan, *Murder and Mayhem*, p. 8; Launay, *Cochinchine*, vol. 1, pp. 67–69.
[25] Leclère, *Histoire de Cambodge*, p. 208.
[26] Sakurai and Kitagawa, 'Hà Tiên or Banteay Meas,' p. 156.
[27] Mak, *Chroniques royales*, pp. 87, 133–134, 140–142, 165, 192, 259–260, 292, 297, 299, 301, 355.
[28] Mikaelian, *Royauté d'Oudong*, p. 348.

border, Fortress River widens considerably as it pursues a southwesterly direction. Eventually, it merges into a lagoon before narrowing again and flowing into the Gulf of Siam. The lagoon, known as East Lake (C: Donghu V: Đông Hồ), formed an ideal harbor for ships to congregate.[29]

The administrative center of Banteay Meas lies to the northeast of Touk Meas Mountain, one of the sources of Fortress River. The settlement fulfilled a vital role as an inland hub for land transportation, given its location midway between Phnom Penh and The Port. A water route also passed through during the rainy season, from April to November. Canals would form from flooding near the other origin of Fortress River, on a mountain situated amid a swampy marshland.[30] They provided access for vessels from The Port to Banteay Meas and Moat Chrouk, where they could sail onward to Phnom Penh via the Bassac.[31] Banteay Meas was traditionally the commercial center, and the area of The Port served as a thoroughfare for goods.

However, when deemed strategically necessary, such as defense against a Siamese invasion, Seashore would be separated into its own province, where important military installations would be placed. Together with Sacred Pond, next to the South China Sea, it would be given an honor ranking of nine. This was just one level below the strategic super-provinces of Santuk, Ba Phnom, Tbaung Khmum, Pursat, and Treang. Known as the "Four Columns," these provinces of the highest tenth rank functioned in a cosmological sense like cardinal points of a mandala, providing balance and stability to the kingdom. In practical terms, they formed a core inner ring of defense around Phnom Penh. Their governors assumed the highest noble rank of *oknha*. Provinces of the ninth rank also had strategic significance. They stood in the outermost of the concentric circles of the mandala, surrounding the super-provinces and forming the frontiers of the kingdom's projection of power. Seashore guarded the other provinces along the Gulf of Siam and collected duties from trade, while Sacred Pond was responsible for the South China Sea. The customs revenues went to the central Ministry of Justice (Yomreach), since the office's income came from its cosmological direction facing the southeast.[32]

---

[29] Aymonier, *Cambodge*, vol. 1, pp. 156–157; Nguyễn Dynasty, *Nhất thống chí*, vol. 3, p. 278.
[30] Sakurai and Kitagawa, 'Hà Tiên or Banteay Meas,' p. 156; Mak, *Histoire du Cambodge*, p. 366.
[31] Aymonier, *Cambodge*, pp. 156–157.
[32] Mikaelian, *Royauté d'Oudong*, pp. 221–230; Leclère, *Les codes*, vol. 1, pp. 115–116; *Tamrathamnieb bandasak Krung Kamphucha*, p. 31.

According to the Cambodian Royal Chronicles, a Chen Chong Tok, who was based at The Port and either held the highest noble rank of *oknha* or the third highest *chaoponhea*, led troops each time conflict broke out with Siam. The name appears in the chronicles on at least three occasions from the 1570s to 1630s. "Chen" means Chinese in Khmer, while "Chong Tok" is a corruption of *zongdu* (governor-general). It must refer to a generic title rather than any specific individual since Chen Chong Tok was documented to have been killed in action two times. Their task was to lead Chinese troops and handle maritime defense. They were probably the prototypes for the Mo later on.[33] The presence of this prominent position shows that there was already a substantial Chinese population in the water world, including Banteay Meas and its surroundings. Joining the Chinese were war captives from Siam and Laos, who were resettled in the area, along with Cham and Malay.[34]

The Cambodian court increasingly depended upon foreigners to supervise and protect its vital maritime linkages. Overseas trade came under the supervision of the Ministry of Foreign Affairs (Kralahom), whose head held the *oknha* rank. It, in turn, appointed two officials, both of Minnan origin, to take overall charge of trading vessels and the foreign communities. One of them, Srey Sramut (Master of the Seas) supervised the Chinese, Japanese, and junks from the rest of Asia, while the other, Desa Nayok (Master of Foreigners), handled the European ships. They both possessed the rank of *chaoponhea*.[35]

The individual foreign communities were each placed under a headman, known as a shahbandar (port master), appointed from among the individual groups and who answered directly to the two officials. At Phnom Penh, which contained the highest concentration of foreigners in the kingdom, the shahbandars resided in separate neighborhoods in the suburbs or satellite towns. The court also allowed the Chinese, Japanese, Austronesians, and Iberians to organize their armed forces to be placed under their own commanders, like Chen Chong Tok, and serve as mercenaries.[36]

Between Two Powers

The militarization of the foreign communities reflected the fragile foundations of Cambodia's prosperity. Domestically, it had much to do with

---

[33] Mak, *Histoire du Cambodge*, pp. 321–323; Mak, *Chroniques royales*, p. 167.
[34] Leclère, *Histoire de Cambodge*, pp. 208, 368–369.
[35] Mikaelian, *Royauté d'Oudong*, pp. 341–344.
[36] Mikaelian, *Royauté d'Oudong*, pp. 341–344; van der Kraan, *Murder and Mayhem*, pp. 12–13; Iwao, *Nanyō Nihonmachi*, p. 106.

the structural weaknesses in the kingdom's political structure. In fact, four formal centers of power coexisted uneasily with one another. Besides the king, there was a viceroy (*oupareach*), usually a brother or son who would be next in the line of succession. An abdicated ruler or a royal relative ineligible to inherit the throne would become a co-king (*oupayureach*). These rules did not always apply. In some cases, the co-king could also qualify for the succession. Then came the queen-mother. Each maintained a palace and personnel in a replica of the royal court. The king oversaw a bureaucratic apparatus consisting of over 100 *oknha*. The court of the co-king, on the other hand, had 51 *oknha*, while the viceroy had 40, and the queen-mother, 25. In addition, 7 provinces out of some 30 to 60 served as the appanage of the co-king, 5 belonged to the viceroy, and 3 to the queen-mother. Of course, the total number of provinces and officials fluctuated over time.[37] This dispersal of power created significant ambiguity, especially when determining the succession.

Moreover, the organizational structure of the kingdom became ossified, since its basis of legitimacy depended primarily upon ordering society in a rigid, predictable hierarchy. As Grégory Mikaelian shows, Khmer identity became equated with the peasant-cultivator, and imbued with a sacred quality celebrated and reinforced in myths and legends. Non-servile commoners attached themselves to high-ranking patrons of their choice in the capital, whether an *oknha* or a prince or princess. They would pay their taxes and render labor and military obligations through these elites. In exchange, the elites protected their clients and served as advocates during disputes. Commoners could switch patrons at will. A good patron could not only retain clients, but those with a large number of them could also attain greater influence at court. The water world, on the contrary, was characterized by greater cosmopolitanism, mobility, orientation toward trade, and vulnerability to invasion. There, foreign groups became more important as they specialized in mercantile and protection services. The court depended upon them for a large share of its income.[38]

After 1594, when Siamese troops invaded and sacked the old capital of Longvek, near Phnom Penh, Cambodia submitted to the suzerainty of Ayutthaya. The increased disadvantage in the competition with its neighbor both in the lead-up to and aftermath of this traumatic event

---

[37] Leclère, *Histoire de Cambodge*, p. 283; Mikaelian, *Royauté d'Oudong*, p. 226; Theam, 'Cambodia in the Mid-Nineteenth Century,' pp. 15–16.

[38] Mikaelian, *Royauté d'Oudong*, pp. 76, 265–274; Theam, 'Cambodia in the Mid-Nineteenth Century,' pp. 20–22.

exacerbated power struggles at the court, especially over the succession. The conflicts, in turn, exposed and widened the structural problems faced by Cambodia, creating opportunities for outsiders to intervene in its affairs. Siam, of course, constituted the most persistent external presence in the kingdom. It sought to fully control the throne and determine the succession by keeping princely heirs as hostages at Ayutthaya and providing refuge for pro-Siamese royal relatives who were on the losing side in power struggles.[39]

The Cambodian rulers understood their neighbor's intentions, and some of them enlisted the support of the kingdom's multiethnic mercantile communities to counter the threat. Often, the solution proved far worse than the problem. Separatist tendencies emerged in the water world, as the rift with the agrarian interior grew. Several times during the sixteenth and seventeenth centuries, Cham and Malay Muslims and Lao, sometimes with the support of the Japanese and Iberians, rebelled or backed Khmer warlords who forged independent power bases. Mercenaries from these groups, along with the Chinese, also took advantage of the decentralized power structure at the court to participate in intrigues and succession struggles.[40]

In seeking a more reliable counterbalance to Siam, other Cambodian rulers turned toward the recently established state of Cochinchina in south-central Vietnam. The area once belonged to several Cham kingdoms, but in 1471 the Lê dynasty had exterminated all but one of them and occupied their territories, extending from the north of Huế to Quy Nhơn. Over the sixteenth century, the Lê gradually disintegrated amid internecine struggles among its leading clans. The Trịnh became the real power behind the Lê rulers in Hanoi. The Nguyễn, on the other hand, exiled themselves to the northern edge of former Cham territory. At the dawn of the seventeenth century, they established a seat of power at Huế. They relied upon overseas trade for much of their revenue. Nearby Hội An became a lively cosmopolitan port, with diverse Chinese, Japanese, Iberian, and Dutch mercantile communities. Over the next few decades, the Nguyễn lords grew independent of the north and stopped forwarding taxes to Hanoi. Their state came to be called Cochinchina, as opposed to Tonkin, under the de facto control of the Trịnh. Both entities, however, maintained a nominal allegiance to the Lê rulers, the only ones who received recognition and investiture from China, Vietnam's tributary overlord.[41]

---

[39] See, for instance, Mak, *Histoire du Cambodge*, pp. 129, 160, 308.
[40] Mikaelian, *Royauté d'Oudong*, pp. 278–294; Leclère, *Histoire de Cambodge*, pp. 330–331, 352–353; Mak, *Histoire du Cambodge*, pp. 89–91, 119–120, 307; van der Kraan, *Murder and Mayhem*, pp. 16–17, 69–70.
[41] K. W. Taylor, *History of the Vietnamese*, pp. 249–257; Li Tana, *Nguyễn Cochinchina*, pp. 19–21.

From 1611 to 1653, through a series of military campaigns, combined with marriage alliances, the Nguyễn succeeded in pushing their boundaries down the coastline of the South China Sea at the expense of the rump Cham state of Panduranga (1471–1697). They organized the Frontier Suppression camp (Trấn Biên *dinh*) to administer the newly conquered areas and forced the Cham to submit as subordinate vassals. As a result of this round of expansion, Cochinchina directly shared a northern border with Cambodia.[42] During the 1620s, the Trịnh reacted to Cochinchina's growing independence and assertiveness by launching a war that dragged on inconclusively along their border for the next fifty years. Since the Mekong Delta became an important source of rice for troop provisions in the struggle against Tonkin, it became imperative for the Nguyễn to establish and maintain friendly ties with Cambodia.[43]

In 1619, Chey Chettha (1576–1628, r. 1618–1628) ascended the Cambodian throne. He made three decisions that would have a profound impact on the subsequent historical trajectory of his kingdom. For one, he established a permanent royal capital at Oudong, about fifty kilometers up the Tonle Sap River from Phnom Penh. Secondly, he sent an embassy to Huế to ally with the Cochinchinese regime and free himself from dependence upon Siam. He took the hand of a daughter of the Nguyễn lord, a princess known in the Cambodian records as Ang Chov. Thirdly, in 1623, Chey Chettha granted the Nguyễn lord a lease on the port of Saigon. Located at the edge of the water world, in a hazy, undefined border zone with the Cham territory to the north, the Khmer had only established a province there at the dawn of the seventeenth century. Now, Chey Chettha allowed the Cochinchinese to freely sail their ships to Saigon to procure grain and station their troops and officials to protect and tax their merchants and settlers.[44]

Chey Chettha's pursuit of closer ties with Cochinchina had three important consequences. The outpost at Saigon became a conduit for the large-scale influx of Cochinchinese migrants into Cambodia. Some of them settled down in "two grand villages" close to Phnom Penh. By the 1660s, their population numbered around 400.[45] Many more went into the water world. The majority of these "wandering people" (*lưu dân*) came from Quy Nhơn, the southernmost frontier of Cochinchina at the time. Since the area had not long been conquered

---

[42] Wong Tze Ken, *Nguyen and Champa*, pp. 112–114, 119–122.
[43] K. W. Taylor, *History of the Vietnamese*, pp. 279–300, 307–318.
[44] K. W. Taylor, *History of the Vietnamese*, pp. 300, 302–303, 307; Leclère, *Histoire de Cambodge*, pp. 339–340.
[45] Launay, *Cochinchine*, vol. 1, pp. 67–69.

from Champa, Cham also participated in the southward migration. They were escaping poverty, warfare, famine, and onerous government impositions.[46] Most of the settlements were clustered around Saigon, in the surrounding, sparsely populated countryside of Donay. A few, however, filtered out farther onto the Gulf of Siam coastline and Phú Quốc and other offshore islands. Like elsewhere in the water world, they formed small communities that cultivated rice and fished.[47]

The new settlements received the active support of the Vietnamese princess, Ang Chov, at the court in Oudong. Her influence rapidly grew. She was elevated to the position of queen-mother and continued to hold this position after her husband's death. She had her own officials and provinces. On several occasions, different Cambodian rulers requested the return of Saigon, but each time she was able to use her influence to persuade them to drop the matter, gradually making the Cochinchinese occupation permanent.[48]

Ang Chov further paved the way for direct Cochinchinese intervention in Cambodia when renewed crises rocked the court. The reigning king, Ponhea Chan (1614–1659, r. 1642–1658), had converted to Islam and displayed great favor toward the Austronesian communities. In doing so, he alienated the influential Theravada Buddhist clergy and much of the court and elites. These elements rallied around two royal princes with close ties to the queen-mother, Ang Chov. She sent a request to the Nguyễn for military assistance. In 1658, Lord Hiền dispatched troops into Cambodia and captured Ponhea Chan, who was brought back to Cochinchina in a cage and died shortly thereafter. The Cochinchinese then turned upon the two princes, Barom Reachea (1628–1672, r. 1658–1672) and his brother Reameatipadey, but the invaders were defeated and forced to retreat. Barom Reachea then assumed the throne, and Reameatipadey became co-king.[49]

This intervention showed that Cochinchina had joined Siam as a formidable outside player in Cambodian affairs. The Cambodian king, Barom Reachea, soon found himself having to strike a delicate balance between the two. Most of the retinue of the former Muslim king, Ponhea Chan, had taken refuge in Siam. Cochinchina, on the other hand, backed Reameatipadey. Under the patronage of the co-king, large numbers of Viet migrants continued to flow into the kingdom, congregating in

---

[46] Li Tana, *Nguyễn Cochinchina*, pp. 24–28.
[47] Sakurai, 'Chinese Pioneers,' p. 37; Huỳnh, 'Sự Tích Giếng Tiên.'
[48] Mak, *Chroniques royales*, pp. 120–122, 148–149, 353–354.
[49] Leclère, *Histoire de Cambodge*, pp. 351–353; Mak, *Chroniques royales*, pp. 192–202.

Phnom Penh and around Saigon.[50] Barom Reachea, needing a firmer base of support, turned toward an emerging third power: an organized maritime Chinese regime.

The Rise of Maritime Chinese Power

During this period, innovations in social organization across maritime East Asia bolstered the autonomy and durability of overseas Chinese communities. During the sixteenth century, smugglers and pirates from South China roamed the seas and traded in various parts of Southeast Asia. Wheeler speaks of the island of Hainan as a point where the maritime routes diverge. For junks from Guangdong, they tended to pass through the northern part of the island and enter the Gulf of Tonkin. Ships from Fujian would venture farther, rounding the southern end and crossing the open sea to central Vietnam, the water world, and beyond. The pirates provided much of the maritime infrastructure for more elaborate forms of networks and organizations. In fact, the successful Nguyễn establishment of Cochinchina owed much to the help of Fujianese armed traders, who supplied them with weapons and goods for the Japanese market.[51]

Meanwhile, in the coastal areas of China, the need for residents to distinguish themselves as upright subjects from the smugglers and pirates before central and local authorities stimulated the growth of lineages tied together by a common ancestor and genealogy.[52] Serving as mediators between local society and officialdom, these organizations, led by prominent gentry, proved highly successful in forwarding revenues and ensuring compliance with laws. Moreover, they could pool, preserve, and redistribute capital, making them ideal vehicles for overseas investment and immigration. Ironically, these activities often brought them into collaboration with smugglers and pirates.

Once overseas, Chinese immigrants benefited from the policies of East Asian rulers and the European colonial authorities. Headmen, such as the shahbandar in Cambodia and the kapitan in Batavia, governed their communities according to their own laws and customs. These leaders and the wealthiest merchants and tax farmers formed an elite class that replicated the gentry and lineage organizations in their native places. The stability of their position in Southeast Asian society drew large numbers of them away from purely overseas trade toward the long-term investment in internal trading networks. They also played a key role in

---

[50] Mak, *Histoire du Cambodge*, pp. 308–309, 313.   [51] Wheeler, 'Placing,' pp. 42–44.
[52] See Lim, *Lineage Society*, pp. 239–246.

recruiting more immigrants to open land for agricultural exploitation. Andrade uses the term "co-colonization" to speak about this mutually beneficial partnership with the Chinese in the case of the VOC and other European outposts in Asia. However, this term equally applies to states in maritime East Asia, such as Cambodia.[53]

Despite their numbers, the Chinese initially coexisted with other mercantile communities in a multipolar environment. To compete with the Japanese, Iberians, and Dutch more effectively, and protect themselves during disputes and conflicts, southern Fujianese (Minnanese) gentry, merchants, smugglers, and pirates consolidated into armed trading organizations. The biggest and most successful of them came under the leadership of the Zheng family, whose members officially joined the Ming as officials in 1628. They then used their new positions in the Fujian and Guangdong bureaucracy to forge a private military force with a formidable naval fleet. Besides conducting lucrative trade with Japan and Southeast Asia in their own capacity, the Zheng required all merchants sailing abroad to purchase their passes and fly their flag or risk predation from their patrols.[54]

Two major events provided a further boost to maritime Chinese power. One was the decision of Japan's Tokugawa shogunate to severely restrict private trade and linkages to maritime Asia. Over the 1630s, the shogunate issued a series of edicts that expelled the Iberians and banned Japanese subjects from leaving or returning to the country. The remaining private trade was confined to Nagasaki and left exclusively in the hands of the VOC and Chinese merchants, both from China and Southeast Asian ports. The measures marginalized and eventually completely removed the Japanese as commercial rivals of the Chinese and the VOC and greatly weakened the Iberian trading network.[55]

The second significant event was the downfall of the Ming in 1644 and the occupation of China by the Manchus, a process that lasted for almost half a century. The newly proclaimed Qing dynasty ran into fierce resistance from various Ming loyalist groups in southern China. The Zheng organization joined their ranks. Under the leadership of Zheng Chenggong (1624–1662), the organization forged a base on the islands of Fujian and Guangdong. Its overseas commercial network continued to operate and expand with the protection of his navy. The Qing tried to cut off this crucial source of income by reviving the Ming-era sea ban in 1656 and, starting in 1660, undertaking a brutal removal of coastal residents into the interior to

---

[53] Chang, 'Rise of Chinese Mercantile Power,' 10–15; Andrade, *Taiwan Became Chinese*, ch. 6; van der Kraan, *Murder and Mayhem*, p. 13.
[54] Andrade, *Lost Colony*, pp. 21–43; Hang, *Conflict and Commerce*, pp. 73–110.
[55] van der Kraan, *Murder and Mayhem*, p. 7.

cut off sources of food and products for trade. Unable to survive on the mainland, Zheng Chenggong attacked Taiwan in 1661 and forced the Dutch to surrender and leave the island. He and his descendants ruled over a maritime kingdom based on Taiwan for the next two decades. The draconian Qing sea ban left the Zheng as the largest and most important intermediaries to China. They succeeded in bringing most of the Chinese merchants in maritime East Asia under their authority.[56]

During the 1660s, the Zheng appeared to have the ambition of expanding their territory beyond Taiwan. Besides their core Minnanese constituency, they forged ties with smugglers and pirates in neighboring Guangdong. Other than the fertile Pearl River Delta around Guangzhou, the province tended to be deficient in arable land and resources. Many of the rebel bands operated around the Leizhou Peninsula, located to the west of the Pearl River Delta and directly facing Hainan across a narrow strait about twenty kilometers long. The peninsula proper, along with the adjacent mainland from Yangjiang westward to Qinzhou, was a vast desert of barren grasslands, an economic backwater that suffered persistent demographic decline. The complex Gulf of Tonkin coastline, full of small islands and passageways, made the area hard to access and an ideal piratical den. Moreover, its proximity to the Vietnam border provided easy avenues of escape in the event of attack from government forces.[57]

After the collapse of the Ming, a chaotic situation prevailed along the Guangdong coastline. As Robert Antony shows, lawless elements sometimes fiercely resisted entering Manchu forces under the banner of Ming loyalism, while at other times collaborating with the Qing, switching back and forth between the two, or proclaiming new, short-lived dynasties of their own. The leaders opportunistically appropriated different symbols to legitimize their local political economy based on plunder. One of the strongmen, Deng Yao (d. 1660), established a base at Dragon Gate during the 1650s. His subordinate commanders included Yang Yandi and Huang Jin, the protagonists who make their appearance at the start of the chapter. There was another figure, Xian Biao, who later played a key role in linking the two to Cambodia. Relentless attacks from the Qing dislodged Deng Yao and his followers from Dragon Gate in 1660. They subsequently fled across the Vietnam border. In 1661, a combined Qing-Tonkin offensive resulted in the capture of Deng, who was promptly executed.[58]

[56] Andrade, *Lost Colony*, pp. 68–297; Hang, *Conflict and Commerce*, pp. 146–175.
[57] Marks, *Tigers*, pp. 97–99; Antony, 'Righteous Yang,' pp. 10–13.
[58] Antony, *Rats*, pp. 46–59; Wheeler, 'Placing,' p. 43; Hao, *Yongzheng Guangdong tongzhi*, juan 42, p. 3a, https://ctext.org/library.pl?if=gb&res=5155&remap=gb; *Zhongguo difangzhi jicheng*, Sheng zhiji: Liaoning 8, Liu Jinzhi, *Qianlong Shengjing tongzhi*, p. 284.

Xian, Yang, and other followers took refuge with a semi-autonomous local strongman in Tonkin, who furnished them with ships and weapons. Around this time, they also joined the Zheng maritime network. Through this connection, the Hainan routes merged into an integrated trading system, as Guangdong-based traders went beyond their traditional haunts near the Vietnamese border to become an increasingly influential presence in maritime East Asia. At least from the 1660s, the Dragon Gate conducted significant trade with Cambodia and Batavia. The Qing soon doubled down on its demand for Tonkin to extradite Xian and his group. Moreover, the VOC, in retaliation for its loss of Taiwan to the Zheng, launched a blockade of Tonkinese ports from 1663 to 1664 in an attempt to monopolize its key exports and deny them to the Chinese, many of them Zheng-affiliated merchants.[59]

Under these pressures, the Dragon Gate contingent relocated to Taiwan. Xian, Yang, and others lost some of their autonomy from their earlier days as opportunistic predators. As Zheng Chenggong's successors set out to forge a maritime state on the island by establishing bureaucratic institutions, the Dragon Gate became more integrated into the military hierarchy as subordinate commanders. Yang Yandi's unit, for instance, was named the Propriety and Martial Company (*Liwu zhen*). They became what Wheeler calls "client military entrepreneurs."[60] The Zheng wanted to utilize the Dragon Gate to open new land for natural resource exploitation and control strategic ports in maritime East Asia. Since Xian, Yang, and others already had close trading ties with Vietnam and Cambodia, this area was a direction where they could spearhead the expansion. Their interests would be in full alignment with the Zheng.[61]

In 1666, Xian Biao led a fleet of eight or nine junks and fifty-six men to the mouths of the Mekong. They settled down at Donay, the Cambodian province surrounding the Cochinchinese enclave of Saigon. It was a fertile area that could supply the needs of Taiwan and control the maritime approach to Phnom Penh and the flow of deerskin to the Japanese market. The settlements under Xian and his Dragon Gate associates prospered as a result. Vietnamese sources claim that the area only became a major commercial center during the 1680s. In fact, since the early seventeenth century, Donay had been a congregation point for the mercantile groups active in maritime East Asia, including Chinese, Austronesians, Europeans, and Japanese. The Dragon Gate brought

---

[59] *Qing shilu*, vol. 4: *Shengzu Renhuangdi shilu*, p. 270; Hoàng, *Silk for Silver*, pp. 113–114; Cheng (Zheng), *War, Trade and Piracy*, pp. 220–221.
[60] Wheeler, 'Placing,' p. 45; *Qing dai guan shu*, p. 33; Antony, *Rats*, pp. 59–60.
[61] Li Qingxin, 'Xi zei,' pp. 152–153.

these groups under its oversight. They also recruited Viet settlers to open new land, allowing Donay to achieve greater agricultural self-sufficiency.[62]

King Barom Reachea invited Xian Biao and his followers to Phnom Penh in the beginning of 1667. Over the course of the year, under Xian's patronage, some 3,000 more Chinese arrived, becoming the first organized Cantonese community in Cambodia. They may have been the forces of his subordinates or units from Taiwan, along with merchants. The newcomers quickly matched the original Fujian population in numbers. In fact, the ruler amended the code on the regulation of overseas trade. In addition to the Fujian shahbandar, he created a post specially for Xian as head of the Guangdong community.[63] Xian and his men soon got involved in the power struggles at the court. With the king's encouragement, they initiated a massacre of the Cochinchinese throughout the country, killing about 1,000 of them, including 500–600 in Phnom Penh. Through these brutal means, they helped Barom Reachea remove the influence of the Cochinchinese-backed co-king, Reameatipadey, the patron of the hapless victims.[64]

Xian exploited his favorable position to wage a personal vendetta against the VOC for blockading his ships at Tonkin and not repaying a debt owed to him. On the night of July 9, he, along with an armed band, broke into the Dutch trading lodge and murdered the head of the factory and some of his employees. Several months later, Barom Reachea wrote a letter of apology to Batavia. He reported the arrest and execution of Xian's alleged co-conspirators, the Fujian shahbandar, known in the Dutch records as Pavie, and six of his subordinates and the imprisonment of three Dutch turncoats who had joined in their massacre.[65]

Xian, on the other hand, had already fled Cambodia, since Chinese sources reveal that he was once again preying off the coasts of Guangdong and Hainan during the 1670s. In 1674, the Rebellion of the Three Feudatories, a revolt of three generals based in southern China, broke out against the Qing. The Zheng allied with the turncoat

---

[62] Cheng (Zheng), *War, Trade and Piracy*, pp. 220–221; Mak, *Histoire du Cambodge*, pp. 134–135; Trịnh, *Thông chí*, p. 202; Leclère, *Histoire de Cambodge*, p. 356.
[63] Mikaelian, *Royauté d'Oudong*, p. 345.
[64] Mak, 'Deuxième intervention,' pp. 234–235; Cheng (Zheng), *War, Trade and Piracy*, pp. 221–222.
[65] Mak, 'Deuxième intervention,' pp. 234–235; Cheng (Zheng), *War, Trade and Piracy*, pp. 221–222; van der Chijs, Colenbrander, and de Hullu, *Dagh-register*, p. 5. In my previous work, I had assumed that it was Xian Biao whom the Cambodian ruler executed. However, Xian goes by Piauwja or Pioja in the Dutch records. Pavie appears to be a different individual, given the transcription of the name and responsibility over the Fujian community.

Qing commanders and returned to their old mainland coastal bases. In 1677, Xian Biao and Yang Yandi left Taiwan and recaptured Dragon Gate. Antony explains that they may have abandoned the Zheng cause, which was on the verge of defeat. However, during 1676 and 1677, the Zheng and the feudatories were enjoying significant successes. They reoccupied coastal Fujian and penetrated as far as the Pearl River Delta. Their defeat would only become apparent two years later. Moreover, Yang left his wife and family behind in Taiwan. Seen in this context, Xian and Yang acted as vanguards for a seemingly imminent Zheng expansion into western Guangdong. By connecting the mainland acquisitions to the China Seas, including trade and communication routes between Taiwan and the water world, the Zheng could forge a more integrated commercial empire.[66]

The Enigma of Mo Jiu

Meanwhile, the situation in Cambodia rapidly deteriorated. In 1672, Barom Reachea was assassinated by his ambitious son-in-law. The co-king, Reameatipadey, fled to Cochinchina, where he soon passed away. Remeatipadey's nephew, Ang Nan (1654–1691), succeeded him in this role. The same year, Cochinchina reached a ceasefire with its northern neighbor of Tonkin that ended open hostilities and fixed a mutual boundary. The two sides would maintain a tense but peaceful coexistence for over a century. The Nguyễn now had the manpower and resources to devote entirely toward the southern frontier. In 1674, when the deceased king Barom Reachea's son, Ang Chee (1652–1677, r. 1673–1676), overthrew the son-in-law usurper, Lord Hiền dispatched an army to assist the new co-king, Ang Nan. The Cochinchinese initially made significant gains until King Ang Chee called for help from Siam. Siamese aid turned the tide of the war. In 1675, the bulk of the Cochinchinese forces withdrew. Ang Nan went along with them to Donay, where, under Cochinchinese protection, he continued to control a smaller portion of Cambodia, mostly the coastal areas.[67]

According to the *Việt Nam khai quốc chí truyện*, the same historical novel that mentions Yang Yandi's dramatic quest for asylum from the Nguyễn lord at the beginning of this chapter, the person who suggested that King Ang Chee appeal for aid from Siam was an *oknha* at his court. The

---

[66] Antony, *Rats*, pp. 59–60; Hang, *Conflict and Commerce*, pp. 200–223; *Zhongguo difangzhi jicheng*, Guangdong fuxian zhi ji 42, Mao and Wang, *Guangxu Wuchuan xianzhi*, pp. 376–377; *Qing dai guan shu*, p. 33.
[67] Mak, 'Deuxième intervention,' pp. 236–256.

nobleman was called Lạc Chi Gia, a "man of the Great Ming." The name corresponds to the Khmer title of Reachea Setthi, meaning "wealthy man of the kingdom." In the Cambodian hierarchy, he was the official in charge of customs at the ports.[68] Combined with other records, there is good reason to believe that he was, in fact, none other than Mo Jiu.

By his time, the diversity and cosmopolitanism of Cambodia's foreign population had decreased significantly. In 1672, five years after Xian Biao's massacre, the VOC closed its factory and left the country. There were still Austronesian traders and the mixed descendants of Japanese and Iberians who formed small but privileged creole communities. However, the vast majority were Minnanese and Cantonese merchants and sojourners.[69] Besides the shahbandar assigned to these two groups, a new Taiwan shahbandar handled ships and personnel from Zheng and rebel feudatory-held areas. King Ang Chee further elevated the Guangdong shahbandar to the role of general supervisor over all foreign groups. He received the prestigious rank of *oknha*, as opposed to the customary *chaoponhea*. The Khmer code that stipulated the appointment called him Oknha Siv. Mikaelian equates him to Mo Jiu. Indeed, one of Siv's main duties was to collect customs revenues in ports full of foreign traders. The job description fits well with the title of Reachea Setthi mentioned in the historical novel, the *Việt Nam khai quốc chí truyện*. The genealogical biography of the Mo by Vũ Thế Dinh (d. 1819), a military commander in The Port, provides additional backing, recounting that the Cambodian ruler allowed Jiu to handle "all matters related to trade and merchants."[70]

These findings constitute the first step toward uncovering and piecing together the early life and career of Mo Jiu, much of which remains wrapped in an enigma. The sources give different and often contradictory dates and narratives of when he arrived in Cambodia, his activities there, and how and at what point he came into possession of The Port. An effort will be made here to construct what I believe to be the most logical sequence of events based, as much as possible, on a comparative reading of Vietnamese, Qing, Cambodian, Siamese, and European accounts. I also consider how they synchronize with the relevant developments elsewhere in maritime East Asia. Of course, given the ambiguity of the records, alternative ways of conceptualizing the events are also conceivable.

---

[68] Nguyễn, *Việt Nam khai quốc*, p. 245; *Prachum phongsawadan* 1: *Phongsawadan khamen*, p. 235.
[69] Iwao, *Nanyō Nihonmachi*, pp. 113–116; Groslier, *Angkor and Cambodia*, p. 43; Buch, 'La Compagnie des Indes néerlandaises' 2, pp. 233–237.
[70] Mikaelian, *Royauté d'Oudong*, pp. 345–346, 350; Vũ, *Gia phả*, p. 93.

Figure 1.1 The Mo clan shrine in Dongling Village, in present-day Leizhou, Guangdong.
Photograph by author.

Mo Jiu was born on June 11, 1655, in the village of Dongling, Leizhou County (see Figure 1.1). The local Mo genealogy lists his original name as Shaoyuan. He came from one of the most prominent gentry clans on the peninsula, whose members enjoyed consistent success in the civil service examinations, with some becoming high officials in the late Ming. We can assume that Jiu, as a young man, received at least some education and achieved proficiency in Classical Chinese. However, the dynastic transition abruptly and permanently altered his life. The Mo, along with other gentry, supported local resistance leaders such as Deng Yao and helped fence their goods. To cut off these sources of aid, the Qing rigorously enforced the removal of the coastal population when its troops entered western Guangdong. As Li Qingxin highlights, the draconian measures ruined the fortunes of the local elites. Along with the ideological disinclination to shave one's head in the Manchu style, Mo Jiu, "unable to bear the chaos brought by the invasion of the Manchu barbarians, crossed the seas and went to Cambodia." He arrived in Phnom Penh in 1671, at the age of sixteen.[71]

For a teenage boy to make this lengthy journey, he had to work through the existing networks operated by the Dragon Gate contingent

---

[71] Li Qingxin, 'Mao Jiu,' pp. 172–184; Vũ, *Gia phả*, p. 93.

and the Zheng organization. Although no direct evidence can yet be located, Jiu most likely served under Xian Biao for some years before his arrival in Cambodia. According to the French traveler and missionary Pierre Poivre (1719–1786), Jiu once traded at Batavia and Manila. Interestingly, Xian also had close business ties with the Dutch to the point that there were unsettled debts. Manila was a major trading partner of the Zheng. Moreover, Jiu gained a prominent position and the title of *oknha* within three to four years of his arrival in Cambodia. His own charisma may have captured the attention of the king and gained him great royal favor, as Dinh's genealogical biography points out. However, this meteoric rise must have owed much more to the recommendation of Xian and the Dragon Gate. Jiu was probably Xian's replacement as Guangdong shahbandar after the latter fled the country.[72]

Jiu seemed to handle his tasks capably. King Ang Chee placed great trust in him as an adviser and adopted his suggestion to seek Siamese troops, if we are to trust the *Việt Nam khai quốc chí truyện*, the Cochinchinese historical novel. In 1676, after the withdrawal of the main Cochinchinese forces, Jiu was probably also behind the ruler's decision to recruit "Chinese from the island of Formosa" in launching a renewed attack on the co-king, Ang Nan. This information, drawn from a first-hand report of a French missionary, shows that the Dragon Gate continued to maintain a presence in Cambodia after Xian Biao's debacle. Some units likely arrived directly from Taiwan. They manned a total of three ships that joined Ang Chee's forces.[73]

However, the alliance failed in its objectives and nearly brought Jiu's blossoming career to an end. The co-king received renewed Cochinchinese assistance in launching a successful counterattack that forced King Ang Chee to abandon Oudong and flee for Siam. He died along the way in 1677. During this moment of crisis, his younger brother, Ang Sor (1656–1725), succeeded to the throne. Ang Sor turned out to be a vigorous and capable ruler who dominated Cambodian politics for the next fifty years. During this lengthy period, he either reigned directly or abdicated and exercised power from behind the scenes. He would, moreover, flexibly alter the various roles according to prevailing circumstances. In this manner, Ang Sor provided much-needed stability and continuity to the troubled kingdom.[74]

---

[72] Cheng (Zheng), *War, Trade, and Piracy*, pp. 222–227; Poivre, *Ouevres complettes*, p. 138; Vũ, *Gia phả*, p. 93; Mikaelian, *Royauté d'Oudong*, pp. 345–346.
[73] Mak, 'Deuxième intervention,' p. 254.
[74] Mak, 'Deuxième intervention,' pp. 254–256. Ang Sor reigned formally as king during the years of 1677–1695, 1696–1700, 1701–1702, and 1705–1706.

One of Ang Sor's first acts as new ruler was to send a desperate appeal for help from King Narai (1632–1688, r. 1656–1688) of Siam. Narai promptly responded by sending an expeditionary force. The Siamese troops advanced along two established routes, one on land from the western border and the other by ship on the Gulf of Siam. The second path would naturally bring them to the shores of The Port. Apparently, the Siamese fleet sailed up to Banteay Meas, where they discovered Mo Jiu and carried him off to Ayutthaya. He remained a hostage in the capital for the next decade, where we leave him as he pondered his options.[75]

Great Transitions

Whatever the nature of Mo Jiu's earlier ties to the Dragon Gate, he largely missed out on a series of events in which this Ming loyalist contingent took center stage and paved the way for his establishment of The Port. Antony, Wheeler, and other scholars have correctly pointed out that the Dragon Gate did not seek asylum under the Nguyễn lord in 1679, as claimed by many Vietnamese sources. At the time, Yang Yandi and Xian Biao were still entrenched in their home base, while their ships alternated among Hainan, Guangzhou, Taiwan, and Cambodia, conducting trade, patrolling, and raiding and plundering in the South China Sea. The area of their activities naturally included the long, winding coastline of Vietnam. It would not be surprising if a large contingent of vessels docked near Đà Nẵng from time to time, whether to escape harsh weather or even to engage in plundering sprees. And, of course, the Nguyễn lord viewed them with a great degree of wariness, as Wheeler has shown. In fact, the Zheng and their affiliates, including the Dragon Gate, had trading relations with Cochinchina through the port of Hội An since at least the 1630s. So, these were an ongoing, familiar menace rather than a sudden intrusion.[76]

Wheeler correctly suspects that the relationship between Cochinchina and the Dragon Gate was initially characterized more by rivalry than any sort of alliance. Indeed, the commanders supported Cambodian kings who had opposed the Nguyễn and leaned toward Siam. However, the situation in China drastically altered the existing configuration. In 1681, the Qing defeated all the rebel feudatories and drove the Zheng from

---

[75] Mak, 'Deuxième intervention,' pp. 256–261; Nguyễn Dynasty, *Thực lục*, vol. 1, p. 273; Vũ, *Gia phả*, pp. 95–96.
[76] Antony, *Rats*, p. 58; Cheng (Zheng), *War, Trade and Piracy*, pp. 98, 235; Wheeler, '1683,' pp. 144–146.

their mainland possessions. In the process, the court secured the surrender of Xian Biao, who, along with his men, received seeds and tools and settled into an agricultural colony in Guangdong. Yang Yandi and Huang Jin now became the leading figures in the contingent. In 1682, the Qing occupied the stronghold of Dragon Gate, forcing them into permanent exile abroad.[77]

According to the report of a Chinese junk captain to the Tokugawa authorities in Nagasaki that year, Yang Yandi evacuated his troops, numbering some 3,000 men, from the Leizhou Peninsula and Hainan on seventy ships to Mesar, in Donay. Many scholars have spoken of this exile as a permanent break with the Zheng on Taiwan. They are correct, but to be precise, a severe disagreement broke out among Zheng partisans over whether to surrender to the Qing or relocate to a new colony abroad. In 1683, a Qing naval expedition into the Taiwan Strait forced the issue. The main Zheng leadership chose to surrender and relocate to mainland China, yielding Taiwan to Qing control. However, an influential faction, consisting of Dragon Gate commanders such as Yang Yandi, chose to sail to the water world, where a base had already been established during the 1660s. According to an unofficial or "wild" history (*yeshi*) sympathetic to the Ming cause, ships from Taiwan carried Zheng Chenggong's younger brother, Lushe, and his entourage to a place called "Dongboshe Island," meaning Donay.[78] There appeared to have truly been an effort to restore the Zheng organization overseas.

Despite the grand intentions, Zheng Lushe evidently lacked the influence and leadership skills to reconstitute the exiles into a cohesive force, and he soon disappeared from the historical records. The Dragon Gate became the instrument of other players in the geopolitics of mainland Southeast Asia. Since Donay came under the control of the Cambodian co-king, Ang Nan, Yang Yandi entered an alliance with him. It lends credence to the claim in the *Việt Nam khai quốc chí truyện*, the Cochinchinese historical novel, of him becoming sworn brothers with the ruler, except the ruler in question was the co-king and not Ang Sor, the main king. The brotherhood probably had concrete substance, since Ang Nan took a Chinese wife, who may have been a sister or cousin of Yang, or someone drawn from the Dragon Gate community. There is little evidence of direct contact between the Dragon Gate and the

---

[77] Wheeler, '1683,' p. 144; Hao, *Yongzheng Guangdong tongzhi*, *juan* 42, p. 49b, https://ctext.org/library.pl?if=gb&res=5155&remap=gb; Hayashi, *Ka'i hentai*, vol. 1, pp. 366–367.

[78] Hayashi, *Ka'i hentai*, vol. 1, pp. 366–367; Zheng, *Yeshi wuwen*, p. 168. Dongboshe Island is an alternative manner of writing Dongpuzhai, the Chinese transcription of Donay, and the Vietnamese equivalent, Đông Phố.

Nguyễn at that point. Nonetheless, the Cochinchinese benefited, since they did not have to expend resources of their own to support the co-king in his struggle with the Siamese-backed king, Ang Sor.[79]

Yang and his units joined Ang Nan in a renewed offensive soon after their arrival in 1682. The alliance initially occupied the entire length of the Mekong and its tributaries up to the outskirts of Phnom Penh. In fear, Ang Sor abandoned Oudong and fled westward. The offensive soon ground to a halt, especially after a Siamese force came to the aid of the king. In the wake of another failed attack in 1684, Yang sent envoys to Ang Sor, claiming that the Dragon Gate forces merely wanted to borrow territory as a staging ground to prepare for an imminent return to the Chinese coast. They had no long-term ambitions to occupy Cambodia. Meanwhile, King Narai of Siam, Ang Sor's protector, dispatched envoys to the Dragon Gate. Narai, claiming that he enjoyed friendly ties with Taiwan, invited Yang and his men to permanently reside in Siam. He promised the Dragon Gate forces a more secure base and the privilege of controlling maritime trade as before. Yang refused the offer, but he eventually grew apart from the Cochinchinese-backed co-king, Ang Nan, and left his patron. The Dragon Gate appeared to have then paid tentative allegiance to Ang Sor.[80]

The fragile equilibrium broke down three years later, in 1687, because of broader developments in maritime East Asia. The Qing victory over the Zheng and annexation of Taiwan in 1683 owed much to the construction of a formidable navy from scratch. Overnight, China once again became the biggest naval power in East Asia, a position that it had not held since the fifteenth century. However, this success depended, in large part, upon the assistance of Zheng defectors, who provided much of the leadership, expertise, and sailors. After the incorporation of Taiwan, they formed an influential maritime faction that the court in Beijing could not entirely control. Its leading figure, Shi Lang (1621–1696), a former Zheng partisan, had commanded the expedition on Taiwan. He had the ambition to dominate the newly occupied island as his personal fiefdom and recreate the maritime hegemony of the Zheng.[81]

In 1684, Shi organized an expeditionary fleet under his subordinate, Chen Ang, a merchant from an educated gentry background. In a period of five years, Chen and his ships sailed, off and on, to different ports

---

[79] *Prachum phongsawadan* 1: *Phongsawadan khamen*, p. 187; Hán-Nôm A. 832: Phạm, *Cao Man ki lược*, n. p.; Trịnh, *Thông chí*, p. 202; Leclère, *Histoire de Cambodge*, pp. 355–356.
[80] Hayashi, *Ka'i hentai*, vol. 1, pp. 366–367, 398–399; Launay, *Cochinchine*, vol. 1, pp. 320–321.
[81] Zheng Weizhong (Cheng Wei-chung), 'Shi Lang,' pp. 37–69.

across the China Seas. The stated purpose was to inform Zheng merchants and military remnants still abroad of the news of Taiwan's fall and persuade them to lay down their arms and return. A more hidden motive involved spying on the overseas Chinese communities and identifying recalcitrant Ming loyalist groups, with the possible aim of launching a large-scale campaign against them at a later point.[82]

Chen Ang's itinerary included Cochinchina and Cambodia. During his journey, he apparently achieved contact with the Dragon Gate leadership and handed over a written demand from the Fujian governor-general to surrender to the Qing and return to Fuzhou, the provincial capital, in exchange for clemency. Yang Yandi must have learned then that the Qing had taken diligent care of his wife and the rest of his family and resettled them from Taiwan to the mainland. Undoubtedly moved by this assurance, Yang hoped to give up and leave Cambodia. His second-in-command, Huang Jin, adamantly insisted upon staying. He wanted to preserve the Dragon Gate's fighting power overseas and double down on its gains. The disagreement between the two intensified over 1688, when they once again teamed up with Ang Nan to revolt against Ang Sor. They got as far as Phnom Penh, but a Siamese-backed counteroffensive halted their further advance to Oudong and routed them.[83]

After fleeing back to the Dragon Gate base at Mesar, Huang Jin assassinated Yang Yandi and took command of the entire contingent. With five ships and 500 men, Huang initiated a blockade of the Mekong. They would often raid villages situated along the banks of the waterways and canals, kidnapping Khmer commoners and holding them for ransom. All vessels, even royal Cambodian ships on official business on the domestic routes, were forced to stop and pay prohibitive duties. His actions so upset King Ang Sor that the ruler set up barricades and chains on the Mekong and Bassac near Phnom Penh and planned an offensive to dislodge them.[84]

Amid the chaos, the co-king, Ang Nan, fled to Cochinchina and appealed to Lord Hiền's successor, Nguyễn Phúc Thái (Lord Nghĩa, 1649–1691, r. 1687–1691) for assistance. This request took place around the time when the Qing fleet under Chen Ang paid a call at Cochinchina. Chen had another letter from the governor-general of Guangdong and

---

[82] Hayashi, *Ka'i hentai*, vol. 1, pp. 415–417, 419, 431; Salmon, 'Réfugiés Ming,' pp. 179–180.

[83] Hayashi, *Ka'i hentai*, vol. 1, pp. 367, 784; *Taiwan guanxi*, p. 31; *Qing dai guan shu*, p. 33; *Prachum phongsawadan* 1: *Phongsawadan khamen*, p. 187; Hán-Nôm A. 832: Phạm, *Cao Man ki lược*, n. p.

[84] Nguyễn, *Việt Nam Khai quốc*, pp. 261–262; Nguyễn Dynasty, *Thực lục*, vol. 1, pp. 89–90.

Guangxi, Guangdong being the Dragon Gate contingent's home province. In it, the governor-general condemned Huang Jin for his unrighteous deeds, which brought misery and suffering upon foreign countries and endangered the Chinese coastline. The letter requested the Nguyễn lord to launch a punitive expedition against him. Whether the Qing knew it or not, the Nguyễn had long coveted Donay. Occupying it would connect the enclave of Saigon to the Cham rump state of Panduranga, which was already under Cochinchinese domination, and directly tap into part of the resource-rich Mekong Delta. Moreover, the area had seen a huge influx of Viet and Chinese migrants, whose numbers had diluted the original Khmer and Cham populations.[85]

The governor-general's request provided Lord Nghĩa with the legitimacy and moral right to act. In 1689, a Cochinchinese force of over 6,000 men and seventy ships came to the aid of Ang Nan. The commanders of the expedition pretended to enlist Huang Jin's support, calling upon him to serve as the vanguard for an upcoming expedition against King Ang Sor, who was already poised to attack the Dragon Gate. In reality, the Cochinchinese prepared an ambush. When their forces met up with Huang, they pounced upon him. Huang fled into the interior, disappearing from the historical records, but his wife and family members were rounded up and killed. With the backing of Ang Nan and the Cochinchinese, Chen Shangchuan emerged as the new commander of the Dragon Gate contingent.[86]

According to Wheeler, Chen "never served the Zheng regime at all and was probably nothing more than a career brigand." Indeed, Qing documents show that he was never garrison commander of Gao-Lei-Lian, the title given to him in the Vietnamese records. Before the Qing permanently occupied the three prefectures in 1680, the position was held almost continuously by Zu Zeqing (1632–1680), who constantly changed sides among the Qing, the feudatory generals, and the Zheng. Chen may have later appropriated this title to increase his prestige and standing. Moreover, Chen does not get mentioned at all in the *Việt Nam khai quốc chí truyện*, the eighteenth-century Cochinchinese historical novel. His name first appears in Trịnh Hoài Đức's gazetteer in the early nineteenth century and then gets picked up in official Nguyễn dynasty compilations. Đức may have wanted to cultivate a legitimate lineage and founding legend for Minh Hương elites such as himself through an

---

[85] Hayashi, *Ka'i hentai*, vol. 1, p. 431; vol. 2, pp. 1127–1128; Nguyễn, *Khai quốc*, p. 262; Nguyễn Dynasty, *Thực lục*, vol. 1, p. 90; Leclère, *Histoire de Cambodge*, p. 356; Choi, *Southern Vietnam*, pp. 39–40.
[86] Nguyễn Dynasty, *Thực lục*, vol. 1, pp. 90–92.

association with the Dragon Gate and whitewashing its shadier aspects. Chen proved perfect for the task, since prior to his arrival in Cochinchina, he was relatively unknown compared to Yang and Huang, whose reputations were tarnished. Besides his legacy as a Ming loyalist pioneer, he also acknowledged the dominant position of the Cochinchinese rulers.[87]

However, Chen Shangchuan was not entirely an upstart, even if his credentials were exaggerated. Accounts contemporary to his time confirm that he was a subordinate of Yang Yandi and had connections to Taiwan. Moreover, there may have been a marriage alliance with the top Dragon Gate leaders. According to the clan genealogy from Chen Shangchuan's native village of Tiantou, in Wuchuan County of western Guangdong, one of his two wives had the surname of Xian, most likely a relative of Xian Biao. However, Chen's position in the Dragon Gate hierarchy was probably minor compared to Yang and Huang Jin. The troops under Chen's leadership settled near present-day Biên Hòa, a remote and sparsely populated part of Donay north of Saigon. It must be pointed out that his base was subordinate to Yang Yandi at Mesar farther to the south, and not a separate force, as implied by Đức and the official Nguyễn dynasty narrative.[88]

Despite the massive Cochinchinese intervention, the invasion of Cambodia once again failed, as King Ang Sor, with Siamese assistance, drove out the combined forces. Nonetheless, the Cochinchinese gained much more than they lost from the campaign. In exchange for their support, Chen Shangchuan had ceded to the Nguyễn lord his original area of settlement at Biên Hòa and proceeded to occupy the main Dragon Gate base of Mesar.[89] Ang Nan, who relied heavily on both men, had no choice but to approve.

In 1699, the Nguyễn set up administrative divisions in the recently acquired territory. Like the rest of Cochinchina, and perhaps more so because of the recent nature of the annexation, the militarized institution of the camp (*dinh*) administered all affairs, including tax collection, law enforcement, and frontier defense. The lord ordered the transfer of the Frontier Suppression camp, previously located to the north of Champa, to Biên Hòa. Another camp, Border Garrison (Phiên Trấn), operated from Saigon. True to its name, it would serve as the vanguard for future

---

[87] Hao, *Yongzheng Guangdong tongzhi*, juan 7, pp. 19b, 22a, 23b; *juan* 42, p. 49b, https://ctext.org/library.pl?if=gb&res=5155&remap=gb; Wheeler, '1683,' pp. 143–145.
[88] Hayashi, *Ka'i hentai*, vol. 2, p. 1265; Nguyễn Dynasty, *Thực lục*, vol. 1, pp. 90–92; *Tiantou cun Chen shi*, n. p.
[89] Nguyễn Dynasty, *Thực lục*, vol. 1, pp. 90–92, 103.

expansion to the south and west. Biên Hòa became the seat of a parallel civilian administration, Gia Định prefecture, which, in turn, oversaw two districts encompassing the scope of both camps. However, these units, based on the Lê model used in the north, appeared to be largely symbolic at the time of their establishment and for some time afterward, with no record of any civil officials serving in these roles.[90]

At this point, after decades of warfare in Cambodia and devastated by the internecine conflict between Yang Yandi and Huang Jin, the ranks of the Dragon Gate had severely diminished. Soldiers were killed off or deserted, with many of them going back to China. According to a report from a captain of a junk from Cambodia to the Nagasaki authorities, Chen's following had dwindled to 400–500 men and six or seven ships, and there were no longer fresh recruits. Chen was so strapped of revenues to administer his part of Donay that he resorted to periodic blockades of the Mekong and the extortion and plundering of passing vessels.[91] Capitalizing upon his growing weakness, the Nguyễn made him an offer that he could not refuse. In 1699, Chen was appointed the military governor (đô đốc) of the Frontier Garrison camp in Saigon. However, he could maintain his autonomous base at Mesar and center his activities around there. A junk captain from Cochinchina confirmed Chen's submission to the Nagasaki authorities, saying that Chen had become a "military headman" for the Nguyễn. This dependence was mirrored in the economic realm. Both Saigon and Mesar, the areas under Chen's oversight, gradually declined as commercial hubs and became subsidiary ports to Biên Hòa, with which a frequent communication was maintained.[92]

A similar consolidation occurred across the border in Cambodia under Ang Sor. The king's old archnemesis, Ang Nan, had passed away in 1691. Through skillful negotiations, Ang Sor persuaded the former co-king's half-Chinese son, Ang Em (1674–1736), to return from exile in Cochinchina. The long-standing political division between maritime and inland Cambodia had temporarily healed. However, the issue of succession continued to plague the king. In 1695, he tried abdicating in favor of another royal relative, but the young man died after sitting on the throne for a mere ten months, and Ang Sor was forced to become king again.[93]

---

[90] Nguyễn Dynasty, *Thực lục*, vol. 1, p. 103; Trịnh, *Thông chí*, p. 205. For more on the relationship between the camp and civilian administrative units, see Yang Baoyun, *Principauté des Nguyễn*, pp. 33–37.
[91] Hayashi, *Ka'i hentai*, vol. 2, p. 1266.
[92] Nguyễn Dynasty, *Thực lục*, vol. 1, p. 119; K. W. Taylor, *History of the Vietnamese*, p. 323; Hayashi, *Ka'i hentai*, vol. 3, p. 2088; Trần, *Nam Bộ*, pp. 173–182.
[93] *Prachum phongsawadan 1: Phongsawadan khamen*, pp. 188–190; Hán-Nôm A. 832: Phạm, *Cao Man ki lược*, n. p.

Ang Sor then faced a conflicted choice between Ang Em, the deceased co-king Ang Nan's son, who received the backing of Cochinchina, and his own son, the pro-Siamese Ang Tham (1690–1747). Given the heavy involvement of the two outside powers, Ang Sor had to strike a delicate balance, while anticipating where the winds blew in the larger geopolitical environment. In 1699, after defeating a Cochinchinese-backed insurgency, he probably decided to placate the Nguyễn lord by abdicating in favor of Ang Em. The designated heir reigned for only a year before he gave the throne back to Ang Sor. In 1702, Ang Sor signaled a leaning toward the Siamese side when he placed twelve-year-old Ang Tham on the throne. But two years later, Ang Tham followed Ang Em's example and returned the throne to his father.[94]

While tackling the thorny issue of succession, Ang Sor enacted major institutional and judicial reforms aimed at achieving greater centralization and consolidation, especially in response to external threats. Their most visible and important legacy involved the creation and compilation of a vast corpus of legal codes that meticulously regulated the operations of bureaucracy and society. These laws continue to influence the Cambodian legal system to the present day. Another important measure involved the reassertion of control over the provinces of the water world, whose administration had languished amid the continuous chaos and warfare of the past decade. He ordered the restoration of customs stations at Sacred Pond, Bassac, Black Water, and Kramoun Sar.[95]

Because the Dragon Gate dominated the mouths of the Mekong through blockade and piracy for years, the Gulf of Siam coast became Cambodia's only reliable means of accessing the trading networks of maritime East Asia. Many merchants had redirected their business to Banteay Meas. Accordingly, a series of tollhouses were established "along the river" and "river promontory of Banteay Meas." These would correspond to the land route and Fortress River culminating in The Port.[96]

The Return of Mo Jiu

Let us now return to Mo Jiu in Ayutthaya. After years of serving as a hostage, he was able to bribe an influential official at the court into granting him permission to relocate to a Siamese dependency known as

---

[94] *Prachum phongsawadan* 1: *Phongsawadan khamen*, pp. 188–191; Hán-Nôm A. 832: Phạm, *Cao Man ki lược*, n. p.; Leclère, *Histoire de Cambodge*, pp. 366–369.
[95] Mikaelian, *Royauté d'Oudong*, pp. 175–181, 355; Eng, *Mahaboros khmer*, vol. 4, p. 54.
[96] Mikaelian, *Royauté d'Oudong*, p. 348.

Vạn Tuế Sơn in the Vietnamese records. It was most likely C: Wanfosui **T: Bang Pla Soi**, a busy commercial port and a center of Chinese settlement in present-day Chonburi, situated along the Gulf of Siam coast.[97] From there, it would be easier for him to make an escape when the opportune conditions arose. An unspecified "internal incident" mentioned in the Vietnamese sources gave Jiu the opening to act. It most likely referred to the palace coup in 1688 in which Phetracha (1632–1703, r. 1688–1703), a royal councillor, took advantage of a popular uprising to usurp the throne from Narai, who died shortly afterward. Jiu took advantage of this chaotic situation to flee Siam, disguised as a commoner.[98]

He took refuge at Ream, an island right across the Cambodian border, around 1690. According to Dinh's genealogical biography, Jiu sent rich bribes to the "favored consort of the kingdom and her ministers." The source must be referring to Ang Sor's wife, whom the ruler elevated to the title of queen the same year. Because of her influence, Jiu recovered his original position as supervisor of foreign merchants. Given the importance of the Gulf of Siam, he and some of the other shahbandar were stationed at Banteay Meas rather than Phnom Penh.[99] In a manner like the Chinese garrison commanders, or Chen Chong Tok, before his time, he acquired his own mercenary army, consisting of several hundred officers and soldiers.[100] They would probably include his relatives, associates from his Leizhou hometown, and professional warriors recruited locally or from China. Their task was to oversee the defense of the coastline. Apparently, the Dragon Gate's activities had severely destabilized the Gulf of Siam littoral, exacerbating the preexisting predation from multiethnic piratical bands. In exchange for a promise to combat piracy,

---

[97] Vũ, *Gia phả*, pp. 95–96; Nguyễn Dynasty, *Thực lục*, vol. 1, p. 273; Macauley, *Distant Shores*, p. 53.

[98] The Vietnamese sources do not specify how long Mo Jiu stayed in Siam. Trương Minh Đạt believes that it was from 1689 to 1699. See Trương, *Nghiên cứu*, vol. 1, pp. 76–79; Trương, *Nghiên cứu*, vol. 2, pp. 102–104. I believe, however, that Jiu went to Siam earlier, since the circumstances of his captivity described in the Vietnamese sources accord nicely with the defeat of King Ang Chee in 1677. And the only time when a political crisis in Siam serious enough to generate the widespread chaos allowing Mo Jiu to escape unnoticed was 1688. See Vũ, *Gia phả*, p. 96; Baker and Phongpaichit, *History of Ayutthaya*, pp. 167–170.

[99] According to a Franciscan missionary report from 1770, Banteay Meas served as the "first residence of the governors" of The Port. It can be assumed that Mo Jiu spent most of his time there, even as he administered Ream as his personal fief. See AMEP, Cochinchine, vol. 745: 'Relation des Franciscains,' p. 180.

[100] Nguyễn Dynasty, *Thực lục*, vol. 1, p. 273; Trịnh, *Thông chí*, p. 304; Vũ, *Gia phả*, p. 94; Mikaelian, *Royauté d'Oudong*, pp. 219, 349; *Prachum phongsawadan* 1: *Phongsawadan khamen*, p. 235; Lê Quang Định, *Hoàng Việt*, p. 989.

Jiu was given a revenue farm in the provinces along the Gulf of Siam coastline.[101] Moreover, he could keep Ream as his personal base. He soon transformed the place into a bustling site for trade.[102]

In the entrepreneurial spirit of finding new sources of revenue, Jiu sponsored the opening of the sparsely populated hinterlands of the water world beyond the coastal areas. Tonkin literati Phạm Nguyễn Du (1739–1786) describes these places as "completely uncultivated. Vicious snakes and strange creatures, swampy water and poisonous weeds congregate. Fishermen and woodcutters rarely visit, and there [are] no traces of habitation."[103] Mo Jiu's son, Tianci, when describing the original condition of the Hà Tiên area as a "remote wilderness," was probably referring to these hinterlands.[104] Jiu drained the swamps, cleared the foliage, and constructed canals. He tried recruiting migrants from other parts of Cambodia but appeared to have little success. On one occasion, he took in a large group of Lao refugees. Fleeing disorder and civil war in their homeland, they had settled in villages south of Phnom Penh. Since they frequently caused trouble and harassed the residents in their new locale, the court arranged for Mo Jiu to settle them on Ream. The newcomers did not stay there for long. They launched a rebellion that Jiu crushed. Some fled into the forests, while others went to Cochinchina.[105]

The most sustainable source of labor for exploiting the new land was the land-hungry Viet and Cham migrants, who had streamed into the core of the water world starting from the late seventeenth century. After Phú Quốc and the islands of the Gulf of Siam coast, they established several farming communities in the hilly area west of The Port's center. The Cambodians collectively called the hills around which they congregated Phnom Yuon (Viet Mountain). Jiu further established seven villages and communes for the Viet in Phú Quốc, Black Water, Kramoun Sar, Kampot, Ream, and Kampong Som.[106] Since the Cochinchinese settlers

---

[101] Sellers, *Princes of Hà-Tiên*, pp. 16–17; Pérez, 'Españoles en el imperio de Annam' 11, p. 201.
[102] Sellers, Trương Minh Đạt, and others portray Mo Jiu's stay in Ream as a separate event from his involvement in The Port or the Cambodian court. While it is certainly true that Ream often served as a shelter of last resort during times of crisis until the 1710s, the admittedly fragmented evidence from different primary records points to Jiu concurrently engaging in other activities in and around The Port. See Trương, *Nghiên cứu*, vol. 1, pp. 76–77; vol. 2, pp. 103–105; Sellers, *Princes of Hà-Tiên*, pp. 20–25.
[103] Hán-Nôm A. 2939: Phạm, *Nam hành*, n. p.
[104] Hán-Nôm A. 441: Mao, *Hexian shiyong*, n. p.
[105] Eng, *Mahaboros khmer*, vol. 5, p. 74; Luang, *Racha phongsawadan*, pp. 107–108; Hán-Nôm A. 832: Phạm, *Cao Man ki lược*, n. p.; Leclère, *Histoire de Cambodge*, pp. 368–370.
[106] Nguyễn Dynasty, *Thực lục*, vol. 1, p. 273; Trịnh, *Thông chí*, p. 304; Trương, *Nghiên cứu*, vol. 2, pp. 21–23.

were entirely dependent on his patronage, they formed a solid base of support separate from the Cambodian court.

He cemented the connection by marrying a Viet woman named Bùi Thị Lẫm, whose native place was a settlement near Biên Hòa. At some point in the first decade of the eighteenth century, on the night of April 7, his new wife conceived their son and heir to his enterprise at their residence in Ream, located next to a lagoon. As local lore would have it, auspicious rays of light suddenly brightened up the dark sky at the moment of his birth. Then, a statue of the Buddha over a meter high emerged from the water close to the shoreline, and its radiance reflected across the lagoon's surface. Witnessing the miraculous spectacle, some Khmer monks went to Mo Jiu and congratulated him on his immense fortune. It was a sign that his son would become a leader of tremendous wisdom and capability, they told him. Overjoyed, Jiu tried to move the Buddha statue, but could not lift it up no matter how hard he tried. In the end, he ordered the construction of a Theravada temple along the shoreline to house it. The son's personal name was Cong, and his style name was Shilin, but he was most commonly and popularly known as Tianci, a "gift from Heaven." The couple would go on to have a daughter named C: **Mo Jinding** V: Mạc Kim Định, who would play an influential role in the governance of The Port.[107]

Jiu's settlement at Ream continued to prosper. The number of vessels from different lands multiplied to the point that its harbor and markets became highly congested. Needing a more spacious commercial settlement, he again made use of his connections to the Cambodian court. It could be about this time that Mo Jiu formed a close relationship with Ang Em. Later, Jiu would outfit a mission to Japan under his name. Perhaps with Ang Em's assistance, as well as additional promises of fighting piracy and ensuring maritime security, King Ang Sor granted Jiu administrative control over The Port, separating Seashore as a province from Banteay Meas for the final time. The Port was already becoming a bustling crossroads where merchants could conduct trade directly after disembarking from their ships and without having to travel upriver. Soon after Mo Jiu took over and with his encouragement, the new settlement not only surpassed his former base of Ream, but also

---

[107] Vũ, Gia phả, p. 96; Nguyễn Dynasty, Nhất thống chí, vol. 3, pp. 286–287; Trịnh, Thông chí, pp. 184–185; Chen Jinghe (Chin Kei-wa), 'Hexian Mao shi,' 217–218. The primary records provide different years for Mo Tianci's birth, ranging from 1706 to 1718. I avoid a conclusive decision but feel that the years between 1700 and 1710 seem more convincing. Lê Quý Đôn's record, published in 1776, contemporary to Tianci's later years, asserts that Tianci was already "over seventy years of age." See Lê Quý Đôn, Tạp lục (Giáo dục), vol. 2, p. 398.

Figure 1.2 Statue of Mo Jiu, situated at the current Hà Tiên city limits southeast of the city center on National Road 80.
Photograph by author.

Banteay Meas to become the preeminent commercial center along the Gulf of Siam littoral.[108]

In 1707, Ang Sor, ailing and in no mood to reign any further, abdicated once again in favor of his son, Ang Tham, this time for good. With Ang Sor gradually fading out of the picture, tensions between Ang Tham and Ang Em rapidly escalated.[109] Mo Jiu sensed renewed danger on the horizon. Since Ang Tham had Siamese protection, he feared a repeat of his earlier experience of captivity in Ayutthaya. He decided to act upon the suggestions of a close adviser and seek protection from Cochinchina.[110] He sent two envoys to Huế, where they received the warm reception of Nguyễn Phúc Chu (Lord Minh, 1675–1725, r. 1691–1725). The lord, eager to acquire whatever bargaining chips he

---

[108] Vũ, *Gia phả*, p. 97; Trịnh, *Thông chí*, p. 304; Kondo, *Gaiban tsūsho*, vol. 1, pp. 137–138; Pérez, 'Españoles en el imperio de Annam' 11, p. 201.
[109] *Prachum phongsawadan* 1: *Phongsawadan khamen*, pp. 190–191; Hán-Nôm A. 832: Phạm, *Cao Man ki lược*, n. p.; Leclère, *Histoire de Cambodge*, pp. 369–370.
[110] Vũ, *Gia phả*, p. 98; Trịnh, *Thông chí*, p. 304.

could to expand his influence over Cambodia, readily recognized Jiu as the vassal of an independent Hà Tiên Kingdom (C: *Hexian guo* V: *Hà Tiên quốc*) (see Figure 1.2).[111]

The name of Hà Tiên, which Jiu devised for The Port, actually had earlier antecedents. A similar term had appeared in 1682, when French missionaries traveling by cart from Banteay Meas boarded a boat at a coastal hamlet that they called Atiam.[112] At the time, Mo Jiu was probably still a hostage in Siam. Moreover, the place was most likely not The Port itself, which already had a fortress, because of its historic role as an established bastion of defense against a Siamese invasion by sea.[113] The term Atiam was probably derived from Peam, the Khmer for "seashore." The French might be referring to the location of the hamlet within the province of Seashore or, literally, being next to the sea along the Gulf of Siam. What Mo Jiu did was to Sinicize Atiam to C: Hexian **V: Hà Tiên**, meaning "River of Fairies," a name laden with mystique, legend, and rich historical allusions. He then applied the name both to his newly acquired realm and its main urban center, the former Seashore provincial seat. So, most likely, the etymology of Hà Tiên came through the mediation of a European language, perhaps Portuguese, who were a sizable community in Cambodia, and in this order: Peam → A Peam → Atiam → Hà Tiên.

Jiu's Viet wife, Bùi Thị Lẫm, appeared to have played a vital role in initiating contacts with Cochinchina. A brief report transmitted to Frederick Pigou (d. 1792), director of the English East India Company (EIC), in 1771 mentions that she was "a considerable woman … the better to focus his conquest." She either came from a wealthy family that acquired great fortune from trade or landholdings or had valuable political connections. It may very well have been at least the latter, since the vice-commander of the Frontier Suppression garrison at Biên Hòa, where her family came from, was Nguyễn Cửu Vân. He, in turn, cooperated closely with Chen Shangchuan.[114] Bùi Thị Lẫm's father may have served as an officer under Vân. Vân would play an instrumental role in the events that followed.

In 1713, open warfare broke out between Ang Tham and Ang Em. The Port may have been the key reason for the hostilities. Ang Tham was furious at Mo Jiu for sharing control over a vital and strategic part of the

---

[111] Nguyễn Dynasty, *Nhất thống chí*, vol. 3, p. 334; Vũ, *Gia phả*, p. 98.
[112] Mak, *Histoire du Cambodge*, pp. 365–366.
[113] Trương, *Nghiên cứu*, vol. 2, pp. 308–309; Sellers, *Princes of Hà-Tiên*, pp. 27–28.
[114] BL, IOR/G/4/1: Borneo, p. 347; Trịnh, *Thông chí*, p. 185; Nguyễn Dynasty, *Thực lục*, vol. 1, p. 115.

country's coastline with a foreign power, especially the patron of his bitter rival for the throne. According to Phạm Nguyễn Du, "the Khmer, in anger, attacked Jiu and his troops." Since Jiu had just acquired The Port, he did not have time to build an adequate defensive infrastructure other than relying upon the antiquated fortress in the heart of the city. Unable to mount an effective resistance, he fled to Huế.[115] Narratives of him drawn from nineteenth-century Nguyễn dynasty sources make no mention of the escape. They claim that Jiu traveled to Huế voluntarily to express his gratitude to the Nguyễn lord. But a careful analysis of events occurring in Cochinchina, Siam, and Cambodia at the time lends greater credence to Phạm Nguyễn Du's version. The Nguyễn dynasty sources probably omitted mention of the exact circumstances of Jiu's visit as a face-saving measure for the Mo clan.

During his exile, he had a personal audience with Lord Minh. Perhaps anticipating that the ruler would take advantage of his adversity to demand more concessions from him, Jiu preemptively asked to place The Port under direct Cochinchinese rule. Highly pleased, Lord Minh gave Hà Tiên the status of garrison (*trấn*), and appointed Jiu its commander (*tổng binh*). He would pay tribute to the lord once every two years. Jiu was also incorporated into the Cochinchinese nobility, receiving the title of Cửu Ngọc marquis (*hầu*).[116] The rank and title roughly corresponded to his Cambodian assignment as a military governor.

Having sealed this deal, the lord arranged for Nguyễn Cửu Vân to escort Jiu and help him recover The Port. He must have been a witness to the Cochinchinese attack on King Ang Tham in 1714 or 1715, led by Vân and Chen Shangchuan, along with mobilized Lao refugees and highlanders who had fled to Saigon. This event had to have occurred first before completing the land journey to The Port. The combined force overwhelmed enemy resistance and surrounded Oudong. Trapped inside for three months, Ang Tham, his son, and his younger brother escaped from the southern gate of the capital to Ayutthaya. Ang Em then ascended the throne.[117]

It must have been during this journey that Mo Jiu got to know Chen Shangchuan, if the two had not already met. After accompanying him back to The Port, part of the Cochinchinese forces remained behind. There must have also been members of the former Dragon Gate, who

---

[115] Hán-Nôm A. 2939: Phạm, *Nam hành*, n. p.; Trịnh, *Thông chí*, p. 305; Sellers, *Princes of Hà-Tiên*, pp. 27–28; Nguyễn Dynasty, *Thực lục*, vol. 1, p. 273.
[116] Trịnh, *Thông chí*, pp. 304–305; Nguyễn Dynasty, *Nhất thống chí*, vol. 3, p. 334; Nguyễn Dynasty, *Thực lục*, vol. 1, p. 111.
[117] Hán-Nôm A. 2939: Phạm, *Nam hành*, n. p.; Nguyễn Dynasty, *Thực lục*, vol. 1, p. 115, 119; *Prachum phongsawadan* 1: *Phongsawadan khamen*, p. 192.

would later become incorporated into the militarized hierarchy of The Port. Combined with Jiu's existing mercenary army of a few hundred, he probably had at most a thousand troops and a handful of war junks at his disposal. Clearly, the cost of Jiu's exile was the acceptance of closer supervision and greater interference in the internal affairs of his realm to serve the Nguyễn lord's strategic aims toward Cambodia. But in the more immediate term, they helped Jiu repel a predictable backlash from Siam in 1717, when it launched a full-scale attack on land and sea in an attempt to reinstate Ang Tham.[118]

The key maritime pathway toward the political and commercial heartland of Cambodia went through The Port. It became the initial target of an invasion force consisting of 5,000 troops led by Phraya Kosa, himself an ethnic Chinese noble. Mo Jiu, his wife, and some of his other family members and followers fled to the safety of his old base in Ream. The Siamese sailed unimpeded into Fortress River and charged into the city. They plundered, set fire, and laid waste to it. They then ran into an ambush from a joint Cochinchinese and Cambodian fleet waiting for them at the mouth of Fortress River. The Siamese were forced to flee. Many of their ships were sunk at sea on the way back because of storms.[119]

However, the Siamese enjoyed much greater success on land. Together with Ang Tham and two other princes, they advanced as far as the gates of Oudong. The Cochinchinese-backed Ang Em was forced to sue for peace. In exchange for the return of Ang Tham and his retinue to exile in Ayutthaya, he agreed to subject the western part of his kingdom, centered upon the Tonle Sap Great Lake, to Siamese influence. Concurrently, he would defer to Cochinchina in matters related to Phnom Penh and the water world. Since this area was much more integrated with the maritime East Asian trading networks and formed a more vital component of Cambodia's economy, the Nguyễn lord still had the greatest voice in its affairs. In fact, the Scottish trader and explorer Alexander Hamilton, who visited the area of The Port in 1720, observed that the Cochinchinese court made the major decisions in foreign affairs, including the types of commercial partners that Cambodia could engage with.[120]

In 1722, Ang Em yielded the throne to his son, Satha (1702–1749). Ang Em's position received a further boost three years later, when Ang

---

[118] *Prachum phongsawadan* 1: *Phongsawadan khamen*, pp. 192–193; Hán-Nôm A. 832: Phạm, *Cao Man ki lược*, n. p.; Nguyễn Dynasty, *Thực lục*, vol. 1, pp. 119–120; Lê Quang Định, *Hoàng Việt*, p. 989.
[119] *Prachum phongsawadan* 1: *Phongsawadan khamen*, p. 193; Wyatt and Cushman, *Royal Chronicles*, pp. 397–402; Eng, *Mahaboros Khmer*, vol. 5, p. 78; Trịnh, *Thông chí*, pp. 184–187; Hamilton, *New Account*, vol. 2, pp. 196–198.
[120] *Prachum phongsawadan* 1: *Phongsawadan khamen*, p. 194; Eng, *Mahaboros Khmer*, vol. 5, p. 79; Hamilton, *New Account*, vol. 2, p. 203; Nguyễn Dynasty, *Thực lục*, vol. 1, p. 281.

Sor, the old king who had been the preeminent figure in Cambodia's political life since 1675, passed away at the age of sixty-nine. In 1729, Ang Em, confident in his newly acquired power, made his son abdicate in his favor. However, his reign of seven months was not popular, and he was forced to return Satha to the throne and assume the role of co-king instead.[121] Despite the minor turbulence, the situation in Cambodia had stabilized. Ang Em and Satha adopted a largely pro-Cochinchinese stance. Naturally, both rulers also tolerated Mo Jiu, who had come to his own, independent arrangement of vassalage with Cochinchina.

Wheeler, Antony, Li Qingxin, and other scholars have challenged the notion that the arrival of Ming loyalist Chinese in the water world depended upon the patronage of the Nguyễn. Indeed, merchants, sojourners, and immigrants from Fujian had been active across maritime East Asia since at least the sixteenth century, forming networks and colonies in their own right. State actors, such as Cambodia and Cochinchina, and European enterprises such as the VOC recruited them to obtain domestic and regional advantages. As we have seen, the Chinese became mercenaries in Cambodia and, at times, commanded strategic garrisons in the area of The Port. The Ming loyalists were established in Cochinchina since the 1650s and integrated into local society through intermarriage, trade at ports such as Hội An, and serving in the bureaucracy. This was almost thirty years before 1679, when nineteenth-century Vietnamese sources claim that Yang Yandi and Chen Shangchuan requested asylum from the Nguyễn. Moreover, the Dragon Gate's permanent exile to the water world only occurred in 1682 and independently of Cochinchina.[122]

Initially, the Chinese networks operated in a multipolar and multi-ethnic environment. The withdrawal of Japan from the sea-lanes and the Ming–Qing transition were crucial turning points in maritime East Asian history. For Wheeler, the 1683 Qing annexation of Taiwan "signals an unprecedented projection of Chinese sovereignty into the sea" through control over the crucial shipping lanes of the Taiwan Strait.[123] However, it must be pointed out that the Qing built upon the foundations of the Zheng organization, whose merchants filled up most of the vacuum once occupied by the Japanese. The Zheng expulsion of the Dutch from Taiwan in 1662 deprived the VOC, their fiercest competitor, of a forward

---

[121] *Prachum phongsawadan* 1: *Phongsawadan khamen*, pp. 194–195; Eng, *Mahaboros Khmer*, vol. 5, p. 81; Leclère, *Histoire de Cambodge*, p. 374.
[122] Wheeler, '1683,' p. 146; Antony, 'Righteous Yang,' pp. 4–5, 18; Li Qingxin, 'Xi zei,' pp. 154–155.
[123] Wheeler, '1683,' pp. 136–137.

base for penetration into Japan, China, and mainland Southeast Asia. The loss of the island marked the beginning of the company's gradual divestment from active involvement north of the Malay Peninsula. Macao and Manila remained under the control of Portugal and Spain, respectively. But like Batavia, these isolated outposts could only survive by integrating into the existing intra-Asian trading networks.[124] The Zheng maritime hegemony halted the first round of European global expansion.

In the process, the Chinese, initially from southern Fujian but later including Cantonese groups, became the preeminent mercantile presence on the seas. States in the region came to see them as an indispensable third force to harness and employ for their own geopolitical objectives. The Dragon Gate commanders tried to leverage their position between Siam, Cambodia, and Cochinchina to obtain a new base in the water world after their withdrawal from the Chinese coast. However, internecine conflicts severely weakened them to the point that Chen Shangchuan, the eventual winner, had no choice but to accept subordination under Cochinchina. Mo Jiu would learn from their lesson, carefully forging ties to both horizontal networks and hierarchically structured state actors to ensure his own legitimate and independent space at The Port.

---

[124] Massarella, 'Chinese, Tartars,' p. 425; Cramer-Byng and Wills, 'Trade and Diplomacy,' pp. 186–198; Cheong, 'Canton and Manila,' p. 237.

2 Managing Hybridity

衣錦登高望北京 (In splendid garb, I climb up high to view Beijing from afar)

心中常眷故鄉情 (In my heart, how I yearn for my native place)

千言萬語憑難訴 (Even with infinite words, it is difficult to describe my emotions)

獨坐樓頭待日明 (I sit in solitude on top of the gate and await the dawn)

Double meaning: (I sit in solitude on top of the gate and await the sun to become Ming)

—Chen Shangchuan[1]

The demise of the Zheng organization in 1683 meant the disappearance of a higher Han authority for the southeastern Chinese coast, and the Fujianese and Cantonese mercantile settlements in maritime East Asia. For the overseas Ming loyalist exiles in the wake of Taiwan's annexation, different sects of **C: Chan** V: Thiền Buddhism became important in preserving an overseas Chinese identity without a physical homeland. According to Wheeler, religion could sustain connections within a particular Chinese settlement, link these communities to others across the sea, and forge bonds with the hierarchies and bureaucracies where they resided. Temples and itinerant monks also created a platform and safe space for the expression of Ming loyalist sentiments and Chinese elite culture.[2]

Mo Jiu embraced this religious network in forging a Buddhist-Daoist synthesis for his realm. It conformed to the prevailing ideology of his Cochinchinese overlord, which was itself influenced by the same southern Chinese Chan sects. More importantly, the patronage of Buddhism deepened his alliance with Chen Shangchuan and the Dragon Gate and allowed Jiu to benefit from their military prowess and connections to

---

[1] Chen Guohao, 'Lü Yue huaqiao,' in Chen Jihua, *Annan wang*, p. 70.
[2] Wheeler, '1683,' p. 147.

Qing literati in Guangzhou. The syncretic beliefs further provided inspiration for Jiu to transform the core area of The Port in the idealized elite image of a nostalgic China of old that had been lost forever to the Manchu conquest.

On a practical level, the Sinicization of the landscape aimed to create a welcoming and familiar environment for Qing merchants, sojourners, and immigrants, who flooded maritime East Asia after the court's legalization of private trade and travel abroad in 1684. Besides their business, Jiu attracted other ethnic groups and religions by throwing open The Port to free trade and developing it into a center of money creation and finance. His skillful associations with various horizontal networks balanced out Cochinchinese attempts to subordinate him in a hierarchical relationship and secured his independence.

Cochinchinese Strategies of Control

Sellers correctly points out that Mo Jiu's submission to Cochinchina remained largely symbolic in nature, because he was too far away from even its new possessions in Saigon and Donay. Although this was the ultimate outcome, Cochinchina did take advantage of his initial weakness to seriously try to control The Port. Mo Jiu originally had a small mercenary force numbering several hundred granted to him by the Cambodian court. They were led by members of his clan and others from western Guangdong.[3]

One of them was an individual known only by the surname of Xu. Before his death in 1754, he served as the Great General of the Five Arms (*Wurong dajiangjun*), implying a role as commander-in-chief. The Cochinchinese court bequeathed upon him the noble title of Marquis of the Han Sun (C: Hanyang V: Hàn Dương). It was an obvious reference to the ethnically Han Ming, which, like the sun, would rise and shine once again over his homeland someday. Moreover, two large, horizontally placed characters for "Imperial Ming" (*Huang Ming*) are emblazoned across the top of his tombstone.[4] Perhaps Xu had been active in the Ming loyalist resistance while still in China. If so, he must have maintained many connections with the Dragon Gate and served as a mediator with them on Jiu's behalf. As can be seen by the conferment of marquis upon Xu, the Cochinchinese court was making subtle attempts

---

[3] Sellers, *Princes of Hà-Tiên*, p. 24; Lê Quang Định, *Hoàng Việt*, p. 989.
[4] Phạm Đức Mạnh, 'Cổ mộ,' p. 1297; Chen Jinghe (Chin Kei-wa), 'Hexian Mao shi,' p. 200.

68   Managing Hybridity

to balance out Mo Jiu by granting his subordinate commanders the same noble title as had been given to him.

The Nguyễn lords also installed their own military apparatus into The Port. As late as the early 1740s, the French naturalist and adventurer Pierre Poivre (1719–1786) notes that over a hundred Cochinchinese troops were still stationed there, ostensibly to protect the Mo leaders.[5] Cochinchina further exploited Jiu's marriage connection. Lord Minh bestowed the royal surname of Nguyễn upon his wife, Bùi Thị Lam, and her entire family as a means of enhancing her prestige and standing.[6] An individual whose tombstone inscription bears the name of Nguyễn Văn Túc (d. 1743) served as a staff officer (*tham mưu*), indicating a role as chief adviser to Jiu. Chen Ching-ho believes that he was a brother of Jiu's wife. At the very least, Túc oversaw the Cochinchinese forces at The Port and probably was the main supervisor over the entire military apparatus, including Jiu's personal troops. The Trương seemed to be another prominent Cochinchinese clan in The Port. One Trương man had married the widow of someone from the Bùi clan, indicating a close bond with the relatives of Jiu's wife.[7]

The Nguyễn further sought to bind the Mo ritualistically to Huế in a deeper manner than the payment of tribute. Soon after Jiu acquired The Port, he began to establish his own independent source of authority. The spirit tablet of his deceased mother, dedicated by Jiu and his son Tianci, provides valuable insight into how both men viewed themselves and their polity in its early days (see Figure 2.1). I discovered it while visiting the Temple of Three Treasures (C: Sanbao V: Tam Bảo), constructed on the orders of Jiu to house his mother, who, at the age of eighty, sailed all the way from her Leizhou hometown to be with her offspring. The first observation is the title line of the tablet: The Mo of Hà Tiên, protectors of the kingdom. No reference is made to Cochinchina or Cambodia, Jiu's overlords, leaving the interpretation of "kingdom" ambiguous, and most likely, purposefully so.

Secondly, Jiu favored the character for Heaven (C: *tian* V: *thiên*) in referring to himself and naming his son, Tianci. The two individuals appear on their maternal ancestor's spirit tablet as "filial son ... Tianjiu and filial grandson ... Tianci." Tianjiu, meaning a jade-like black stone from Heaven, may have been what Mo Jiu originally called himself. Tianci translates into a bestowal or gift of Heaven. The use of Heaven

---

[5] Poivre, 'Journal d'un voyage,' p. 414.
[6] Trương, *Nghiên cứu*, vol. 2, pp. 120–124; Trịnh, *Thông chí*, p. 185.
[7] Phạm Đức Mạnh, 'Cổ mộ,' pp. 1295–1296, 1298; Chen Jinghe (Chin Kei-wa), 'Hexian Mao shi,' p. 189.

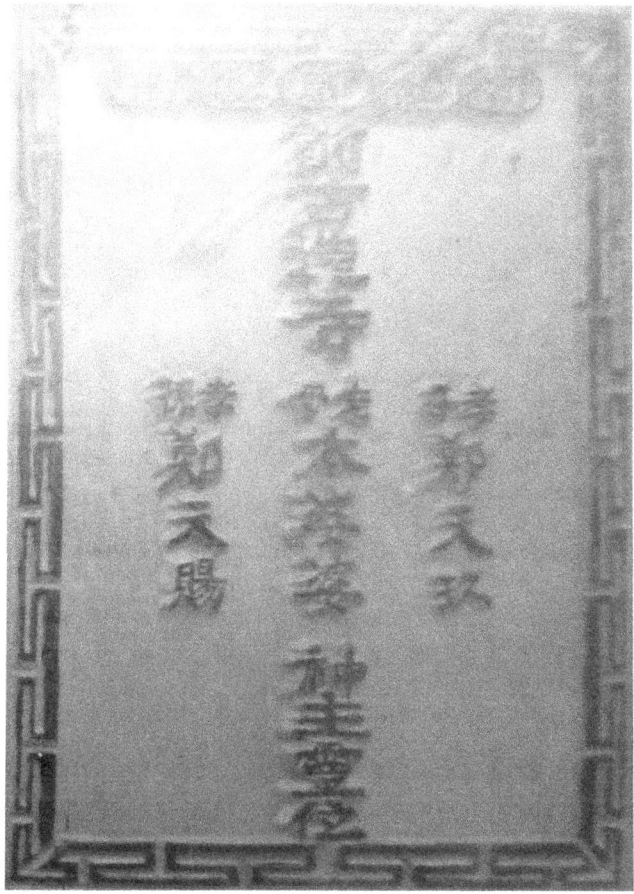

Figure 2.1 The spirit tablet of Mo Jiu's mother, housed at the Temple of Three Treasures.
Photograph by author.

in both their chief preference of names seems to indicate an association with the Heavenly Mandate granting them absolute authority and legitimacy as rulers over an independent polity. Jiu may have wanted to include this character not just in the name of his son but also for later generations in perpetuity in the manner of a dynastic line.

What the Nguyễn did was to alter this naming practice to highlight the Mo's subordination and symbolically diminish the clan's power over time. At some point after his submission to Huế, Mo Jiu dropped the Heaven character from his name. The Nguyễn lord allowed Tianci to keep Heaven in his name but bequeathed upon his descendants their own middle characters down to the seventh generation. They included all of the ranks in the Cochinchinese noble hierarchy in descending order:

> 天 C: Tian V: Thiên (Heaven)
> 子 C: Zi V: Tử (Used together with 天 to form 天子, or Son of Heaven)
> 公 C: Gong V: Công (Duke)
> 侯 C: Hou V: Hậu (Marquis)
> 伯 C: Bo V: Bá (Earl)
> 子 C: Zi V: Tử (Viscount)
> 男 C: Nan V: Nam (Baron)

As John Wong argues, these seven characters embedded the feudal ranks of nobility into the personal names of each generation. As a result, future generations, out of filial piety, would be unable to use them again. The Nguyễn lord thus intended for the Mo to become increasingly dependent upon Cochinchina over time until their full incorporation as commoner subjects.[8]

Finally, Jiu had to alter the character of his surname from 莫 (Mo) to 鄚 (Mao). The difference in pronunciation only applies to standard Mandarin. Both characters are pronounced Mok in Minnanese and the dialects of Guangdong, and Mạc in Vietnamese. However, the additional double-ear radical (阝) distinguished him and his clan from a dynasty that had usurped the Lê rulers in Hanoi in the mid-sixteenth century. The ancestors of both the Nguyễn and Trịnh lords had risen to prominence and obtained their legitimacy to govern in the struggle against those Mạc in the name of restoring the Lê. By having The Port's leaders alter their surname, the lord was integrating them into the Cochinchinese and Vietnamese hierarchy, with its conventions for ideological conformity.[9]

Mo Jiu had no choice but to submit to Cochinchinese expectations, at least in appearance. But he and his son found ways to reinterpret the ritual subordination in subtle ways favorable to their clan and The Port. The modified surname of Mao 鄚, with the double-ear radical, had an intrinsic meaning of its own. It was an abbreviation for Maocheng in Hebei Province, northern China, where the Mo surname first emerged during remote antiquity.[10] Both the modified surname character and the

---

[8] J. D. Wong, 'Improvising Protocols,' pp. 257–258.
[9] Ang, *Poetic Transformations*, p. 5, n. 8.   [10] Zhang Xuexian, *Huaxia baijiaxing*, p. 157.

characters for nobility assigned by the Nguyễn primarily appeared on public documents, especially ones that involved the Cochinchinese state or subjects. Even then, their use was far from consistent. In private and on many public occasions, Jiu and his son retained their original surname of Mo 莫. Other than Tianci, the name given by his father, the other Mo clan members usually omitted their middle characters indicating a descending order of nobility. Besides ritual and symbolism, Jiu made use of The Port's commercial potential to forge ties with horizontal networks as a means of balancing out Cochinchinese penetration.

Chan Buddhists and the Dragon Gate

As his control over The Port stabilized, Mo Jiu embraced Buddhism. On the one hand, this act reflected a pragmatic adaptation to the governing ideologies and structures of his new Cochinchinese overlord. As Li Tana points out, Mahayana Buddhism, in particular the **C: Linji V: Lâm Tế** sect of Chan, combined with Daoist beliefs and folk rituals of the Cham and other peoples of mainland Southeast Asia to form a synthesis in Cochinchina that tied the court to its diverse elites and commoner subjects. This eclectic faith proved well-suited for a regime that, in contrast to the bureaucratic orientation of Tonkin, derived its basis for rule primarily on military camps and personalized chains of command.[11] At the same time, Buddhism allowed for the preservation of overseas Chinese communities by keeping them in communication with one another. The religious connections allowed Jiu to cement his ties to the Dragon Gate contingent, now led by Chen Shangchuan, and, through Chen's clan, establish contacts with lower-level Qing elites in the home province of Guangdong.

The monk **C: Yuanshao** V: Nguyên Thiều (1648–1728) proved crucial in bringing all of these vertical and horizontal elements together. A native of Chaozhou, he had arrived at Quy Nhơn, in south-central Vietnam, in 1677. He established on the site of ten old Cham stupas a monastery named the Ten Stupas Amitabha Temple (C: Shita mituo V: Thập Tháp Di-Đà). Five years later, he journeyed to Huế, where he became the Buddhist adviser to the court at the invitation of Lord Minh. His C: Huangbo V: Hoàng Bích branch of the Linji sect of Chan Buddhism quickly caught on among Cochinchinese elites. With official support, Yuanshao was able to send his disciples to establish new

---

[11] Li Tana, *Nguyễn Cochinchina*, pp. 99–116.

temples across southern Vietnam, making his teachings the most influential and widely accepted in the realm.[12]

Although, according to the official Vietnamese records, Yuanshao remained in Huế until his death, Nguyễn Hiền Đức has discovered that the monk, in fact, sailed for Donay sometime after 1694. Besides cultivating relations with the ruling authorities, the monk evidently wanted to expand his reputation and stature among the translocal Ming loyalist networks. In 1698, he established the Diamond Temple (C: Jingang V: Kim Cang) and served as its head abbot until his death in 1728.[13] There, he must have come into contact with Chen Shangchuan. In fact, one clan genealogy of Chen's home village of Tiantou mentions that the commander sponsored the construction of an "Anqing Temple at the harbor of Donay."[14] Could it have been the same as Diamond Temple, where Yuanshao presided? The location mentioned in the genealogy appears to be consistent with that of the Diamond Temple, close to the shores of the Donay River.

Regardless of the association between the two men, there is conclusive evidence to tie both to Mo Jiu. Between when he took over The Port and the Siamese invasion, Jiu had the Temple of Three Treasures constructed for his eighty-year-old mother. A monk named Yellow Dragon (C: Huang Long V: Hoàng Long) (d. 1737) served as its first head abbot. He came from Quy Nhơn, site of the Temple of Ten Stupas established by Yuanshao. Nguyễn Hiền Đức argues that he was probably a disciple of the great master. More likely, he served under Yuanshao's successors, either at the temple in Quy Nhơn or the Diamond Temple at Donay. The records of the Temple of Three Treasures indicate that he was a Chan master of the thirty-fifth generation (see Figure 2.2). Yuanshao, on the other hand, belonged to the thirty-third generation. The records also indicate that he originally came from China as a Ming loyalist. Yellow Dragon was his monastic title. His dharma name was **C: Yincheng** V: Ân Trừng.

Under the care and spiritual guidance of Yellow Dragon, Jiu's mother spent her final years in the temple. She passed away one day while engaged in meditation. Jiu had a statue erected in her honor and placed it on the temple grounds. It evidently did not survive the Siamese invasion, which laid waste to the entire city, including the temple itself. After the Siamese withdrew, the Temple of Three Treasures was rebuilt

---

[12] Wheeler, '1683,' pp. 139–140.
[13] Nguyễn Hiền Đức, *Lịch sử Phật Giáo*, pp. 60–97.
[14] *Tiantou cun Chen shi*, n. p.

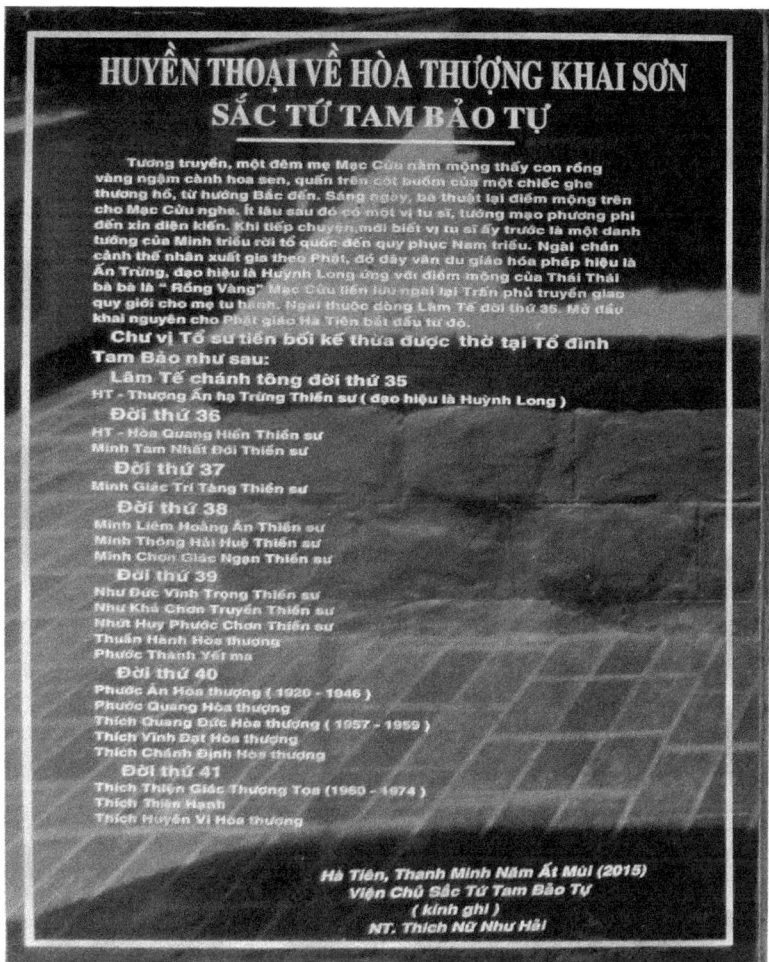

Figure 2.2 Inscription at the Temple of Three Treasures explaining Yellow Dragon's background and how he came to know Mo Jiu's mother. Following it is a list of the successive generations of patriarchs, starting with him as the thirty-fifth generation. The inscription also shows that Yellow Dragon's dharma name was Yincheng.[15] Note that Huỳnh, used here to spell the first part of his monastic title in Vietnamese, is an alternate spelling of Hoàng common to southern Vietnam because of naming taboos. Hoàng is a homophone of the personal name of a Nguyễn lord. Photograph by author.

---

[15] Thích Nữ Như Hải, 'Hòa Thượng Khai Sơn.'

Figure 2.3 A bronze bell from the Temple of Three Treasures, now on the grounds of Thonburi Palace, Bangkok (left). Given the date of the cast in 1816, it is likely that the Siamese had taken it away from its original home during their war with Vietnam from 1841 to 1845. The inscription on the bell (right) reads:
Master Yincheng of the Temple of Three Treasures in Hà Tiên Garrison attests that in front of me, the sins of all of you, men and women devotees of Buddha, are extinguished and your fortunes are increased. When your time has reached its limit, you will all be reborn in the Pure Land.
Photograph by author.

in a more makeshift form.[16] A bronze bell belonging to the temple contains Yellow Dragon's message to his believers (see Figure 2.3). Although the bell was cast in 1816, the inscription appears to be a faithful reproduction of his original words.

Through the Buddhist connection, Mo Jiu actively worked to recruit members of the Dragon Gate contingent. After arriving in the water world, Chen Shangchuan either renewed or forged new ties with elites

---

[16] Trương, *Nghiên cứu*, vol. 2, pp. 325–326; Trịnh, *Thông chí*, pp. 536–537; Nguyễn Dynasty, *Nhất thống chí*, vol. 3, p. 286.

Figure 2.3 (cont.)

in his home province of Guangdong. He donated ten bars of gold to his native village of Tiantou to fund the construction of a grand clan shrine in honor of his ancestors (see Figure 2.4). This generous act boosted his reputation among his fellow villagers and kin, who called him the "King of Annam," the name of Vietnam in the Chinese official records.[17] Chen also gained a reputation for being an accomplished poet and composed a total of eighty verses in his lifetime. Many of them, such as the verse quoted at the beginning of this chapter, expressed yearning for his native place. In particular, the last line consists of a pun using the character bright, which carries the double meaning of Ming. It could either describe him waiting for the sun to shine on the land or for the Ming to return.[18]

Chen appears to have maintained a lively long-distance exchange with gentry based at Guangzhou, where the ships of either him or his agents frequently paid calls. The most prominent among them was She Xichun. Xichun hailed from Shunde, on the outskirts of Guangzhou, and held a

---

[17] *Tiantou cun Chen shi*, n. p.; Chen Guohao, 'Lü Yue huaqiao,' in Chen Jihua, *Annan wang*, pp. 65–66.
[18] Chen Guohao, 'Lü Yue huaqiao,' in Chen Jihua, *Annan wang*, pp. 70–72.

Figure 2.4 The Chen clan shrine at Tiantou Village, Wuchuan County, Guangdong, constructed with funds supplied by Chen Shangchuan. Photograph by author.

senior licentiate (*gongsheng*) degree from passing the civil service examinations, the second-highest rank after presented scholar (*jinshi*). He served on editorial boards commissioned by the governor-general of Guangdong and Guangxi to compile both the Qingyuan county and Guangdong provincial gazetteers. He also once had an official position as an instructor for the Confucian Academy of Yangjiang County, west of Guangzhou.[19]

Xichun was a member of a poetry society that frequently gathered in West Garden, south of the Guangzhou city gate in present-day Panyu. On one occasion, he dedicated a poem to Chen Shangchuan. In it, Xichun praised the general's martial accomplishments in a foreign land. He also verified that Chen was a skilled poet and "every month, he climbs a mountain and, in solitude, longs for his Guangdong homeland."[20] An associate of Xichun was Chen Zhikai, a merchant who frequently plied the waters between Guangzhou and ports across the South China Sea. He would later become a close poetry companion of Mo Jiu's successor, Tianci.[21]

---

[19] Wen, *Yuedong shihai*, vol. 3, p. 1254. She Xichun is often mistakenly referred to as Yu Xichun, because the character for She (佘) bears a striking resemblance to Yu (余).
[20] Chen Jianhua, *Guangzhou dadian*, vol. 444: She, *Yushan tang*, p. 157.
[21] Chen Jianhua, *Guangzhou dadian*, vol. 89: Ling, *Haiyatang*, p. 336; Hán-Nôm A. 441: Mao, *Hexian shiyong*, n. p.

The intermediary between these elites and the Mo was almost certainly Chen Shangchuan. Chen's death in 1715 precipitated a series of events that would culminate in The Port's control and consolidation over the bulk of the Dragon Gate forces. Shangchuan's successor as leader of the contingent, and the Frontier Garrison camp at Saigon, was **C: Chen Dading** V: Trần Đại Định (d. 1732). The Vietnamese records claim that he was Shangchuan's son. The reality was more complex. According to two genealogies of the Chen from their native Tiantou, Shangchuan had passed away childless. He had adopted Dading, a younger cousin, as his son and successor to his enterprise.[22]

In 1725, the Nguyễn lord, Minh, passed away. His son, Nguyễn Phúc Thụ (Lord Ninh, 1697–1738, r. 1725–1738), ascended the throne in Huế. The new lord wanted to consolidate his power in Saigon and the water frontier, and constantly sought some pretext to realize this aim. His chance came in 1730, when rebellious Lao descendants of Cambodia united around a holy man and massacred substantial numbers of Viet settlers. At one point, they briefly occupied Saigon and laid waste to it in an orgy of looting, burning, and killing. Although the pro-Cochinchinese Cambodian court of King Satha quelled the insurgency, Lord Ninh decided to send Chen Dading and Cochinchinese troops against the ruler anyway to punish him for allowing the rebellion to occur. To better coordinate the campaign, Lord Ninh placed the two camps of Border Suppression and Frontier Garrison under a unified controller of the camps (*Điều Khiển Dinh*) headquartered in Saigon.[23]

When the offensive failed in the face of fierce resistance from the Cambodians, the lord capitalized upon the setback to hold Chen Dading accountable. In 1732, Dading was relieved of his command and recalled to Huế, where he languished in a prison until his death shortly afterward. Through this move, the lord stripped him of his power base, bringing the two camps of Border Suppression and Frontier Garrison, including Chen Shangchuan's old base at Mesar, entirely under his own Cochinchinese commanders. The withdrawing Cochinchinese forces also seized much of the thinly defended Cambodian province of **K: Longhor** V: Long Hồ, whose population had largely been evacuated after the Siamese invasion. A new Longhor camp was established at present-day Cái Bè and placed under the

---

[22] *Tiantou cun Chen shi*, n. p.; *Tiantou qi zhi shijiu shi*, p. 20b; Chen Guohao, 'Lü Yue huaqiao,' in Chen Jihua, *Annan wang*, pp. 64–65.

[23] *Prachum phongsawadan* 1: *Phongsawadan khamen*, p. 195; Eng, *Mahaboros khmer*, vol. 5, p. 83; Nguyễn Dynasty, *Thực lục*, vol. 1, p. 128; Pérez, 'Españoles en el imperio de Annam' 5, p. 326.

controller, along with a corresponding civilian administration of Stabilizing the Far (Định Viễn) subprefecture under Gia Định prefecture. The occupation extended Cochinchina's territorial limits beyond Mesar westward to the interior, along the northern bank of the main Mekong branch.[24]

Some of the Dragon Gate remnants became absorbed into the Cochinchinese hierarchy. But it appears that the vast majority took refuge in The Port under the leadership of Chen Dading's son, **C: Chen Dali** V: Trần Đại Lực (d. 1770). Chen Ching-ho and Trương Minh Đạt both argue, based upon their meticulous studies of the Vietnamese sources, that he was the son of Mo Jiu's younger daughter, Jinding, who the sources claim, had married Dading.[25] The Tiantou genealogies, however, reveal a vastly different narrative. Dading, in fact, never took a Mo wife. Instead, he first married a woman with the surname of Zheng, and, later, another from the Yang clan, perhaps a relative of Yang Yandi. He had five sons from both unions. Chen Dali was Dading's second son from his marriage to Zheng and was identified as the third-generation Dragon Gate commander.[26]

Dali's trajectory was far more convoluted and fascinating than a conventional, straightforward inheritance. After his father's death at the hands of Cochinchina, both he and his elder brother fled back to his native Wuchuan in western Guangdong. Dali, the Tiantou genealogies and local gazetteers claim, passed the civil service examinations and acquired the prestigious rank of senior licentiate (gongsheng). He also became an accomplished poet and compiled two anthologies of verses. But he, together with his elder brother, refused to serve in the Qing bureaucracy and eventually set sail for The Port. The elder brother, frail in composition and in ill-health, passed away soon after arriving at The Port. Both men must have cultivated ties with local gentry in Wuchuan, since one of them composed a verse in memory of Dali's deceased brother. It described him as a "junior licentiate (zhusheng) who abandoned his post and became a sojourner again."[27]

But why did the two descendants of Chen Shangchuan choose The Port, in particular? The genealogies reveal additional details. One of Dali's clan members from the same generation, Chen Ruishu (d. 1754)

---

[24] Eng, *Mahaboros khmer*, vol. 5, p. 83; Nguyễn Dynasty, *Thực lục*, vol. 1, p. 130; Trịnh, *Thông chí*, pp. 206–207.
[25] Chen Jinghe (Chin Kei-wa), 'Hexian Mao shi,' pp. 217–218; Trương, *Nghiên cứu*, vol. 2, p. 59; Vũ, *Gia phả*, p. 113.
[26] *Tiantou qi zhi shijiu shi*, p. 28b; Chen Guohao, 'Lü Yue huaqiao,' in Chen Jihua, *Annan wang*, p. 64.
[27] *Tiantou qi zhi shijiu shi*, p. 28b; Chen Jihua, 'Annan wang Chen Shangchuan shiliao' and Wei, 'Huaqiao xianqu,' in Chen Jihua, *Annan wang*, pp. 94, 163–164.

was already serving as "a general of the Wu unit in Hà Tiên." His profile appears to match the occupant of a tomb located inside the Mo clan cemetery. The inscription does not give his full name but labels him the Great Dragon-Tiger General (*Longhu dajiangjun*), with the title of C: Huanwu V: Hoàn Vũ Marquis, matching the "Wu unit" mentioned in the genealogy.[28] Both the genealogies and the tombstone confirm that this Chen clan member married a Mo woman.

I believe that Chen Ruishu was, in fact, the husband of Mo Jiu's daughter Jinding. The marriage ties provided Dali with a welcoming and familial environment at The Port. The most likely scenario is that Jinding adopted him as her own son to enhance the prestige and legitimacy of the Mo by tying the clan to the illustrious legacy of Chen Shangchuan. And the attempt was successful. Dali was able to use his authority and influence to reconstitute the Dragon Gate as a formidable fighting force, this time in The Port's service.

Making Memories Real

The linkages forged with Buddhist networks, along with the addition of Chen Shangchuan's descendants, enhanced the military prowess and symbolic capital of Mo Jiu. Both sources further provided him with a substantial knowledge base in Chinese culture that he could use to highlight the distinct character of his realm, especially in relation to Cochinchina. And he did not aim for a simple imitation of his native Leizhou. Instead, he sought to recreate what he believed to be an idealized China of old, unblemished by the corruption and cultural mutilation visited upon it at the hands of the "barbarian" Manchu hordes. He appears to have looked up to the Tang dynasty (618–907) as his model of a golden age to replicate, in particular the copious poetical productions of the period.[29]

It started with his decision to use the name of Hà Tiên. Although most likely a Portuguese corruption for the Khmer word for Seashore, Peam, he claimed to the Nguyễn lord that it came from a local myth of fairies roaming around Fortress River and the East Lake lagoon. In fact, Jiu had partially fabricated the legend. Precisely speaking, he derived it from two historical allusions, both from the Tang. One was the Maiden of Hexian (Hexiangu), a fairy who lived during the seventh century. The mountains and hills were her favorite haunts, and she would fly from one peak to another, gathering medicine and elixirs to cure the sick. She was the only female out of a group of eight Daoist immortals who crossed the seas to

---

[28] *Tiantou qi zhi shijiu shi*, p. 29a; Phạm Đức Mạnh, 'Cổ mộ,' p. 1300.
[29] Trương, *Nghiên cứu*, vol. 2, p. 17.

visit a faraway land of magic.[30] The geographic configuration of Hà Tiên, endowed with mountains and seas, certainly seemed like the ideal abode for a fairy such as her.

The other allusion comes from a lengthy verse written by the great Tang poet Bai Juyi (772–846). Entitled "Song of Unending Sorrow," it celebrates the relationship between Emperor Xuanzong (685–762, r. 712–756) and his favorite consort, Yang Guifei (719–756), adapting it into a tragic ballad of romance and enchantment. After Yang was put to death for distracting the emperor from his duties and causing a massive rebellion, the verses speak of her transforming into a fairy who lived in "an enchanted isle at sea." It was "a part of the intangible and incorporeal world, with pavilions and fine towers in the five coloured air, and of exquisite immortals moving to and fro."[31] Mo Jiu had likewise expressed his wish to depart the disorder and chaos of his homeland to join the fairies in a mysterious land afar.

Jiu drew from other frequent geographic references mentioned in Tang poetry to name and categorize the distinctive features of his realm. The mountains lying opposite the harbor from The Port's urban center to its east, came to be called **C: Suzhou** V: Tô Châu after the southern Chinese commercial center and a bastion of elite high culture. The tallest of the hills known as Viet Mountain (Phnom Yuon), west of The Port center around which the Viet settlements clustered, had its name changed to the Sinicized Hibiscus Mountain (C: Furong V: Phù Dung). The inspiration came, once again, from the "Song of Unending Sorrow," which compares the flowers to the fair facial complexion of Yang Guifei.[32]

The Big Golden Islet (C: Da Jinyu V: Đại Kim Dữ), consisting of a single hill, and the Small Golden Islet (C: Xiao Jinyu V: Tiểu Kim Dữ), which was shaped like a golden turtle, once stood opposite one another along the mouth of Fortress River. They served as landmarks for incoming vessels and guarded The Port's maritime approach. Their names draw inspiration from Golden Mountain (Jinshan), an islet that stood in the middle of the Yangzi upriver between Suzhou and Nanjing.[33] East Lake, the lagoon where Fortress River intersects with the Gulf of Siam, was a conscious juxtaposition to West Lake, the famed tourist attraction outside Hangzhou.

After driving away the Siamese, Mo Jiu rearranged the layout of The Port, both to ensure a stronger defense and to accord with Chinese

---

[30] Trịnh, *Thông chí*, p. 304; Ni, *From Kuan Yin to Chairman Mao*, pp. 192–196.
[31] Birch and Keene, *Anthology of Chinese Literature*, pp. 266–269.
[32] Trương, *Nghiên cứu*, vol. 2, p. 16, 20–23; Birch and Keene, *Anthology of Chinese Literature*, pp. 266–269.
[33] Nguyễn Dynasty, *Nhất thống chí*, vol. 3, p. 275; Trịnh, *Thông chí*, pp. 175, 533–534; Trương, *Nghiên cứu*, vol. 2, p. 16.

Figure 2.5 A surviving section of Seashore Fortress on the grounds of the Temple of Three Treasures.
Photograph by author.

geomantic principles. The original inner fortress, known as Seashore Fortress (C: Fangcheng K: Srok Peam V: Phương Thành), was the traditional seat of power in Seashore Province. It included the governor's residence and offices, shrines and temples, and key military installations. However, it was entirely situated on flat terrain and only protected by a rectangular stone wall about 0.6 meter thick. A small section survives and can still be seen on the grounds of the Temple of Three Treasures, which it once enclosed (see Figure 2.5). Naturally, the meager fortifications made the city vulnerable to a direct attack from any enemy that managed to seize the nearby high points. Accordingly, after the Siamese left, Jiu abandoned the old site and never bothered to restore its devastated buildings. Even as late as 1869, after the French colonized Hà Tiên, the first-known European map of the city center that they commissioned labeled the area as "Ruins."[34]

---

[34] Trương, *Nghiên cứu*, vol. 2, pp. 309–310; Sellers, *Princes of Hà-Tiên*, p. 33.

Instead, Jiu constructed a grander, rectangular citadel farther to the southeast. It was surrounded by a moat some four meters wide. Then came the walls. Stacked together with bamboo, logs, and twigs, they stood two meters high on three sides. A left and right gate, made of masonry, punctured the walls on the east and west, respectively. Located outside were military barracks that housed troops. At the very center of the citadel stood the garrison office, where Jiu conducted formal business.[35]

The citadel made better use of natural barriers to protect the approach to the city center from land and sea. They were also given Sinicized names. The citadel opened to Fortress River to its southeast. The Mount of Five Tigers (C: Wuhu V: Ngũ Hổ) acted as a shield to the north and made a wall there unnecessary. Screen Mountain (C: Pingshan V: Bình San) guarded the citadel from the rear. The slopes functioned as a cemetery where the tombs of the Mo and their main commanders and officials are concentrated. Jiu also built a personal residence at the foot so he and his family could enjoy time away from the noisy bustle of the city. Southwest of Screen Mountain was Hibiscus Mountain. Despite having "mountain" in their names, all of them were, in reality, a series of relatively low-lying hills. Farther to the west was a stretch of unnavigable marshes all the way to the Gulf of Siam coast. Another belt of marshlands lies along the north to northeast of the city. A small canal, the Water Station (C: Shuichang V: Rạch Ụ), dug by the Mo cuts through the area, flowing from the west into the lagoon.[36]

Like elsewhere in the water world, The Port suffered from a persistent shortage of fresh water, especially during the dry season, when the southward flow of Fortress River weakens and retreats before the mass encroachment of the saline seawater from the Gulf of Siam into the East Lake lagoon. For at least half of the year, residents had to rely upon wells dug upstream and in the hills and from ponds. They could also purchase water from specialized carriers who earned their living making round trips to and from these sources.[37] Another method would be to trap rain at home using large basins.[38]

To alleviate the water shortage, Jiu ordered the construction of two huge, open-air reservoirs. They were dug out of the ground at the foot of

---

[35] Trương, *Nghiên cứu*, vol. 2, pp. 309–310, 323; Vũ, *Gia phả*, p. 98; Nguyễn Dynasty, *Nhất thống chí*, vol. 3, p. 280; Trịnh, *Thông chí*, pp. 170, 317, 532–533.
[36] Nguyễn Dynasty, *Nhất thống chí*, vol. 3, p. 280; Trịnh, *Thông chí*, pp. 170, 317, 532–533; Trương, *Nghiên cứu*, vol. 2, p. 323.
[37] Giá Khê, 'Sự tích Đồi Ngũ Hổ' http://tuanbaovannghetphcm.vn/su-tich-doi-ngu-ho/.
[38] Mộng, *Chậu úp*, pp. 157–164.

Screen Mountain and drew water from its springs. Known as the Lotus Pond (C: Lianchi V: Ao Sen), the two were impressive endeavors that Sellers describes as "each nearly a modern city-block in size." Square stone blocks line the sides of both reservoirs. They were chiseled out of the Seven Mountains and brought to The Port on barges by way of the seasonal canals and Fortress River.[39] Besides potable water, the project provided sufficient irrigation for agricultural cultivation around the city center. As the name of the reservoirs imply, there was also a cosmological element to their construction. Lotuses, symbols of purity in the Buddhist faith, grew out of the mud on the bottom of the ponds. Moreover, the reservoirs were located almost directly west of the Temple of Three Treasures, a visual representation of the Western Paradise in the popular Pure Land sects.[40]

The Challenge of Diversity

Mo Jiu's design and choice of names for the various places in The Port's center and its vicinity aimed at taming what had once been a "barbarian" wilderness and redefining it as a land of literature and arts. He could transform his inspiration from Tang poetry into a reality of his own imagination to alleviate his nostalgia for a lost homeland. Yet, there was also a pragmatic purpose to his symbolism. By the first decades of the eighteenth century, the composition of overseas Chinese society in the water world had grown increasingly complex. A century had passed since the fall of the Ming, and the flood of political refugees from China had run its course. Some had originally brought along their entire families. Others, who came as single men, intermarried with Viet or Khmer women. They and their offspring might completely melt into one of these more locally based ethnic groups. Or, more commonly, they might hold onto their Chinese roots and forge creolized communities that still came under heavy influence from Viet and Khmer and adaptation to the local ecology.[41]

Complicating things further, in 1684, the Qing court completely repealed its sea ban and established customs houses throughout the coast to regulate private trade and travel abroad. Soon afterward, large numbers of merchants and immigrants from China flooded to overseas destinations. This massive outflow was sustained by fundamental

---

[39] Nguyễn Dynasty, *Nhất thống chí*, vol. 3, p. 280; Trịnh, *Thông chí*, pp. 532–533; Trương, *Nghiên cứu*, vol. 2, pp. 309–310, 323; Sellers, *Princes of Hà-Tiên*, p. 28.
[40] Ning, *Art, Religion, and Politics*, pp. 30–31.
[41] Choi, *Southern Vietnam*, pp. 39–40; P. Taylor, *Khmer Lands*, pp. 209–210.

changes occurring within the Qing and the trading structure of maritime East Asia. In China, the return to peace after the cataclysm of dynastic transition led to renewed demographic growth and commercialization. These developments contributed to a highly efficient and specialized economy that generated significant surpluses of manufactured goods. Domestic competition intensified, as population growth came up against mounting ecological pressures, especially acute in the resource-poor southern provinces of Fujian and Guangdong. As a result, there was heavy demand for essential primary products and commodities and, for the elite and wealthy, exotic items that fulfilled high-end consumption. More than ever before, China in the long eighteenth century, or the High Qing, depended on interregional and global linkages to support its complex agrarian economy.[42]

Authorities across maritime East Asia sought to take advantage of the lucrative opportunity presented by the Qing while containing the potential dangers. Although little documentation exists, the arrival of Qing subjects contributed to tensions with preexisting overseas settlements, which tended to sympathize with the Ming cause. Not only did the newcomers differ in outward appearance, since they adopted the Manchu queue, but Qing merchants also presented stiff competition and lowered profit margins in the trade across maritime East Asia.[43] The primary effort of most regional political actors involved keeping the two groups of Chinese separate. The Qing aimed to prevent the spread of subversive Ming loyalist ideas to its shores and forestall potential collusion with foreign powers to disturb domestic security. Accordingly, the Kangxi Emperor (1654–1722, r. 1661–1722) gradually tightened his supervision over the maritime zone. He stripped away the privileges of surrendered Zheng commanders, in particular Shi Lang, and ended their ambition to follow the footsteps of their former Zheng masters in cornering overseas trade.[44] In 1694, the Qing court promulgated a new law that essentially banned overseas Chinese sporting the Ming attire from sailing to ports in China.[45]

Other state and non-state actors sought to form common cause with the pro-Ming Chinese creoles, maintaining them as a separate and often privileged community whose linguistic and cultural skills would be used to mediate with the more numerous Qing arrivals and the Qing state. In Cochinchina, the Nguyễn lords organized a Minh Hương commune

---

[42] Myers and Wang, 'Economic Developments,' p. 564; Zhao Gang, *Qing Opening*, pp. 79–136.
[43] Zhao Gang, *Qing Opening*, pp. 158–160; Holroyd, 'Rebirth,' pp. 96–97; Zheng Weizhong (Cheng Wei-Chung), 'Shi Lang,' pp. 67–68.
[44] Hayashi, *Ka'i hentai*, vol. 2, p. 698, 707–709.   [45] Holroyd, 'Rebirth,' pp. 93–94.

for the first time at Hội An during the 1650s. In 1699, similar settlements were established near Saigon and at Biên Hòa. Over time, Minh Hương gradually lost its Ming loyalist political connotation, as Qing subjects settled down in the communes and extensive intermarriage with local women took place. Eventually, it became a generic label for Chinese creoles. The Minh Hương maintained self-rule under their own headmen and were eligible to take the Cochinchinese civil service examinations. Usually, they served as port officials dealing with incoming vessels, primarily from the Qing. The Qing merchants, on the other hand, forged their own associations, later known as assemblies (*bang*), which were at a greater remove from the local population.[46] Both the creolized groups, whether Ming loyalist or more recent Qing immigrants, and the Qing merchants and sojourners, enjoyed legal privileges and exemption from tax and labor obligations.

Mo Jiu adopted an opposite approach from his maritime East Asian neighbors in reacting to the explosion in Chinese junk traffic. Instead of separating the Ming loyalists from the Qing subjects, his purposeful Sinicization of The Port's landscape aimed at providing a welcoming and inclusive environment for all Chinese, regardless of ideological persuasion or level of creolization. They could view the place as a home away from home, where they could do business without being subject to harsh restrictions and policies of segregation. The symbolism and rhetoric were accompanied by concrete policies. Jiu proclaimed The Port to be duty free and open to everyone. During the 1720s, priests of the Franciscan order traveling between Cambodia and Cochinchina through The Port confirm that "it is easy to enter and leave from one kingdom to another without passing through customs." In another measure aimed at increasing the appeal of The Port as a stopover or destination and fund the lost income from duties, Jiu opened casinos for gambling.[47]

His open policies had much to do with fundamental changes in the structure of trade in maritime East Asia. The arrangement since the sixteenth century, centered upon the exchange of Chinese silk for Japanese and New World silver, gradually unraveled as rapid growth in the demand for the precious metal outpaced its supply. After 1684, the flood of vessels arriving to trade in Nagasaki and Manila overwhelmed the capacity of both ports to provide markets for the products that the merchants brought along. The slow, cumbersome galleons from the New World simply could not

---

[46] Choi, *Southern Vietnam*, pp. 40–41; Salmon, 'Réfugiés Ming,' pp. 181–183; Wheeler, '1683,' p. 145.
[47] Trịnh, *Thông chí*, p. 304; Vũ, *Gia phả*, p. 97; Sellers, *Princes of Hà-Tiên*, pp. 33–34; Pérez, 'Españoles en el imperio de Annam' 4, pp. 170–173.

supply adequate quantities of silver in a timely manner to Manila. Meanwhile, Japan, faced with a surge in bullion outflow and depletion in its mines, began to impose quotas on the number of junks arriving at Nagasaki and the silver value of exports during the 1690s.[48]

Unable to find sufficient outlets in Nagasaki and Manila, Chinese merchants turned to the South China Sea littoral, penetrating deeper into its markets through sales of such prized luxuries as silk, porcelain, and tea. Guangzhou, Batavia, and Ayutthaya emerged as the three most important commercial emporia in the area. As the eighteenth century progressed, British country traders and, to a lesser extent, French, Armenian, and Muslim merchants began to directly ply the long-distance route between Indian Ocean ports and China. After attempts at a commercial presence at numerous ports along the Chinese coastline, Guangzhou and the Pearl River Delta became their most preferred destination. The British East India Company and its French counterpart (*Compagnie des Indes*), established in 1719, presently set up their factories in the city, followed by more European companies and merchants. The direct economic ties that they forged between Europe, South Asia, and the Qing quickly blossomed, as tea became the leading Chinese export, enjoying a hugely popular market across Eurasia.[49]

Batavia provided the only legal means of access to the rest of island Southeast Asia, from the southern Malay Peninsula to the Indonesian archipelago. Pepper, spices, tin, tropical forest and marine products, and medicinal ingredients constituted the major products for sale. In its attempt to dominate trade over this vast area, the Dutch East India Company pursued a vision of a closed sea (mare clausum) under its exclusive economic domination. To this effect, it signed treaties with various kingdoms and principalities across island Southeast Asia, and issued licenses strictly regulating where and when certain ships could sail and what products could be carried onboard. VOC patrols roamed the strategic channels and straits, ready to intercept and confiscate goods from vessels caught without a proper pass.[50]

Ayutthaya, on the other hand, became important as a provider of essential natural resources. Rice from the fertile Chao Phraya River plain around Bangkok helped alleviate grain shortages in Fujian and Guangdong and level the soaring prices. Ayutthaya also served as the gateway to mainland Southeast Asia. Siam, Laos, western Cambodia,

---

[48] Holroyd, 'Rebirth,' pp. 50–55, 57–66.
[49] Holroyd, 'Rebirth,' pp. 142–149, 162–180; Van Dyke, *Canton Trade*, pp. 5–18.
[50] Holroyd, 'Rebirth,' pp. 76–79, 89.

and the northern Malay Peninsula offered a similar mix of products as the VOC-dominated areas. But compared to Batavia, there were fewer regulations.[51]

All three hubs initially procured South Asian goods, especially textiles, for the maritime East Asian market. Eventually, however, the only major product from outside the region consisted of New World silver sourced through Europe. Much of it went to procure Chinese goods, a testament to the renewed centrality of China in global trade flows. Within the region, Chinese junks came to dominate the main routes between Guangzhou, Ayutthaya, and Batavia, as well as many secondary ones. Vessels of the VOC and private Dutch citizens of Batavia (*vrijburgers*), Portuguese, Spanish, and Iberian creole were also involved for certain segments. Austronesians, such as the Malay and Bugis, were more locally focused, plying the sea-lanes within island Southeast Asia and connecting to certain ports along the Gulf of Siam.[52]

The Port stood at the crossroads of these different maritime routes. As Chinese compass charts and navigational guides written during the seventeenth and eighteenth centuries reveal, its vicinity served as a natural and often necessary transit point for ships. Given the navigational technology at the time, which depended upon monsoon winds and ocean currents, the vessels often stopped there midway during their journeys from China and Japan to island Southeast Asia, and vice versa.[53] But for the area to maximize its potential, the waters had to be cleared of the rampant piracy that made navigation exceedingly dangerous. The pirates included Viet and Chinese, as well as Cham and locally based sea peoples, both with long traditions of maritime predation. There were also Malay, Bugis, and other Austronesians from farther south in island Southeast Asia. The pirate bands could consist of a single ethnicity but were more often mixed between the diverse groups. Some might turn to predation occasionally, whether driven by desperation or attracted by lucrative and low-risk opportunities for gain, such as chancing upon a ship in distress or one that lacked the means to protect itself. Others were more organized and professional.[54]

The root of the predation had much to do with violence and political instability in the broader China Seas. As Li Tana and Wong Tze Ken show, the rapid pace of Cochinchinese expansion into Champa and the

---

[51] Holroyd, 'Rebirth,' pp. 80–82; Yang Kaijian and Tian, 'Zhongguo yu Xianluo de dami maoyi,' p. 82.
[52] Holroyd, 'Rebirth,' pp. 80–90, 98–105.
[53] Xiang, *Liangzhong haidao zhenjing*. See, for instance, pp. 35–36, 50–51, 82–83, 174–175; Li Qingxin, 'Mao shi,' pp. 115–117.
[54] Trịnh, *Thông chí*, p. 168; *Nouvelles lettres*, vol. 6, p. 191.

Mekong Delta far exceeded the capacity of the court in Huế to follow up with adequate institutions and regulations.⁵⁵ Meanwhile, in island Southeast Asia, a fierce succession struggle broke out within the powerful Sultanate of Johor. The Malay commercial center and political hegemon in the Strait of Melaka zone, Johor comprised both the peninsula and the island of Sumatra across the strait and was seen as the successor state to Melaka. The city of Melaka itself had come under the direct control of the VOC according to a bilateral agreement. In 1718, Raja Kecil (d. 1746), the Minangkabau ruler of Siak, on Sumatra, took advantage of the political disorder in Johor to invade and seize the throne. Sulaiman, son of the deposed sultan, formed an alliance with the Bugis, who had migrated in large numbers from their homeland in southern Sulawesi. With their support, he drove Kecil back to Siak in 1721. Sulaiman and his Bugis allies forged a new political and commercial center for Johor on the Riau Islands, south of Singapore.⁵⁶

In response to the persistent maritime threat, the Port dispatched patrols every year, during the southern monsoon, to seek out and destroy pirate dens along the Gulf of Siam.⁵⁷ Although never entirely successful, Mo Jiu's efforts managed to keep the seas in the vicinity relatively peaceful. At the same time, by making The Port a free port and opening entertainment facilities, he was removing a pretext for the geopolitical belligerents and their mercenaries or outlaw elements to cause trouble in his neighborhood. Instead, he could forge ties with the different mercantile networks that came to his shores.

Much of The Port's trade at the time occurred with Cochinchina. Besides formal vassalage, Qing policies worked to bolster this relationship. In the early decades of the eighteenth century, the Kangxi Emperor walked away from his previously tolerant attitude toward private maritime trade. In 1717, he imposed a limited sea ban on Chinese junks from sailing to Batavia and elsewhere in Southeast Asia. Vietnam, including Cochinchina, was exempt from the prohibitions. According to Poivre, ships from Cochinchina often arrived at The Port to purchase ivory, rice, and wax, primary products acquired from the hinterlands of the water world. Mo Jiu took advantage of the continued influx of Viet migrants and, together with preexisting or newly arrived Cham and Khmer, harnessed their skills and experience in intensive agricultural cultivation, extraction, or fisheries. The control and exploitation of natural resources

---

⁵⁵ Li Tana, *Nguyễn Cochinchina*, pp. 141–142; Wong Tze Ken, *Nguyen and Champa*, pp. 151–162.
⁵⁶ Vos, *Gentle Janus*, pp. 64–67.
⁵⁷ Trịnh, *Thông chí*, p. 181; Nguyễn Dynasty, *Nhất thống chí*, vol. 3, p. 278.

was making The Port into a competitor with Ayutthaya in the Gulf of Siam littoral. In exchange, ships from Cochinchina brought along some manufactures from around Huế, such as lacquerware and silk. But the majority were transshipped Chinese products from the port of Hội An.[58]

For the rest of Southeast Asia, The Port became the most convenient place to acquire Chinese goods within the context of the Qing maritime ban. The Austronesian networks included it as an important stopover point. For instance, in 1733, the Guangdong authorities reported rescuing thirty-four men and women who had floated onto the shores of the province. They identified themselves as subjects of Cambodia, possibly Khmer but more likely Cham or Malay residents, who had far more experience with seafaring. Their ship had set sail from The Port and was on its way to the Riau island of Siantan when fierce winds punctured a hole in it. They had no choice but to transfer to a smaller backup boat that was then carried by the southwestern monsoon to the Guangdong coast.[59] Through crews like this one, The Port could obtain goods directly from island Southeast Asian ports other than Batavia, often in violation of VOC policy.

The Austronesians also enjoyed the casinos of The Port, and they often used the venues as arenas for settling their own political differences in relative peace. One popular game was cockfighting. According to a semi-legendary account from the Johor and Bugis chronicles, a Minangkabau prince, Raja Chulan, possessed a cock renowned for its martial prowess and undefeated track record. He happened to be visiting Cambodia. A Bugis nobleman, Daeng Rilaka, heard about Chulan's reputation and decided to challenge him. Rilaka and his sons set sail from Siantan to Cambodia. They were warmly received by the king and given a house to reside in. A shahbandar took care of their daily needs. Raja Chulan accepted the challenge and bet his entire belongings, including a ship filled with goods and its crew. As the objects of wager reveal, the arena of the competition must have taken place at The Port. Rilaka's cock won the fight. Accepting defeat, Chulan surrendered the ship and other belongings, and he and his wife departed with only sarongs wrapped around their loins. Rilaka and his sons returned to Siantan. Around that time, the wife of one of his sons gave birth to a baby boy. He was given the name of Daeng Cambodia (d. 1777) in honor of the kingdom where they won the cockfight.[60]

---

[58] Poivre, 'Journal d'un voyage,' p. 414; Wheeler, 'Cross-Cultural Trade,' pp. 173–174; Holroyd, 'Rebirth,' p. 105; Lê Quý Đôn, Tạp lục (Giáo dục), vol. 2, pp. 476, 505–506; Trịnh, Thông chí, p. 181, 304; Nguyễn Dynasty, Thực lục, vol. 1, p. 273.
[59] Shizong xian huangdi zhupi yuzhi, juan 255, pt. 4, pp. 19b–20a.
[60] Al-haji, 'Silsilah Melayu dan Bugis,' pp. 346–347; Ibn Ahmad, Precious Gift, pp. 45–46.

Portuguese creoles based in Phnom Penh became another important network that Mo Jiu tapped into. Many of them migrated to The Port, where they helped him establish a mint to forge copper coins. Under their guidance, skilled Chinese blacksmiths made imitations of older Chinese, Vietnamese, and Japanese coins, particularly in the use of dynastic reign names. As Li Tana shows, some of the more popular objects of imitation included coins bearing the Thiệu Bình reign name (1434–1439) of the Lê dynasty and the Kan'ei (1624–1644) period of Tokugawa Japan. The coins circulated locally as currency and gambling tokens for the casinos. However, as seen in their design and choice of reign names, they were deliberately made for export to Cochinchina, which suffered from an acute shortage of copper coins. Private workshops had already proliferated there, although it is unclear whether they emerged under the influence of The Port or separately.[61]

The Portuguese creoles maintained frequent trading connections with Macao, Siam, and Melaka. Initially, after settling down at The Port, the small but cohesive community built a chapel to serve as the center of their activities. They relied upon chaplains on board visiting ships to administer to their spiritual needs on an irregular basis. Only after 1722 did the Spanish Franciscans establish a permanent presence by maintaining a regular dispatch of missionaries from Phnom Penh and Saigon.[62]

Besides religious purposes, the Portuguese creoles probably obtained their copper for the mints from the visiting ships, which, in turn, sourced them at their ports of origin from Chinese junks sailing from Japan. Because of the huge demand for coinage in the Qing and both Vietnamese regimes, copper had replaced silver as Japan's most important export after 1683. The Dutch at Batavia purchased the metal as well and transported it to South Asia, where it was used for a variety of utensils, such as pots and statues of deities. However, copper went the way of silver in the rapid depletion of Japanese mines. Starting from 1698, the Tokugawa imposed a quota on exports of slightly under four million kilograms per year. In 1715, a stringent new licensing system took effect, aimed at reducing Japan's foreign trade in favor of a policy of import substitution and the promotion of domestic manufactures. The strict regulations stipulated the reduction in the numbers of arriving Chinese ships from seventy to thirty.[63]

---

[61] Li Tana, 'Cochinchinese Coin Casting,' in Tagliacozzo and Chang, *Chinese Circulations*, pp. 132–141; Pérez, 'Españoles en el imperio de Annam' 11, pp. 201–202.
[62] BL, IOR/G/12/35, p. 99; Pérez, 'Españoles en el imperio de Annam' 11, pp. 201–202.
[63] Shimada, *Intra-Asian Trade*, pp. 86–88; Prakash, *Dutch East India Company and the Economy of Bengal*, pp. 130–136; Holroyd, 'Rebirth,' pp. 55–56; Zhao Gang, *Qing Opening*, p. 143.

In 1727, Mo Jiu decided to obtain more direct access to copper by cooperating with the retired Cambodian king, Ang Em, in outfitting a royal mission to Japan. The delegation was led by Oknha Sneha Metrei and consisted of three Khmer; six "Javanese," a reference to Malay, Cham, and other Austronesians; and fifty-six Chinese. They carried along twenty articles of tribute, together with Ang Em's letter requesting a license. These passes had become increasingly hard to obtain, since the majority went to ships from the Chinese mainland. Southeast Asian-based junks, on the other hand, would have a much-improved chance of accessing Japan if they sailed as part of official missions dispatched by rulers. As Mark Ravina shows, the Tokugawa authorities would treat these delegations in a semiformal manner. They would be hosted on-site in Nagasaki rather than in the shogunal seat of Edo, while the ship captain would naturally receive a pass to trade. As luck would have it, the shogunal government agreed to grant the license, although it returned the gifts.[64] In reality, the privilege went entirely to Mo Jiu, who controlled the most convenient and accessible maritime route to Cambodia.

Two years later, in 1729, a vessel belonging to Mo Jiu once again made the journey successfully to Nagasaki. However, subsequent attempts in 1731 and 1732 ended in disaster, as fierce winds blew the ships off course and forced the crews to take refuge in Guangzhou, one after the other. Jiu undoubtedly sustained heavy financial losses from these disasters, and eventually, the license granted by the Tokugawa lapsed.[65] Nonetheless, the missions reveal that Jiu never relinquished his connections to Cambodia even after his submission to Cochinchina, although the exact way he participated in Oudong's hierarchy remains poorly understood. Another important outcome was the establishment, for the first time, of communications with Qing officialdom. Let us revisit the shipwrecked crew that was sailing from Siantan to the Cambodian coast but was blown off course to Guangzhou in 1733. The captain somehow got word that Mo Jiu's two damaged junks were docked at the harbor and planned to sail back to The Port after repairs. Through the mediation of the Guangdong authorities, the crew members were able to board his vessels for their return journey.[66]

In 1735, after over thirty years of rule, Mo Jiu passed away peacefully at the ripe old age of 80. Upon receiving the news, the Cochinchinese ruler, Lord Ninh, bequeathed upon him the posthumous honor of Great

---

[64] Ravina, *To Stand*, p. 34; Kondo, *Gaiban tsūsho*, vol. 1, pp. 137–138.
[65] Kondo, *Gaiban tsūsho*, vol. 1, p. 138.
[66] *Shizong xian huangdi zhupi yuzhi*, *juan* 255, pt. 4, p. 29a.

General and Superior Pillar of the State, Founder of the Garrison (*Khai trấn Thượng trụ quốc Đại tướng quân*). The lord authorized Jiu's son, Mo Tianci, who had reached maturity, to succeed him as garrison commander of Hà Tiên.[67] Although the clan still depended to a certain extent upon Cochinchina for legitimacy and trade, Jiu managed to achieve greater autonomy by cultivating ties with various horizontal networks. His patronage of Linji Chan Buddhism gave him the cultural tools to recreate his imagination of a pure China from the glorious Tang onto the landscape of his realm. The descendants of Chen Shangchuan and the Dragon Gate contingent gave him a modest but experienced military force independent of the Cochinchinese garrison. Their mediation would also lay the foundations for future exchanges with lower-level Qing gentry.

Other networks had became attracted to The Port because of Jiu's favorable mercantile policies, combined with the Qing court's contradictory decisions, first to legalize private trade in 1684 and then, in 1717, to impose a renewed ban on junks from sailing to Southeast Asia outside Vietnam. There is still little evidence for merchants from Qing-held territory coming to conduct business during this period. However, the Austronesians and Portuguese mestizos provided direct access to Batavia, one of the three major hubs of maritime East Asia, as well as many secondary routes where their ships were dominant. They also helped him start up a mint to forge coinage. In his quest for copper, Jiu had strengthened his ties to the Cambodian court and secured a license to export the metal from Nagasaki. And then, after a few disasters at sea, the ships from several of the missions had ended up in Guangzhou and obtained contact with the Qing authorities.

By the time of his death, Jiu had forged a successful but increasingly complex enterprise. A Buddhist-Daoist synthesis certainly allowed him to conform ritualistically to the Cochinchinese hierarchy while maintaining his Ming loyalist connections, which, in turn, underpinned a creolized overseas Chinese identity. However, this ideological outlook proved unable to keep up and encapsulate the sheer diversity of his realm, from Portuguese mestizos and Austronesians to the new Qing arrivals around the time of his death. His son and successor, Mo Tianci, needed to conceive of a more inclusive vision for The Port.

---

[67] Vũ, *Gia phả*, pp. 99–100; Trịnh, *Thông chí*, p. 305; Nguyễn Dynasty, *Thực lục*, vol. 1, p. 274.

3   Situating Space through Verse

鱸溪泛泛夕陽東 (Sea Perch Creek leisurely flows eastward from the setting sun)

冰線閑拋白練中 (I close my eyes, and hurl the icy line into the white silken water)

鱗鬣頻來黏玉餌 (Fish, like hair coiled into a knot, often come and stick to the jade bait)

煙波長自控秋風 (The misty waters flow afar, lamenting the autumn winds)

霜橫碧篷虹初霽 (The frost forms patterns on the boat's canopy, as the rainbow comes out and the sky starts to clear)

水浸金鉤月在空 (The water envelops the golden hook and reflects the moon in the sky)

海上斜頭時獨笑 (In the middle of the sea, I tilt my head and sometimes laugh in solitude)

遺民天外有漁翁 (Among the leftover subjects far, far away, there is a fisherman)[1]
　　—Mo Tianci, *Luxi xiandiao* (Idle fishing at Sea Perch Creek), Poem 1, 1736

I draw my literary talents from my roots in the Central Plains, but my enterprise will be celebrated in a foreign land.[2]
　　　　　　　　　　　　—Mo Tianci to Liang Luan, c. 1742

After Mo Tianci took over the helm of The Port's leadership in 1735, he set out to craft a more inclusive vision for his realm that could factor in the tremendous growth in its commercial connections and the diversity and complexity of its visitors, sojourners, and long-term residents. He came to embrace Wang Yangming's neo-Confucian teachings, which were themselves heavily influenced by the Chan and Daoist practices espoused under his father. The Heart-Mind school's decentralized character and emphasis

---

[1] Chin Kei-wa (Chen Jinghe), 'Kasen Maku-shi,' p. 169.　　[2] Luo, *Wushan zhilin*, p. 58.

on subjectivity could better harmonize the different religious and ideological inclinations of his realm, while justifying a focus on trade and profits.[3]

Tianci began with a quest to forge a Confucian commonwealth able to transcend the boundaries of the Sinosphere states, in particular Vietnam and China. His literary society, the Pavilion for Summoning Worthies, joined Tianci and his elites at The Port together with those from both countries to produce and publish anthologies of poetry and prose. Their projects inherited the tradition of late-Ming gentry, who wrote prolifically about scenic landmarks, especially mountains, during visits to monasteries. The landscape poetry was doubly intended as a visual guide toward spiritual enlightenment.[4] The unique feature of the works sponsored by Mo Tianci's literary society was that a substantial portion of the exchange took place remotely, relying upon the same junks that circulated goods and labor throughout maritime East Asia.

Đông Hồ, Chen Ching-ho, Liam Kelley, and Claudine Ang have meticulously examined these collaborations. They take particular interest in an anthology of poetic descriptions penned by Tianci and thirty-one other poets in 1737, soon after he came to power. The poems uniformly take as their theme ten scenic views from The Port handpicked by Tianci, or the "Ten Scenic Views of Hà Tiên" (C: *Hexian shijing* V: *Hà Tiên thập cảnh*). The collection was entitled the "Ten Verses of Hà Tiên" (C: *Hexian shiyong* V: *Hà Tiên thập vịnh*) and was the most well-known and best-preserved out of all the output of the literary society. Ang has undertaken a detailed, line-by-line analysis of Mo Tianci's own contribution of ten poems to the "Ten Verses." She has also provided highly precise translations of each poem into English.[5] I largely use her version for my analysis of Tianci's ten poems with some modifications to account for greater accuracy in the translations of certain lines.

Ang argues that Tianci's poetry reveals subtle and encoded expressions of nostalgia for the Ming. From her reading of the lines, she further detects a conversation between him and other like-minded, dispersed dissidents from across the China Seas. There were, in particular, allusions to members of the Dragon Gate. Ang believes that Tianci aimed to create a network and platform enabling them to maintain these long-distance exchanges.[6] And, indeed, the historical evidence validates much of her analysis. Dragon Gate members found refuge at The Port. Being

---

[3] Wheeler, '1683,' p. 147; Brook, *Praying for Power*, p. 62.
[4] Brook, *Praying for Power*, p. 110.
[5] Đông, *Văn Học*, pp. 157–302; Kelley, 'Chinese Diaspora,' pp. 79–90; Chin Kei-wa (Chen Jinghe), 'Kasen Maku-shi'; Ang, *Poetic Transformations*, pp. 121–222.
[6] Ang, *Poetic Transformations*, pp. 150–162.

adept at poetry themselves, they joined his literary society. Tianci also sponsored the journeys of other men of letters to come and compose verses with him.

The lyrical conversations, conducted both remotely and on-site, provide a valuable window into the profound crisis of authenticity that engulfed the Sinosphere amid the Ming–Qing transition, whose impact continued to be felt well into the eighteenth century. Wu Jiang, Ge Zhaoguang, and Ronald Toby have spoken about how China's civilizational centrality came under severe scrutiny and doubt from both its elites and neighbors, as they grappled with how to come to terms with its domination by "barbarian" Manchu outsiders. Ming loyalist exile communities and many inside the Qing held onto the nostalgic memory of a pure China dominated by the Han. Partly because of their influence, a proto-national awareness emerged in the elite and a segment of commoner discourse in Korea, Japan, and Vietnam that redefined their own countries to be the new Middle Kingdom. The "crisis of authenticity," Wu argues, created "a fragmented and inconsistent chaos that led to the collapse of the Sinosphere."[7]

The exchanges between Mo Tianci and the members of his literary society, however, appear to reveal a strengthened Sinosphere. Despite the Manchu conquest and the skepticism it engendered about an authentic China, political and intellectual developments within the Qing had a profound impact on its neighbors. The spread of books and print culture and the circulation of Ming loyalist refugees and religious figures followed and reinforced the trading networks. The ideas that they brought along penetrated deeper and more widely into Sinosphere societies than before, at least reaching the lower elite stratum. Naturally, the more intense level of participation would translate into a greater divergence of opinions, but these were disagreements within a common, cross-border conversation.[8]

The Mo leaders and Chinese creoles of The Port unquestionably shared sentiments of nostalgia and some disdain for the Manchus. However, Ang reminds us, a Ming loyalist platform did not necessarily translate into an active movement to resist or topple the Qing. In Mo Jiu's later years and especially under Tianci, Ming loyalism, like elsewhere in maritime East Asia, functioned more as a marker of Chinese ethnic and generational continuity outside China.[9] It was a largely

---

[7] Wu, *Rising Sun*, pp. 5–7, 244–267; Toby, *State and Diplomacy*, pp. 168–230; Ge, *What Is China?*, pp. 122–133.
[8] Elman, *Cultural History of Modern Science*, pp. 85–87.
[9] Reid, *Age of Commerce*, vol. 2, p. 314.

depoliticized personal identification that "by no means came at the exclusion of one's participation in the society of the supporters of the Qing dynasty."[10]

It must be pointed out that this tolerance was incomplete and only achieved through a gradual process. On the part of the Qing court, it remained suspicious of subversive activities among the diaspora, who might activate any latent hostilities if given the opportune conditions. Indeed, in Chen Shangchuan's poetry, as seen earlier, and a set of poems written by Tianci a few years before the famous "Ten Verses," the ideal of a restored Ming was openly expressed. For many of the lower-level Qing literati who eventually participated in the "Ten Verses" project, they found it to be a refreshing channel for public opinion. Certainly, they did not have to face the severe restrictions in what they could express back home amid the literary inquisition against written materials deemed subversive to the state.[11]

Over time, however, such sentiments became far more subdued and tucked away in cryptic poetic lines. Tianci had to deal with the reality of increasingly widespread acceptance of Qing political and economic primacy in maritime East Asia. His anthology included pro-Qing contributors. Some of the poets even tried to find common ground and reconcile the different political stances. Wang Yuanfei's assertion of a shared imagined empire, subject to alternate interpretations from various strata of Chinese society, continued to apply for much of the eighteenth century, and in expanded form among the overseas communities, whether for creolized diaspora or merchants, sojourners, and immigrants who identified as Qing subjects.[12]

Judging from the verses supplied by Viet or long-term residents of Vietnam, they likewise came to terms or felt comfortable with a world order centered upon the Qing. The prevailing attitude appears consistent with that of the Viet tributary envoys to the Qing, who, Kelley shows, expressed in their poetry "a profound identification with the cultural world which found its center at the Chinese capital."[13] And this attitude was fairly widespread across the Sinosphere. Even among intellectuals in Tokugawa Japan, which had stood outside of any official affiliation with the tributary system since the mid-Ming, "Sinophilia was by no means a minor intellectual current."[14] Of course, elites in Sinophere states focused on the Han component of the Qing and either ignored or

---

[10] Ang, 'Writing Landscapes,' pp. 628–629.
[11] Brokaw, *Commerce in Culture*, pp. 496–498.
[12] Wang Yuanfei, *Writing Pirates*, pp. 140–141.
[13] Kelley, *Beyond the Bronze Pillars*, p. 2.   [14] Ng, *Imagining China*, p. xiv.

disdained its Manchu ruling class. While nativism did acquire a following among certain segments of society, it would not become a major trend until the late eighteenth century.

Tianci's literary project tapped into this integrative trend in the Sinosphere. He hoped to forge an ideological commonwealth founded upon Confucian values and classical elite Chinese culture. The conception had practical benefits, since a common community would remove barriers to trade and lower transaction costs, allowing his fledgling commercial network to operate more smoothly and efficiently. His command over cross-border cultural capital would make him more powerful than territorial governments in his ability to set the rules for the sea-lanes.

Seeking Authenticity

After he came to power, Mo Tianci initially inherited his father's ideological framework, based upon a Buddhist-Daoist synthesis. He appeared to lean more to the Daoist side, imagining himself to be a recluse and dissident exile. The Linji monk Yellow Dragon, who had been close to Mo Jiu and provided connections to temples and Ming loyalist networks in Cochinchina, remained an important influence during Tianci's early years in power.[15] He and a group of locally based literary figures appear to have constituted an informal advisory council, providing recommendations on matters of policy and administration.

After conducting formal business, they would recount historical tales and compose verses. The conversations often lasted through the night, driven by a shared passion for literature and copious quantities of tea and wine. They usually met in an open-air pavilion in the courtyard of the family mansion on Screen Mountain. Tianci called it the Pavilion for Summoning Worthies. The gatherings soon became formalized under the auspices of a permanent literary society that would be named after the meeting venue.[16]

Tianci's literary society was modeled upon the ones in Guangzhou, which met in the courtyards and gardens of elite mansions and religious establishments and drew much of their inspiration from Daoist influences and themes.[17] In fact, a Daoist shrine was located not far away from the site of the Pavilion for Summoning Worthies. It houses the statues of the Jade Emperor and his attendants, the northern and southern polar stars (see Figure 3.1). They date from 1752, according to the

---

[15] Trịnh, *Thông chí*, p. 307.
[16] Trịnh, *Thông chí*, pp. 306–307; Nguyễn Dynasty, *Thực lục*, vol. 1, p. 274.
[17] For more on the connection between Daoism and poetry in Guangzhou literary societies, see Honey, *Southern Garden*, pp. 3–92.

Figure 3.1 Statue of the Jade Emperor and his attendants at the Daoist shrine that overlooks the site where Mo Tianci's literary society held its gatherings.
Photograph by author.

written descriptions displayed within the shrine, when Mo Tianci employed craftsmen from China to mold the deities. Great care was taken in their design and decoration, with colorful paint and gold leaves applied to their exteriors.

Tianci would often take "two or three close companions" on journeys to explore the natural wonders of The Port. One scenic spot was the Stone Grotto (C: *Shidong* V: *Thạch Động*), located northwest of The Port center (see Figure 3.2). It is a strange rock formation protruding upward in the midst of an otherwise flat terrain. A path made out of bamboo leads into a cave. Deep inside, a Buddhist temple is situated in a relatively open space. There, a small hole at the top of the cave allows one to gaze up at the open sky. During dawn and dusk, a misty fog rises through this passage into the air from its subterranean reaches.[18] The place provided much in the way of literary inspiration:

[18] Trịnh, *Thông chí*, pp. 168–169.

Figure 3.2 The Stone Grotto, situated on the side of National Road 80, about three kilometers from the present Cambodian border.
Photograph by author.

隨時花草供詩句 (At any moment, the flowers and grass provide poetic lines)
到處風雲入酒杯 (Everywhere, the wind and clouds enter the wine cups).[19]

A place where Mo Tianci preferred to spend his personal time in complete solitude from his companions in the pavilion was Sea Perch Creek, located some five kilometers to the east of The Port's urban center in present-day Thuận Yên commune. Its highlight was a winding creek that connected directly to the Gulf of Siam. Huge quantities of sea fish would swim into the brackish waterway, which naturally trapped them within a narrow, confined space and made them easy prey for anglers. Tianci spent much of his leisure time on the creek, fishing from

---

[19] Hán-Nôm A. 2939: Phạm, *Nam hành*, n. p.

his boat. In fact, his first major literary composition was achieved as he awaited his catch.[20]

"Idle Fishing at Sea Perch Creek" (*Luxi xiandiao*) consists of one rhapsody and thirty poems. It was arguably the earliest publication of the Pavilion for Summoning Worthies, appearing in 1736. Some of the verses might have been penned before his father's death. Evidently, Mo Tianci spared no expense in having the collection printed. Each poem was written in a distinctive style of calligraphy and accompanied by a beautiful landscape painting that added a visual and emotional component to the text.[21] Unfortunately, no complete copies of the anthology have survived. A few of the poems and the rhapsody have been recovered from handwritten manuscripts. Two of the verses and parts of the rhapsody were painted onto the walls of the Mo clan shrine when it was constructed in Hà Tiên in 1845 (see Figure 3.3).[22]

"Idle Fishing at Sea Perch Creek" provides a rare glimpse into Mo Tianci's inner thoughts and sentiments as an idealistic young man right on the cusp of becoming involved in the complex commercial and political world of maritime East Asia. It also reflects The Port's own public face that had taken shape under his father.

The verse provided at the opening of this chapter, which has been identified as the first poem in the collection, emphasizes the Daoist theme of seclusion and withdrawal from a disordered and immoral world. Tianci begins by taking the setting sun as the location of The Port, his point of reference, a place far away in a distant corner of the earth from the vantage point of China. He then writes about fishing in the creek, but he was not just describing a hobby. In traditional Chinese poetry, the angler, along with the woodcutter, functioned as stock images of the recluse. And the imagery and adjectives that he uses reinforce this sense of isolation and loneliness.[23] In the final two lines, Tianci openly refers to himself as a "leftover subject," meaning a holdover of a former dynasty: the Ming. He was a political exile overseas, who sometimes tilted his head and looked in the direction of his distant homeland.[24] Ironically, it was an imagined homeland that he had personally never visited and only heard about from his father and other diaspora.

---

[20] Trịnh, *Thông chí*, pp. 182–183, 357; Thanh, 'Theo dấu văn thơ kỳ' 5, https://thanhnien.vn/van-hoa/theo-dau-van-tho-ky-5-lu-khe-nhat-dau-365747.html; Hán-Nôm A. 2939: Phạm, *Nam hành*, n. p.

[21] Ngạc, 'Minh Bột Di Ngư,' pp. 7–8; Chin Kei-wa (Chen Jinghe), 'Kasen Maku-shi,' pp. 167–168.

[22] Trương, *Nghiên cứu*, vol. 2, pp. 72–79.   [23] Cai, *How to Read Chinese Poetry*, p. 339.

[24] Chin Kei-wa (Chen Jinghe), 'Kasen Maku-shi,' p. 169.

Figure 3.3 Fragments from "Idle Fishing at Sea Perch Creek" on a wall of the Mo clan shrine in Hà Tiên. Two of the poems are situated in the center, while the two flanks contain a part of the rhapsody. Written in beautiful calligraphy and accompanied by landscape paintings, they appear to have been drawn straight out of the pages of the lost original text. Unfortunately, much of the paint has peeled off because of age and the lack of preservation.
Photograph by author.

In lines from the rhapsody, Tianci gives off similarly clear signals regarding his political inclinations:

> 宜浮游於天外兮,恆出沒乎江洋 (Oh! I am suited to roam the distant corners of the earth, to eternally come and go in the rivers and seas)
>
> …
>
> 繫此生於南海 (I tie myself to the Southern Seas for my lifetime)
>
> …
>
> 思美人兮渺何之,懷故國兮徒引領 (Time and again, like thinking about a beautiful woman, oh! how tiny and distant! My old country, oh how I miss it! I stretch my neck out in vain to catch a glimpse from afar)[25]

Again, Mo Tianci presented himself as a lonely Ming loyalist exile who remained keenly focused on his ancestral land despite having never been there.

Undoubtedly, from these verses, Tianci identified primarily as Chinese. But unlike Chen Shangchuan, for instance, there was no embrace of a specific native place or province, whether Leizhou or Hainan or Guangdong. Instead, Tianci fully subscribed to the classical elite culture of the Central Plain as he imagined it before the Manchu occupation. This affiliation becomes highly obvious in the later "Ten Verses" anthology. All the other contributors listed their native places in Fujian, Guangdong, Vietnam, or elsewhere next to their names. Tianci, on the other hand, indicated that he was a man of Maocheng, in Hebei Province.[26] It was the place where the Mo surname originated. The first character of "Mao" in Maocheng was also the official surname used by his father and him in front of the Cochinchinese court. It was an identification with a historical allusion rather than a concrete geographic location. Little wonder that he would have felt lonely at times, just like a Daoist recluse.

Tianci's own upbringing contributed to this unique worldview. From an early age, he had "thoroughly read and memorized all the Confucian classics and works of the Hundred Schools of Thought" in ancient China. He mastered the martial strategies from Sunzi's *Art of War* and other military manuals.[27] Ironically, perhaps because of his embrace of the classical tradition, he never wanted to set foot on Qing territory. As he disclosed to Liang Luan, a contributor to one of his later

---

[25] Chin Kei-wa (Chen Jinghe), 'Kasen Maku-shi,' p. 170; Hán-Nôm A. 2939: Phạm, *Nam hành*, n. p.

[26] Hán-Nôm A. 441: Mao, *Hexian shiyong*, n. p.   [27] Vũ, *Gia phả*, p. 102.

anthologies, he hoped to remain a sojourner in a foreign land, where he could realize his vision of a Chinese utopia.[28]

This message was also a recognition that his Chinese identity would be creolized and localized, heavily colored by the hybrid, multiethnic environment where he resided in spite of any quest for purity and authenticity. He certainly spoke Vietnamese at a native level through his mother's side and was also at least fluent in Khmer. He may have been proficient in Siamese as well. During the 1770s, a resident of The Port who translated for him on behalf of a Spanish Franciscan missionary was identified to be "a native of Siam."[29] Given his background, and depending on his ethnicity, this individual may have either spoken Chinese or Siamese to Tianci.

Confucian Marketing

Under the influence of his background and prior education, Mo Tianci moved beyond the Buddhist networks, with their Ming loyalist associations, to espouse Confucianism in his governance. It was not really a replacement of one ideology by another. Rather, it aimed to broaden The Port's horizons, being inclusive of the previous associations but also encapsulating as much as possible the growing complexity of the realm. Indeed, the kind of Confucianism that he espoused built upon the foundations of Chan Buddhism and Daoism.[30] As Nguyễn Ngọc Thơ and Nguyễn Thanh Phong point out, Wang Yangming's Heart-Mind school was also decentralized enough to accommodate horizontal ties with different networks and allowed space for individual interpretation.[31] It provided the ideological justification for the Pavilion of Summoning Worthies to engage in long-distance associations beyond The Port.

The individual who played a crucial role in these linkages was the merchant Chen Zhikai. He stood at the heart of several distinct yet overlapping networks. On the one hand, he traded at ports from Guangzhou to Vietnam. At the same time, he had an appreciation for literature and culture and was an active member of the West Garden poetry club, where he had the opportunity to mingle with the gentry class. These elites, including She Xichun, enjoyed close ties to the Ming loyalist diaspora, including the Buddhist networks and the Dragon Gate

---

[28] Luo, *Wushan zhilin*, pp. 57–58.
[29] Perez, 'Los españoles en el imperio de Annam' 13, pp. 183–184.
[30] Swain, *Confucianism in China*, pp. 149–151.
[31] Nguyễn Ngọc Thơ and Nguyễn, 'Philosophical Transmission,' p. 104.

contingent.[32] Through them, both Chen Zhikai and She Xichun could maintain contacts with elites in Vietnam. Most importantly, from the perspective of Mo Tianci, The Port was a major, and probably the terminal, stop on the merchant's journey. Whenever Chen Zhikai arrived, he would get together with Tianci to drink, converse, and compose verses.[33]

It was Chen Zhikai who made Tianci aware of She Xichun's existence, if the two did not know of each other before. She Xichun sent along a sample of his poetry on board Chen Zhikai's ship for Tianci to read. Tianci loved it so much that when the following sailing season came along, he sent a ship filled with luxury goods to "purchase Xichun's new verse."[34] Through Chen Zhikai's mediation, She Xichun welcomed Tianci into their club and worked to spread his name beyond The Port. It was probably at the encouragement of She Xichun and Chen Zhikai that Tianci decided to publish the output from the literary exchanges centered upon the Pavilion for Summoning Worthies. The merchant likely arranged for a workshop in the Guangzhou area to carve out woodblocks and print their contents. Perhaps Tianci's earlier "Idle Fishing" collection was the first to be published.

Around 1736, Tianci and Chen Zhikai conceived of the idea of selecting ten of the most scenic views in The Port and recruiting poets locally and from China and Vietnam, including Tianci himself, to write verses about each landmark. Unlike the previous "Idle Fishing" collection, Tianci had more practical aims this time around. He primarily composed the verses as a marketing ploy to promote his realm before gentry and merchant-scholars in the Sinosphere. Of course, he made use of the opportunity to express his ideals and search for like-minded individuals, as Ang correctly highlights.[35] Still, the ultimate aim was to attract more business to his shores and assure merchants that it was a safe place to be. By portraying The Port as an exotic but civilized space on par with its Sinosphere neighbors, he could create a horizontal bond of trust across state boundaries and the traditional maritime divide, thereby lowering transaction costs and creating the equivalent of a free trade zone. And he enjoyed successful results.

Mo Tianci's set of poems on the "Ten Scenic Views" reveals the influence of a literary technique used since the Song that combines the

---

[32] Chen Jianhua, *Guangzhou dadian*, vol. 444: She, *Yushan tang*, p. 157; vol. 89: Ling, *Haiyatang*, p. 336.
[33] Hán-Nôm A. 441: Mao, *Hexian shiyong*, n. p.
[34] Chen Jianhua, *Guangzhou dadian*, vol. 89: Ling, *Haiyatang*, p. 295; Wen, *Yuedong shihai*, vol. 3, p. 1254.
[35] Ang, *Poetic Transformations*, p. 161.

travel guide, landscape painting, and poetry to describe noteworthy locations and the integration of human activities with nature. The most famous example of this genre is the "Ten Scenic Views of West Lake" in Hangzhou. Hangzhou and Suzhou, the two cities of Jiangnan, the commercial and cultural heartland of China, had been the sources of inspiration for The Port since the days of Mo Jiu. Both he and his son had referred to the rich historical allusions related to these sites from the classical Chinese tradition to tame what was once considered a remote, barbarian-infested frontier. Whereas Jiu sought to reshape the physical landscapes of the realm through the discovery and identification of noteworthy locations, Tianci celebrated them in text.[36]

One group of verses in Tianci's contribution to the "Ten Verses" highlights the imposing natural wonders of The Port. However, their beauty had to fit the aesthetic tastes of the gentry literati. In "Stone Grotto Swallows Clouds" (Scene 5), Tianci associates the strange cave formation northwest of The Port center with a similar natural wonder in China: the Linglong Mountains outside Hangzhou. Likewise, the title of his poem on East Lake lagoon, "Moon's Reflection on East Lake" (7), deliberately juxtaposes it to the "Moon's Reflection on the Three Pools," a famed scene of Hangzhou's West Lake (see Figure 3.4).[37]

Certain sites were celebrated for their pristine natural beauty. These were great selling points for adventurous Sinosphere tourists, but their wildness and exoticism had to be restrained and channeled. Take the example of Pearl Cliff, a towering, craggy network of caves along the shoreline east of The Port, in present-day Thuận Yên. Many poker-chip venus clams lived in their subterranean waters. According to a local legend, Mo Jiu had retrieved a giant pearl from one of these clams while touring the area. He immediately arranged to have this rare, priceless treasure sent to Huế as tribute to the Nguyễn lord.[38] Tianci, too, visited this site and dedicated a poem to a steep waterfall tumbling downward from the precipitous cliffs of one cave formation. Ang shows how his focus on the mists and spray given off by the splashing water in "An Egret Descends from Pearl Cliff" (6) blunt its loud noise, while the gentle descent of an egret substitutes for its far more tumultuous crash.[39] Both the pearl and the falls knew their place in the peaceful and orderly framework established by the Mo.

---

[36] Duan, *Rise of West Lake*, pp. 156–182; Ang, *Poetic Transformations*, p. 126.
[37] Hán-Nôm A. 441: Mao, *Hexian shiyong*, n. p.; Trịnh, *Thông chí*, p. 182.
[38] Trương, *Nghiên cứu*, vol. 1, pp. 287–298; Trịnh, *Thông chí*, pp. 171–172.
[39] Hán-Nôm A. 441: Mao, *Hexian shiyong*, n. p.; Ang, *Poetic Transformations*, pp. 141–143.

Figure 3.4 The East Lake lagoon. Suzhou Mountain lies on the other side.
Photograph by author.

Other natural landscapes combine their inherent aesthetic qualities with their practical value for The Port's protection. "Golden Islet Blocking Waves" (1) extols the Big Golden Islet's usefulness in breaking and calming the tempestuous waves as they entered the harbor (see Figure 3.5). It was a "wondrous beauty" that "strengthens Hà Tiên." "Verdant Folds of Screen Mountain" (2) compares the mountain to an opened, colorfully decorated screen. It was a place full of life, teeming with lush and verdant trees, and fauna roaming about. But it also served as an important barrier on land. Its peaks, like folds in a screen, pressed up to the sky, blocking the path of advance from hostile infantries.[40]

Then, there are the poems that focus on human activity, with the landscape forming the backdrop. The sound of the "Dawn Bell at the Temple of Seclusion" (3) from outside town awakens "the thousand households." This religious establishment was dedicated to the Bodhisattva Ksitigarbha (C: Dizang V: Địa Tạng) and located about a

---

[40] Hán-Nôm A. 441: Mao, *Hexian shiyong*, n. p.; Trịnh, *Thông chí*, pp. 166–167, 174–175.

Figure 3.5 The Big Golden Islet, once standing isolated in the middle of the Fortress River mouth, has now integrated with the mainland. Photograph by author.

kilometer east of the Stone Grotto. According to Trịnh Hoài Đức's gazetteer, it occupied an ethereal world of its own. When people passed through its gates, they "immediately shed off their greed and discontent and their lowly ambitions" to enter a higher spiritual realm. The lines in Tianci's poem, however, purposely break down this barrier between sacred and profane. He highlights the ringing of the temple bell at dawn to symbolize both the advent of a physical new day and a state of spiritual enlightenment: "purified region and human destiny awaken to the world." Even as the holy Buddhist teachings are transmitted afar, the cocks crow and ordinary people join the hustle and bustle and go about their everyday business.[41]

A formidable fortress situated near the headwaters of Fortress River, where it connects to the seasonal canals leading to Moat Chrouk, marks the start of a lengthy series of defensive fortifications built to protect

---

[41] Hán-Nôm A. 441: Mao, *Hexian shiyong*, n. p.; Ang, *Poetic Transformations*, pp. 137–139; Trịnh, *Thông chí*, p. 168.

against threats from the Cambodian interior. In "Night Drum of River Wall" (4), guards stood watch through the darkness and regulated the passage of time to ensure a smooth transition to daylight without any incident. South Bay lies to the south of Suzhou Mountain, across the harbor from The Port's center. From its sandy beaches, one can view the busy traffic of merchant junks and fishing vessels parting the tides in the gulf as they enter and exit the harbor. This scene forms the main topic of "Clear Waves on South Bay."[42]

"Rustic Dwellings at Deer Cape" (9) celebrates the rustic settings of Deer Cape (C: Luqi, K: Phnom Nay, V: Mũi Nai), a picturesque peninsula about six kilometers to the west of The Port's center that sticks out into the Gulf of Siam. Here, Tianci skillfully strikes a balance between a portrayal of the exotic and a moral affirmation of the Confucian-Daoist romanticization of the idyllic rural life. He describes peasant dwellings made from bamboo mixed in with lush, fertile paddies and gardens full of dense trees, all perched perilously on top of a steep cliff overlooking the sea. Nearby were forests where gibbons and deer roamed. Around the time for meals, the scent of fragrant rice and millet pervaded the air. Meanwhile, a young boy sat on a water buffalo, playing a flute as he watched over the fields.[43]

The very last poem takes the reader back to Sea Perch Creek, the site featured in the previous "Idle Fishing" publication. In "Anchored Fishing Boat at Sea Perch Creek" (10), Tianci, the solitary fisherman, once again appears with his boat. As he patiently waits for his catch in the frosty mist, his gaze remains fixed in the distance toward the sea. The sun gradually sets, and darkness envelops the realm that he has recently inherited.[44]

Taken together, Mo Tianci's poems on the "Ten Scenic Views" excites potential visitors with a romantic touch of the distant, mysterious, and foreign. In fact, in Line 7 of "Verdant Folds of Screen Mountain," he self-consciously describes The Port as unusual (*yi*):

敢道河仙風景異 (I dare say that in Hà Tiên the scenery is unusual)[45]

But this quality had to be placed within a format that draws upon China's rich literary tradition, familiar to the entire Sinosphere.

---

[42] Hán-Nôm A. 441: Mao, *Hexian shiyong*, n. p.; Trịnh, *Thông chí*, pp. 181–182; Nguyễn Dynasty, *Nhất thống chí*, vol. 3, p. 282.
[43] Hán-Nôm A. 441: Mao, *Hexian shiyong*, n. p.; Trịnh, *Thông chí*, pp. 167–168; Nguyễn Dynasty, *Nhất thống chí*, vol. 3, p. 272.
[44] Hán-Nôm A. 441: Mao, *Hexian shiyong*, n. p.
[45] Hán-Nôm A. 441: Mao, *Hexian shiyong*, n. p.

The style and imagery of Mo Tianci's poems follow a famous, eighth-century Tang poem by Zhang Ji on Suzhou, entitled "A Night Mooring by Maple Bridge":

> 月落烏啼霜滿天 (Moon set, a crow caws, frost fills the sky)
> 江楓漁火對愁眠 (River, maple, fishing-fires, cross my troubled sleep)
> 姑蘇城外寒山寺 (Beyond the walls of Suzhou from Cold Mountain Temple)
> 夜半鐘聲到客船 (The midnight bell sounds reach my boat)[46]

References to the moon, darkness yielding to dawn, the cries of a crow, frost, fishing boats, a temple bell, a river, and more appear throughout Tianci's verses, and he expands upon them in describing The Port's scenic views. In doing so, he was displaying a prosperous, well-ordered realm in the Confucian sense, where everything, from human beings to inanimate objects, contributed their part in agriculture, fishing, trade, and defense.

Aside from the main themes of his scenic descriptions, Mo Tianci did not forget to pitch his Ming loyalist ideals. Ang and Kelley show how he incorporated them in the form of double interpretations or coded messages underneath the direct description of a certain landmark. The first poem, "Golden Islet Blocking Waves," which functions as a sort of introduction to the entire "Ten Scenic Views," contains the densest concentration of these allusions. Take lines 3 and 4:

> 波濤勢截東南海 (The power of waves and tempests are cut off in the southeastern sea)
> 日月光迴上下天 (The radiance of the sun and moon permeates the sky above and below)[47]

When the characters for sun (日) and moon (月) are combined, the result becomes Ming (明). Ang additionally points out that if the two characters of 下天 (*xiatian*) in the last line were pronounced in Cantonese, they would be a homophone of the Vietnamese Hà Tiên. Thus, an alternative interpretation for these two lines can be that the power of the Manchus, whose onslaught was unstoppable like the stormy waves, has been blocked in front of the Golden Islets. At The Port, the radiance of the Ming freely permeates the landscape.[48]

---

[46] Mair, *Shorter Columbia Anthology*, p. 100; Kelley, 'Chinese Diaspora,' pp. 89–90.
[47] Hán-Nôm A. 441: Mao, *Hexian shiyong*, n. p.
[48] Ang, *Poetic Transformations*, p. 161; Kelley, 'Chinese Diaspora,' pp. 85–86.

The final line of the poem contains another encoded message:

濃淡山川異國懸 (In this landscape of shadow and light, an unusual kingdom, distant)[49]

Ang offers a second reading: "In this landscape of shadow and light, distant from that heterodox kingdom."[50] Especially when read in conjunction with the previous lines, one can interpret Tianci as denying the legitimacy of the Qing and emphasizing that his realm lay at a safe distance away.

Yet, compared to his more open, straightforward expression of Ming loyalist sentiment in "Idle Fishing," Tianci took greater care to disguise his political loyalties. And even the subdued statements sought to achieve more pragmatic ends. A distant Ming loyalist land could excite the nostalgic memories of Sinosphere elites who wished to fulfill their quest for authenticity. At the very least, it presented an interesting and exotic spectacle able to attract tourists, merchants, sojourners, and immigrants to his shores.

Where the Bright Moon and Crisp Breeze Form Friendships

The merchant Chen Zhikai took Mo Tianci's poems on the "Ten Scenic Views" onto his ship. Wherever he visited, he solicited responses from local elites he knew. He appeared to have also brought along a guest named Mao Yunyang. Judging from his surname, modified from Mo, he was a close relative of Tianci and probably traded as a trusted personal agent on behalf of the clan. Like Zhikai, he was also a man of cultural refinement and had valuable connections of his own to recruit for the project. Presently, Zhikai introduced Yunyang to his fellow poetry society members at Guangzhou. They celebrated the meeting with a poem bearing the lengthy but highly informative title: "Presented to the Envoy from Hà Tiên Garrison Mao Yunyang after Joyfully Meeting Him and Spontaneously Responding to His Prompt Request for Poems and Rhapsodies."[51]

As the title implies, at least a few members gladly responded to the call for contributions to the "Ten Verses" anthology and wrote them on the spot. Besides a spontaneous method of composition, others whom Zhikai

---

[49] Hán-Nôm A. 441: Mao, *Hexian shiyong*, n. p.; Ang, *Poetic Transformations*, p. 128.
[50] Ang, *Poetic Transformations*, p. 161.
[51] Ang, *Poetic Transformations*, p. 15; Chen Jianhua, *Guangzhou dadian*, vol. 445: Yang, *Luxi shichao*, pp. 176–177.

and Yunyang approached might be given more time, until the next sailing season for the merchant vessels to collect their works. Through these means, thirty-one poets wrote their own ten poems in response to Tianci's description of the "Ten Scenic Views" of The Port.[52] The "Ten Verses" anthology, published in 1737, contains a total of 320 poems, along with Tianci's preface and postscripts penned by Chen Zhikai and She Xichun, both of whom did not contribute any poems to the project.[53]

Each set of ten verses starts off by listing the author's native place and his given and style names. The twenty-five Chinese poets largely claimed affiliation with Fujian and Guangdong, although a few may have origins in other provinces. It is not clear how many of them resided in their listed native places or whether they lived elsewhere but continued to maintain the identity of their homelands. The China-based contributors predominantly came from the ranks of the lower-level elite, who would have been the most approachable for someone of Chen Zhikai's background. Wang Chang, for instance, was a native of Guangzhou and obtained a junior licentiate (*zhusheng*) degree after passing the lowest level of the civil service examinations. He never acquired a government post and instead devoted his energy toward composing verse. Eventually, he compiled and published his own anthology.[54] He and many of the other contributors never stepped foot in The Port. In fact, one poet, Zhu Pu of Guangdong, openly admitted in his reaction to "Golden Islet Blocking Waves" that he was "yet to ride the winds and come to this land."[55] In other words, he was describing this famous scene entirely with his own imagination!

Two of Zhu Pu's fellow Guangdong contributors, Chen Ruifeng and Chen Yinsi, were either long-term residents of The Port or had close connections to it. They identified themselves as natives of Wuyang, the county seat of Wuchuan, the hometown of Chen Shangchuan. And there is conclusive evidence to prove this connection. Chen Ruifeng's name appears in one of the clan genealogies. He belonged to the same generation as Chen Ruishu and Chen Dali, the commanders of the Dragon Gate contingent in The Port.[56] Chen Yinsi, on the other hand, was probably a distant clan relative or a close associate.

Two of the contributors to the anthology are documented to have resided in Cochinchina. C: Chen Mingxia V: Trần Minh Hạ and

---

[52] Ang, *Poetic Transformations*, p. 15.
[53] Chin Kei-wa (Chen Jinghe), 'Kasen Maku-shi,' pp. 162–165.
[54] Wen, *Yuedong shihai*, vol. 3, p. 1466.
[55] Hán-Nôm A. 441: Mao, *Hexian shiyong*, n. p.   [56] *Tiantou qi zhi shijiu shi*, p. 26b.

C: Sun Tianzhen V: Tôn Thiên Trân self-identified as Minh Hương.[57] Sun Tianzhen appears to be related to another poet, Sun Tianrui of Xiamen. As Chen Ching-ho surmises, the two may have been brothers and lived in Cochinchina together. They simply used their native-place affiliations in a flexible manner.[58]

Among the six Viet literati, only one of them, Phan Thiên Quảng, had roots in Cochinchina, or more precisely, from the area north of Huế. The other five listed native places in Tonkin. A traditional center of bureaucracy and Confucian education, northern Vietnam naturally had a larger pool of educated elites with the literary refinement to compose verse in Classical Chinese.[59] But they probably had already migrated to Cochinchina or were the descendants of migrants. Perhaps this explains why Trịnh Hoài Đức's gazetteer lists all the Viet contributors as being instead from places controlled by Cochinchina, four of them from the north of Huế, while the other, Trịnh Liên Sơn, came from Saigon.[60]

The content of the 310 poems submitted by the thirty-one contributors to the "Ten Verses" reflected the diversity of opinion within the Sinosphere. Some were apolitical and simply chose to sing praises to the different scenic marvels of The Port. Chen Ruifeng, who had close ties to the Dragon Gate, unquestionably embraced the Ming loyalist messages within Mo Tianci's poetry. In his response to "Golden Islet Blocking Waves," he writes:

> 古今每見風雲變 (It has seen the winds and clouds change every time from past to present)
> 朝夕常教日月懸 (From dawn to dusk, it keeps the sun and moon hanging over the sky)[61]

Recall that the characters for sun and moon put together make Ming. The author is saying that the Golden Islets fulfill the important defensive function of preserving Ming institutions and customs in The Port. The geographic features also keep out the "wind and clouds," representing political turbulence and dynastic change.

The use of the sun and moon characters to stand for "Ming," or the "Ming" character itself, appears in the poems of several other contributors. These Qing elites participated in Mo Tianci's literary

---

[57] Trịnh, *Thông chí*, pp. 306–307 labels Chen Mingxia a person from Fujian, while Sun Tianzhen came from Guangdong.
[58] Chin Kei-wa (Chen Jinghe), 'Kasen Maku-shi,' pp. 162–165. Trịnh, *Thông chí*, pp. 306–307 claims that Sun Tianrui and Sun Tianzhen both originated from Guangdong.
[59] Li Tana, *Nguyễn Cochinchina*, pp. 99–116.   [60] Trịnh, *Thông chí*, pp. 306–307.
[61] Hán-Nôm A. 441: Mao, *Hexian shiyong*, n. p.

project as an opportunity to voice pro-Ming sentiments and other forms of political dissent that they could not safely express within their own society. After the death of the Yongzheng Emperor (1678–1735, r. 1722–1735) in 1735, his successor, Qianlong (1711–1799, r. 1736–1799), gradually intensified the literary inquisition of his predecessors. Over the course of his lengthy reign, the Qianlong Emperor targeted written texts and punished their authors for even the merest hints of anti-Qing sentiment.[62] Indeed, the court had good reason to view Han gentry, including the contributors to the "Ten Verses" anthology, with suspicion. They either could not find a stable government position or served in ones that offered little compensation and slim chances for upward advancement.[63] Moreover, the southeastern Chinese coastline, where most of the poets came from, had been a hotbed of anti-Qing military resistance and continued to view the dynasty with ideological ambivalence or outright hostility.

Wang Chang of Panyu was one of these discontented elites, and we can gauge his personal feelings in several of his poems. He wrote in "Golden Islet Blocking Waves":

> 書生獨抱梯航志 (This scholar specially desires to climb mountains and cross seas)
> 空對文瀾枕硯田 (But meaninglessly, he faces a wave of essays cushioned under an inkstone)[64]

He laments being caught in a dead-end career, with little room for further advancement and with no hope other than daydreaming about journeying to distant lands. The issue was not just about social mobility. In fact, in 1736, around the time he would be writing these lines, he received a recommendation from a high-ranking official to sit for the special "broad learning and vast erudition" (*boxue hongru*) examination. Held outside the regular schedule of civil service examinations, it was the second and final time it was offered after 1678. If Wang had taken it, he would have enjoyed a much higher rate of success and, if he passed, he could have obtained a stable position working for imperially sponsored scholarly projects in Beijing. But Wang rejected the offer.[65]

More than career advancement, his ideals prevented him from advancing in the hierarchy of the ruling dynasty. As his poetic response to "Verdant Folds of Screen Mountain" reveals:

---

[62] For a detailed look at the Qing literary inquisition, see Guy, *Four Treasuries*, pp. 16–37, 203–204.
[63] Rowe, *China's Last Empire*, pp. 111–114 explains more about literati relations with the government during the Yongzheng and Qianlong periods.
[64] Hán-Nôm A. 441: Mao, *Hexian shiyong*, n. p.
[65] Wen, *Yuedong shihai*, vol. 3, p. 1466; Guy, *Qing Governors*, p. 242.

我有詩心無處托 (I have the heart to write poetry but have no place to express my mind)
直從天外寄情遙 (My emotions are focused in the distance upon the outer lands)

Wang places hope in The Port as a place where he could express his true sentiments, unfettered by the censorship that he faced at home. In "Clear Waves on South Bay," he writes:

煙消雲斂接天清 (After the smoke and clouds dissipate, the sky becomes clear)
聖人有道昭明世 (A sage lightens up the way for this world)[66]

The character for "clear" (清) contains the double meaning of the Qing dynasty, while bright and Ming (明) share the same character. Therefore, "lightens up the way for the world" (昭明世) can stand for "following the path of the Ming rulers." The smoke and clouds serve as metaphors for chaos and warfare. The lines could alternatively be interpreted as the Qing coming to power after the disorder of the dynastic transition had ended. However, a sage has appeared who opens another way, one that follows the Ming house. He was none other than Mo Tianci.

Perhaps the most unique anti-Qing allusion comes from Lin Weize of Chaozhou. His poem on Screen Mountain speaks of it being so high and forbidding that "wild horses filling up an entire road cannot fly over" (野馬滿途飛不到).[67] The character for "wild" (野) is synonymous with "barbarian," while "full" (滿) carries the double-meaning of Manchu, who were renowned for their fast and fierce cavalry. Therefore, the line can also say that the "path of the barbarian Manchu hordes cannot fly over" Screen Mountain.

Although Ming loyalism was a popular theme among the contributors, it had its detractors. Tang Yuchong of Chaozhou openly supported the Qing. In his response to "Clear Waves on South Bay," he credits the peace and prosperity of The Port to the protective power of the dynasty:

河仙寧靖頌河清 (Hà Tiên, at peace, sings praises to the clearness of its river)
謾言獻瑞無征驗 (To those who deceive, saying that auspicious omens cannot be verified)
先兆中華萬載清 (Here is an indication that China will for ages onward be Qing)[68]

The character for "clear" is the same as Qing, and he does not bother to disguise his political loyalties after the first line. Tang Yuchong goes on

---

[66] Hán-Nôm A. 441: Mao, *Hexian shiyong*, n. p.
[67] Hán-Nôm A. 441: Mao, *Hexian shiyong*, n. p.
[68] Hán-Nôm A. 441: Mao, *Hexian shiyong*, n. p.

to accuse those who continue to harbor Ming loyalist sentiments of deception, not only of others but also of themselves, since they could not adapt to the times and come to terms with a new, powerful dynasty that was there to stay.

Others, out of respect for Mo Tianci, avoided a direct disagreement with him. In the case of Chen Zhikai's poetry companions at West Garden in Guangzhou, we can discover their attitude in their poem dedicated to Mao Yunyang, Tianci's envoy who came to solicit poems from them:

> 浮槎東指海天遙 (A hawthorn leaf floats eastward into the distant ocean sky)
> 星使來王奉朔朝 (The royal envoy comes to pay tribute to our dynasty)
> 文教久推成化俗 (Prolonged exposure to civilization has transformed customs)
> 騷壇今喜接清標 (Now our poetry society happily receives an extraordinary individual)
> 麈揮夷甫寰中論 (Like Wang Yan, he will speak about the affairs of the world while waving a stag's tail)[69]
> 才邁玄虛筆下描 (His ability surpasses what are described in empty and deceitful writings)
> 心折瞻韓羨年少 (In great admiration, we first meet him and envy his youth)
> 雞林聲望溢雲霄 (Jilin's reputation has spilled over to the far corners of the earth)[70]

It is readily apparent that the members of the poetry society were deeply impressed by the young man's talent. While highly laudatory of Yunyang as an individual, their verse was patronizing in its tone about where he came from. They viewed The Port as an originally "barbarian" frontier that had only recently embraced civilized practices. Jilin, in the last line, originally the name of an ancient kingdom in present-day Northeast China and Korea, broadly referred within this context to China's Sinosphere neighbors. Yunyang's visit to Guangzhou thus resembled a tributary mission from a kingdom that aspired to participate in the Qing order. The attitude expressed here resembles that of Tang Yuchong's poem.

---

[69] Wang Yan (256–311) was a politician of the Jin dynasty (266–420). He was known for being a master rhetorician who often participated in lengthy discussions on cosmology and metaphysics. In order to express his ideas more smoothly, he would wave a stag's tail in one hand while speaking. See Zhang Chengzong, *Liu chao minsu*, p. 81.

[70] Chen Jianhua, *Guangzhou dadian*, vol. 445: Yang, *Luxi shichao*, pp. 176–177.

Although The Port was a vassal of Cochinchina, the "Ten Verses" collection contains few explicit assertions of it being a part of Vietnam or sharing a distinct Vietnamese identity. The Minh Hương Sun Tianzhen probably comes closest in likening Screen Mountain to "a minister who pays respect to the Southern dynasty on every side" (如臣面面拱南朝). Xu Xiemin of Guangdong likens the same mountain to the ceremonial tablets used by ministers at court audiences. And they were held in the direction of the Southern dynasty, a gesture of subordination. But this theme was much more subdued and marginal compared to the Chinese historical allusions. Surprisingly, the self-identified Viet contributors make no direct mention of their country except a few vague references to The Port being a vassal of a faraway court.[71] These allusions are themselves subject to multiple interpretations, as explained later.

The Viet poets, together with many of their Chinese counterparts, preferred instead to celebrate The Port as a new member of a broader interstate Sinosphere community. In his response to "Rustic Dwellings at Deer Cape," Trần Trinh describes the prosperous and well-fed Khmer residents of the village:

> 人人皷腹東皋外 (With protruding bellies, they all gather in the eastern marshes)
> 翹首中華慶帝星 (With heads raised toward the Central Efflorescence, they say their blessings to the emperor)[72]

In this context, Central Efflorescence (中華), or the Middle Kingdom, does not appear to be referring to Vietnam as a replacement for China but rather to the actual China. Trinh makes this point more explicit in "Clear Waves on South Bay":

> 應識越裳頻入貢 (You should know that the Việt Thường frequently pay tribute)
> 中華天子更廉明 (The Chinese Son of Heaven has greater integrity)

Trinh uses an archaic, Han-period term for the Viet people to show that they, too, admired China since ancient times, as seen in their regular tribute missions. He and the other Viet poets appeared to accept the country's continued centrality regardless of the actual dynasty in power.

And it was Mo Tianci's wise governance and focus on maintaining a just Confucian order that had allowed for the smooth incorporation of an unfamiliar territory and people into the Sinosphere. As Chen Zilan, a native of Xiamen, writes about Screen Mountain:

---

[71] Hán-Nôm A. 441: Mao, *Hexian shiyong*, n. p.
[72] Hán-Nôm A. 441: Mao, *Hexian shiyong*, n. p.

此中並入中華地 (The land [embraced by the mountain] has now joined the territory of the Central Efflorescence)
鑿石分光有霍姚 (It benefits from the merit of Huo Yao, who chisels away at the stone)

Chen consciously compares Mo Tianci's feat to the famous Han general Huo Qubing (140–117 BCE). Also known as the Piaoyao commander, he opened the Western Regions for China.

In this spirit of interstate Sinosphere community, many of the contributors explored ways of reconciling the ideological divide between Ming and Qing. Lin Weize writes in his response to "Anchored Fishing Boat at Sea Perch Creek":

清風明月為知識 (The crisp breeze and bright moon are close friends)
綠水青山作友朋 (The green water and verdant mountain find common cause)[73]

The character for crisp (清) is the same as Qing, while bright stands for Ming. Lin was highlighting that proponents of either can coexist in harmony and friendship, just like other pairings in nature, such as the rivers and mountains.

The emphasis here is on friendship and integration rather than division and antagonism. It appears to be a broad consensus among the contributors despite whatever beliefs they held. The tribute-bearing ship (*gongchuan*) was one prominent theme used to highlight the connections. In the Sinosphere, tributary relations served as a prerequisite or cover for trade.[74] Three poets mention this kind of vessel in their responses to "Golden Islet Blocking Waves." Tang Yuchong speaks of "the massive tribute ships, motivated by profits, traveling back and forth." Xu Xiemin describes them "breaking through the smoky mist as they sail far away." The Cantonese poet Wu Zhihan imagines an envoy on board charged with transmitting messages to the "superior country" (*shangguo*), or China.[75] Regardless of who sat on the throne in the Central Plain, it remained the repository of civilization. Recognition of its standards served as a prerequisite for The Port to participate in the lively trading network of maritime East Asia.

But Mo Tianci wanted to be the arbiter of what constituted Chinese culture and control the linkages between the different Sinosphere states. Perhaps he would most be able to identify with the verses of two

---

[73] Hán-Nôm A. 441: Mao, *Hexian shiyong*, n. p.
[74] For more on the relationship between trade and tribute under the Qing, see Gipouloux, *Asian Mediterranean*, pp. 84–86.
[75] Hán-Nôm A. 441: Mao, *Hexian shiyong*, n. p.

contributors. Tang Yuchong, in his response to "Anchored Fishing Boat at Sea Perch Creek," mentions that a fisherman, gazing at the creek, "envies the fish and thought of making a net" (江上羨魚思結網) to catch them for their tasty meat. The line carries a double meaning, however. We can also equate the fisherman with Tianci, who loved to spend his idle time there, and the fish would be human beings whom he wanted to recruit into his network.

And Tang Yuchong was not the only poet to see through Tianci's intentions. The Viet poet Mạc Triều Đán writes in his reaction to "Clear Water at South Bay":

江上清風沙若岸 (The crisp breeze on the river, the sanded banks)
舟中明月水如晶 (The bright moon on the boat, the crystal water)
持竿獨釣溪頭客 (The guest who fishes alone with a pole at the head of the creek)
長詠滄浪可濯纓 (Always sings that he can wash his hat in the waters of Canglang)[76]

The first two lines, like Lin Weize's contribution, speak about the harmony of the Qing, represented by the crisp breeze, and the Ming, symbolized by the bright moon, at The Port. The guest would refer to Tianci, an ethnic Chinese residing far away from his native homeland.[77] The final line is especially intriguing, since it refers to an ancient song by a fisherman that was often quoted in classical Chinese works:

沧浪之水清兮 (When the Canglang's waters are clear)
可以濯吾纓 (I can wash my hat in them)
沧浪之水污兮 (When the Canglang's waters are muddy)
可以濯吾足 (I can wash my feet in them)[78]

True to his subscription to the decentralized Heart-Mind school of Confucianism, Tianci was willing to be pragmatic, just like the angler. His main goal was to de-emphasize the differences among translocal elites and build consensus as being part of the same world order, while spreading word of his realm across the Sinosphere.

And Tianci enjoyed much success. After the publication of the "Ten Verses," the Pavilion for Summoning Worthies continued to flourish, and the number of its participants multiplied. Evidently, the poems had circulated quite widely among literati in the Qing and Vietnam, and many of them were motivated to contribute their own creativity and insights. Trịnh Hoài Đức's gazetteer lists eight poets beyond the thirty-

---

[76] Hán-Nôm A. 441: Mao, *Hexian shiyong*, n. p.
[77] I borrow from Ang's interpretation. See Ang, *Poetic Transformations*, p. 136.
[78] Translation from Murck, *Poetry and Painting*, p. 115.

one contributors to the original "Ten Verses."[79] There were also at least five other literary compilations that appeared in print throughout Tianci's lengthy career.[80] Only fragments have survived the devastation and destruction across mainland Southeast Asia during the late eighteenth century.

The project that immediately followed the "Ten Verses" was an anthology on the four seasons of The Port. Its publication took place sometime in the 1740s. The Tonkin scholar Lê Quý Đôn lists thirty-two contributors, who composed eighty-eight verses. Most of the poems, including Mo Tianci's own piece, have been lost to us. Nine of them have survived by being included in Lê Quý Đôn's work, including a verse by Chen Zhikai on autumn reflections.[81]

This time around, Chen Zhikai introduced Tianci to more members of his poetry society and other Cantonese literati. Compared to the participants in the "Ten Verses" project, many of them enjoyed greater fame as poets, and their works circulated more widely, at least in Guangdong. Some of them also either once served in government office or had connections to the regular Qing bureaucracy. One of the contributors, Wang Houlai, had passed the military examinations and become a low-ranking company commander (*qianzong*). He led forces against rebels in Fujian and Guangdong before his retirement at around the age of sixty in the 1730s. Over the course of his duties, he cooperated closely with the governor-general.[82]

Because this project required a sensitivity and appreciation of the changing of seasons, participants had to be physically present at The Port. Mo Tianci funded all the costs related to their visit. He housed them at his own residence at the foot of Screen Mountain and feasted them and showered them with expensive gifts. Material enticements certainly motivated Wang Houlai to accept his invitation and contribute a poem on wintertime. Similarly, Liang Luan of Shunde, "a poor Confucian scholar who, at seventy, did not have any offspring," benefited from this opportunity. When Tianci learned of his plight, he dispatched four of his envoys to accompany Chen Zhikai's junk back to Guangzhou. They hauled a heavy piece of furniture made of firwood to Liang's residence. After his return, the poor poet sold it on the market for 200 pieces of gold, allowing him to spend the rest of his life in comfort.

---

[79] Trịnh, *Thông chí*, pp. 306–307.
[80] Chin Kei-wa (Chen Jinghe), 'Kasen Maku-shi,' p. 168; Ngạc, 'Minh Bột Di Ngư,' p. 10.
[81] Lê Quý Đôn, *Tiểu Lục*, vol. 1, pp. 704–709.
[82] Chen Jianhua, *Guangzhou dadian*, vol. 89: Ling, *Haiyatang*, p. 287. Lê Quý Đôn, *Tiểu Lục*, vol. 1, pp. 704–705 erroneously lists Wang Houlai as Wang Xilai.

Despite being well-advanced in years, at over ninety, She Xichun somehow made the journey as well, since he, too, wrote a verse, but like Liang's, it is not recorded in Lê Quý Đôn's work.[83]

For the Sinosphere literati, Tianci's translocal cultural platform helped broaden their horizons and made available opportunities that were unimaginable solely within their own societies. Although gentry loved to travel, their sphere of activities mostly occurred domestically between provincial lines. For instance, Chen Zhikai's poetry companion Fang Qiubai had roamed the empire, going as north as Beijing and as far south as Hainan. Although Tianci's lavish patronage certainly helped, Fang loved adventure and would have jumped at the opportunity to sail abroad using his own means. During his stay at The Port, he contributed a poem on springtime and was given the honor of writing the preface for the entire anthology, a surviving copy of which has not been located.[84] For Fang and others, The Port became an extension of their own domestic travels. There, they could revel in the scenery and engage in literary pursuits without being associated with merchant sojourners and immigrants, who were beneath them in social status, or having to adapt to strange "barbarian" customs.

Cochinchinese literati also came as guests of Tianci, although probably not as participants in the anthology on the four seasons. The Huế-based poet and recluse Ngô Thế Lân visited him at Sea Perch Creek on at least one occasion and wrote a brief verse on it.[85] Combined with the content of the Viet contributors to the "Ten Verses" project, it is apparent that these elites viewed The Port as a surrogate China. It was closer and more easily accessible from Cochinchina, especially since, unlike Tonkin, Huế could not send any official tributary missions to the Qing. The Port, with its Chinese creoles and concentration of Qing gentry visitors, was an exotic but not entirely foreign destination for them, given its hybridity.

Even if the Qing and Viet literati did not meet in person, Tianci's network ensured that they could maintain a long-distance connection. Guangzhou native Zhang Taichu cultivated a remote friendship with his Viet counterpart, Lâm Kỳ Tảo. Because neither of them could meet in person, they each drew a self-portrait and sent it to the other, thereby "pretending to meet." Every season, the two men exchanged gifts carried by a trading vessel, perhaps belonging to the merchant Chen Zhikai.[86]

Mo Tianci's literary projects reveal a gradual evolution in his clan's ideological vision for The Port. In "Idle Fishing," he expressed his

---

[83] Trương, *Nghiên cứu*, vol. 1, p. 195; Luo, *Wushan zhilin*, p. 58.
[84] Chen Jianhua, *Guangzhou dadian*, vol. 89: vol. 445: Yang, *Luxi shichao*, p. 160.
[85] Hán-Nôm A. 2939: Phạm, *Nam hành*, n. p.   [86] Luo, *Wushan zhilin*, p. 58.

nostalgia for the Ming quite openly, and the sentiments seem genuine. But he was writing under the framework of a Buddhist-Daoist synthesis that held together overseas Ming loyalist networks, while affirming ties with Cochinchina. Subsequent collections reflected the increasingly complex composition of The Port's maritime linkages that could not be contained within the original ideological framework. In the "Ten Verses" project, Ming loyalism constituted just one, albeit prominent, voice. Undoubtedly, many literati, especially from the Qing, cherished the opportunity to express and engage with ideas deemed subversive to Manchu rule. But there were many contributors who espoused a pro-Qing view or found ways to reconcile the different opinions. For this reason, Tianci toned down his rhetoric in his poems for the "Ten Verses."

Despite the diversity of opinions, the anthology reflects the continued coherence of the Sinosphere, at least from the perspective of elites in Vietnam and China. There was a recognition of a common civilization based in the Central Plains, although not necessarily the Manchus who ruled over it. Mo Tianci's main goal was to de-emphasize the differences among these translocal elites and cast his realm as a neutral mediator, haven, and clearinghouse for all kinds of information circulating across the Sinosphere. A common cultural language and friendly ties with elites helped lower the costs of doing business, providing a safer environment for merchant vessels to maneuver between different political jurisdictions. On a broader scale, the evolution of the literary projects accords with Tianci's embrace of the Heart-Mind school of neo-Confucianism. It provided the flexibility and tolerance to form connections with different networks and authorities. As time went on, he proved able to use this decentralized framework to maneuver both within and outside the Sinosphere. He could integrate himself into the hierarchies of different states and attempt to shape and influence their policies in a manner favorable to himself and his realm.

4 Ambiguous Associations

> The prince, who rules the place despotically, does not take the title of king, so as not to offend the sovereigns of Cochinchina and Cambodia, whose friendship he still maintains out of politics. It is this policy that supports him on the throne.
> —Nicolas-Jacques-Gervais Levavasseur (1741–1777), 1768[1]

> The Port, or Hà Tiên Garrison, is a place in Annam abutting Siam. It has always paid tribute to both countries.
> —Mo Wu, envoy of Mo Tianci, to Li Shiyao (d. 1788), governor-general of Guangdong and Guangxi, September 4, 1772[2]

Through his sponsorship of translocal literary projects, Mo Tianci enjoyed much success in forging an integrated cultural community among elites in China and Vietnam. Moreover, his embrace of the decentralized Confucian teachings of Wang Yangming allowed him to flexibly adapt to a complex external environment. Although Tianci maintained a formal vassalage toward Cochinchina, he became increasingly confident that it needed The Port at least as much, if not more, than the other way around. His realm served as a strategic maritime gateway that guarded the approach to Huế from adversaries in Cambodia and Cochinchina's foremost geopolitical rival: Siam. Multiple military successes against serious threats to the security of The Port, achieved primarily using Tianci's own resources, appeared to validate this perspective. Moreover, he came to see himself as an important cultural intermediary for Cochinchina through his privileged access to Sinosphere elites. Like his father, Tianci concurrently continued The Port's traditional subordination to Cambodia and actually increased his involvement in the kingdom. At the same time, he integrated his realm into the VOC hegemony, allowing him to deepen ties with the Austronesian and Batavia Chinese mercantile networks.

---

[1] AMEP, Cochinchine, vol. 744: 'Relation,' p. 966.
[2] Grand Council Archives, Qianlong Reign, 017970: Li Shiyao, n. p.

The secret to Tianci's ability to juggle simultaneous identities and allegiances lay in his understanding and manipulation of the conventions of the Sinosphere and the Southeast Asia mandala system. The two worldviews shared sufficient commonalities to allow for some level of synchronization. They both conceived of political order and diplomacy in an unequal manner, a hierarchy extending outward from an administrative and ritual center, where power was most concentrated, toward the peripheries as authority gradually becomes diluted. Both worldviews emphasize the role of the ruler as a semidivine figure responsible for mediating between the heavenly and mortal realms. He would be the Son of Heaven in China or a universal king of kings responsible for upholding a religious precept, whether Buddhism or Islam, in Southeast Asia. Lesser rulers within his sphere of control or influence would render vassalage through the regular dispatch of missions and payment of tribute. These gestures would be reciprocated by ranks and honors and generous gifts.[3]

The key distinction between the Sinosphere and the mandala system lies in their respective degrees of centralization and institutionalization. In the Sinosphere states, elaborate bureaucracies staffed by officials selected through rigorous examinations formalized and rationalized the Confucian hierarchy of familial and social obligations. In theory, they took responsibility for the implementation of a huge body of laws and moral regulations that covered every aspect of human behavior. The emperor sat atop this intricate machinery and, in principle, had the absolute and final say over its operation. Diplomacy represented an extension of the vision of domestic harmony and order, with a clear hierarchy placing China at the pinnacle and regulating the rank and status of each vassal kingdom. Meticulous instructions governed the arrivals and departures of tributary missions, the number and variety of gifts, and protocol.[4]

It should be noted that this is a description of an idealized model. As Peter Perdue and others have shown, the tributary system was only one of several kinds of foreign relations that the Qing dynasty pursued that also included purely trading partners and interactions based on status parity. Moreover, tribute-bearing states conceived of their vassalage in flexible ways and often not in accordance with their overlord.[5] The

---

[3] For an overview of the Sinocentric tributary system, see Kang, *East Asia*, pp. 17–24. More on the Southeast Asian mandala can be found in Wolters's *History, Culture, and Region*, pp. 27–40; Tambiah, *World Conqueror*, pp. 46–70.

[4] Kang, *East Asia*, pp. 54–81.

[5] Perdue, 'Tenacious Tributary System'; Chia, 'Lifanyuan,' pp. 158–168.

rulers of the Lê dynasty in Vietnam recognized Chinese supremacy but concurrently maintained their own set of subordinate vassals among the highland tribes, Laos, and Champa. Domestically and toward the Lê's Southeast Asian neighbors, its monarchs assumed the role of emperor of Đại Việt, while they transformed into vassal kings of Annam in front of China.[6] After the seventeenth century, Tokugawa Japan flatly refused to recognize the Ming and the succeeding Qing as its overlords. Instead, it set out to create a Japanocentric tributary system involving its close trading partners of Ryukyu, Korea, and the VOC.[7] Despite the differences in interpretation and practice, the tributary model gave the Sinosphere states a shared cultural and ideological vocabulary and predictability in the form of lengthy periods of peace, stable boundaries, and regularized relations.[8]

The mandala mode of diplomacy prevalent in Siam and Cambodia and island Southeast Asia, by contrast, relied far more on the individual charisma, energy, and interpersonal skills of the supreme ruler. According to Wolters and Tambiah, he resembled more of a mediator trying to resolve problems and maintain an equilibrium among cohesive, powerful nobility and clients, themselves welded together by real or fictive kinship ties. This personal element, which tended to supersede formal bureaucratic structures, effectively limited the size of the ruler's area of direct control and, by extension, his sphere of influence. The mandala system, accordingly, facilitated the emergence of volatile, competing centers of power. This environment gave vassals, especially the ones on the peripheries, opportunities to switch loyalties and choose the supreme ruler best able to grant them benefits and serve their interests.[9]

As with the Sinosphere, the reality was often more nuanced. Mandala centers, such as Ayutthaya, implemented reforms aimed at greater institutional continuity and sought to control its outer provinces and frontier areas to prevent the switching of allegiances. Ministries specialized in aspects of governance, while society was ranked into hierarchies that spelt out distinct levels of obligations and privileges. However, the entire system often depended upon strong personalities to work.[10] Cochinchina was a special case in that it had elements of both the Sinosphere and mandala. Dependence upon marriage alliances,

---

[6] Baldanza, *Ming China and Vietnam*, pp. 77–211; Li Tana, *Nguyễn Cochinchina*, p. 16.
[7] Ravina, *To Stand*, pp. 26–35; Clulow, *Company and the Shogun*, pp. 95–134.
[8] Kang, *East Asia*, pp. 158–171.
[9] Wolters, *History, Culture, and Region*, pp. 27–40; Tambiah, *World Conqueror*, pp. 112, 138–157.
[10] Hall, *Early Southeast Asia*, pp. 234–235; Gesick, 'Kingship,' pp. 14–48.

patronage, and kinship coexisted with and sometimes superseded the formal, Chinese-style bureaucratic structures.[11]

The Port functioned more as a crossroads than a transition zone like Cochinchina. By flexibly exploiting and alternating between the Sinosphere and mandala frameworks, Mo Tianci achieved outside recognition of the autonomous status of his realm without the need to declare a formally independent state. As the French missionary Nicolas-Jacques-Gervais Levavasseur notes, his equidistant diplomacy allowed him to acquire unchecked power at home.[12] At the same time, Claudine Ang shows, he made himself useful as a mediator, becoming an essential force for stability and peace in maritime East Asia.[13]

Balancing Cochinchina

After Mo Tianci ascended to power in 1735, he promptly dispatched an envoy to Huế with news of the succession. The Nguyễn lord employed a combination of methods to establish his authority over the young heir. On the one hand, Lord Ninh elevated Tianci's position above his deceased father, promoting him to the rank of military governor (Đô đốc) and bequeathing upon him the title of Tông Đức marquis.[14] On the other hand, Cochinchina continued to exercise influence by stationing troops in The Port and manipulating marriage and kinship ties. Tianci's wife, Lady Nguyễn, may have emigrated from Cochinchina or was a daughter of migrants. Alternatively, since her grave on the slopes of Screen Mountain had the characters for "Imperial Ming" inscribed on the tombstone, she may have been of Chinese creole background.[15]

She bore Tianci four sons, all of whom would play important roles in The Port's administration and military affairs. They were **C: Mo Hao** V: Mạc Tử Hạo, **C: Mo Huang** V: Mạc Tử Hoàng (d. 1821), C: **Mo Tang** V: Mạc Tử Thắng (d. 1780), and **C: Mo Rong** V: Mạc Tử Dung (d. 1780). She also gave birth to four daughters. In addition, Tianci took in at least seven concubines and had ten sons with them.[16]

Within the Sinosphere, Mo Tianci officially portrayed his realm as being a part of Annam, the traditional way of referring to Vietnam in relation to its tributary ties with China. Indeed, in the preface to his "Ten Verses" anthology, he opens with "Hà Tiên garrison of Annam" as a way

---

[11] Li Tana, *Nguyễn Cochinchina*, pp. 37–41.
[12] AMEP, Cochinchine, vol. 744: 'Relation,' p. 966.
[13] Ang, *Poetic Transformations*, p. 183. [14] Vũ, *Gia phả*, p. 100; Trịnh, *Thông chí*, p. 305.
[15] Phạm Đức Mạnh, 'Cổ mộ,' p. 1297.
[16] Chen Jinghe (Chin Kei-wa), 'Hexian Mao shi,' pp. 217–218; Trương, *Nghiên cứu*, vol. 2, p. 49.

of introducing the land that would serve as the topic of the landscape poems.[17] Qing sources elsewhere similarly speak of an "Annamese Port."[18] Affiliation with Annam served as a necessary prerequisite for The Port's participation in the political, economic, and cultural circles of the Sinosphere. Vietnam ranked third in the hierarchy of the Qing's vassal kingdoms, behind only Korea and Ryukyu, and was hence seen as constituting part of a common civilized community. Siam enjoyed a fairly privileged position, coming right after Vietnam in rank, but it was portrayed as being more barbarous in its customs. Claiming vassalage to Cambodia did not seem to be an attractive alternative, either. The Qing did not consider Cambodia to be a tribute-bearing state at all, since it had not sent any mission to China since the early Ming.[19]

It would also be difficult for Tianci to obtain recognition as ruler of an independent state. The Qing recognized the Lê in Hanoi as the sole rulers of Vietnam. As James Anderson has shown in the case of relations between the Song and earlier Viet dynasties, the Lê presided over their own nested hierarchy of lesser entities, which would include Tonkin and Cochinchina. The two, in turn, would each have their set of vassals. This rigid arrangement proved almost impossible to alter even though the Lê no longer exercised any real power. The Trịnh lords had to rule through Lê puppets. Tianci's Cochinchinese overlords made several attempts to portray themselves as rulers of Annam or an entirely separate kingdom but failed every time and therefore had to maintain their largely fictional subordination.[20]

On the positive side, the highly pro-Chinese outlook of Cochinchina held appeal for Tianci. Chinese merchants, immigrants, and religious figures played a key role in shaping its hybrid society. Many of them were also recruited to serve in the bureaucracy. Like Mo Tianci, they subscribed to Confucianism and applied its principles in their work. Although Buddhism remained dominant in Cochinchinese society, the ethnic Chinese presence undoubtedly contributed to growing inroads made by Confucian ideas over the eighteenth century.[21]

By the time Mo Tianci initiated his "Ten Verses" project, he had become increasingly confident of The Port's military and cultural strength, the result of the solid foundations laid by his father. In "Night

---

[17] Hán-Nôm A. 441: Mao, *Hexian shiyong*, n. p.
[18] Grand Council Archives, Qianlong Reign, 007528: Pan Siju, n. p.
[19] Fuheng, *Huang Qing zhigongtu*, vol. 1, pp. 61–62, 77, 167.
[20] Anderson, *Rebel Den*, p. 8; Yang, *Principauté des Nguyễn*, pp. 156–162.
[21] Nguyễn Ngọc Thơ and Nguyễn, 'Philosophical Transmission,' p. 91; Wheeler, 'Cross-Cultural Trade,' pp. 150–151; Ang, *Poetic Transformations*, pp. 83–84.

Drum of River Wall," Tianci writes in ambivalent language of a relationship of vassalage to a faraway court:

> 【客】仍【警】夜銷金甲 (A guest, armor decaying, continues to stay on alert at night)[22]
> 人正幹城擁錦袍 (An upright, heroic defender upholds the one in silken robes)
> 武略深承英主眷 (A brilliant ruler views his military ability with keen interest)
> 日南境宇賴安牢 (All of **C: Rinan** V: Nhật Nam depends on him for peace and security)[23]

As Ang points out, the guest mentioned here is Mo Tianci himself, a Chinese general in a distant land. Day and night, he stood on guard to the point that his armor was corroding to protect "the one in silken robes," a reference to a person of high rank and authority. That individual, the next line reveals, was a wise and capable ruler, who viewed Tianci's military prowess with admiration. Rinan, at the end of the poem, was the name of the southernmost commandery of the Han dynasty, with its administrative seat near present-day Huế.[24]

In similar fashion, a few other contributors use their descriptions of the Golden Islets, Screen Mountain, and the fortress in highlighting the strategic usefulness of these landmarks to a distant court and ruler. Mạc Triều Đán compares Screen Mountain to Mo Tianci himself, a "vassal holding up the distant heavenly court on high" (籓翰擎天萬仭朝).[25] The Viet poet Trịnh Liên Sơn writes of the Golden Islets:

> 帶礪山河分異域 (Splitting the uninterrupted mountains and rivers into a different realm)
> 屏藩海宇峙同天 (Under the same sky, a protective barrier faces the territorial waters)
> 日南於此稱奇勝 (Here in Rinan, this place can be called a majestic wonder)
> 不負探奇到客傳 (Let's satisfy our curiosity and book a hotel!)[26]

---

[22] The first character in brackets is missing in Hán-Nôm A. 441: Mao, *Hexian shiyong*, n. p. However, both Chin Kei-wa (Chen Jinghe), 'Kasen Maku-shi,' p. 336, and Ang, *Poetic Transformations*, p. 133, use the character for guest (客), and I borrow from them. Hán-Nôm A. 441: Mao, *Hexian shiyong*, n. p., lists the second character in brackets as 警, or staying on alert. I will use it instead of 竟, found in Chin (Chen) and Ang.
[23] Hán-Nôm A. 441: Mao, *Hexian shiyong*, n. p. The translation here is my own because I use a different base source from Chin (Chen) and Ang.
[24] Rinan is discussed in greater depth in Li Tana, 'Jiaozhi,' pp. 48–49.
[25] Hán-Nôm A. 441: Mao, *Hexian shiyong*, n. p.
[26] Hán-Nôm A. 441: Mao, *Hexian shiyong*, n. p.

Here, the Rinan metaphor appears again. Other poems refer to the Southern Sky (C: *Nantian* V: *Nam Thiên*), often in juxtaposition to the North Sea (C: *Beihai* V: *Bắc Hải*). Tang Yuchong praises the garrison at Fortress River:

南天德化銷煙警 (Its transformative virtue snuffs out signal fires in the Southern Sky)[27]
北海波恬靖海鼇 (It calms the waves and pacifies the giant turtle in the North Sea)

Elsewhere, both Tianci and some of the contributors describe Fortress River as a long river (C: *Changjiang* V: *Trường Giang*).[28]

These passages can be interpreted on two levels, depending on the connotations of Rinan, the distant court, Southern Sky and North Sea, and the long river. It is entirely conceivable to equate Rinan with Cochinchina, since its original location was around present-day Huế. The long river would simply be Fortress River, which stood on the front lines with Cambodia and Siam beyond. Southern Sky was a traditional term for Vietnam. The North Sea, on the other hand, refers to the South China Sea from the perspective of The Port.[29] The distant ruler would be the Nguyễn lord. Mo Tianci, who appears as the frontier general or vassal in the poems, would take on the role of Cochinchina's protector, vigilantly keeping its enemies at bay, ensuring peace within its boundaries, and calming its waters of tempests and monsters.

There is another way to read these poems. Rinan could serve as a figurative term for The Port itself. The merchant Chen Zhikai mentions in his postscript to the "Ten Verses" that "in 1736, I went on board a junk and arrived in Rinan. I stayed for six months, singing and composing poetry with" Tianci.[30] The Guangzhou poet Wang Houlai spoke of receiving lavish gifts from the "rulers of Rinan," here an obvious reference to the Mo leaders.[31] By using Rinan in this context, the contributors to Tianci's anthologies were consciously connecting The Port to the Han dynasty's southernmost frontier outpost. Far away from major political centers and surrounded by various barbarian tribes at its peripheries, it constantly had to defend against raids and invasions. Other poems compare The Port's defenses to the Willow Camp, which guarded the Han capital of Chang'an (present-day Xi'an) from the formidable Xiongnu hordes of the northern steppes during the first century BCE. The camp

---

[27] These were fires lit from beacons on high hills to warn of an imminent invasion.
[28] Hán-Nôm A. 441: Mao, *Hexian shiyong*, n. p.
[29] *Vùng đất Nam Bộ*: Nguyễn, vol. 4, p. 144.
[30] Hán-Nôm A. 441: Mao, *Hexian shiyong*, n. p.
[31] Chen Jianhua, *Guangzhou dadian*, vol. 89: Ling, *Haiyatang*, p. 287.

acquired fame for its strict regulations, superior military training, and effective leadership.³² Similarly, the North Sea can serve as an archaic term for Lake Baikal in Siberia, the homeland of the Xiongnu.

Given the appearance of Ming loyalist references in many of the poems, the North Sea can additionally refer to the Manchus, who originated in the same area. The long river would then be the Yangzi.³³ After 1644, the region south of the river, South China, or the Southern Sky, became a bastion for the Ming loyalists in their futile attempt at restoration from the Qing. But now, since the Manchu "barbarians" firmly controlled the entire heartland of civilization in China, Fortress River had become the new Yangzi, and the Southern Sky would be localized to The Port. The distant court would be the Han or Ming, remote in the sense that they no longer exist except as historical memory. Mo Tianci could thus cast himself as the leader of a completely independent polity, the final bastion of authentic Chinese civilization. His task would be to defend the southernmost frontier of the Sinosphere from the forces of barbarism, whether the Manchus in China or neighboring Siam and Cambodia.³⁴

Regardless of the interpretation, the "Ten Verses" anthology reveals a growing confidence on the part of Tianci and his collaborators in The Port's military power and cultural reputation, which gave it distinct advantages in the relationship with Cochinchina. His position received a significant boost when he successfully defused a major existential threat to his realm using primarily his own resources. In 1736, a year after he came to power, instability broke out again in Cambodia when Ang Em, the Mo clan's patron who had dominated Cambodian affairs for the past thirty years, passed away. His archnemesis, Ang Tham, took advantage of this opportunity to return from exile in Ayutthaya and attack the reigning king Satha. On land, Siamese forces helped him capture Oudong and force Satha to flee to Saigon. Ang Tham went by sea. Together with the Siamese fleet, he landed at Kampot. In 1738, Ang Tham's nephew, **K: Ang Mei Bhen** V: Nặc Bồn, led a contingent of troops from Oudong to welcome him. Ang Tham then returned to the capital and proclaimed himself king.³⁵

The bulk of Ang Tham's forces continued their advance toward Saigon and engaged in fierce battles with the Cochinchinese defenders in the surrounding province of Donay until at least 1740, when they were

---

³² Đông, *Văn Học*, pp. 158, 199–200.   ³³ Hán-Nôm A. 441: Mao, *Hexian shiyong*, n. p.
³⁴ Kelley, 'Chinese Diaspora,' p. 87.
³⁵ Hán-Nôm A. 832: Phạm, *Cao Man kỉ lược*, n. p.; EFEO Khmer: *Preah reach pongsavatar*, p. 105.

Figure 4.1 Touk Meas Mountain, viewed from the center of Banteay Meas, around where Mo Tianci's forces successfully counterattacked and defeated Ang Mei Bhen's invasion in 1739.
Photograph by author.

defeated and withdrew.[36] Meanwhile, Ang Mei Bhen set his sights upon The Port, since it seemed isolated and vulnerable, given the recent death of Mo Jiu and with the bulk of Cochinchinese forces engaged near Saigon. He therefore saw an opportunity to exact revenge upon a key supporter of Ang Tham's rival. In 1739, Ang Mei Bhen reached the walls of The Port, and placed the defenses under heavy pressure. Tianci resisted with all his strength. His forces managed, with great difficulty, to drive the enemy out of the urban center, toward the northwest. At the head of Fortress River near Touk Meas Mountain, he launched a fierce counterattack (see Figure 4.1). The two sides battled day and night. With food and supplies running dangerously low, Tianci's wife personally took charge of the planning. She prepared rice and procured necessities and supervised their timely

[36] Favre, *Lettres édifiantes et curieuses*, p. 141.

delivery to the soldiers on the front lines. Her effort paid off in the end; Tianci's forces smashed and routed the enemy.[37]

The ability to mount a successful resistance using The Port's own means made Tianci valuable to the Nguyễn lord, especially at a time when the Siamese and their Cambodian allies were making massive gains in mainland Southeast Asia and rolling back Cochinchinese influence. Shortly after the victory over Ang Mei Bhen, the new lord, Nguyễn Phúc Khoát (1714–1765, r. 1738–1765), who came to power in 1738 after the death of Lord Ninh, took active measures to appease Tianci. Tianci received a promotion to military governor-general (Đô đốc tướng quân) and the corresponding insignia of a red robe and cap. His wife became a royal consort as a reward for her demonstration of selfless bravery. If Nguyễn was not her original surname, the Cochinchinese court may have bequeathed it upon her on this occasion in the same manner as Mo Jiu's wife.[38]

Tianci further obtained preferential trade policies. The lord granted formal approval for him to open a mint and forge his own coinage. It was more a recognition of a fait accompli, since Tianci's father had already started doing so with the help of the Portuguese creoles. Tianci received "dragon passes" that entitled three of his ships to trade duty-free at Cochinchinese ports.[39] The rest of the vessels from The Port only had to pay a duty of 300 strings of cash (quan) upon arrival at Hội An and 30 strings of cash when departing. In comparison, ships from Guangdong and Shanghai had to pay 3,000 strings of cash and 300 for returns, while the ones from the "Western Ocean," which would include the British and Dutch, contributed 8,000 and 800, respectively.[40] With these generous concessions, Huế was beginning to treat Tianci more as a peer and ally rather than a subordinate political unit.

Motivated, in part, by this relative weakness in status toward the Mo and other frontier vassals, Nguyễn Phúc Khoát initiated, in 1744, sweeping political and social reforms with significant geopolitical ramifications. He mandated that the rulers of Cochinchina would henceforth no longer be called lords but heavenly kings (thiên vương). He proclaimed himself to be the Martial King (Võ Vương) and elevated the ranks and titles of his entire bureaucracy from those of a militarized frontier authority to a royal court. He replaced the relatively austere office buildings at

---

[37] Nguyễn Dynasty, Thực lục, vol. 1, pp. 134, 274; Vũ, Gia phả, p. 101; Nguyễn Dynasty, Nhất thống chí, vol. 3, pp. 273–274.
[38] Nguyễn Dynasty, Thực lục, vol. 1, p. 134; Vũ, Gia phả, p. 101.
[39] Trịnh, Thông chí, p. 306; Nguyễn Dynasty, Thực lục, vol. 1, p. 132.
[40] Lê, Tạp lục (Giáo dục), vol. 2, pp. 324–325.

the capital with lavish palaces befitting of their new status. He further issued an edict calling upon elites and commoners alike to abandon their old fashions, akin to northern Vietnam, and adopt costumes based upon former Chinese dynasties, particularly the Han and Ming.[41]

Wong Tze Ken believes that the reforms proved disastrous for Cochinchina in the long term, since the existing personnel lacked the competence and training to take on the more complex and expanded responsibilities of the upgraded offices. The need to project external legitimacy and power served as the primary motivations for the Martial King's policies. For one, they provided a boost to the prestige of him and his successors. These rulers now enjoyed parity with the Trịnh in Tonkin, who similarly possessed the title of king. More importantly, the Martial King hoped to use his elevated status in tandem with the creation of a tributary system between Cochinchina and its immediate neighbors that made subordination a prerequisite for commercial exchange.[42]

The measures were sufficient to make Mo Tianci dispatch envoys to Huế in the late spring of 1747, after a hiatus of over a decade. They brought along his tribute, consisting of European and Indian cloth and jade, five parakeets of unusual colors, a mastiff, a turkey, ornaments made from crane skulls, and rattan. He promised, in the future, to search out and procure the finest "treasures and most beautiful things from overseas" specially for the Martial King. During that audience, the visits to Huế became institutionalized. According to the official statutes for Cochinchinese tributary vassals, The Port was required to send one large mission every three years and present a tribute worth 3,000 strings of silver coins, and a small annual mission carrying 200 to 300 strings. After the return of the envoys, Mo Tianci further agreed to enact the Martial King's new law on changing fashion.[43] Presumably, the order applied solely to the Viet population of The Port, but he certainly welcomed this development, since their idealized outward appearance would now resemble more the Ming-style outfits of him and his Chinese creole subjects.

The high-profile nature of the tribute mission undoubtedly presented a satisfactory spectacle of submission before the newly proclaimed king and stoked his ego. Tianci received tangible benefits in exchange. The Martial King "enjoyed and praised his loyalty and sincerity," and gifted him with bolts of silk and earthenware. More importantly, Tianci

---

[41] Nguyễn Dynasty, *Thực lục*, vol. 1, pp. 136–139.
[42] Wong Tze Ken, *Nguyen and Champa*, pp. 141–146, 151–162.
[43] Vũ, *Gia phả*, pp. 103–105; Trịnh, *Thông chí*, p. 308; EFEO, A. 586: Lê, *Nam Hà*, p. 37a; Nguyễn Dynasty, *Thực lục*, vol. 1, pp. 140, 275.

received authorization to upgrade his military force by adding four company units (đội). Just like the minting of coinage, it was a belated recognition that the size and sophistication of his troops had expanded substantially since his victory over Ang Mei Bhen.[44]

What happened next would once again put The Port's defensive capabilities to the test. Through the chaos, it emerged even stronger as a formidable power that had the ability to set the terms of engagement in the water world. In the early fall of 1747, as Tianci's tribute ship made its return journey from Huế, it ran into pirates from Quy Nhơn led by Big-Bellied Đức (Đức Bụng) in the waters near the Black Water peninsula. Đức and his band ambushed the junk and stripped it of its cargo. Tianci responded by dispatching a fleet of ten war vessels under the command of Xu Youyong, son of Jiu's trusted commander, the marquis of the Han Sun, to chase down the pirates. Xu caught up with Đức and captured and promptly beheaded four of his men. However, the leader and his remaining crew slipped away and fled northward. Tianci informed the Nguyễn commander in Saigon, who sent a fleet of ships that stood ready to cut off their retreat. Đức and his pirate followers were seized and brought back to The Port for execution.[45]

The predation was, in large part, a spillover from the widespread unrest along the southern frontier of Cochinchina during this period. It was a good thing for the Martial King that Mo Tianci could subjugate the pirate fleets. The ruler already had his hands full putting down a revolt of the Cham in Panduranga in 1746. Then, in the following year, a group of Chinese merchants based at Biên Hòa led by Li Wenguang proclaimed an independent kingdom and nearly succeeded. They were eventually defeated and captured, but they managed to kill one of the Martial King's top commanders.[46]

Around this time, King Ang Tham of Cambodia passed away, and a fierce succession struggle broke out. The Martial King backed the former king Satha, who had resided in Saigon since his overthrow in 1736. He was the son of Ang Tham's old archnemesis, Ang Em. In early 1748, Satha's retinue of Khmer exiles, accompanied by a Cochinchinese expeditionary force, seized Oudong, and he was reinstated on the throne. Six months later, Siam mobilized its own Khmer allies, both in Ayutthaya and Cambodia, and waged a successful counterattack. Forced again into exile, Satha passed away a few months later at the age of forty-five. Ang Sngoun (1698–1755, r. 1748–1755),

---

[44] Vũ, *Gia phả*, pp. 104–105; Trịnh, *Thông chí*, pp. 307–308.
[45] Trịnh, *Thông chí*, p. 308; Nguyễn Dynasty, *Thực lục*, vol. 1, p. 275.
[46] Nguyễn Dynasty, *Thực lục*, vol. 1, p. 140; Wong Tze Ken, *Nguyen and Champa*, p. 161.

who had previously fled to Ayutthaya, now returned and assumed the throne with the blessing of the Siamese king.[47]

The chaos in Cambodia started to affect The Port by 1750. It was three years after Mo Tianci's visit to Huế. Although it was time for him to present another large tribute to Cochinchina, the Vietnamese records, both northern and southern, contain no mention of any further missions from The Port. A 1751 report by Pan Siju (1695–1752), governor of Fujian, to the Qing court on news from Southeast Asia, most likely gleaned from Chinese junk crews, reveals that Cochinchinese envoys were starting to make the journey to Tianci instead.[48] The Franciscan priest Francisco Hermosa de San Buenaventura (1711–1771), in a letter written in 1763, confirms that "an emissary of the court" in Huế would stay for a period of time at The Port to collect tribute.[49]

For the journey in 1750, the Cochinchinese envoy took the land route, probably to avoid the pirate-infested seas. However, The Port was surrounded by Cambodia, which had also become hostile territory after the ascendance of the pro-Siamese Ang Sngoun. Fortunately for the envoy, the Cambodian king granted him passage through the country and allowed him to rest at Oudong before continuing on his way. Upon his arrival at the capital, he received a grand and generous reception. The Cambodian officials and ordinary subjects tried to appease him and cater to his every whim. The envoy, on the other hand, conducted himself in an overbearingly arrogant manner. The last straw occurred when he took out a whip and viciously flogged one of the Khmer who was serving him over a minor issue. His action incited widespread popular outrage. Reports of the incident soon reached the king. The equally furious ruler promptly had the envoy executed. He then mobilized the xenophobic rage of his subjects, calling for the wholesale massacre of "all the Annamese [Viet] in The Port." He ordered his forces to launch an attack upon The Port, but they encountered stiff resistance and were beaten back.[50]

At this point, Ang Sngoun decided to escalate. He gave permission for his subjects to massacre any Viet that they came across throughout Cambodia. As the French missionary Guillaume Piguel (1722–1771), who resided at The Port, remarked, the order was "very exactly and very cruelly executed." The killing spree went on for one and a half months,

---

[47] EFEO Khmer: *Preah reach pongsavatar*, pp. 109–110; *Prachum phongsawadan* 1: *Phongsawadan khamen*, pp. 202–203; Hán-Nôm A. 832: Phạm, *Cao Man ki lược*, n. p.; Nguyễn Dynasty, *Thực lục*, vol. 1, p. 141.
[48] Grand Council Archives, Qianlong Reign, 007528: Pan Siju, n. p.
[49] Pérez, 'Españoles en el imperio de Annam' 12, p. 188.
[50] Grand Council Archives, Qianlong Reign, 007528: Pan Siju, n. p.

sparing nobody, not even the women and children. The demographic destruction was so thorough that, years later, Piguel claimed being no longer able to meet any Viet person in Cambodia as opposed to previously, when they constituted a highly visible presence.[51]

To punish The Port's stubborn resistance, Ang Sngoun reached out directly to Siam. Since the Port obtained most of its grain and other essential supplies from Cambodia by land and Siam from the sea, he proposed imposing a joint blockade. Although the Siamese king agreed to the idea, he had broader ambitions in mind. He first dispatched several ships loaded with rice and thousands of troops to call at The Port. The visit amounted to a highly visual ultimatum. If Tianci agreed to submit to Siam and launch a joint offensive on Cochinchina, he could have the grain. On the other hand, if he refused, then starvation and internal collapse and extermination by conquest awaited him. However, the Siamese display of might quickly transformed into a farce. According to Governor Pan's report, "the Annamese" launched a surprise raid on the ship, stole all the rice, and killed many of the crew while forcing the rest to flee.[52] It is not clear whether Tianci organized this successful ambush with his official troops or if it was only Viet residents at The Port who took matters into their own hands.

Upon hearing the news, the Siamese king fell into a fit of rage. He bluntly informed Tianci in a sharply worded letter that "the two of us cannot coexist (*bu liangli*)" and prepared to launch a campaign to chastise him.[53] The Port had already suffered a severe economic downturn because of the disorder. Trading vessels, afraid of the blockade, turned away. Moreover, severe food shortages hit, aggravated by the onset of a drought throughout Cambodia and Cochinchina. In desperation, Tianci appealed to Huế for military assistance. The Martial King responded by mobilizing 5,000 troops and 150 elephants from camps across his realm and sending them to The Port's rescue.[54] Meanwhile, the Siamese came to the aid of Ang Sngoun. The combined force and the Cochinchinese fought several battles near The Port, but neither of them obtained a decisive advantage. In the end, the Cambodians, despite Siamese assistance, failed to exterminate Tianci. Likewise, the Cochinchinese failed to reinforce him and had to withdraw when the drought triggered famine back home.[55]

---

[51] Launay, *Cochinchine*, vol. 2, pp. 366, 370.
[52] Grand Council Archives, Qianlong Reign, 007528: Pan Siju, n. p.
[53] Grand Council Archives, Qianlong Reign, 007528: Pan Siju, n. p.
[54] AMEP, Cochinchine, vol. 743: 'M. D'Azema à Mgr. Lefevre,' p. 718.
[55] Launay, *Cochinchine*, vol. 2, p. 368.

Subsequent events spared The Port's fate. In fact, the intervention of Siam and Cochinchina aggravated the severe internal fissures within the Cambodian royal hierarchy. As Piguel notes, the dispute over the envoy had not only blown up into a full-scale "outside war"; it also had developed into a "constant inside war."[56] Ang Sngoun faced a serious challenge to his rule from the co-king, Preahbat Reameatipadey (1691–1758). Then, there was the viceroy, Outey (1708–1753). Although Outey adamantly refused to take part in any intrigues, an ambitious relative, Preah Kse Ek (d. 1753), plotted to place the viceroy's teenage son, Ang Tan (1740–1777), on the throne. When the conspiracy was discovered, Preah Kse Ek and his followers rebelled.[57] Ang Sngoun, fearing for his life, fled Oudong to seek refuge at The Port. Piguel wrote in April 1751 that the ruler and his entire court were there and undoubtedly with the blessing of Mo Tianci.[58] Ironically, the very place that Ang Sngoun once tried in vain to subjugate now became a haven precisely because of its alienation from the rest of Cambodia.

The Cochinchinese saw in these bitter internal divisions and conflicts another opportunity for intervention.[59] According to Piguel, hostilities erupted again in 1752. This time, he claimed, the Cochinchinese succeeded in installing their choice of king on the Cambodian throne.[60] However, neither the Vietnamese nor Cambodian sources make any mention of such a momentous change of regime. Likely, the Cochinchinese backed one of the contenders, who, at most, only controlled part of the Mekong Delta. At any rate, the scheme failed. Piguel writes that the "Cambodians won over the Cochinchinese who were killed or chased from this kingdom."[61] The Cambodian Royal Chronicles notes that by 1753, Ang Sngoun had exterminated Preah Kse Ek and his rebels, subduing all his rivals. Afterward, the king was able to move back to Oudong and reign in relative security. The Cochinchinese offensive was not entirely in vain, however. During the campaign, they seized the remainder of Longhor Province still in Cambodian hands and appended it to their Longhor camp.[62]

---

[56] Launay, *Cochinchine*, vol. 2, p. 368.
[57] EFEO Khmer: *Preah reach pongsavatar*, pp. 111–112; *Prachum phongsawadan* 1: *Phongsawadan khamen*, pp. 204–205; Hán-Nôm A. 832: Phạm, *Cao Man ki lược*, n. p.
[58] Launay, *Cochinchine*, vol. 2, p. 368.
[59] From this point onward until 1760, the sources related to The Port, whether Khmer, Siamese, Vietnamese, or Western, provide mutually contradictory narratives of dates and events. An effort will be made to sort out the historical progression by synthesizing the sources and arranging the information according to the most logical sequence.
[60] AMEP, Cochinchine, vol. 744: 'M. Piguel à Messrs. les Directeurs,' p. 11.
[61] Launay, *Cochinchine*, vol. 2, p. 373.
[62] EFEO Khmer: *Preah reach pongsavatar*, pp. 111–112; *Prachum phongsawadan* 1: *Phongsawadan khamen*, pp. 204–205; Hán-Nôm A. 832: Phạm, *Cao Man ki lược*, n. p.

Ang Mei Bhen's invasion, Big-Bellied Đức's piratical raid, and the crisis in Cambodia bolstered the political and military position of The Port in relation to Huế. Of course, the protection of Cochinchina, a preeminent mainland Southeast Asian power, remained important to Tianci as a deterrence to potential enemies from attacking him. And as long as its forces remained engaged in his vicinity, attention would be deflected away from him, especially from any ambitious Cambodian or Siamese kings who would, under ideal circumstances, try to fully restore control over The Port and its lucrative access to the sea. Despite the guarantees of Cochinchinese support, Tianci proved able to fend off even the most serious threats to his survival with his own resources. The Port had become "a strategic garrison and protective screen" for Cochinchina, ensuring that Huế's vital yet vulnerable coastal shipping routes remained in friendly hands and safe from disruption.[63] The cost of this reliance for Cochinchina was a greater degree of independence and strategic initiative on the part of Tianci.

Cultural Contestations

Perhaps because the war in Cambodia did not go entirely according to plan, the Martial King turned to one of his most trusted officials, Nguyễn Cư Trinh (1716–1767). In 1753, Trinh was transferred to Saigon to become the controller of the camps. The functions of the office underwent significant expansion under him. It provided a permanent unified command structure to direct the maneuvers of all five camps along the southern frontier, with the specific purpose of intervening in highlander and Cambodian affairs.[64]

Nguyễn Cư Trinh and Mo Tianci came to know each other very well. It is unclear whether the two men ever met in person, but they certainly maintained a regular written exchange. They were probably introduced to each other by a scholar and official named Lê Bá Bình, who contributed to Tianci's literary anthologies. Bình had served in the Royal Academy at Huế and later relocated to Saigon. Trinh, too, held an office in the capital for several months in 1752, after his return from an assignment in Quảng Ngãi, a tiny province south of Huế on the south-central coast, and before his own transfer to Saigon at the end of the year.[65]

---

[63] Vũ, *Gia phả*, p. 100. [64] Trịnh, *Thông chí*, pp. 207–208.
[65] Nguyễn Dynasty, *Thực lục*, vol. 1, pp. 141–143, 253–254. Little is known about Lê Bá Bình other than the information acquired from the biography of his son in Nguyễn Dynasty, *Thực lục*, vol. 4, p. 1141 (129).

The personal touch in the relationship between Tianci and Trinh was hugely important in smoothing over their significant divergence in interests and conflicting visions for the water world. Indeed, the two men came from vastly divergent backgrounds. As Ang argues, Trinh was an ethnic insider of Cochinchina, a powerful, semi-legitimate state, and adopted the perspective of its political center at Huế. As governor of Quảng Ngãi from 1749 to 1752, he organized a mobilization of lowland peasants to build walls, both to defend against raids from Mon Khmer-speaking highlanders and clearly demarcate what were once fluid ethnic boundaries. On similar lines, he had authored the *Sãi Vãi* (Monk and Nun), a satirical vernacular play that called for social reforms to maintain and strengthen the loyalty of Viet subjects as a means of sharpening their separation from hostile "barbarian" highlanders.[66]

For Trinh, the water world was another distant southern frontier to be conquered and absorbed into the larger entity. Sellers and Ang point out that he was probably the first person on record to openly celebrate the Vietnamese occupation and opening of new lands as a preordained and inevitable "Southern Advance." Trinh advocated state support on a political and military level to ensure a systematic, long-term strategy of territorial expansion.[67] Without an organized structure in place, he believed, the migrants would be left entirely at the mercy of others, even to be slaughtered at will like lambs, as happened during the wars of 1750 and 1751.[68]

Mo Tianci, on the other hand, was an outsider to both the Qing and his neighborhood, including Cambodia and Cochinchina. A self-proclaimed "leftover subject," his imagined homeland, the Ming, had long ceased to exist.[69] He had no true political center outside of The Port. He envisioned his realm to be a nexus of commerce and Chinese culture over a horizontally integrated, translocal maritime sphere.

Nonetheless, what the two men shared was a passion for philosophy and poetry. At Tianci's invitation, Trinh joined the Pavilion of Summoning Worthies. Since Tianci was preoccupied with the business of managing his realm, his son Huang had taken oversight of its activities. Around this time, the pavilion circulated a second round of calls for responses to the original "Ten Scenic Views."[70] Trinh was among those

---

[66] Ang, *Poetic Transformations*, pp. 112–117; Nguyễn Dynasty, *Thực lục*, vol. 1, p. 253.
[67] Sellers, *Princes of Hà-Tiên*, p. 51; Ang, *Poetic Transformations*, pp. 108–109, 164–170.
[68] Launay, *Cochinchine*, vol. 2, p. 368.
[69] Chin Kei-wa (Chen Jinghe), 'Kasen Maku-shi,' p. 169.
[70] *Zhongguo difangzhi jicheng*, Shanghai fuxian zhi ji 8, Cheng and Fan, *Jiading xianzhi*, p. 653.

who submitted their set of ten poems, and his was the only contribution that has survived.

Trinh's poetic response and the surviving fragments of his letters to Tianci provide a valuable window into the complex interplay of friendship between the two men on the micro level, and the geopolitical competition between The Port and Cochinchina on a broader scale. The verses express much admiration for Tianci's literary refinement and military skills, and praise for the successful management of such a flourishing settlement. Couched within the platitudes, however, was a subtle attempt to subvert The Port's self-definition of cultural centrality and the legitimacy of its leader. In his poems for each of the ten scenes, Trinh deconstructs the paradox of strange yet cultivated natural features and restores them to an untamed, pristine state. He further strips The Port of its Ming loyalist connotations and connections. In "Verdant Folds of Screen Mountain," he praises the city as a little Guangzhou.[71] Vibrant and teeming with life, it was, nonetheless, a typical, apolitical trading port with a large Chinese population like elsewhere in maritime East Asia. Accordingly, it could be safely put back in its place as a frontier garrison far away from the main political and civilized centers.

Other poems gently but firmly emphasize Trinh as the unquestionable superior in the relationship between the two men. He recognized Tianci's special status as an autonomous leader but viewed him as a transitional figure. In "Dawn Bell at the Temple of Seclusion," Trinh likens him to a monk who withdrew from the world and became a recluse once he brought enlightenment to his people. In "An Egret Descends from Pearl Cliff," he referred to Tianci as a "guest in the halls of Black Robe Lane," an allusion to a formerly prosperous neighborhood where elite families maintained their residences. However, it had, over the course of centuries, fallen into decay and disrepair. Similarly, Ang points out, Tianci's Ming loyalist-based ideals belonged to a bygone age. If he did not adapt to the changed reality, he, too, risked the decline in his own fortunes. In contrast, Trinh identified himself in a line of "Clear Waves on South Bay" as a government frontier inspector. He surveys the landscape of The Port and notes with satisfaction a realm at peace with "no questions about sword sounds."[72] This line places him, rather than Tianci, in the position as the ultimate arbiter of local conditions.

---

[71] Lê, *Tạp lục* (Giáo dục), vol. 2, p. 350; Ang, *Poetic Transformations*, pp. 196–198, 206–207.

[72] Lê, *Tạp lục* (Giáo dục), vol. 2, pp. 350, 352–353; Ang, *Poetic Transformations*, pp. 207–216.

To drive this point across more emphatically, Trinh's letters to him raised many examples from Chinese history of loyal ministers serving their rulers.[73] On one occasion, he sent a harquebus to Tianci's son, Huang. In a letter accompanying the gift, Trinh praises the weapon for its reliability, effectiveness, and deadliness. He compares these qualities to the Confucian virtues of trustworthiness and benevolence, since it only strikes those whom its owner targets, and once it fires, it can always bring down the enemy without fail. Trinh was thus voicing his hope that The Port's leadership, just like the harquebus, would faithfully listen to Cochinchina's directives and implement them, especially in regards to its geopolitical rivals.[74] Through subtle literary methods, Trinh delineated The Port as Cochinchinese space and positioned Tianci as a temporary caretaker who took orders from him and, by extension, the court in Huế.

Mo Tianci pushed back at his counterpart's subtle attempts to territorialize his realm by exploiting the translocal literary space of the Sinosphere. His son, Mo Huang, who took charge of the "Ten Verses 2.0" project, became friends with Guo Jie, a native of Haicheng County, in Fujian. Guo was probably like Chen Zhikai, a merchant who had a passion for literature and mingled with gentry. In 1756, he introduced Huang to Zhao Pilie, a *zhusheng* degree holder from Shanghai, in the Jiangnan heartland. Zhao enjoyed fame throughout the empire for his literary refinement and artistic skill, especially in landscape paintings. However, like She Xichun, he never held any official post.[75]

The biography of Zhao in the Jiading County gazetteer of Shanghai states that Huang humbly requested to become his disciple and forwarded a copy of "Ten Verses 2.0" for him to read over and judge its value, and make necessary corrections. To ensure a favorable reaction, Huang gifted him with a shipload of cinnamon and a massive, rare limestone for the decoration of his garden.[76] Although it appeared to be Zhao Pilie who set the standards for aesthetic taste and literary refinement, in reality, Mo Tianci possessed the ultimate authority through his control over substantial financial resources. On the other end, Nguyễn Cư Trinh and his fellow contributors to the "Ten Verses 2.0" anthology effectively subjected their literary output to the judgment

---

[73] Lê, *Tạp lục* (Giáo dục), vol. 2, pp. 360–368; Ang, *Poetic Transformations*, pp. 184–185.
[74] Hán-Nôm A. 2939: Phạm, *Nam hành*, n. p.; Ang, *Poetic Transformations*, pp. 184–185, in meticulously examining two other letters, has come to this same conclusion.
[75] *Zhongguo difangzhi jicheng*, Shanghai fuxian zhi ji 8, Cheng and Fan, *Jiading xianzhi*, p. 411.
[76] *Zhongguo difangzhi jicheng*, Shanghai fuxian zhi ji 8, Cheng and Fan, *Jiading xianzhi*, p. 653.

of a faraway anonymous peer reviewer. The very act of participation from Trịnh, a high-profile scholar and commander, regardless of his motivations, signaled his subordination to Tianci's translocal cultural mediation.

The Port's strategic importance, significant military resources, and cultural capital meant that Trịnh could not treat it in the same condescending manner as the highlanders or Cambodia to achieve the aims of his political center, especially the use of force. On Tianci's part, he could directly deal with one of Cochinchina's most powerful men, who enjoyed the full trust of the Martial King. "Only you," the ruler once wrote in an edict assigning Trịnh to Quảng Ngãi, "know everything about military affairs and the needs of the common people. So, I defer to what you decide to do" on the ground.[77] The friendship between Tianci and Trịnh and the proximity of Saigon and The Port allowed them to quickly sort out disagreements and arrive at a mutual understanding. They could also avoid being overly subject to the interference of Huế, which was much more distant and less sensitive to the changing power balance in the water world.

The two men would prove their usefulness to one another after Trịnh initiated a fresh campaign against Cambodia in the summer of 1753. The Cochinchinese got as far as the eastern outskirts of Phnom Penh and forced King Ang Sngoun to abandon the capital. However, autumn floods caused the Mekong to overflow its banks, making troop movements difficult and forcing the Cochinchinese to withdraw. The following year, Trịnh renewed his offensive on the pretext that the Khmer had attacked a convoy of highlander tribal forces allied to his army. The Cochinchinese enjoyed much greater success this time around. They reoccupied the areas they had captured during the previous campaign and continued to press forward. Again, Ang Sngoun fled the capital, this time for The Port, where he sought refuge from Mo Tianci for the second time. The king requested Tianci's assistance in persuading the Martial King to end the campaign.[78]

In 1754, Tianci approached Huế with an offer to secure Cambodian recognition of the cession of Longhor Province in exchange for the withdrawal of Cochinchinese forces. The Martial King initially opposed the proposal since it only granted to him what he and his predecessors had already seized through force of arms. He wanted to continue the campaign in Cambodia, perhaps to conquer more land or subjugate the

---

[77] Launay, *Cochinchine*, vol. 2, p. 391; Nguyễn Dynasty, *Thực lục*, vol. 1, p. 141.
[78] Nguyễn Dynasty, *Thực lục*, vol. 1, pp. 145–146; Trịnh, *Thông chí*, pp. 208–210, 308–309.

kingdom entirely. For Ang, the ruler's reluctance is revealing, since it shows that he did not entirely trust Tianci, whom he saw more as a separate third party rather than a subordinate vassal.[79]

At this point, Tianci turned to Nguyễn Cư Trinh to petition on his behalf. Trinh sought to help his friend while ensuring his ruler that the proposal best suited Cochinchinese interests. In his memorial to the Martial King, he advocated a go-slow approach toward frontier expansion. For the time being, Saigon and the newly taken areas of the water world lacked sufficient manpower to maintain garrisons and defend Viet settlement and agricultural exploitation on a large scale. Trinh instead suggested a policy of limited retrenchment, patiently waiting for these places to fill up with people and the requisite increase in productivity to support a large military presence before moving on toward the next target. He famously likened this incremental yet full digestion of conquered land to "a silkworm nibbling away at mulberry leaves." Although time-consuming, this approach would enhance the security and permanence of Cochinchinese control. The joint intercession of Trinh and Tianci persuaded the Martial King to agree to the terms. Ang Sngoun acknowledged the complete Cochinchinese occupation of Longhor Province, and, in addition, coughed up three years' worth of tribute.[80]

Cambodia's Preeminent Statesman

Besides the cooperation and competition with Cochinchina, Mo Tianci made full use of his realm's location at the crossroads of Southeast Asia to maintain multiple allegiances to the major centers. Outside of the Sinosphere, The Port was still considered a part of Cambodia. The narratives of the Franciscans and French missionaries, who were physically present there, make this point clear. In fact, far from detaching himself, Tianci sought deeper integration into the Khmer social and political hierarchy. He did not seem to have inherited his father's position as governor of Seashore Province or, if he did, he soon gave it up. According to the Royal Chronicles, a person named Chov held the title of Oknha Reachea Setthi during the 1750s and was identified as a separate individual from Tianci. Chov operated out of Moat Chrouk, which appears to have become the new seat of Seashore Province. He

---

[79] Nguyễn Dynasty, *Thực lục*, vol. 1, p. 147; Trịnh, *Thông chí*, pp. 210, 308–309; Ang, *Poetic Transformations*, p. 169.

[80] Nguyễn Dynasty, *Thực lục*, vol. 1, p. 147; Trịnh, *Thông chí*, pp. 208–210, 308–309. The present-day place-names and territorial extent of these concessions can be found in Nguyễn Văn Hầu, 'Tầm Phong Long,' p. 9.

may have been the Austronesian known in Trịnh Hoài Đức's gazetteer as Captain Sa. He supposedly possessed supernatural powers, having acquired a special martial arts technique that made him invincible to knives and guns.[81]

Tianci himself assumed a new and more prestigious title: Preah Sotoat. Literally meaning "lord of wealth," it refers to the protagonist of a Buddhist allegory tale, a fabulously wealthy individual. The man, out of faith, donated generously to beggars and the needy and showered his gold upon the king to buy land for the construction of a temple. Tianci's first documented use of Preah Sotoat occurred in 1740, when he dispatched a ship to Japan with a request for a trading permit, which had lapsed under his father because of repeated failures to reach Nagasaki on account of shipwrecks and inclement weather. Unlike Jiu, who passed off his junk as belonging to the former king, Ang Em, Tianci directly claimed to be the reigning king of Cambodia. The full title that prefaced his greeting to the shogun reads: Guardian and Supreme Controller of Cambodia over All Military and Civil Matters in Angkor Thom and Land and Water Zhenla, Rewarded with the Noble Title of King Neak Samdech Preah Sotoat Mao (*Jianpuzhai guo zhenguo dazongzhi Zhenla Jinta shuilu deng chu difang junguo zhu wushi jin Lu Sanlie Basizhe Wang Mao* 柬埔寨國鎮國大總制真臘金塔水陸等處地方軍國諸務事進六參烈巴司哲王鄭). "Neak Samdech" was an honorific used to address kings and members of the royal family.[82]

The letter closed off with the traditional Sinic sexagenary cycle of years (*ganzhi*), preceded by the enigmatic characters of *tianyun* (Heavenly Movement): *tianyun gengshen*, fourth month.[83] This dating convention, derived from Daoism, was commonly used in Chinese popular religion as a marker of the passage of time in the underworld. Because it could take the place of the imperial reign name that counted the years of the monarch on the throne and was used in an official capacity in Sinosphere states, it also served as a symbolic refusal to recognize the Qing. As scholars have shown, rebels and secret societies during the eighteenth century and beyond that idealized the restoration of the Ming often dated their

---

[81] Trịnh, *Thông chí*, p. 318; Eng, *Mahaboros khmer*, vol. 6, p. 14.
[82] Chuon, *Dictionnaire Cambodgien*, pp. 800, 1010; Kondo, *Gaiban tsūsho*, vol. 1, p. 138. When Kondo transcribed this document, he wrote down Tianci's surname as Zheng (鄭), which is quite easily confounded with Mao (鄭). Zhenla is the traditional Chinese name for Cambodia. It is customarily divided into Land or Mountain Zhenla, referring to the agrarian interior, and Water Zhenla, representing the trade-oriented maritime zone, a legacy of the old Funan civilization. See Mikaelian, *Royauté d'Oudong*, pp. 274–275, 292–293.
[83] Kondo, *Gaiban tsūsho*, vol. 1, p. 138.

communications according to the *tianyun*-sexagenary combination.⁸⁴ In mainland Southeast Asia, on the other hand, this convention became applied toward a vastly different cultural context. According to a nineteenth-century preface to the Vietnamese translation of the Cambodian Royal Chronicles, *tianyun* referred to the years since Buddha's birth, the dating system used in Cambodia and Siam.⁸⁵ In this context, Tianci was simply adopting the Cambodian calendar in a Sinic format.

Two years later, Tianci sent another mission consisting of twelve Khmer noblemen in his service led by Oknha Bavar Metrei. This time, he prepared two versions of his letter to the Tokugawa authorities. The Chinese letter opened with a title similar to two years ago. The Khmer version used a shorter, more straightforward introduction: "Neak Samdech Preah Sotoat, King of Cambodia" (*reachea krong Kampucea tiptei* អ្នកសម្តេចព្រះសោទត្តរាជាក្រុងកម្ពុជាធិបតី). In it, he used words specially reserved for royalty. For instance, the very first phrase, "Letter from ..." (*sopheak aksor* សុភអក្សរ) identifies the sender as someone having the same power as the ruler of an independent state. The date that closed off the correspondence was clearly the original Cambodian calendar: Sunday, eighth day of the waxing moon, Chesth (seventh) month, year of the dog, fourth year of the decade.⁸⁶

Passing himself off as royalty was the only legitimate way for Tianci to obtain passes for ships from The Port to legally sail to Japan at a time when the Tokugawa was imposing ever more stringent quotas and restrictions on Chinese junks at Nagasaki. However, the titles that he used in his letters were not completely fictional. They highlight his position as a chief commander of Cambodia's military forces and member of the royal family. Indeed, Preah Sotoat belonged to the same category as twelve other titles in the Cambodian nobility, all of them denoting minor relatives of the king. They were addressed using the honorific term of Samdech.⁸⁷ They had a retinue of Khmer and Austronesian noblemen, including many who held the rank of *oknha*.⁸⁸

---

⁸⁴ For more on the different usages of *tianyun* during the Qing, see Zhao, '"Tianyun" jinian,' pp. 484–495.

⁸⁵ Hán-Nôm A. 832: Phạm, *Cao Man ki lược*, n. p. Letters from the Siamese king and nobility translated into Chinese frequently end with the *tianyun* date. See, for instance, Kondo, *Gaiban tsūsho*, vol. 1, pp. 102–105.

⁸⁶ Péri, 'Japon et l'Indochine,' pp. 131–132; Tokyo University, *Higashi Ajia to Nihon*, pp. 16–17; *Codes anciens du Cambodge*, pp. 52–53; Chuon, *Dictionnaire Cambodgien*, p. 858.

⁸⁷ Kondo, *Gaiban tsūsho*, vol. 1, p. 138; *Tamrathamnieb bandasak Krung Kamphucha*, pp. 1–2.

⁸⁸ Eng, *Mahaboros khmer*, vol. 6, p. 4; EFEO Khmer: *Preah reach pongsavatar*, p. 112; *Prachum phongsawadan* 1: *Phongsawadan khamen*, p. 205.

The Cambodian Royal Chronicles also speak of an earlier Preah Sotoat who lived during the sixteenth century and was based at Banteay Meas. This individual commanded an army of 3,000 soldiers and sixty-six ships. In addition, he supervised the defenses in all the maritime zone provinces along the South China Sea and Gulf of Siam and could mobilize about a thousand troops from each of them.[89] Tianci fulfilled a similar role as this predecessor. The Port and surrounding Seashore Province functioned as his military headquarters and private fief, and he could station troops or recruit soldiers from other coastal provinces, from Bassac to Kampong Som.

The responsibilities denoted by Preah Sotoat roughly equaled the position of military governor-general granted to Tianci by Cochinchina. This coordination was certainly not coincidental. The conferral of Preah Sotoat was probably a concession granted by a weakened Cambodian court, which could no longer assert effective control over the maritime zone after his victory over Ang Mei Bhen. Only then did Huế follow up with the promotion to military governor-general to keep his loyalty as a vassal. As a result, a subtle difference developed in the respective attitudes of Mo Tianci and the Cochinchinese toward Cambodia. Unlike the Martial King, Tianci was perfectly willing to defer to whichever ruler sat on the throne, regardless of political affiliation. If Ang Sngoun paid tribute to Siam, Tianci, by extension, would also submit. For this reason, the entry on The Port in the Qing dynasty's official encyclopedia of institutions and statecraft (*Qing chao wenxian tongkao*) mentions it as a vassal of both Cochinchina and Siam. Published in 1784, this compilation reflects the observations of travelers, perhaps the participants in Tianci's poetry society, during the 1740s.[90] Other sources, including the testimony of Tianci's envoy, Mo Wu, in 1772 say the same thing.[91]

Relations were not always smooth with King Ang Sngoun and Siam, as seen with the open conflict that broke out over the abuse of the Khmer by the arrogant Cochinchinese representative in 1750. Nonetheless, incidents such as this were exceptions to the largely cordial interactions with the Cambodian and Siamese courts, especially compared to the antagonism during the days of Mo Jiu and Tianci's early years in power. In 1747, as The Port's naval fleets relentlessly hounded Big-Bellied Đức, the pirate and the remnants of his fleet sailed into the port of Bassac. The powerful governor of the province, Oknha Norean Tok, was a bitter enemy of Cochinchina. The same year, he had launched an offensive that expelled

---

[89] Khin, *Chroniques royales*, pp. 33, 337–338.
[90] Zhang, *Wenxian tongkao*, vol. 2, p. 7463.
[91] Grand Council Archives, Qianlong Reign, 017970: Li Shiyao, n. p.

the Cochinchinese from his borders and almost captured Mesar. The *oknha* also had Siamese troops stationed at Bassac. Intriguingly, the official Nguyễn biography of Mo Tianci notes that it was Siamese soldiers who seized Đức and his core followers and handed them over for execution back at The Port.[92]

Then, in 1751 and 1754, King Ang Sngoun sought refuge with Tianci. Remarkably, on the first occasion, the ruler's flight occurred, in part, because of his own antagonism toward The Port. During times of duress, he viewed Tianci's multiple allegiances as a positive characteristic. Tianci could serve as a neutral mediator who could soften or even push back against the demands of a stronger adversary. He may have pioneered the idea of buying off invasions with territorial concessions, which could achieve the best compromise for all parties in accordance with the power balance on the ground. Ang Sngoun's agreement in 1754 to relinquish Cambodia's claim to Longhor presented little immediate loss for the ruler, since it merely recognized a fait accompli.[93] In the long term, however, the granting of territories set a damaging precedent that only served to whet the Cochinchinese appetite for more Cambodian land in the future and showed them how to achieve it without firing a shot.

For Tianci, his generous treatment of the court and tireless mediation provided a boost to his personal prestige and indispensability in Cambodia. He formed crucial alliances with the nobility in Oudong, as well as the governors of several of the super-provinces surrounding Phnom Penh and the capital.[94] These connections served him well when the death of Ang Sngoun in 1755 sparked a renewed crisis. An intense power struggle broke out among the co-king, Preahbat Reameatipadey, who never formally assumed the throne; the viceroy, Srey Sauryopor (d. 1757), who had replaced Outey in this position after his death in 1753; and Outey's son, Ang Tan. The rivalry was fiercest between Sauryopor and Ang Tan. Although Preahbat Reameatipadey commanded the most authority, he was, at the age of sixty-six, frequently ill and lacking in vigor. It would only be a matter of time before this precarious balance collapsed. The tipping point occurred in 1757, when Sauryopor plotted with his followers to assassinate Ang Tan. However, Ang Tan heard about the conspiracy and made a hasty departure from Oudong on foot, with soldiers hot on his trail.[95]

---

[92] EFEO Khmer: *Preah reach pongsavatar*, pp. 108–109; *Prachum phongsawadan* 1: *Phongsawadan khamen*, pp. 201–202; Nguyễn Dynasty, *Thực lục*, vol. 1, pp. 140–141, 275.
[93] Launay, *Cochinchine*, vol. 2, p. 376.
[94] Mikaelian, *Royauté d'Oudong*, p. 222; Aymonier, *Cambodge*, vol. 1, pp. 70–71.
[95] EFEO Khmer: *Preah reach pongsavatar*, p. 112; *Prachum phongsawadan* 1: *Phongsawadan khamen*, p. 205; Hán-Nôm A. 832: Phạm, *Cao Man ki lược*, n. p.

Like Ang Sgnoun before him, the young man took refuge at The Port. Mo Tianci had the influence and strength to at least protect him from harm, if not give him the decisive edge over his rivals. Tianci, on his part, welcomed the young man with joy and open arms. Needless to say, if he could successfully place Ang Tan on the throne, he would become the most powerful man in Cambodia. Aside from mutual interests, a genuine bond appeared to have formed between the two. Tianci must have taken pity on Ang Tan, who, from a young age, had been used and manipulated by scheming factions in Oudong for their own interests. Not too long ago, he had also lost his own father, Outey. Tianci appeared to be the perfect replacement for the deceased prince, feeding and sheltering the lonely orphan during his greatest time of need and putting his troubled mental faculties at ease. At Ang Tan's request, Tianci adopted him as a son and became his surrogate father, literally a "first father" (*bothoam beida*) in Khmer. He further promised to help the young man get rid of his opponents and take the throne.[96]

Tianci made effective use of his allies in both Cambodia and Cochinchina to get the job done. He requested and received approval for military assistance from Nguyễn Cư Trinh. Tianci's troops, numbering over 10,000, escorted Ang Tan and his followers to Moat Chrouk, where they met up with Cochinchinese forces coming in from Saigon. They all got on board ships and proceeded up the Bassac to Phnom Penh. Meanwhile, Tianci successfully persuaded the governors of seven provinces to raise soldiers and launch an attack on land. The two-pronged offensive defeated Sauryopor and forced him to flee the capital. The pretender was later hunted down and killed.[97]

In 1758, Mo Tianci and his soldiers escorted Ang Tan back to Oudong, where the young man was crowned king. Tianci, Ang Tan's adoptive father, succeeded his biological father, Outey, in the official role of viceroy. This rank was revealed in two missives written to Tianci from the VOC governor-general and High Government (*Hoge Regeering*) in Batavia in 1771. They addressed him as: "Sam Liet Pa Soe Tjetto Gie Moho Palet Bok." It was a transcription of a Chinese transcription of the Khmer original: Samdech Preah Sotoat Sri Maha Oupareach

---

[96] Vũ, *Gia phả*, p. 105; Trịnh, *Thông chí*, p. 309; EFEO Khmer: *Preah reach pongsavatar*, p. 112; *Prachum phongsawadan* 1: *Phongsawadan khamen*, p. 206; Hán-Nôm A. 832: Phạm, *Cao Man ki lược*, n. p.; Sakurai and Kitagawa, 'Hà Tiên or Banteay Meas,' pp. 167–168.

[97] EFEO Khmer: *Preah reach pongsavatar*, pp. 112–113; *Prachum phongsawadan* 1: *Phongsawadan khamen*, pp. 206–208; Hán-Nôm A. 832: Phạm, *Cao Man ki lược*, n. p.; Vũ, *Gia phả*, pp. 105–106; Sakurai and Kitagawa, 'Hà Tiên or Banteay Meas,' pp. 167–168; Nguyễn Dynasty, *Thực lục*, vol. 1, p. 148; Trịnh, *Thông chí*, p. 211.

Mo (សម្តេចព្រះសុន្ធរាធិបតីមហាឧបរាជម៉ាក់), his new title as viceroy.[98] In reality, he had replaced Siam and Cochinchina as the direct overlord of Cambodia, even though he remained nominally subordinate to both.

The Siamese reacted by throwing their support behind Sauryopor's widow. Driven by revenge, she gathered her late husband's partisans and rebelled against Ang Tan. Although the new king's troops crushed the insurgency and massacred her and her followers, one prince in her retinue, Ream Reachea (1739–1779), son of the former king Ang Sngoun, got away to Ayutthaya with the help of a nobleman. Siam backed him as their preferred candidate-in-waiting for the Cambodian throne.[99]

The Cochinchinese friends of Ang Tan and Mo Tianci demanded a heavy price for their assistance, making them just as much, if not more, of a threat as the Siamese. When the fierce conflicts over succession were only beginning to unfold in Cambodia, the co-king, Preahbat Remeatipadey, had, according to Vietnamese records, requested Cochinchinese protection from his domestic rivals. The Martial King, not satisfied with the previous terms of peace under Ang Sngoun, wanted Preahbat Remeatipadey to give up the provinces of Sacred Pond and Bassac, along with their two strategic ports, as a precondition. The demand went unanswered since the situation in Cambodia soon descended into chaos. After Ang Tan fled to The Port in 1757, Mo Tianci once again became a mediator with the Cochinchinese court. He started out in a weakened position, since he had to work with the previous conditions imposed upon Preahbat Reameatipadey. This time, on top of Sacred Pond and Bassac, the Martial King demanded the cession of the entire southwestern bank of the main Mekong River branch.[100]

According to the Vietnamese sources, Ang Tan agreed to the draconian terms. The Cambodian records, on the contrary, make no mention of any transfer of territory. The voluntary surrender of such a massive expanse of land, including two ports of strategic significance for Cambodia, should have generated much more controversy and documentation, not to mention moral castigation of the ruler who allowed it to happen.[101] Sources contemporary to the events in the mid-eighteenth century reveal a much clearer narrative. The French missionary Urbain Lefebvre (1725–1792), who was accompanying Ang Tan and his court, observes that the ruler stubbornly refused to give up Bassac.

---

[98] ANRI, K66a: 3686, p. 227; 3688, p. 366.
[99] EFEO Khmer: *Preah reach pongsavatar*, pp. 113–114; *Prachum Phongsawadan* 1: *Phongsawadan khamen*, pp. 207–208; Hán-Nôm A. 832: Phạm, *Cao Man ki lược*, n. p.
[100] Nguyễn Dynasty, *Thực lục*, vol. 1, p. 148; Trịnh, *Thông chí*, p. 211; Nguyễn Văn Hầu, 'Tầm Phong Long,' pp. 11–12.
[101] Mikaelian, *Royauté d'Oudong*, p. 222.

In Lefebvre's words, it was "the only port that remains with the king of Cambodia ... The Cochinchinese want to seize it, and the Cambodians absolutely do not want to let it go."[102] And indeed, no transfer of territory took place. Around a decade later, in 1768, Levavasseur confirmed that in Bassac, "the government is Cambodian," during his visit.[103] According to Siamese narratives, its governor during the 1770s was Oknha Athivongsa, who had replaced Oknha Norean Tok and enjoyed close relations with both Tianci and Ang Tan.[104]

Sacred Pond, too, was not ceded. Several close relatives of Ang Tan took refuge there during the war with Sauryopor.[105] Trịnh Hoài Đức's 1820 gazetteer admits that Sacred Pond, "in former times, formed an integral part of Cambodia." It further identified its governor as Oknha Suất, possibly a transcription of his title, Senathipdey.[106] According to the Cambodian codes, he was an official with an honor ranking of 9,000.[107] It is clear that Ang Tan refused to cede any of the two provinces, at least not in their entirety or core areas.

As Ang Tan's advocate and negotiator, Mo Tianci, in his eagerness to expedite an agreement and secure Cochinchinese aid, may have purposefully withheld or obfuscated information from both parties. Moreover, the Vietnamese records might have also exaggerated or provided an anachronistic interpretation of the actual terms. In reality, Ang Tan probably agreed to some transfer of territorial rights along the main branch of the Mekong. The nineteenth-century French missionary and explorer Charles-Emile Bouillevaux (1823–1913) more accurately describes the Cochinchinese as establishing "forward posts in the middle of the Cambodian population."[108] Besides stationing troops, Cochinchina would provide administration for Viet settlers in this area and, at most, force the Khmer local leaders to pay some regular tribute.[109]

After the agreement was reached, the Longhor camp headquarters relocated from Cái Bè, on the eastern bank of the main Mekong branch, to present-day Vĩnh Long, on the other side. From there, the Cochinchinese constructed fortresses and outposts upriver. They established the circuits (C: *dao* V: *đạo*) of Đông Khẩu at **K: Phsar Dek** V: Sa Đéc, Tân Châu at K: Koh Russei Prei V: Cù lao Giêng, and

---

[102] Launay, *Cochinchine*, vol. 2, p. 376.   [103] *Nouvelles lettres*, vol. 6, pp. 213–214.
[104] *Prachum phongsawadan* 66: *Krao prab mueng Phutthaimat*, pp. 13, 20.
[105] EFEO Khmer: *Preah reach pongsavatar*, p. 112; *Prachum phongsawadan* 1: *Phongsawadan khamen*, p. 205.
[106] Trịnh, *Thông chi*, p. 132.   [107] Leclère, *Les codes*, vol. 1, p. 116.
[108] Bouillevaux, *L'Annam et le Cambodge*, p. 371.
[109] Nguyễn Dynasty, *Thực lục*, vol. 2, p. 315 (25).

Moat Chrouk, all lying to the northwest of Sacred Pond.[110] As Sakurai Yumio shows, the Cochinchinese managed, with this concession, to acquire rights over trade and navigation on the main branch of the Mekong.[111]

But it must be noted that these places remained Cambodian territory well into the late eighteenth century. As late as 1784, one Franciscan missionary, for instance, claimed to be writing his letter from Phsar Dek in Cambodia.[112] Moreover, the circuit of Moat Chrouk does not correspond to the river port bearing the same name. The intersection of the Bassac River, flowing south from Phnom Penh, and its tributary, the Moat Chrouk River, coming in from the northwest, creates three pieces of land facing one another on the east, north, and west. According to Trịnh Hoài Đức's gazetteer, the urban area itself was situated on the northern peninsula. The Cochinchinese garrison lay on the eastern shore, connected to the main branch of the Mekong. The western shore only came under settlement during the early nineteenth century at the initiative of the Nguyễn dynasty. Before then, and certainly during the 1750s, it remained an "open and empty space."[113]

At the time, the Cochinchinese sphere of influence reached, at most, to the northeastern banks of the Bassac. The river itself remained off-limits for Viet navigation. The Viet boatmen whom Levavasseur met during his stay in the city of Bassac refused to take him to The Port, because "of the prohibition against the Cochinchinese to enter the interior of Cambodia." Moat Chrouk was a place where one must pass to reach The Port, since a canal connected the two.[114]

The Martial King was obviously unsatisfied at his inability to project power into the Bassac, and his greed was insatiable. On March 2, 1759, undoubtedly at the ruler's instigation, the Cochinchinese soldiers that had accompanied Ang Tan and assisted him in gaining the throne suddenly turned violent and began torching buildings in Oudong. According to Lefebvre, they came "with arms not to escort him, but to get rid of him." After staunchly resisting until nightfall, the king and his entourage were forced to flee. A few days later, the commanders of the Cochinchinese expeditionary army tricked two Cambodian officials into meeting with them to discuss the incident. During the session, their soldiers seized the two men. They killed one of them, but the other tore

---

[110] Nguyễn Dynasty, *Thực lục*, vol. 1, p. 148; Trịnh, *Thông chí*, pp. 212, 285; Nguyễn Văn Hầu, 'Tầm Phong Long,' p. 10.
[111] Sakurai, 'Chinese Pioneers,' p. 44.
[112] Pérez, 'Españoles en el imperio de Annam' 14, p. 349.
[113] Trịnh, *Thông chí*, p. 142; Nguyễn Dynasty, *Nhất thống chí*, vol. 3, p. 296.
[114] Launay, *Cochinchine*, vol. 2, p. 388; *Nouvelles lettres*, vol. 6, p. 216.

away and escaped, leaving a sizable piece of his hair in the hands of his captors. These events precipitated another war between Cambodia and Cochinchina. However, just three months later, the entire Cochinchinese expeditionary force withdrew, ostensibly because of the heavy monsoon rains.[115] It was likelier that some Cambodian battlefield victories, along with Mo Tianci's intervention and mediation, persuaded them to leave.

Piguel wrote in July 1760 that Ang Tan "had routed all his adversaries," from domestic contenders to foreign invaders.[116] Amid the chaos, the old co-king, Preahbat Reameatipadey, had passed away out of sickness and despair at the devastation visited upon his country.[117] With all potential challengers dead or exiled, Ang Tan finally obtained recognition from the Martial King in the form of an edict proclaiming him a vassal of Huế and royal robes and gifts of gold and silver. Interestingly, the Cochinchinese ruler first handed over these instruments of authority to Mo Tianci, who then bequeathed them upon the new Cambodian ruler. Around the same time, the king of Laos, a Siamese vassal, sent back the cremated ashes of Ang Tan's deceased mother, who had passed away there while in exile. This friendly gesture could not have taken place without the blessing of the court in Ayutthaya and shows that relations had also normalized earlier with Siam, even if it continued to harbor Ang Tan's political enemies.[118]

For the rest of the decade, Cambodia realized relative peace and stability under the reign of Ang Tan, a remarkable shift away from the perennial political volatility of previous years. He himself certainly lacked the capability to pull off such a feat on his own. According to Lefebvre, he was frequently ill and easily prone to panic when faced with danger.[119] Chen Ching-ho characterizes the regime of Ang Tan as "pro-Vietnamese" and only secondarily "Pro-Ha-tien" (*sic*).[120] In reality, he was not pro-Vietnamese, just as he was not pro-Siamese. Ang Tan's emergence owed almost entirely to Mo Tianci's consummate skill as a strategist, mediator, and diplomat. By integrating into the hierarchy of Cambodia, he presented himself as a valuable third force able to balance out the influence of both neighbors. In this manner, Tianci became the true overlord of the kingdom, its preeminent statesman.

---

[115] Launay, *Cochinchine*, vol. 2, pp. 375–376.   [116] Launay, *Cochinchine*, vol. 2, p. 377.
[117] EFEO Khmer: *Preah reach pongsavatar*, pp. 113–114; *Prachum phongsawadan* 1: *Phongsawadan khamen*, pp. 207–208; Hán-Nôm A. 832: Phạm, *Cao Man ki lược*, n. p.
[118] Vũ, *Gia phả*, pp. 106–107; EFEO Khmer: *Preah reach pongsavatar*, p. 114; *Prachum phongsawadan* 1: *Phongsawadan khamen*, p. 210; Eng, *Mahaboros khmer*, vol. 6, p. 9.
[119] Launay, *Cochinchine*, vol. 2, p. 376.
[120] Chen Ching-ho (Chen Jinghe), 'Mac Thien Tu and Phrayataksin,' p. 1567.

Malay Port Principality

Besides Cochinchina and Cambodia, Mo Tianci continued to build upon the foundations of his father and actively sought to integrate The Port as a node in the VOC-dominated economic network of island Southeast Asia. In one of his first official communications with the High Government in Batavia in 1771, he introduced himself as the governor of "my *negeri*, which my father has passed on to me." This Malay term implies a particular type of polity consisting of a major port centered upon a river enclosure. Indeed, the Malay name for The Port, Kuala, means river mouth.[121] The Dutch translated the term as *landschaap* and labeled Tianci "governor of the *negeri* of The Port" (*Gouverneur van het Landschaap Kankhauw*) or simply, "chief of The Port" (*Hoofd van Kankhauw*).[122]

According to Trocki, the *negeri* oversaw a hierarchy of minor ports and interior hinterlands and associated with similar centers within a broader network of trade and communication lanes stretching across maritime Asia.[123] These entities conformed to the classic definition of the Southeast Asian mandala model of politics and diplomacy. Although loosely subordinated to larger inland state hierarchies and dependent to a certain degree on their ranks and titles, the *negeri* were, in effect, self-governing. Indeed, the term nicely characterizes the nature of The Port, its relationship with its neighbors, and Tianci's form of governance.

Since the Portuguese creole and Austronesian networks traditionally included the Gulf of Siam coast as a stopover point in their trading voyages, the VOC permitted their ships to travel as far as Siam and Cambodia. They might pay call at several ports, but The Port was undoubtedly the most important and popular destination for them, since they could avoid dealing with the VOC, which had a factory in Ayutthaya, the other prominent location in the area. For Mo Tianci, their presence provided him access to product sources and markets in island Southeast Asia outside of the Dutch-held entrepôts of Melaka and Batavia.[124]

But Tianci concurrently cultivated linkages to the colonial center at Batavia. Although his first official communication with the VOC authorities occurred only in 1771, he had already forged a close relationship

---

[121] Li Tana and Van Dyke, 'Canton,' p. 12; Ibn Ahmad, *Precious Gift*, pp. 126, 335n1; Andaya, *Brothers*, p. 218; Li Tana, 'Mekong Delta,' p. 157.
[122] ANRI, K66a: 3574b, p. 110; 3686, p. 227; 3688, p. 366; Li Tana and Van Dyke, 'Canton, Cancao, and Cochinchina,' p. 12.
[123] Trocki, *Prince of Pirates*, p. 9; Li Tana, 'Mekong Delta,' pp. 159–160.
[124] ANRI, K66a: 3657, p. 904.

with the influential Chinese network based in the city. In a missive to a Siamese official in 1772, VOC Governor-General Petrus Albertus van der Parra (1714–1775) identifies one Lin Houqua as "lieutenant of the Chinese" at The Port before the 1770s. He lived there with his entire family, including his mother, wife, children, and extended relatives.[125] Incredibly, Lin Houqua was the grandson of Lin Jiguang (Lim Tjipko), one of the most powerful and longest-serving Chinese kapitans at Batavia, whose term lasted from 1755 to 1774.[126]

One of the key duties of the kapitan was to supervise trade and maintain peace and order among the people of his ethnic community. He held court on a weekly basis to resolve civil disputes and referred criminal cases to the VOC authorities. The kapitan was supposed to discuss his decisions with the lieutenants, who served under him. There were a few based locally in Batavia.[127] Despite being far away, Lin Houqua, too, can be assumed to answer directly to Lin Jiguang, given the concentration of the kapitan's relatives at The Port.

The lieutenant's presence served two important purposes for Mo Tianci. On the one hand, Lin Houqua helped reinforce The Port's role as a transshipment point by connecting Chinese merchants and sojourners to both Batavia and the Qing. For this reason, Tianci's letters to the VOC were all dated in the Qing reign name, for instance: "Written in the year *gengyin* (Kei-ien), Qianlong (Khi-en Lijong) 35: the twenty-fifth of the twelfth month," or February 10, 1771.[128] As Robert Batchelor points out, dating systems provided unified standards for keeping accounts and credit transactions across long distances. Most overseas Chinese communities, with their complex commercial ties to ports in southern China and with each other, adopted the calendar of the Qing.[129] Mo Tianci, too, had to follow this convention if he were to participate in these important commercial exchanges.

At the same time, Lin Houqua provided him with the service of an international criminal and mediation court that could ensure the safe and smooth operation of long-distance trade. Civil litigation was probably handled exclusively within the Chinese network. Criminal matters, however, had to go through the High Government. And it occurred on only one documented occasion in 1771, an opportunity that Tianci exploited to write to the governor-general for the first time.[130]

---

[125] ANRI, K66a: 3689, pp. 292–293. [126] Blussé and Nie, *Chinese Annals*, p. 249.
[127] Rush, *Opium to Java*, pp. 85–86. [128] ANRI, K66a: 3574b, pp. 108–111.
[129] Batchelor, *London*, p. 188; Salmon, 'Réfugiés Ming,' p. 205.
[130] ANRI, K66a: 3574b, pp. 108–112.

This case, which has been preserved in the High Government records of the Indonesian National Archives, gives us a fascinating glimpse into how the translocal justice system functioned. On December 17, 1770, a local junk belonging to the merchant Oeij Tshing was sailing to The Port center from Black Water when the craft became stranded at the river mouth next to the South China Sea because of a lack of wind. Several days later, another vessel from Siam on its way to Batavia happened to sail by. It belonged to Lauw Wo, who, like Oeij, resided at The Port. Oeij accused Lauw of seizing him and his crew of eight people and plundering their ship of their cargo. Oeij claimed that he and two other men escaped by jumping overboard and swimming to shore. They caught onto the wreckage of a vessel and floated with it back to Black Water, where they obtained transportation to return to The Port.[131]

According to Lauw Wo, however, he had discovered Oeij Tshing's junk in a terrible condition; the craft was sinking, and most of it had already submerged underwater. The eight people on board were waving and calling out for help. Moved to compassion, Lauw Wo took them in and provided them food and shelter. But his ship could not move anywhere since no favorable winds appeared. Oeij Tshing grew impatient and, he, along with two others, requested to be brought ashore by boat, where they would hail another vessel to take him and his crew back to The Port. The remaining passengers stayed with Lauw Wo while awaiting their return. When a good wind finally started to blow one seamy afternoon, and Oeij and his companions still did not show up, Lauw Wo feared that he would soon run out of food and water. He persuaded the rest of the crew to sail with him to Batavia, where they could easily find a ship bound for The Port. His vessel arrived at Batavia on January 5, 1771.[132]

Oeij Tshing reported the incident to the authorities after making his way back to The Port center. Since the dispute involved the criminal act of piracy, and part of the crew was at Batavia, Mo Tianci turned over its adjudication to Governor-General van der Parra. He arranged for a junk captain to transport the three men at The Port to Batavia. The ship carried Tianci's letter, dated February 10, 1771, in which he requested the individuals involved in this case, accusers and accused, to be repatriated back to his polity after the appropriate punishments were recommended. Before departure, Oeij and his shipmates were questioned by two officials whom the VOC sources called grandees (*groote*): Tscheiwan Kauw Kei Sien Tik Tsoe and Tscheiwan Sieuwhabien Hoeij Lam.

---

[131] ANRI, K66a: 3574b, pp. 109–114.
[132] ANRI, K66a: 3574b, pp. 120, 123–124, 129–130.

In these transcriptions, the office title and rank precede the surname of the bearer in the last word, but it is difficult to precisely identify either of them. The second of the two officials may have been Lin Houqua, Lam being the Cantonese pronunciation of the surname. The transcripts of the testimonies were sent along with the ship.[133]

Meanwhile Lauw Wo, his passengers, and the rest of Oeij's crew underwent questioning from the lieutenants at Batavia. After the arrival of Oeij and the other two men, a second round of interrogation was directed at them. A secretary of the Chinese community translated the interviews into Dutch for the High Government, and the kapitan made his recommendation.[134] On June 25, 1771, Governor-General van der Parra replied to Mo Tianci. He dismissed Oeij Tshing's accusations, finding them "to be devoid of all truth." Therefore, van der Parra decided not to pursue the charges against Lauw Wo and his men for piracy. Oeij and all eight members of his crew would accompany the junk captain, who was deputized by Tianci for this mission, back to The Port.[135] Although Oeij's case was the only documentation for the existence of a cross-border justice system, the procedures and interrogations appear to be part of a highly regularized and mature arrangement between the Chinese communities of The Port and Batavia. The fact that the Dutch authorities only got involved in these deliberations on one occasion also attests to the rarity of piratical activities among long-distance Chinese merchants.

However, the same cannot be said of the Austronesian networks, which were plagued by predation because of perennial political instability in island Southeast Asia. On the one hand, the rivalry between the Minangkabau of Siak and the sultanate of Johor continued. At the same time, struggles occurred among factions within these polities. In Johor, the Bugis won over the Malays and had emerged as the power behind the throne by 1760. In Siak, Raja Alam (1714–1779, r. 1761–1779) and his brother, Raja Mahmud (r. 1723–1760), had engaged in a protracted conflict for the leadership since the death of their father, Raja Kecil, in 1746. Eventually, with the aid of VOC forces based at Melaka, Alam emerged victorious. Mahmud's son, Raja Ismail, forged a base on the Tujuh islands, off the eastern coast of Sumatra.[136]

During their decades-long conflict, Johor and Siak and their internal factions had all competed to enlist the support of the nomadic sea peoples (Orang Laut). Besides plundering ships of their cargoes, the

---

[133] ANRI, K66a: 3574b, pp. 109–112.   [134] ANRI, K66a: 3574b, pp. 115–132.
[135] ANRI, K66a: 3688, p. 367.
[136] Ibn Ahmad, *Precious Gift*, pp. 124–136; Vos, *Gentle Janus*, pp. 73–114.

Orang Laut, Andaya shows, long engaged in the practice of seizing the passengers and selling them into slavery. The involvement of Malay, Minangkabau, and Bugis political actors caused predation in the straits zone to grow to such alarming levels that it frequently disrupted trade for prolonged periods of time.[137]

Moreover, just like during the days of Mo Jiu, the predation continued to spill over into the Gulf of Siam, where multiethnic pirate bands harassed passing vessels. In 1762, Raja Ismail went as far as to plan the military conquest of The Port with his sea people allies. He and his fleet were already sailing northward when a request from the Malay faction in Johor to fight the Bugis convinced him to abandon the offensive.[138] It is not clear whether Mo Tianci was ever aware of Ismail's intentions, but if he was, it was one additional reason for him to join the VOC's sphere of influence. Unlike the Gulf of Siam, he could not directly combat piracy so far away from his shores. The VOC, on the other hand, could use its influence and military power as leverage to ensure that the disorder in the straits zone did not get too out of hand, even if the polities in the area often defied its directives.[139]

Equidistant Diplomacy

As The Port increased in power and influence, Tianci came to deemphasize its status as a part of "Annam." References to him and his realm grew increasingly ambivalent over time. Take the example of the Qing sources. The official Veritable Records continue to mention The Port as being "under the administrative jurisdiction of Annam" during the 1760s. However, others, such as the *Wenxian tongkao*, labeled it the "Kingdom of The Port" (*Gangkou guo*) and a tributary of both Annam and Siam. Tianci, its "king" (*wang*), resided in a Chinese-style palace.[140] The gazetteer of Jiading County, in present-day Shanghai, speaks of his son Mo Huang as "crown prince (*wangzi*) of the Hà Tiên Kingdom (*Hexian guo*)."[141] Not only in the Sinosphere, but, according to the adventurer Pierre Poivre, Tianci's "barbarian neighbors," perhaps referring to the Khmer and Siamese, also called him a king.[142]

---

[137] Vos, *Gentle Janus*, pp. 82–114; Barnard, *Multiple Centres*, pp. 93–116; Andaya, *Brothers*, pp. 95–97.
[138] Ibn Ahmad, *Precious Gift*, pp. 126–136.   [139] Vos, *Gentle Janus*, pp. 207–208.
[140] *Qing shilu*, vol. 18: *Gaozong Chunhuangdi shilu*, p. 711; Zhang, *Wenxian tongkao*, vol. 2, p. 7463.
[141] *Zhongguo difangzhi jicheng*, Shanghai fuxian zhi ji 8, Cheng and Fan, *Jiading xianzhi*, p. 653.
[142] Poivre, *Ouevres complettes*, p. 142.

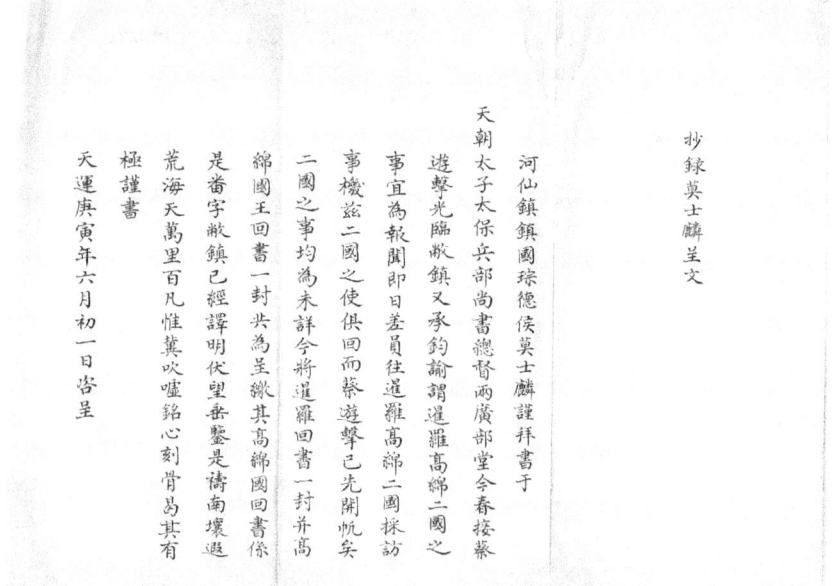

Figure 4.2 Mo Tianci's memorial to the Qianlong Emperor, c. 1770. ©National Palace Museum

Much of the confusion resulted from Mo Tianci's own pragmatic self-representations before different political actors according to different circumstances. In his memorials to the Qing court during the 1770s, preserved in the Palace Museum archives, he always addressed himself as "Tông Đức Marquis of Hà Tiên Garrison, Defender of the Country, Mo Shilin" 河仙鎮鎮國琮德侯莫士麟 (see Figure 4.2). The name that he used to refer to The Port and his noble title all came from the conferral of Annam, or Cochinchina in particular. Yet, references to the larger state entity do not appear anywhere in his memorial. In none of his communications does he ever write "Hà Tiên Garrison of Annam," which was the more appropriate usage. As a result, it becomes unclear which country he is helping to safeguard, or whether he considered The Port to be a country. Note also that he used his style name of Mo Shilin, with his original surname of Mo (莫) rather than the Mao (鄚) mandated by the Cochinchinese court.[143] The act of directly pursuing ties with China, the central overlord, served as a classic strategy within the Sinosphere for the

---

[143] Grand Council Archives, Qianlong Reign, 013221: Mo Shilin, n. p.

vassals of lesser tributary states.[144] Tianci could assert a greater level of independence, while checking any ambitions of Cochinchina, his immediate overlord, on his domain.

More intriguing was a map of the navigational route from Guangdong to Siam commissioned by him and presented to the Qianlong Emperor in 1769. It presented a rare view of maritime East Asia from the perspective of The Port. First, The Port, or Hà Tiên Garrison, was marked off separately from all its neighbors by highlighting its domain in a different, brighter color (see Figure 4.3). Tianci evidently viewed the entire northern littoral of the Gulf of Siam as constituting the territorial dimensions of his realm. Siam also appears on the map, as does Cochinchina, coming under the label of Kingdom of Annam. Curiously, Cambodia gets completely ignored, probably because it did not constitute a legitimate participant in the Qing tributary system. However, Tonkin and Champa are shown separately from Cochinchina even though the two did not have official Qing recognition. Perhaps their inclusion diminishes the size and influence of Cochinchina, and makes it appear more distant from The Port on the map than was actually the case.[145]

Despite being a vassal of Huế, there is no documentation of Tianci ever using the Vietnamese Lê dynasty reign names, even though he adopted the Qing and Cambodian calendars in a pragmatic fashion for certain occasions. Most of the time, including at the end of his preface to the "Ten Verses," one of his earliest writings, he simply wrote down the date according to the sexagenary cycle. In some of his correspondences with the Qing court and officials, such as the one in Figure 4.2, he put in *tianyun* before the sexagenary combination. It could be a subtle statement of Ming loyalist defiance to the Qing. Or it could be the Sinic rendering of the Buddhist calendar used in Siam and Cambodia to serve as a balance to his titles from Cochinchina at the opening.

But Tianci never proclaimed his own reign name, a necessary symbol for assuming the throne and establishing his own dynasty. Within The Port, the characters for "soaring dragon" (*longfei*) often appear before dates, most commonly on the tombstones in the cemetery on Screen Mountain. Mo Tianci inscribed the characters onto the grave of his own father (see Figure 4.4).[146] Similar to *tianyun*, it was not a reign name. Instead, it functioned as a stand-in to refer to whichever ruler or government currently held power, especially amid an unclear political situation or to provide a sense of timelessness that goes beyond an individual

---

[144] Anderson, *Rebel Den*, p. 67.
[145] Grand Council Archives, Qianlong Reign, 013221: Mo Shilin, n. p.
[146] Phạm Đức Mạnh, 'Cổ mộ,' pp. 1294–1295, 1298, 1300–1303.

Figure 4.3 A map of the maritime route from Guangdong to Siam, presented to the Qianlong Emperor by Mo Tianci, 1769.
©National Palace Museum

monarch. This convention could be found in other parts of Southeast Asia, particularly among Chinese creole communities with Ming loyalist attachments. According to Claudine Salmon and Li Qingxin, its use allowed them to safely express their dissident sentiments while not upsetting the Qing or clashing with local dating systems, such as Vietnam's own reign names.[147]

Tianci's purposeful ambiguity shows that he was less interested in forging an independent state than maintaining an equidistant diplomacy with the major powers in maritime East Asia. Pierre Poivre confirms that he "never pretended to reign but only to establish an empire of reason" and was "very content to be the chief laborer and merchant of his

---

[147] Salmon, 'Réfugiés Ming,' pp. 204–205; Li Qingxin, 'Haishang Ming chao.'

Figure 4.4 Tomb of Mo Jiu on Screen Mountain. The epitaph contains the *longfei* dating system.
Photograph by author.

realm."[148] Similarly, as one of the contributors to Tianci's original "Ten Verses," Sun Tianrui of Xiamen, comments in his response to "Night Drum of River Wall," "it is difficult to exchange a suit of armor for the silken robe of the palace."[149] Tianci preferred to remain, at least nominally, a military commander rather than becoming a king. The French missionary Levavasseur believes that Tianci refused to proclaim his own dynasty to avoid offending Cochinchina or Cambodia, whose friendship "sustains him on his throne."[150] There might be another explanation. By leaving his precise status ambiguous, he did not have to territorialize his area of control over a confined polity like The Port. He could instead exercise authority and influence beyond his official boundaries, especially over the trading networks that spanned maritime Asia.

In the end, perhaps the Qing came up with the most precise definition for Mo Tianci's realm. The court and its officials most commonly

[148] Poivre, *Ouevres complettes*, p. 142. [149] Hán-Nôm A. 441: Mao, *Hexian shiyong*, n. p.
[150] AMEP, Cochinchine, vol. 744: 'Relation,' p. 966.

referred to him as an "aboriginal official" (*tuguan*) or "aboriginal headman" (*tumu*), "barbarian headman" (*yimu*), or "garrison headman" (*zhenmu*). These terms meant that they largely considered him the equivalent to the hereditary tribal rulers (*tusi*) in the liminal frontier of southwestern China.[151] As C. Patterson Giersch shows in his study of Yunnan around the same period, chieftains in the borderlands frequently switched loyalties among competing and often antagonistic neighboring states. At times, they maintained multiple allegiances according to the prevailing geopolitical situation. Anderson argues that this arrangement allowed them also to intervene and take territory from their neighbors.[152]

Indeed, through his pragmatism and the decentralized character of his ruling ideology, Mo Tianci successfully manipulated the loopholes and points of intersection between the Sinosphere and the Southeast Asian mandala system. He was able to make The Port indispensable to his Nguyễn overlords as a guardian of their vulnerable southern maritime frontier. It was also a crucial conduit for access to elite Chinese culture that Cochinchina otherwise could not obtain in a formal manner since it did not have direct tributary access to the Qing. Meanwhile, The Port increased its involvement in a mandala centered upon Siam, through its vassal: the Cambodian court at Oudong. Tianci participated actively in the Khmer hierarchy and emerged to become the viceroy and power behind the throne. He also integrated The Port as a petty principality within the VOC's hegemony in island Southeast Asia. This allowed him to forge linkages to the Austronesian and Chinese networks. He could thereby access destinations beyond Batavia and benefit from a translocal mechanism for resolving commercial disputes. He maintained official communications with the VOC authorities as well since they could play a vital role in combating piracy and other criminal activities far beyond his shores.

His calculated ambiguity and equidistant diplomacy allowed him to enjoy the full benefits of being a ruler of an independent state without any formal recognition as such. To some degree, Tianci's strategy was typical of many other ports in the water world and beyond, such as Bassac. As Li Tana convincingly argues, this "pre-nation-state world of shifting and multiple alliances was the necessary condition" for trade to flourish.[153] It was the best means for him to survive and maintain friendly relations within a fragmented and conflict-ridden neighborhood, especially if he

---

[151] See, for instance, *Qing shilu*, vol. 18: *Gaozong Chunhuangdi shilu*, pp. 711–712; vol. 19, p. 174.
[152] See Giersch, *Asian Borderlands*, especially pp. 64–127; Anderson, *Rebel Den*, p. 67.
[153] Li Tana, 'Mekong Delta,' p. 152.

wanted to trade as widely as possible and therefore earn money from everyone. What was distinct about Tianci's approach was that he did not merely seek to join different vertically organized hierarchies. He also sought to harness their systems and achieve dominant positions within them, not so much to become their rulers, but to be able to set the rules to benefit The Port's position as a translocal node of commerce. He adopted a similar approach in the management of The Port's domestic affairs, which mirrored the maritime East Asian world in its geographic, ethnic, and religious diversity.

5 A Port with Many Faces

> All of this is the result of Mo [Tianci's] management. Alleyways crisscross one another, lined throughout with shops. Viet, Chinese, Khmer, and Javanese reside in their communities. Long-distance junks and river vessels come and go, their density as thick as silk on a loom. It is truly a metropolis by the sea.[1]
>
> —Trịnh Hoài Đức

迯景河仙溫有情 *Mười cảnh Hà Tiên rất hữu tình* (The Ten Scenes of Hà Tiên are full of sentiment)

嫩嫩渃渃嚼㦖樟 *Non non nước nước gẫm nên xinh* (Mountains and waters, do ponder their beauty)

東湖鹿峙竜涌沚 *Đông Hồ, Lộc Trĩ luôn dòng chảy* (East Lake, Deer Cape, [the waters] always flow)

南浦鱸溪乂脈生 *Nam Phố, Lư Khê một mạch xanh* (South Bay, Sea Perch Creek, a flash of green)

蕭寺江城鐘皷煨 *Tiêu Tự, Giang Thành, chuông trống ỏi* (Temple of Seclusion, Fortress River, the noise of bells and drums)

珠岩金嶼魟鴼迋 *Châu Nham, Kim Dự cá chim quanh* (Pearl Cliff, Golden Islet, fish and birds circle about)

屏山石洞羅梁榾 *Bình San, Thạch Động là rường cột* (Screen Mountain, Stone Grotto are supports and columns)

啾啾闆秋景底名 *Sừng sững muôn năm cảnh để dành* (Standing motionless, the scenes remain this way for eternity)

—General Summary of the Ten Views of Hà Tiên (*Hà Tiên thập cảnh tổng luận*)[2]

Just as Tianci integrated his realm into the prevailing hierarchies across maritime East Asia, he adopted multiple methods of governance in front of the diverse residents and sojourners of The Port. Sakurai and

---

[1] Trịnh, *Thông chí*, p. 534.
[2] Đông, *Văn Học*, pp. 301–302. A scanned reproduction of the demotic *nôm* version is found in Trương, *Nghiên cứu*, vol. 2, p. 188.

163

Kitagawa characterize The Port as having "two faces: one for the Khmer people and another for the Chinese, as well as two faces for internal and external affairs."[3] More precisely, Tianci enacted two forms of domestic administration that coexisted and commingled. He preserved the Cambodian noble hierarchy and official positions, while selectively adopting and adapting Sino-Viet institutions. In addition, he utilized religions and ethical systems and devised some of his own practices for specific situations and depending on his constituency.

Ultimately, he aimed to achieve two interrelated objectives: territorial expansion into the resource-rich hinterlands and the recruitment and retention of the population necessary to exploit the new acquisitions. Accordingly, he welcomed migrants to his realm, regardless of ethnic or social background or religious affiliation. Chinese creoles formed the core of the polity's identity. But he also welcomed Qing, Viet, Khmer, Siamese, Austronesian, and European sojourners and settlers. Tianci employed the religious and ethical systems prevalent among them, including Confucianism, Mahayana and Theravada Buddhism, Islam, and Christianity, to give them a sense of belonging and organize them for easier administration. In particular, he worked closely with Catholic missionaries to attract dissident Viet migrants, who became a major source of labor and qualified officials as The Port's territory underwent tremendous expansion during the late 1750s.

Despite his flexibility in accommodating his diverse population, Tianci ultimately depended upon native place ties, marriage alliances, and a militarized chain of command to ensure his own dominance. The Mo's style of governance resembled the role of the gentry in the grassroots societies of Ming and Qing China but transplanted onto an overseas setting without a strong centralized authority to oversee them or certify their legitimacy through civil service examinations. Eventually, Tianci sought to provide a more unified ideology for his realm. In this respect, he targeted the Chinese creole, Qing, and Viet, who constituted most of his population. Important measures involved the establishment of Confucian schools, patronage of Buddhism, and the possible rendering of his original "Ten Verses" project into the Vietnamese vernacular to reach a larger audience underneath the elite level.

Military Rule with Civilian Characteristics

The leadership core of The Port consisted of Mo Tianci and his family members, with whom he was close. After his eldest son, Hao, passed

---

[3] Sakurai and Kitagawa, 'Hà Tiên or Banteay Meas,' p. 207.

away during the 1750s, he designated his second son, Huang, as the successor to his enterprise. Huang received the position of assistant garrison commander (*Hiệp trấn*) from the Cochinchinese court. According to the Franciscan father Julián de Nuestra Señora del Pilar (1733–1779), Tianci loved him dearly and entrusted him with successively greater responsibilities over time. Huang came to handle most of The Port's daily administration, leaving his father to attend to larger matters, including diplomacy and trade, or to the pastime of fishing in Sea Perch Creek. The other important individual in Tianci's family was his sister Jinding, who had an important input in making decisions. Tianci also consulted his small circle of advisers in the Pavilion of Summoning Worthies.[4]

His subjects, at least those in The Port's center, must have seen him quite frequently, since they knew him well in person, and he enjoyed a wide degree of popularity among them. There was another side to him, however. Like the stern gentry patriarch of any prominent East Asian lineage, whatever he said had the effect of law and must be unconditionally obeyed. Both the Franciscans and French missionaries claim that he was the "absolute owner" of the realm, a petty king (*régulo*) who "ruled despotically."[5]

Mo Tianci exercised power through a highly militarized bureaucratic structure. In fact, both his position of military governor-general of Hà Tiên Garrison, granted by Cochinchina, and the Cambodian title of Preah Sotoat highlighted his official responsibility for frontier defense. True to his task, Tianci worked to bolster the defensive infrastructure established under his father's rule. He maintained and repaired the walls of the original citadel. As the urban area grew because of increased population and commercial activity, Mo Tianci widened and expanded the roads, constructed new buildings, and opened additional marketplaces.[6]

In a perimeter around the citadel, a second line of fortifications was constructed that took full advantage of The Port's natural protective barriers. Walls about three meters high extended for 3.3 kilometers along the backbones of Hibiscus Mountain to the southwest, Screen Mountain to the west, and the Mount of Five Tigers on the north. They were mostly made of bamboo stockades and logs, like the citadel, but several locations were reinforced by stone. On water, a heavily fortified stone

---

[4] AMEP, Cochinchine, vol. 745, 'Relation des Franciscains,' pp. 176, 180; Trương, *Nghiên cứu*, vol. 2, p. 49; Hán-Nôm A. 2939: Phạm, *Nam hành*, n. p.
[5] AMEP, Cochinchine, vol. 744: 'Relation,' p. 966; Pérez, 'Españoles en el imperio de Annam' 11, p. 201.
[6] Trịnh, *Thông chí*, p. 306.

stockade was constructed at the highest point of the Big Golden Islet overlooking the Gulf of Siam and safeguarding the busy harbor. A third, outermost layer of defense consisted of watchtowers and trenches manned by guards and patrols. They ran from the gulf eastward along hills until they converged at a fortress situated on the shores of Fortress River, near its headwaters.[7] Collectively, these defensive works delineated and separated The Port's core area from the rest of Cambodia.

The troops under his command witnessed a substantial increase in size and capability over time. From barely being able to repel Ang Mei Bhen's invasion in 1739, Tianci could put together a fleet of ten ships to suppress the pirate band of Big-Bellied Đức in 1747 and mobilize enough soldiers to handily beat back another attack on The Port in 1751. By the end of the 1760s, he could organize an invasion of Siam consisting of 50,000 soldiers and over a hundred ships.[8] At the height of his power, Tianci probably possessed on regular occasions about half the figures provided for this expeditionary force. In comparison, the entire Cochinchinese military around the same time consisted of 100,000 to 150,000 men, with 50,000 of them being regular units and the rest, militia to be mobilized for war. It was a little more than double the size of The Port's armed forces and spread out over a larger area. Tianci's military power was thus formidable. He also maintained a systematic routine of drills to keep his men prepared for contingencies.[9]

After Tianci's succession, the Cochinchinese military presence at The Port gradually disappeared. Nguyễn Văn Túc, the likely relative of his mother who had served in an important advisory position during the time of Mo Jiu, passed away in 1743. The commander of another unit identified only by his surname of Nguyễn died in 1751.[10] Tianci apparently used the occasion of these deaths and the Martial King's authorization for him to establish four company units in 1747 to undertake a drastic reorganization of his military.

The resulting arrangement took on hybrid characteristics from the Ming and Cochinchina. According to Lê Quý Đôn, there were two specialized naval companies, the Left and Right, and an infantry named Heroic Treasure (C: Xiongbao V: Hùng bảo).[11] An individual with the

---

[7] Zhang, *Wenxian tongkao*, p. 7463; Trịnh, *Thông chí*, pp. 166–167, 174–175; Nguyễn Dynasty, *Nhất thống chí*, vol. 3, p. 282; Sellers, *Princes of Hà-Tiên*, p. 42; Trương, *Nghiên cứu*, vol. 2, pp. 306–307, 310.

[8] Trịnh, *Thông chí*, pp. 308–312; Vũ, *Gia phả*, pp. 101, 112–113; Grand Council Archives, Qianlong Reign, 007528: Pan Siju, n. p.

[9] Yang Baoyun, *Principauté des Nguyễn*, p. 103; Nguyen Thanh-Nha, *Tableau économique*, pp. 20–21; Trịnh, *Thông chí*, p. 306.

[10] Phạm Đức Mạnh, 'Cổ mộ,' pp. 1297–1298, 1302.

[11] Lê Quý Đôn, *Tạp lục* (BNF), https://archivesetmanuscrits.bnf.fr/ark:/12148/cc912795.

surname of Zhou (d. 1765) led one of the companies, while a Mo clan member who passed away in 1766 and whose relationship to Tianci remains unclear took charge of another one. The third likely came under the command of Chen Ruishu, the clan relative of Chen Shangchuan who probably married Tianci's sister. In addition, the Dragon Gate formed their own specialized company led by Chen Dali, Shangchuan's nephew and Dading's son. To keep alive the Dragon Gate memory, his unit acquired a special name for itself: the Victorious Naval Company (C: *Shengshui dui* V: *Thắng Thuỷ đội*).[12]

Just as in Cochinchina, each company was divided into three smaller units known as boats (*thuyền*). In the standard Cochinchinese military organization, each boat contained around forty troops and, if applicable, three warships.[13] But according to the anecdotal evidence, the size of The Port's basic units were certainly far larger. One clue to the true figures lies in the title given to the company commanders: Great General of Manifest Valor (*Zhaowu dajiangjun*), which appears on their tombstone inscriptions. It was most likely derived from the precedent of the Ming, in which each commander holding this title led 5,600 men.[14] This translates into over 1,800 soldiers per boat. With four companies in total, the total regular troop size comes out to around 22,000 men, close to my earlier estimate.

In addition, Mo Tianci directly commanded six independent boats. These were probably the original forces that he and his father had at their disposal before the Martial King's authorization to establish additional companies. One of them, named the Dragon Banner (C: *Longqi* V: *Long kỳ*), was the Mo clan's personal bodyguard unit. Besides standard infantry, some boats specialized in specific weapons, such as harquebuses or big knives, while others served as an elite crack force. One independent boat belonged to his son, Mo Huang. Another came under General Xu's son, Youyong, who inherited the title and position of his father, the marquis of the Han Sun, and served as commander-in-chief of The Port's military.[15] He had demonstrated great skill and bravery during the battles against Big-Bellied Đức's piratical band. Tianci placed Xu in high esteem, giving him the hand of his second daughter in marriage.[16] The total troop sizes of these independent boats remain unknown.

---

[12] Trịnh, *Thông chí*, p. 312; Vũ, *Gia phả*, p. 113; Phạm Đức Mạnh, 'Cổ mộ,' pp. 1298, 1302.
[13] Lê Quý Đôn, *Tạp lục* (BNF), https://archivesetmanuscrits.bnf.fr/ark:/12148/cc912795.
[14] Phạm Đức Mạnh, 'Cổ mộ,' pp. 1298, 1302; Yu, *Zhongguo guanzhi da cidian*, p. 1156.
[15] Lê Quý Đôn, *Tạp lục* (BNF), https://archivesetmanuscrits.bnf.fr/ark:/12148/cc912795.
[16] Trịnh, *Thông chí*, p. 312; Vũ, *Gia phả*, pp. 111–112; Phạm Đức Mạnh, 'Cổ mộ,' p. 1298, 1302; Trương, *Nghiên cứu*, vol. 2, p. 49.

Mo Tianci's commanders concurrently took charge of the most important civil affairs, whose administration was simple and pragmatic. There were two principal areas of focus. One of them involved the maintenance of social stability and the prevention of crime and rebellion. The tombstone of the company commander Zhou reveals that, during his lifetime, he concurrently served as a punishment official (*tixing*), a title derived from a Ming bureaucratic office. He and whoever was his successor oversaw at least two judges who tried criminal cases and handled litigation. One of them was, perhaps, the occupant of a tomb surnamed Trần (d. 1775), a Viet who held the noble title of marquis, the same as Tianci and the generals. But he appears to have had no military rank. The judges always kept Tianci informed of the progress of each case. Ultimately, he was the one who decided and signed off on the outcome, often after discussion with his son, Huang, his advisers in the pavilion, and his officers.[17] For civil and criminal cases with implications beyond The Port, Tianci would refer them to the lieutenant Lin Houqua, who would, in turn, cooperate with the Chinese kapitan in Batavia.[18]

There was also an entire unit of jailers. They staffed The Port's prisons, with the main one located west of the city center. The jails were intentionally constructed to inflict the greatest degree of discomfort upon their occupants. Half-naked prisoners were entirely exposed to the elements and for the full view of the public. Interrogations often took place under torture, while serious offenders wore heavy cangues around their necks. The severest penalties, reserved for cases of sedition and rebellion, included decapitation and exile to the hinterlands.[19]

The second main purpose of civil administration was to secure revenues. Xu Youyong's father, as indicated on his tombstone, served as treasurer (*cai bạ*). His tasks would involve supervising the collection of taxes and maintenance of household registries and the allocation of revenues acquired from overseas trade. He would spend these funds on feeding, equipping, and paying the salaries of officers and soldiers and for public works and other necessary outlays.[20] His son, Youyong, most likely took over these responsibilities after his death. Although deriving much of its institutional framework from Cochinchina, The Port, at its core, consisted of a Chinese creole military elite held together by

---

[17] *Nouvelles lettres*, vol. 6, pp. 471–475; Phạm Đức Mạnh, 'Cổ mộ,' pp. 1298–1299.
[18] ANRI, K66a: 3689, pp. 292–293.
[19] *Nouvelles lettres*, vol. 6, pp. 470–473, 476–477; AMEP, Cochinchine, vol. 745: 'Relation des Franciscains,' p. 180.
[20] Phạm Đức Mạnh, 'Cổ mộ,' pp. 1297, 1301; Trương, *Nghiên cứu*, vol. 2, p. 49; Đỗ Văn Ninh, *Từ Điển Chức Quan*, p. 110.

Leizhou/Hainanese native place clan ties and Ming loyalist credentials and perpetuated through the hereditary transfer of titles and offices.

Ming Memories, Qing Reality

Let us now join a group of Qing travelers, who later contributed to the entry on The Port in the *Wenxian tongkao*, and imagine what they saw and experienced after their arrival during the 1740s. Strolling through the streets of the city center, they commented on how "everyone lived in houses made of tiles and bricks" level with the ground surface, just like in their homeland. In reality, these structures were rare, and only officials, wealthy merchants, and other prominent individuals could afford them.[21] Perhaps what they saw was the interior of the citadel, where the Chinese creole elites were concentrated.

The most prominent of these buildings, situated at the center of the citadel, was a Chinese-style "palace" where the "king" lived. This was actually the garrison office where Mo Tianci conducted public business and not his actual residence. It doubled as a shrine to Confucius (551–479 BCE). Open to the public for "everybody to pay their respects," it symbolized the exalted status of the great sage's teachings. Education also proved to be an important medium for propagating Confucian doctrines and ensuring the preservation and generational continuity of Chinese creole identity. Tianci established a network of public schools throughout the realm. Teachers mostly consisted of local creoles proficient in reading and writing the language and trained in the Confucian classics.[22]

The most promising and brightest young people in The Port were eligible to attend the schools. Usually, they came from the families of Tianci and his inner circle. These privileged descendants would, one day, take over the positions of their fathers. However, the schools also took great care to select students from the most impoverished backgrounds. After finishing their studies, they might become functionaries and recordkeepers in the garrison offices, and, perhaps, obtain the chance for further upward mobility.[23]

In front of the garrison office and Confucian shrine were a spacious courtyard and garden situated between the eastern gate and moat.

---

[21] Zhang, *Wenxian tongkao*, p. 7463; AMEP, Cochinchine, vol. 745: 'Relation des Franciscains,' p. 174.

[22] Zhang, *Wenxian tongkao*, p. 7463; Nguyễn Dynasty, *Nhất thống chí*, vol. 3, p. 280; Trịnh, *Thông chí*, pp. 532–533.

[23] Zhang, *Wenxian tongkao*, p. 7463; Nguyễn Dynasty, *Nhất thống chí*, vol. 3, p. 280; Trịnh, *Thông chí*, pp. 532–533.

Crossing over the waterway on a stone bridge, one encountered on the righthand side a hostel for visiting emissaries, whether from Cochinchina, Cambodia, China, or other lands. On the left stood an office that managed civilian affairs. North of the citadel, at the foot of the Mount of Five Tigers, the only side not enclosed by walls, was the office of the assistant garrison commander, Tianci's son Mo Huang.[24]

The area south of the citadel constituted the heart of the city, filled with shops and open-air stalls that lined the busy streets and narrow alleyways. Here, the scenery was more typical of Southeast Asia. Houses and makeshift markets with elevated stilt structures and thatched roofs made from straw permeated the banks of several canals and the drawbridges built above them. Smaller craft could sail directly into town with their wares. Still, amid the chaotic noises and crowds, the visitors would have come across a shrine dedicated to Guan Yu (d. 220 CE), the famous Eastern Han dynasty (25–220 CE) general who later became worshipped as a god of war in China and Vietnam. His presence demonstrated the preponderant power of the military elite. Moving along in a counterclockwise direction, they would have passed a fish market and warehouse. Farther east, there was a shrine to the protector god of the city (*chenghuang*). The tourists would end up on the shores of East Lake, and continuing northward, stop at a shipyard close to the main citadel gate that constructed junks for trade and the navy. Once completed, the vessels could be launched directly into the water from a jetty that extends into the lagoon. From there, one could also take a ferry to the foot of Suzhou Mountain, on the other side.[25]

Tracing their steps back, the travelers would have encountered a wooden-plank bridge along a canal next to the Guan Yu shrine. Following the waterway to its head, the bridge would cross a stretch of sea and connect to the Big Golden Islet, a remarkable feat of engineering for its day. There, on the shoreline beneath the stone stockade, another canal and drawbridge filled with vendors and people greeted them. Nearby was a fishing pavilion where anglers could perfect their catch. If one ventured a bit further inland, one could escape the hustle and bustle of the never-ending conversations and commercial transactions at a Buddhist temple offering a quiet haven for relaxation and meditation.[26]

---

[24] Zhang, *Wenxian tongkao*, p. 7463; Nguyễn Dynasty, *Nhất thống chí*, vol. 3, p. 280; Trịnh, *Thông chí*, pp. 532–533.

[25] Nguyễn Dynasty, *Nhất thống chí*, vol. 3, p. 280; Trịnh, *Thông chí*, p. 170, 533; Trương, *Nghiên cứu*, vol. 2, pp. 310–318.

[26] Nguyễn Dynasty, *Nhất thống chí*, vol. 3, p. 280; Trịnh, *Thông chí*, pp. 174–175, 533–534.

Evidently, the Qing visitors had an enjoyable stay. They seemed to have prioritized the landmarks and features that reminded them the most of their homeland. The comments appended to the entry on The Port in the *Wenxian tongkao* praised it as a place that, "out of all the barbarian lands, most closely resembles us" in its customs. Despite its remote distance, it "voluntarily submitted to the rites and teachings of China." Everything, from marriage customs and the divination of auspicious dates and times to the use of white as the color of mourning during funerals, exhibited striking similarities with practices back home. This spread of civilization afar served as a testament to the triumph of the way of Confucius and the "miraculous transformative influence of our holy dynasty."[27]

At the same time, observers from the Qing would have witnessed one striking difference from their homeland: open displays of political and ideological affiliation toward the defunct Ming. They could instantly recognize that the Chinese creoles adopted "the dress and institutions of the previous dynasty."[28] The men, in particular, grew out their hair long, in contrast to the shaven pates and queue imposed by the Manchu rulers in China on pain of death. They wore loose, flowing robes with wide sleeves rather than the tight riding jackets of the Qing. The Qing visitors must have additionally seen many Viet who donned a similar fashion, although they might notice some minor differences in detail. The Viet were complying with the Martial King's edict to change the dress, also based primarily upon Ming precedents and which Tianci adopted for his realm. These sights, both familiar and exotic, would later leave a deep impression on the Qing court and officials during the 1770s, when they started having frequent contacts with The Port. According to the Mo clan biography, the Qianlong Emperor profusely praised the attire of Tianci's envoys, claiming that their "gowns and caps resembled the Han dynasty."[29]

Memories of the Ming were also embedded into the physical landscape of The Port. On Screen Mountain, the tombstones of the core female relatives of the Mo ruling family bore the characters for "Imperial Ming" (*Huang Ming*) at the start of their epitaphs. When Tianci's wife passed away around 1752, their sons, Hao, Huang, and Tang, had them inscribed onto her tombstone (see Figure 5.1). Later, Tianci married another woman from the C: Huang V: Hoàng clan. Like his main wife, it is not clear whether she was Chinese or Viet. But she, too, had "Imperial Ming" inscribed on her tomb by her four sons after her death in 1767.

---

[27] Zhang, *Wenxian tongkao*, p. 7463.   [28] Zhang, *Wenxian tongkao*, p. 7463.
[29] Vũ, *Gia phả*, pp. 104, 132.

Figure 5.1 The epitaph on the tomb of Lady Nguyễn, Tianci's principal wife, on the slopes of Screen Mountain identifies her to be a subject of the Imperial Ming.
Photograph by author. 'From: Hang Xing/Kenneth Swope, © 2019 Routledge. Reproduced by permission of Taylor & Francis Group.'

Another example is Lady Xu 許, the wife of Mo Huang, the assistant garrison commander, and likely a Chinese creole herself. After she died in 1776, her five sons and her grandsons erected a tomb for her. Her epitaph begins with "Deceased Ming Subject" (*Ming gu*).[30] Commemoration of the matriarchs of the Mo clan allowed for the preservation and continuity of the Ming memory, especially since their offspring would leave their names on the tombstones and retain this identity out of filial piety.

Tianci and the other main Chinese creole officials and commanders themselves, however, consciously avoided an open political affiliation. Doing so would go against his purposeful ambiguity in regards to state and non-state actors across maritime East Asia that had successfully secured the independence of his realm. Accordingly, they used the sexagenary cycle and, at most, placed the ambivalent "soaring dragon" in front of it to refer to a vague ruling emperor.[31] In particular, Tianci did not want to antagonize the Qing and jeopardize the flourishing trading connections that formed a backbone of The Port's commerce. He also actively welcomed Qing immigrants to settle in his realm and had contact with gentry and officials.

A memorial by the Qing governor-general of Guangdong and Guangxi, Li Shiyao, in 1772 states that "there are many people from China making their living at The Port."[32] Much of this influx took on a partially temporary character. Merchants and travelers from the Qing would come and stay briefly or for extended periods of time before departing for their homeland. Chinese merchants also came from other ports. Lauw Wo, who was accused of pirating Oeij Tshing's junk, appeared to have divided his time between The Port and Batavia. Because of The Port's close linkages with China and Batavia and the high degree of fluidity between all three places, Lin Houqua, grandson of the Chinese kapitan of Batavia, served as the lieutenant of this community.[33] The position obviously entailed responsibility over merchants and sojourners who were more or less considered Qing subjects and not the creole descendants of the Ming loyalists.

We can obtain a snapshot of the people who went to The Port from the depositions before Qing officials of several followers of Li Wenguang, who rebelled at Biên Hòa in 1747. The Cochinchinese held them in captivity until they were repatriated to China together with a shipwrecked

---

[30] Phạm Đức Mạnh, 'Cổ mộ,' pp. 1297, 1303.
[31] See, for instance, the tomb of Mo Jiu in Phạm Đức Mạnh, 'Cổ mộ,' p. 1294.
[32] Grand Council Archives, Qianlong Reign, 017970, 1772: Li Shiyao, n. p.
[33] ANRI, K66a: 3689, pp. 292–293; 3574b, pp. 118–119.

Zhejiang official ten years later.³⁴ Wang Xian, Lin Wenbao, and Mo Qin all came from Chaozhou and its vicinity, and they all originally sailed to The Port for the purpose of doing business (*shengli*). Wang and Lin voluntarily left for Biên Hòa because they failed to earn a profit. While Mo Qin was on his way to The Port, his ship got blown off course to Donay. Eventually they found employment in the construction of Li's ships or as sailors onboard.³⁵ Presumably, they would engage in similar lines of work as artisans and merchants at The Port.

Like at Manila, Batavia, and elsewhere, these Chinese outsiders had their own quarters. They resided in several seaside suburbs east of Suzhou Mountain that represented an extension of The Port's city center, across the river mouth, in their endless profusion of shops and markets that spilled out of their narrow alleyways. There, they could market their wares and outfit their junks with goods and provisions. These suburbs were known as **C: Mingbo** V: Minh Bột commercial districts. The sources identify at least three of them, namely, the Mingbo Grand Commercial District (C: Mingbo Dabu V: Minh Bột Đại Phố), the Mingbo New Commercial District (C: Mingbo Xinbu V: Minh Bột Tân Phố), and the Mingbo Majestic Tree Commercial District (C: Mingbo Qishubu V: Minh Bột Kỳ Thọ Phố). The prefix Mingbo clearly marked them as Chinese settlements. Literally meaning Ming Rising Tide or Ming Shoreline, it referred to the vast nautical distance from China and the physical location where Qing subjects stayed while at The Port. At the same time, it also served as a form of propaganda or statement of defiance, a metaphor for the future return and restoration of the Ming in China.³⁶

The Chinese merchants and sojourners were not segregated from the rest of The Port. They could freely move about and mingle with other communities. Quite a few, for whatever reason, never left and took up permanent residence, even if they claimed to be staying temporarily. As Governor-General Li remarked, The Port "has always had a large population of sojourners. Commercial junks carrying wandering migrants onboard sail there in an endless stream."³⁷ After their arrival, they might intermarry with Viet or Khmer women. The inscription on

---

[34] Yang Baoyun, *Principauté des Nguyên*, pp. 158–162.
[35] China First Historical Archives, Junjichu, 1387-020, pp. 000302–000303.
[36] Đặng, 'Đô thị cổ Hà Tiên,' pp. 74, 76; Trịnh, *Thông chí*, p. 357; Nguyễn Dynasty, *Nhất thống chí*, vol. 3, pp. 280–281. Although both gazetteers were compiled in the early nineteenth century, they undoubtedly referred to a system of governance devised by the Mo. The Nguyễn dynasty, which at the time had newly unified Vietnam, inherited the old administrative units to help its consolidation over this new frontier.
[37] Grand Council Archives, Qianlong Reign, 017970: Li Shiyao, n. p.

Figure 5.2 Joint tomb of Mo Bang, who identified as a subject of the Qing, and his wife, a self-identified Viet.
Photograph by author.

the tomb of Mo Bang on Screen Mountain indicates that he "resided in Dongling," the home village of Tianci's father. He was probably the individual identified as Mo Dingbang in the Dongling clan genealogy. He was one generation younger than Tianci and passed away in 1773. Although the tomb inscription states that he was merely sojourning, his move was clearly permanent, since he married a Viet woman. She bore him two daughters, the very ones who erected a joint tomb for the couple (see Figure 5.2).[38]

Chen Junqing and Liang Shangxian, two peasants originally from Haifeng, in eastern Guangdong, chose to bring their entire families with them. Chen, along with seventeen of his relatives, both male and female, old and young, set sail together with Liang and his group of eighteen, making a total of thirty-five people.[39] Young women from upstanding families and at least some level of education were also brought into The Port to join Mo Tianci's harem or to serve as the wives and concubines of

[38] Phạm Đức Mạnh, 'Cổ mộ,' pp. 1298–1299; *Dongling Mo shi zupu*, n. p.
[39] Grand Council Archives, Qianlong Reign, 017970: Li Shiyao, n. p.

his sons and members of his inner circle.⁴⁰ Compared to other parts of Southeast Asia, where the Chinese population was overwhelmingly male and single, The Port enjoyed a more balanced gender ratio.⁴¹

Not surprisingly, the Mo clan's native place of Leizhou became an important source of migrants. Mo Bang was one person who made the move. The clan genealogy placed footnotes beside several more individuals from his home village, indicating that they had "gone to The Port" or "gone to The Port in Annam" around this period. Another person simply "went to Annam," but his specific destination may have been The Port as well.⁴²

In addition to native place ties, Mo Tianci appeared to have put in place a sophisticated system for recruiting and retaining immigrants in Guangdong and elsewhere. Whether through word of mouth, agents, or some form of advertisement, he was able to promote The Port quite widely among common people. Haifeng, where Chen Junqing and Liang Shangxuan came from, was subject to overpopulation and overdevelopment. Competition over ever scarcer land and resources took the form of violent intervillage and interdialect feuding, secret society and sectarian infiltration, rampant banditry and piracy, and outright rebellion.⁴³ In their testimony before Governor-General Li, the two men made the decision to leave Haifeng in 1765 after they heard glowing descriptions of The Port as being "a wide and spacious land suitable for us to open up and cultivate." They departed for their destination by boarding a commercial junk at Guangzhou.⁴⁴ Mo Tianci must have provided generous subsidies or advances on loans to defray the substantial costs associated with the journey for Chen and Liang and the thirty-three other people on board.

The support for the new arrivals extended to their settlement and cultivation of land. Chen and Liang, for instance, received a plot around the Lotus Pond reservoir in the countryside immediately northwest of the city center.⁴⁵ An agricultural Mingbo settlement was established, known as the Mingbo Dirt Hill Hamlet (C: Mingbo Tuqiu Dian V: Minh Bột Thổ Khâu Điếm) (see Figure 5.3).

Another site was located right next to Tianci's favorite fishing haunt at Sea Perch Creek, east of the Mingbo commercial districts. There, he established the Mingbo Sea Perch Creek Settlement (C: Mingbo Luxi suo V: Minh Bột Lư Khê Sở). As can be imagined, many Chinese anglers

---

⁴⁰ Phạm Đức Mạnh, 'Cổ mộ,' pp. 1299–1300.
⁴¹ Kuhn, *Chinese among Others*, pp. 70–73.   ⁴² *Dongling Mo shi zupu*, n. p.
⁴³ Antony, *Unruly People*, pp. 12–38.
⁴⁴ Grand Council Archives, Qianlong Reign, 017970: Li Shiyao, n. p.
⁴⁵ Grand Council Archives, Qianlong Reign, 017970, Li Shiyao, n. p.

Figure 5.3 One of the two Lotus Pond reservoirs, built during the days of Mo Jiu. Its water supply allowed for settlement and widespread agricultural cultivation and formed the basis of a nearby suburban village.
Photograph by author.

established residences and made a living off the creek and the gulf to the south. Perhaps they became fishing buddies with Tianci, who spent more of his time there as he got older and delegated successively greater responsibilities to his son Huang.[46]

To facilitate communications between the different settlements, Tianci constructed a road that extended from the city center through the Mingbo commercial districts and then continued eastward until reaching the C: Jishan K: Phnom Mlou V: Hòn Chông peninsula, in present-day Kiên Lương. The picturesque route runs along the coast between the sea on one side and a series of hills on the other. Along the way, voyagers would pass by the sandy beaches of South Bay, Sea Perch Creek, and the dense network of caves that constitute Pearl Cliff. These were three of the "Ten Scenic Views" of The Port. As the travelers

---

[46] Trịnh, *Thông chí*, pp. 182–183, 357; Hán-Nôm A. 2939: Phạm, *Nam hành*, n. p.

reached the terminus, a cape at the tip of the peninsula, they would encounter a spectacular cluster of limestone formations that jut out from the middle of the water. Here, one can take in this magnificent view and gaze out farther toward the numerous islands fanned out across the sea in the distance.[47]

Another group of Chinese immigrants to whom Tianci paid special attention were the elites. They probably started out as participants in the projects of his literary society and received invitations to The Port as his guests and at his expense. Quite a few of them decided never to go back. Xie Zhang (d. 1758) was a native of Fujian. He had passed the civil service examinations and qualified for official posts at the chief upper fifth rank in the Qing bureaucratic hierarchy, such as vice-prefect.[48] Given the fiercely competitive nature of official positions in China, he may not have found any employment, at least none that provided a stable livelihood. He was listed as a participant in the Pavilion for Summoning Worthies. The epitaph on his tomb on Screen Mountain labels him a "master" (*xiansheng*). Similarly, Zhang Xianying's tombstone inscription, made after his death in 1773, praises him as a man of "tremendous virtue" (*shuode*), usually used in reference to a morally upright Confucian.[49] As the inscriptions of both men reveal, the two found employment as teachers in the public schools, since they came directly from China and had a better command of the language and knowledge of the classical tradition. They also became a part of Tianci's trusted body of advisers.

In contrast to the Chinese creoles, the newly arrived immigrants, regardless of social standing, in almost all cases identified with the Qing and its institutions. Tianci did not suppress expressions of loyalty to the reigning dynasty, as the epigraphic evidence from Screen Mountain reveals. The characters, "Imperial Qing" (*Huang Qing*), graced the top of Zhang Xianying's tombstone, while Xie Zhang's son prefaced his epitaph with "Great Qing" (*Da Qing*).[50] The epitaph of Tianci's own concubine, one Lady Wu, closed off with the reign name of the Qianlong Emperor. Even Mo Bang, a fellow native-place kinsman, had "Imperial Qing" inscribed on his tombstone (see Figure 5.2).[51]

---

[47] Trần, *Trung Học*: Trương, 'Đường Hòn Chông,' https://trunghochatienxua.wordpress.com/2021/03/19/tu-nhung-buc-anh-tram-nam-phan-b-quang-nguyen/.
[48] For more on Qing official titles and ranks, see Xie, *Official System in China*, pp. 158–195.
[49] Trịnh, *Thông chí*, pp. 306–307; Phạm Đức Mạnh, 'Cổ mộ,' pp. 1297, 1299.
[50] Phạm Đức Mạnh, 'Cổ mộ,' pp. 1297, 1299.
[51] Phạm Đức Mạnh, 'Cổ mộ,' pp. 1299–1300.

A Haven for Dissident Viet

Because of the proximity of Cochinchina and, to a lesser extent, Tonkin, Viet migrants continued to stream into the water world under The Port's authority. Initially, they integrated into the city center and reinforced their previous areas of settlement, including the "Viet villages" around Hibiscus Mountain in the western suburbs and the outlying islands of the Gulf of Siam. They also began to cluster along the seaside ridge east of the Mingbo commercial districts. Sea Perch Creek, Tianci's favorite getaway, was a popular destination. Among those who settled down there were the ancestors of local scholar Trương Minh Đạt. During the second half of the eighteenth century, they formed a village around an ideal fishing ground. His ancestors, like most of the migrants, came from central Vietnam. In fact, the Vietnamese vernacular name for the place, Rạch Vược, derives its origins from the word for sea perch (*vược*) in the central dialect spoken around Quy Nhơn.[52]

Few Viet seemed to have occupied military positions in The Port after the 1750s. The tombs on Screen Mountain reveal that a sizable number of Viet women entered the households of Tianci, his sons, and subordinates to serve as principal wives or concubines. Because of the personal relationship, they could have quite some influence in decision-making. For instance, Tianci held in high esteem the widow of one of his favorite officials. Her intercession secured the release of a Franciscan missionary who was put in jail because of a dispute with the servant boy of a military commander.[53]

The Viet also handled important aspects of civil administration, especially in relation to the daily livelihood of The Port. The highest ranking of them was someone whom the Spanish Franciscan missionary Julián del Pilar labeled Tianci's "principal mandarin." This individual had served at Tianci's side at least since he assumed leadership of The Port in 1735, the first documented mention of the official. Father Julián's narrative spoke of the mandarin again in reference to events in 1768. He was, at that point, "already well-advanced in age."[54] The French missionary Jacques-Nicolas Morvan (d. 1776) confirms that the official

---

[52] Trần, *Trung Học*: Trương, 'Họ Trương ở Rạch Vược,' https://trunghochatienxua .wordpress.com/2021/04/30/tu-nhung-buc-anh-tram-nam-phan-g-ho-truong-o-rach- vuoc-quang-.nguyen.

[53] Pérez, 'Españoles en el imperio de Annam' 11, p. 206; Trương, *Nghiên cứu*, vol. 2, p. 49; Phạm Đức Mạnh, 'Cổ mộ,' pp. 1295–1303.

[54] *Nouvelles lettres*, vol. 6, pp. 474–475; AMEP, Cochinchine, vol. 745: 'Relation des Franciscains,' pp. 175, 178; Pérez, 'Españoles en el imperio de Annam' 11, pp. 207–208.

had passed away by 1771.⁵⁵ A survey of the tombstones on Screen Mountain reveals that the likeliest match, given these brief descriptions, belonged to an occupant with the surname of Tống, erected by his son in 1770. His epitaph does not reveal his full name but indicates his position as a prefect (*tri phủ*). He could be readily identified as Viet from the characters, "Imperial Viet" (*Hoàng Việt*), etched onto his tombstone. The date of the inscription was also recorded according to the Lê dynasty reign name of Cảnh Hưng.⁵⁶ As prefect, he probably handled The Port's urban administration.

Tianci formed a cooperative relationship with Catholic missionaries to exercise more effective control over the Viet and recruit reliable officials from among their ranks. In fact, Prefect Tống was himself a Christian. In late 1735 to 1736, soon after Tianci assumed power, Tống hosted at his mansion the Spanish Franciscan missionary José de la Concepción (1687–1761). After a fifteen-year absence, he had come to The Port again to visit his old converts among the local Portuguese creole community. Now, a new opportunity awaited the man of faith. The prefect encouraged Father José to establish a new church in the center of the city to attract Viet converts and promised protection for its construction and operation. Tianci granted his seal of approval to the contracts for the missionary's purchase of property associated with the proposed place of worship on behalf of the Franciscans.⁵⁷

The king of Spain funded the construction. Local Christians paid for the transportation of materials and carpenters and craftsmen from Donay. The church, completed in 1745, was massive even by European standards. It had three naves supported by columns, along with oval arches. Three altars and reliefs and sculptures graced the interior. Nearby was a dormitory able to house six to eight people. In the garden was a huge fountain, which, besides its aesthetic value, provided a reliable supply of water and saved on the cost of sourcing it from carriers, like much of the city. At the celebration of the first mass, Father José named it the Church of Saint Mary and Saint Joseph.⁵⁸ The establishment of such a grand structure symbolized The Port's welcoming attitude toward Christians.

For Tianci, the Catholic Church provided a mature network and institutions for regulating grassroots communal life and moral values for the

---

⁵⁵ Launay, *Cochinchine*, vol. 2, p. 415. ⁵⁶ Phạm Đức Mạnh, 'Cổ mộ,' p. 1303.
⁵⁷ AMEP, Cochinchine, vol. 745: 'Relation des Franciscains,' p. 175.
⁵⁸ AMEP, Cochinchine, vol. 745: 'Relation des Franciscains,' p. 175; AMEP, Cochinchine, vol. 744: 'Relation,' p. 966; Pérez, 'Españoles en el imperio de Annam' 8, pp. 311–314.

mobile Viet immigrants. The Port's Christians came under the oversight of the mission of Cochinchina, which handled the propagation of the faith in both Cochinchina and Cambodia. By the mid-eighteenth century, many religious orders, such as the Jesuits, the Paris Foreign Missions Society (*Société des Missions Etrangères de Paris*, MEP), and Franciscans conducted their work in different provinces. Since their activities quite often overlapped, conflicts frequently broke out over turf and influence, disguised as disputes over matters of doctrine. In 1740, a fragile settlement was reached that assigned each order its own district, consisting of parts of several provinces. The Franciscans took charge of the southern frontier of Cochinchina and Cambodia, an area including The Port.[59]

The Church of Saint Joseph and Saint Mary became the principal place of worship for the district of Cambodia and the main residence of the missionaries. It also served as the chief establishment of its own parish. Congregations served as the most basic units of organization in the parish. They might include a gathering of like-minded believers within a city or village or encompass an entire neighborhood or village. Although the missionaries would visit and coordinate the affairs of the congregations, local ministers, known as catechists, handled the religious instruction, charitable works, and other daily affairs of their communities. Large congregations established their own churches, most notably the main church of Saint Mary and Saint Joseph. In addition, a Church of the Third Order of Saint Francis was founded within the urban center. Smaller congregations might gather at the homes of catechists, where an altar was set up for worship. There were also informal chapels in the suburbs and countryside.[60]

This arrangement functioned well even without the long-term presence of the European missionaries. Before the 1750s, Father José was the only missionary responsible for The Port. But he utilized the place more as a base for his efforts to convert new souls in Cochinchina and was thus absent for lengthy periods of time, leaving the Christians at The Port unattended. Nonetheless, the chief catechist at the main church of Saint Joseph and Saint Mary faithfully served his congregation for decades without fail. He ministered in Vietnamese and piously observed the rituals and feasts.[61]

---

[59] Favre, *Lettres édifiantes*, pp. 97–98; Huerta, *Estado geográfico*, pp. 679–680; Pérez, 'Españoles en el imperio de Annam' 7, 186–187.

[60] Huerta, *Estado geográfico*, pp. 679–680; Keith, *Catholic Vietnam*, p. 22; Pérez, 'Españoles en el imperio de Annam' 8, p. 322; AMEP, Cochinchine, vol. 744: 'Relation,' p. 966.

[61] AMEP, Cochinchine, vol. 745: 'Relation des Franciscains,' p. 175; Platero and Portillo, *Catálogo Biográfico*, pp. 528–529.

The parish also funded and operated The Port's main hospital, which served Cambodia and the adjoining districts of Cochinchina. Many Catholic orders placed tremendous importance on healing and charitable works as a temporal demonstration of spiritual salvation. The Franciscan order and MEP almost made it a requirement for their missionaries to master "science, medicine, and surgery."[62] The Franciscans provided a much-needed public health service in The Port and its vicinity. Father José and Francisco Hermosa de Buenaventura both expressed shock at the rudimentary practices of Cochinchinese doctors, who combined unreliable folk remedies with a highly imperfect understanding of Chinese medical texts. The missionaries obtained a formal rank in The Port's bureaucracy as medical officials and served residents, rich and poor alike. They prescribed medicines and performed surgical operations, skills that made them particularly in demand. High-ranking commanders and officials and even Tianci himself sought their expertise.[63]

The Catholic Church had a holistic system of administration, welfare provision, and personnel management for its converts. Promising young men and women could live with the missionaries and catechists and study under them, learning how to read and write, and acquiring basic knowledge of theology. Eventually, they could become catechists or receive ordination as priests, who could proselytize the faith in their own right.[64] Another way would be to apprentice as a medical practitioner. For women, they could serve as sisters who aided and housed the poor and cared for the sick.[65]

Because the Church offered an alternative hierarchy and avenue for social advancement, East Asian states from Japan to Siam and Cochinchina viewed it with a great degree of suspicion and often deemed it subversive.[66] For Tianci, however, it was precisely what he needed. The Church could provide order and discipline to the considerable number of migrants flowing into his realm at a far lower cost than with his own resources. Moreover, the congregations generated their own talented individuals. Tianci appeared to have recruited the main officials of The Port from among them. The epitaph on the tomb of Prefect Tống, his trusted mandarin, indicates that he was once a lay doctor or someone who served at the hospital (y viện).[67]

---

[62] Alberts, *Conflict and Conversion*, pp. 108–111.
[63] Alcobendas, 'Religiosos médico-cirujanos' 5, pp. 206–210, 221–222.
[64] Keith, *Catholic Vietnam*, pp. 22–24; Alberts, *Conflict and Conversion*, pp. 44–45.
[65] Keith, *Catholic Vietnam*, p. 22.
[66] For the reasoning behind the famous persecution of Christians in Japan, see Boxer, *Christian Century*, pp. 317–318.
[67] Phạm Đức Mạnh, 'Cổ mộ,' p. 1303.

The very fact that these Viet were Christians also made them naturally suspicious or hostile toward the Cochinchinese and Tonkinese regimes. In this regard, they resembled the Minh Hương communities of Cochinchina. As Wheeler observes, the Ming hairstyle and dress, which were prohibited in the Qing, ensured the dependence of the Minh Hương upon the Nguyễn rulers "for their continued status, because they had no other monarch to turn to."[68] Likewise, Tianci could be assured of the loyalty of the Viet Christians, especially after 1750, when the Martial King proscribed the religion and launched a severe crackdown on worship and proselytizing. Someone like Prefect Tống would have found it difficult to survive back home if he did not fully renounce his faith. He and others would have faced an environment of unpredictable danger, including the destruction of their places of worship, harassment from soldiers, imprisonment, and horrendous punishments and possible execution.[69]

As a sign of just how much the Viet Christians of The Port hated the Martial King, when false rumors of his death circulated in 1762, Prefect Tống organized a grand mass. In a strong show of support, Tianci's son Huang attended. The liturgical music was played with "the instruments of the palace" of the Mo. Although it was claimed that the joyful occasion was intended to pray to God for the health of Tianci, everyone interpreted it as "a sign of joy at the death of the said persecutor," the Martial King.[70]

Despite Mo Tianci's subordination to Cochinchina, which implied a commitment not to contravene its laws and diplomatic stance, he defied its regulations concerning Christianity. It was one of the ways he demonstrated his independence. When the Martial King's edict of prohibition arrived at The Port, he indefinitely delayed its execution. After the ruler really died in 1765, confusion over his successor's attitude toward the religion generated significant panic among the Franciscans and their Cochinchinese converts, especially when the new king briefly promulgated and then retracted a ban in 1767. Faced with these uncertain circumstances, Mo Tianci's sister, Jinding, whose words carried significant weight in the ruling household, reassured the Franciscans. She told them "not to have any doubts" about their safety and freedom. She stated emphatically that "the order of the king cannot take place here, because

---

[68] Wheeler, 'Cross-Cultural Trade,' pp. 150–151.
[69] Through the letters of missionaries, Launay has compiled a detailed narrative of the persecution across Cochinchina in: Launay, *Cochinchine*, vol. 2, pp. 209–310.
[70] Pérez, 'Españoles en el imperio de Annam' 12, p. 188.

we are a free port."[71] As a result, Franciscan missionaries flocked to The Port, viewing it as a haven and a base for clandestine activities in neighboring Cochinchina. An ailing Father José de la Concepción returned in 1754. Francisco Hermosa de Buenaventura and Pedro Salazar (1729–1763) had arrived by 1760, followed by two others, one of whom was a trained surgeon.[72]

Tianci encouraged activities that served to publicly display and promote the contrast between his tolerance of Christianity and the restrictive attitude of the Nguyễn rulers. In 1761, Father José passed away. His funeral was a lavish affair. Throngs of Viet Christians gathered in the center of the city to see him off. His body was exposed for the public to view for three days, before being interred in a grand mausoleum inside the Church of Saint Joseph and Saint Mary, which he had founded.[73]

A year later, according to Father Julián's account, Tianci came down with an illness so severe that it nearly took away his life. A team of doctors attended to him day and night, while Buddhist monks chanted nonstop in the temples, but to no avail. Eventually, at the advice of his Cochinchinese prefect, he sought the help of the Franciscans. Under the supervision of soldiers from the garrison office, Pedro Salazar, together with his catechists, sponsored a grand feast at the main church. They used the occasion to chant prayers and liturgical songs throughout the evening. Meanwhile, Tianci fell soundly asleep as he sweated profusely. The next morning, he woke up feeling much better and fully recovered shortly thereafter.[74]

Was Tianci really as sick and close to death as the missionary narrative claimed and had the Christians saved his life through their prayers when other methods had all failed? Judging from his actions in the wake of his recovery, the story of his miraculous cure appeared to form part of a consistent strategy of flattering the Catholic community and keeping it reliant upon his favor. Soon afterward, Tianci summoned Father Pedro and ordered him and his fellow Franciscans to shed their Chinese-style robes, which they wore out of respect for local customs. Henceforth, they were authorized to adopt the garments of their own religious order in public. Tianci also ordered the construction of a church bell for their use, a treatment equivalent to the Buddhist temples in the realm.

---

[71] AMEP, Cochinchine, vol. 745: 'Relation des Franciscains,' p. 176. Julián del Pilar mentions her as Tianci's "elder sister." This was probably an error on his part, since there is no documentation of an elder female relative of Tianci's generation.
[72] Alcobendas, 'Religiosos médico-cirujanos,' 5, pp. 321–335; Pérez, 'Españoles en el imperio de Annam' 11, pp. 224–227.
[73] AMEP, Cochinchine, vol. 745: 'Relation des Franciscains,' p. 176.
[74] AMEP, Cochinchine, vol. 745: 'Relation des Franciscains,' pp. 176–178.

Remarkably, these and the other open displays of support for Christianity occurred at the height of the persecution in Cochinchina and before anyone could have predicted the change toward a more tolerant policy. Enticed by the prospects of a new life in keeping with their principles, Viet Christians flooded into The Port's jurisdiction. By 1770, a Franciscan missionary estimated that there were over 3,200 resident active Catholics, compared to 1,300 at some point in the past.[75]

The Awkward Austronesians

Not far away from the Church of Saint Joseph and Saint Mary, the symbol of Catholic presence at The Port, was a mosque. According to the Franciscan narratives, a prominent man had sponsored its construction. He fit the category of an "Arab priest." These individuals traced their origins from several religious lineages in the southern Arabian peninsula that claimed descent from Mohammed, hence the namesake. They had migrated in large numbers and settled throughout Southeast Asia during this period. Because of their connection to the Prophet and command of the holy language of the Koran, sultans of strait polities such as Palembang considered them to be valuable assets and held them in high esteem. The rulers employed the Arabs as advisers and diplomats. The Arab priests used this protection and privilege to capture a major share of the foreign trade of these polities and engage in commerce in different ports.[76]

The individual at The Port had the mosque constructed to serve the needs of long-established communities of Cham, Malay, Javanese, and other ethnic groups from island Southeast Asia. Despite the different labels, they were interrelated with one another, all of them speaking Austronesian languages and practicing the common religion of Islam. In fact, one could argue, as Philip Taylor does, that the place of origin, whether from coastal mainland or island Southeast Asia, and recentness of arrival served as the determining factors behind the different designations.[77] Some were indigenous to the water world, living for generations in villages along the river mouths and beach ridges of the mainland and the islands scattered across the gulf, and usually took up fishing as a

---

[75] AMEP, Cochinchine, vol. 745: 'Relation des Franciscains,' pp. 175–178; AMEP, Cochinchine, vol. 744: 'Relation,' p. 966; Platero and Portillo, *Catálogo Biográfico*, p. 507.

[76] Pérez, 'Españoles en el imperio de Annam' 8, p. 312; Locher-Scholten, *Sumatran Sultanate*, p. 139; Andaya, *Brothers*, pp. 219–221.

[77] P. Taylor, *Cham Muslims*, pp. 45–54.

living. Others had moved more recently from Champa and island Southeast Asia. These two groups were, in turn, closely linked to the Austronesian mercantile networks that covered crucial legs of the intra-Asian trade. Bugis traders frequented the Cambodian coastline, including The Port, as part of regularly undertaken journeys whose destinations typically also included Siam, the Malay Peninsula, and Java. Moreover, a large group of Minangkabau people resided for the long term at The Port.[78]

Their physical and cultural fluidity made them difficult to control. Since the Gulf of Siam and the South China Sea witnessed some of the liveliest trade and busiest traffic in maritime East Asia, many of them engaged in piracy. Seaside villages doubled as piratical lairs, where they would store weapons and booty. However, much of the predation occurred far from The Port's shores and beyond the reach of its regular patrols. The intensification of conflict between Malay, Minangkabau, and Bugis political actors in the straits zone led to such alarming levels of competitive piracy that it frequently disrupted trade for prolonged periods of time. A letter from the VOC authorities at Melaka to Batavia in 1755 remarked that, as a result, ships from The Port and Cambodia had been unable to proceed beyond present-day Singapore for the past two years.[79]

Mo Tianci sought to incorporate Austronesian residents and sojourners into his administration, especially in matters related to trade. Oknha Reachea Setthi, the governor of Seashore Province, was himself of Malay background. In addition, Mo Tianci recruited and organized Austronesians into their own military unit, which was called the Java Company (Đồ Bà đội). Their base was located at the back of Suzhou Mountain on the northern shore opposite The Port's urban center across Fortress River. Given their knowledge of the waters of the Gulf of Siam and connections to island Southeast Asia, the Austronesians formed a vital component in naval expeditions against both pirates and more organized enemies.[80] However, they might not always be loyal or reliable. When Raja Ismail planned to launch an expedition against The Port in 1762, a group of 500 Minangkabau residents offered him their full support. If he attacked, they promised, "we will desert to you."[81] They probably served in none other than the Java Company of Mo Tianci.

---

[78] Ibn Ahmad, *Precious Gift*, pp. 126, 335: Folio 89n1.
[79] Vos, *Gentle Janus*, pp. 82–114; Andaya, *Brothers*, pp. 95–97; *Nouvelles lettres*, vol. 6, p. 191.
[80] *Nouvelles lettres*, vol. 6, p. 191; Trịnh, *Thông chí*, pp. 170, 181, 318.
[81] Ibn Ahmad, *Precious Gift*, pp. 126–136.

The Cambodian Face

Like the Austronesians, Khmer had, for generations, resided in the city center and its surrounding hinterlands. However, as with the Viet, a substantial number of destitute and starved migrants, fleeing civil war and foreign invasion, sought asylum in The Port. Among the more notable refugees were two kings, Ang Sngoun and Ang Tan, and the members of their entourage. It would not be surprising if many of the commoners and slaves who served them, or certain members of the court, chose not to leave. Regardless of rank, Tianci fed them from his granaries and aided those who wished to stay.[82]

A few Khmer settlements were interspersed with the Chinese and Viet villages east of the city center, in present-day Thuận Yên, but they dominated the rural areas lying to the west and northwest. The largest and most famous of these was Deer Cape, the scenic peninsula that constituted one of the "Ten Scenic Views."[83] The Qing travelers visited and recorded their impressions of this seaside landscape, where the suburbs of The Port gradually blended into the rural countryside beyond. They saw peasants hard at work underneath the scorching sun. Since the weather was warm year-round, they went naked except for a piece of cotton cloth wrapped around their waists. When they greeted the travelers, they would clasp their hands in prayer and raise them upward. This description of their action conforms to the *sampeah*, the Cambodian salutation. The Khmer must have considered the travelers to be individuals of high status or faraway guests since they raised their clasped hands high rather than directly in front of their chests as usual.[84]

One of the Qing visitors must have been the poet Zhuang Huiyao, whom Tianci had invited to participate in his poetry anthology on the four seasons of The Port. This collection was quite unique in that all the verses can be read in both directions: forward and backward, each containing a set of slightly different meanings. So, they were essentially two poems in one. In his description of spring, Zhuang observed with fascination the rowdy festive atmosphere during the Khmer New Year, which fell in the middle of April:

---

[82] Vũ, *Gia phả*, pp. 104–105.
[83] Trịnh, *Thông chí*, pp. 357–358; Trương, *Nghiên cứu*, vol. 1, p. 28.
[84] Zhang, *Wenxian tongkao*, p. 7463; Howard, *Textiles and Clothing*, pp. 79–80; Klepeis, *Cambodia*, p. 16.

縈帶錦飄風弄杏 (Twirling ribbons, silken gowns afloat, wind blowing at apricot petals)

染衣班妒雨搖筠 (Clothes stained with water droplets, beauties to make even Concubine Ban jealous, playing bamboo flutes in the rain)[85]

Read backwards, the lines read:

杏弄風飄錦帶縈 (The fluttering apricot petals swaying with the wind, silken gowns floating and ribbons twirling)

筠搖雨妒班衣染 (Bamboo trees swaying, the jealous rain stains the colorful costumes)

Local scholar Trương Minh Đạt believes that these lines refer to the female *apsara* dancers, whose graceful movements, intended to recount religious stories and myths, are compared to the involuntary swaying of bamboo trees or apricot petals in response to natural phenomena. Water is liberally sprinkled upon them and among members of the audience as a symbol of ritual purification and renewal.[86]

Zhuang goes on to speak about the wild partying and drinking that accompanied the holiday:

迎輦玉尘披拂拂 (Welcoming the carriages, water splashes in the air)

城西醉遍踏歌人 (In the western suburbs, drunkenness accompanies the dancing folks)[87]

The lines, read backwards, go:

拂拂披尘玉輦迎 (The wind blows up dust, welcoming the jade carriage)

人歌踏遍醉西城 (People, singing, walking all over drunk west of the city)

Zhuang was describing activities that the Khmer engaged in during the New Year, including oxcart racing, the splashing of water on each other, and drunken revelry and dancing. The "jade carriage" mentioned in the first line of the poem read in reverse alludes to an exalted authority, which could mean the Cambodian king, the Martial King of Cochinchina, the Chinese emperor, or Mo Tianci. For Zhuang, the wild celebrations speak to the peace and prosperity of the realm under an orderly administration such as The Port.

---

[85] A reference to the Concubine Ban, a favorite consort of a Han dynasty emperor. She observed propriety and ritual and never got jealous of anyone. See Idema and Grant, *Red Brush*, pp. 78–79.

[86] Lê Quý Đôn, *Tiểu Lục*, vol. 1, p. 707; Trương, *Nghiên cứu*, vol. 1, pp. 197–198, 218–219.

[87] Lê Quý Đôn, *Tiểu Lục*, vol. 1, p. 707.

The maintenance of these Khmer traditions depended upon a holistic cultural and religious framework centered upon the Theravada Buddhist wat. These temples contained large ponds (*sras*) lined with stone or clay that stored water used for drinking and irrigation. It was an especially precious commodity during the dry season.[88] The wats were also the repositories of knowledge, where literary works and historical memory were stored. All Khmer men spent time in them as monks at some point in their youth. Besides performing their religious duties, they could receive an education, and learn how to read and write. Like other monks, they went out daily, ringing a bell on the streets. When laypeople heard the sound, they would come and pay their respects, and then, on their knees, place food and other necessities into the alms bowls of the holy men.[89] Theravada Buddhism was so intertwined with Khmer cultural practices that the Catholic missionaries found it almost impossible to convert them, in contrast to their stunning success with the Viet.[90]

Accordingly, in his treatment of the Khmer, Mo Tianci chose to preserve their integration with the rest of Cambodia, not only in the realm of religion, but also in the social and political hierarchy. He ruled over them as Preah Sotoat, a delegate of the royal court whose duties were parallel to his Cochinchinese assignment as military governor-general, tasked with overseeing foreign trade and defense in the water world. Although evidence is lacking, it would not be surprising if his commanders and officials had noble ranks and titles from the Cambodian court of their own that, like him, delineated responsibilities equivalent to their Sino-Viet positions. It appears that he delegated the administration of Khmer affairs to Oknha Reachea Setthi Chov, the governor of Seashore Province at Moat Chrouk. He first appears in the records in the mid-1750s but likely assumed office earlier. Tianci frequently made major decisions in joint consultation with him. The two men enjoyed such a close relationship that the Cambodian Royal Chronicles often list their names together, as if they were the same person.[91]

Chov would, like the governors of other Cambodian provinces, maintain the population registers and forward taxes. He would be assisted in his duties by a vice-governor and several secretaries. Judges stood ready to enforce laws and punish crimes. These officials worked with the village

---

[88] P. Taylor, *Khmer Lands*, pp. 174–175.
[89] AMEP, Cochinchine, vol. 745: 'Relation des Franciscains,' p. 174; Theam, 'Cambodia in the Mid-Nineteenth Century,' p. 12.
[90] Launay, *Cochinchine*, vol. 1, p. 70.
[91] Eng, *Mahaboros khmer*, vol. 6, pp. 4, 14–19; Sakurai and Kitagawa, 'Hà Tiên or Banteay Meas,' pp. 167, 182, 185, 197.

chiefs and the head of corvée to mobilize commoners and slaves for public works and military service. It is not clear how much of the revenues went to the court in Oudong or directly entered the coffers of Mo Tianci, but he must have taken a substantial cut. Moreover, during campaigns, Chov would be among the first to raise troops from among his subjects on behalf of Tianci.[92] His scope of authority included Khmer who lived in The Port's core area. Besides Deer Cape, there was the Khmer quarter in the city center, concentrated around a marketplace next to East Lake. One important characteristic of this district was a wat that also functioned as a shrine to a tutelary ancestral spirit (*neak ta*).[93]

During the conflicts of the 1750s, Tianci possessed sufficient influence to become the main patron of choice for Khmer from several neighboring provinces. As a result, he proved able to secure the cooperation of their governors in raising revenues and troops. They included a super-province, Treang, and the lower-ranked Banteay Meas, Bati, Samrong Tong, Kampot, and Prey Krabas. Banteay Meas, although now a landlocked province of middling importance with an honor ranking of 8,000 after being separated from Seashore, contains the headwaters of Fortress River, and marked the terminus of the land and canal routes from the Bassac. Treang, known as Chuncuchung or Chiconchong to the Franciscan and French missionaries, was their starting point, intersecting with the Bassac a little beyond Moat Chrouk.[94]

After becoming the adoptive father of Ang Tan and successfully placing the young man on the throne in 1757, Tianci acquired an official status within the court as viceroy. According to the Vietnamese sources, the young ruler, out of gratitude, handed over to him five provinces. Besides Seashore, Tianci acquired Banteay Meas, Kampot, Kampong Som, and Treang. Trịnh Hoài Đức's gazetteer claims that upon receiving the new territories, Mo Tianci immediately offered them up to the Martial King. The Cochinchinese ruler refused and authorized him to retain the acquisitions.[95] In reality, it was standard practice, according to the Cambodian codes, for the viceroy to have his own appanage

---

[92] Leclère, *Les codes*, vol. 1, pp. 117–118; Sakurai and Kitagawa, 'Hà Tiên or Banteay Meas,' pp. 185–186.

[93] Trương, *Nghiên cứu*, vol. 2, pp. 331–332.

[94] Mikaelian, *Royauté d'Oudong*, p. 226; Theam, 'Cambodia in the Mid-Nineteenth Century,' p. 19; Sakurai and Kitagawa, 'Hà Tiên or Banteay Meas,' pp. 167–169; Eng, *Mahaboros khmer*, vol. 6, p. 4; EFEO Khmer: *Preah reach pongsavatar*, p. 113; *Prachum phongsawadan* 1: *Phongsawadan khamen*, p. 206; Launay, *Cochinchine*, vol. 2, p. 435; Pérez, 'Españoles en el imperio de Annam' 11, p. 218; AMEP, Cochinchine, vol. 745: 'Relation des Franciscains,' p. 178.

[95] Trịnh, *Thông chí*, p. 309; Vũ, *Gia phả*, p. 107; Nguyễn Dynasty, *Nhất thống chí*, vol. 3, p. 335.

consisting of five provinces. He would also be able to supervise forty *oknha*, and many more *chaoponhea* and nobles of lower ranks.[96]

Most of the privileges amounted to a fait accompli. The Martial King was merely recognizing Tianci's new position and his expanded area of authority. In addition to his influence over the provinces, Tianci already had a large corps of Khmer nobles serving under him. However, his legitimate possession of the provinces amounted to a recognition of his domination over the entire southern maritime approach to Phnom Penh, Cambodia's busiest and most convenient foreign trade route.[97]

One Realm, Two Systems

After becoming viceroy, Mo Tianci imposed a dual mode of administration over the northwestern and southeastern parts of his realm, respectively, with the line of division running through The Port's core area. Starting from Deer Cape until the Siamese border, the Cambodian system of governance was retained. As the Spanish Franciscan Francisco Hermosa de Buenaventura described the arrangement in the case of Treang, it belonged to Cambodia, but Tianci "took part of the tribute and governance."[98] Similar to Seashore, he presumably exercised administration and appointed officials to handle those aspects involving the non-Khmer population, while the governor took care of the rest.[99]

The five provinces were no strangers to ethnic diversity. The governors themselves may have had foreign roots. Both Oknha Reachea Setthi and the governor of Treang were Autronesian. Treang was probably typical in that it was majority Khmer, but there were substantial numbers of Chinese with their own quarters and some Cochinchinese. The Viet were more numerous in Banteay Meas and Kampot, particularly Kampong Trach, Damnak Chang'aeur, and White Horse (C: Baima K: Kep V: Bạch Mã). In Kampot and Kampong Som, there were also sizable Siamese communities, including Chinese and Viet from Siam. They were primarily Christians fleeing persecution and refugees from the chaos that engulfed the country during the invasion of Myanmar forces in the 1760s.[100]

---

[96] Aymonier, *Cambodge*, vol. 1, p. 61; Theam, 'Cambodia in the Mid-Nineteenth Century,' p. 16.
[97] AMEP, Cochinchine, vol. 745: 'Relation des Franciscains,' p. 178.
[98] Pérez, 'Españoles en el imperio de Annam' 11, p. 218.
[99] Leclère, *Les codes*, vol. 1, pp. 114–115.
[100] Trịnh, *Thông chi*, pp. 170, 183–188, 318; Pérez, 'Españoles en el imperio de Annam' 11, p. 218; Launay, *Cochinchine*, vol. 2, p. 422.

Southeast of The Port, an entirely different arrangement prevailed. In name, the area comprised the Cambodian provinces of Kramoun Sar, Black Water, and parts of Bassac. But aside from the marketing centers of Royal Market and Black Water, and the Viet villages from Mo Jiu's days, the rest was a vast, "desolate Khmer wasteland." Any preexisting Cambodian structure had been destroyed because of warfare and evacuations from the Siamese invasions during the 1720s.[101] Even in the early nineteenth century, Trịnh Hoài Đức's gazetteer describes the 100 kilometer route from the western shores of the Bassac River to the Gulf of Siam as "difficult and taxing for voyagers." They had to traverse for days along an irregular path that cut through endless swamps, with no sign of any human habitation as far as the eyes could see. During the best times for travel in late winter and spring, they had to tread on foot through a light coat of wet mud. From summer to autumn, the constant downpours flooded the road and made it impassable. One could only make the journey by boat, using a machete to cut through the lush outgrowth of vegetation. It felt like sailing on top of wild grass. At all times, the traveler would have to endure harassment from mosquitoes, worms, and leeches.[102]

Mo Tianci had exercised an informal control over this frontier, especially the sea routes around it, before he became viceroy. He now used the occasion to formalize his occupation, establishing institutions to exploit the land. He divided the area into four circuits, according to the model of the Cochinchinese frontier outposts along the main branch of the Mekong. He renamed Kramoun Sar the Solid River (C: Jianjiang V: Kiên Giang) Circuit. Black Water came to be known as Dragon Stream (C: Longchuan V: Long Xuyên). He appropriated for himself the largely empty quarters of Bassac Province, farther to the north. He made the port of C: Qinju K: Kampoul Meas **V: Cần Thơ**, on the western bank of the river, the seat of River Defense (C: Zhenjiang V: Trấn Giang) Circuit. Farther downstream, close to the mouth of the Bassac, he founded the Barbarian Suppression (C: Zhenyi V: Trấn Di) Circuit, perhaps a not-too-subtle reference to Bassac Province, still under nominal Cambodian control, which it surrounds.[103]

As a result of this round of expansion, The Port shared a contiguous boundary, for the first time, with Cochinchina through its tenuously held frontier circuits. Tianci also acquired a foothold on the shores of the

---

[101] Vũ, *Gia phả*, p. 107; Hamilton, *New Account*, vol. 2, pp. 196–198.
[102] Trịnh, *Thông chí*, pp. 150–151.
[103] Trịnh, *Thông chí*, pp. 309–310; Vũ, *Gia phả*, p. 107; Nguyễn Dynasty, *Nhất thống chí*, vol. 3, p. 335.

South China Sea. True to the administrative form of a circuit, an itinerant governor (*cai đạo*) would make routine rounds to handle affairs in each of them. They appeared to have been drawn from among the generals of Tianci's companies. Xu Youyong was documented to have served as circuit governor, although it remains unclear over which one.[104]

These frontier circuits became the ideal arena for Mo Tianci to further pursue a strategy of recruiting manpower to open the new land, increase agricultural productivity, and provide a solid material base for the commercial activities of The Port. Given the military background of the circuit administrators, they probably organized their own troops to break ground in their places of oversight to support their needs when they did not have to take up arms. Certainly, during the early nineteenth century, this area saw quite a few military colonies, including some that belonged to ethnically Khmer units. Their presence may have built upon Mo Tianci's precedents.[105]

Over the following decades, land-hungry peasants, artisans, merchants, and other skilled laborers joined the soldiers in expanding upon or founding new settlements and commercial centers. It appears that a substantial plurality, if not a majority, of the newcomers were Chinese. Besides the administrative centers and ports, such as Royal Market and Black Water, they filtered out into the countryside, where they intermarried extensively with the Khmer, most of whom were probably themselves migrants rather than original residents. Instead of forming a creole population, they blended into the local landscape as Khmer peasants. During Philip Taylor's fieldwork in the water world, he discovered that many self-identified Khmer from the Bassac to the Gulf of Siam were actually of mixed Chinese descent. And they were the ones who obtained prominent social status as priests in the wats or teachers at the temple schools. In Steadfast River, nearly all of the Khmer were Chinese-Khmer mestizos, and they remained an exclusive presence in the rural areas until well into the twentieth century, with the intensification of French colonization. As late as 1940, one elderly resident recalled to Taylor, "there were just one to two Viet people per hundred Khmer in this stretch of coast."[106]

Because of the proximity of Cochinchina, Tianci also sought to bring in more Viet. Although they had settled large parts of the water world, their presence in much of the land beyond the Bassac remained comparatively limited. The Catholic Church network became an important

---

[104] Trịnh, *Thông chí*, pp. 150, 308.   [105] Trịnh, *Thông chí*, p. 151.
[106] P. Taylor, *Khmer Lands*, pp. 63–64, 209–210.

194   A Port with Many Faces

intermediary in organizing their widespread migration and settlement. When Father Francisco Hermosa de Buenaventura visited Cần Thơ in 1761, he observed that "every day, Christians came from within Cochinchina for confession, and some stayed."[107] Of course, the Franciscans mostly did so to expand their own congregation of the faithful. But their interests aligned with Tianci's perfectly. As the father mentioned, one important reason for the toleration of missionary activity was to "populate this land with Cochinchinese, which is what he desires."[108]

In one of his first meetings with Tianci in 1759, Tianci, at the persuasion of his trusted prefect, proclaimed that he had set aside Phú Quốc as an exclusive domain for Christians, and banned nonbelievers from residing on the island. With their encouragement, the father and several families sailed there. They cut down trees for building houses and a church and making space for gardens. Eventually, around 350 believers settled down. At Earthen Mount (C: Tushan K: Phnom Dei V: Hòn Đất), an island some seventy kilometers from The Port center in the Steadfast River Circuit, the priest sited a place that was suitable for sowing and located in a healthy environment. He built a church, Ascension of Our Lady, which came to oversee its own parish of 700 Christians during its heyday. A similar pattern emerged in other places, whereby the Franciscans would locate a place suitable for agriculture or fishing and clear the land and build a church and dwelling. Their followers would join and build their own residences around them.[109]

It must be pointed out that many of these pioneering projects were ultimately unsuccessful and lost much of their population within a decade. The grand vision for Phú Quốc to become an exclusively Christian haven was shattered a year after its founding in 1762 because of miserable conditions, especially the brackish water supply. The entire community ultimately relocated to another island, farther to the east. Although Father Francisco constructed another church and parish, the effort was again short-lived. During the late 1760s, when Julián del Pilar passed through Earthen Mount, the largest and most flourishing of the Franciscan projects, he found no more than eighty Christians still living there. In fact, the majority of Viet Catholics eventually abandoned their

---

[107] Pérez, 'Españoles en el imperio de Annam' 15, p. 84.
[108] Pérez, 'Españoles en el imperio de Annam' 11, p. 208.
[109] Pérez, 'Españoles en el imperio de Annam' 11, pp. 212–217; AMEP, Cochinchine, vol. 445: 'Relation des Franciscains,' pp. 177–178; Huerta, *Estado geográfico*, p. 680.

faith. According to Father Julián, there were around 7,000 "apostates" at The Port, outnumbering the 3,200 active believers.[110]

More important than their deliberate designs for new areas of residence and cultivation, the efforts of the Catholic missionaries had the unintended consequence of vastly expanding the scope of Viet settlement for Christians and nonbelievers alike. Their methods provided a precedent and model that the Viet could build upon and at their own initiative. Father Julián discovered that most of the original Christian residents on Phú Quốc and its adjacent islands had moved to the mainland, at the mouth of the river running along the boundary of the two circuits of Steadfast River and Dragon Stream. He described this countryside as incredibly fertile. Đức's gazetteer concurs, calling it a place that abounds with rice and fish. Both observers speak of a growing concentration of people, with Father Julián claiming 500 Christians had settled there since 1763.[111] The larger number of former believers or non-Christians expanded the area of settlement even more. Although the Phú Quốc project was abandoned by the Catholic missionaries, the island came to have one of the largest concentrations of Viet on the Gulf of Siam littoral. During the early nineteenth century, it counted ten Viet villages, more numerous than The Port's center, along with Chinese creole and Qing quarters.[112]

The vastly expanded area of The Port allowed it to project influence over the provincial seat of Bassac. Although it remained in direct Cambodian hands, he probably had a power-sharing arrangement with the governor like Treang, in other words, oversight of the non-Khmer residents. And they happened to constitute most of the population. The biggest group were the Chinese, many of them sojourning merchants engaged in trade with Guangzhou. There were also Viet Christians and Portuguese creoles. Tianci appeared to have stationed troops in Bassac. In April 1768, the French missionary Levavasseur noted in his journal that two soldiers in The Port's military accompanied his boat as it left the place.[113]

Even if boundaries seemed somewhat hazy, they still existed. After the boat sailed away from Bassac and entered the waterway bearing its namesake, Levavasseur assumed that "we would always be under the dominion of Cambodia." But as he learned that very night, just a few hours after his

---

[110] AMEP, Cochinchine, vol. 445: 'Relation des Franciscains,' pp. 175–178; Trịnh, *Thông chí*, p. 177.
[111] AMEP, Cochinchine, vol. 445: 'Relation des Franciscains,' p. 178; Trịnh, *Thông chí*, pp. 188–189.
[112] Trịnh, *Thông chí*, p. 357; Crawfurd, *Journal of an Embassy*, vol. 1, p. 65.
[113] *Nouvelles lettres*, vol. 6, pp. 215–216; Launay, *Cochinchine*, vol. 2, p. 390.

departure, he had entered the territory of The Port. After all, the province was now surrounded by the Barbarian Suppression Circuit. A day later, farther upriver, the boat stopped for dinner at Moat Chrouk. Although a typical Khmer town, it belonged to Oknha Reachea Setthi, who answered to Mo Tianci. The two soldiers disembarked and got on board another boat that entered the canal to The Port on the other end.[114] Similarly, when Tianci sent off Father Francisco and several other Franciscan missionaries and Viet Christians to Phnom Penh in 1749, he prepared passports for them and an escort of armed men. The soldiers accompanied them as far as Treang. There, the Cambodian governor took charge of the group, and the troops returned, having reached the limits of their jurisdiction.[115] Although the journey occurred about a decade before Treang formally became Tianci's appanage as the viceroy, it was already within his sphere of actual domination.

Homogenizing the Realm

Mo Tianci's promotion of Confucianism, especially the decentralized Heart-Mind variant, did not conflict with the tremendous proliferation of ethnic groups and belief systems at The Port. The relativism implied by its teachings allowed for tolerance and a significant degree of mutual interaction. In the city center, as Đức's gazetteer describes, people from all backgrounds lived in mixed neighborhoods and rubbed shoulders with one another as they went about their business. They would traverse the crowded alleyways, canals, and streets that stretched out like a maze into the distance.[116]

The case of suspected piracy referred to Batavia involving Oeij Tshing and Louw Wo reveals interesting details about the hybrid environment of The Port. Eight armed "Mohammedans," referring to Malay or Cham sailors, formed part of Lauw Wo's crew. They were armed with short guns (*korte geweeren*) strapped onto their waists. They served as bodyguards to protect his ship in case of a pirate raid, a common practice.[117] Lauw must have known how to speak their language. According to Father Francisco, Malay was often the only means by which the Chinese in the water world could communicate with the Europeans.[118]

---

[114] *Nouvelles lettres*, vol. 6, pp. 216–217; Launay, *Cochinchine*, vol. 2, pp. 390–391.
[115] Pérez, *Diario*, pp. 17–18.
[116] Trịnh, *Thông chí*, p. 534; Nguyễn Dynasty, *Nhất thống chí*, vol. 3, pp. 280–281; AMEP, Cochinchine, vol. 745: 'Relation des Franciscains,' pp. 173–174.
[117] ANRI, K66a: 3574b, p. 125.   [118] Pérez, *Diario*, p. 68.

Two of the crew members on Oeij Tshing's vessel, Lang Kaij and Lang Tshauw, were women. Like elsewhere in Southeast Asia, women were heavily involved in markets and the circulation of goods and were often passengers on board ships. Lang Tshauw was one of the largest owners of the merchandise consigned on the junk. Lang Kaij, on the other hand, was doing business at Black Water when her husband sent her a letter, carried to her by her son, informing her that he had received a prestigious appointment to serve under Fingkijie, some general or official. So, she accompanied her son back to The Port on Oeij's ship.[119]

The woman Lang Kaij was Viet. She had struck up a conversation with Lauw Wo and some of his Chinese crew members in the "Cochinchinese languages" (*Coechimse taalen*), ostensibly referring to different dialects of southern Vietnamese. Oei Tshing "understood nothing of the conversation being held." Later, Lang Kaij had to explain to him what they had been talking about. Curiously, the language differences revealed through this episode did not occur strictly along ethnic lines. Evidently, Lauw Wo and his crew had extensive dealings with the Viet, whether through business or intermarriage, or growing up in a creole background. They at least felt comfortable speaking the language. Oeij Tshing, on the other hand, was either a recent Qing immigrant or someone whose family more strictly adhered to a traditional Chinese upbringing. Interestingly, both Lang Tshauw and Lang Kaij could communicate with him directly in Chinese. Lang Kaij had married into a Chinese official's household, while Lang Tshauw was either a native speaker or must have picked up the language through marriage or business.[120]

Interethnic interactions and mutual influence were unescapable facts in The Port, even for those who wished to withdraw from the world of mortals. In the empty spaces of the hinterlands, especially in the hilly area to the north, which connects to the Seven Mountains, wandering Khmer and Viet mendicants found a place of refuge in the forested slopes, where they were able to cultivate an aura of mystique. The monk Yellow Dragon, for instance, left the Temple of Three Treasures after the death of his client, Mo Jiu's mother. Perhaps inspired by the Khmer hermits, he wandered around aimlessly until he came upon a mountain on the extreme northern edge of The Port's core area. In this still largely uninhabited place, he passed away in 1737. His disciples constructed a seven-storied white pagoda in his memory that housed part of his remains. As legend would have it, every year during the Ghost Festival and Buddha's Birthday, a stork would dutifully fly over to his mountain retreat and visit his White Pagoda,

---

[119] ANRI, K66a: 3574b, pp. 113, 117; Reid, *Age of Commerce*, vol. 2, pp. 49, 92–93.
[120] ANRI, K66a: 3574b, pp. 112–114.

while a monkey left fruit at the altar and lingered for meditation.[121] Similarly, tombs of Nguyễn Đình Tú and Nguyễn Hữu on Screen Mountain identify them as religious recluses (*cư sĩ*), although, compared to Yellow Dragon, not much of their lives and deeds are known.[122]

Of course, relations were not always harmonious between the diverse groups. A Chinese barber who cut the hair of the Franciscan Pedro Salazar accused him of not giving enough money for the service, because "he was a rich European and should pay more." On another occasion, the servant boy of a captain of the night watch taunted Father Pedro and called him names, probably because he looked different. When the father threatened to beat the boy with his staff, the servant ran off to the captain. The captain used his influence to briefly imprison the hapless missionary. A more serious conflict occurred during the 1740s, while Father José was having his church built in the center of The Port. The Arab priest did not like having the building situated at such proximity to his mosque. So, he tried, albeit unsuccessfully, to obstruct the construction by throwing stones at the church. These disputes occurred mostly out of ignorance and cultural misunderstanding. Eventually, compromises were worked out in each case, such as the intervention of the widow of Tianci's favorite official, which secured the release of Father Pedro Salazar from prison.[123] There were no serious conflicts until the 1770s.

Although the Heart-Mind school allowed for a high degree of eclecticism, Mo Tianci sought to achieve greater homogeneity over the realm. He could not hope to integrate his entire diverse constituency, ranging from short-term merchant visitors to long-term residents from around the world. Accordingly, he focused his efforts upon the Chinese groups and the Viet, who shared many cultural commonalities. Although it is true that Mo Tianci espoused Confucian teachings as the guiding belief for his governance of The Port, he did not walk away from his father's patronage of Buddhism, as some scholars, such as Trương Minh Đạt, claim. In fact, Buddhist institutions, especially the Mahayana Linji Chan sect, flourished under his rule. Tianci sponsored the construction of Hibiscus Temple, which was situated on the southwestern slopes of the old Viet Mountain. The main hall housed a magnificent statue of Buddha installed in 1758. Tianci had made it to order from China, where artisans had cast it out of pure bronze (see Figure 5.4). Visitors recalled the temple to be a surreal place, where the sound of monks chanting mixed with the noises from the shops and markets emanating

---

[121] Trịnh, *Thông chí*, p. 169; P. Taylor, *Khmer Lands*, pp. 167–168.
[122] Phạm Đức Mạnh, 'Cổ mộ,' pp. 1296, 1303.
[123] Pérez, 'Españoles en el imperio de Annam' 8, pp. 311–314; 11, pp. 206–207.

Figure 5.4 A statue of the Shakyamuni Buddha purchased by Mo Tianci from China in 1758. It was cast out of pure bronze. The statue stands in the main hall of Hibiscus Temple.
Photograph by author.

from the city center below, as if one had a foot each in the realms of the sacred and profane.[124]

Tianci also maintained ties with the Ming loyalist Buddhist network of his father's days that, by now, had largely been depoliticized and, to a certain extent, stripped of its ethnic Chinese associations. He probably made use of his connections to the Shanghai literati to arrange for the publication of a copy of the Jiaxing Tripitaka (*Jiaxing zang*), a Ming-period compilation of the Buddhist canon sponsored by gentry in the Jiangnan region. He then donated the collection to the Temple of the

---

[124] Trịnh, *Thông chí*, p. 167; Nguyễn Dynasty, *Nhất thống chí*, vol. 3, p. 286; Trương, *Nghiên cứu*, vol. 2, pp. 150–156. As Trương Minh Đạt shows, the Hibiscus Temple no longer survives in its original location, having been destroyed by Siamese troops in 1833. In 1846, a new Hibiscus Temple was constructed on the slopes of Screen Mountain on the remains of Tianci's poetry society. Trương Minh Đạt believes that the two temples, despite sharing the same name, had no prior connection to one another. However, the new structure contains many of the relics from the old, including the Buddha statue from the days of Mo Tianci.

Ten Stupas in Quy Nhơn, the former base of the monk Yuanshao and, most likely, the deceased Yellow Dragon.[125]

Tianci's continued patronage of Buddhism intended to provide an alternative instrument of grassroots management and social bonding to the Catholic Church. The missionaries were not able to manage all the Viet migrants, and many Christians left the Church after settling down. As a faith more anchored in Sinosphere traditions, Buddhism could provide Tianci greater control over Viet and Chinese commoners. A sizable number of those who apostatized embraced Buddhism. One of them was the widow of Tianci's trusted official, whose intercession secured the release of the Franciscan Pedro Salazar. She had once been Catholic but later turned to Buddhism and became a nun.[126]

The promotion of Buddhism integrated well into Tianci's Confucian framework. There was concurrently a greater effort to expand Confucian teachings beyond the elites and Chinese creoles at The Port. His public schools admitted bright or needy Viet students, who studied alongside their Chinese counterparts. Such was the case with Vũ Thế Dinh. After losing his father at the age of eight, Tianci took him into his household and reared him like his own son. Dinh mastered the Chinese language and Confucian classics. He wrote his genealogical biography of the Mo clan in his later years in an act of gratitude and remembrance for Tianci, whose own records were destroyed because of warfare. Dinh seems to have become highly acculturated toward a Chinese cultural lifestyle. His tombstone inscription indicates that he took for his main wife a woman from the Kong family and a concubine, Lady Wang. Their surnames identify them clearly as being Chinese or Chinese creole.[127]

Another initiative involved the circulation of the "Ten Verses" project in the Vietnamese vernacular. This companion version to the Classical Chinese anthology is entitled *Hà Tiên thập cảnh khúc vịnh* (Musical ballads of the ten scenes of Hà Tiên). Each scene opens with a ballad of thirty-four lines with a rhythmic structure of 7/7/6/8. It concludes with a regulated verse of eight lines of seven words, influenced by Tang poetic conventions. The ballad amplifies, elaborates upon, clarifies, or repeats the descriptions, sentiments, and allusions related to the scenes mentioned in the poem proper. The "Musical Ballads" are not direct translations of the Chinese originals but are similar in content and theme.

---

[125] Thích Không Nhiên, Thích Pháp Hạnh, and Lê Thọ Quốc, 'Gia Hưng Đại tạng kinh,' pp. 110–113.
[126] Pérez, 'Españoles en el imperio de Annam' 8, pp. 311–314.
[127] Vũ, *Gia phả*, pp. 185–186; Phạm Đức Mạnh, 'Cổ mộ,' p. 1296.

In fact, taken together, they provide a summary of all the contributions of the Chinese and Viet poets to the original anthology.[128]

According to Kelley and Nguyễn Huệ Chi, the vernacular verses, compared to their Classical Chinese counterparts, present the content in a straightforward manner and with greater emotion.[129] The purpose of the two versions was also different. The original "Ten Verses" intended to advertise The Port as an ideal place to visit, trade, and settle down before a Sinosphere elite audience. The "Musical Ballads," on the other hand, places greater focus on the domestic Viet population. It provides them with a compact, readily accessible introduction to the essential elements of Chinese culture and Confucian value system. Much of the content consists of references to famous Chinese figures and places, literal translations of proverbs and historical allusions, and loanwords arranged in a Vietnamese grammatical format.[130]

Collectively, the lines praise the beautiful scenery of The Port and extol its well-ordered society, where farmers, merchants, fishermen, woodcutters, shepherds, and soldiers busily went about their pursuits, content with their stations. As a line in the vernacular "Anchored Fishing Boats at Sea Perch Creek" goes, "although a river village, it has become another Chang'an" (tuy giang thôn nào khác Trường An), the capital of the glorious Han and Tang.[131] The "Musical Ballads" drives home the point that The Port was a complete embodiment of Confucian virtues and enjoyed glory and prosperity as a result. In addition to the individual descriptions of the "Ten Scenes," another vernacular poem, the Hà Tiên thập cảnh tổng luận (General summary of the ten views of Hà Tiên), sums up all of the above in a general introduction.[132] Succinct and easy to memorize, the lines, shown in the beginning of the chapter, inscribe the key landmarks of The Port into the minds of its Viet residents, cultivating a deep attachment to The Port as their home.

The "Musical Ballads" has been a subject of much academic controversy within and outside Vietnam, particularly over whether Tianci had actually authored the work or whether it at least could be dated to his lifetime. Indeed, no versions of the vernacular or records attesting to its

---

[128] Đông, Văn Học, pp. 143–148, 157–301; Chin Kei-wa (Chen Jinghe), 'Kasen Maku-shi,' p. 333.
[129] Kelley, 'Chinese Diaspora,' p. 86; Nguyễn Huệ Chi, Từ điển Văn học, pp. 935–936.
[130] Đông, Văn Học, pp. 25–44. Chen Jinghe praises the "Musical Ballads" as a unique masterpiece that mixes Chinese and Vietnamese lyrical styles. See Chin Kei-wa (Chen Jinghe), 'Kasen Maku-shi,' p. 333.
[131] Đông, Văn Học, p. 290.
[132] Đông, Văn Học, pp. 301–302; Trương, Nghiên cứu, vol. 2, p. 188.

existence appeared before the early twentieth century. Detractors such as Kelley rightly suspect that it may have been a substantial embellishment of the original Classical Chinese or a creation entirely from the imagination of contemporary authors.[133] Trương Minh Đạt's opinion is representative of the other view. He points out that although the vernacular descriptions appeared only in the early twentieth century, they were recorded by many different authors who did not know of each other or the existence of a Classical Chinese base text. However, their contents retained a surprising degree of coherence, whether internally, between the various versions that they published, and the original "Ten Verses."[134]

Overall, Vietnamese scholars have moved toward a broad consensus that the "Musical Ballads" originated from Mo Tianci or his literary society, and their assessment appears to be convincing. Its publication accorded with Tianci's overall strategies and intentions for The Port's governance. Perhaps another way to explain the problematic nature of the sources is that the "Musical Ballads" was never primarily meant to be preserved in written form. After all, Đông Hồ observes, the target audience consisted of Viet commoners, most of them poor and illiterate migrants.[135] The vernacular verses were meant to be sung, read aloud, or performed as theater during festivals or other public occasions. As such, the written texts, despite inheriting a standardized content much later, came after and remained subordinate to oral methods of transmission and thus evolved together with the changes in spoken vocabulary and usage.

If the "Musical Ballads" is indeed authentic, then its value lies in its successful transmission and interpretation of the content, meaning, and spirit of the original "Ten Verses" beyond a limited circle of elites. The Viet population of The Port subscribed to Christianity, Buddhism, and popular spiritual cults. Many of them readily renounced or switched between different faiths at whim. By having the Classical Chinese anthology rendered into the vernacular, Tianci could instill a greater sense of ideological stability, just as Nguyễn Cư Trinh attempted with his own fictional narrative during his governance of Quảng Ngãi. In the case of The Port, it would provide a medium for the mass penetration of Chinese culture and popularization of Confucianism among Viet commoners.[136] And this effort proved quite successful not only in The Port but,

---

[133] Kelley, 'Chinese Diaspora,' p. 86. Ang largely concurs, calling the "Musical Ballads" an example of Mo Tianci-style poetry that aimed to situate Hà Tiên and the Mo clan within the narrative of an emergent Vietnamese nation. See Ang, *Poetic Transformations*, p. 229.
[134] Trương, *Nghiên cứu*, vol. 1, pp. 120–129.   [135] Đông, *Văn Học*, p. 140.
[136] Ang, *Poetic Transformations*, pp. 83–84.

eventually, also in Cochinchina as a whole. It perhaps explains why the Classical Chinese "Ten Verses" anthology continues to circulate in its complete version, while other literary collections have either vanished or survive in fragments.

Mo Tianci maintained a contradictory coexistence of institutions and arrangements in the governance of his complex, multiethnic realm. At its core, however, was a militarized gentry regime that ensured the defense of The Port's boundaries and expansion into the sparsely populated hinterlands. Tianci never attempted to alter established hierarchies where they already existed but chose to work within them, while importing new institutions, such as Christianity, to facilitate grassroots control and settlement into new areas. After 1758, by virtue of his position as viceroy of Cambodia, his area of control extended from the shores of the Bassac to the Siamese border. Within his vastly enlarged realm, he tried to ensure greater coherence by promoting Confucianism and Buddhism among the Chinese and Viet populations beneath the elite level. In the end, it was all about business. The Port, as an integrated unit, could more effectively exploit and market the agricultural produce and natural resources of its hinterlands, while bolstering its established role as a transit point for ships and products across maritime Asia.

6   The Business of Business

> 西園把臂動高唫 (In the West Garden, we hold each other's arms and cry aloud)
>
> 社事虛期歲月深 (We have long spent leisurely time together in the society)
>
> 海角片帆慈母夢 (A solitary ship in the remote seas dreams of a compassionate mother)
>
> 天涯卮酒故人心 (A wine vessel in the far corners of the sky carries the heart of an old friend)
>
> 竹城翠擁煙千疊 (In the City of Bamboo, treasures accumulate like a thousand layers of smoke)
>
> 銀市花開月一林 (When flowers in Silver Market bloom for a month, they become a forest)
>
> 此去河仙春漸暖 (When you go to Hà Tiên, the spring gradually brings warm weather)
>
> 多君風雅重南金 (The vassal ruler there is elegant and prizes southern talent)
>
> —Tan Xiang, "Sending Off Chen Zhikai to Annam"[1]

The pragmatism of Wang Yangming's teachings, especially the emphasis on the unity of knowledge and action, provided a sound basis for Mo Tianci to promote the pursuit of profits as a necessary means of nurturing his people and ensuring their widespread prosperity.[2] Indeed, trade formed the lifeblood of The Port's economy. Franciscan Father Julián described The Port as a Livorno of the East, and it shared many commonalities with the early modern Italian principality.[3] Ruled by prominent families, namely, the Mo and the Medici, both adopted a

---

[1] Chen Jianhua, *Guangzhou dadian*, vol. 89: Ling, *Haiyatang*, p. 336.
[2] Nguyễn Ngọc Thơ and Nguyễn, 'Philosophical Transmission,' p. 90. For the connection between Heart-Mind and trade, see Lufrano, *Honorable Merchants*, pp. 43–50.
[3] AMEP, Cochinchine, vol. 745: 'Relation des Franciscains,' p. 174.

policy of neutrality in their commercial dealings, transacting with friend and foe alike. Thriving within a fiercely competitive climate of multiple competing ports, the two succeeded by divorcing trade from ethnic privilege and protecting the property and livelihoods of merchants. Both managed, as a result, to substantially lower transaction costs.[4] As Father Julián shows, just like Livorno, The Port provided favorable conditions to attract diverse groups of people from all lands to do business and reside for the long term.

Besides sound policies, The Port owed much of its success to its ability to fulfill three important economic functions in maritime East Asia. It provided natural resources to China and Southeast Asia. In addition, The Port and a group of other ports under its dominance, particularly Bassac, became transit points for ships and products between Northeast and Southeast Asia and mainland and island Southeast Asia. The Port also functioned as a center for money creation and finance.

All three components had already started to develop under Mo Jiu. But Tianci integrated them more firmly into the flourishing Chinese junk trade in maritime East Asia. As a result, The Port functioned as a key go-between for a vibrant offshore Chinese economy. Between 1760 and 1770, when the most complete quantitative data is available, The Port and its sphere of influence accounted for around half of the trade between Southeast Asia and Guangzhou alone. As Paul van Dyke estimates, the junk trade with Southeast Asia, in turn, made up 31 percent of Guangzhou's total foreign commercial ties, including with European firms.[5] The Port thus occupied an important albeit overlooked node in the emergent eighteenth-century global economic system. The Myanmar invasion and destruction of Siam in 1767 presented tremendous challenges to the continued viability of Mo Tianci's network in the form of renewed insecurity and the return of large-scale piracy close to his shores. But The Port gained far more than it lost by filling the void left by a formerly formidable competitor in the water world. By the late 1760s, Tianci had reached the height of his economic, political, and military fortunes.

Water World Emporium

The Port provided convenient access to the resource-rich hinterlands of the water world. The forests on the surrounding hills contained timber for shipbuilding. Bamboo could be found in abundant quantities and varieties and was used for the construction of houses and large parts of

---

[4] For more on the qualities of early modern Livorno, see Tazzara, *Free Port*, pp. 11–12.
[5] Van Dyke, *Merchants*, vol. 1, pp. 68–73.

the city walls. Allusions to it occur frequently in the contributions to Tianci's poetic anthologies. As many of the primary records, including the poem sending off Chen Zhikai, reveal, a popular nickname for The Port was "City of Bamboo."[6]

Rattan was another famed local product. In particular, a special type about a meter in diameter could securely bind and fasten ship masts. The resins of some trees yielded a special type of amber, which "resembled a piece of bronze, its color as black as iron."[7] It was marketed as a talisman to repel bad luck. Ivory was extracted from the large herds of elephants that roamed about in the forests. Already, when the Siamese invaded The Port in 1717, during the days of Mo Jiu, the warehouse that they burned down contained some 200 short tons of ivory. With the price for the largest elephant tusks at the time being fifty to fifty-five Spanish dollars, the value of the stored ivory alone came to at least 75,000 dollars.[8] At Bassac, the proximity to the South China Sea, along with low levels of precipitation, formed an ideal environment for the drying and processing of red salt.[9]

Rice and other crops, such as taro and wheat, could be grown extensively on the Mekong floodplain around Cần Thơ. In the swampy terrain of Black Water, where most of the water was saline, farming made use of captured rainwater. There were also cultivation zones on the coastal dune belts along the South China Sea, the beach ridges next to the Gulf of Siam, and manmade terraces from the hills. Along the slopes of the hills, various fruit trees and pepper were grown. By the early nineteenth century, some 1,000 piculs (60,000 kg) of pepper were being harvested each season.[10]

The seas and rivers of the water world and the offshore islands abound with an astoundingly diverse variety of fish and other seafood. The richest catches can be obtained from around Phú Quốc. Many of the anchovies caught around the island would be fermented and processed into fish sauce, a clear and potent liquid used to season food. Other sea products included ambergris, drawn from the intestines of the sperm whale and made into a perfume. Sea cucumbers, considered a delicacy among Chinese, both at home and abroad, came in black and white

---

[6] Nguyễn Dynasty, *Nhất thống chí*, vol. 3, pp. 291, 333; Trịnh, *Thông chí*, pp. 430–431; Trương, *Nghiên cứu*, vol. 2, p. 26; Chen Jianhua, *Guangzhou dadian*, vol. 89: Ling, *Haiyatang*, p. 336.
[7] Lê, *Tạp lục* (Giáo dục), vol. 2, p. 503; Nguyễn Dynasty, *Nhất thống chí*, vol. 3, p. 291.
[8] Hamilton, *New Account*, vol. 2, pp. 196–198.
[9] Trịnh, *Thông chí*, p. 414; Li Tana, 'Mekong Delta,' p. 151.
[10] Trịnh, *Thông chí*, pp. 411–417; Poivre, 'Journal d'un voyage,' p. 414; Nguyễn Dynasty, *Nhất thống chí*, vol. 3, p. 293; P. Taylor, *Khmer Lands*, pp. 43, 102–104, 140, 169, 202.

colors. During the early nineteenth century, about 25,000 kilograms were caught on average each year. The hawksbill turtle was a unique and prized export item. Not only could its meat be consumed but its shell could also be crafted into ornaments and decorative items.[11] Mo Tianci had presented a living turtle as a gift to the Tokugawa shogun in 1740. The creature created a sensation in Nagasaki. The crew of the junk that transported his envoys spent two months teaching two Japanese guards of the Chinese quarter, where they were confined during their stay, how to raise and care for the turtle. The guards, in turn, transmitted this knowledge to two foot-soldiers responsible for escorting it to the shogun while they traveled together on the road to Edo.[12]

The natural resources from The Port's hinterlands went north and south. In particular, rice came into strong demand in China to satisfy a growing population and commercial economy. In 1742, the Qianlong Emperor expanded the Qing court's official incentive program for grain imports, which had previously applied only to Siamese vessels on a case-by-case basis. He decreed that starting from the following year, all junks from abroad bringing in at least 5,000 piculs (300,000 kg) of rice would have their customs duties cut by a third. Those carrying 10,000 piculs (600,000 kg) would receive a discount of a half.[13] From the 1740s, memorials to the Qianlong Emperor highlighted The Port as one of the places in Southeast Asia where "harvests are abundant, and prices are low." Rice was shipped to Guangdong and Xiamen and other ports in Fujian, traditionally the most resource-deficient of the coastal provinces.[14]

Rice also went the other way to destinations in island Southeast Asia. Much of the hinterlands of the Malay Peninsula and Sumatra had been cleared for the cultivation of pepper. Polities such as Palembang and Jambi depended heavily upon rice shipments from Cambodia and Siam to feed the laborers who worked the plantations, often slaves captured in piratical raids.[15] The other major source of grain from Java often proved to be more expensive and subject to shortages. One reason was because it primarily went to source the vicinity of Batavia, which increasingly specialized in the cultivation of sugar.[16]

The Port faced significant competition in rice and natural resource exports, since many ports in neighboring Cambodia, Siam, and south-

---

[11] Trịnh, *Thông chí*, p. 417; Sellers, *Princes of Hà-Tiên*, p. 8.
[12] Tanabe, *Nagasaki jitsuroku taisei*, p. 271.
[13] *Qing shilu*, vol. 11: *Gaozong Chunhuangdi shilu*, p. 566.
[14] Yang Kaijian and Tian, 'Zhongguo yu Xianluo de dami maoyi,' pp. 84–86.
[15] Andaya, *Brothers*, pp. 95–97.
[16] Vos, *Gentle Janus*, p. 37, 42; Andaya, *Brothers*, pp. 52–127; Shimada, 'Southeast Asia and International Trade,' pp. 61–62.

central Vietnam could fulfill the same function, despite some unique local species and varieties. Ayutthaya had the greatest overlap in terms of the product mix with The Port. Ships carried to China and Japan both Siamese and Cambodian sappanwood, a plant used as an ingredient in herbal medicine.[17] There appears to be no distinction between the two other than their ports of origin, with the Cambodian variety most likely coming from The Port, given Mo Tianci's control over its coastline.

Ayutthaya held the edge in the production and shipment of rice. In 1758, merchants from Siam forwarded 23,500 piculs (1,414,200 kg) to Xiamen, the largest on record. A more representative quantity was probably 1753, when 7,020 piculs (421,200 kg) were shipped out. In 1763, a total of 2,000 piculs (120,000 kg) went to Guangzhou, the last documented year for this destination. The earliest data that I can locate for The Port is for 1766. The Dutch recorded the export of 500 piculs (30,000 kg) of rice to Guangzhou from Cambodia, which would include The Port and its hinterlands.[18] Much larger quantities were probably shipped to Xiamen, although the precise figures remain unknown. It is an imperfect comparison, but the Qing sources of this period prioritized Siam as the chief source of the grain and mentioned other places like The Port only in passing. Until the mid-1750s, The Port also depended upon Siamese rice during periods of famine, as occurred during the crisis over the Cochinchinese envoy.[19]

In other respects, however, The Port appeared to enjoy a slight advantage. During the late seventeenth century, Ayutthaya was a convenient transit point for South Asian goods, especially cloth, which once enjoyed high demand in island Southeast Asia. The VOC also brought in cloth through its channels of procurement in India. Over the eighteenth century, local production in Southeast Asia picked up and catered to the tastes and needs of all classes, while gradually displacing the imported varieties. Besides Javanese fabrics, cloth produced in Cambodia enjoyed the greatest success. There is no evidence whether the Mo were involved in establishing the industry, but its export went through the coastal areas under their domination. Kwee Hui Kian shows that in 1759, Cambodian vessels brought 515 corge (10,300 pieces) to Sumatra compared to just one corge (20 pieces) forty years earlier. Similar cloth production sites in

---

[17] Dalrymple, *Oriental Repertory*, vol. 1, pp. 287–288; NA, 1.04.21: Deshima, 152, pp. 124–127.
[18] Yang Kaijian and Tian, 'Zhongguo yu Xianluo de dami maoyi,' pp. 84–86; Van Dyke, *Merchants*, vol. 1, Appendix 4D, p. 272.
[19] Grand Council Archives, Qianlong Reign, 007528: Pan Siju, n. p.

Siam also emerged, but they lagged in production. In the same year of 1759, they supplied 255 corge (5,100 pieces) to Sumatra.[20]

Tianci also promoted the deeper integration of his realm with the official VOC world centered upon Batavia. Jan Taijko, a Chinese tax farmer in Batavia with close connections to Lin Jiguang, the Chinese kapitan of the city, owned a fleet of junks that made frequent trips to Siam and Cambodia to purchase "dried, salted, or pickled fish" and other preserved seafood. Most of the items were undoubtedly shipped out from The Port, since Lin Jiguang's own grandson, Lin Houqua, and other relatives resided there to supervise Qing merchants and sojourners. Perhaps one important reason for their presence was to ensure the smooth operation of Batavia's fish market, whose operations Jan Taijko administered. The city came to depend entirely upon the water world for its supply of dried seafood.[21]

Although Mo Tianci had considerable influence and informal control over his realm's hinterlands after 1739, he obtained a greater say over how to use the territory after it was granted to him in his official capacity of viceroy in the late 1750s. Besides imposing new administrative divisions and encouraging frontier settlement, he opened land and sea routes to ensure that a substantial portion of the natural resources in mainland Southeast Asia would flow through his area of control. Because Bassac was located on the shores of the South China Sea, it emerged as a second, and often more important, center for trade with China. Although strictly speaking still an integral part of Cambodia, Bassac was, in fact, surrounded by The Port's territory. It was probably a free port under the joint authority of the Cambodian king; the governor, Oknha Athivongsa, a subject of the court who retained significant autonomy; and Mo Tianci, who was himself a member of the Khmer royalty. Tianci maintained a military presence in the city and controlled navigation along the river.[22]

Bassac's hazy political status contributed to a rowdy, freewheeling atmosphere conducive to the specialization in trade. The French missionary Levavasseur describes the town as a makeshift settlement that surrounded both sides of a canal extending in an elongated fashion for two kilometers. Wood cut down from the nearby forests, along with branches of the coconut palm, served as the primary construction material for houses. There was almost no public infrastructure to speak of. The

---

[20] Kwee, 'End of the "Age of Commerce",' in Taglicozzo and Chang, *Chinese Circulations*, p. 288.
[21] ANRI, K66a: 3689, pp. 292–293. See, for example, ANRI, K66a: 1560, pp. 913, 919–920; 1567, p. 97; 1570, p. 564; 1573, pp. 509, 527.
[22] *Prachum phongsawadan* 66: *Krao prab mueng Phutthaimat*, p. 13; *Nouvelles lettres*, vol. 6, pp. 215–217; Launay, *Cochinchine*, vol. 2, pp. 390–391.

lack of walls made it vulnerable to damage to lives and property from tigers and elephants. The water was dirty and brackish. Because so little rain fell, the canal's water level could only allow vessels to sail in and out during high tide. Nonetheless, Levavasseur describes Bassac as a place of tremendous prosperity, where Chinese ships as big as their European counterparts were densely packed together. He must be referring to the junks from Guangzhou, since they were the largest compared to vessels from elsewhere in China. At Bassac, he recounts with amazement, all kinds of goods could be found in abundance.[23]

Tianci also encouraged the development of a hierarchy of smaller ports underneath The Port and Bassac that would service local connections and handle certain long-distance shipments. In a list of the imports and exports of Guangzhou, Alexander Dalrymple (1737–1808), a Scottish geographer and employee of the British East India Company, identifies a place that he calls New Port (New Kang-kow) and groups it under the same section as The Port (Kang-kow).[24] Although the location remains undetermined, it most likely referred to Cần Thơ, farther up the river from Bassac. Like Bassac, it was situated close to the South China Sea and could attract junks from China. Cần Thơ was also in the heart of the Mekong River Delta and could more easily access and ship out its abundant rice harvests. The VOC factory at Guangzhou documents another port of call for ships known as Tsou geth or Tju-hot. Van Dyke believes that this enigmatic place was located somewhere in Cochinchina. Likely, it was C: Haoji **K: Prek Prahut** V: Gành Hào, situated midway between Bassac and Black Water, within The Port's area of jurisdiction.[25] Black Water, too, was a fairly sized local port. Oeij Tshing, who accused Lauw Wo of pirating his ship, was originally carrying goods from it to The Port's center.[26]

One major focus after Tianci's appointment as viceroy involved the development of Treang into a land and riverine transportation hub. Situated at the intersection of the Bassac and Moat Chrouk rivers, the seasonal canal from Moat Chrouk to the Gulf of Siam, and roadways; it connected Cambodia proper, Cochinchina, and the highland areas with each other and with The Port and Bassac. It became a congregation point for natural resources before they were transported to the coast for shipment overseas or for distributing imported items along the same

---

[23] *Nouvelles lettres*, vol. 6, pp. 213–214; Li Tana and Van Dyke, 'Canton,' p. 13; Li Tana, 'Mekong Delta,' p. 151.
[24] Dalrymple, *Oriental Repertory*, vol. 1, pp. 281–282.
[25] Trịnh, *Thông chí*, p. 191; Van Dyke, *Merchants*, vol. 1, p. 277.
[26] ANRI, K66a: 3574b, pp. 109–114.

channels. For this reason, there was a sizable marketplace in town occupied by Chinese merchants.[27]

With Tianci's encouragement, Franciscan missionaries built a church and started a parish at Treang, transforming the place into a frontier recruitment center for migrants coming in from Cochinchina. The newcomers would be welcomed, treated for any illnesses, and settled down locally or sent to other places to break land. In a sign of its growing centrality, Tianci arranged to have the Catholic district headquarters of Cambodia transferred from The Port's urban center to Treang in 1769.[28] By then, the Franciscan fathers Julián del Pilar and Martín Robles de Zugarramurdi (1729–1783) had taken over the mission, replacing Francisco Hermosa de Buenaventura. Father Martín, in particular, was a trained surgeon and treated many sick people, improving their chances for survival amid the continued exploitation of the disease-filled tropical frontiers. His skills impressed Tianci and his officials, and he acquired considerable influence among them, since they "granted him whatever he asked for."[29]

One major reason Tianci promoted the interior routes to his ports was because of the rampant piracy throughout the Gulf of Siam and beyond. Starting from the 1750s, much of the predation up to the northern Malay coast was undertaken by Viet migrants residing within The Port's authority. In addition to being fishermen, perhaps they were farmers who failed in their attempt to break new land or ran away from the Church as apostates. Or they were underpaid sailors in Tianci's navy who viewed the passing merchant junks as opportunities to strike it rich. Father Francisco encountered at least four instances of predation from Cochinchinese pirates when his ship, which was sailing from Phnom Penh to The Port in 1753, ran off course and ended up on the shores of Chumphon in southern Siam. During his stay there, he met a Chinese junk captain who was robbed of everything while at sea. And the poor captain was stranded at Chumphon, living in abject penury. He was almost naked, since his own clothes had been taken away from him, and he had no money to pay for his return journey.[30]

To prevent the Viet from using the seas and therefore potentially becoming predators and colluding with other piratical groups like the Austronesians, Tianci slapped a 10 percent duty on all vessels from

---

[27] Pérez, 'Españoles en el imperio de Annam' 11, pp. 217–218; AMEP, Cochinchine, vol. 745: 'Relation des Franciscains,' pp. 178, 180.
[28] Alcobendas, 'Religiosos médico-cirujanos' 5, pp. 221–222.
[29] Alcobendas, 'Religiosos médico-cirujanos' 6, pp. 337–338.
[30] Pérez, *Diario*, pp. 40–41, 48–49.

Cochinchina sometime in the late 1750s, after he became viceroy. He encouraged them instead to enter The Port's authority from land or Bassac. As a result, the Franciscan father observed in 1763 that Cochinchinese ships no longer came to The Port itself.[31] The decision to impose duties on The Port's overlord epitomizes the decreased economic interdependence between the two. In fact, just like with Siam, competition came to characterize the relationship. There was a similar overlap of natural resources, especially from the highlands. As Mo Tianci developed closer ties to the Qing, Cochinchinese ports like Hội An were becoming less useful as intermediaries for Chinese products.

However, we must keep in mind that despite the competition that existed between The Port's sphere of influence, Cochinchina, and Siam, there was also a significant degree of integration between them. Ships often stopped at more than one port of call to supplement their cargo, take advantage of better deals, or exchange certain products. Lauw Wo, whom Oeij Tshing accused of pirating his ship, was returning to The Port, where he resided, from a trip to Siam and intended, shortly afterward, to proceed to Batavia.[32] Although fewer ships from Cochinchina went to The Port because of the added duties, they did pay call at Bassac.[33]

Transshipment Center

The Port had already become a place to concentrate goods from China, Japan, and Southeast Asia under Mo Jiu. The Qing maritime ban of 1717, which practically made all trade with Southeast Asia illegal aside from Vietnam, facilitated its emergence as a transshipment point. The prohibitions were completely lifted in 1729 at the orders of the Yongzheng Emperor. But The Port retained its significance as a key node in the regional sea-lanes because of four other major developments in maritime East Asia.[34]

Starting from the middle of the 1740s, the VOC attempted to put more teeth into its monopoly on pepper and impose exclusive rights over tin, especially after the discovery of rich mines on the island of Bangka, a dependency of Palembang. Tin was a lucrative export, as it enjoyed tremendous popularity in China. It was used in the sacred paper that was burned in Chinese shrines and temples to communicate with deities. It also went into the production of canisters for the storage of tea, China's largest export item. The Dutch sought to restrict the marketing of tin and

---

[31] Pérez, 'Españoles en el imperio de Annam' 11, p. 218.
[32] ANRI, K66a: 3574b, p. 109.   [33] Launay, *Cochinchine*, vol. 2, p. 388.
[34] Zhao Gang, *Qing Opening*, pp. 166–167.

pepper to exclusive VOC channels at Batavia and VOC ships to bring them to Guangzhou. They aimed to prevent direct linkages between China and the sites of production in the straits zone. Besides increasing the number and frequency of patrols, the VOC successfully pressured the sultan of Palembang to refuse junks from China access to his domain. In 1753, the VOC further banned the ships from calling at Melaka, which was under its direct control.[35] The measures were, for the most part, able to deter long-distance junks and curb much of the direct southbound trade between China and the Malay Peninsula and Sumatra.

Rulers, their clients, and merchants based in the straits zone came upon the alternative of outfitting their own ships with tin and pepper and sending them northward. They could either sail straight to China or, more securely, to an intermediate location, where their goods would be loaded onto junks bound for Guangzhou.[36] Located midway between China and the straits, The Port proved to be an ideal stopover point. The VOC recognized this loophole and initially tried to enforce the ban on tin and pepper on ships headed for the water world. In 1757, for instance, its patrols confiscated three vessels suspected of carrying these items that were returning to Palembang from The Port and Cambodia, perhaps a reference to Kampot and Kampong Som, situated farther west on the Gulf of Siam coast.[37] But such heavy-handed measures ran into strong opposition from the rulers of island Southeast Asian polities, who depended on rice from Cambodia and Siam to feed the laborers on their pepper plantations and tin mines. Two years later, after intensive lobbying from the sultan of Palembang, the VOC released the captured ships and issued passes for them to proceed northward.[38]

The crews of the vessels found ways to evade the VOC patrols. If discovered, they could try outrunning them or hide the contraband items amid the legal products on board, making it almost impossible to discover when searched. In the end, the VOC gave up its attempts at enforcement. In 1759, after releasing the vessels that they had confiscated two years earlier, Batavia instructed the Dutch residents at Palembang to henceforth "turn a blind eye" toward ships sailing to and from the straits zone and The Port. The VOC prohibited ships on this route from carrying tin and pepper, but it was unwilling or simply unable to enforce its regulations, since it had to issue these directives repeatedly.

---

[35] Vos, *Gentle Janus*, pp. 7, 36–42; Andaya, *Brothers*, pp. 52–127; Van Dyke, *Merchants*, vol. 1, pp. 68–73; Bulbeck et al., *Southeast Asian Exports*, p. 81.
[36] Vos, *Gentle Janus*, pp. 33–42.   [37] ANRI, K66a: 3668, p. 219.
[38] ANRI, K66a: 3670, pp. 687–688.

Moreover, ships under the license of the sultan of Palembang could travel unmolested whatever they carried on board.[39]

Another key factor behind The Port's growth was the massacre of the Chinese population of Batavia in 1741, which severely damaged the VOC's reputation as a reliable business partner. In subsequent years, the number of junks sailing to the city from Xiamen, Ningbo, and Guangzhou experienced a significant and steady decline, from an average of 15.6 vessels per year between 1735 and 1740 to 8.1 in the 1740s, and between 6 and 7 from the 1750s. Ships leaving Batavia to these places recorded a similar drop. The VOC spent much effort reassuring the Chinese merchants and persuading them to return. However, memorials from Qing officials reveal that other destinations, including The Port, increased in popularity because of perceived Dutch brutality and because merchants did not have to pay monopoly prices.[40]

The third major development occurred in Johor, on the tip of the Malay Peninsula. During the 1740s, on the Riau Islands, the Bugis and Malay introduced gambier and cultivated the plant on a large scale. Most of it went to Java, where it was exchanged for rice. The gambier was then shipped onward to China for use as a tanning agent and additive to food and medicine. Both tin and gambier required tremendous inputs of labor, and local Southeast Asian slaves could not readily fulfill the need. At first, Chinese refugees fleeing the massacre at Batavia were recruited to work the mines and plantations. When those sources dried up, men shipped directly from China, which possessed a large and steady pool of surplus labor, replaced them.[41] The two decades from the late 1750s to late 1770s marked a peak of Chinese migration. On Bangka alone, the population of laborers was estimated to be 25,000–30,000.[42]

From the 1750s, most of these migrants set sail from Guangzhou, where a substantial portion of China's foreign trade became concentrated. By then, the debates over policy between the maritime faction and more conservative elements in Qing official circles had settled into a rough equilibrium. On the one hand, the court maintained a tolerant attitude toward Chinese sojourning in Southeast Asia, even if their time

---

[39] s' Jacobs, *Generale missiven*, vol. 13, p. 380; Vos, *Gentle Janus*, pp. 41–42; Andaya, *Brothers*, p. 218.
[40] Blussé and Nie, *Chinese Annals*, pp. 220–227; Li and Van Dyke, 'Canton,' p. 17. Data on ships between China and Batavia is compiled from the monthly lists of incoming and outgoing vessels at Batavia found scattered across the documents in ANRI, K66a: 2567–2591, 2593–2597.
[41] Ibn Ahmad, *Precious Gift*, pp. 90–91, 340: Folio 118n3; Trocki, *Prince of Pirates*, pp. 33–34.
[42] Andaya, *Brothers*, p. 218.

abroad assumed a permanent character. On the other hand, with the neutralization of the most serious maritime threats to Manchu rule, such as the Zheng and, for the time being, the Europeans, the Qing gradually retreated from the forward naval posture adopted by Shi Lang in the late seventeenth century. The Qing switched back to the Ming-period emphasis on coastal defense, which focused on fighting pirates, deterring invasion, and supervising trade within its territorial waters.[43]

As part of this shift toward a more passive management of the seas, the court restricted the access of foreign merchants to its shores and placed their activities under increased surveillance. In 1757, it banned them from visiting other ports in China and mandated that they could only trade at Guangzhou, which was already tightly integrated into regional and global networks and had a sophisticated infrastructure in place to handle their business. European chartered enterprises, including the Dutch, British, Danish, and Swedish East India Companies, had established their factories on the outskirts of the city several decades prior. As Guangzhou's commercial exchanges with India and Europe grew, the companies invested substantial capital into the procurement of Chinese goods, especially tea, silk, and porcelain.[44]

The court outsourced the management of Western traders to the Hong merchants, whose firms specialized in their business. The Hong merchants guaranteed their payment of duties and fees to the customs superintendent, commonly known as the Hoppo, and the Guangdong authorities. These officials then forwarded the sums to Beijing. The Hong merchants also stood in security for one another in repaying debts generated among the foreign community and ensuring lawful behavior.[45]

Burdened with heavy financial and political obligations, the Hong merchants often turned to their Western counterparts for loans and advances on products. But a reliance upon these sources of credit only threatened to drive them further into debt. Many of the Hong merchants also formed partnerships that could allow them to better weather unexpected shortfalls and crises over the longer term. The Qing court offered its support to this initiative. In 1760, the formation of an officially sanctioned alliance of Hong merchants, the Co-hong (*Gonghang*), or public guild, granted them greater bargaining power before the European companies. Of course, as Van Dyke argues, Qing policy involved a delicate balance between the different parties in Guangzhou to ensure a competitive environment in which none of them could acquire a monopoly over trade, whether on the supply or demand side.

---

[43] Po, *Blue Frontier*, pp. 135–143; Zhao Gang, *Qing Opening*, pp. 183–185.
[44] Zhao Gang, *Qing Opening*, pp. 169–186. [45] Van Dyke, *Merchants*, vol. 1, pp. 9–24.

Bringing the Hong merchants underneath a common umbrella and regulating their activities proved to be a more ideal alternative compared to powerful private partnerships operating outside official channels.[46]

Southeast Asia figured prominently in the consideration of the Hong merchants. They viewed the junk trade as an important source of revenue generation to offset the expenses and debts incurred in their dealings with the Europeans. Financing from the European companies, in turn, fueled greater levels of commercial activity between Guangzhou and Southeast Asian ports. During the 1760s and 1770s, when comprehensive documentation is available, about 31 percent of Guangzhou's total exports in volume went through the junk trade to Southeast Asia. About 10–15 percent of what the Hong merchants purchased in exchange would be reexported to the Europeans, according to Van Dyke's estimate. Wax, for instance, was used for candles and as a lubricant and seal for the repair and maintenance of ships. Sago could pack porcelain or serve as ballast. Other items might be exotic consumer novelties.[47]

The Port took full advantage of the opportunities brought about by the larger political and economic climate in maritime East Asia. It sourced pepper from island Southeast Asia in addition to growing its own, although little information is available regarding shipments. The path of tin, on the other hand, is better documented. According to the fragmented import figures at Guangzhou compiled by Li and Van Dyke for 1758, 1767 to 1769, 1770, and 1774, ships listed as coming from The Port and Bassac supplied 4,807 piculs (288,470 kg) of tin on average per documented year. Most of this amount probably represented what was brought in on ships authorized by the sultan of Palembang, who sourced the metal from his dependency on the island of Bangka.[48] The Malay Peninsula served as another source of tin for vessels from Cambodia, including The Port, and Siam. In 1749, for instance, four junks from these places and Xiamen sailed to Kedah, on the northwestern coast, and purchased 90 bahars, equal to 270 piculs (16,200 kg), of tin.[49]

At Guangzhou, the available data for 1762 to 1765, 1767, and 1774 also indicates that some 8,500 piculs (510,000 kg), twice the quantity of tin reported from The Port's jurisdiction, was imported from vessels claiming to be from Palembang. Since junks from China had largely stopped going to Palembang, the ships, in reality, originated from

---

[46] Van Dyke, *Merchants*, vol. 1, pp. 49–66.
[47] Van Dyke, *Merchants*, vol. 1, pp. 68–73; Dalrymple, *Oriental Repertory*, vol. 1, pp. 281–282.
[48] Data on tin quantity comes from Li Tana and Van Dyke, 'Canton,' p. 18.
[49] ANRI, K66a: 3659, p. 743.

Bangka. There, agents of the sultan, his courtiers, the Chinese and Chinese creole kapitans of its mining communities, and even the laborers themselves secretly outfitted their own vessels. They might have the covert support of the sultan or be entirely smuggling operations for personal gain. Some of the ships probably risked the VOC patrols and went directly to Guangzhou, but Li and Van Dyke believe that most chose to pass through The Port first. Besides Bangka, they could also smuggle the tin to nearby Riau, taking advantage of its mounting hostility toward the VOC as Daeng Cambodia and his Bugis subjects became the de facto rulers of Johor. During this period, Riau became an emporium where ships from many lands, including the water world, came to trade.[50]

The selling price of tin at Guangzhou ranged from 12 to 19 taels per picul in the two decades from 1758 to 1778. This translates into a mean of 15.5 taels. Multiplying 15.5 by the total available estimates of yearly average tin quantity reported for ships from The Port, Bassac, and Palembang yields 206,259 taels. We can assume that this amount serves as a ballpark figure for the revenues from tin that passed through The Port's jurisdiction in a typical year.[51]

Although The Port's waters contained marine products such as sea cucumbers and tropical luxuries such as birds' nests, it also became a transit point for similar items farther away from its shores. The Franciscans noted that Chinese junks frequented Chumphon, in southern Siam. Their crews would go on shore to extract birds' nests.[52] In 1762, Dalrymple, who at the time headed the British factory on the island of Balambagan, between the Philippine Islands and Borneo, noted the arrival of a vessel from Cambodia at Abai, on the northern Borneo coast.[53] It is unclear whether it was a Chinese junk or an Austronesian vessel, or whether it came from The Port, Kampot, or Kampong Som, but it sought after sea cucumbers. Clandestine trade flourished in this contested border zone between the Dutch, British, and Spanish spheres of influence on the eastern edge of the Indonesian archipelago, taking advantage of the inability of any one political actor to fully impose its rules.[54]

Although the VOC suffered a loss in profits from the private selling and smuggling of its monopoly products, it gained much more from its ties with the Gulf of Siam coast. The Chinese and Austronesian networks, through the mediation of Mo Tianci, gave the VOC access to a

---

[50] Li Tana and Van Dyke, 'Canton,' pp. 18–19; Andaya, *Brothers*, pp. 218–219; Vos, *Gentle Janus*, pp. 26–28.
[51] Data on prices are derived from Appendix 1 in Vos, *Gentle Janus*, pp. 213–215.
[52] Pérez, *Diario*, p. 40.   [53] BL, IOR/G/4/1: Borneo, p. 169.
[54] Sutherland, 'Sino-Indonesian Commodity Chain,' in Taglicozzo and Chang, *Chinese Circulations*, pp. 174–178.

greater variety of product sources and markets in mainland Southeast Asia than was possible through its own formal system of factories. These had all shut down except for the one at Ayutthaya. Moreover, ships from The Port did not avoid Batavia altogether. In fact, from 1735 to 1770, the daily journals (*dagregisters*) of Batavia record the arrival of 135 ships from Cambodia, including The Port, while 151 came from Siam. Over the same period, a total of 102 vessels went the other direction to Cambodia, and 162 to Siam.[55] Batavia became a secondary source of Chinese and Japanese products, including silk, copper, gold thread, and tobacco. Traders could also procure Javanese tobacco and sugar, opium, and many types of Indian and Javanese cloths, including batik, which Bugis traders supplied to the Cham and Malay communities of The Port.[56]

The Port became the primary receiving point and distribution center for goods from China and Japan, on the other end. It was a major consumer in its own right of all kinds of products, ranging from luxuries to items for daily use. Mo Tianci, for instance, imported religious items, such as Buddhist statues and sutras, and all manner of books. He frequently drank tea with guests, including the Franciscan missionaries. From their narratives, sharing the beverage with him was considered to be a special mark of honor and favor. When Father Francisco visited Tianci, he would also be served grape wine, which originated from the Europeans in Guangzhou and was most likely brought over by the Hong merchants.[57] Li and Van Dyke have shown that many of the prominent Hong merchants outfitted ships that frequently paid call at The Port and Bassac. In addition, their agents also traveled directly to Batavia, where they must have encountered the kapitan, Lin Jiguang. Given his connections to The Port and the integrated nature of the Chinese commercial networks, it would not be surprising if there were also interactions between the Hong merchants and Lin Jiguang's grandson, Lin Houqua, the lieutenant of The Port's Chinese merchants and sojourners.[58]

The Port's area of authority played a crucial role as a transit point for ships sailing from China. The most important and lucrative imports were the Chinese themselves, who sold their own labor. Some would settle down in The Port and its vicinity. Others would stop at The Port's

---

[55] The monthly lists of incoming and outgoing vessels at Batavia are recorded across the documents in ANRI, K66a: 2571–2589.
[56] Reid, 'Southeast Asian Consumption,' p. 40; Clarence-Smith, 'Production of Cotton Textiles,' pp. 140–141.
[57] Alcobendas, 'Religiosos médico-cirujanos' 5, p. 224; Pérez, *Diario*, p. 17.
[58] ANRI K66a. 3689: pp. 292–293; Van Dyke, *Merchants*, vol. 1, p. 163; Li Tana and Van Dyke, 'Canton,' p. 15.

domain while on their way to the tin mines and gambier plantations of Sumatra and Riau. In 1764, for instance, the daily journal of Batavia reported the arrival in Palembang of a junk from Cambodia carrying sixty Chinese on board. They had come at the invitation of the sultan and intended to go onward to Bangka, where they would work the tin mines.[59] Some might have been drawn directly from among the Chinese already in the water world, who were most commonly seized and trafficked by pirates. However, the majority came from China.[60]

Because of their almost complete specialization in mining, the laborers became, after the pepper planters, another, and even larger, captive market for rice. These communities had to import as much as 150,000 piculs (9 million kg) per year, along with condiments, such as fish, salt, and vegetables to sustain themselves. There was also demand for broadcloths and woolens, probably to be worn as work clothes. Because of the comparatively scarcer labor supply and high wages in island Southeast Asia, the migrants had significant consumption ability relative to their counterparts back home. Other products on their purchase list included tea, porcelain cups and dishes, herbal remedies, paper, candies and sweetmeats, dried fruits, lacquerware, silk, and assorted items for daily use.[61]

The migrants could source their goods while in transit at The Port, which could produce some of them locally, such as the salt of Bassac, or import them from China. Alternatively, Chinese junks could supply their needs on-site. Vos compares them to "floating supermarkets supplying much of Southeast Asia with miscellaneous cheap merchandise."[62] The consumption of the laborers facilitated the creation of an offshore Chinese economy, one that had much more spending power compared to the domestic market.

Thanks to the detailed records of the VOC factory in Guangzhou, we can obtain a quantitative picture of the trade between Guangzhou and The Port's authority in seven documented years between 1760 and 1770, and how it compared to the rest of the region. Over the decade, a total of 234 vessels from across Southeast Asia are recorded to have arrived at Guangzhou. Of these, 82 vessels came from The Port's sphere of influence, including 24 from its core area, 49 from Bassac, 7 from Cambodia (probably Kampot and Kampong Som), and 2 from Prek Prahut (probably in Black Water). The Port's area of authority made up 41 percent of

---

[59] ANRI, K66a: 2594, p. 5.
[60] Andaya, *Brothers*, p. 218; Li and Van Dyke, 'Canton,' p. 17.
[61] Dalrymple, *Oriental Repertory*, vol. 1, pp. 283–286; Li Tana and Van Dyke, 'Canton,' pp. 21–23.
[62] Vos, *Gentle Janus*, p. 26.

the number of arrivals in Guangzhou. The figure exceeds those of competitors in mainland Southeast Asia, namely Siam and, increasingly, Cochinchina, especially after Mo Tianci slapped duties on its ships. Over the same period, junks originating from Cochinchina numbered 53, while a total of 20 ships sailed from Siam, which here meant Ayutthaya and Bangkok.[63]

Dalrymple, in his survey of trade in maritime East Asia, provides a chart that lists the values of the trade for the sole year of 1767. He shows that junks from The Port, New Port (maybe Cần Thơ), Bassac, and Cambodia earned 248,711 taels of silver from exports. Tin, timber, sea cucumbers, and medicinal products contributed the largest share of the revenues. In exchange, The Port and its sphere of influence purchased 64,214 taels' worth of goods from Guangzhou, yielding a surplus of 184,497 taels. In comparison, ships from Cochinchina realized a revenue of 194,271 taels, mainly achieved through sugar and pepper.[64] They purchased imported goods valued at 132,733 taels, or a surplus of 61,538 taels. Dalrymple did not provide any data for Siam. The Port's area of authority made up roughly 41 percent of exports and a quarter of imports.

We should keep in mind that these figures are only for junks that sailed directly from their points of origin to Guangzhou. During the decade from 1760 to 1770, there were other vessels identified as coming from places in island Southeast Asia, such as Batavia, Makassar, Palembang, and the Sulu Islands. Most of them transited at The Port's area of authority, Siam, and Cochinchina before docking at Guangzhou. Van Dyke estimates that 80 percent of all vessels at Guangzhou included ports in these three places in their itineraries, or 187 out of a total of 234 documented arrivals from Southeast Asia.[65] Accordingly, the actual ship numbers and monetary value that The Port's area of authority handled would be much larger, and, judging from the empirical evidence, they still exceeded Cochinchina and Siam. Conservatively speaking, The Port and its sphere of influence made up around half of the trade between Guangzhou and Southeast Asia. This proportion is impressive, especially given the smaller size, population, and domestic production of The Port compared to Cochinchina and Siam.

---

[63] Ship numbers are derived from Van Dyke, *Merchants*, vol. 1, Appendix 4C–4H, pp. 269–281.
[64] Calculations of total revenue employ a multiplication of unit prices by the quantity of imports into Guangzhou, which are based upon the weights of individual products in piculs and catties, or pieces of items listed in Dalrymple, *Oriental Repertory*, vol. 1, pp. 281–282.
[65] Van Dyke, *Merchants*, vol. 1, pp. 68–76, Appendix 4C–4H, 269–281.

Besides Guangzhou, Mo Tianci maintained ties with ports farther north along the Chinese coastline. Dalrymple's chart reveals that two junks from The Port's core area and one from Bassac sailed to Ningbo in 1767. Their cargoes consisted of comparable items to the vessels bound for Guangzhou. There was, in addition, another ship from Palembang carrying tin and wax. At the nearby Zhoushan Islands, off the coast to the northeast of Ningbo, Dalrymple documents the arrival of a junk from Batavia and another from the Philippines. Most of these vessels probably transited at The Port's jurisdiction.[66]

From there, they might return to their places of origin, or they could accompany ships based locally or at Shanghai and sail to Japan. At Nagasaki, they would market the remainder of their original cargo, primarily sappanwood and other medicinal ingredients and the newly acquired products from China. In exchange, the vessels would obtain copper, the most prized Japanese export. Because junks from China held the largest share of the trading licenses issued by the Tokugawa, The Port and other Southeast Asian polities found it more convenient and practical to sail from Ningbo and Shanghai. These places enjoyed the closest commercial ties with Japan and being there would increase the chances of getting a pass.[67]

It was becoming increasingly difficult for ships from Southeast Asian ports to directly access Nagasaki. Although Mo Tianci was lucky enough to secure a trading permit, he discontinued the official missions to Japan after 1743. An unfortunate mishap occurred that summer, as his envoy, Oknha Bavar Metrey, and his crew set out on their return journey. Their junk ran into a severe storm and capsized off southern Kyushu, drowning fourteen. The remaining sixty survivors were repatriated to Nagasaki together with their cargo. What happened next remains unknown, including the fate of Oknha Bavar Metrey, but, barring other contingencies, the survivors of the shipwreck would have made their way back to The Port, maybe on another junk.[68] This incident marked the third severe disaster in The Port's attempt to open direct trade with Japan, the first two occurring under Tianci's father. The formation of a connection with Ningbo completely removed the need for such missions.

A Center of Finance

The demand for Japanese copper reflected The Port's growing attractiveness as a site for the accumulation and flow of capital. Over time, the

---

[66] Dalrymple, *Oriental Repertory*, vol. 1, p. 287.
[67] Dalrymple, *Oriental Repertory*, vol. 1, p. 288; Holroyd, 'Rebirth,' pp. 101–103.
[68] Kondo, *Gaiban tsūsho*, vol. 1, pp. 139–140.

urban center appeared to have taken on more financial functions, while much of the actual trade in products or artisan production moved to Bassac and a handful of minor ports. In fact, the intriguing poem at the beginning of the chapter points to this focus on money. Tan Xiang, a prominent Guangzhou literati, composed the verse on the occasion of sending off his friend, Chen Zhikai, on one of his frequent business trips to The Port. The final line mentions Tianci, the Port's ruler, as prizing "southern talent" (*nanjin*).[69] On the surface, Tan appears to be praising Chen for his literary skill, which was formidable enough to attract the esteem of Tianci. However, the two characters could also mean "southern gold," another term for copper, used for coinage.

Under Tianci's rule, The Port's area of authority continued to serve as a major production center of coins. Besides the official mint at The Port proper, private workshops proliferated at Bassac, which lacked any kind of meaningful regulation.[70] A portion of the casts was inscribed with the characters for "Great Peace" (*Thái Bình*), which the Nguyễn lords would issue every time a successor assumed the throne. Two other frequent inscriptions include "Sacred Origins" (*Thánh Nguyên*) and "Peace and Law" (*An Pháp*). The first was originally the reign name of Hồ Quý Ly (1336–1407, r. 1400–1401), founder of a short-lived dynasty before the brief Ming conquest of Vietnam, from 1407 to 1428. The second, which was never used for any legitimate reign in the Sinosphere, appears to be an imitation of coins cast by the usurper Mạc dynasty.[71] The coins served as legal tender in The Port for small-scale, localized transactions.[72]

However, as Tianci's difficulty in achieving direct access to Nagasaki demonstrates, the supply of copper from Japan gradually dried up in the face of Tokugawa restrictions and the strict licensing system. Although some copper could still be sourced from Batavia, since the VOC had an exclusive channel for its procurement at Nagasaki, the company marketed most of its supply to South Asia, where profit margins were greater.[73] A larger and more reliable source came from the licensed Chinese ships that went to Japan. Even then, most of the copper was brought back to China and absorbed into its massive domestic economy.[74]

---

[69] Chen Jianhua, *Guangzhou dadian*, vol. 89: Ling, *Haiyatang*, p. 336.
[70] Li Tana, 'Cochinchinese Coin Casting,' in Taglicozzo and Chang, *Chinese Circulations*, p. 138.
[71] Li Tana, *Nguyễn Cochinchina*, p. 93; Li Tana, 'Cochinchinese Coin Casting,' in Taglicozzo and Chang, *Chinese Circulations*, p. 138; Phạm Quốc Quàn, *Vietnamese Coins*, pp. 119–120, 263, 265–266.
[72] Milburn, *Oriental Commerce*, p. 444.
[73] For VOC resale of copper from Japan, see Shimada, *Intra-Asian Trade*, pp. 94–99.
[74] Jansen, *China in the Tokugawa World*, pp. 33–34; Shimada, *Intra-Asian Trade*, pp. 24–28.

Starting from the 1750s, The Port followed the precedent of Cochinchina and adulterated its coins with zinc. A cheaper and more abundant substitute to copper, it allowed for the growth of money to better keep up with commercial expansion in maritime East Asia. China became the main source for procuring the metal. By 1767, ships from The Port's sphere of influence, including its core area, Bassac, and Cambodia, were taking out 8,495 piculs (509,675 kg) of zinc from Guangzhou, while Cochinchina-bound vessels procured 9,868 piculs (592,080 kg). Li Tana estimates that at least 616,929 strings of coins could be cast with this quantity.[75]

As in the days of Mo Jiu, many of the coins serviced Cochinchina. Their export exacerbated Huế's loss of control over its monetary policy, especially in its faraway Mekong Delta possessions. Already, the large-scale counterfeiting of official coins by private foundries in Cochinchina starting from the 1750s, undertaken with the connivance or even active participation of officials at the court, had resulted in rampant inflation and severely affected its foreign trade.[76] In 1770, Ngô Thế Lân, who had fished with Tianci at Sea Perch Creek, memorialized the Nguyễn ruler. Lân highlighted the seriousness of the situation in the Longhor camp, where the persistent lack of motivation on the part of commoners to save coins of little intrinsic value had resulted in their widespread impoverishment. Although he avoided direct mention, he placed the blame squarely upon Longhor's neighbors: The Port and Bassac. These places essentially held Cochinchina hostage through their monetary policies. Perhaps because the court knew that it could do little about the casting of coinage beyond its effective jurisdiction, his petition received no response.[77]

Under Mo Tianci, the coins, whether pure copper or adulterated with zinc, circulated beyond Cochinchina. They were found in Cambodia and large parts of Siam. Their reach often extended further, with discoveries as far as southern China and the eastern Indonesian archipelago. Just as at The Port and its sphere of influence, they mostly served the needs of localized exchanges. For instance, Li Tana shows, they were used to purchase slaves in Bali and as small change and gambling tokens in Batavia itself.[78]

The poem by Tan Xiang speaks of silver as another and, perhaps more important, monetary instrument. The lines provide clear evidence of a silver market in the city center. This exchange must have consisted of

---

[75] Li Tana, 'Cochinchinese Coin Casting,' in Taglicozzo and Chang, *Chinese Circulations*, pp. 132–139; Dalrymple, *Oriental Repertory*, vol. 1, p. 286.
[76] Li Tana, 'Cochinchinese Coin Casting,' in Taglicozzo and Chang, *Chinese Circulations*, p. 134; Li Tana, *Nguyễn Cochinchina*, pp. 95–98.
[77] Nguyễn Dynasty, *Thực lục*, vol. 1, pp. 156–157; Hán-Nôm A. 2939: Phạm, *Nam hành*, n. p.
[78] Li Tana, 'Cochinchinese Coin Casting,' in Taglicozzo and Chang, *Chinese Circulations*, pp. 132–142.

many financial houses or banks occupying one or several street blocks that specialized in handling deposits and loans based upon the metal. The poem describes the beautiful natural surroundings of the market. But it also contains the double meaning of principal investment accumulating interest to grow into a forest of money after a month.[79]

The surplus obtained from trade constituted the primary source of silver inflow. Most of the bullion came from the New World, but it took different routes to reach The Port. European firms, such as the Swedish East India Company, procured the specie from European ports, such as Cadiz in Spain. They sold it to the Hong merchants in Guangzhou as payment for goods, advances, or loans. The Hong merchants, in turn, sent the silver on their junks to Southeast Asia. Another source was Manila, from where, during the 1760s, at least one ship sailed to Bassac each year. The owner was Gregorio Chan, a partner of Pan Qiguan (1714–1788), one of the wealthiest and most influential Hong merchants. Chan was also a Catholic who spent part of his time at Macao and enjoyed close ties with the Spanish.[80] In addition to imports, the hills of Treang contained rich silver mines, giving The Port a useful domestic reserve of the metal to supplement and even out fluctuations in imports.[81]

Silver penetrated deeply into The Port's everyday life. The Spanish peso served as the second official currency within the realm, used for large-scale transactions. Oeij Tshing's vessel, which was stranded at Black Water, carried 191 silver coins on board. The woman trader Lang Tshauw had 160 pieces.[82] The smooth circulation of silver within The Port down to the level of localized exchanges points to the existence of a mature, efficient financial infrastructure. Besides trade, the silver market alluded to in Tan's poem allowed Mo Tianci to raise the funds for investment in territorial expansion and the recruitment of settlers, patronage of Qing elites, literary projects, and the maintenance of his troops.

The Port also became a center for financial settlements. Payments were exchanged and cleared even for transactions occurring far away from its shores and having little to do with its own affairs. Sometime in the late 1750s or early 1760s, the pirate and exile from Siak, Raja Alam, and his sea people allies seized a ship from Tegal, on the northern coast of central Java. According to the VOC documents, the passengers on board included a "Christian woman" with her two children. Since there was a small community of Chinese Christians at Tegal, she probably came from that background. The sea people enslaved her and sold her to the ruler of the

---

[79] Chen Jianhua, *Guangzhou dadian*, vol. 89: Ling, *Haiyatang*, p. 336.
[80] Van Dyke, *Merchants*, vol. 2, pp. 75–77, 253.   [81] Trịnh, *Thông chi*, p. 413.
[82] Milburn, *Oriental Commerce*, p. 444; ANRI, K66a: 3574b, pp. 115–117; Ibn Ahmad, *Precious Gift*, p. 23.

south-central Sumatran polity of Inderagiri, probably as an addition to his harem. The VOC authorities first learned of her plight in 1762 in exchanges with Jambi, the native land of Raja Alam's mother. The Christian woman evidently had to endure significant hardship, since missives from Batavia to Palembang two years later mention her as having only one small son. Presumably, the other sibling had passed away.[83]

Subjects of Palembang at The Port paid a ransom in the amount of 100 Spanish coins to the Arab priest there. He was certainly the same individual that, according to the Franciscan narratives, oversaw the mosque and threw stones at the nearby church while it was still under construction. The priest departed The Port and, on November 25, 1764, arrived at Inderagiri, where, ironically, he purchased the freedom of the Christian woman and her son. After he had paid the ransom, the hostages were transferred to a ship from Jambi that headed for Palembang. The unfortunate woman and her son were handed over to the VOC authorities for repatriation to Tegal. Batavia reimbursed the ransom amount to the crown prince of Palembang.[84] Because merchants throughout island Southeast Asia, including the Malay, Minangkabau, and Bugis, all had extensive trading connections at The Port, it was much easier to handle payments on-site rather than individually sailing with the money to each other's territories, which may also be mutually hostile. The resolution of this incident was but one of undoubtedly many more transacted at The Port. It provides a fascinating glimpse into its mature financial system, including the ready availability of massive quantities of coinage and silver and the efficiency of their transfer.

Crisis and Opportunity

The Port's position as a natural resource exporter, transshipment hub, and financial center underwent further solidification because of a dramatic development in its immediate neighborhood. At the same time, it was a major crisis, and Tianci had to confront the potentially negative implications for his realm. In 1765, forces from the newly established Konbaung dynasty (1752–1885) of Myanmar, under its third king, Hsinbyushin (1736–1776, r. 1764–1776), invaded Siam. Within a year, they handily crushed the armies sent to resist him and surrounded Ayutthaya. In desperation, the Siamese ruler, Ekkathat (1718–1767, r. 1758–1767), mobilized whatever troops he could put together to

---

[83] ANRI, K66a: 3674, pp. 123, 143; s' Jacobs, *Generale missiven*, vol. 17, p. 765; Balk, Van Dijk, and Kortlang, *Archives of the Dutch East India Company*, p. 78.

[84] Pérez, 'Españoles en el imperio de Annam' 8, pp. 312–313; ANRI, K66a: 3675, p. 193; ANRI, K66a: 3677, pp. 1054–1055; s' Jacobs, *Generale missiven*, vol. 17, pp. 765, 768.

defend the capital. The ethnic Chinese proved to be the most organized of these volunteers, and they put up a staunch resistance.[85]

The governor of the northwestern Siamese province of Tak, on the border with Myanmar, had fled together with the other scattered forces to Ayutthaya. He was the son of a Chaozhou immigrant and a Siamese woman who went by the Chinese name of Zheng Zhao (1734–1782, r. 1767–1782), Trịnh Quốc Hoa in Vietnamese, and the Siamese Sin, meaning money or wealth. Since he governed the province of Tak, he also became known as Phraya Tak Sin, or the governor of Tak named Sin. Let us call him Taksin, the standard academic usage in Thailand (see Figure 6.1). Taksin soon realized the potential of cooperation with the Chinese and recruited them into his ranks. Late in 1766, he, along with a contingent of a thousand Siamese and Chinese troops, broke through the Myanmar encirclement and fled eastward.[86]

The water world became an ideal base for him to build up a larger following. Since the seventeenth century, immigrants from Chaozhou, Taksin's native place, had settled down in large numbers in southeastern Siam, close to the Cambodian border, at Bang Pla Soi, Trat, and C: Jianzhuwen K: Chan Borei **T: Chanthaburi**. Over the eighteenth century, their presence expanded along the Cambodian coastline, and large numbers began migrating to The Port. The various documents from the Qing archives reveal that many of the Qing sojourners and settlers in The Port's area of authority during this period came from Chaozhou or the adjacent prefectures between it and the Pearl River Delta. These places, such as Haifeng, consisted of mixed and often mutually hostile communities of Chaozhou, Cantonese, and Hakka speakers.[87]

The Myanmar invasion and the collapse of Ayutthaya's central oversight contributed to the militarization of the Siamese water world. The Chaozhou mercantile community organized into autonomous bands. They invested capital in armaments, primarily procured from the Dutch at Batavia, and mobilized soldiers from among the large destitute population of commoners. Some ambitious groups hoped to wrest control over the trading routes and access to natural resources on the northern littoral of the Gulf of Siam away from The Port.[88]

---

[85] Wyatt and Cushman, *Royal Chronicles*, pp. 492–514.
[86] Wyatt and Cushman, *Royal Chronicles*, pp. 512–515; Pombejra, 'Chinese in Siam,' p. 343; Baker and Phongpaichit, *History of Ayutthaya*, p. 262.
[87] Sakurai, 'Chinese Pioneers,' p. 45; Grand Council Archives, Qianlong Reign, 017970: Li Shiyao, n. p.; China First Historical Archives, Junjichu, 1387-020, pp. 000302–000303.
[88] Pombejra, 'Chinese in Siam,' pp. 347, 350.

Figure 6.1 Portrait of Taksin and his spirit tablet, housed at a Chinese shrine near the Temple of Dawn (Wat Arun) in Bangkok.
Photograph by author.

One Chaozhou leader named Huo Ran built a fortress on the island of Koh Kong.[89] Situated at the edge of Kampong Som, the westernmost limit of The Port's territory, it was mountainous and heavily

---

[89] From 1766 to 1771, the chronology of events and some of the details of what happened vary according to different sources. As before, I choose the most logical sequence through a reading and synthesis of these accounts. Of course, others might come up with a different chronological narrative based on the same materials.

forested and contained a long, deep bay ideal for anchorage. From this base, Huo and his ships raided north–south maritime traffic between China and island Southeast Asia, and kidnapped Siamese war refugees on the adjacent shore and held them for ransom.[90] Piracy in the waters surrounding The Port was nothing new, as plenty of examples have shown us already. However, Huo's level of organization and sophistication went beyond the occasional raiding and plundering of ad hoc armed bands. His activities seemed to have posed an existential threat to The Port's economic lifeblood.

More alarmingly for Mo Tianci, he heard reports from spies whom he had earlier sent to scout out conditions in Siam that King Ekkathat, unable to repel the Myanmar invaders, had, in desperation, amassed troops and ships to attack The Port. Perhaps the ruler wanted to plunder it of its wealth and manpower to replenish his own depleted reserves. Tianci probably saw Huo as the vanguard for an upcoming campaign directed from Ayutthaya, especially since the pirate himself also had designs on The Port's territory. Unsure about confronting the Siamese army alone, Tianci activated the military alliance with Cochinchina for the first time since 1751. The controller of the five camps in Saigon promptly dispatched two naval regiments consisting of a thousand soldiers and twenty war junks to his aid. They arrived at The Port on December 4, 1766, and took up defensive positions. Then, in April of the following year, Mo Tianci again wrote to Saigon with a sudden request for the controller to pull back the reinforcements. Although he was supremely grateful for the assistance, he claimed, the danger of an invasion from Ekkathat had passed and he should not burden them further by keeping them around. They should return and rest.[91]

But the threat had not subsided and the situation in Siam continued to deteriorate. In April 1767, Myanmar forces seized Ayutthaya and destroyed the venerable city in a spree of wanton killing, raping, plundering, and burning. King Ekatthat perished amid the chaos. The crown prince and most of the royal household, along with tens of thousands of residents, were carried off to Myanmar. Mo Tianci feared that the invaders would capitalize upon their victory and continue to press eastward into the Gulf of Siam littoral. And indeed, Myanmar forces tried to pursue Taksin into the Siamese water world, although he successfully repulsed and routed them.[92] Given what happened, it seems that Tianci would have a much greater need for the Cochinchinese reinforcements and want them to stay longer, rather than requesting them to leave. How can this counterintuitive behavior be explained?

---

[90] Trịnh, *Thông chí*, pp. 312–313.
[91] Trịnh, *Thông chí*, pp. 310–311; Nguyễn Dynasty, *Thực lục*, vol. 1, p. 153.
[92] Wyatt and Cushman, *Royal Chronicles*, pp. 516–517, 519–522.

On the one hand, relations with Cochinchina had deteriorated significantly after a turbulent transition in leadership. In 1765, the Martial King passed away. Before his death, he had designated as his successor his second and eldest surviving son. The Martial King's maternal uncle, Trương Phúc Loan (d. 1776), was entrusted to serve as the heir's regent. However, the power-hungry Loan felt that the new ruler was much too mature and independent to manipulate. Accordingly, Loan orchestrated a palace coup that toppled him and replaced him with a much more pliable candidate: Nguyễn Phúc Thuần (1754–1777, r. 1765–1777), the deceased Martial King's sixteenth son and a boy of twelve years old. Thuần became the Stable King (Định Vương). The original legitimate heir soon died while under house arrest, and Loan emerged as the real power behind the throne. He was appointed to the position of chief advisor (quốc phó), giving him control over the treasury and military.[93]

More than his predecessors, Loan adopted an interventionist approach toward local society and frontier expansion, all for the purpose of obtaining more revenue for the cash-starved state and his personal benefit. He launched detailed surveys and registrations of landholdings and, on that basis, increased the rates and varieties of taxes. He sold offices to the highest bidder. He also proved to be highly corrupt and venal, spending the proceeds on lavish building projects, such as new palaces for himself and his cronies. Soon after Loan's ascent to power, Nguyễn Cư Trinh, the controller at Saigon and Tianci's close friend, was recalled to Huế. Since he had been a harsh critic of Loan's policies, the chief adviser probably thought it wise to marginalize him from his frontier power base and keep him closely supervised by promoting him to a central office. Trinh passed away in 1767, two years after his return.[94]

Mo Tianci experienced significant personality differences with Trinh's replacement as controller of the five camps at Saigon, Tống Văn Khôi (1733–1775). Vũ Thế Dinh's genealogical biography of the Mo clan explicitly singled out Khôi as a corrupt individual whose "greedy desires, as deep as a canyon, cannot be satiated."[95] And this nineteenth-century source was already heavily sanitized and restrained in its criticism of an official who had served the ancestors of the ruling Nguyễn dynasty. In contrast, the official biography of him compiled by the Nguyễn Dynasty Historiographical Institute spoke of Khôi in positive terms as "brave and decisive."[96] The Cochinchinese soldiers stationed at The Port likely demonstrated rapacious behavior and severely disrupted the livelihoods of the local people. They surely must have annoyed Tianci to the point that he would find any excuse to let them go.

[93] Nguyễn Dynasty, Thực lục, vol. 1, pp. 151–152.
[94] Nguyễn Dynasty, Thực lục, vol. 1, pp. 255–256; Dutton, Tây Sơn Uprising, pp. 34–36, 37–38.
[95] Vũ, Gia phả, p. 116.   [96] Nguyễn Dynasty, Thực lục, vol. 1, p. 249.

More importantly, around this time, Tianci came to view the chaos in Siam as an opportunity to expand his own sphere of influence. He welcomed refugees fleeing the Myanmar invasion to settle down in his realm. Among them were French missionaries of the MEP, along with their staff of Siamese, Chinese, and Viet catechists. Toward the end of 1765, with the approval of the Franciscans, they relocated their theological seminary from Chanthaburi, where it had temporarily been based after they fled from Ayutthaya, to a new compound at the seaside parish of Earthen Mount. Later, in 1767, following the fall of Ayutthaya, two Siamese princes, Chao Chui (d. 1770), the second son of the crown prince, and the third son, Chao Sisang, and hundreds in their retinue, fled to The Port. Tianci treated them with great honor and respect, feeding them and providing them accommodations befitting the standards of royalty.[97] He viewed the exiles as vital symbolic assets and manpower that could facilitate a reconquest of Siam in the name of restoring its rightful ruling house.

At this conjuncture, two major developments strengthened Tianci's resolve to intervene. On the one hand, he received a letter from Ayutthaya, probably from Ekkathat before the city's fall, with a plea for assistance.[98] Secondly, Tianci and the Qing established regular communications with one another at Guangzhou, undoubtedly with the help of the Cantonese literati who participated in his literary projects. Both sides had the motivation to work together against a common enemy. Since 1765, the Qing had engaged in a border war against Myanmar forces on the southwestern Yunnan frontier. In 1767, after suffering a series of heavy defeats, the Qianlong Emperor decided to escalate into a full-scale invasion and conquest of the country. His elite Manchu banner forces planned to penetrate deep into the Ayeyarwady River valley and seize the capital of Inwa.[99]

In October, Li Shiyao, governor-general of Guangdong and Guangxi, ordered the patrolling admiral (*youji*), Xu Quan, to board a merchant ship bound for The Port. The Qing did not know whether someone had succeeded Ekkathat or, if a new king had ascended the throne, where he was located or what was his identity. Therefore, Li drafted a proclamation directed at a hypothetical ruler and ordered Xu to deliver it into the hands of Tianci. Tianci would then forward it to whomever ruled over Siam.[100]

Meanwhile, Tianci alerted the Cochinchinese court of his intention to restore the Siamese ruling house. Trương Phúc Loan responded favorably, again offering him troops from the five camps under the controller at

---

[97] Launay, *Siam*, vol. 2, pp. 241–243; Vũ, *Gia phả*, pp. 107–109.
[98] *Prachum phongsawadan* 65: *Krung Thonburi*, p. 10.
[99] Dai, 'Disguised Defeat,' 156–159.
[100] *Qing shilu*, vol. 18: *Gaozong Chunhuangdi shilu*, pp. 711–712.

Saigon to accompany the expedition. However, Tianci explicitly refused and emphasized that he could handle the operation on his own.[101] He probably wanted to monopolize any fruits of victory for himself. This motivation could serve as an additional reason for his earlier demand for the Cochinchinese soldiers stationed at The Port to depart.

From this point, there appears to have been close coordination between The Port, the Qing, Cochinchina, and Cambodia. A letter later written by the two exiled princes, Chao Chui and Chao Sisang, to the High Government at Batavia on May 3, 1770, mentioned that Tianci held periodic joint consultations with envoys from all three governments. He further established contact with the governor of Chanthaburi, known in the Qing records as Pulan. According to the famous Thai historian Nidhi Eoseewong, this individual most likely took advantage of the disorder to seize power in the province without the approval of the Ayutthaya court. Indeed, the VOC data on trade put Chanthaburi in a separate category from Siam starting from 1764, meaning that it had become autonomous at least three years before the fall of Ayutthaya. Until 1769, when it was last mentioned, a total of twelve junks sailed to Guangzhou. Pulan maintained a calculated and cunning neutrality toward all sides of the conflict, simultaneously negotiating with Tianci, Taksin, and Myanmar. Now, the Qing joined in, with Governor-General Li instructing the envoy Xu Quan to sail onward to Chanthaburi to talk to Pulan after his visit to The Port.[102]

The result of these multilateral consultations was a consensus for Tianci to answer the appeal for aid from Ayutthaya. The chances for success certainly seemed high. After the destruction of the capital, Myanmar exhibited little interest in establishing durable control over Siam. Hsinbyushin left behind a small contingent in Ayutthaya, along with scattered garrisons in a few strategic locations. He appointed a puppet governor based at Thonburi, farther down the west bank of the Chaophraya River, lying opposite Bangkok along the coast. Then, Hsinbyushin withdrew most of the Myanmar troops to deal with the Qing onslaught. A power vacuum ensued, as autonomous local power-holders, such as Pulan and many of the other governors along the Gulf of Siam littoral provinces, emerged in their place and scrambled for territory and influence.[103] Mo Tianci was confident that he could use at least

---

[101] Vũ, *Gia phả*, p. 109.
[102] ANRI, K66a: 3574a, p. 300; *Qing shilu*, vol. 18: *Gaozong Chunhuangdi shilu*, pp. 711–712; *Prachum phongsawadan* 65: *Krung Thonburi*, p. 10; Eoseewong, *Wang Phaendin*, pp. 133–134.
[103] Baker and Phongpaichit, *History of Ayutthaya*, pp. 262–263; Pombejra, 'Chinese in Siam,' p. 346.

one of the Ayutthaya princes in his custody to rally these fragmented forces and unite Siam under his overall protection.

Tianci fired the opening salvo of the expedition with an attack on Koh Kong, the base of the Chaozhou pirate Huo Ran and his band. During the engagement, crack forces from The Port fired harquebuses at the ships of the enemy, causing them to scatter. Huo jumped overboard and tried to get away, armed with only a short knife. But before he could swim to shore, he was surrounded and stabbed to death by Tianci's soldiers. They cut off his head and presented it in public, while the corpse submerged into the sea. After his defeat, The Port's military extended its control into the islands and coastal areas west of Kampong Som. Elite forces under Chen Dali, the grand nephew of the famed commander Chen Shangchuan, occupied Trat and established a base for regular patrols on the nearby seas. His forces could now link up with the autonomous governors on the Siamese side of the gulf and control the kingdom's lucrative trade flows in a manner favorable to The Port (see Figure 6.2).[104]

As Siam degenerated into disorder, it was forced to readjust or abandon its areas of comparative advantage in the maritime East Asian and global trading system. In an ironic twist of fate, Siam, which was once a leading exporter of rice, transformed overnight into an importer. Warfare had laid waste to wide swathes of the country, including some of its most productive paddy fields and labor power. Moreover, the occupation and destruction of Ayutthaya in 1767, along with the civil war that ensued, incapacitated ports in the Chaophraya plain, such as Bangkok. As a result, the price of rice was dear in Siam.[105]

The acute shortage of grain is reflected in the dramatic expansion of trade between Siam and Batavia. In 1769, an unprecedented 18 vessels headed for Siam. They imported 475 kojang (around 855,000 kg) of rice from Batavia. In 1770, the number had increased to a staggering 34, more than any year on record. The ships carried 682.5 kojang (1,228,500 kg) of rice and almost nothing else. To balance out the voracious grain imports, Siam apparently engaged in a frenzied selling of its natural resources. For instance, in 1770, 12 ships from there sent 4,912 piculs (294,720 kg) of sappanwood to Batavia, compared to a few hundred to a thousand in most years. On board these vessels were also thirty-five slaves, who were probably taken as prisoners of war.[106] The trafficking of

---

[104] Trịnh, *Thông chí*, pp. 312–313; Nguyễn Dynasty, *Thực lục*, vol. 1, p. 153.
[105] Li Tana and Van Dyke, 'Canton,' p. 23; Pombejra, 'Chinese in Siam,' p. 344.
[106] ANRI, K66a: 2597, pp. 199–201, 220–227.

Figure 6.2 Wat Buppharam, a Theravada Buddhist temple in Trat, dates to the seventeenth century. A mural on one of the walls of its main chapel, although of unknown provenance, perfectly highlights the complex backgrounds and affiliations of Chinese in the water world, including The Port, which briefly occupied Trat. The warriors, all dressed in Ming garb, on the left and the woman on the right are likely Chinese creoles, and they formed the core of the soldiers and residents of The Port. The individual who is smoking a pipe on the right is obviously dressed in Manchu clothing. He fits the profile of a Qing merchant or sojourner.
Photograph by author.

humans proved to be extraordinary for Siam, where labor was scarce, and warfare revolved around the capture and possession of manpower.[107]

Along with Batavia, The Port and its area of authority replaced Siam as the leading supplier of rice in the region. The tables were turned in the competition to export grain to China. There was no longer any record of ships sailing from Siam to Guangzhou, the last time being the 2,000

[107] Rungswadisab, 'War and Trade,' pp. 8–9.

234   The Business of Business

Figure 6.2 (cont.)

piculs (120,000 kg) in 1763. Voyages to Xiamen continued in 1767, when 8,160 piculs (489,600 kg) were exported. It was a major decline from the previous decade when exports of over 10,000 piculs (600,000 kg) were the norm. Moreover, this only occurred after a four-year hiatus and was followed by a much longer gap of seven years when no grain shipments were documented. In 1774, the next shipment to Xiamen had declined to 3,100 piculs (186,000 kg). In contrast, the Dutch recorded 2,000 piculs (120,000 kg) of rice to Guangzhou from Bassac in 1767 and 4,000 piculs (240,000 kg) from The Port in 1770.[108] The shipments to Xiamen must have been much larger, but no documentation has yet been found.

Another destination for rice shipments was obviously Siam itself. Lauw Wo, who was accused of piracy, apparently followed a route that maximized his ability to profit from both The Port's area of authority and Batavia. His vessel had first traveled to Siam, where it unloaded its cargo

[108] Lin, 'Taiguo jinkou dami,' pp. 17, 25–26; Van Dyke, *Merchants*, vol. 1, Appendix 4C–4H, pp. 269–281.

of rice from the Mekong Delta and Cambodia. Carrying just a bit of the leftover grain and water for subsistence, the ship's next intended destination was Batavia. There, Lauw Wo and his crew would procure more rice and sell it in Siam, before returning to The Port and starting the entire process over again.[109]

Since Siam's natural resource endowment largely overlapped with The Port's area of authority, it had to pay steep prices for rice in silver. In 1768, for instance, Taksin procured grain from The Port's vessels at three to five baht of silver per *thang* (20 L), considered by contemporary records to be an exorbitant rate.[110] By 1770, even small-time local merchants such as Oeij Tshing and others who consigned their products on his ship at Black Water carried twenty baht with them.[111] Unsurprisingly, a massive outflow of specie from Siam resulted and enhanced The Port's silver surplus and its position as a center of finance.

Since Mo Tianci's accession to power in 1735 to the 1760s, The Port witnessed a dramatic growth in its economic functions and influence. Its role as a transit point between the Qing, Tokugawa Japan, and Southeast Asia, and between mainland and island Southeast Asia became enhanced and solidified. Rice, tin, and other natural resources flowed northward, while labor and its associated consumption demands went in the other direction. Fundamentally, The Port's area of authority serviced the "Chinese century" in maritime East Asia as an intermediary for the creation of an offshore Chinese economy. The key difference of this Chinese economy compared to its domestic counterpart was the scarcer and more expensive cost of labor, which boosted spending power. The Port's transshipment functions resulted in resource relief for China's commercialized core areas and greater markets and profit margins for its products. The Port further supported the offshoring with crucial financial functions, such as becoming a center for coin-casting and the accumulation and relatively free movement of capital.

Mo Tianci owed his success to his sound policies and a cautious sensitivity to changes in the larger geopolitical environment, including loopholes in the VOC monopoly, the emergence of the Guangzhou system, and Siam's descent into chaos. Measuring his achievements according to Douglass North's definition of innovations that can lower transaction costs, Tianci removed barriers to the flow of capital and information, while spreading out the risks.[112] His policy of calculated

---

[109] ANRI, K66a: 3574b, p. 109.
[110] Li Tana, 'Cochinchinese Coin Casting,' in Taglicozzo and Chang, *Chinese Circulations*, pp. 138, 140.
[111] ANRI, K66a: 3574b, pp. 115–117.   [112] North, Institutions, p. 125.

ambiguity in diplomacy allowed him to remain on friendly terms with East Asian and European state and non-state actors. By espousing tolerance for ethnic and religious groups, he provided a welcoming climate for ships from all countries to trade at his shores. The Port thereby became a haven where capital could congregate in relative security from the warfare and exactions that characterized its neighbors. However, he subsequently abandoned his customary prudence and made bold gambles to dominate, first, the throne of Siam and then of Cochinchina, repeating what he successfully did with Cambodia. He failed spectacularly, and he and his realm would never fully recover from the ensuing disasters.

7   Clash of the Titans

> We have served as ministers of the Southern Heaven for two generations. My heartfelt resolution, as steadfast as iron, will not change even if I die. How can I conspire against Heaven with you bandits![1]
>
> —Mo Tianci to Tây Sơn envoy, 1777

> I made a compact with the masses to eliminate the tyrant so that the people can live. We will select someone with virtue from our race and uphold him in restoring our country. How can we depend upon those Chinamen to raise and nurture us?[2]
>
> —Khun Kaew to Phraya San, 1782

The end of the 1760s ushered in a period of profound transition in mainland Southeast Asia. As Victor Lieberman argues, economic growth and the expansion of overseas trade stimulated population growth and migration to the peripheries. The influx of newcomers, the expansion of their operations, and intense competition for products and markets, severely strained the capacity of existing political and social hierarchies in each of the established mainland Southeast Asian states. Severe chaos and even wholesale collapse occurred in Myanmar, Siam, Vietnam, and Cambodia. On the other hand, the disruptions removed many barriers for interactions across class and geographic divisions inside these countries. With the continued spread and infiltration of neo-Confucianism in Vietnam and Theravada Buddhism elsewhere beneath the elite level and the rise in literacy, there was a broader homogenization of ethnic characteristics, political and institutional allegiances, and popular culture. Ambitious rulers built upon these elements in forging more powerful, consolidated states characterized by clearer identities and boundaries.[3]

The state-building process had occurred earlier in a parallel manner in other parts of Eurasia, including the Qing and Tokugawa Japan. In Southeast Asia, it heralded the decline of the cosmopolitan "Age of

---

[1] Vũ, *Gia phả*, p. 134. [2] Vũ, *Gia phả*, p. 146.
[3] Lieberman, *Strange Parallels*, vol. 1, pp. 41–43, 299–337, 406–456.

Commerce."[4] The Port, which had thrived off of its ambiguity and the smooth functioning of translocal networks, faced threats from growing nativism among its multiethnic constituency and the emergence of territorially focused regimes in its neighborhood. Ironically, the success of ambitious state-builders in mainland Southeast Asia during the 1770s depended, in large part, upon the support of Chinese mercantile groups such as the Mo. In fact, Tianci himself was presented with several contingent opportunities to dominate the thrones of Siam and Cochinchina. And he nearly succeeded in securing Qing support for his endeavors. But Mo Tianci's efforts ultimately came to naught, and he died tragically as an exile in Siam. Despite his failure, his descendants managed to play on the rivalry between Siam and Vietnam to ensure the survival of The Port as a distinct entity well beyond its prime.

The Struggle for Siam

Emboldened by his prior successes, Tianci decided to take advantage of the power vacuum in Siam to make a bold move into its heartland. He evidently hoped to dominate the fertile rice-producing hinterlands and control the distribution of grain by seizing the ports along the entire littoral of the Gulf of Siam. He believed that the coastal governors, including Pulan at Chanthaburi, would eagerly respond to his call, especially with the two Ayutthaya princes at his side. Sometime in the latter half of 1767, Tianci sent a fleet consisting of over a hundred ships, which he placed under his commander-in-chief, Xu Youyong. The ships also carried a substantial quantity of food and provisions to recruit any loyalists of the Ayutthaya court against Myanmar that the troops could find. However, at the mouth of the Chaophraya River near Bangkok, the fleet endured a heavy attack from the Myanmar garrison. A typhoon wreaked additional devastation. Xu was forced to retreat after ten days and losing forty of his ships. He and his fleet retired to Bang Pla Soi, where he soon passed away from illness. The ships then withdrew completely to The Port. The soldiers brought back Xu's body, which was interred on the slopes of Screen Mountain during the autumn.[5]

Around this time, Tianci started to take notice of Taksin, who was achieving significant success in the Siamese water world. Through native place ties, Taksin acquired the allegiance of the Chaozhou community and nobility of the coastal provinces, especially after he took control over

---

[4] Sakurai, 'Chinese Pioneers,' pp. 35–36.
[5] Vũ, *Gia phả*, p. 112; *Prachum phongsawadan* 65: *Krung Thonburi*, p. 11; Phạm Đức Mạnh, 'Cổ mộ,' p. 1301.

the crucial port of Bang Pla Soi. Initially, he and Tianci treated each other with great respect and cordiality. Taksin may have established contact with Tianci through Xu Youyong, who spent his last days at Bang Pla Soi. In fact, Taksin probably provided refuge to Xu's fleet. After learning about the failed expedition, Taksin dispatched envoys to The Port with a gift of Western cloth and his message, which contained a request to send additional troops against the Myanmar puppet governor at Thonburi. Tianci responded positively with his own presents and a promise to initiate another expedition during the next monsoon season.[6]

Despite the potential for cooperation, he concurrently viewed Taksin's rapid expansion along the Gulf of Siam littoral with increasing concern. In June 1767, Taksin attacked and captured Chanthaburi, forcing the governor, Pulan, to flee to The Port. Shortly afterward, his forces occupied Trat after a minor skirmish in the harbor with some armed Chinese junks. They were probably a group of local pirate-merchants, since the remnants of Xu Youyong's fleet had earlier withdrawn from the area after the debacle outside Bangkok. Taksin avoided venturing further into The Port's sphere of influence and thereby directly confronting Tianci. Instead, Taksin went the opposite direction. In October, he captured Thonburi and expelled its Myanmar-appointed puppet governor. A month later, he crushed the Myanmar forces around Ayutthaya and seized the royal capital itself. In December, he proclaimed himself king and set out to unify the entire country. In this indirect manner, he became a formidable obstacle to Tianci's own ambitions.[7]

On Taksin's part, he perceived Tianci's continued asylum for the Ayutthaya princes and the Chanthaburi governor as grave threats to his legitimacy. Accordingly, he sent another letter to The Port demanding the repatriation of Chao Chui and Chao Sisang to Siam. In exchange, he offered generous territorial concessions and promised to pay a regular tribute. As a preview for what he could provide, he sent along two Western cannons, which he had acquired from the Dutch, as gifts. Tianci had a shortage of these heavy arms and highly coveted them. To obtain more, he appeared willing to hand over Chao Sisang, the younger of the two princes, and the one with the lesser claim to the throne. But Chao Sisang refused to become a diplomatic pawn. At this critical juncture, he secretly slipped away one night to Earthen Mount and sought refuge at the Catholic seminary. The director, Pierre-Joseph-Georges Pigneau de

---

[6] *Prachum phongsawadan* 65: *Krung Thonburi*, p. 12.
[7] *Qing shilu*, vol. 18: *Gaozong Chunhuangdi shilu*, pp. 711–712; Rungswadisab, 'War and Trade,' p. 80; Pombejra, 'Chinese in Siam,' pp. 347–348; *Prachum phongsawadan* 65: *Krung Thonburi*, pp. 14–21; Baker and Phongpaichit, *History of Ayutthaya*, p. 263.

Béhaine (1741–1799), hoping to avoid political entanglements, refused to extend assistance. The prince then trekked farther along the coast until he sneaked into a boat docked along the shore and fled to Phnom Penh, where he came under the protection of King Ang Tan.[8]

Chao Sisang's flight deprived Tianci of a useful bargaining chip that could offer a mutually beneficial settlement with Taksin. As a sign of just how devastating this loss was to him, Tianci took out his anger at Pigneau and the main faculty of the seminary. He ordered their arrest in January 1768 and subjected them to harsh interrogation. He then clamped them in prison, only to release them several weeks later when one of the missionaries offered to travel to Phnom Penh and persuade Chao Sisang in person to return. Chao Sisang predictably refused, and the priests were again clamped into jail, this time with heavy cangues placed around their necks. As Tianci's fury subsided, he ordered their release and allowed them to return to the seminary in February. His actions against the clerics could not salvage his relationship with Taksin, who issued ever more stringent calls for Chao Sisang to be delivered to him, dead or alive. When Tianci could not deliver anything, Taksin likely viewed him as dishonest and treacherous, especially given his influence over the Cambodian king.[9] Combined with their deeper, structural competition for territory, commercial networks, and manpower along the gulf, their relations grew openly hostile.

The Qing envoy Xu Quan arrived at The Port toward the end of 1767. Tianci used this opportunity to acquaint Xu with the political situation and advance his personal agenda of placing one of the Ayutthaya princes on the throne. Taksin, knowing this consultation would harm his interests, preemptively dispatched his own envoy, a fellow Chaozhouese, to Guangzhou with a formal petition for investiture as king of Siam. The Qianlong Emperor rejected his request. In instructions to Li Shiyao, the governor-general of Guangdong and Guangxi, the emperor labeled Taksin "a lowlife from China who floated on the seas and became a barbarian chieftain abroad."[10] Besides the questionable character of his ascent to power, Taksin's control over Siam was incomplete. The capital and the political and economic heartland belonged to him, and he had proclaimed himself king. But four other warlords had carved out power bases of their own and claimed royal prerogatives in the wake of Ayutthaya's fall.[11]

---

[8] Launay, *Siam*, vol. 2, pp. 245–246.   [9] Launay, *Siam*, vol. 2, pp. 246–254.
[10] *Qing shilu*, vol. 18: *Gaozong Chunhuangdi shilu*, p. 1069.
[11] Baker and Phongpaichit, *History of Ayutthaya*, p. 262; Pombejra, 'Chinese in Siam,' p. 346.

The Qianlong Emperor issued a harsh pronouncement to Taksin that reproached him for taking "advantage of the chaos to violently establish yourself. You wildly sought enfeoffment and you appropriated the title of king. You violated your place and your status, ignored propriety, and turned your back on grace. What can be more evil than this?" By brashly requesting investiture while eligible heirs of the ruling house were still alive, he had willingly become a usurper. As someone who "was originally a commoner from China, you must be familiar with the principles of righteousness." The emperor was insinuating that because of his Chinese origins, he should have known better compared to the other ignorant "barbarians" around him, making his actions even more unjust and unforgivable. The emperor implored Taksin to rally the other warlords under the banner of Chao Chui and Chao Sisang.[12] After all, restoring the two princes to their rightful status conformed to Confucian standards of loyalty and righteousness.

In another pronouncement, the Qianlong Emperor heaped praise upon Mo Tianci. Although situated "in a remote maritime corner, your heart desires to be transformed" by Chinese values. Tianci also "understands propriety and righteousness, and this is a praiseworthy quality." The emperor ordered bolts of silk to be given to him as a sign of the imperial favor.[13] It was a diplomatic triumph for Mo Tianci. He now had the moral authority to wage war against not only the Myanmar invaders but also opportunistic usurpers such as Taksin, who was becoming his main adversary. On Taksin's part, the questions about his ethnicity, his humble class origins, and the legitimacy of his rule, not only from the Qing but also from other states and even his own subjects, would plague him for the rest of his life. In addition to enemies on the battlefield, this constant skepticism of his identity placed severe mental strains upon him and contributed to extreme behavior and overreaction toward the slightest offense. The situation was bound to rapidly escalate between Tianci and Taksin to the point of no return.

Cooperation between the Qing and The Port subsequently deepened. In one letter to Governor-General Li, Tianci flatteringly referred to the Qing as the "Celestial Dynasty" (*tianchao*) and the Qianlong Emperor as the "Great Emperor" (*dahuangdi*). Mention of these and any other terms related to the court were always shifted to begin a new line and placed at least one character above the standard margins of the paper. Within the Sinosphere, this literary device, known as "raising the head" (*taitou*), was a typical format used by tributary vassals in addressing the Son of

---

[12] J. K. Chin, 'King Taksin and China,' pp. 175–177.
[13] *Qing shilu*, vol. 18: *Gaozong Chunhuangdi shilu*, p. 1071.

Heaven. The content of his correspondences also gushed with praise. The "Celestial Dynasty," he wrote in one line, "takes pity on its tributary vassals and soothes and pacifies the outer lands. Even parents do not treat their offspring so well." Referring to himself as "a humble garrison commander (*bizhen*) tucked away in a remote seacoast," Tianci "sincerely desires to submit and be transformed" by Chinese civilization (see Figure 4.2 for another example of a similarly worded letter).[14]

There was certainly a genuine element in these expressions, reflecting admiration and pride at the power and influence wielded by his ancestral land abroad. Tianci's genealogical biography, which presents a more personal side to him, records him as commenting that the Qianlong Emperor possessed the "virtue to transform others" according to civilized values.[15] However, perhaps as a subtle gesture of his principled defiance of Manchu rule, he never used the Qianlong reign name in his correspondences to the court and its officials. Instead, he preferred the ambiguous sexagenary cycle of years or combined them with *tianyun*, an adaptation of the Cambodian or Siamese dating systems. Some of the letters did not contain any date.[16]

His flattering remarks also had the more practical purpose of persuading the Qing to intervene in some manner in mainland Southeast Asia. Throughout 1768, he dispatched ships to Guangzhou with letters containing detailed intelligence on Myanmar and Siam. Attached were maps of mainland Southeast Asia that he had commissioned based upon extensive consultations with Siamese exiles at The Port and Cambodian officials. He specially checked them against Dutch maps and geographical records, probably imported from Batavia, for accuracy.[17]

The Qianlong Emperor carefully read over his letters and maps and seriously considered the possibility of an alliance. The Manchu banner forces had, not long ago, in late 1767, suffered a massive debacle outside of the Myanmar capital of Inwa. Their commander had not bothered to study local conditions and paid a heavy price for his ignorance and overconfidence. Surprise attacks from Myanmar forces and devastating

---

[14] Grand Council Archives, Qianlong Reign, 010189: Mo Shilin, n. p. For more on the conventions of communications between tributary kings and the Chinese emperor, see Wang Yuanchong, *Remaking*, p. 40. Wang refers specifically to Korea, but since it was the premier Qing tributary kingdom, it can serve as a model for how Sinosphere overlord-vassal relations worked.

[15] Vũ, *Gia phả*, p. 129.

[16] See, for instance, Grand Council Archives, Qianlong Reign, 010189: Mo Shilin, n. p.; Grand Council Archives, Qianlong Reign, 013221: Mo Shilin.

[17] Grand Council Archives, Qianlong Reign, 013988: Li Shiyao; Grand Council Archives, Qianlong Reign, 014670: *Chaxun Guangdong zhi Xianluo*; *Qing shilu*, vol. 18: *Gaozong Chunhuangdi shilu*, p. 1070.

tropical diseases decimated the ranks of the Manchu bannermen. Only a few dozen out of an original expeditionary army of 10,000 soldiers made it back to Yunnan. Although shaken by the defeat, the Qianlong Emperor decided to organize another, larger campaign against Myanmar. In April 1768, he appointed three top generals, seasoned veterans of the frontier wars against the Zunghars in Xinjiang and the Tibetan tribes of western Sichuan, to lead the banner forces.[18]

The emperor conceived of the idea of synchronizing his campaign with Tianci's own designs on Siam. Since Xu Quan, the envoy previously dispatched to The Port, had died at sea from illness on his way back to Guangzhou, Qianlong ordered Governor-General Li to appoint another patrolling admiral, Zheng Rui, to take his place. In late 1768, Zheng boarded a merchant ship bound for The Port. After his arrival, he and Tianci met frequently.[19] Apparently, the two of them were jointly planning an expedition on Siam.

The timing was opportune. Earlier in 1768, Taksin had taken the northeastern region of Khorat, the independent base of an Ayutthaya prince who was an uncle of Chao Chui and Chao Sisang. Taksin had captured and executed him. His death removed the only surviving senior member in the line of succession before the two exiled princes and cleared the way for Tianci to fully support the elder brother, Chao Chui, as the new ruler. Tianci acquired an additional pretext in early 1769, when Taksin invaded Cambodia after King Ang Tan rejected his demand for recognition as overlord and turned away his envoys. Taksin attempted to have his troops escort the monarch's archnemesis, Ream Reachea, who resided in exile in Siam at the time, back to Oudong and forcibly assume the throne. Tianci, as viceroy and Ang Tan's adoptive father, could now claim to chastise Taksin on behalf of the rightful king.[20]

The proposed expedition received the blessing of the Qianlong Emperor. After Zheng Rui returned to Guangzhou in July 1769 and reported the outcome of his discussions at The Port, Governor-General Li promptly dispatched Patrolling Admiral Cai Han.[21] In August, Cai set out, carrying with him Li's instruction, issued in the name of the emperor, that authorized Mo Tianci to lead troops against Taksin to punish him for usurping the throne and killing a royal relative. The Qianlong Emperor further called upon the provinces along the Gulf of

---

[18] Dai, 'Disguised Defeat,' pp. 161–163.
[19] *Qing shilu*, vol. 18: *Gaozong Chunhuangdi shilu*, pp. 1069, 1181.
[20] *Prachum phongsawadan* 65: *Krung Thonburi*, pp. 26–27; Eng, *Mahaboros khmer*, vol. 6, pp. 12–14.
[21] Grand Council Archives, Qianlong Reign, 012083: Li Shiyao, n. p.

Siam littoral to rise up and uphold the legitimate princes in exile. He went on to announce his intention to chastise Myanmar. He ordered the Siamese provinces and the rulers of neighboring polities to guard against any attempts by Myanmar units to infiltrate and forge bases of resistance on their territories.[22]

However, Cai did not arrive at The Port until March 1770, a full six months after his departure from Guangzhou and much longer than the standard two or three months for the journey. As a later investigation revealed, he was so scared of the sea that he ordered his junk to stay as close to shore as possible. Whenever a strong wind started to blow and the waves started to feel rough, the ship would dock, and he and his crew would disembark and stay on land for prolonged periods of time. More seriously, Cai arrived at The Port too late for Li Shiyao's official notice to make a decisive impact.[23]

After the departure of Zheng Rui from The Port in April 1769, Mo Tianci prepared a force consisting of 50,000 soldiers and sailors. An additional 10,000 Khmer were mobilized with the coordination of Oknha Reachea Setthi Chov at Moat Chrouk and the governors of Treang, Banteay Meas, Kampot, and Kampong Som. The war junks that Tianci assembled were so numerous that they stretched out for over five kilometers. It was the largest mobilization that he had ever carried out. Chen Dali, head of the Victorious Naval Company, led the campaign, replacing the deceased Xu Youyong. He brought along Prince Chao Chui. Tianci and Zheng Rui had successfully secured promises from nine Siamese provincial governors to contribute their forces toward the restoration of the Ayutthaya court. At first, everything went according to plan. Chen Dali attacked and seized Chanthaburi, routing the 3,000 troops sent by Taksin to defend the city and killing their commander. Then, to Dali's great dismay, none of those who had earlier pledged their support came to greet his troops, nor did they surrender their positions despite the presence of the legitimate prince, Chao Chui.[24]

Dinh's genealogical biography of the Mo clan ascribed this frosty reception to cowardice and fear on the part of the Siamese elites when faced with Taksin's ruthlessness.[25] There is some truth to this

---

[22] Grand Council Archives, Qianlong Reign, 010253: Li Shiyao, n. p.
[23] Grand Council Archives, Qianlong Reign, 012083: Li Shiyao, n. p.; Grand Council Archives, Qianlong Reign, 012446: Li Shiyao, n. p.; *Qing shilu*, vol. 18: *Gaozong Chunhuangdi shilu*, p. 1181.
[24] *Qing shilu*, vol. 19: *Gaozong Chunhuangdi shilu*, pp. 217–218; Vũ, *Gia phả*, pp. 112–113; Eng, *Mahaboros khmer*, vol. 6, p. 14; Grand Council Archives, Qianlong Reign, 010253: Li Shiyao, n. p.
[25] Vũ, *Gia phả*, pp. 113–114.

explanation. As Nidhi Eoseewong argues, Taksin placed his trusted inner circle of mostly Chaozhouese merchants and military men in charge of his recently conquered territories in the north and east of the country. These areas contained a substantial source of revenues and manpower that Taksin could draw upon to overpower and ensure compliance from the nobility in the old Ayutthaya core zone.[26] But this narrative of brute intimidation, like the Qianlong Emperor's denunciation of him as a usurper, was a Confucian view. Lorraine Gesick shows that Taksin worked within the Theravada tradition by convincing the fence-sitting governors that he possessed the merit accumulated from previous reincarnations to assume the role of a righteous and upright monarch (*dhammaraja*), whose task was to protect and spread the laws of Buddha. In contrast, the heirs of Ayutthaya had lost this position because of weakness and corruption.[27] Taksin's recent victories and the submission of new territories as tributary vassals served as proof of his charisma.

Meanwhile, troops from The Port, although numerous, mostly consisted of newly conscripted multiethnic recruits. Coordination between the units was poor. Out of fear of sustaining heavy losses, Chen Dali did not launch any organized offensives on the other, more heavily fortified cities and installations that stood between them and Bangkok. After three months in Chanthaburi, epidemics, a product of the unsanitary environment caused by the breakdown of social order in the wake of the Myanmar invasion, plagued his base. The disease soon decimated his ranks, with over a hundred soldiers dying each day. Dali himself grew seriously ill and eventually succumbed. Unable to bear the losses any longer, Mo Tianci ordered a withdrawal. Chanthaburi was plundered and completely evacuated. The Port's troops carried away 5,000 families when they departed. At this point, Taksin arrived with reinforcements and aggressively pursued them, attacking and inflicting more casualties upon their ranks.[28]

Only 10,000 out of an original 50,000 soldiers returned. In mainland Southeast Asia, where political and economic survival depended upon the possession of large reserves of manpower, the heavy losses severely affected The Port's revenues and productivity. The 5,000 abducted families compensated to a certain extent. Still, the campaign resulted in the obliteration of entire companies, which served as the cornerstone for the militarized bureaucracy. The effect was felt almost immediately,

---

[26] Eoseewong, *Karn Muang Thai*, pp. 141–149.
[27] Gesick, 'Kingship,' pp. 47–57, 103–105.
[28] Grand Council Archives, Qianlong Reign, 012083: Li Shiyao, n. p.; Vũ, *Gia phả*, pp. 113–115; Eng, *Mahaboros khmer*, vol. 6, p. 14.

when Tianci had to pull back much of his remaining troops to defend The Port's center. He could no longer secure large parts of its hinterlands. Fortunately for him, Taksin, whose forces had just been repulsed by Ang Tan in western Cambodia and who was now busily planning a new, major campaign against the autonomous southern vassal state of Nakhon Si Thammarat, decided to turn back.[29]

The envoy Cai Han arrived with more unwelcome news. Besides his delivering a long overdue imperially sanctioned proclamation from Li Shiyao that could no longer make any difference on the ground, the much-anticipated Qing offensive against Myanmar had stalled into a bloody stalemate south of Bhamo, close to the Yunnan border. Again, Manchu banner forces succumbed to tropical diseases by the thousands. At the start of 1770, a truce was finally declared. A relative calm returned to the Qing-Myanmar border, with both sides no longer in any mood to continue the fighting.[30]

Cosmopolitanism Challenged

The Myanmar destruction of Ayutthaya and Taksin's emergence appeared to have both reflected and facilitated a trend of nativism and ethnic exclusivity that had been building on the popular level across mainland Southeast Asia. Successful state-builders would harness these sentiments to forge more consolidated political units. Of course, Lieberman correctly emphasizes, these kingdoms still differed from the modern nation-state, since they remained "hierarchic, anti-entropic, obsessed with innumerable particularities of status and privilege determined by one's distance from the sovereign." Despite the vertical approach to governance, they nonetheless provided, through the intensification of trade and the spread of religious and ethical systems, the domestic horizontal linkages necessary for greater cultural uniformity, and clearer boundaries between states and ethnic groups.[31]

Perhaps the first stirrings of this nativist sentiment could be found among the Khmer, as seen in their periodic massacres of Viet migrants, often with royal encouragement, since the late seventeenth century. Yet, King Ang Tan went beyond these occasional xenophobic outbursts, targeted specifically at the Viet, to articulate a more comprehensive sense

---

[29] Vũ, *Gia phả*, p. 115.
[30] Grand Council Archives, Qianlong Reign, 012083: Li Shiyao, n. p.; Grand Council Archives, Qianlong Reign, 012446: Li Shiyao, n. p.; Dai, 'Disguised Defeat,' pp. 166–170.
[31] Lieberman, *Strange Parallels*, vol. 1, pp. 41–44.

of ethnic separateness. In late 1768, when Taksin demanded that he submit to Siam as a vassal, the king replied, "I cannot resolve to place myself on the foot of equality with a man who, whatever his own value, was, after all, the product of a union between a Chinese merchant and a Siamese commoner." Considerations of class and hierarchy certainly came into play. Although Taksin came from humbler origins than the royal family of Ayutthaya, Ang Tan was concurrently prejudiced against him on ethnic grounds. He made this point clear when he told Taksin's envoys that "the friendly relations between Siam and Cambodia have stopped from the moment a foreign adventurer puts himself on the throne of the ancient kings of your country." These insults infuriated Taksin and became a primary factor behind his invasion in 1769. Ang Tan successfully beat back his commanders in battles around Angkor, close to the Siamese border.[32]

The king's ire against the Chinese did not stop with Taksin. The close bond that formerly existed between Ang Tan and his ally and adopted father, Mo Tianci, also appeared to have dissipated. Although the records do not reveal much information about their split, part of the reason may have to do with Ang Tan's disappointment at the outcome of the expedition to Siam. He no longer felt that Tianci could guarantee his security. In the Theravada worldview, Tianci had fallen short on merit and charisma. But perhaps like the attitude toward Taksin, the Cambodian king also came to detest what he perceived to be foreign interference in his own country. Ang Tan's opposition may have explained why Tianci could not secure the return of Chao Sisang to The Port. In fact, at some point after the failed invasion of Siam, Ang Tan replaced Tianci with a new Khmer viceroy related by blood to the royal household.[33]

Meanwhile, tensions between Tianci and Taksin continued to escalate. Sakurai characterizes their rivalry in terms of a struggle between the dialect groups and clan networks of Leizhou/Hainan and Chaozhou.[34] Puangthong Rungswadisab places the emphasis more on competition for natural resource exports and control over the maritime routes along the Gulf of Siam.[35] Both perspectives are correct, but there appears to be an additional, deeper layer of animosity.

---

[32] Nguyễn Dynasty, *Thực lục*, vol. 1, p. 154; Trịnh, *Thông chí*, p. 314; Leclère, *Histoire de Cambodge*, p. 386; Moura, *Royaume du Cambodge*, vol. 1, pp. 86–87; Eng, *Mahaboros khmer*, vol. 6, pp. 12–13; Hán-Nôm A. 832: Phạm, *Cao Man ki lược*, n. p.

[33] Nguyễn Dynasty, *Thực lục*, vol. 1, p. 154; Trịnh, *Thông chí*, p. 314; Eng, *Mahaboros khmer*, vol. 6, p. 14; Hán-Nôm A. 832: Phạm, *Cao Man ki lược*, n. p.

[34] Sakurai, 'Chinese Pioneers,' p. 45.   [35] Rungswadisab, 'War and Trade,' pp. 81–82.

The primary records reveal much antagonism between Chinese creoles of the water world and recent Qing immigrants, who were less acclimated to local society and culturally "purer." Most of the newcomers hailed from Chaozhou, and they not only migrated in large waves to Siam, but also appeared to constitute the dominant Qing group in The Port. They had good reasons to support Taksin, a Chaozhou compatriot. The division was not absolute, however. Some Chinese creoles also felt predisposed to Taksin. He was himself of mixed parentage and therefore a more ideal overlord than the completely foreign Cochinchinese or Khmer, or someone "tainted" by association like Tianci. These factors probably explain why Taksin was successful in recruiting and maintaining an extensive network of spies from among The Port's residents. One of them worked as a servant in the household of Tianci's younger sister, Jinding, and was able to report on the troop movements of Chen Dali during the failed expedition to Siam.[36]

These nativist Chinese elements capitalized upon Tianci's preoccupation with the campaign and plotted to topple him. A Chaozhou adventurer named Chen Tai, along with a band of armed followers, established a base at White Horse, about thirty kilometers to the northwest of The Port center (see Figure 7.1).[37] He secretly conspired with two members of the Mo clan to stage an uprising. On the afternoon of July 15, 1769, they set fire to the city center as a cover for their actions. Fanned by high winds, the flames engulfed the packed storefronts and religious establishments near the garrison office. Entire blocks were devastated before the fire was put out after midnight. Tianci, who had learned of the plot, took advantage of the confusion to ambush and exterminate the two rogue clan members and their followers. With the bulk of his forces still engaged in Siam, he depended entirely on Austronesian troops of the Java Company to confront Chen Tai at White Horse.[38] In the end, they defeated Chen and forced him to flee westward to Chanthaburi, where he joined Taksin

---

[36] Vũ, *Gia phả*, pp. 112–113; Pombejra, 'Chinese in Siam,' p. 346; *Prachum phongsawadan 66: Krao prab mueng Phutthaimat*, p. 7.

[37] Sakurai and Kitagawa place the Chen Tai revolt before Mo Tianci's failed expedition against Siam. They see the event as a preemptive attack on the part of Tianci against Tai and a prelude to the subsequent campaign on Siam. See Sakurai and Kitagawa, 'Hà Tiên or Banteay Meas,' pp. 178–183. However, the suppression of Huo Ran's piracy marked an extension of The Port's power into the Siamese water world. Chen Tai, on the other hand, had penetrated deep into Tianci's sphere of influence in one of the provinces given to him as viceroy. Moreover, Dinh's clan genealogy states that he launched his revolt at a time when the troops in Siam had not yet returned. See Vũ, *Gia phả*, p. 115.

[38] For the origin of the name of White Horse, refer to the caption of Figure 7.1 and 'Kep Travel Guides,' www.tourismcambodia.com/travelguides/provinces/kep.htm.

Figure 7.1 The name of White Horse comes from a Khmer legend of a Cambodian prince who stole a commander's white horse from Angkor and fled to the Gulf of Siam coast. For this reason, the Chinese and Vietnamese call the place, literally, White Horse. In Khmer, it is Kep, which translates into a horse saddle. A statue of a white horse at a roundabout reminds visitors of the namesake. Chen Tai and his band made their base in this area, especially the hills overlooking the beaches of the Gulf of Siam.
Photograph by author.

right about the time when the ruler was giving chase to the retreating expeditionary troops of The Port.[39]

A week later, a new rebellion broke out among Khmer deserters and decommissioned soldiers from the Siam campaign at Kampong Som and Kampot. They soon drew in their Chinese and Austronesian counterparts and assembled a force consisting of 800 troops and fifteen ships. The Khmer and the Austronesians did not necessarily hate the Chinese creoles, but they harbored hostile sentiments toward the Cochinchinese, whom they accused of taking away their land and exacting heavy tribute.

---

[39] Nguyễn Dynasty, *Thực lục*, vol. 1, p. 154; Trịnh, *Thông chí*, pp. 314–315; Vũ, *Gia phả*, p. 115; AMEP, Cochinchine, vol. 745: 'Relation des Franciscains,' pp. 178–179.

Their grievances aside, the rebellion also received the support of King Ang Tan, who was all too willing to weaken Mo Tianci to the point where the ruler could regain the Gulf of Siam coastline. According to the Franciscan missionary Father Julián, Ang Tan secretly dispatched a commander to organize and provide coordination for the insurgents.[40] The multiethnic rebels, unified by a common hatred, went on a rampage in the hinterland Viet settlements. They rounded up and massacred large numbers of people to the point that the streams flowed red with blood. In gruesome public spectacles, they shot their muskets at the bellies of pregnant women in contests to see which one would be the first to accurately hit the fetus inside. The expectant mothers perished from the loss of blood.[41]

The rebels also took aim at Christians, most of them Viet, and the missionaries who exercised leadership over their communities. In October 1769, a band burst into the home of a French missionary at Earthen Mount. When they heard some words of Vietnamese uttered from the mouth of the housekeeper, they cut him down and left behind the cleric to comfort and cry over the poor man as he lay dying. The following month, a hundred armed men arrived at the seminary. After making sure there were no Chinese, they proceeded to massacre any Viet whom they could find on the grounds. They even had designs to kill the instructors at the seminary and mortally wounded one of them, Father Jean-Baptiste Artaud (d. 1769). The director, Pigneau, and the other missionaries fled to The Port center, abandoning the seminary for good. The Franciscan father Martín Robles provided them shelter until December, when they boarded a junk bound for Melaka. From there, they returned to the MEP mission in Puducherry.[42]

At the end of 1769, the insurgents, whose numbers had expanded to 1,300 men, attacked The Port center. A Chinese-Austronesian fleet sailed up Fortress River, while the Khmer reached the city gates from Screen Mountain. The Port's bolstered defenses in the wake of the defeat at Siam repulsed the offensive, and the leaders from each ethnic group were killed in action or captured and executed. Fighting continued outside of The Port into January 1770, as the rebel remnants retreated to Kampot. In the end, the main commander fled back to the Cambodian interior.[43]

---

[40] Nguyễn Dynasty, *Thực lục*, vol. 1, p. 156; Trịnh, *Thông chí*, p. 315; AMEP, Cochinchine, vol. 745: 'Relation des Franciscains,' pp. 180–181.
[41] AMEP, Cochinchine, vol. 745: 'Relation des Franciscains,' pp. 179–180.
[42] Launay, *Siam*, vol. 2, pp. 255–257; Alcobendas, 'Religiosos médico-cirujanos' 6, pp. 339–340.
[43] AMEP, Cochinchine, vol. 745: 'Relation des Franciscains,' pp. 180–181; Nguyễn Dynasty, *Thực lục*, vol. 1, p. 156; Trịnh, *Thông chí*, p. 315.

But the internal disturbances only marked the beginning of Tianci's misfortunes. From 1769 to 1771, both the residents of The Port and European missionaries witnessed strange occurrences that they believed carried ominous portents for the future. A fierce tiger was discovered one day roaming around the garrison office. When soldiers came to capture it, the beast gave out a great yell, jumped outside of the walls, and disappeared without a trace. For fifteen days in August 1769, Father Julián observed a comet with a long tail flying through the sky. Then, on October 18, a solar eclipse occurred at dawn. For ten minutes, everything went black to a degree that he had never experienced before, even at nighttime. On September 29, 1771, a fiery red cross was seen in the southern sky. Two days later, a strong sandstorm swept through the city and blocked the sunlight. Suddenly, the wind stopped and the sand that it carried dropped onto the ground and created the exact same form of a cross. Many superstitious people interpreted these signs to mean that the city would soon fall.[44]

Meanwhile, in Siam, through a series of campaigns in 1769 and 1770, Taksin successfully defeated his remaining warlord rivals at Phitsanulok in the north and Nakhon Si Thammarat in the south. Having achieved complete unification of the country under his unchallenged rule, he could direct his focus entirely upon Cambodia. Not only did it constitute Siam's traditional sphere of influence, but he also wanted to remove the remaining threats to his legitimacy in the form of the two Ayutthaya princes. Then, there was personal vengeance. Taksin wanted to get back at Ang Tan for the insults to his class and ethnic background and place Ream Reachea on the throne instead. He additionally wanted to teach Tianci a lesson for trying to overthrow him.[45]

In 1771, Taksin mobilized 300 large and small vessels and 15,000 Chinese, Siamese, and Western soldiers and sailors. He adopted the classic strategy used by his Ayutthaya predecessors in invading Cambodia. Some of the troops would accompany the contender for the Cambodian throne, Ream Reachea, on land. Taksin would personally travel with the bulk of his forces, consisting of 10,866 men, on sea to attack The Port. The commander of the naval expedition, bearing the title of Phraya Phiphit, was a Chaozhou native named Chen Lian (1741–1782).[46] Sakurai and Kitagawa posit that he may have been the

---

[44] AMEP, Cochinchine, vol. 745: 'Relation des Franciscains,' p. 179; Trịnh, *Thông chí*, pp. 314–316.
[45] *Prachum phongsawadan* 65: *Krung Thonburi*, pp. 29–35.
[46] *Prachum phongsawadan* 65: *Krung Thonburi*, p. 40; *Prachum phongsawadan* 66: *Krao prab mueng Phutthaimat*, pp. 1–5; Eoseewong, *Karn Muang Thai*, pp. 127–128.

same person as Chen Tai, leader of the conspiracy against Mo Tianci in 1769. Indeed, Phraya Phiphit was the title of the governor of Chanthaburi, which would include Trat, where Tai had fled. But all of the primary records mention the two names separately and performing different tasks even when the same event was occurring.[47] Therefore, I avoid a conclusive judgment and follow the lead of the sources in treating them as different individuals.

Before departure, Taksin had Phraya Phiphit issue an ultimatum to Mo Tianci demanding that he recognize Ream Reachea as king of Cambodia and hand over the exiled princes and noblemen of Ayutthaya. Tianci should either come out in person or, if he was too old, send his son Huang to surrender. If they refused or resorted to dilatory tactics, they and their followers would be completely exterminated. Tianci sent a simple reply that he would meet with his officials and consider the matter. However, Taksin received no further response.[48]

Tianci could not give any answer, since he had no options other than making a stand. Besides a severe loss of face, submission would only mean the complete loss of his already shattered influence over The Port's neighboring Cambodian provinces. He frantically tried to secure military aid from any source able to provide it. In early 1770, he sent the Qing envoy Cai Han home with a bizarre plea for the Qianlong Emperor to encourage Myanmar to invade Siam once again and defeat Taksin. The emperor rejected it out of hand as a preposterous idea. And, indeed, he was in no mood to allow Myanmar to accumulate more territory and power than it already had and become an even greater threat on the doorstep of his empire. The level of Qing communications with Mo Tianci subsided after Cai Han's departure. On the contrary, relations with Taksin improved over the 1770s, as the Qing gradually adjusted to the reality that he had become the unchallenged ruler of Siam and took steps to accord him formal recognition.[49]

In 1770, Mo Tianci concurrently sent envoys to Batavia, making official contact with the High Government of the VOC for the first time. He sent along letters from himself, as well as the two Ayutthaya princes, Chao Chui and Chao Sisang. He either translated what they wrote into Chinese or outright assumed their identities without their knowledge. The letters, dated May 3, 1770, requested the VOC to provide weapons or other forms of aid, promising, in the event of victory,

---

[47] Sakurai and Kitagawa, 'Hà Tiên or Banteay Meas,' p. 183.
[48] *Prachum phongsawadan* 65: *Krung Thonburi*, pp. 40–41.
[49] *Qing shilu*, vol. 19: *Gaozong Chunhuangdi shilu*, pp. 587–588; J. K. Chin, 'King Taksin and China,' pp. 180–183.

to restore its factory at Ayutthaya, which it was forced to shut down in 1765 after the onset of the Myanmar invasion. On February 10 of the following year, 1771, Tianci sent three more letters to Batavia. This was the background behind his request to the company to prosecute the case of suspected piracy involving Oeij Tshing and Lauw Wo.[50]

The VOC agreed to provide some armaments. A letter from Governor-General van der Parra, dated June 25, 1771, mentioned that Tianci still had an outstanding balance for his order of four heavy iron cannons with balls. These were not the only weapons that he bought, but the amount of his purchases was certainly dwarfed by Taksin, who paid much more dearly with sappanwood and other natural resources from his kingdom. On July 11 of the same year, a total of seven junk captains from Siam procured a staggering 3,000 pieces of matchlock muskets (*snaphaan*) on behalf of Taksin's minister of finance (Phra Klang). Despite the heavy cost, Taksin got better access to firearms and European mercenaries able to operate them with precision. As the larger consumer, Batavia naturally favored him in deals and pricing.[51]

In addition, Tianci appealed several times to the controller of the five camps in Saigon. However, the earnest petitions were all rebuffed by the commander, Tống Văn Khôi. Not even rich bribes could change his mind. Khôi continued to harbor resentment at being sent away the last time when his forces came to the aid of The Port. Moreover, his inaction may have reflected the will of Trương Phúc Loan, who stood to benefit from sitting on the sidelines and playing Taksin off against Tianci, thereby weakening both of them.[52] King Ang Tan of Cambodia probably harbored a similar attitude. Tianci sent envoys to Oudong to request troops as well, but again received no reply. The loss of his status as viceroy made him no longer able to mobilize forces from the Cambodian provinces in his hinterland.[53]

On November 9, 1771, Taksin attacked The Port. Chen Tai, the former rebel leader who had joined him at Chanthaburi, served as the guide to the main forces. Taksin's men formed three lines of encirclement around the city center. But they ran into fierce resistance from just over a thousand outnumbered yet determined defenders inside the citadel, whose muskets picked apart anyone who tried to approach. An infuriated Taksin gathered 111 men and ordered them to storm the city or face execution if they fell back. To soften up the enemy positions,

---

[50] ANRI, K66a: 3574a, pp. 299–303; 3574b, pp. 108–109.
[51] ANRI, K66a: 3688, pp. 366–368, 447–448.
[52] Nguyễn Dynasty, *Thục lục*, vol. 1, p. 157; Trịnh, *Thông chí*, p. 316; Vũ, *Gia phả*, p. 116.
[53] Eng, *Mahaboros khmer*, vol. 6, p. 16.

one Siamese unit charged up Suzhou Mountain. From this vantage point, its cannons pounded away at the citadel on the other side, inflicting heavy damage. Then, on the night of November 16, a small force infiltrated into the city and blew up the munition depot located at the assistant garrison commander's camp on the Mount of Five Tigers. With the support of this contingent, the bulk of the Siamese troops charged in through a small unwalled portion of the citadel on land, where the Water Station Canal met Fortress River. Tianci's men, having lost their source of ammunition, were killed off in large numbers by the superior firepower of the Siamese.[54]

Tianci's sons, Huang, Tang, and Rong broke through the encirclement with over ten war junks and got away by sea. They rounded the Black Water Peninsula, sailed through the mouth of the Bassac, and reached Cần Thơ, where they came under the protection of the neighboring Longhor camp of Cochinchina. Tianci, who personally joined the fight through the streets and alleyways, escaped by boarding a small vessel that sailed at full speed for Moat Chrouk. Others were not so fortunate. Countless people, including over ten from Tianci's household, perished as they trampled over each other to reach the limited boats for escape or drowned in the sea. The Siamese troops discovered Tianci's two young daughters and concubines and took them captive. They also hunted down the pretender Chao Chui, who tried to escape on a boat. At midnight, The Port fell entirely to the Siamese, and Taksin entered the city.[55]

At Moat Chrouk, Tianci joined up with Oknha Reachea Setthi Chov. Before they had time to organize an effective defense, however, the Siamese under Phraya Phiphit Chen Lian, whom Taksin had dispatched to chase after Tianci, caught up and attacked the town. Chov was killed amid the fighting along with six to seven hundred families. Evidently, the superhuman ability to dodge bullets and knives attributed to him failed to save him this time. Tianci escaped to the Cochinchinese frontier garrison of Tân Châu, where he reported what happened. The garrison troops came to his aid and attacked Phraya Phiphit. They forced him and his men to abandon their ships and flee back to The Port on land. He sustained heavy losses, including 300 killed. After Chen Lian's return, Taksin made The Port once again the seat of Seashore Province

---

[54] *Prachum phongsawadan* 65: *Krung Thonburi*, pp. 40–41; *Prachum phongsawadan* 66: *Krao prab mueng Phutthaimat*, p. 7; Nguyễn Dynasty, *Thực lục*, vol. 1, p. 157; Trịnh, *Thông chí*, pp. 317–318; Vũ, *Gia phả*, pp. 116–118; Eng, *Mahaboros khmer*, vol. 6, p. 17; Hán-Nôm A. 832: Phạm, *Cao Man ki lược*, n. p.

[55] *Prachum phongsawadan* 66: *Krao prab mueng Phutthaimat*, pp. 9–11; Nguyễn Dynasty, *Thực lục*, vol. 1, p. 157; Trịnh, *Thông chí*, p. 318; Vũ, *Gia phả*, p. 119.

and appointed him its governor. Lian's title, K: Preah Reachea Setthi T: **Phraya Racha Setthi**, was exactly the same as his deceased predecessor, Chov.[56]

Having secured The Port, Taksin sailed with 5,000 men and sixty boats to Phnom Penh. He met up with the Siamese land forces marching in from the west, which had encountered little resistance. The combined troops accompanied Ream Reachea to Oudong. King Ang Tan, along with the Ayutthaya prince Chao Sisang, fled to Donay, where they appealed for aid from Cochinchina. The Siamese chased after them, while making plans to continue their offensive until they reached Saigon. Taksin sent another naval detachment to Bassac with a message to the Cambodian governor, Oknha Athivongsa, informing him about The Port's fall and ordering him to submit to Siam, as his province had done in past. The letter further commanded him to capture Tianci's relatives and commanders if he discovered them fleeing in his direction. In exchange, Taksin promised not to harm him. This correspondence provides additional evidence that Bassac formerly came under The Port's authority.[57]

Things were now escalating into a full-scale war between Siam and Cochinchina. The Cochinchinese controller at Saigon launched a three-pronged counterattack against Taksin. Two contingents, in coordination with Tianci's subordinates, struck from Royal Market and Moat Chrouk. However, they were repulsed after encountering heavy resistance. The third Cochinchinese army, which accompanied Ang Tan, met with much greater success. It drove Ream Reachea out of Oudong and Phnom Penh and forced him to withdraw to Kampot. Taksin, on the other hand, retreated to The Port.[58]

Meanwhile, on Trương Phúc Loan's orders, Mo Tianci was brought to Saigon, where, in January 1772, he gave a full written report of his defeat to Huế. He took this opportunity to exact vengeance upon the controller of the five camps, Tống Văn Khôi, for failing to come to his aid and shifted the blame entirely upon the commander's dilatory tactics and inaction in response his earnest appeals. Loan took the side of Tianci and demoted and removed Khôi as controller. His replacement provided

---

[56] Nguyễn Dynasty, *Thực lục*, vol. 1, p. 157; Trịnh, *Thông chí*, p. 318; Vũ, *Gia phả*, p. 119; *Prachum phongsawadan 66: Krao prab mueng Phutthaimat*, p. 12.

[57] *Prachum phongsawadan 66: Krao prab mueng Phutthaimat*, p. 13; Trịnh, *Thông chí*, p. 320; Eng, *Mahaboros khmer*, vol. 6, pp. 17–18.

[58] *Prachum phongsawadan 66: Krao prab mueng Phutthaimat*, pp. 16–17; Nguyễn Dynasty, *Thực lục*, vol. 1, p. 158; Trịnh, *Thông chí*, pp. 321–323; Eng, *Mahaboros khmer*, vol. 6, pp. 18–19.

provisions and armaments, including 3,000 pieces of cannon, to Tianci and escorted him to Cần Thơ, where he joined his sons.[59]

Probably during this mission, fifty Cochinchinese ships confronted the Siamese fleet that was carrying Taksin's message to Bassac, decimating it and causing its crew to scatter. Nonetheless, some of the escaped men managed to deliver Taksin's letter to the governor, Oknha Athivongsa, who promptly sent along five Khmer monks to The Port as envoys. They transmitted his agreement to uphold Ream Reachea as his king and, through him, Siam as the new overlord.[60] But the submission came too late to forestall Tianci's sons from sailing past the governor's territory to establish a new line of defense at Cần Thơ, farther upriver.[61]

At this point, the conflict descended into a stalemate. The Cochinchinese proved unable to dislodge the Siamese from the Gulf of Siam coast. But Phraya Racha Setthi was also having a difficult time administering The Port. Although Taksin gave specific instructions not to harm the mercantile community and allow trade to occur as before, the governor and his officials and soldiers proved to be rapacious and corrupt. They destroyed the city walls and frequently blackmailed, plundered, and killed merchants at will. Constant shortages of food accompanied widespread destitution and impoverishment resulting from warfare and famine. Many residents chose to abandon the city and relocate to Bangkok or Saigon. Even after the chaos ended, the outflow was irreversible. In the subsequent decades, these two places would replace The Port as the main commercial centers of mainland Southeast Asia. Taksin also felt pressure to return to Siam when he learned of a renewed Myanmar threat to its northern areas, which contained the largest concentration of resources and manpower under his direct control.[62]

Yet, both Taksin and Trương Phúc Loan were too proud to break their impasse. As a face-saving measure, they collectively forced Mo Tianci to take the blame for the conflict, which had, after all, started with The Port. In the spring of 1772, after repeated overtures from both parties, Tianci dispatched a clan relative along with tribute gifts to Thonburi to surrender to Taksin. He also handed over the former governor of Chanthaburi, Pulan. Greatly pleased, Taksin accepted the submission and ordered

---

[59] Nguyễn Dynasty, *Thực lục*, vol. 1, pp. 157–158; Trịnh, *Thông chí*, pp. 320–321; Vũ, *Gia phả*, pp. 120–121, 123.
[60] *Prachum phongsawadan* 66: *Krao prab mueng Phutthaimat*, pp. 16, 19–21.
[61] Nguyễn Dynasty, *Thực lục*, vol. 1, p. 158; Trịnh, *Thông chí*, pp. 320–321; Vũ, *Gia phả*, p. 123.
[62] *Prachum phongsawadan* 66: *Krao prab mueng Phutthaimat*, pp. 11–12, 17–18, 22, 25–26, 32–33; Trịnh, *Thông chí*, p. 323; Eoseewong, *Karn Muang Thai*, p. 189.

Phraya Racha Setthi to withdraw from The Port and return it to Tianci's control. Taksin further released Tianci's concubines and little girls. They had been carried off to Siam during the offensive on The Port. Taksin also recognized Ang Tan as the rightful king of Cambodia in a concession to Cochinchina. The deal allowed Taksin to cement formidable gains. He eliminated or neutralized the remaining challengers to his rule. He rounded up and executed Chao Chui and Pulan, along with their retinues. Chao Sisang passed away around this time in exile at Donay. Moreover, the Taksin-backed pretender, Ream Reachea, could maintain an independent power base along the Gulf of Siam, backed by 5,000 Siamese troops.[63] Cambodia was effectively partitioned between the two Southeast Asian powers.

Mo Tianci recovered The Port but at a tremendous cost. The defeat dealt a severe blow to his relationship with Batavia's Chinese community. Lin Houqua fled to Batavia and rejoined his grandfather, Kapitan Lin Jiguang, but the rest of his family went missing. A missive from the VOC to one of Taksin's officials in 1772 specifically requested Siam's assistance in locating them. The war further bankrupted the tax farmers in charge of Batavia's fish market. Unable to acquire any dried fish for the next few years, Jan Taijko and his successor, Ko Kinko, both accumulated heavy debts. They and their families had to repeatedly petition the VOC authorities for extensions and forgiveness of several months at a time of rents and fees owed to the High Government.[64] Moreover, the Siamese invasion destroyed the Franciscan mission and its network of parishes and congregations in The Port. Father Julián del Pilar managed to flee with Tianci to Cần Thơ. Father Martín Robles, on the other hand, was captured by the Siamese. They treated him cordially and sent him to Bangkok. He was released in 1774 and eventually made his way back to Manila.[65]

On the geopolitical level, Tianci failed to become the power behind the throne in Siam and lost his sizable territories in the water world and sphere of influence in Cambodia. Vietnamese narratives portray him being so saddened and humiliated at the tragic outcome that he chose to stay in his new base at Cần Thơ and refused to return to The Port. Instead, his son, Assistant Garrison Commander Huang, took charge of

---

[63] *Prachum phongsawadan* 66: *Krao prab mueng Phutthaimat*, p. 21; Trịnh, *Thông chí*, pp. 322–323; Vũ, *Gia phả*, pp. 123–124; Eng, *Mahaboros khmer*, vol. 6, pp. 19–23.

[64] ANRI, K66a: 1560, pp. 913, 919–922; 1567, p. 97; 1570, p. 564; 1573, pp. 509, 527–529; 3689, pp. 292–293.

[65] Alcobendas, 'Religiosos médico-cirujanos' 5, p. 226; 6, pp. 341–343.

The Port's affairs.[66] Tianci's relocation, Sakurai argues, eroded his autonomy and placed him more firmly under Cochinchinese power.[67]

However, this claim needs to be qualified. The Mekong Delta, centered upon Cần Thơ, came under greater Cochinchinese influence. The Port's core area along the Gulf of Siam littoral submitted to the suzerainty of Siam, a condition for Taksin's withdrawal. The line of division between their respective jurisdictions roughly went through the circuit of Steadfast River, the former Cambodian province of Kramoun Sar. To its east and northeast, up to the shores of the Bassac, this area remained under Mo Tianci's direct control, although he had to pay tribute to Cochinchina. The territory southwest of The Port, from Kampot to Kampong Som, was ceded to Ream Reachea. Mo Huang took charge of The Port proper and a part of Steadfast River, and paid Siam a modest annual tribute of eaglewood, whose aromatic resin was used to make perfumes.[68] Hence, Tianci's decision to send his son to The Port represented a strategy of diversification adapted from the arrangement during the height of his power. This modified dual allegiance allowed the Mo to maintain their autonomy and reestablish their authority over much of their hinterlands at a time of military weakness.

Contesting Cochinchina

One key reason behind Cochinchina's decision to compromise with Siam through Mo Tianci, even at the expense of sharing the role of overlord of him and the king of Cambodia, was because of the outbreak of a massive domestic rebellion. As Li Tana and George Dutton have shown, the continued Nguyễn southward expansion into the Mekong Delta had led to severe overextension, as the costs of consolidation grew increasingly prohibitive. Yet, the delta had also become crucial in terms of the rice and other natural resources necessary to sustain the rest of the state. Trương Phúc Loan's onerous taxation and labor demands and the shortage of imported copper coins led to the widespread debasement of coinage. Then came rampant inflation and corruption, which killed confidence in the economy and the entire political system. The bulk of the exactions fell upon the central-southern provinces around Quy Nhơn, which served as a necessary passageway for the flow of resources from the delta to Huế.[69]

---

[66] Trịnh, *Thông chí*, p. 323; Vũ, *Gia phả*, p. 124. [67] Sakurai, 'Chinese Pioneers,' p. 46.
[68] König, 'Journal,' p. 160.
[69] Dutton, *Tây Sơn Uprising*, pp. 29–36; Li Tana, *Nguyễn Cochinchina*, pp. 139–154.

In 1771, the Tây Sơn rebellion broke out in the central-southern highlands. Led by three brothers, Nhạc (1743–1793, r. 1778–1788), Huệ (1753–1792, r. 1788–1792), and Lữ (d. 1787), their movement quickly amassed a huge following, and they defeated government forces in battle after battle. In 1773, they seized Quy Nhơn. Taking advantage of the disorder, troops from Tonkin invaded the south a year later under the pretext of helping the Nguyễn put down the uprising. By the end of 1774, they had taken the royal capital of Huế. The officials of the city handed Trương Phúc Loan to the Trịnh commander, who carried him off to Hanoi. Loan died along the way. Meanwhile, the Stable King and many members of the royal family fled south to Saigon. Among the entourage was a teenage boy named Nguyễn Ánh, the third son of the original successor to the throne whom Loan had displaced in favor of the Stable King. The Tonkin forces, already overextended, did not press farther southward. Instead, in May 1775, they secured the submission of the Tây Sơn brothers, who feared the prospect of fighting both the Trịnh and the Nguyễn. The Tây Sơn could now focus their entire attention upon the extermination of the exiled Nguyễn court in Saigon.[70]

The chaos that engulfed Cochinchina opened opportunities for resident Chinese. What resulted was an intense competition similar to the Chaozhou, Leizhou/Hainan, and creolized communities along the Gulf of Siam, except the groups involved were more numerous and spread out along the country's lengthy coastline. In 1773, Chinese merchants based at Hội An formed the Loyal and Righteous (C: Zhongyi V: Trung Nghĩa) Army and the Harmonious and Righteous (C: Heyi V: Hòa Nghĩa) Army. Both units, comprised entirely of Chinese soldiers, served as crucial pillars of support for the Tây Sơn during their early years. In late 1775, another merchant named Xi invested "countless sums of his fortune" in two Cochinchinese princes in Quảng Nam, south of Huế. However, the Tây Sơn leader, Nhạc, defeated them. One of the princes, Tôn Thất Xuân (d. 1780), escaped to Saigon.[71] These Chinese groups benefited from the continued robust growth of trade in maritime Asia, driven by increased demand from China, along with greater capacity to export its surplus population. These trends, in turn, generated vast pools of capital and manpower to fund the different warring factions in Cochinchina.

Mo Tianci, too, despite the defeat of his Siam adventure, continued to prosper from his overseas commercial linkages. Under the management

---

[70] Dutton, *Tây Sơn Uprising*, pp. 39–44; Nguyễn Dynasty, *Thực lục*, vol. 1, pp. 155–165, 290.
[71] Dutton, *Tây Sơn Uprising*, pp. 199–201; Nguyễn Dynasty, *Thực lục*, vol. 1, p. 167.

of his son Huang, The Port quickly recovered its traditional role as a flourishing transshipment point between China and Southeast Asia. In 1774, 5,000 piculs (300,000 kg) of tin arrived on ships from The Port at Guangzhou. Another 7,000 piculs (420,000 kg) came from Palembang, most of them by way of transit through Tianci's sphere of influence. In 1779, two junks from The Port arrived at Palembang from Bangka with 3,000 piculs (180,000 kg) of tin.[72] These were some of the best documented years for tin shipments.

One important reason for Tianci's move to Cần Thơ, Sakurai and Kitagawa suggest, was his effort to create a new emporium closer to the most fertile lands for rice cultivation in the Mekong Delta. From there, he could conveniently ship the harvests via the Bassac to the South China Sea and compete more effectively with the other rice bowl in the Chaophraya River plain and its port of Bangkok.[73] The empirical evidence shows that he enjoyed quite a bit of success. He recruited 3,000 Viet peasants from Saigon and Longhor, along with refugees from The Port, to open new land in the surrounding circuit of River Defense.[74]

He must have received assistance in this endeavor from the Franciscan mission under Julián del Pilar, which relocated to Cần Thơ after the Siamese invasion. With funds provided by the King of Spain, the Franciscans reconstituted their network on a grander scale. Like at The Port, they built a church and residences for missionaries and lay Christians. They also constructed a hospital. Medical professionals, such as Father Martín, had become much more important to Tianci since the late 1760s. Besides battling diseases and epidemics, they treated wounded soldiers from the frontlines during the numerous engagements of The Port against rebels and Siam. After Father Martín was taken away to Bangkok, no other European doctor replaced him at Cần Thơ. The presence of a hospital, however, shows that a competent staff of local doctors and surgeons could handle the tasks alongside amateur Western missionaries. In addition, Father Julián established a school for little children.[75] At minimal cost to himself, Tianci laid down the infrastructure for welcoming and absorbing new migrants to fuel his rice-based economy.

With Cochinchina descending into chaos, Mo Tianci saw an opportunity to turn the tables on his disadvantaged political situation and, in a

---

[72] Li Tana and Van Dyke, 'Canton,' pp. 18–21.
[73] Sakurai, 'Chinese Pioneers,' p. 46; Sakurai and Kitagawa, 'Hà Tiên or Banteay Meas,' pp. 201–202.
[74] Vũ, *Gia phả*, pp. 122–123; Trịnh, *Thông chí*, p. 325.
[75] Alcobendas, 'Religiosos médico-cirujanos' 5, p. 226; 6, pp. 336–338; Pérez, 'Españoles en el imperio de Annam' 13, p. 192.

repeat of his earlier attempt in Siam, aimed to become the power behind the throne. As befitting someone with a classical Confucian education, he chose to back whom he believed to be the individual with the most legitimate claim: the Stable King. Already in mid-1774, Tianci had expressed his support by sending a ship laden with rice to aid Huế. However, it was confiscated by pirate allies of the Tây Sơn in the waters outside Quy Nhơn.[76]

In 1775, after the Stable King fled to Saigon, Mo Tianci, together with all his sons, paid him a high-profile visit. During the audience, the ruler promoted Tianci from the rank of marquis to prefectural duke (*quận công*) and honored him as an elder of the country (*quốc lão*). The Stable King further upgraded the Mo clan's military units from companies to regiments (*cơ*). Tianci's sons took over their command after the deaths of his main generals. His heir Huang became commander-in-chief (*chưởng cơ*) and remained the assistant garrison commander in charge of The Port. His third son, Mo Tang, replaced the deceased Chen Dali as head of the renamed Victorious Naval Regiment. The fifth son, or the fourth from his principal wife, Rong, became the staff officer and chief adviser and oversaw the governance of River Defense Circuit and Cần Thơ (see Figure 7.2).[77] Tianci succeeded in concentrating more power into the hands of his clan than ever before.

However, the exiled Nguyễn court was not easily manipulated like the Ayutthaya princes. It attracted support from a broad social base in Saigon and the delta, which were relatively unaffected by the fiscal policies of Trương Phúc Loan and the Tây Sơn offensives. Many Chinese mercantile groups competed fiercely with Tianci and each other for influence over the exiled court. Saigon-based merchants organized and outfitted the Eastern Mountain (Đông Sơn) army, so named as a conscious juxtaposition to the Tây Sơn (Western Mountain) rebels. A commander of Chinese descent, C: Du Qingren **V: Đỗ Thanh Nhơn** (d. 1781), recruited a formidable corps of motivated officers and soldiers who fought fiercely and loyally for the Stable King. They successfully beat back a Tây Sơn attempt to capture Saigon in late 1775. Around this time, Li Cai, commander of the Harmonious and Righteous Army, defected from the Tây Sơn and also arrived in Saigon.[78]

Joining Li several months later was the crown prince, Nguyễn Phúc Dương (d. 1777), a royal relative who was adopted by the Stable King because he had no son of his own. The Tây Sơn leader Nhạc had held

---

[76] Nguyễn Dynasty, *Thực lục*, vol. 1, p. 160.
[77] Vũ, *Gia phả*, p. 125; Trịnh, *Thông chí*, p. 325; Nguyễn Dynasty, *Thực lục*, vol. 1, p. 165.
[78] Trịnh, *Thông chí*, pp. 326–327; Nguyễn Dynasty, *Thực lục*, vol. 1, pp. 167–169; Dutton, *Tây Sơn Uprising*, pp. 201, 204–205.

Figure 7.2 This part of central Cần Thơ was formerly the site of the citadel and garrison office, which Mo Tianci relocated from The Port. The road is named after Mo Tianci. The creek and a nearby bridge and market are all called Tham Tướng, or staff officer, a reference to the position of his fifth son, Mo Rong.
Photograph by author.

Dương hostage in an attempt to provide a prestigious figurehead for the rebel movement. The prince managed to flee from captivity to Saigon in 1776. Li Cai quickly brought Dương under his protection. Severe disagreements and outright hostility soon broke out between Li and Đỗ Thanh Nhơn and the Eastern Mountain Army, which backed the Stable King. To prevent the Tây Sơn from exploiting their differences and to maintain a unified resistance, the Stable King yielded the throne to Dương, who became the Reformation King (Tân chính vương). The Stable King assumed the role of king-father (Thái thượng vương).[79]

Vietnamese sources portray Tianci as being saddened by everything that had happened. They describe him constantly "pounding his chest and gnashing his teeth and heaving huge sighs, ashamed of his lack of

---

[79] Vũ, Gia phả, p. 125; Trịnh, Thông chí, pp. 327–328; Nguyễn Dynasty, Thực lục, vol. 1, pp. 165–166, 169–170.

soldiers. He could only watch helplessly as the country descended into disaster."⁸⁰ Although meant to project an image of him as the tragically heroic loyal minister, the narratives inadvertently reveal the fact that Tianci did not send any of his troops to assist the Nguyễn restoration in Saigon. Instead, he chose to prioritize the maintenance of his own vast power base, stretching from the southern banks of the Bassac to the Cambodian coastline. He only planned to use his forces if he could direct the restoration in a manner favorable to himself.

A valuable window of opportunity opened for him in May 1777, when Tây Sơn forces led by Nhạc's younger brother, Huệ, captured Saigon. The Nguyễn court and its sponsors quickly disintegrated, but this outcome resulted more from severe internal differences than the strength of the enemy. The Tây Sơn certainly wanted to eliminate all opposition to their rule, which could involve anything from the surrender of the Nguyễn to their complete extermination. Still, the brothers were reluctant to carry out extended campaigns in an unfamiliar frontier far away from their base in Quy Nhơn. Moreover, the monsoons only allowed large-scale long-distance movements of troops by sea during parts of the year, compounding the logistical difficulties.⁸¹

The war in the water world was just as much about a struggle for leadership and consolidation over the loyalist forces as resisting the Tây Sơn. Seizing the occasion of the fall of Saigon, Đỗ Thanh Nhơn attacked and routed the Harmonious and Righteous Army and killed its leader, Li Cai. Li's former patron, the Reformation King, joined up with the remnants of the old controller of the five camps south of Saigon. Nhơn and his 4,000-strong Eastern Mountain Army escorted the rest of the royal court, including the former Stable King, Tôn Thất Xuân, and Nguyễn Ánh, to Cần Thơ. There, they received the warm welcome of Mo Tianci.⁸²

Initially, Tianci and the Eastern Mountain forces jointly participated in engagements against the Tây Sơn along the north bank of the Bassac around Phsar Dek, opposite his base. However, Tianci would not commit troops to assist the Reformation King despite the earnest pleas of the former Stable King and Đỗ Thanh Nhơn. He further erected defensive barricades around the city and river. His main intention was apparently to control the former Stable King and use him as a figurehead to establish an independent regime based in the water world. He would then decide whether to continue expanding his territory into

---

⁸⁰ Trịnh, *Thông chí*, p. 328.   ⁸¹ Dutton, *Tây Sơn Uprising*, p. 44.
⁸² Vũ, *Gia phả*, pp. 125–126; Trịnh, *Thông chí*, p. 328; Nguyễn Dynasty, *Thực lục*, vol. 1, pp. 171–172.

Cochinchina or Siam. Đỗ Thanh Nhơn saw through Tianci's ambition, and dissension soon broke out between them. Nhơn tried to persuade the former Stable King to abandon Cần Thơ altogether and escort him to the camp of the Reformation King. Undoubtedly under tremendous pressure from Tianci, the former Stable King refused, claiming that he had grown tired of being chased by the rebels and desired to stay where he was.[83]

Nhơn decided to act unilaterally. Claiming that Tianci was "too isolated and weak to mount an effective resistance against the rebel bandits," Nhơn forced the former Stable King to issue an edict ordering his Eastern Mountain troops to leave Cần Thơ to reinforce the Reformation King. But they either never went to the camp of the Reformation King or stayed there only briefly, for soon, they were on their way northward to join forces with another anti-Tây Sơn army in the former Cham territories. If Nhơn was genuinely concerned that Tianci lacked the strength to face the rebels, the departure of the Eastern Mountain troops only further depleted the available manpower at Cần Thơ, while doing nothing to aid the Reformation King. Huệ's Tây Sơn forces, seeing through the disunity of the loyalist lines, pressed onward from Saigon. They hunted down the Reformation King south of the city, and, in September 1777, captured and killed the ruler and his followers.[84]

Two months before the ruler's tragic end, Huệ attacked Cần Thơ. Unable or unwilling to risk a direct conflict with the Tây Sơn, Tianci evacuated the city. Once again, the Franciscan mission scattered. In 1776, before all this happened, Father Julián had boarded a Portuguese vessel and left for Macao. The only missionary who remained behind was Juan de Jesús (1732–1778). He wrote in one of his letters about being cramped in a small boat in the middle of the harbor at Bassac together with the former Stable King, awaiting further instructions from Tianci. Father Juan eventually found a ship for Macao. Already gravely ill, he passed away in 1778.[85]

By then, Tianci was trying to find a way to get rid of the former Stable King, whose presence, after all, had made Tianci an obvious target of the Tây Sơn. He ordered some troops to escort the former Stable King and members of the royal court farther south to Black Water. One of Tianci's envoys, he assured the ruler, would soon return from Guangdong and accompany the king-father's entourage to China, where they could appeal for Qing aid. In the meantime, Tianci and the bulk of his forces

---

[83] Vũ, *Gia phả*, pp. 125–126; Trịnh, *Thông chí*, p. 328; Nguyễn Dynasty, *Thực lục*, vol. 1, pp. 171–172.
[84] Vũ, *Gia phả*, pp. 126–127; Nguyễn Dynasty, *Thực lục*, vol. 1, pp. 172–173.
[85] Pérez, 'Españoles en el imperio de Annam' 13, p. 193; 14, pp. 344–345.

withdrew westward to Royal Market, in Steadfast River Circuit, to forge a new line of naval defense. Apparently, the troops sent to guard the former Stable King soon left or were too few in number to begin with. Tianci effectively abandoned the former Stable King to the Tây Sơn, who dispatched a small crack contingent that penetrated Black Water in October 1777 and captured the king-father without any documented resistance. The former Stable King and many of the royal relatives accompanying him were brought to Saigon and then executed.[86]

Defeat, Exile, Death

Soon afterward, the Tây Sơn leader, Huệ, dispatched an envoy, along with fifty soldiers, to Royal Market with a menacing ultimatum to Tianci calling upon him to surrender. Tianci adamantly rejected it, insisting that his clan had faithfully served the Nguyễn for two generations. He opposed submission to the rebels on Confucian grounds, calling them illegitimate bandits and usurpers who did not deserve the throne.[87] In reality, with the former Stable King out of the way and knowing that the Tây Sơn were too overstretched to fully control the Mekong Delta, Tianci felt confident of carving out an independent domain without answering to any higher authority. And he could achieve this aim while preserving a moral reputation for steadfast loyalty.

As he accurately predicted, the Tây Sơn could not sustain their offensive momentum and soon withdrew to Saigon. But events in Cambodia worked against him. Khin Sok believes that the Khmer were uniformly the victims of the vicious Vietnamese civil war; they were forced to choose among one of the many different sides and endured most of the devastation and suffering.[88] There is much truth to this claim. With the Nguyễn preoccupied with quelling domestic disorder, they could no longer form an effective counterbalance to Siam in Cambodia. In late 1775 and early 1776, Ang Tan was forced to abdicate in favor of Taksin's client, Ream Reachea. The former king assumed the title of co-king. In 1777, Ream Reachea accused the viceroy who was appointed by Ang Tan of sedition and had him executed. Greatly stricken, Ang Tan himself passed away shortly thereafter.[89] Ream Reachea now had a full monopoly on power.

---

[86] Vũ, *Gia phả*, pp. 127–133; Trịnh, *Thông chí*, pp. 328–329; Nguyễn Dynasty, *Thực lục*, vol. 1, pp. 172–173, 277.
[87] Vũ, *Gia phả*, p. 134.   [88] Khin, *Cambodge*, p. 51.
[89] Eng, *Mahaboros khmer*, vol. 6, pp. 27–31; Leclère, *Histoire de Cambodge*, pp. 390–392; Moura, *Royaume du Cambodge*, vol. 1, pp. 89–91; Hán-Nôm A. 832: Phạm, *Cao Man ki lược*, n. p.; Trịnh, *Thông chí*, p. 329.

Yet, the 1770s were also a tremendously advantageous time for Cambodia. The powerful governor of Bassac, Oknha Athivongsa Pok, apparently entered into an alliance with the overextended Tây Sơn, who were all too willing to delegate power to him. The governor took advantage of the collapse of the Nguyễn and Mo Tianci's regime at Cần Thơ to reestablish direct Cambodian control over large swathes of the water world. The Bassac forces, led by Mou, a nobleman in Pok's service, seized control of Black Water and Royal Market, where Tianci and his troops were stationed. They then pressed onward, poised to strike The Port. As a result of these successes, the Bassac nobility rapidly acquired influence at the Oudong court. Ream Reachea initially welcomed them, seeing this group as a useful pro-Viet element in counterbalancing Taksin.[90]

The records are unclear about whether Mou's forces occupied The Port. They probably did, since Tianci and his family, as well as his entire officialdom and military, ended up living on his fleet of naval ships on the sea. Moreover, his son Huang, who was supposed to oversee The Port, joined Tianci with his own contingent. They took refuge on Phú Quốc and the other islands in the Gulf of Siam and attracted a sizable following from among the Viet settler population. They continued their withdrawal until they reached the waters around Nakhon Si Thammarat. There was hesitation about what to do next, with some officials suggesting that they continue onward to take refuge in the Malay Peninsula and the straits zone.[91]

At this conjuncture, a delegation from Taksin arrived and invited Tianci to reside in Siam. Tianci readily acquiesced and landed with his retinue at Chanthaburi. The Siamese escorted them to Thonburi, where they received the warm welcome of Taksin at his palace. During the audience, the two men agreed to put aside the bygone animosity between them. Taksin treated him and his retinue with tremendous hospitality, feasting them lavishly for over a week. Not long afterward, Tôn Thất Xuân and the remnants of the Nguyễn royal family members and officials, who had similarly sought refuge on islands off the coast, also arrived in Siam.[92]

Taksin settled the exiles on the opposite bank of the Chaophraya River from Thonburi, in and around the present-day royal palace in central Bangkok. The place was already the site of a Chaozhou enclave. But the

---

[90] Eng, *Mahaboros khmer*, vol. 6, pp. 31–33; Pérez, 'Españoles en el imperio de Annam' 14, pp. 343–344; Leclère, *Histoire de Cambodge*, p. 390; Hán-Nôm A. 832: Phạm, *Cao Man ki lược*, n. p.
[91] Vũ, *Gia phả*, p. 136. [92] Vũ, *Gia phả*, pp. 137–138; Trịnh, *Thông chí*, p. 329.

Sino-Viet exiles played a crucial role in the opening and development of the modern city. Tianci and Xuân were accorded a status equivalent to visiting royal dignitaries, and all their needs and expenses were paid out of the official coffers. Their followers, both Chinese creole and Cochinchinese, resided around the guesthouses of the two men. Eoseewong estimates that the total number of exiles amounted to 3,000, constituting a substantial community in its own right. During a voyage to Siam in 1779, the German naturalist and physician Johann Gerhard König (1728–1785) paid visits to Tianci and Xuân. According to him, they and their followers were led by "a chief of their own nation." König does not provide any detail about this individual, but Siamese accounts identify him as Phraya Racha Setthi. He was probably none other than Chen Lian, who once administered The Port after Mo Tianci's defeat. Besides overseeing his own Chaozhou compatriots, Chen had experience and familiarity with the exiles. By a twist of fate, former enemies literally found themselves within the same camp.[93]

König has left behind a detailed description of the part of Bangkok where the exiles stayed. It was land mostly reclaimed from swamps and crisscrossed by canals. Vendors, markets, and the workshops of shoemakers, blacksmiths, and other artisans lined the waterfronts. The houses were almost all made of bamboo and placed on stilts, since inundations from rainstorms were frequent and flooded over the largely unpaved roads, crudely raised above the ground. The palaces where Tianci and Xuân stayed, along with other mansions of the rich, had the luxury of wooden plank flooring. The Buddhist wats were the only permanent structures, made from brick.[94] Despite the rudimentary environment, it was a thriving and increasingly prosperous settlement where the Chinese creole and Cochinchinese exiles spent three years in relative peace.

However, the welcoming attitude of Taksin gradually transformed into suspicion and outright hostility. Sources from across mainland Southeast Asia are uniform in saying that his actions grew more erratic and violent over time as his mental health took a turn for the worse. König's account largely echoes their narrative but in more vivid terms. According to him, Taksin subjected his people to onerous taxes and exactions and meted out heavy punishments regardless of social rank. He beheaded suspected wrongdoers for the smallest of infractions. He spared not even his own sons and highest officials, often viciously whipping them with a heavy

---

[93] König, 'Journal,' pp. 157–158; Sng and Bisalputra, *Thai-Chinese*, p. 107; Eoseewong, *Karn Muang Thai*, p. 198.
[94] König, 'Journal,' pp. 157–158.

rattan stick. Meanwhile, he indulged in religious fanaticism, spending long hours in intense meditation and then imagining himself to be a supernatural being who could fly and bleed white blood.[95]

His erratic behavior should be interpreted in light of the formidable internal and external challenges that he was facing at the time. The Myanmar invasion of northern Siam in 1774 and 1775 destroyed a huge part of his direct power base, along with its revenue and manpower potential. As a result, Taksin had to levy more onerous burdens on the Siamese heartland around the capital. This measure threatened to alienate the old Ayutthaya nobility. He also harmed the interests of his Chaozhou inner circle by levying higher duties and placing heavier restrictions on overseas trade. As a result, Taksin lived in constant fear of rebellion and sedition. According to Gesick, his claim to supernatural powers and the increased frequency and severity of his punishments were attempts to bolster his Theravada Buddhist credentials as a charismatic ruler amid the deterioration in his actual power base. After all, without proof of merit, his Chinese background and low class origins placed him at a relative disadvantage to other potential competitors for the throne. Seen in this context, Tianci and Xuân naturally came under suspicion, since they and their exiled followers were a formidable potential political force.[96]

Subsequent developments in Cambodia intensified Taksin's insecurity and volatile behavior. After the flight and demise of the Stable King, the fifteen-year-old Nguyễn Ánh, the only surviving member of the Cochinchinese royal household, had escaped the clutches of the Tây Sơn by hiding in the swamps and jungles of Black Water. By the end of 1777, he returned to Phsar Dek, on the northern bank of the Bassac, and met up with the Eastern Mountain Army under Đỗ Thanh Nhơn and the remnants of the forces of the controller of the five camps. They all upheld him as Grand Marshal, and the combined forces were placed under Nhơn's command. In early 1778, the Nguyễn restorationists recaptured Saigon from the Tây Sơn.[97]

The Bassac Cambodians under Oknha Athivongsa Pok, once allied with the Tây Sơn, now switched sides to Ánh. Pok's influence had been growing rapidly at Oudong. He became the adoptive father of Neareay Reachea (1773–1796, r. 1779–1796), the orphaned son of the deceased Ang Tan and rival of the ruling king, Ream Reachea. Similarly, the

---

[95] Eng, *Mahaboros khmer*, vol. 6, p. 48; *Prachum phongsawadan* 65: *Krung Thonburi*, pp. 85–89; Trịnh, *Thông chí*, p. 332; König, 'Journal,' pp. 164–165.
[96] Eoseewong, *Karn Muang Thai*, pp. 186–198; König, 'Journal,' p. 165; Gesick, 'Kingship,' pp. 105–107.
[97] Nguyễn Dynasty, *Thực lục*, vol. 2, pp. 310 (20)–312 (22).

brothers of Pok's top subordinate, Mou, became governors of several provinces. In 1778, Taksin forced Ream Reachea to agree to onerous requisitions of food, ships, and soldiers from Cambodia to assist in an upcoming campaign against Laos. Mou and Pok used the popular discontent around this issue to organize and revolt. With the assistance of Nhơn's forces, they chased Ream Reachea out of the capital and, in the following year, hunted him down and had him drowned. Neareay Reachea became the new king. But because he was only a boy of six years old, Mou served as his regent and became the most powerful man behind the throne. Pok, as the adoptive father of Neareay Reachea, came in second as the viceroy.[98]

Ánh's support for this new governing body came at a price. Mou was forced to accept the appointment of a Viet protector (*bảo hộ*), who would have overall supervision over Cambodian affairs. Moreover, a power-sharing arrangement seemed to have been reached in the water world. The Khmer could continue to rule over their subjects from Oudong, while paying Ánh a regular tribute. Ánh would establish direct military administration over cities and nearby settlements with a high concentration of Viet and Chinese. Accordingly, an Eastern Mountain regiment commander named Thăng was stationed at The Port and the Steadfast River Circuit.[99]

Taksin was not too pleased at seeing his choice of king toppled from the throne of Cambodia. More alarmingly for him, the revival of the Nguyễn under Grand Marshal Ánh marked the return of an established rival that had posed a formidable impediment to his designs toward the east. With Cambodia becoming a Cochinchinese protectorate, all his gains there, achieved through years of struggle, threatened to be in vain. Taksin's suspicions became directed toward his exiled guests at Bangkok when, in 1778, Ánh sent a mission to reestablish diplomatic ties with Siam. This friendly gesture seemed odd, since it was in stark contrast to the mutual hostility by proxy escalating around the same time in Cambodia. Moreover, during the visit, Ánh's mission met with Mo Tianci and Tôn Thất Xuân and tried to secure their release from Taksin. Unsure about the intentions of the envoys, Taksin politely rejected their request and sent them away.[100]

---

[98] Eng, *Mahaboros khmer*, vol. 6, pp. 33–44; Nguyễn Dynasty, *Thực lục*, vol. 2, p. 313 (23); Leclère, *Histoire de Cambodge*, pp. 393–395; Moura, *Royaume du Cambodge*, vol. 1, pp. 91–94; Hán-Nôm A. 832: Phạm, *Cao Man kỉ lược*, n. p.
[99] Nguyễn Dynasty, *Thực lục*, vol. 2, pp. 313 (23), 315 (25); Trịnh, *Thông chí*, p. 331; Vũ, *Gia phả*, p. 141.
[100] Nguyễn Dynasty, *Thực lục*, vol. 2, p. 313 (23); Trịnh, *Thông chí*, p. 331; Vũ, *Gia phả*, p. 141.

In 1780, Ánh sent another mission to Siam with a similar request for Tianci and Xuân to return to Saigon. At this point, Taksin began to wonder whether something more sinister was going on behind the scenes. His fears appeared to be confirmed when Thăng, the garrison commander of The Port, seized and plundered a Siamese tribute ship that was on its way back from Guangzhou and massacred its crew of over fifty. The sole survivor made it to Thonburi and reported the matter to Taksin. Taksin was infuriated at this egregious insult, especially since this act of predation occurred while Ánh's envoys were still being hosted at his court! He promptly had them clamped in chains and put in prison. The final straw for Taksin occurred not long afterward when an exiled Khmer nobleman in his service claimed to have intercepted a secret letter from Saigon. It contained instructions for Tianci and Xuân to await the arrival of Đỗ Thanh Nhơn's navy and collaborate in seizing Bangkok. From there, they would launch an offensive on the rest of Siam. One of Taksin's spies further reported the presence of over a hundred warships belonging to Nhơn docked along the Cambodian coastline.[101]

Taksin then rounded up Xuân, Tianci and all his family members, and their subordinates and incarcerated them outside Bangkok. He subjected them daily to severe interrogations, while viciously whipping their backs with his infamous rattan stick. Tôn Thất Xuân, unable to bear the pain and bleeding from the blows, admitted to the conspiracy. However, Mo Tianci and his retinue vociferously denied the charges. Taksin then had a mental meltdown. One day, he rushed over to Tianci's fifth son and chief staff officer, Mo Rong, and killed him with his bare hands. As the tragedy unfolded before Tianci, he lost all hope in himself and the future of his enterprise. On November 1, 1780, Mo Tianci committed suicide. He was over seventy years of age. Three weeks later, Taksin had Tôn Thất Xuân; all but the youngest of Tianci's sons and grandsons; their officials; and the two envoys dispatched by Nguyễn Ánh, a total of fifty-three people, put to death. Subsequently, he ordered all the surviving Chinese creole and Cochinchinese residents of their quarter in Bangkok to be banished to the faraway frontiers of Siam.[102]

Did Mo Tianci plot with the Nguyễn to attack Siam? Were Taksin's fears justified? Naturally, Tianci's genealogical biography fiercely defended him. He and Tôn Thất Xuân, it claims, were framed by the Tây Sơn, who did not want to see an alliance develop between the

---

[101] Nguyễn Dynasty, *Thực lục*, vol. 1, p. 278; vol. 2, p. 315 (25); Trịnh, *Thông chí*, p. 331; Vũ, *Gia phả*, p. 141.
[102] Nguyễn Dynasty, *Thực lục*, vol. 1, p. 278; vol. 2, p. 315 (25); Trịnh, *Thông chí*, pp. 331–332; Vũ, *Gia phả*, pp. 143–145.

Nguyễn and Siam against them. The rebels forged the letter and purposely allowed it to fall into the hands of the Khmer nobleman. The biography further justifies the presence of over a hundred ships in Cambodia as a measure to guard against a Tây Sơn offensive by sea. This version of events holds credibility, especially since the Tây Sơn were planning another offensive on Saigon and the water world. But why were those vessels parked next door to Siam? Also, Tianci had a past record of backing contenders for the throne and using them to expand his own power base. It would have benefited him enormously if Tôn Thất Xuân replaced Taksin and accorded Tianci autonomous leadership over The Port and its hinterlands in the water world.[103]

There is, possibly, a third explanation. Đỗ Thanh Nhơn took charge of the campaign against Ream Reachea in Cambodia. It would not be surprising if he and his Eastern Mountain Army had divergent interests from Nguyễn Ánh. Nhơn may have had designs to take his campaigns farther into Siam and topple Taksin and replace him with Tôn Thất Xuân. From the perspective of Nhơn and his Saigon-based Chinese mercantile backers, this expansion would have positive effects for their business interests. But obviously, the move threatened Nguyễn Ánh's legitimacy and monopoly on power. Indeed, Nhơn demonstrated increasing arrogance and insubordination in his actions around this time. The seizure of the Siamese tribute ship by his commander at The Port directly contradicted Ánh's friendly overtures to Taksin. Incidents like this probably prompted Ánh to order Nhơn's arrest and execution in April 1781.[104]

Taksin certainly believed that the Viet were up to no good, and he felt hurt and betrayed, especially after treating their exiles with such compassion and generosity. Soon after his rampage against the exiles, he ordered another offensive against the Nguyễn-backed Cambodian protectorate. Two commanders, Thongduang (1737–1809), the chancellor (Chaophraya Chakri), and his younger brother Bunma (1744–1803), the governor of Phitsanoluk (Chaophraya Surasi), took leading roles in the fresh attack. Taksin had come to rely heavily upon them for their military capabilities. They had played a significant role in helping him fight off the Myanmar invasion of the northern provinces in 1775.[105]

By this point, however, the years of almost nonstop warfare and expansion, which brought Siam's territory and sphere of influence to the largest

---

[103] Vũ, *Gia phả*, pp. 142–144.
[104] Nguyễn Dynasty, *Thực lục*, vol. 2, pp. 315 (25)–316 (26).
[105] *Prachum phongsawadan* 65: *Krung Thonburi*, pp. 67–68; Nguyễn Dynasty, *Thực lục*, vol. 2, p. 317 (27).

ever in its history, had stretched the resources of the kingdom and its people to the breaking point. More seriously, as Taksin's personal power base eroded and his style of rule increasingly depended upon terror and charisma, he alienated the Siamese nobility in the heartland and his own Chaozhou mercantile constituency. Many of these elites rallied around the chancellor. Thongduang and his brother had a powerful base in the Khorat area and replaced Taksin as the leading influence in the northern provinces. According to Eoseewong, Thongduang and Bunma had already made plans to overthrow the ruler before their dispatch to Cambodia.[106] Although growing divisions were occurring among the elites, one cannot ignore the groundswell of discontent against Taksin on the part of commoners. And nativism became the unifying element that mobilized individuals across class divisions.

It was this platform that provided the critical mass necessary for the outbreak of a massive rebellion at Ayutthaya in 1781. Its leader was a discontented nobleman named Phraya San (d. 1782). As the conversation between him and his younger brother, Khun Kaew, reveals, they wanted a man of virtue from "our race," the Siamese, to recover "our country." They simply could not place their fates upon outsiders like the Chinese, who had brought them nothing but disaster. In 1782, the rebels entered Thonburi and forced Taksin to abdicate. Taksin was imprisoned in a Buddhist temple, where he took up vows and became a monk. Word of the coup soon reached Thongduang and Bunma while they were still on campaign in Cambodia. They quickly made peace with their Nguyễn rivals and rushed back to Thonburi. They captured and killed Phraya San on the spot. Then, they brought Taksin out of the temple and had him executed. Thongduang then ascended the throne as Rama I (r. 1782–1809), while his younger brother Bunma (r. 1782–1803) became viceroy (*upparat*).[107] Their coronation marked the start of the Chakri dynasty, which remains the ruling house of Thailand.

Meanwhile, renewed Tây Sơn offensives in 1782 and 1783 succeeded in reoccupying Saigon. Nguyễn Ánh barely managed to escape by sea to Siam, whose new regime had become his ally. He attempted, with the help of Siamese troops, to recapture Saigon, but the joint offensive ended in disaster. In 1785, he again fled to Bangkok, where he spent the next four years. Free, for the time being, from the threat of the Nguyễn restorationists, the Tây Sơn brothers turned northward against Tonkin

---

[106] *Prachum phongsawadan* 65: *Krung Thonburi*, pp. 88–91; Pombejra, 'Chinese in Siam,' p. 352; Eoseewong, *Karn Muang Thai*, pp. 204–245.
[107] *Prachum phongsawadan* 65: *Krung Thonburi*, pp. 89–95; Nguyễn Dynasty, *Thực lục*, vol. 2, p. 317 (27); Vũ, *Gia phả*, pp. 146–150; Pombejra, 'Chinese in Siam,' p. 352.

and, in 1786, captured Hanoi, ending both the Lê dynasty and the Trịnh lords who exercised de facto power in its name. Northern and southern Vietnam were unified for the first time since the sixteenth century. In 1788, the Tây Sơn leader Huệ beat back a large Qing expeditionary force that tried to capture Hanoi in the name of restoring the exiled Lê ruler. Afterward, however, internal rivalries between the Tây Sơn siblings severely weakened their regime. The deaths of the main leaders, starting with the youngest brother Lữ in 1787, and followed by Huệ in 1792 and Nhạc in 1793, struck further blows, along with continued discord among their successors.[108]

Nguyễn Ánh, with the support of Siamese and European advisers and weaponry, took Saigon again in 1789, this time permanently. From there, he gradually pushed northward in the face of fierce Tây Sơn resistance. In 1802, his forces finally entered Hanoi and unified the country. He proclaimed the Nguyễn dynasty at Huế and became its founding ruler, adopting the reign name of Gia Long. He further obtained the recognition of the Qing emperor as a tributary vassal.[109]

After numerous rounds of battles and intrigues, Vietnam and Siam came to a consensus in Cambodia. They recognized Neareay Reachea as king, and he would become a vassal to both countries. After his death in 1796, his adoptive father, Oknha Pok, became regent for the deceased ruler's eldest son, Ang Chan (1791–1835, r. 1806–1835), until the young man reached maturity. In 1806, Ang Chan was formally enthroned in a coronation ceremony held in Siam. Shortly afterward, Gia Long received a tributary mission from the new ruler.[110]

By the nineteenth century, the contours of modern mainland Southeast Asia had taken shape. The area came to be dominated and defined by the bounded territorial states of Myanmar, Cambodia, Vietnam, Laos, and Siam. Of course, significant ambiguity still thrived at their fringes. The surviving descendants of Mo Tianci, after their return from exile in Siam with the forces of Nguyễn Ánh, skillfully took advantage of this intermediate zone to restore and stubbornly hold onto their realm. Until the middle of the nineteenth century, their survival depended upon acting as a fulcrum and balancing force for Vietnam and Siam, while avoiding complete incorporation by any of them. To the northwest of The Port, the Khmer hierarchy prevailed under Siamese

---

[108] Dutton, *Tây Sơn Uprising*, pp. 45–53.
[109] Dutton, *Tây Sơn Uprising*, pp. 53–56; Woodside, *Vietnam and the Chinese Model*, pp. 16–18, 120.
[110] Eng, *Mahaboros khmer*, vol. 6, pp. 67–76; Moura, *Royaume du Cambodge*, vol. 1, pp. 99–100.

supervision. To the east were the Sino-Viet circuits, now administered by Vietnamese governors. They included Bassac and Sacred Pond, long the sites of fierce contestation among The Port, Cochinchina, Siam, and Cambodia.[111]

After an inconclusive war fought between Vietnam and Siam over Cambodia during the 1840s, firmer boundaries between the three states were established as part of the settlement. The area northwest of The Port up to Kampong Som and Koh Kong were definitively ceded to Cambodia. The seat of the Cambodian Seashore Province relocated from Moat Chrouk, which came under Vietnamese control, to Kampong Trach. Located about twenty kilometers inland and to the northwest of The Port, it was no longer much of a seashore since it did not have any harbors of significance. The Port's core area became gradually incorporated into Vietnam as its province of Hà Tiên.[112]

Lê Quý Đôn, sent to administer Huế after its occupation by Tonkin forces in 1774, wrote admiringly of how Mo Tianci, despite being "well over seventy years of age," was still steadfastly upholding the Nguyễn and resisting the "fake Nhạc."[113] The early nineteenth-century narratives include more dramatic scenes that bear traces of embellishment, such as how Tianci would frequently get up at night and sigh, lamenting his inability to more effectively serve his king.[114] As Ang shows, these accounts successfully established his reputation in later Vietnamese scholarly and popular circles as a loyal minister of the Nguyễn.[115] Mo Tianci, too, probably promoted this image later in his life, as it was the best way for him to prosper in a world characterized by increasing contradictions. On the one hand, the 1770s marked a peak in trade between China and Southeast Asia, driven by the growth in exchange between China and the West and the expansion of Western credit at Guangzhou.[116] On the other hand, the impulse toward greater cultural homogenization and nativist sentiments across mainland Southeast Asia provided the basis for forging more centralized territorial states. They posed an increasing impediment to the flourishing translocal Chinese mercantile networks that Tianci promoted.

Nonetheless, contingencies existed for him to bridge these contradictions. He seized upon the chaos in Siam to support two of its exiled princes and placed his money upon the Stable King when the ruler fled to

---

[111] Sakurai, 'Chinese Pioneers,' pp. 47–49.
[112] Sellers, *Princes of Hà-Tiên*, pp. 131–139; Aymonier, *Cambodge*, vol. 1, pp. 154–155.
[113] Lê Quý Đôn, *Tạp lục* (Giáo dục), vol. 2, p. 398.
[114] Trịnh, *Thông chí*, p. 328; Vũ, *Gia phả*, pp. 134, 136.
[115] Ang, *Poetic Transformations*, p. 171.
[116] Van Dyke, *Merchants*, vol. 1, pp. 45–48, 68–71.

Saigon. After the tragic death of the former Stable King, Tianci appeared to have wanted to form an independent state. When that failed and he ended up an exile in Siam, he became implicated in a conspiracy to topple Taksin and replace him with Tôn Thất Xuân. In all cases, Tianci lost to the other claimants. In fact, his greatest obstacle was not competing rulers but rather Chinese merchants, who likewise supported influential patrons in exchange for security and influence, albeit on a lesser scale than Tianci.

One fundamental reason for this internecine competition was the lack of support from the Qing court. Tianci tried to secure the intervention of the Qianlong Emperor in his Siam adventure by appealing to the Myanmar threat to China's borders and acting as a model Confucian. And he came close to success. Yet, as James Kong Chin shows, the Qing ultimately did not provide any substantial assistance to him, especially after the situation in Siam turned unfavorable toward him. To be fair, it treated his rival, Taksin, in a comparable manner, only granting recognition when Taksin had, with force of arms, changed the reality on the ground.[117] The Qing proved highly pragmatic in its dealings with overseas Chinese and supported them if doing so aligned with its interests. But territorial expansion in the service of their trading networks was not among them.

Despite their often-adverse relationship, Taksin and Tianci were very much alike, the products of a similar environment responding in their own ways to a fluid situation. Of the two, Taksin went the farthest, to the point of forging his own state. However, the need to balance out overseas trading interests with territorial governance so strained his capabilities that he ultimately lost control over both. Although Tianci's tragic suicide preceded Taksin's violent downfall, the Mo clan may have ended up with the last laugh, since their descendants would return to administer The Port again. And they retained significant autonomy until the French occupied and colonized the realm in 1867.[118] In the end, however, the state triumphed over the more loosely organized and semiformal translocal Chinese networks and conditioned and limited their scope of action.

---

[117] J. K. Chin, 'King Taksin and China,' pp. 185–186.

[118] Sellers, *Princes of Hà-Tiên*, pp. 127–139 remains the most comprehensive study of Hà Tiên under Mo Tianci's descendants.

Conclusion

The fortunes of the Mo clan overlapped with the "Chinese century" in maritime Asia. This long eighteenth-century period marked a transitional phase from the multipolar cosmopolitan environment of the Age of Commerce to the nineteenth-century world of more firmly defined territorial states and a global trading system centered upon Western Europe.[1] Mo Jiu's founding of The Port coincided with two large-scale waves of Chinese migration to Southeast Asia. The first occurred in the aftermath of the Ming collapse in 1644 and was made possible by the Zheng family's commercial and naval dominance in maritime East Asia. The Qing legalization of private overseas trade in 1684 heralded a second, much larger, and steadier influx.

The Port's emergence around this period further owed to a power vacuum in the water frontier of mainland Southeast Asia, extending from the Mekong Delta to the Gulf of Siam littoral. Cambodia, the owner of this vast territory, experienced constant internal struggles amid a broadening rift between the agrarian-centered interior and the outwardly oriented maritime zone.[2] The situation invited intervention from various foreign forces, but Siam and Cochinchina had the most substantial and sustained impact. Throughout the seventeenth and eighteenth centuries, the two powers fought each other in proxy wars for domination over Cambodia, with neither side gaining a decisive advantage. Mo Jiu founded his autonomous polity precisely at the weak and volatile intersection of the spheres of influence of all three countries.

He and his son, Mo Tianci, transformed The Port into a key collection point for natural resources from its hinterlands, such as rice, timber, seafood, and medicinal ingredients, to China and island Southeast Asia. It also became a transit point where tin and other minerals from island Southeast Asia stopped over on their way to Qing ports, while Chinese laborers went in the opposite direction to work the mines and

---

[1] Reid, *Age of Commerce*, vol. 2, pp. 1–61; Lieberman, *Strange Parallels*, vol. 1, pp. 15–66.
[2] Mikaelian, *Royauté d'Oudong*, pp. 76, 295–298.

plantations.³ The Port and its hinterlands developed sophisticated financial capabilities, especially as the supply of copper and silver from Japan declined because of restrictions on their export from the Tokugawa. The Port's area of authority became a center for the minting and distribution of zinc coins and a clearinghouse for silver. The formation of the Guangzhou System during the 1750s brought more prosperity from the large-scale participation of the Hong merchants in the junk trade with Southeast Asia. Western capital funded some of the expansion, especially in the reexports of products to Europe.⁴

For most of their time in power, the Mo did not seek to establish a separate state so much as acquire the "territoriality," in Macauley's terms, for the opening of new land and growth of trade.⁵ To this effect, they practiced a calculated ambiguity toward the major players of maritime Asia. They subscribed to Sinosphere norms in becoming vassals of Cochinchina and used this relationship to engage in diplomacy with the Qing. They manipulated the Southeast Asian mandala, positioning The Port as an outer frontier province that could maintain multiple loyalties to Cochinchina, Cambodia, and Siam. Toward the VOC, the Mo, especially Tianci, actively participated as an integrated member of its monopolistic economic framework in island Southeast Asia, often bending or breaking its rules.

In similar fashion, the Mo adapted the administrative hierarchies of both Cochinchina and Cambodia to govern their diverse and polyglot Chinese creole, Qing, Viet, Khmer, and Austronesian communities. They also forged ties with the various horizontal networks that made The Port their crossroads. The Linji Buddhist temples allowed Jiu and Tianci to make initial contact with other overseas Chinese communities, as well as Qing gentry. The remnants of the Dragon Gate contingent built the foundations for a strong and seasoned military force. Through the VOC, the Mo tapped the mercantile and legal resources of the Chinese kapitan of Batavia and the Austronesian networks. The Roman Catholic orders became an important vehicle for the recruitment and management of Viet settlers within The Port. The Portuguese mestizos contributed their financial and monetary expertise.

The Port resembled, in many aspects, the VOC to its south. The primary purpose of the VOC and of their British and other counterparts for that matter was to increase their value for investors in the trade with Asia. To achieve this aim, the Dutch maintained a far-flung network of

---

[3] Li Tana and Van Dyke, 'Canton,' pp. 12–20.
[4] Van Dyke, *Merchants*, vol. 1, pp. 45–48, 68–71.
[5] Macauley, *Distant Shores*, pp. 12–13.

trading posts stretching from the Cape of Good Hope to Japan and engaged with a range of state and non-state actors. The chief difference between the Mo and the VOC involved the degree of centralization and formality. The VOC or even the more organizationally dispersed EIC had charters that set out the parameters of their autonomy and privileges and their relationship to the mother country. They had a clear hierarchical division of the roles and responsibilities of shareholders and the board of directors and coordinated the activities of their factories and colonies. They also regulated the participation of private country traders.[6]

The Mo had formal institutions of governance, but only if they could not be substituted by personal and native place ties or adaptation to the existing practices of the localities where they conducted business. Within maritime Asia, the dense commercial interactions and proximity of supply sources and markets made the costs of these informal mechanisms much lower than a centralized arrangement, which was suited for coordination of trade over longer distances.[7] Accordingly, The Port's administration functioned like a gentry-operated local society in southern China lifted across space onto an overseas setting. Nonetheless, Mo Tianci, in particular, sought to achieve greater control and consolidation over his realm and its translocal linkages by backing his own candidates onto the thrones of neighboring kingdoms. Although it worked spectacularly with Ang Tan in Cambodia, he became overextended in the case of Siam and simply encountered too much competition in a disintegrating Cochinchina.

More successful were his efforts to promote the decentralized Wang Yangming school of neo-Confucianism. As Nguyễn Ngọc Thơ and Nguyễn Thanh Phong point out, it proved flexible enough to support his trade-oriented policies and tolerance for the coexistence of often mutually antagonistic political actors, ethnicities, religions, and corporate entities.[8] Confucian teachings were also a sound method of indoctrinating and homogenizing the diverse inhabitants of his realm. His sponsorship of literary projects and public schools allowed him to hone his moral and cultural credentials as a Confucian role-model for society, just like gentry in China. At the same time, he provided a de-stateified platform for Qing and Viet elites of all persuasions to freely express themselves in poetry and prose and voice out their mutual disagreements. This was an especially valuable asset for them amid the ongoing literary inquisitions of the Qianlong court. Fundamentally, Tianci aimed to achieve a horizontal translocal integration by devising a common

---

[6] Adams, 'Principals and Agents,' pp. 19–20.
[7] Rosenthal and Wong, *Before and Beyond Divergence*, pp. 67–98.
[8] Nguyễn Ngọc Thơ and Nguyễn, 'Philosophical Transmission,' pp. 88–92.

ideological consensus to minimize elite and commoner opposition to his business of business and thereby lower transaction costs.

Inadvertently, The Port had a tremendous and long-lasting impact on southern Vietnam. Unlike Tonkin, where regular tributary missions to China and contacts at the official level influenced the bureaucracy and hierarchy, Cochinchina received Chinese influence in a decentralized manner and at all levels of society, often in unfiltered form. The Port allowed this momentum to continue and even intensify. Its concentrated presence of Chinese creoles, Qing merchants and long-term sojourners, and more importantly, Qing elite visitors and permanent residents made it a surrogate China. Its existence had immense value for Cochinchina, which did not have official recognition in the Sinosphere. The most prominent statesmen and cultural figures of the day, including Ngô Thế Lân and Nguyễn Cư Trinh, participated in the literary conversations of Tianci's translocal society. They willingly subjected their works to the aesthetic judgments of gentry in Jiangnan, in the Chinese heartland. Regardless of whether the vernacular version of the "Ten Verses of Hà Tiên" actually came from Mo Tianci's period or was a more recent creation, its existence attests to how Chinese cultural elements also penetrated on a large scale among Viet commoners and far beyond the confines of The Port.

After Mo Tianci's tragic suicide, The Port's legacy continued to bear a heavy imprint on a newly unified Vietnam under the Nguyễn dynasty. The Chinese creole Minh Hương based in the neighboring Cochinchinese water world played a vital role in Nguyễn Ánh's rise to power and the consolidation of his governance in the early nineteenth century. Besides serving as the ruler's close advisers, prominent Minh Hương officials, among them Trịnh Hoài Đức, followed the example of Tianci and formed their own literary society in Saigon, known as the Bình Dương Poetry Club (thi xã).[9] Đức himself was a huge fan of Mo Tianci's works, and he took the initiative to preserve, recover, and recopy them. One example of the fruit of his endeavors was "Idle Fishing at Sea Perch Creek," probably Tianci's earliest anthology. Đức's own writings drew inspiration from The Port. In a conscious imitation of the "Ten Scenic Views of Hà Tiên," he selected landmarks of significance in Saigon and wrote poetry on the "Thirty Scenic Views of Gia Định" in 1797. He also left behind verses directly commemorating Chen Shangchuan and The Port.[10]

---

[9] Choi, *Southern Vietnam*, pp. 40–41.   [10] Hán-Nôm A. 780: Trịnh, *Thi tập*, n. p.

The Port's contribution to the character of southern Vietnam as a distinct space from its northern counterpart adds an additional layer of complication to the notion of an uninterrupted Southern Advance, especially in the water world. Hopefully, as this narrative has shown, the process whereby the Mo became incorporated into a unified Vietnam was fraught with contingencies. Holroyd argues that they could have founded an independent state.[11] But it is just as likely that The Port would remain in Cambodia or be incorporated into Siam, or it could have become a Dutch dependency. In fact, much of its western territories were ceded to Cambodia during the mid-nineteenth century. And, in the end, when the Southern Advance stopped at The Port, it was the outcome of a bidirectional process. Just as Viet migrants entered the Gulf of Siam littoral, Chinese culture flowed the other way.

The story of the Mo and their prosperous emporium allows for a clearer understanding of how the broader eighteenth-century world operated. It was a world characterized not just by surprising similarities, as Pomeranz's path-breaking study has shown, but also increased convergence on both ends of Eurasia.[12] The major core areas stood at rough parity to one another and influenced each other through points of interaction in the China Seas and Indian Ocean. The eighteenth century also marked a transitional period in which long-distance translocal monopolies, whether formal corporations, clans, or ethnic or linguistically based networks, coexisted with intense and widespread state-building.

Political unification enhanced the growth of trade and accumulation of capital by decreasing transaction costs, while contributing to a homogenization of cultures within the different states. Yet, this process, ironically, stimulated the emergence of exclusive nativist sentiments. Of course, these were nothing new within the context of maritime East Asia. The ethnic Han resistance against the Manchus was certainly one example and had far-reaching repercussions, including the emergence of the Mo clan. Cambodia, too, experienced several waves of anti-Cochinchinese xenophobia. But the nativism of the eighteenth century was comparatively less accommodating. It appeared to form part of a systematic policy of state-building emanating from the core areas, especially the capitals, and extended, albeit unevenly and in a diluted fashion, to the limits of their capacity to set boundaries.[13] The exclusivity can be detected in the animosity of the newly arrived Chaozhou migrants to the Gulf of Siam littoral, who probably identified more as Qing subjects, toward the Chinese creoles and Viet of The Port. It was expressed much more

---

[11] Holroyd, 'No Man's Borderland.'   [12] Pomeranz, *Great Divergence*, pp. 29–108.
[13] Lieberman, *Strange Parallels*, vol. 1, pp. 62–65.

explicitly in the contempt of Siamese and Khmer nobility toward both Taksin and Mo Tianci.

Perhaps because of the politically fragmented nature of Vietnam and, as Kelley shows, a higher affiliation of its elites to the Qing-centered Sinosphere, a coherent nativism was slower to take root.[14] Nonetheless, the stirrings of such sentiments arguably occurred with the Tây Sơn movement. Dutton has correctly deemphasized the status accorded to the Tây Sơn in Vietnamese communist historiography as a popular revolution centered upon the peasant class. As he shows, the brothers opportunistically responded to circumstances and appealed to different segments of society with the purpose of seizing and holding onto power. For instance, after they occupied Saigon in 1782, they conducted a ruthless massacre of its large Chinese population, killing over 10,000. For Dutton and other scholars, the Tây Sơn actions did not represent a systematic anti-Chinese stance. Rather, the Tây Sơn were venting their frustration at the lack of support from this community, including the defection of one of their most important subordinates, Li Cai, to the Nguyễn and their failed attempts to secure Mo Tianci's submission. Indeed, the rampage did not hamper their cooperation later with other Chinese groups, like the pirates who ravaged the coastline from central-southern Vietnam to the Pearl River Delta of Guangdong.[15]

Still, the fact that the Tây Sơn could mobilize and target such widespread hatred at a specific ethnic group does speak to at least some level of popular anger against the Chinese. Perhaps it was a reaction to perceived economic exploitation, as Choi points out. But there seems to be a deeper pattern of othering involved, especially if subsequent actions by the Tây Sơn are seen in conjunction with the Saigon massacre. After the second brother, Huệ, occupied northern Vietnam in the late 1780s, he promoted the use of the demotic *nôm* characters in place of Chinese script. Although this measure could be explained as an expedient means of popularizing and disseminating neo-Confucian texts, the use of the vernacular as a medium facilitated greater cultural homogenization and cohesion of nativist tendencies. Huệ also had irredentist notions of reclaiming what he considered to be historically Viet territories in southern China.[16] The Tây Sơn were certainly opportunistic, but they played upon existing or latent aspirations within society, and among them was a rudimentary form of nationalism.

---

[14] Kelley, *Beyond the Bronze Pillars*, p. 90.
[15] Dutton, *Tây Sơn Uprising*, pp. 13–17, 202–204; Choi, *Southern Vietnam*, pp. 35–37.
[16] Dutton, *Tây Sơn Uprising*, pp. 27–29, 113–116; Choi, *Southern Vietnam*, pp. 35–36.

Even as the world became more similar and interacted with each other in a dynamic fashion, distinct differences in trajectory had started to emerge between the two ends of Eurasia. Maritime Asia served as an ideal venue for observing how this divergence gradually widened until it became a huge chasm. As Andrade shows, Europeans had acquired a distinct edge in military technology over the rest of the world in the sixteenth century through innovations such as heavy artillery, muskets, regular drills, sturdy and powerful ships, and the Renaissance fortress. The Chinese and other East Asians managed to quickly bridge this gap by adopting, imitating, and adapting Western weapons and techniques, and made up for any remaining disadvantages through superior organization, leadership, and logistics.[17] A rough military parity subsequently prevailed in maritime East Asia, allowing for first the Zheng and then the Qing to establish naval dominance over the China Seas. Mo Jiu and Mo Tianci owed their emergence and prosperity to the resulting balance of power in the region.

During the late eighteenth century, however, the differential had developed once again. Andrade lists many examples of obsolete weaponry used by the Qing military. A comparable situation prevailed in mainland Southeast Asia, which was heavily influenced by the warfare techniques of China and India. The records document Mo Tianci's shortage of heavy cannons, which explains why he chose to negotiate with Taksin and initiate official contacts with the VOC. On the other hand, Taksin's ability to procure large numbers of armaments from Batavia played a decisive role in his successful occupation of The Port and his victories against other enemies. Likewise, one key reason for Nguyễn Ánh's ability to overcome the Tây Sơn and establish a unified Vietnam owed much to European advisers, mercenaries, and weaponry. The different trajectories of these Southeast Asian state-builders reflected their growing dependence upon Western weaponry for the success of their endeavors.[18]

In a related development, European ships and navigational methods underwent dramatic improvement. Van Dyke shows that new sail and hull designs increased the speed of vessels, while the invention of the chronometer in 1765 allowed for greater precision in pinpointing locations and avoiding hazards. Mariners charted new routes to Guangzhou farther to the east of the well-trodden pathways of the junk trade, starting in the waters of Java and New Guinea and traversing northward through the Philippine Islands. The technological advances led to faster, more

---

[17] Andrade, *Gunpowder Age*, pp. 75–236.
[18] Andrade, *Gunpowder Age*, pp. 239–240; Charney, *Southeast Asian Warfare*, pp. 239–242.

reliable, and predictable long-distance transport. Ships could sail to Guangzhou at all times of the year, without being constrained by the seasonal patterns of the monsoons. They could also stop at ports that were previously unreachable or inconvenient. These innovations came to be reflected in the interest rates on bottomry loans for junks sailing between China and Southeast Asia, which far exceeded those on European vessels traveling the same route. Investors evidently considered junk voyages to be riskier and more vulnerable to damage from storms, dangerous shoals, or pirate attacks.[19]

Besides better equipped militaries and navigational breakthroughs, a sophisticated financial infrastructure allowed the West to dictate the terms of trade. Substantial amounts of credit facilitated the expansion and prosperity of commercial exchange at Guangzhou and other ports across maritime Asia. At the same time, the Hong merchants grew increasingly dependent upon Western loans and advances to operate their firms and cover shortfalls resulting from sudden contingencies. Faced with steep interest rates, most firms became highly leveraged and eventually went under because of permanent debt or bankruptcy. Yet, the continued willingness of the merchants to take out loans from Westerners epitomized their lack of access to cheaper, more efficient sources of funding.[20] As a result, trade between China and Southeast Asia gradually declined relative to commerce between China and India and Europe.

Fundamentally, after the closure of the Japanese silver mines, Europeans dominated the world's bullion production, which the Qing depended upon as currency for large transactions. The Europeans transported silver through the sea-lanes that they dominated with their ships into ports under their control, such as Cadiz and Manila.[21] The Qing also could never resolve shortfalls in its other currency for daily exchange: copper; especially when faced with increasingly stringent restrictions from Japan.[22] Because much of the available silver and copper became absorbed within China, the shortages afflicted Southeast Asia more acutely.[23] Cochinchina and The Port had to experiment with substitutes, such as casting zinc coins. Although they circulated widely, their overproduction, Li Tana points out, contributed to rampant inflation in the prices of real goods, a key reason behind the popular discontent that resulted in the Tây Sơn uprising.[24]

---

[19] Van Dyke, *Merchants*, vol. 1, p. 47, 70; Van Dyke, *Canton Trade*, p. 110.
[20] Van Dyke, *Merchants*, vol. 1, pp. 18–21; vol. 2, pp. 214–215.
[21] Van Dyke, *Merchants*, vol. 2, p. 95.   [22] Zhao Gang, *Qing Opening*, pp. 140–152.
[23] Shimada, *Intra-Asian Trade*, pp. 24–28.
[24] Li Tana, 'Cochinchinese Coin Casting,' pp. 131–139; Li Tana, *Nguyễn Cochinchina*, pp. 95–98.

The lead exhibited by Western Europe emanated from an environment of almost continuous warfare between states and equally fierce competition among their antagonistic elites. The need for survival stimulated official encouragement of long-distance trade and overseas expansion, scientific research and experimentation, and innovative ways to fund these projects, such as public debt. The political economy of Western Europe proved conducive to the integration of vertical hierarchies, with their clearly defined categories and boundaries, with horizontal, boundary-crossing mercantile activities.[25] The formation of the long-distance trading companies effectively consolidated the advantages in firearms, shipping, and finance; and weaponized overseas trade as a means of enriching and enhancing the power of the home country.

A similar climate of competition and warfare characterized mainland Southeast Asia. However, as a crossroads of Eurasia, it was constantly exposed to outside influence and intervention. The ready availability of European weapons and expertise led to a dependence upon them when waging war. The result was an uneven and often poorly integrated mix of Westernized and Western, non-Western mercenary, and indigenous military units. It made the creation of domestic infrastructures to produce firearms and, more importantly, keeping up with the fast pace of innovations, highly difficult.[26]

Qing state-building, on the other hand, had largely concluded in the middle of the eighteenth century with the establishment of dominance over the steppes and neutralization of the nomadic groups that had been a persistent threat to Inner China for thousands of years. For many decades afterward, the external political climate was generally peaceful, and trade flourished, as vessels flocked to its shores to purchase the products from its highly efficient market economy. Andrade's data reveals that the period from 1760 to 1830 saw the "lowest level of armed conflict" in China between 900 and 1900.[27] Accordingly, the overall orientation of its institutions and policies aimed at the preservation and perpetuation of a satisfactory status quo.

Commerce was essential for the livelihood of coastal Chinese residents, and the Qing court understood their priorities and supported their activities. As Po shows, the Qing operated customhouses along the coast that supervised and taxed incoming and outgoing ships. Its navy protected merchants and ensured the safety of their ships by rescuing shipwreck survivors and combating pirates. Beyond the Inner Seas, which the

---

[25] Rosenthal and Wong, *Before and Beyond Divergence*, pp. 209–221.
[26] Charney, *Southeast Asian Warfare*, pp. 243–247.
[27] Andrade, *Gunpowder Age*, pp. 238–239.

Qing territorialized and administered just like on land, it used its fleets to project power through the implied threat of force, while relying primarily upon diplomacy to ensure compliance from polities across the region.[28] As the more restrictive Guangzhou System took shape over the 1750s, the Qing ensured that prices remained competitive at the city so as to encourage continued growth in the trade and more foreigners to come and do business. In fact, the court came to depend upon the revenues forwarded from Guangzhou for a sizable part of its annual budget.[29]

However, for an empire committed to internal maintenance and stability, the biggest potential threat that the Qing faced was domestic subversion, often in connivance with foreign forces. While it depended upon the Hong merchants for its revenues, the Qing kept close watch over their activities to ensure that none of them would grow powerful enough to translate their commercial wealth into political influence, especially in a sensitive frontier such as Guangzhou. The court purposely set up a system that encouraged competition with one another. The Hong merchants were made collectively responsible for each other's debts and took responsibility for repaying loans from foreigners even if borrowing from them was illegal. Debt gave the Qing more leverage over the Hong merchants and weakened their power and influence as a group. Moreover, they were not allowed to directly contact foreign governments, nor could they outfit missions of their own beyond Southeast Asia.[30]

Toward Chinese immigrants and their descendants outside the legal reach of the Qing, the court could be highly pragmatic, but it could never overcome a deep-seated fear of their intentions and actions. As Zhao Gang highlights, the court remained suspicious of the persistence of Ming loyalist sentiments among the overseas communities and feared that they would conspire with discontented Han subjects at home to foment insurrection. This security concern motivated the Kangxi Emperor's renewal of the sea ban in 1717 and the court's subsequent attempts to restrict long-term residence abroad.[31] It could also explain why, beyond the apparent alarm about the legitimacy of Taksin's seizure of the throne in Siam, the Qianlong Emperor seems to have been unsettled by his Chinese creole background. The Qing withheld official recognition of Taksin as king until 1777, five years after it permitted him to pay tribute.[32]

Cognizant of the sensitivity of the issue, Mo Tianci consciously downplayed assertions of Ming loyalism. Instead, he projected himself to both

---

[28] Po, *Blue Frontier*, pp. 71–76, 176–177, 211.   [29] Van Dyke, *Merchants*, vol. 1, p. 85.
[30] Van Dyke, *Merchants*, vol. 1, pp. 85, 102; vol. 2, pp. 213–214.
[31] Zhao Gang, *Qing Opening*, pp. 156–160; Kuhn, *Chinese among Others*, pp. 20–21.
[32] J. K. Chin, 'King Taksin and China,' pp. 180–185.

the Qing court and officials and gentry as a model Confucian. He also showered praise upon the Qianlong Emperor and Li Shiyao, the governor-general of Guangdong and Guangxi. By keeping merchants confined within a limited scope and area of operations and overseas Chinese groups at arm's distance, the Qing did not effectively integrate trade, military innovation, and capital into a cycle of political and economic expansion. Given its political economy, there was simply no need.

There were, however, two contingent circumstances centered upon Southeast Asia that might have altered this direction. Although improvements in navigational technology allowed Western ships to acquire a decisive advantage in many parts of maritime Asia, junks continued to dominate the routes to and from the water world. The area's proximity to China and island Southeast Asia made it well-suited to the trading pattern of the junk, and it continued to occupy one of the largest shares of Guangzhou's foreign commerce. The dense concentration of Chinese, Malay, Minangkabau, and Bugis merchants proved conducive to capital accumulation. A financial center emerged in The Port, and there were reserves of silver in its hinterlands.

During the late 1760s, moreover, the Qing, faced with disastrous setbacks in its campaign against Myanmar, seriously attempted an alliance with Mo Tianci. The Qianlong Emperor wanted to use him as a means of consolidating control over the Chinese maritime networks. They would prove useful for the Qing in asserting a more interventionist role in mainland Southeast Asian affairs, especially in the recruitment of kings, pretenders, governors, and other persons of influence to form a second front against Myanmar. Ultimately, the plan did not materialize because of fortuitous circumstances, such as the unexpected rise of Taksin and Tianci's failed invasion of Siam. The Qing envoy, Cai Han, out of sheer incompetence, also arrived too late for the official instructions that he carried to make a dramatic impact on the ground.

More fundamentally, however, Myanmar simply could not threaten the Qing at an existential level. The Qianlong Emperor persisted in the campaign more for his own pride since the repeated defeats represented a serious loss of face and a blight on his previous record of victories. In the end, a negotiated truce was agreed upon in 1770. About twenty years later, Myanmar sent a tribute mission to Beijing, providing the pretext for the emperor to spin the disaster into a glorious victory.[33] There was thus no compelling reason for him to continue in his advocacy for Mo Tianci. Taksin, too, defeated Myanmar and established his dominance in Siam

---

[33] Dai, 'Disguised Defeat,' pp. 169–182.

without any help from the Qing.³⁴ The Qianlong Emperor accorded recognition to him only after his status as ruler over the kingdom had become indisputable.

Lacking meaningful support from the home country, Chinese mercantile groups from Cochinchina to Siam were forced to expend their huge sums of capital in backing local rulers whom they believed were the most capable of providing them protection and privileges. When warfare and chaos broke out within and among states, these business interests turned against each other in vicious internecine competition. The support of the Chaozhou community for Taksin against Mo Tianci can be seen in this light, as well as the more numerous and enterprising Chinese merchants who backed various contenders for the throne during the Tây Sơn uprising. And, Sakurai argues, once successful local rulers had completed their unification and consolidation of their states, they readily abandoned the Chinese.³⁵ Even Taksin, who was half-Chaozhou and employed many Chinese officials, presented himself as a wholly Siamese ruler and built his kingdom according to Theravada symbols of legitimacy and authority.³⁶

Toward the end of the eighteenth century, new elements became involved in the China Seas. This development occurred in tandem with the decline of Spain, Portugal, and The Netherlands, the powers that participated in the first wave of European maritime expansion, from the sixteenth to the seventeenth centuries. Starting from the 1770s, British country traders flooded into the Straits. They traded with Johor, Kedah, and other polities on the Malay Peninsula, using weapons and opium and cloth from South Asia to buy into the rest of the intra-Asian trade. In particular, opium, which enjoyed robust demand from Chinese laborers in the plantations and mines, provided a means for country traders to reap significant profits.³⁷ Equipped with the latest naval technology and generous capital from the EIC, they struck the final blow to the VOC's commercial dominance in island Southeast Asia, which was already severely punctured by rampant smuggling outside official channels. British shipping also managed to out Chinese junks from many of their established routes.³⁸

The activities of the country traders paved the way for the EIC's establishment of colonies at Penang in 1786 and Singapore in 1819.

---

³⁴ J. K. Chin, 'King Taksin and China,' p. 186.   ³⁵ Sakurai, 'Chinese Pioneers,' p. 36.
³⁶ Pombejra, 'Chinese in Siam,' pp. 348–349.
³⁷ Miller, *British Traders*, pp. 51–150; Hanser, *Mr. Smith*, pp. 47–49; Trocki, *Opium*, pp. 50–52.
³⁸ Vos, *Gentle Janus*, pp. 28–29.

The duty-free status of the two and their location at the crossroads of South and East Asia resembled The Port during its heyday. As with The Port, the Chinese creoles and Qing merchants and sojourners played a significant role in their settlement and commercial development. They were also home to a cosmopolitan population from across Eurasia. The key difference is that Penang and Singapore, and later, Hong Kong after 1842, formed integrated nodes in the British strategy of worldwide economic and imperial expansion centered upon control of the sea-lanes.[39] Neither The Port nor its mainland Southeast Asian neighbors or China arrived at a similarly comprehensive vision that could take the Mo clan's enterprise beyond the China Seas and into the contest for global markets. But The Port undoubtedly became a prototype for how the later Asian emporia functioned.

During the period from 1780 to 1830, the significant degree of autonomy and agency enjoyed by overseas Chinese, as epitomized by The Port's own status as an independent entity, gradually eroded. As a result of the intensification of European colonialism and imperialism, they were faced with three choices. Many went to more remote, sparsely populated frontiers still outside the reach of centralizing states and the European trading systems. In places such as West Borneo and the interior of the Malay Peninsula, they formed organizations known as *gongsi* that were primarily centered around laborers engaged in mining, planting, and natural resource extraction. Merchants, on the other hand, tended to join local states or the British or Dutch trading systems, settling down at ports under their control and subordinating the junk trade under their supervision.[40] The cost was to give up significant political autonomy, especially the maintenance of their own armed forces. Both choices effectively constrained and gradually marginalized the Chinese commercial networks and their scope of activities.

Faced with this situation, many Chinese opted for a third path, forming secret societies that perpetuated the original long-distance commercial networks underneath the proliferation of new boundaries and clarified jurisdictions set by emergent states on land and European naval power on the seas. As Mary Heidhues convincingly argues, secret societies and the *gongsi* constituted two sides of the same coin. Both had organizational structures based on sworn brotherhoods, usually from the same native place, and leaders chosen by the popular votes of members. They monopolized occupations in local economies and controlled the labor supply. They also shared religious elements, such as worshipping a

---

[39] Kuhn, *Chinese among Others*, pp. 99–103.   [40] Trocki, *Opium*, pp. 30, 33–34.

common patron deity, and ideological convictions, particularly nostalgia for the Ming.[41] In many ways, they represented an evolution from the privileges and autonomy enjoyed by Chinese communities across Southeast Asia, including independent polities such as The Port, during the heyday of the Chinese century.

The only difference between them was the mark of illegality given by state authorities. The secret societies' possession of weapons and the kind of trade that they engaged in, involving opium and other items considered to be contraband, took place outside officially sanctioned channels. Moreover, their activities often crossed boundaries between mutually hostile territories, such as from the Dutch to British spheres of influence in island Southeast Asia. Secret societies further created corridors to the homeland in China but in ways potentially or openly subversive to Qing rule. The late eighteenth century witnessed a proliferation of rebellions involving partisans with secret society connections in Taiwan and the southeastern mainland coast.[42] The Qing, in turn, had less motivation to support or find common cause with these autonomous overseas Chinese elements.

The tragic outcomes of both Mo Tianci and Taksin in the 1780s therefore marked the beginning of the end of the Chinese century in maritime Asia. It coincided with the decline of Qing sea power and its definitive replacement by the Europeans, particularly the British. The West proved increasingly able to set the rules for economic integration and derive the greatest benefit from it. China, on the other hand, gradually transformed into a periphery as it fell behind in technology and experienced severe capital outflows from the rapid growth in opium imports and global silver shortages.[43] China's outdated military proved unable to defend its lengthy coastline and ports, its most vital and lucrative linkages to the outside world, from the influx of illegal drugs and threats to its sovereignty from powerful Western warships and armies. Nor could China control the money supply or devise a new, widely accepted currency on its own terms. Over the nineteenth century, China's surplus labor, combined with Southeast Asia's natural resources, came to primarily supply the voracious demand of an industrializing West.[44]

---

[41] Heidhues, 'Chinese Organizations,' pp. 80–82.
[42] Heidhues, 'Chinese Organizations,' pp. 81–82; Kuhn, *Chinese among Others*, pp. 56–57, 69–70.
[43] Lin, *China Upside Down*, pp. 29–95.
[44] Kuhn, *Chinese among Others*, pp. 97–196; Pan, *Sons of the Yellow Emperor*, pp. 43–172.

In sum, The Port's downfall as a fully autonomous entity resulted from the confluence of firmer territorial boundaries in Southeast Asia and Western domination of the sea routes. These, in turn, constrained the Mo's ability to exploit their key advantages of translocal connections and integration into multiple state hierarchies. Nonetheless, The Port and its hinterlands, which gradually transformed into liminal borderlands, continued to shape modern mainland Southeast Asia well past their prime. On the one hand, they offered havens and rich troves of capital and manpower that aspiring state-builders could draw upon to realize their ambitions. By mobilizing the Chaozhou community that had become at least a sizable plurality in the water world, Taksin could take over the Siamese throne. His remarkable trajectory of conquest, expansion, and consolidation paved the way for his successors, the Chakri, to establish a durable rule over the kingdom. Also in this water frontier, Nguyễn Ánh managed to survive the Tây Sơn onslaught and later defeat them to bring Cochinchina and Tonkin under his new dynasty.[45] It can be argued that the non-state space of The Port became the cradle of modern Thailand and Vietnam.

At the same time, the descendants of Mo Jiu and Mo Tianci proved able to stubbornly hold onto their realm and prevent full domination from state actors. Although they could never bring back the glorious days of their ancestors, they continued to serve as hereditary governors and enjoyed a significant degree of autonomy. It was only in 1867, with the arrival of the French as part of their occupation of the Mekong Delta and Gulf of Siam littoral, that The Port, a frontier holdover from the Chinese century, finally lost its unique status.[46] Its subsequent history would be integrated, in a marginal way, into the narratives of French empire and Vietnamese nation.

---

[45] Li Tana, 'Mekong Delta,' p. 154.   [46] Sellers, *Princes of Hà-Tiên*, pp. 131–139.

Glossary

Khmer terms are cross-checked and verified by Choeurn Kim Heng. Thai terms are cross-checked and verified by Pisut Phonglaohaphan.

An Nam	安南
Ạn Pháp	安法
Ân Trừng	印澄
Ang Chan	អង្គចន្ទ
Ang Chee	អង្គជី
Ang Chov	អង្គជូវ
Ang Em	អង្គអឹម
Ang Mei Bhen	អង្គម៉ែ ប៉េន
Ang Nan	អង្គនន់
Ang Sngoun	អង្គស្ងួន
Ang Sor	អង្គស៊ូ
Ang Tan	អង្គតន់
Ang Tham	អង្គធម្ម
Angkor	អង្គរ
Angkor Thom	អង្គរធំ
Annan	安南
Anqing	安慶
Ao Sen	沟蓮
apsara	អប្សរា
Athivongsa	អធិវង្សា
Ayeyarwady	ဧရာဝတီ
Ayutthaya	อยุธยา
Ba Phnom	បាភ្នំ
Bắc Hải	北海
Bạch Mã	白馬
baht	บาท
Bai Juyi	白居易
Baima	白馬

291

Ban	班
bang	幫
Bang Pla Soi	บางปลาสร้อย
Banteay Meas	បន្ទាយមាស
bảo hộ	保護
Barom Reachea	បរមរាជា
Bassac	បាសាក់
Bati	បាទី
Bavar Metrey	បវរមេត្រី
Bảy Núi	罷凸
Beihai	北海
Beijing	北京
Bendi	本底
Bhamo	ဗန်းမော်
Biên Hòa	邊和
Bình Dương	平陽
Bình San	屏山
bizhen	敝鎮
bothoam beida	បឋមបិតា or *brothoam beida* ប្រឋមបិតា
boxue hongru	博學鴻儒
bu liangli	不兩立
Bùi	裴
Bùi Thị Lẫm	裴氏凜
Bunma	บุญมา
Cà Mau	哥毛
cai bạ	該薄
Cái Bè	丐舥
cai đạo	該道
Cai Han	蔡漢
Cần Thơ	芹苴
Cảnh Hưng	景興
Chakri	จักรี
Chan	禪
Chan Borei	ចន្ទបុរី
Chang'an	長安
Changjiang	長江
Chanthaburi	จันทบุรี
Chao Chui	เจ้าจุ้ย
Chao Sisang	เจ้าศรีสังข์ (modern Thai academic usage) or Chao Sesang เจ้าเสสัง (historical records)

Chaophraya	เจ้าพระยา
Chaophraya Chakri	เจ้าพระยาจักรี
Chaophraya Surasi	เจ้าพระยาสุรสีห์
chaoponhea	ចៅពញា
Chaozhou	潮州
Châu Đốc	朱篤
Chen Ang	陳昂
Chen Chong Tok	ចិនចុងតុក
Chen Dading	陳大定
Chen Dali	陳大力
Chen Junqing	陳俊卿
Chen Lian	陳聯
Chen Mingxia	陳鳴夏
Chen Ruifeng	陳瑞鳳
Chen Ruishu	陳瑞書
Chen Shangchuan	陳上川
Chen Tai	陳太
Chen Yinsi	陳寅泗
Chen Zhikai	陳智楷
Chen Zilan	陳自蘭
chenghuang	城隍
Chesth (month)	ខែជេស្ឋ
Chey Chettha	ជ័យជេដ្ឋា
Chiêu Anh Các	招英閣
Chonburi	ชลบุรี
Chov	ជូរ
chúa	主
Chumphon	ชุมพร
chưởng cơ	掌奇
cơ	奇
Cù lao Giêng	岣崂崰
cư sĩ	居士
Cửu Ngọc	玖玉
Da Jinyu	大金嶼
Đà Nẵng	沱瀼
Da Qing	大清
dahuangdi	大皇帝
Đại Kim Dữ	大金嶼
Đại Việt	大越
Damnak Chang'aeur	ដំណាក់ចង្អេរ
Đàng Ngoài	塘外

Đàng Trong	塘中
dao	道
đạo	道
Deng Yao	鄧耀
Desa Nayok	ដេសានាយក
dhammaraja	ธรรมราชา
Địa Tạng	地藏
Điều Khiển Dinh	調遣營
dinh	營
Định Viễn	定遠
Định Vương	定王
Dizang	地藏
Đồ Bà đội	闍問隊
Đô đốc	都督
Đô đốc tướng quân	都督將軍
Đỗ Thanh Nhơn	杜清仁
đội	隊
Donay	ដូនណៃ
Đông Hồ	東湖
Đông Khẩu	東口
Đông Kinh	東京
Đồng Nai	狪狔
Đông Phố	東浦
Đông Sơn	東山
Dongboshe	東波社
Donghu	東湖
Dongling	東嶺
Dongpuzhai	東埔寨
Du Qingren	杜清仁
Đức Bụng	德脝
Dương Ngạn Địch	楊彥迪
Edo	江戶
Ekkathat	เอกทัศ
Fang Qiubai	方秋白
Fangcheng	芳城
Fuguo	富國
Funan	扶南
Furong	芙蓉
Fuzhou	福州
Gangkou	港口
Gangkou guo	港口國

Gành Hào	矿蠔
ganzhi	干支
Gao-Lei-Lian	高雷廉
Gaozhou	高州
gengshen	庚申
gengyin	庚寅
Gia Định	嘉定
Gia Long	嘉隆
Giang Thành	江城
Giao Chỉ	交趾
gongchuan	貢船
Gonghang	公行
gongsheng	貢生
gongsi	公司
Guan Yu	關羽
Guangdong	廣東
Guangxi	廣西
Guangzhou	廣州
Guo Jie	郭傑
Hà Nội	河內
Hà Tiên	河仙
Hà Tiên quốc	河仙國
Hà Tiên thập cảnh	河仙十景
Hà Tiên thập cảnh khúc vịnh	河仙十景曲詠
Hà Tiên thập cảnh tổng luận	河仙拾景總論
Hà Tiên thập vịnh	河仙十詠
Haicheng	海澄
Haifeng	海豐
Hainan	海南
Han	漢
Hàn Dương	漢陽
Hangzhou	杭州
Hanyang	漢陽
Haoji	蠔磯
hầu	侯
Hebei	河北
Hexian	河仙
Hexian guo	河仙國
Hexian shijing	河仙十景

Hexian shiyong	河仙十詠
Hexiangu	何仙姑
Heyi	和義
Hiền	賢
Hiệp trấn	叶鎮
Hồ Quý Ly	胡季犛
Hòa Nghĩa	和義
Hoàn Vũ	桓武
Hoàng	黃
Hoàng Bích	黃檗
Hoàng Long	黃龍
Hoàng Tiến	黃進
Hoàng Việt	皇越
Hội An	會安
Hòn Chông	圫蓯
Hòn Đất	圫坦
Hsinbyushin	ဆင်ဖြူရှင်
Huang	黃
Huang Jin	黃進
Huang Long	黃龍
Huang Ming	皇明
Huang Qing	皇清
Huangbo	黃檗
Huanwu	桓武
Huế	化
Huệ	惠
Hùng bảo	雄寶
Huo Qubing	霍去病
Huo Ran	霍然
Huỳnh	黃
Inwa	အင်းဝ
Jiading	嘉定
Jiangcheng	江城
Jiangnan	江南
Jianjiang	堅江
Jianzhuwen	尖竹汶
Jiaozhi	交趾
Jiaxing zang	嘉興藏
Jin	晉
Jingang	金剛
Jinshan	金山

jinshi	進士
Jishan	戢山
Jundaima	君代嗎
Kampong Som	កំពង់សោម
Kampong Trach	កំពង់ត្រាច
Kampot	កំពត
Kampoul Meas	កំពូលមាស
Kampuchea Krom	កម្ពុជាក្រោម
Kan'ei	寬永
Kangxi	康熙
Kep	កែប
khaet	ខេត្ត
Khai trấn Thượng trụ quốc Đại tướng quân	開鎮上柱國大將軍
Khorat	โคราช
Khun Kaew	ขุนแก้ว
Kiên Giang	堅江
Kiên Lương	堅良
Kim Cang	金剛
Kochi	കൊച്ചി
Koh Kong	កោះកុង
Koh Russei Prei	កោះឫស្សីព្រៃ
Koh Tral	កោះត្រល
Konbaung	ကုန်းဘောင်
Kong	孔
Kralahom	ក្រឡាហោម
Kramoun Sar	ក្រមួនសរ
Ksitigarbha	क्षितिगर्भ
Lặc Chi Gia	勒之加
Lâm Kỳ Tào	林其藻
Lâm Tế	臨濟
Lê	黎
Lê Bá Bình	黎伯評
Lê Quý Đôn	黎貴惇
Leizhou	雷州
Li Cai	李才
Li Shiyao	李侍堯
Li Wenguang	李文光
Lianchi	蓮池
Liang Luan	梁鸞
Liang Shangxian	梁上選

Lianzhou	廉州
Lin Jiguang	林緝光
Lin Weize	林維則
Lin Wenbao	林文寶
Linglong	玲瓏
Linji	臨濟
Liwu zhen	禮武鎮
Lon Nol	លន់ នល់
Long Hồ	龍湖
Long kỳ	龍旗
Long Xuyên	龍川
Longchuan	龍川
longfei	龍飛
Longhor	លង់ហោ
Longhu dajiangjun	龍虎大將軍
Longmen	龍門
Longqi	龍旗
Longvek	លង្វែក
Lữ	侶
Luqi	鹿崎
lưu dân	流民
Luxi xiandiao	鱸溪閑釣
Mạc	莫、鄚
Mạc Cửu	莫玖、鄚玖
Mạc Kim Định	莫金定、鄚金定
Mạc Thiên Tứ	莫天賜、鄚天賜
Mạc Triều Đán	莫朝旦
Mạc Tử Dung	鄚子溶
Mạc Tử Hạo	鄚子灝
Mạc Tử Hoàng	鄚子潢
Mạc Tử Thảng	鄚子尚
Mao Tianci	鄚天賜
Mao Tianjiu	鄚天玖
Mao Yunyang	鄚雲陽
Maocheng	鄚城
Mesar	ម៉េ ស
Ming	明
Ming gu	明故
Mingbo	明渤
Mingbo Dabu	明渤大庯
Mingbo Luxi suo	明渤鱸溪所

Mingbo Qishubu	明渤奇樹庯
Mingbo Tuqiu Dian	明渤土丘玷
Mingbo Xinbu	明渤新庯
Minh	明
Minh Bột	明渤
Minh Bột Đại Phố	明渤大庯
Minh Bột Kỳ Thọ Phố	明渤奇樹庯
Minh Bột Lư Khê Sở	明渤鱸溪所
Minh Bột Tân Phố	明渤新庯
Minh Bột Thổ Khâu Điếm	明渤土丘玷
Minh Hương	明香、明鄉
Minnan	閩南
Mo	莫
Mo Bang	莫邦
Mo Cong	莫琮
Mo Dingbang	莫定邦
Mo Hao	莫灝
Mo Huang	莫潢
Mo Jinding	莫金定
Mo Jiu	莫玖
Mo Qin	莫欽
Mo Rong	莫溶
Mo Shaoyuan	莫紹原
Mo Shilin	莫士麟
Mo Tang	莫尙
Mo Tianci	莫天賜
Mo Wu	莫武
Moat Chrouk	មាត់ជ្រូក
Mou	មូ
Muang Kham	ມ່ວງຄຳ
Mũi Nai	堳狔
Mỹ Tho	美湫
Nặc Bồn	匿盆
Nagasaki	長崎
Nakhon Si Thammarat	นครศรีธรรมราช
Nam Bộ	南部
Nam Thiên	南天
Nam tiến	南進
nanjin	南金

Nanjing	南京
Nantian	南天
Narai	นารายณ์ or Somdet Phra Narai สมเด็จพระนารายณ์ฯ
Neak Samdech	អ្នកសម្ដេច
neak ta	អ្នកតា
Neareay Reachea	នារាយណ៍រាជា
Nghĩa	義
Ngô Thế Lân	吳世鄰
Ngũ Hổ	五虎
Nguyễn	阮
Nguyễn Ánh	阮映
Nguyễn Cư Trinh	阮居貞
Nguyễn Cửu Vân	阮久雲
Nguyễn Đình Tú	阮廷秀
Nguyễn Hữu	阮祐
Nguyễn Phúc Chu	阮福凋
Nguyễn Phúc Dương	阮福暘
Nguyễn Phúc Khoát	阮福濶
Nguyễn Phúc Tần	阮福瀕
Nguyễn Phúc Thái	阮福溙
Nguyễn Phúc Thụ	阮福澍
Nguyễn Phúc Thuần	阮福淳
Nguyên Thiều	元韶
Nguyễn Văn Túc	阮文肅
Nhạc	岳
Nhật Nam	日南
Ningbo	寧波
Ninh	寧
nôm	喃
Norean Tok	នរេន្ទ្រ តុក
oknha	ឧកញ៉ា
Oudong	ឧដុង្គ
oupareach	ឧបរាជ
oupayureach	ឧភយោរាជ
Outey	ឧទ័យ
Pan Qiguan	潘啟官
Pan Siju	潘思矩
Panyu	番禺
Peam	ពាម

Phạm Nguyễn Du	范阮攸
Phan Thiên Quảng	潘天廣
Phetracha	เพทราชา or Somdet Phra Phetracha
	สมเด็จพระเพทราชา
Phiên Trấn	藩鎮
Phitsanulok	พิษณุโลก
Phnom Dei	ភ្នំដី
Phnom Mlou	ភ្នំម្លូ
Phnom Nay	ភ្នំណៃ
Phnom Penh	ភ្នំពេញ
Phnom Yuon	ភ្នំយួន
Phra Klang	พระคลัง
Phraya Kosa	พระยาโกษา
Phraya Phiphit	พระยาพิพิธ
Phraya Racha Setthi	พระยาราชาเศรษฐี
Phraya San	พระยาสรรค์
Phraya Tak Sin	พระยาตากสิน
Phsar Dek	ផ្សារដែក
Phsar Reachea	ផ្សាររាជា
Phù Dung	芙蓉
Phú Quốc	富國
Phương Thành	芳城
Phutthaimat	พุทไธมาศ
Piaoyao	嫖姚
Pingshan	屏山
Pok	ប៉ុក
Ponhea Chan	ពញាចន្ទ
Preah Kse Ek	ព្រះខ្សែឯក
Preah Reachea Setthi	ព្រះរាជាសេដ្ឋី
Preah Sotoat	ព្រះសុទាត
Preah Trapeang	ព្រះត្រពាំង
Preahbat Reameatipadey	ព្រះបាទរាមាធិបតី
Prek Prahut	ព្រែកព្រហ្ួត
Prey Krabas	ព្រៃក្របាស់
Prey Nokor	ព្រៃនគរ
Puducherry	புதுச்சேரி
Pulan	普蘭
Pursat	ពោធិសាត់
Qianlong	乾隆
qianzong	千總
Qing	清

Qing chao wenxian tongkao	清朝文獻通考
Qingyuan	清遠
Qinju	芹苴
Qinzhou	欽州
quan	貫
quận công	郡公
Quảng Nam	廣南
Quảng Ngãi	廣義
quốc lão	國老
Quốc ngữ	國語
quốc phó	國傅
Quy Nhơn	歸仁
Rạch Giá	瀝架
Rạch Ụ	瀝塢
Rạch Vược	瀝鱸
Rama I	รัชกาลที่๑ or Somdet Phra Phutthayotfa สมเด็จพระพุทธยอดฟ้าฯ
Reachea Setthi	រាជាសេដ្ឋី
Ream	រាម
Ream Reachea	រាមរាជា
Reameatipadey	រាមាធិបតី
Rinan	日南
Ryukyu	琉球
Sa	沙
Sa Đéc	沙溄
Sài Gòn	柴棍
Sãi Vãi	仕娓
Samdech	សម្តេច
sampeah	សំពះ
Samrong Tong	សំរោងទង
Sanbao	三寶
Santuk	សន្ទុក
Satha	សត្ថា
Senathipdey	សេនាធិបតី
Shakyamuni	शाक्यमुनि
shangguo	上國
Shanghai	上海
She Xichun	佘錫純
shengli	生理
Shengshui dui	勝水隊
Shi Lang	施琅

Shidong	石洞
Shita mituo	十塔彌陀
Shuichang	水場
Shunde	順德
shuode	碩德
Sichuan	四川
Sin	สิน
Siv	ស៊ីវ
Song	宋
sras	ស្រះ
Srey Sauryopor	ស្រីសុរិយោពណ៌
Srey Sramut	ស្រីសាមុត
Srok Peam	ស្រុក ពាម
Suất	率
Sun Tianrui	孫天瑞
Sun Tianzhen	孫天珍
Sunzi	孫子
Suzhou	蘇州
taitou	抬頭
Tak	ตาก
Taksin	ตากสิน or Somdet Phrachao Taksin สมเด็จพระเจ้าตากสินฯ
Tam Bảo	三寶
Tân Châu	新洲
Tân chính vương	新政王
Tan Xiang	譚湘
Tang	唐
Tang Yuchong	湯玉崇
Tây Sơn	西山
Tbaung Khmum	ត្បូងឃ្មុំ
Thạch Động	石洞
Thái Bình	太平
Thái thượng vương	太上王
tham mưu	參謀
tham tướng	參將
thang	艭
Thăng	昇
Thánh Nguyên	聖源
Thắng Thủy đội	勝水隊
Thập Tháp Di-Đà	十塔彌陀
Thất Sơn	七山

thi xã	詩社
thiên	天
Thiền	禪
thiên vương	天王
Thiệu Bình	紹平
Thonburi	ธนบุรี
Thongduang	ทองด้วง
Thuận Yên	順安
thực lục	寔錄
thuyền	船
tian	天
tianchao	天朝
Tiantou	田頭
tianyun	天運
Tiểu Kim Dữ	小金嶼
tixing	提刑
Tô Châu	蘇州
Tokugawa	德川
Tôn Thất Xuân	尊室春
Tôn Thiên Trân	孫天珍
Tống	宋
tổng binh	總兵
Tông Đức	琮德
Tống Văn Khôi	宋文魁
Tonle Sap	ទន្លេសាប
Touk Meas	ទូកមាស
Trà Vinh	榇樑
trấn	鎮
Trấn Biên	鎮邊
Trần Đại Định	陳大定
Trần Đại Lực	陳大力
Trấn Di	鎮彝
Trấn Giang	鎮江
Trần Minh Hạ	陳鳴夏
Trần Thượng Xuyên	陳上川
Trần Trinh	陳禎
Trat	ตราด
Treang	ទ្រាំង
tri phủ	知府
Trịnh	鄭
Trịnh Hoài Đức	鄭懷德

Trịnh Liên Sơn	鄭連山
Trịnh Quốc Hoa	鄭國華
Trung Nghĩa	忠義
Trương	張
Trường Giang	長江
Trương Phúc Loan	張福巒
tuguan	土官
Tuk Khmau	ទឹកខ្មៅ
tumu	土目
Tushan	土山
tusi	土司
upparat	อุปราช
Vạn Tuế Sơn	萬歲山
Việt Nam	越南
Việt Nam khai quốc chí truyện	越南開國志傳
Vĩnh Long	永隆
Võ Vương	武王
Vũ Thế Dinh	武世營
vược	鱥
Wanfosui	萬佛歲
wang	王
Wang Chang	王昶
Wang Houlai	汪後來
Wang Xian	王仙
Wang Xilai	汪溪來
Wang Yan	王衍
Wang Yangming	王陽明
wangzi	王子
wat	K: វត្ត T: วัด
Wat Arun	วัดอรุณ
Wat Buppharam	วัดบุปผาราม
Wu	武
Wu Zhihan	吳之翰
Wuchuan	吳川
Wuhu	五虎
Wurong dajiangjun	五戎大將軍
Wuyang	吳陽
Xi	悉
Xiamen	廈門
Xi'an	西安

Xian	冼
Xian Biao	冼彪
xiansheng	先生
Xiao Jinyu	小金嶼
Xie Zhang	謝璋
Xinjiang	新疆
Xiongbao	雄寶
Xiongnu	匈奴
Xu	徐
Xu	許
Xu Quan	許全
Xu Xiemin	徐叶旻
Xu Youyong	徐有用
Xuanzong	玄宗
y viện	醫院
Yang	楊
Yang Guifei	楊貴妃
Yang Yandi	楊彥迪
Yangjiang	陽江
Yangzi	揚子
yeshi	野史
yimu	夷目
Yincheng	印澄
Yindaima	尹代嗎
Yomreach	ឈមរាជ
Yongzheng	雍正
youji	遊擊
Yuanshao	元韶
Yunnan	雲南
Zhang Ji	張繼
Zhang Taichu	張太初
Zhang Xianying	張憲英
Zhao Pilie	趙丕烈
Zhaowu dajiangjun	昭武大將軍
Zhaoying ge	招英閣
Zheng	鄭
Zheng Chenggong	鄭成功
Zheng Huaide	鄭懷德
Zheng Lushe	鄭祿舍
Zheng Rui	鄭瑞
Zheng Zhao	鄭昭

Glossary

Zhenjiang	鎮江
Zhenla	真臘
zhenmu	鎮目
Zhenyi	鎮彝
Zhongyi	忠義
Zhou	周
Zhoushan	舟山
Zhu Pu	朱璞
Zhu Xi	朱熹
Zhuang Huiyao	莊輝耀
zhusheng	諸生
zongbing	總兵
zongdu	總督
Zu Zeqing	祖澤清

Bibliography

Abbreviations

AMEP   Archives des Missions Etrangères de Paris (Archives of the Paris Foreign Missions Society), Paris
ANRI   Arsip Nasional Republik Indonesia (National Archives of the Republic of Indonesia), Jakarta
BEFEO   *Bulletin de l'Ecole française d'Extrême-Orient* (Bulletin of the French School of the Far East)
BL, IOR   British Library, India Records Office, London
BNF   Bibliothèque nationale de France (French National Library), Paris
EFEO   Ecole française d'Extrême-Orient (French School of the Far East), Paris
NA   Nationaal Archief (National Archive), The Hague

Archives, Manuscripts, Inscriptions

AMEP, Cochinchine (Cochinchina)

vol. 743: 'Copie de la lettre de M. D'Azema à Mgr. Lefevre' (Copy of the letter from Mr. D'Azema to Mgr. Lefevre), 10 April 1751.
vol. 744: 'M. Piguel à Messrs. les Directeurs' (Mr. Piguel to the Directors), 15 July 1752.
'Relation' (Report), 1768.
vol. 745: 'Relation des Franciscains des Iles Philippines dans les royaumes de Cochinchine, Ciampa, Cambodge par le Père Julien de la Saint Vierge, double en Français' (Account of the Franciscans from the Philippine Islands in the Kingdoms of Cochinchina, Champa, and Cambodia by Father Julián de Nuestra Señora, copy in French), Kam-kao, 1770.

ANRI

K66a: Archief van de gouverneur-generaal en raden van Indië (Hoge Regering) van de Verenigde Oostindische Compagnie en taakopvolgers, 1612–1812 (Archive of the governor-general and Council of the Indies [High

Government] of the Netherlands United East India Company and legal successors).
1560, Bijlagen Generale Resoluties (Appendices to the general resolutions), 1771-5-3–1771-6-28.
1567, Bijlagen Generale Resoluties (Appendices to the general resolutions), 1772-3-6–1772-4-28.
1570, Bijlagen Generale Resoluties (Appendices to the general resolutions), 1772-8-4–1772-9-25.
1573, Bijlagen Generale Resoluties (Appendices to the general resolutions), 1772-12-1–1772-12-29.
2567–2591, Dagregisters (Daily registers), 1735-1-1–1761-12-31.
2593–2597, Dagregisters (Daily registers), 1763-1-1–1770-12-31.
3574, Inlandse vorsten ingekomen en uitgaande missiven (Incoming and outgoing missives of the inland princes), 1768-4-11–1771-5-9.
3654, Buitenkantoren ingekomen en uitgaande missiven (Incoming and outgoing missives with outside of the company), 1745-3-2–1745-12-31.
3657, Buitenkantoren ingekomen en uitgaande missiven (Incoming and outgoing missives with outside of the company), 1747-7-25–1747-12-31.
3659, Buitenkantoren ingekomen en uitgaande missiven (Incoming and outgoing missives with outside of the company), 1749-1-1–1749-12-31.
3668, Buitenkantoren ingekomen en uitgaande missiven (Incoming and outgoing missives with outside of the company), 1757-1-4–1757-12-31.
3670, Buitenkantoren ingekomen en uitgaande missiven (Incoming and outgoing missives with outside of the company), 1759-1-8–1759-12-31.
3674, Buitenkantoren ingekomen en uitgaande missiven (Incoming and outgoing missives with outside of the company), 1763-1-4–1763-12-31.
3675, Buitenkantoren ingekomen en uitgaande missiven (Incoming and outgoing missives with outside of the company), 1764-1-6–1764-12-31.
3677, Buitenkantoren ingekomen en uitgaande missiven (Incoming and outgoing missives with outside of the company), 1765-7-5–1765-12-31.
3687, Buitenkantoren ingekomen en uitgaande missiven (Incoming and outgoing missives with outside of the company), 1770-8-3–1770-12-31.
3688, Buitenkantoren ingekomen en uitgaande missiven (Incoming and outgoing missives with outside of the company), 1771-1-10–1771-12-31.
3689, Buitenkantoren ingekomen en uitgaande missiven (Incoming and outgoing missives with outside of the company), 1772-1-4–1772-7-31.

BL

IOR/G/4/1: Borneo.
IOR/G/12/35: China and Japan: Diaries and Consultations of the Council in China, 25 May 1733 – 28 May 1734.

China First Historical Archives, Beijing

Junjichu 軍機處 (Grand Council), 1387-020.

EFEO

A. 586: Lê Đản 黎亶, *Nam Hà tiệp lục* 南河捷錄 (Summary record of Cochinchina).

Khmer Manuscripts, d.888.IV.2, film n° 145: *Preah reach pongsavatar preah maha ksatr* ព្រះរាជពង្សាវតារព្រះមហាកសត្រ (Royal chronicles of the kings and queens).

'Grand Council Archives of the National Palace Museum (Taipei),' Qianlong 乾隆 Reign

007528: Pan Siju 潘思矩, 1751.
010186: Li Shiyao 李侍堯, 1769.
010189: Mo Shilin 莫士麟, undated.
010253: Li Shiyao, 1769.
012083: Li Shiyao, 1770.
012446: Li Shiyao, 1770
013221: Mo Shilin, 1770.
013988: Mo Shilin, undated.
014670: *Chaxun Guangdong zhi Xianluo cheng haidao cheng tu* 查詢廣東至暹羅城海道程圖 (Navigational map drawn upon consultation of the maritime route from Guangdong to Ayutthaya), undated.
017920: Li Shiyao, 1772.
017970: Li Shiyao, 1772.

Hán-Nôm Institute, Hanoi

A. 441: Mao Tianci 鄭天賜, **C: Annan Hexian shiyong** V: *An Nam Hà Tiên thập vịnh* 安南河仙十詠 (Ten verses of Hà Tiên in Annam).

A. 780: Trịnh Hoài Đức 鄭懷德, *Cấn Trai thi tập* 艮齋詩集 (Poetry collection of Trịnh Hoài Đức).

A. 832: Phạm Khắc Trạch 范克宅 (ed.), *Cao Man ki lược* 高蠻紀略 (Narrative of the Khmer barbarians).

A. 2939: Phạm Nguyễn Du 范阮攸, *Nam hành ký đắc tập* 南行記得集 (Collection of memories from the southern journey).

Inscriptions

Huỳnh Phước Huệ, 'Sự Tích Giếng Tiên' (The historical relic of Fairy Well), Dương Đông: descriptive plaque.

Thích Nữ Như Hải, 'Huyền thoại về Hòa Thượng Khai Sơn Sắc Tứ Tam Bảo Tự' (Legend of the founding monk of the Temple of Three Treasures), Hà Tiên: descriptive plaque.

Manuscripts

Dongling Mo shi zupu 東嶺莫氏族譜 (Ancestral genealogy of the Dongling Mo clan), Dongling: unpublished manuscript, n. p.

Tiantou cun Chen shi Nanfang Changzhi zupu 田頭村陳氏南房長枝族譜 (Clan genealogy of the Nanfang Changzhi Chen clan of Tiantou Village), Tiantou: unpublished manuscript, n. p.

Tiantou qi zhi shijiu shi zu shihui pu 田頭七至十九世祖諡諱譜 (Genealogy of the personal and posthumous names of the seventh to the nineteenth generations of Tiantou), Tiantou: unpublished manuscript, n. p.

NA

1.04.21 Archieven van de Nederlandse Factorij in Japan te Hirado (1609–1641) en te Deshima (1641–1860) (Archives of the Dutch factory in Japan at Hirado [1609–1641] and at Deshima [1641–1860]), 1609–1860.
152, Dagregisters (Daily registers), 1741-10-29–1742-10-17.

Primary Printed Sources

Alcobendas, Severiano, 'Religiosos médico-cirujanos de la Provincia de San Gregorio Magno de Filipinas' (Religious doctors and surgeons of the Province of Saint Gregory the Great of The Philippines),
  5: *Archivo Ibero-Americano* (Iberian-American archives), 37.114 (1934): 205–226.
  6: *Archivo Ibero-Americano* (Iberian-American archives), 37.115 (1934): 321–345.
Al-haji, Raja Ali, 'Silsilah Melayu dan Bugis dan Sakalian Raja-raja-nya' (Genealogy of Malay and Bugis princes), Hans Overback (trans.), *Journal of the Malayan Branch of the Royal Asiatic Society* 4.3 (1926): 339–381.
Birch, Cyril, and Donald Keene (eds.), *Anthology of Chinese Literature: From Early Times to the Fourteenth Century*, New York: Grove Press, 1965.
Blussé, Leonard, and Nie Dening (eds.), *The Chinese Annals of Batavia, the Kai Ba Lidai Shiji and Other Stories (1610–1795)*, Leiden: Brill, 2018.
Chen Jianhua 陳建華 (ed.), *Guangzhou dadian* 廣州大典 (The great compendium of Guangzhou), 520 vols, Guangzhou: Guangzhou chubanshe, 2015.
  vol. 89: Ling Yangzao 凌揚藻, *Haiyatang quanji* 海雅堂全集上 (The complete collection from the Hall of Maritime Elegance, Part 1), pp. 223–571.
  vol. 444: She Xichun 佘錫純, *Yushan tang shichao* 語山堂詩抄 (Compendium of the poetry of She Xichun), pp. 137–173.
  vol. 445: Yang Zhenqing 楊霞青, *Luxi shichao* 蘆溪詩抄 (Copies of poetry from Luxi), pp. 61–196.
Les codes anciens du Cambodge: Corpus de 1891 (The ancient codes of Cambodia: Corpus of 1891), Phnom Penh: Krasuong Sethakech nung Heronvottho, 2016.

Crawfurd, John, *Journal of an Embassy from the Governor-General of India to the Courts of Siam and Cochin China: Exhibiting a View of the Actual State of Those Kingdoms*, 2nd ed., 2 vols, London: Henry Colburn and Richard Bentley, 1830.

Dalrymple, Alexander, *Oriental Repertory*, 2 vols, London: Ballintine and Law, 1808.

Eng Soth ឯងសុត, *Akkasar mahaboros khmer* ឯកសារ មហាបុរសខ្មែរ (Documents on Khmer heroes), 7 vols, Phnom Penh, 1969.

Favre, Pierre François, *Lettres édifiantes et curieuses sur la visite apostolique de M. de La-Baume, évêque d'Halicarnasse à la Cochinchine en l'année 1740, où l'on voit les Voyages & les Travaux de ce zélé Prélat, la conduite des Missionnaires Jésuites & de quelques Autres, avec de nouvelles Observations &c. Pour servir de continuation aux Mémoires historiques du R. P. Norbert Capucin* (Uplifting and curious letters about the apostolic visit of Mr. de La-Baume, Bishop of Halicarnasse to Cochinchina in the year 1740, where we see the travels and work of this zealous prelate, the conduct of the Jesuit missionaries and several others, with new observations, etc. To serve as a continuation of the historical memoirs of the Capuchin, R. P. Norbert), Venice: Chez les Frères Barzotti, 1746.

Fuheng 傅恒, *Huang Qing zhigongtu* 皇清職貢圖 (Portraits from the tributary vassals of the Imperial Qing), 2 vols, Taipei: Huawen shuju, 1968.

Hamilton, Alexander, *A New Account of the East Indies*, 2 vols, London: C. Hitch and A. Millar, 1744.

Hayashi Shunsai 林春齋, *Ka'i hentai* 華夷變態 (The transformation from Chinese to barbarian), Ura Ren'ichi 浦廉一 (ed.), 3 vols. Tokyo: Tōyō bunko, 1958.

Ibn Ahmad, Raja Ali Haji, *The Precious Gift (Tuhfat al-Nafis)*, Virginia Matheson and Barbara Watson Andaya (trans. and annot.), Kuala Lumpur: Oxford University Press, 1982.

s' Jacobs, Hugo K. (ed.), *Generale missiven van gouverneurs-generaal en raden aan Heren XVII der Vereinigde Oostindische Compagnie* (General missives from the governors-general and council to the Gentlemen Seventeen of the United East India Company), vol. 14, pt. 1, Amsterdam: Huygens ING, 2016.

Khin Sok (ed. and trans.), *Les Chroniques royales du Cambodge: De Bañā Yāt jusqu'à la prise de Lañvaek* (The royal chronicles of Cambodia: From Ponhea Yat to the capture of Longvek), Paris: EFEO, 1981.

Kondo Morishige 近藤守重, *Gaiban tsūsho* 外蕃通書 (Diplomatic letters with foreign lands), *Kondo Seisai zenshū* 近藤正齋全集 (The complete works of Kondo Morishige), vol. 1, Tokyo: Kokusho kankōkai, 1905.

König, Johann Gerhard, 'Journal of a Voyage from India to Siam and Malacca in 1779,' *Journal of the Straits Branch of the Royal Asiatic Society* 26 (1894): 80–201.

Launay, Adrien (ed.), *Histoire de la Mission de Cochinchine, 1658–1823: Documents historiques* (History of the Cochinchinese Mission, 1658–1823: Historical documents), 3 vols, Paris: Société Générale d'Imprimerie et d'Edition, 1924.

Histoire de la Mission de Siam: Documents historiques (History of the Siamese Mission: Historical documents), 2 vols, Paris: Anciennes maisons Charles Douniol et Retaux, 1920.

Lê Quang Định 黎光定, *Hoàng Việt nhất thống địa dư chí* 皇越一統輿地志 (Unified gazetteer of the Imperial Việt), Huế: Nhà xuất bản Thuận Hoá, 2002.

Lê Quý Đôn 黎貴惇, *Kiến Văn Tiểu Lục* 見聞小錄 (Small record of things seen and heard), 2 vols, Hanoi: Nhà xuất bản Giáo dục, 2008.

Phủ biên tạp lục 撫邊雜錄 (Miscellaneous chronicles of the pacified frontier), 2 vols, Hanoi: Nhà xuất bản Giáo dục, 2007.

Leclère, Adhémard, *Les codes cambodgiens* (The Cambodian codes), 2 vols, Paris: Ernst Leroux, 1898.

Lin Jingzhi 林京志 (ed.), 'Qianlong nianjian you Taiguo jinkou dami shiliao xuan' 乾隆年間由泰國進口大米史料選 (Selections from the archival documents on imported Thai rice during the Qianlong period), *Lishi dang'an* 历史档案 (Historical archives) 3 (1985): 17–27.

Luang Ruengdetanan พันตรี หลวงเรืองเดชอนันต์, *Racha phongsawadan krung kamphucha khong Nak Ong Noppharat* ราชพงษาวดารกรุงกัมพูชา ของ นักองค์นพรัตน (Royal chronicles of Cambodia of Nak Ong Noppharat), Thongdi Thanarat ทองดี ธนรัชน์ (trans.), Bangkok: Phrae Phittaya, 1970.

Luo Tianchi 羅天尺, *Wushan zhilin* 五山志林 (Gazetteer of the Five Mountains), in Wu Qi 吳綺 (ed.), *Qing dai Guangdong biji wuzhong* 清代廣東筆記五種 (Five prose writings from Qing Guangdong), Guangzhou: Guangzhou renmin chubanshe, 2006, pp. 29–178.

Mair, Victor H. (ed.), *The Shorter Columbia Anthology of Chinese Literature*, New York: Columbia University Press, 2001.

Mak Phoeun (ed. and trans.), *Chroniques royales du Cambodge de 1594 à 1677* (The royal chronicles of Cambodia from 1594 to 1677), vol. 3, Paris: EFEO, 1981.

Milburn, William, *Oriental Commerce: Containing a Geographical Description of the Principal Places in the East Indies, China, and Japan, with Their Produce, Manufactures, and Trade*, London: Black, Parry, and Company, 1813.

Nguyễn Dynasty Historiographical Institute, *Đại Nam nhất thống chí* 大南一統志 (Unified gazetteer of the Great South), Tự Đức 嗣德 edition, 6 vols, Chongqing: Xinan shifan daxue chubanshe, 2015.

Đại Nam thực lục 大南寔錄 (Veritable records of the Great South), 20 vols, Tokyo: Keiō gijuku daigaku gogaku kenkyūsho, 1961.

Nguyễn Khoa Chiêm 阮科占, *Việt Nam khai quốc chí truyện* 越南開國志傳 (Chronicle of the founding of Vietnam), Sun Xun 孫遜, Trịnh Khắc Mạnh 鄭克孟, and Chen Yiyuan 陳益源 (eds.), *Yuenan Hanwen xiaoshuo jicheng* 越南漢文小說集成 (Anthology of Vietnamese literature written in Chinese), vol. 7, Shanghai: Shanghai guji chubanshe, 2010.

Nouvelles lettres édifiantes des missions de la Chine et des Indes orientales (New uplifting letters from the missions of China and the East Indies), 8 vols, Paris: Chez Ad. Le Clere, 1823.

Pérez, Lorenzo, 'Los españoles en el imperio de Annam' (Spaniards in the Empire of Annam),

    4: *Archivo Ibero-Americano* (Iberian-American archives), 26.77 (1926): 145–178.

    5: *Archivo Ibero-Americano* (Iberian-American archives), 26.78 (1926): 273–326.

7: *Archivo Ibero-Americano* (Iberian-American archives), 27.80 (1927): 145–195.
8: *Archivo Ibero-Americano* (Iberian-American archives), 27.81 (1927): 289–323.
11: *Archivo Ibero-Americano* (Iberian-American archives), 29.86 (1928): 187–227.
12: *Archivo Ibero-Americano* (Iberian-American archives), 30.89 (1928): 179–240.
13: *Archivo Ibero-Americano* (Iberian-American archives), 35.106 (1932): 161–204.
14: *Archivo Ibero-Americano* (Iberian-American archives), 35.107 (1932): 321–365.
15: *Archivo Ibero-Americano* (Iberian-American archives), 36.109–110 (1933): 49–93.
(ed.), *Diario del P. Francisco Hermosa de Buenaventura: Misionero de Cochinchina, 1744–1768* (Diary of Francisco Hermosa de Buenaventura: Missionary of Cochinchina, 1744–1768), Florence: Collegii S. Bonaventurae, 1934.

Poivre, Pierre, 'Journal d'un voyage à la Cochinchine' (Journal of a voyage to Cochinchina), in Henri Cordier (ed.), *Revue de l'Extrême-Orient* (Far Eastern review), vol. 3, Paris: E. Leroux, 1887, pp. 364–510.

Ouevres complettes (Complete works), Paris: Chez Fuchs, 1797.

Prachum phongsawadan ประชุมพงศาวดาร (Collected chronicles), Bangkok: Khurusapha.
  1: *Phongsawadan khamen* พงศาวดารเขมร (Chronicle of Cambodia), 1963.
  65: *Phongsawadan Krung Thonburi chabab Phanchantanumat Choem* พงศาวดารกรุงธนบุรี ฉบับพันจันทนุมาศ เจิม (Thonburi chronicles, edition of Phanchantanumat Choem), 1960.
  66: *Chotmaihet raiwan thap samai krung Thonburi krao prab mueng Phutthaimat lae Khamen* จดหมายรายวันทัพสมัยกรุงธนบุรี คราวปราบเมืองพุทไธมาศและเขมร (Daily narrative in the Thonburi Era about the subjugation of The Port and Cambodia), 1960.

Qing dai guan shu ji Taiwan Zheng shi wangshi 清代官書記臺灣鄭氏亡事 (The fall of the Zheng family as recorded in the Qing official publications), Taipei: Taiwan yinhang jingji yanjiushi, 1963.

Qing shilu 清實錄 (Qing veritable records), 60 vols, Beijing: Zhonghua shuju, 2008.
  Gaozong Chunhuangdi shilu 高宗純皇帝實錄 (Qianlong veritable records), vols. 9–27, 2008.
  Shengzu Renhuangdi shilu 聖祖仁皇帝實錄 (Kangxi veritable records), vols. 4–6.

Shizong xian huangdi zhupi yuzhi 世宗憲皇帝硃批諭旨 (Rescripts and edicts of the Yongzheng Emperor), 360 *juan*, Taipei: Shangwu yinshuguan, 1983.

Tanabe Mokei 田邊茂啓, *Nagasaki jitsuroku taisei seihen* 長崎實錄大成正編 (Formal compendium of the Veritable Records of Nagasaki), Nagasaki: Nagasaki bunkensha, 1973.

Bibliography

Taiwan guanxi wenxian jiling 臺灣關係文獻集零 (Compilation of documents related to Taiwan), Taipei: Taiwan yinhang jingji yanjiushi, 1961.

Trịnh Hoài Đức 鄭懷德, *Gia Định thành thông chí* 嘉定城通志 (Gazetteer of Gia Định Viceroyalty), Hanoi: Nhà xuất bản Giáo dục, 1998.

van der Chijs, J. A., H. T. Colenbrander, and J. de Hullu (eds.), *Dagh-register gehouden int Casteel Batavia vant passerende daer ter plaetse als over geheel Nederlandts-India* (Daily journal held at Batavia Castle of the things happening in places over the entire Netherlands India), 1668–1669, The Hague: Martinus Nijhoff, 1897.

Vũ Thế Dinh 武世營 (ed.), *Hà Tiên trấn Hiệp trấn Mạc thị gia phả* 河仙鎮叶鎮鄚氏家譜 (Genealogy of the Mo clan, assistant commanders of Hà Tiên Garrison), Hanoi: Nhà xuất bản Thế Giới, 2006.

Wen Runeng 溫汝能 (ed.), *Yuedong shihai* 粵東詩海 (Sea of Cantonese poems), 3 vols, Guangzhou: Zhongshan daxue chubanshe, 1999.

Wyatt, David K. (ed.), *The Royal Chronicles of Ayutthaya*, Richard D. Cushman (trans.), Bangkok: The Siam Society, 2006.

Xiang Da 向達 (ed.), *Liangzhong haidao zhenjing* 兩種海道針經 (Two kinds of compass guides to the sea routes), Beijing: Zhonghua shuju, 1992.

Zhang Tingyu 張廷玉, *Qingchao wenxian tongkao* 清朝文獻通考 (Qing comprehensive examination of literature), 2 vols, Beijing: Shangwu yinshuguan, 1936.

Zheng Da 鄭達, *Yeshi wuwen* 野史無文 (An unspoken wild history), Taipei: Taiwan yinhang jingji yanjiushi, 1965.

Zhongguo difangzhi jicheng 中國地方誌集成 (Anthology of Chinese regional gazetteers)

  Shanghai fuxian zhi ji 上海府縣誌輯 (Collection of Shanghai prefecture and county gazetteers) 8: Cheng Qijue 程其珏 and Fan Zhongxiang 范鐘湘, *Guangxu Jiading xianzhi* 光緒嘉定縣志 (Guangxu Jiading County gazetteer), Shanghai: Shanghai shudian chubanshe, 2010.

  Sheng zhiji 省志輯: Liaoning 遼寧 (Collection of provincial gazetteers: Liaoning) 8: Liu Jinzhi 劉謹之, *Qianlong Shengjing tongzhi* 乾隆盛京通志 (Qianlong comprehensive Shengjing gazetteer), Nanjing: Fenghuang chubanshe, 2009.

  Guangdong fuxian zhi ji 廣東府縣誌輯 (Collection of Guangdong prefecture and county gazetteers) 42: Mao Changshan 毛昌善 and Wang Fuzhi 王輔之, *Guangxu Wuchuan xianzhi* 光緒吳川縣誌 (Guangxu Wuchuan County gazetteer), Shanghai: Shanghai shudian chubanshe, 2003.

Digital Resources

ANRI, *Sejarah Nusantara* (History of the Indonesian archipelago) <https://sejarah-nusantara.anri.go.id/>.

EFEO, Khmer Manuscripts <https://khmermanuscripts.efeo.fr/>.

Giá Khê, 'Sự tích Đồi Ngũ Hổ' (The legend of the Mount of Five Tigers), *Tuần Báo Văn Nghệ Thành Phố Hồ Chí Minh* (Ho Chi Minh City Arts weekly) 432 (2016) <http://tuanbaovannghetphcm.vn/su-tich-doi-ngu-ho/>.

Hao Yulin 郝玉麟, *Yongzheng Guangdong tongzhi* 雍正廣東通志 (Yongzheng comprehensive Guangdong gazetteer), *Chinese Text Project* <https://ctext.org/library.pl?if=gb&res=5155&remap=gb>.

'Kep Travel Guides,' *Tourism of Cambodia*, <www.tourismcambodia.com/travelguides/provinces/kep.htm>.

Lê Quý Đôn 黎貴惇, *Phủ biên tạp lục* 撫邊雜錄 (Miscellaneous chronicles of the pacified frontier), BNF, Archives et manuscrits (Archives and manuscripts), Vietnamien (Vietnamese) A. 18 <https://archivesetmanuscrits.bnf.fr/ark:/12148/cc912795>.

NA, *Ons nationaal geheugen* (Our national memory) <www.nationaalarchief.nl/>.

Thanh Dũng, 'Theo dấu văn thơ kỳ 5: Lư Khê nhạt dấu' (Following the traces of poetry record 5: A light trace of Sea Perch Creek), *Thanh Niên* (Youth), August 2, 2013 <https://thanhnien.vn/van-hoa/theo-dau-van-tho-ky-5-lu-khe-nhat-dau-365747.html>.

Trần Văn Mãnh, *Trung Học Hà Tiên Xưa* (Hà Tiên Secondary School in the past) <https://trunghochatienxua.wordpress.com/>.

Trương Minh Quang Nguyên, 'Từ những bức ảnh trăm năm, phần B: Đường Hòn Chông' (From photographs of a hundred years ago, part B: Hòn Chông Road), March 19, 2021 <https://trunghochatienxua.wordpress.com/2021/03/19/tu-nhung-buc-anh-tram-nam-phan-b-quang-nguyen/>.

Trương Minh Quang Nguyên, 'Từ những bức ảnh trăm năm, phần G: Họ Trương ở Rạch Vược' (From photographs of a hundred years ago, part G: The Trương clan in Sea Perch Creek), April 30, 2021 <https://trunghochatienxua.wordpress.com/2021/04/30/tu-nhung-buc-anh-tram-nam-phan-g-ho-truong-o-rach-vuoc-quang-nguyen/>.

Secondary Scholarship

Adams, Julia, 'Principals and Agents, Colonialists and Company Men: The Decay of Colonial Control in the Dutch East Indies,' *American Sociological Review* 61.1 (1996): 12–28.

Alberts, Tara, *Conflict and Conversion: Catholicism in Southeast Asia, 1500–1700*, Oxford: Oxford University Press, 2013.

Andaya, Barbara Watson, *To Live as Brothers: Southeast Sumatra in the Seventeenth and Eighteenth Centuries*, Honolulu: University of Hawai'i Press, 1993.

Anderson, James, *The Rebel Den of Nùng Trí Cao: Loyalty and Identity Along the Sino-Vietnamese Frontier*, Seattle: University of Washington Press, 2007.

Andrade, Tonio, *Gunpowder Age: China, Military Innovation, and the Rise of the West in World History*, Princeton: Princeton University Press, 2017.

How Taiwan Became Chinese: Dutch, Spanish, and Han Colonization in the Seventeenth Century, New York: Columbia University Press, 2008.

Lost Colony: The Untold Story of China's First Great Victory over the West, Princeton: Princeton University Press, 2011.

Ang Tsu Lyn, Claudine, *Poetic Transformations: Eighteenth-Century Cultural Projects on the Mekong Plains*, Cambridge: Harvard University Press, 2019.

'Regionalism in Southern Narratives of Vietnamese History: The Case of the "Southern Advance [Nam Tiến]",' *Journal of Vietnamese Studies* 8.3 (2013): 1–26.

'Writing Landscapes into Civilization,' T'oung Pao 104.5–6 (2018): 626–671.
Antony, Robert J., *Rats, Cats, Rogues, and Heroes: Hidden Glimpses of China's Past*, Lanham: Rowman and Littlefield, 2023.
'"Righteous Yang": Pirate, Rebel, and Hero on the Sino-Vietnamese Water Frontier, 1644–1684,' *Cross-Currents: East Asian History and Culture Review* 11 (2014): 4–30.
Unruly People: Crime, Community, and State in Late Imperial South China, Hong Kong: Hong Kong University Press, 2016.
Aymonier, Etienne, *Le Cambodge: Le royaume actuel* (Cambodia: The current kingdom), 2 vols, Paris: Ernest Leroux, 1900.
Baker, Chris, and Pasuk Phongpaichit, *A History of Ayutthaya*, Cambridge: Cambridge University Press, 2017.
Baldanza, Kathelene, *Ming China and Vietnam: Negotiating Borders in Early Modern Asia*, Cambridge: Cambridge University Press, 2016.
Balk, Louisa, Frans Van Dijk, and Diederick Kortlang, *The Archives of the Dutch East India Company (VOC) and the Local Institutions in Batavia (Jakarta)*, Leiden: Brill, 2007.
Barnard, Timothy P., *Multiple Centres of Authority: Society and Environment in Siak and Eastern Sumatra, 1674–1827*, Leiden: KITLV Press, 2003.
Batchelor, Robert, *London: The Selden Map and the Making of a Global City, 1549–1689*, Chicago: University of Chicago Press, 2014.
Bellwood, Peter, James J. Fox, and Darrell Tryon, 'The Austronesians in History: Common Origins and Diverse Transformations,' in Peter Bellwood, James J. Fox, Darrell Tryon (eds.), *The Austronesians: Historical and Comparative Perspectives*, Canberra: ANU E Press, 2006, pp. 1–16.
Blussé, Leonard, 'The Chinese Century: The Eighteenth Century in the China Sea Region,' *Archipel* 58 (1999): 107–129.
Bouillevaux, Charles-Emile, *L'Annam et le Cambodge: Voyages et notices historiques* (Annam and Cambodia: Travels and historical records), Paris: Victor Palmé, 1874.
Boxer, Charles Ralph, *The Christian Century in Japan, 1549–1650*, Berkeley: University of California Press, 1967.
Brokaw, Cynthia J., *Commerce in Culture: The Sibao Book Trade in the Qing and Republican Periods*, Leiden: Brill, 2020.
Brook, Timothy, 'Family Continuity and Cultural Hegemony: The Gentry of Ningbo, 1368–1911,' in Joseph W. Esherick and Mary Backus Rankin (eds.), *Chinese Local Elites and Patterns of Dominance*, Berkeley: University of California Press, 1990, pp. 37–47.
Praying for Power: Buddhism and the Formation of Gentry Society in Late-Ming China, Cambridge: Harvard University Press, 1993.
Vermeer's Hat: The Seventeenth Century and the Dawn of the Global World, New York: Bloomsbury Press, 2008.
Bruckmayr, Philipp, *Cambodia's Muslims and the Malay World: Malay Language, Jawi Script, and Islamic Factionalism from the 19th Century to the Present*, Leiden: Brill, 2019.
Buch, W. J. M., 'La Compagnie des Indes néerlandaises et l'Indochine' (The Netherlands East India Company and Indochina) 2, *BEFEO* 37 (1937): 121–237.

Bulbeck, David, Anthony Reid, Tan Lay Cheng, and Wu Yiqi (comp.), *Southeast Asian Exports since the 14th Century: Cloves, Pepper, Coffee, and Sugar*, Leiden: KITLIV Press, 1998.

Cai Zong-qi, *How to Read Chinese Poetry: A Guided Anthology*, New York: Columbia University Press, 2007.

Cao Tự Thanh, *Nho giáo ở Gia Định* (Confucianism in Gia Định), Ho Chi Minh City: Nhà xuất bản Tổng hợp Thành phố Hồ Chí Minh, 1996.

Chang Pin-tsun, 'The Rise of Chinese Mercantile Power in VOC Dutch Indies,' *Chinese Southern Diaspora Studies* 3 (2009): 3–21.

Charney, Michael, *Southeast Asian Warfare, 1300–1900*, Leiden: Brill, 2018.

Chen Ching-ho (Chen Jinghe, Chin Kei-wa) 陳荊和, 'Mac Thien Tu and Phrayataksin: A Survey on Their Political Stand, Conflicts and Background,' *Proceedings: Seventh IAHA Conference, 22–26 August 1977*, Bangkok: Organising Committee, 1979, pp. 1534–1575.

Chen Jihua 陈济华 (ed.), *Annan wang Chen Shangchuan* 安南王陈上川 (Chen Shangchuan, King of Annam), Hong Kong: Zhongguo renmin chubanshe, 2012.

  Chen Guohao 陈国豪, 'Lü Yue huaqiao mingren Chen Shangchuan' 旅越华侨名人陈上川 (Chen Shangchuan, a famous overseas Chinese residing in Vietnam), pp. 54–74.

  Chen Jihua, 'Annan wang Chen Shangchuan shiliao shiyi' 安南王陈上川史料拾遗 (Discoveries of some historical materials related to Chen Shangchuan, king of Annam), pp. 161–164.

  Wei Feng 魏风, 'Huaqiao xianqu Wuchuan ren Chen Shangchuan' 华侨先驱吴川人陈上川 (Chen Shangchuan of Wuchuan, an overseas Chinese pioneer), pp. 90–96.

Chen Jinghe (Chen Ching-ho, Chin Kei-wa) 陳荊和, 'Hexian Mao shi shixi kao' 河仙鄚氏世系考 (An examination of the genealogy of the Hà Tiên Mo clan), *Huagang xuebao* 華岡學報 (Hwakang academic journal) 5 (1969): 179–218.

Cheng Wei-chung (Zheng Weizhong) 鄭維中, *War, Trade and Piracy in the China Seas, 1622–1683*, Leiden: Brill, 2013.

Cheong, W. E., 'Canton and Manila in the Eighteenth Century,' in Jerome Ch'en and Nicolas Tarling (eds.), *Studies in the Social History of China and South-East Asia: Essays in Memory of Victor Purcell*, Cambridge: Cambridge University Press, 1970, pp. 227–246.

Chia Ning, 'Lifanyuan and Libu in the Qing Tribute System,' in Dittmar Schorkowitz and Chia Ning (eds.), *Managing Frontiers in Qing China: The Lifanyuan and Libu Revisited*, Leiden: Brill, 2017, pp. 144–183.

Chin, James Kong, 'King Taksin and China: Siam-Chinese Relations during the Thonburi Period as Seen from Chinese Sources,' in James Kong Chin and Geoff Wade (eds.), *China and Southeast Asia: Historical Interactions*, Abingdon: Routledge, 2019, pp. 174–187.

Chin Kei-wa (Chen Ching-ho, Chen Jinghe) 陳荊和, 'Kasen Maku-shi no bungaku katsudō, toku ni Kasen Jūei ni tsuite,' 河仙鄚氏の文学活動, 特に河仙十詠に就て (The Mo clan of Hà Tiên's literary activities, especially the Ten Verses of Hà Tiên), *Shigaku* 史学 (*History*) 40.2/3 (1967): 149–211.

Choi Byung Wook, *Southern Vietnam under the Reign of Minh Mang (1820–1841): Central Policies and Local Response*, Ithaca: Southeast Asia Program, 2004.

Chuon Nath ជូន ណាត, *Dictionnaire Cambodgien* (Dictionary of Cambodia), Phnom Penh: Buddhasasana Pandity, 1967.

Clarence-Smith, William Gervase. 'The Production of Cotton Textiles in Early Modern South-east Asia,' in Giorgio Riello and Prasannan Parthasarathi (eds.), *The Spinning World: A Global History of Cotton Textiles, 1200–1850*, Oxford: Oxford University Press, 2011, pp. 127–142.

Clulow, Adam, *The Company and the Shogun: The Dutch Encounter with Tokugawa Japan*, New York: Columbia University Press, 2014.

Cramer-Byng, John L., and John E. Wills, Jr., 'Trade and Diplomacy with Maritime Europe,' in John E. Wills (ed.), *China and Maritime Europe, 1500–1800: Trade, Settlement, Diplomacy, and Missions*, Cambridge: Cambridge University Press, 2010, pp. 183–254.

Dai Yingcong, 'A Disguised Defeat: The Myanmar Campaign of the Qing Dynasty,' *Modern Asian Studies* 38.1 (2004): 145–189.

Đặng Hoàng Giang, 'Theo dấu đô thị cổ Hà Tiên' (Tracking the ancient town of Hà Tiên), *Nghiên cứu Đông Nam Á* (Southeast Asian studies) 10 (2008): 69–76.

Đỗ Quỳnh Nga, *Công cuộc mở đất Tây Nam Bộ thời chúa Nguyễn* (The task of opening up the southwest during the time of the Nguyễn lords), Hanoi: Nhà xuất bản Chính trị quốc gia Sự thật, 2013.

Đỗ Văn Ninh, *Từ Điển Chức Quan Việt Nam* (Dictionary of Vietnamese official positions), Hanoi: Nhà xuất bản Thanh Niên, 2002.

Đông Hồ, *Văn Học Hà Tiên* (Literature of Hà Tiên), Saigon: Quinh Lâm, 1970.

Duan Xiaolin, *The Rise of West Lake: A Cultural Landmark in the Song Dynasty*, Seattle: University of Washington Press, 2020.

Dutton, George E., *The Tây Sơn Uprising: Society and Rebellion in Eighteenth-Century Vietnam*, Honolulu: University of Hawai'i Press, 2006.

Edwards, Penny, *Cambodge: The Cultivation of a Nation, 1860–1945*, Honolulu: University of Hawai'i Press, 2007.

Elman, Benjamin A., *A Cultural History of Modern Science in China*, Cambridge: Harvard University Press, 2009.

Eoseewong, Nidhi นิธิ เอียวศรีวงศ์, *Karn Muang Thai Samai Phrachao Krung Thonburi* การเมืองไทยสมัยพระเจ้ากรุงธนบุรี (Thai politics in the era of the Thonburi King), Bangkok: Silpawattanatham, 1986.

Wang Phaendin Prawattisat Preabtheap 'Krung Taek' nai Sam Ratcha Arnachak ว่างแผ่นดิน: ประวัติศาสตร์เปรียบเทียบ 'กรุงแตก' ในสามราชอาณาจักร (Interregna in comparison: Ineffectual adjustment to changes in the 18th Century among three mainland Southeast Asian kingdoms), Bangkok: Munnithi Khrongkan Tamra Sangkhommasat lae Manutsayasat, 2019.

Ge Zhaoguang, *What Is China?: Territory, Ethnicity, Culture, and History*, Michael Gibbs Hill (trans.), Cambridge: Belknap Press, 2018.

Gesick, Lorraine, 'Kingship and Political Integration in Traditional Siam, 1767–1824,' PhD diss., Cornell University, 1976.

Giersch, C. Patterson, *Asian Borderlands: The Transformation of Qing China's Yunnan Frontier*, Cambridge: Harvard University Press, 2006.

Gipouloux, François, *The Asian Mediterranean: Port Cities and Trading Networks in China, Japan and South Asia, 13th–21st Century*, Jonathan Hall and Dianna Martin (trans.), Cheltenham: Edward Elgar, 2011.

Goscha, Christopher, *Vietnam: A New History*, New York: Basic Books, 2016.

Groslier, Bernard Philippe, *Angkor and Cambodia in the Sixteenth Century: According to Portuguese and Spanish Sources*, Bangkok: Orchid Press, 2006.

Guy, R. Kent, *The Emperor's Four Treasures: Scholars and the State in the Late Ch'ien-lung Era*, Cambridge: Council on East Asian Studies, Harvard University, 1987.

Qing Governors and Their Provinces: The Evolution of Territorial Administration in China, 1644–1796, Seattle: University of Washington Press, 2017.

Hall, Kenneth R., 'The Coming of the West: European Cambodian Marketplace Connectivity, 1500–1800,' in T. O. Smith (ed.), *Cambodia and the West, 1500–2000*, London: Springer, 2018, pp. 7–36.

A History of Early Southeast Asia: Maritime Trade and Societal Development, 100–1500, Lanham: Rowman and Littlefield, 2011.

Hang Xing, *Conflict and Commerce in Maritime East Asia: The Zheng Family and the Shaping of the Modern World, c.1620–1720*, Cambridge: Cambridge University Press, 2015.

Hanser, Jessica, *Mr. Smith Goes to China: Three Scots in the Making of Britain's Global Empire*, New Haven: Yale University Press, 2019.

Heidhues, Mary Somers, 'Chinese Organizations in West Borneo and Bangka: Kongsis and *Hui*,' in David Ownby and May Somers Heidhues (eds.), *Secret Societies Reconsidered: Perspectives on the Social History of Modern South China and Southeast Asia*, Armonk: M. E. Sharpe, 1993, pp. 66–88.

Hoàng Anh Tuấn, *Silk for Silver: Dutch-Vietnamese Relations, 1637–1700*, Leiden: Brill, 2007.

Holroyd, Ryan, 'No Man's Borderland: Revisiting Ha Tien on the Eighteenth-Century Water Frontier,' *Monsoon Asia Studies* 11 (2020): 1–32.

'The Rebirth of China's Intra-Asian Maritime Trade, 1670–1740,' PhD diss., Pennsylvania State University, 2018.

Honey, David B., *The Southern Garden Poetry Society: Literary Culture and Social Memory in Guangdong*, Hong Kong: Chinese University of Hong Kong Press, 2013.

Howard, Michael C., *Textiles and Clothing of Việt Nam: A History*, Jefferson: McFarland, 2016.

de Huerta, Félix, *Estado geográfico, topográfico, estadístico, històrico-religioso, de la santa y apostólica provincia de S. Gegorio Magno* (Geographic, topographic statistical, historical-religious state of the holy and apostolic province of Saint Gregory the Great), Manila: M. Sanchez, 1865.

Idema, Wilt L., and Beata Grant, *The Red Brush: Writing Women of Imperial China*, Cambridge: Harvard University Asia Center, 2004.

Iwao Seiichi 岩生成一, *Nanyō Nihonmachi no kenkyū* 南洋日本町の研究 (Research on the Japantowns of Southeast Asia), Tokyo: Minami Ajia bunka kenkyū sho, 1940.

Jansen, Marius B., *China in the Tokugawa World*, Cambridge: Harvard University Press, 1992.

Kang, David C., *East Asia before the West: Five Centuries of Trade and Tribute*, New York: Columbia University Press, 2010.

Keith, Charles, *Catholic Vietnam: A Church from Empire to Nation*, Berkeley: University of California Press, 2012.

Kelley, Liam C., *Beyond the Bronze Pillars: Envoy Poetry and the Sino-Vietnamese Relationship*, Honolulu: University of Hawai'i Press, 2005.

  'Thoughts on a Chinese Diaspora: The Case of the Mạcs of Hà Tiên,' *Crossroads: An Interdisciplinary Journal of Southeast Asian Studies* 14.1 (2000): 71–98.

Khin Sok, *Le Cambodge entre le Siam et le Viêtnam, de 1775 à 1860* (Cambodia between Siam and Vietnam, from 1775 to 1860), Paris: EFEO, 1991.

Kitagawa Takako, '*Kampot* of the Belle Epoque: From the Outlet of Cambodia to a Colonial Resort,' *Southeast Asian Studies* 42.4 (2005): 394–417.

Kleinen, John, 'Towards a Maritime History of Vietnam: Seventeenth-Century Vietnamese-Dutch Confrontations,' in Volker Grabowsky (ed.), *Southeast Asian Historiography: Unravelling the Myths*, Bangkok: River Books, 2011, pp. 276–293.

Klepeis, Alicia Z., *Cambodia*, Hopkins: Bellwether Media, 2019.

Kuhn, Philip, *Chinese among Others: Emigration in Modern Times*, Lanham: Rowman and Littlefield, 2008.

Leclère, Adhémard, *Histoire de Cambodge depuis le 1er siècle de notre ère* (The history of Cambodia since the first century of our era), Paris: Librarie Paul Geuthner, 1914.

Li Qingxin 李庆新, '16–17 shiji Yuexi "Zhu zei," haidao yu "Xi zei"' 16–17世纪粤西"朱贼"、海盗与"西贼" (The 'Pearl River Delta bandits,' pirates, and 'West River bandits' in western Guangdong during the sixteenth to seventeenth centuries), *Haiyang shi yanjiu* 海洋史研究 (Studies of maritime history) 2 (2011): 121–164.

  'Haishang Ming chao: Mao shi Hexian zhengquan de Zhonghua tese' 海上明朝：郑氏河仙政权的中华特色 (Ming dynasty at sea: The Mao Hà Tiên regime and its Chinese characteristics), *Xueshu yuekan* 学术月刊 (Academic monthly) 10 (2008): 133–138.

  'Mao Jiu, Mao Tianci yu Hexian zhengquan (Gangkou guo)' 郑玖、郑天赐与河仙政权（港口国）(Mo Jiu, Mo Tianci and the Hà Tiên regime [Kingdom of The Port]), *Haiyang shi yanjiu* 海洋史研究 (Studies of maritime history) 1 (2010): 171–216.

  'Mao shi Hexian zhengquan ("Gangkou guo") ji qi duiwai guanxi: Jiantan Dongnanya lishi shang de "fei jingdian zhengquan"' 郑氏河仙政权（港口国）及其对外关系：兼谈东南亚历史上的"非经典政权" ('The Hà Tiên polity of the Mo clan ["Kingdom of The Port"] and its external relations: Concurrent discussion of "non-traditional regimes" in Southeast Asian history'), *Haiyang shi yanjiu* 海洋史研究 (Studies of maritime history) 5 (2013): 114–147.

Li Tana, 'The Eighteenth-Century Mekong Delta and Its World of Water Frontier,' in Nhung Tuyet Tran and Anthony J. S. Reid (eds.), *Việt Nam: Borderless Histories*, Madison: University of Wisconsin Press, 2006, pp. 147–162.

  'Jiaozhi (Giao Chi) in the Han Period Tongking Gulf,' in Nola Cooke, Li Tana, and James A. Anderson (eds.), *The Tongking Gulf through History*, Philadelphia: University of Pennsylvania Press, 2011, pp. 39–52.

Nguyễn Cochinchina: Southern Vietnam in the Seventeenth and Eighteenth Centuries, Ithaca: Southeast Asia Program, 1998.

Li Tana and Paul van Dyke, 'Canton, Cancao, and Cochinchina: New Data and New Light on Eighteenth-century Canton and the Nanyang,' *Chinese Southern Diaspora Studies* 1 (2007): 10–28.

Lieberman, Victor, *Strange Parallels: Southeast Asia in a Global Context, c. 800–1830*, 2 vols, Cambridge: Cambridge University Press, 2003.

Lim, Ivy Maria, *Lineage Society on the Southeastern Coast of China: The Impact of Japanese Piracy in the 16th Century*, Amherst: Cambria Press, 2010.

Lin Man-houng, *China Upside Down: Currency, Society, and Ideologies, 1808–1856*, Cambridge: Harvard University Press, 2007.

Locher-Scholten, Elsbeth, *Sumatran Sultanate and Colonial State: Jambi and the Rise of Dutch Imperialism, 1830–1907*, Ithaca: Cornell University Press, 2018.

Lufrano, Richard John, *Honorable Merchants: Commerce and Self-Cultivation in Late Imperial China*, Honolulu: University of Hawai'i Press, 1997.

Macauley, Melissa, *Distant Shores: Colonial Encounters on China's Maritime Frontier*, Princeton: Princeton University Press, 2021.

Mak Phoeun, 'La deuxième intervention militaire vietnamienne au Cambodge (1673–1679)' (The second Vietnamese military intervention in Cambodia [1673–1679]), *BEFEO* 77 (1988): 229–262.

Histoire du Cambodge de la fin du XVIe siècle au début du XVIIIe (History of Cambodia from the end of the sixteenth century to the beginning of the eighteenth century), Paris: EFEO, 1995.

Malleret, Louis, *L'archéologie du Delta du Mékong* (The archaeology of the Mekong Delta), 4 vols., Paris: EFEO, 1959.

Marks, Robert, *Tigers, Rice, Silk, and Silt: Environment and Economy in Late Imperial South China*, Cambridge: Cambridge University Press, 2004.

Massarella, Derek, 'Chinese, Tartars and "Thea" or a Tale of Two Companies: The English East India Company and Taiwan in the Late Seventeenth Century,' *Journal of the Royal Asiatic Society* III.3.3 (1993): 393–426.

Matsuda, Matt, *Pacific Worlds: A History of Seas, Peoples, and Cultures*, Cambridge: Cambridge University Press, 2012.

Mikaelian, Grégory, *La Royauté d'Oudong: Réformes des institutions et crise du pouvoir dans le royaume Khmer du XVIIe siècle* (The royalty of Oudong: Institutional reform and the crisis of power in the seventeenth-century Khmer kingdom), Paris: Presses de l'Université Paris-Sorbonne, 2009.

Miller, W. G., *British Traders in the East Indies, 1770–1820: 'At Home in the Eastern Seas'*, Woodbridge: Boydell and Brewer, 2020.

Mộng Tuyết, *Nàng ái cơ trong chậu úp* (The girl in the upside-down basin), Saigon: Bốn phương, 1961.

Moura, Jean, *Le Royaume du Cambodge* (The Kingdom of Cambodia), 2 vols, Paris: Ernest Leroux, 1883.

Murck, Alfreda, *Poetry and Painting in Song China: The Subtle Art of Dissent*, Leiden: Brill, 2020.

Myers, Ramon H., and Wang Yeh-chien, 'Economic Developments: 1644–1800,' in Denis Twitchett and John King Fairbank (eds.), *The*

Cambridge History of China, vol. 9, pt. 1: *The Ch'ing Empire to 1800*, Cambridge: Cambridge University Press, 2002, pp. 563–646.

Nara Shuichi, 'Zeelandia, the Factory in the Far Eastern Trading Network of the VOC,' in Leonard Blussé (ed.), *Around and about Formosa: Essays in Honor of Professor Ts'ao Yung-ho*, Taipei: Ts'ao Yung-ho Foundation for Culture and Education, 2003, pp. 161–174.

Ng Wai-ming, *Imagining China in Tokugawa Japan: Legends, Classics, and Historical Terms*, Binghamton: State University of New York Press, 2019.

Ngạc Xuyên, 'Minh Bột Di Ngư: Một quyển sách, hai thi xã' (Remaining fishing vessels at Mingbo: One volume, two poetry societies), *Đại Việt Tập Chí* (Great Việt journal) 12 (1943): pp. 6–13.

Nguyễn Hiền Đức, *Lịch sử Phật Giáo Đàng Trong, 1558–1802* (The history of Buddhism in Cochinchina, 1558–1802), Ho Chi Minh City: Nhà xuất bản Tổng Hợp Thành phố Hồ Chí Minh, 2006.

Nguyễn Huệ Chi, *Từ điển Văn học, bộ mới* (Dictionary of literature, new edition), Hanoi: Thế giới, 2004.

Nguyễn Ngọc Thơ and Nguyễn Thanh Phong, 'Philosophical Transmission and Contestation: The Impact of Qing Confucianism in Southern Vietnam,' *Asian Studies* 8(24).2 (2020): 79–112.

Nguyen Thanh-Nha, *Tableau économique du Vietnam aux XVIIe et XVIIIe siècles* (Economic picture of Vietnam in the seventeenth and eighteenth century), Paris: Editions Cujas, 1970.

Nguyễn Văn Hầu, 'Sự thôn thuộc và khai thác đất Tầm Phong Long: Cuối Chặng Cuối Cùng Của Cuộc Nam Tiến' (The acquisition and exploitation of Kampong Long: The final stage of the Southern Advance), *Tập San Sử Địa* (Journal of historical geography) 19–20 (1970): 3–24.

Ni, Xueting Christine, *From Kuan Yin to Chairman Mao: The Essential Guide to Chinese Deities*, Newburyport: Weiser, 2018.

Ning Qiang, *Art, Religion, and Politics in Medieval China: The Dunhuang Cave of the Zhai Family*, Honolulu: University of Hawai'i Press, 2004.

North, Douglass C., *Institutions, Institutional Change and Economic Performance*, Cambridge: Cambridge University Press, 1990.

Nuon Khoeurn ឈន ឃឿន, *Damnaer chhpaohtow tisakheanglich ning Indauchen knong chhnam 2000* ដំណើរឆ្ពោះទៅទិសខាងលិច និង កម្ពុជា 2000 (The journey toward the west and Indochina in the year 2000), Phnom Penh: Rongpoump Sinn Muy, 1971.

Pan, Lynn, *Sons of the Yellow Emperor: The Story of the Overseas Chinese*, New York: Kodansha America, 1994.

Pelley, Patricia M., *Postcolonial Vietnam: New Histories of the National Past*, Durham: Duke University Press, 2002.

Perdue, Peter, 'The Tenacious Tributary System,' *Journal of Contemporary China* 96 (2015): 1002–1014.

Péri, Noël, 'Essai sur les relations du Japon et l'Indochine aux XVIe et XVIIe siècles' (Essay on the relations between Japan and Indochina in the sixteenth and seventeenth centuries), *BEFEO* 23 (1923): 1–136.

Phạm Đức Mạnh, 'Cổ mộ quý tộc Mạc gia trên đất Hà Tiên' (Ancient burials of Mo aristocratic family in the Hà Tiên region), *Kỷ yếu Hội thảo khoa học quốc* tế Việt Nam học lần thứ IV (Proceedings of the Fourth International Academic Conference on Vietnamese Studies), Hanoi: Nhà xuất bản Khoa học xã hội, 2013, pp. 1292–1314.

Phạm Quốc Quân (ed.), *Vietnamese Coins*, Hanoi: Bảo tàng lịch sử Việt Nam, 2005.

Phan Huy Lê, 'Về việc đánh giá họ Mạc ở Hà Tiên' (An assessment of the Mo clan in Hà Tiên), *250 năm Tao đàn Chiêu Anh Các (1736–1986)* (250 year-anniversary of the Pavilion for Summoning Worthies poetry forum [1736–1986]), Rạch Giá: Sở Văn Hóa Thông Tin Kiên Giang, 1986, pp. 33–49.

Platero, Eusebio Gómez, and Fernandez Portillo, *Catálogo Biográfico de los Religiosos Franciscanos de la Provincia de San Gregorio Magno de Filipinas* (Biographic catalogue of religious Franciscans of the Province of Saint Gregory the Great of the Philippines), Manila: Colegio de Santo Tomás, 1880.

Po Chung Yam, Ronald, *The Blue Frontier: Maritime Vision and Power in the Qing Empire*, Cambridge: Cambridge University Press, 2018.

na Pombejra, Dhivarat, 'Administrative and Military Roles of the Chinese in Siam during an Age of Turmoil, Circa 1760–1782,' in Wang Gungwu and Ng Chin-keong (eds.), *Maritime China in Transition, 1750–1850*, Wiesbaden: Harrassowitz Verlag, 2004, pp. 335–353.

Pomeranz, Kenneth, *The Great Divergence: China, Europe, and the Making of the Modern World Economy*, Princeton: Princeton University Press, 2000.

Prakash, Om, *The Dutch East India Company and the Economy of Bengal, 1630–1720*, Princeton: Princeton University Press, 1985.

Ravina, Mark, *To Stand with the Nations of the World: Japan's Meiji Restoration in World History*, Oxford: Oxford University Press, 2017.

Reid, Anthony, 'Flows and Seepages in the Long-term Chinese Interaction with Southeast Asia,' in Anthony Reid (ed.), *Sojourners and Settlers: Histories of Southeast Asia and the Chinese*, Honolulu: University of Hawai'i Press, 1996, pp. 15–50.

Southeast Asia in the Age of Commerce, 1450–1680, New Haven: Yale University Press, 1990,

vol. 1: *The Land Below the Winds*.

vol. 2: *Expansion and Crisis*.

'Southeast Asian Consumption of Indian and British Cotton Cloth, 1600–1850,' in Girogio Riello and Tirthankar Roy (eds.), *How India Clothed the World: The World of South Asian Textiles, 1500–1850*, Leiden: Brill, 2009, pp. 31–53.

Rosenthal, Jean-Laurent, and Roy Bin Wong, *Before and Beyond Divergence: The Politics of Economic Change in China and Europe*, Cambridge: Harvard University Press, 2011.

Rowe, William T., *China's Last Empire: The Great Qing*, Cambridge: Harvard University Press, 2010.

Saving the World: Chen Hongmou and Elite Consciousness in Eighteenth-Century China, Stanford: Stanford University Press, 2001.

Rush, James Robert, *Opium to Java: Revenue Farming and Chinese Enterprise in Colonial Indonesia, 1860–1910*, Ithaca: Cornell University Press, 1990.

Rungswadisab, Puangthong, 'War and Trade: Siamese Interventions in Cambodia, 1767–1851,' PhD diss., University of Wollongong, 1995.

Sakurai Yumio, 'Eighteenth-Century Chinese Pioneers on the Water Frontier of Indochina,' in Nola Cooke and Li Tana (eds.), *Water Frontier: Commerce and the Chinese in the Lower Mekong Region, 1750–1880*, Lanham: Rowman and Littlefield, 2004, pp. 35–52.

Sakurai Yumio and Kitagawa Takako, 'Hà Tiên or Banteay Meas in the Time of the Fall of Ayutthaya,' in Kennon Breazeale (ed.), *From Japan to Arabia: Ayutthaya's Maritime Relations with Asia*, Bangkok: Toyota Thailand Foundation, 1999, pp. 150–218.

Salmon, Claudine, 'Réfugiés Ming dans les Mers du sud vus à travers diverses inscriptions (ca. 1650 – ca. 1730)' (Ming refugees in the southern seas as seen across diverse inscriptions [c. 1650 – c. 1730]), *BEFEO* 90–91 (2003): 177–227.

Schottenhammer, Angela, 'Characteristics of Qing China's Maritime Trade Policies, Shunzhi through Qianlong Reigns,' in Angela Schottenhammer (ed.), *Trading Networks in Early Modern East Asia*, Wiesbaden: Otto Harrassowitz, 2010, pp. 101–153.

Sellers, Nicholas, *The Princes of Hà-Tiên (1682–1867): The Last of the Philosopher-Princes and the Prelude to the French Conquest of Indochina: A Study of the Independent Rule of the Mạc Dynasty in the Principality of Hà-Tiên, and the Establishment of the Empire of Viêtnam*, Brussels: Editions Thanh-Long, 1983.

Shimada Ryūto, *The Intra-Asian Trade in Japanese Copper by the Dutch East India Company during the Eighteenth Century*, Leiden: Brill, 2006.

'Southeast Asia and International Trade: Continuity and Change in Historical Perspective,' in Sugihara Kaoru and Ōtsuka Keijirō (eds.), *Paths to the Emerging State in Asia and Africa*, Singapore: Springer, 2019, pp. 55–72.

Smith, George Vinal, *The Dutch in Seventeenth Century Thailand*, Dekalb: Northern Illinois University Press, 1977.

Sng, Jeffery, and Pimpraphai Bisalputra, *A History of the Thai-Chinese*, Singapore: Editions Didier Millet, 2015.

So Oeur ស៊ អឺរ], *Bravottesastr preah reachea nachakr Kampouchea cheamuoy Ahnam ning Siem chabpi satavots ti 16* ប្រវត្តិសាស្ត្រព្រះរាជាណាចក្រកម្ពុជាជាមួយអណ្ណាមនិងសៀមចាប់ពីសតវត្សទី១៦ (History of the kingdom of Cambodia with Vietnam and Siam from the sixteenth century), Phnom Penh: 1997.

Swain, Tony, *Confucianism in China: An Introduction*, New York: Bloomsbury Press, 2017.

Tagliacozzo, Eric, and Chang Wen-chin (eds.), *Chinese Circulations: Capital, Commodities, and Networks in Southeast Asia*, Durham: Duke University Press, 2011.

　Kwee Hui Kian, 'The End of the "Age of Commerce"? Javanese Cotton Trade Industry from the Seventeenth to the Eighteenth Centuries," pp. 283–302.

　Li Tana, 'Cochinchinese Coin Casting and Circulating in Eighteenth-Century Southeast Asia,' pp. 130–148.

　Sutherland, Heather, 'A Sino-Indonesian Commodity Chain: The Trade in Tortoiseshell in the Late Seventeenth and Eighteenth Centuries,' pp. 171–199.

Tambiah, S. J., *World Conqueror, World Renouncer: A Study of Buddhism and Polity in Thailand against a Historical Background*, Cambridge: Cambridge University Press, 1977.

Tamrathamnieb bandasak Krung Kamphucha ตำราทำเนียบบรรดาศักดิ์กรุงกัมพูชา (Lists of the court titles of the Kingdom of Cambodia), Bangkok: Sophon Phiphatthanakorn, 1922.

Taylor, Keith Weller, *A History of the Vietnamese*, Cambridge: Cambridge University Press, 2013.

'Surface Orientations in Vietnam: Beyond Histories of Nation and Region,' *Journal of Asian Studies* 57.4 (1998): 949–978.

Taylor, Philip, *Cham Muslims of the Mekong Delta: Place and Mobility in the Cosmopolitan Periphery*, Singapore: National University of Singapore Press, 2007.

The Khmer Lands of Vietnam: Environment, Cosmology and Sovereignty, Singapore: National University of Singapore Press, 2014.

Tazzara, Corey. *The Free Port of Livorno and the Transformation of the Mediterranean World, 1574–1790*, Oxford: Oxford University Press, 2017.

Tea Than ទៀ ថាន, *Rueng reav nei tukdei Kampouchea kraom, reo ateitax Kausangsin* រឿងរ៉ាវនៃទឹកដីកម្ពុជាក្រោម, ឬ អតីតកូសាំងសុីន (Stories of Kampuchea Krom, or former Cochinchina), Phnom Penh: Indradevi, 2005.

Theam Bun Srun, 'Cambodia in the Mid-Nineteenth Century: A Quest for Survival, 1840–1863,' MA thesis, Australian National University, 1981.

Thích Không Nhiên, Thích Pháp Hạnh, and Lê Thọ Quốc, 'Về bộ Gia Hưng Đại tạng kinh' (Regarding the Jiaxing Tripitaka), *Liễu Quán* 5 (2021): 109–135.

Thurgood, Graham, *From Ancient Cham to Modern Dialects: Two Thousand Years of Language Contact and Change*, Honolulu: University of Hawai'i Press, 1999.

Toby, Ronald P., *State and Diplomacy in Early Modern Japan: Asia in the Development of the Tokugawa Bakufu*, Princeton: Princeton University Press, 1984.

Tokyo University Historiographical Office, *Higashi Ajia to Nihon, sekai to Nihon* 東アジアと日本, 世界と日本 (East Asia and Japan, the world and Japan), Tokyo: Tōkyō daigaku shiryō hensanjo, 2013.

Tong Chee Kiong, *Identity and Ethnic Relations in Southeast Asia: Racializing Chineseness*, Dordrecht: Springer Netherlands, 2010.

Trần Nam Tiến, *Nam Bộ dưới thời chúa Nguyễn thế kỷ XVII–XVIII* (The southern area during the era of the Nguyễn lords, sixteenth to eighteenth centuries), Ho Chi Minh City: Nhà xuất bản Khoa học xã hội, 2018.

Trocki, Carl A., 'Chinese Pioneering in Eighteenth-Century South Asia,' in Anthony Reid (ed.), *The Last Stand of Asian Autonomies: Responses to Modernity in the Diverse States of Southeast Asia and Korea, 1760–1840*, New York: St. Martin's Press, 1997, pp. 83–102.

'Chinese Revenue Farms and Borders in Southeast Asia,' in Richard M. Eaton, Munis D. Faruqui, David Gilmartin, and Sunil Kumar (eds.), *Expanding Frontiers in South Asian and World History: Essays in Honour of John F. Richards*, Cambridge: Cambridge University Press, 2013, pp. 318–346.

Opium and Empire: Chinese Society in Colonial Singapore, 1800–1910, Ithaca: Cornell University Press, 1990.

Prince of Pirates: The Temenggongs and the Development of Johor and Singapore, 1784–1885, Singapore: National University of Singapore Press, 2013.

Trương Minh Đạt, *Nghiên cứu Hà Tiên* (Research on Hà Tiên),
  vol. 1: *Kỷ niệm 300 năm Hà Tiên trấn* (Commemorating 300 years of Hà Tiên Garrison), Ho Chi Minh City: Nhà xuất bản Trẻ, 2008.
  vol. 2: *Họ Mạc với Hà Tiên* (The Mo clan and Hà Tiên), Ho Chi Minh City: Nhà xuất bản Tổng hợp Thành phố Hồ Chí Minh, 2017.

van der Kraan, Alfons, *Murder and Mayhem in Seventeenth-Century Cambodia: Anthony van Diemen vs. King Ramadhipati I*, Bangkok: Silkworm Books, 2009.

Van Dyke, Paul, *The Canton Trade: Life and Enterprise on the China Coast, 1700–1845*, Hong Kong: Hong Kong University Press, 2007.
  Merchants of Canton and Macao, Hong Kong: Hong Kong University Press,
  vol. 1: *Politics and Strategies in Eighteenth-Century Chinese Trade*, 2011.
  vol. 2: *Success and Failure in Eighteenth Century Chinese Trade*, 2016.

Vos, Reinout, *Gentle Janus, Merchant Prince: The VOC and the Tightrope of Diplomacy in the Malay World, 1740–1800*, Leiden: KITLV Press, 1993.

Vùng đất Nam Bộ, (The southern area), 11 vols. Hanoi: Nhà xuất bản Chính trị quốc gia Sự thật, 2017.
  Nguyễn Văn Kim (ed.), vol. 3, *Từ thế kỷ VII đến thế kỷ XVI* (From the seventh to sixteenth centuries).
  Nguyễn Quang Ngọc (ed.), vol. 4, *Từ đầu thế kỷ XVII đến giữa thế kỷ XIX* (From the start of the seventeenth to the mid-nineteenth centuries).
  Vũ Văn Quân (ed.), vol. 8, *Thiết chế quản lý xã hội* (Institutions for social management), pp. 29–58.

Wang Yuanchong, *Remaking the Chinese Empire: Manchu-Korean Relations, 1616–1911*. Ithaca: Cornell University Press, 2018.

Wang Yuanfei, *Writing Pirates: Vernacular Fiction and Oceans in Late Ming China*, Ann Arbor: University of Michigan Press, 2021.

Wheeler, Charles J., '1683: An Offshore Perspective on Vietnamese Zen,' in Eric Tagliacozzo, Helen F. Siu, and Peter C. Perdue (eds.), *Asia Inside Out: Changing Times*, Cambridge: Harvard University Press, 2015, pp. 135–162.
  'Cross-Cultural Trade and Trans-regional Networks in the Port of Hoi An: Maritime Vietnam in the Early Modern Era,' PhD diss., Yale University, 2001.
  'Placing the "Chinese Pirates" of the Gulf of Tongking at the End of the Eighteenth Century,' in Eric Tagliacozzo, Helen F. Siu, and Peter C. Perdue (eds.), *Asia Inside Out: Connected Places*, Cambridge: Harvard University Press, 2015, pp. 31–63.

Wolters, Oliver W., *History, Culture, and Region in Southeast Asian Perspectives*, Ithaca: Southeast Asia Program, 1999.

Wong, John D., 'Improvising Protocols: Two Enterprising Chinese Migrant Families and the Resourceful Nguyễn Court,' *Journal of Southeast Asian Studies* 50.2 (2019): 246–262.

Wong Tze Ken, *The Nguyen and Champa during 17th and 18th Century: A Study of Nguyen Foreign Relations*, Champaka Monograph No. 5, Paris: International Office of Champa, 2007.

Woodside, Alexander, *Vietnam and the Chinese Model: A Comparative Study of Vietnamese and Chinese Government in the First Half of the Nineteenth Century*, Cambridge: Harvard University Press, 1971.

Wu Jiang, *Leaving for the Rising Sun: Chinese Zen Master Yinyuan and the Authenticity Crisis in Early Modern East Asia*, Oxford: Oxford University Press, 2015.

Xie Baocheng, *Brief History of the Official System in China*, London: Paths International and Social Sciences Academic Press, 2013.

Yang Baoyun, *Contribution à l'histoire de la principauté des Nguyên au Vietnam méridional (1600–1775)* (Historical contribution of the Nguyên lords in southern Vietnam [1600–1775]), Geneva: Editions Olizane, 1992.

Yang Kaijian 杨开建 and Tian Yu 田渝, 'Yong-Qian shiqi Zhongguo yu Xianluo de dami maoyi' 雍乾时期中国与暹罗的大米贸易 (The rice trade between China and Siam during the Yongzheng and Qianlong periods), *Zhongguo jingji shi yanjiu* 中国经济史研究 (Research on Chinese economic history) 1 (2004): 81–88.

Yu Lunian 俞鹿年 (ed.), *Zhongguo guanzhi da cidian* 中國官職大辭典 (Dictionary of Chinese offices and institutions), Hong Kong: Zhonghua shuju, 2020.

Zhang Chengzong 张承宗, *Liu chao minsu* 六朝民俗 (Folk customs of the Six Dynasties), Nanjing: Nanjing chubanshe, 2002.

Zhang Xuexian 张学衔, *Huaxia baijiaxing tanyuan* 华夏百家姓探源 (Exploration into the origins of the Hundred Surnames in China), Nanjing: Nanjing daxue chubanshe, 2000.

Zhao Gang, *The Qing Opening to the Ocean: Chinese Maritime Policies, 1684–1757*, Honolulu: University of Hawai'i Press, 2013.

Zhao Shiyu 赵世瑜, '"Tianyun" jinian de liyong jiqi benxiang: Jianlun Ming Qing yilai minjian jiaomen richang zhuangtai' '天运'纪年的利用及其本相：兼论明清以来民间教门的日常形态 (The fundamental nature and usages of the 'Tianyun' dating system: Together with a discussion of daily practices of popular religious cults since the Ming and Qing), *Nanguo xueshu* 南国学术 (Scholarship from the southern region) 3 (2017): 484–495.

Zheng Weizhong (Cheng Wei-chung) 鄭維中, 'Shi Lang "Taiwan guihuan Helan" miyi' 施琅'臺灣歸還荷蘭'密議 (Shi Lang's secret deliberations on "the return of Taiwan to the Dutch"), *Taiwan wenxian* 臺灣文獻 (Taiwan Historica) 61.3 (2010): 37–69.

Zheng Yangwen, *China on the Sea: How the Maritime World Shaped Modern China*, Leiden: Brill, 2011.

Zhuang Guotu 庄国土, *Zhongguo fengjian zhengfu de huaqiao zhengce* 中国封建政府的华侨政策 (Policies of the feudal Chinese government toward overseas Chinese), Xiamen: Xiamen daxue chubanshe, 1989.

Zottoli, Brian A., 'Reconceptualizing Southern Vietnamese History from the 15th to 18th Centuries: Competition along the Coasts from Guangdong to Cambodia,' PhD diss., University of Michigan, 2011.

Index

Locators in *italic* refer to figures. Locators in **bold** refer to notes.

Andaya, Barbara Watson, 155–156
Anderson, James, 126, 161
Andrade, Tonio
　"co-colonization" used as a term by, 17, 41
　early modern convergence on both ends of Eurasia asserted by, 18
　on the lowest levels of armed conflict in China, 284
　on obsolete weaponry used by the Qing, 282
Ang Mei Bhen (V: Nặc Bồn)
　suppression of his invasion of The Port (1739), 130–131, 133, 137, 145, 166
Ang Tsu Lyn, Claudine
　on Ming loyalism's functioning as marker of Chinese ethnicity, 95–96
　on the "Musical Ballads," **202**
　on Nguyễn Cư Trinh, 138
　on The Port's incorporation into the Vietnamese state, 12
　on Tianci's contribution of ten poems to the "Ten Verses," **94**, 110
　on Tianci's "An Egret Descends from Pearl Cliff," **105**
　on Tianci's incorporation of Ming loyalist ideals into his poetry, 109, 139
　on Tianci's negotiations with Cochinchinese ruler Nguyễn Phúc Khoát, 142
　on Tianci's "Night Drum of River Wall," **127**
　on Tianci's reputation as a loyal minister of the Nguyễn, 274
　on Tianci's role as a mediator, 125
Angkor
　ancient civilization of, 8
　location of, *xvi*
　sacking by Siamese forces, 31
　the water world as a marginal frontier of, 30–31
Antony, Robert J.
　on the arrival of Ming loyalists in the water world, 64
　on strongmen acting under the banner of Ming loyalism, 42
　on Xian Biao and Yang Yandi, 45, 49
Austronesians. *See also* Bugis people; Cham kingdoms
　communities in Ayutthaya, 32
　Java Company (*Đồ Bà đội*) organized by Mo Tianci, 186, 248
　Khmer and Austronesian attacks on hinterland Viet settlements, 249–250
　Khmer and Austronesian attacks on The Port, 250
　mercantile and legal resources tapped by the Mo, 277
　trading voyages in The Port sanctioned by the VOC, 152
　villages along the river mouths and coastline along the Gulf of Siam, 29
　VOC reliance on Chinese and Austronesian traders in Southeast Asia, 17
Ayutthaya Kingdom (1351–1767)
　Ang Sngoun's exile in, 134
　Ang Tham's exile in, 62–63, 129
　Austronesian communities in, 32
　Cambodia's suzerainty to, 36–37
　Ekkathat (1718–1767, r. 1758–1767), 225, 228, 230
　as the gateway to mainland Southeast Asia, 86, 208
　growing power of, 31
　location of, *xvi*
　mandala model of diplomacy, 124
　Mo Jiu as a hostage in, 49, 56

Index

Ayutthaya Kingdom (1351–1767) (cont.)
Myanmar invasion under King
Hsinbyushin (1760s), 4, 17, 191, 225, 228, 231–232, 238, 246
natural resources from, 86, 89, 208
Ream Reachea's exile in, 148
as a secondary source of Chinese and Japanese products, 86
shortage of grain following its occupation and destruction, 232
VOC factory in, 17, 32, 152, 218, 253
Ayutthaya Kingdom (1351–1767) – princes Chao Chui and Chao Si Sang
Chao Chui executed by Taksin, 257
Chao Chui supported by Tianci, 243–244
Chao Si Sang's exile and death in Donay, 255, 257
Chao Si Sang's flight to Phnom Penh, 239–240
letter to the High Government at Batavia, 231, 252–253
refuge in The Port offered by Tianci, 230, 239

Banteay Meas ("golden citadel")
Cambodian court management of, 33
location of, xvii, 34
as one of five provinces given to Tianci by Ang Tan, 190
The Port distinguished from, 33
The Port included in, 1–2
seasonal canals in, 34, 83, 107, 210
Touk Meas Mountain located in, 34, *130*, 130
Bassac Province
Cambodian court management of, 33
customs stations restored by Ang Sor at, 56
Mo Tianci's acquisition of, 192
as a site of contestation among The Port, Cochinchina, Siam, and Cambodia, *148*, 148–149, 274
Bassac River
location in the Gulf of Siam littoral, xvi–xvii, 30, 192
port of. *See under* Moat Chrouk (V: Châu Đốc)
Bassac settlement
French missionary Levavasseur's visit to (1768), 149, 195–196, 209–210
private coin workshops in, 222
Batavia (present-day Jakarta)
fish market overseen by Jan Taijko, 209, 257

Kapitan Lin Jiguang (Lim Tjipko), 153, 209, 218, 257
linkages with The Port, 173, 233–234
massacre of the Chinese population by the VOC (1741), 214
as a secondary source of Chinese and Japanese products, 86, 218
sugar exported from, 207, 218
trade in pepper, spices, tin, tropical forest and marine products, and medicinal ingredients, 86
VOC control of operations at, 17, 86
Batchelor, Robert, 153
Biên Hòa
independent kingdom proclaimed by Li Wenguang in, 133, 173
location of, xvii
Minh Hương commune established in, 85
as the native place of Jiu's Viet wife, Bùi Thị Lẫm, 59
as a refuge for Chen Shangchuan and his troops, 27, 54
as the seat of Gia Định prefecture administered by the Nguyễn, 55
Big-bellied Đức (Đức Bụng)
encounter with Tianci's tribute ship (1747), 133, 145, 166
piratical raids, 137, 167
Big Golden Islet (C: Da Jinyu V: Đại Kim Dữ). *See also* "Ten Scenic Views of Hà Tiên"
location of, xviii, 80, *107*
Black Water (K: Tuk Khmau V: Cà Mau)
Cambodian court management of, 33
customs stations restored by Ang Sor at, 56
farming in, 206
local port in, 210
location of, xvi–xvii, 33, 192
renamed Dragon Stream (C: Longchuan V: Long Xuyên) by Mo Tianci, 192
villages and communes for the Viet established by Mo Jiu in, 58
Blussé, Leonard, 3–4
Bouillevaux, Charles-Emile, 149
British. *See also* East India Company (EIC)
free trade associated with its overseas expansion during the nineteenth century, 1
imperial expansion centered on control of the sea lanes, 19, 288–289
spheres of influence in the Indonesian archipelago, 217, 289
Buch, W. J. M., 17

Index 331

Buddhism. *See also* "Ten Scenic Views of Hà Tiên" – 3. "Dawn Bell at the Temple of Seclusion"
  Mo clan support of, 15
  Mo Jiu's Buddhist-Daoist synthesis, 14, 66, 71, 92, 97
  Tianci's support and patronage of, 3, 198
Buddhism – Mahayana – Chan (V: Thiền). *See also* Yellow Dragon (C: Huang Long V: Hoàng Long) (d. 1737)
  Hibiscus Temple, 198–199, *199*, **199**
  Linji (V: Lâm Tế) sect of, 71, 83, 92, 198, 277
  role along with Daoist beliefs and folk rituals of the Cham in unifying Conchinchinese, 71, 277
  role in preserving an overseas Chinese identity for Ming loyalist exiles, 66, 97
Buddhism – Theravada
  Khmer cultural and religious framework centered on, 189
  Ponhea Chan's alienation of Theravada Buddhist clergy, 39
  spread beneath the elite level in Southeast Asian states, 237
  Taksin's exploitation of its symbols of authority and legitimacy, 245, 268, 287
  temple built by Mo Jiu to house a miraculous Buddha statue, 59
  temples (*wat*) during the Angkor period, 30–31
  Wat Buppharam, *233*
Bugis people
  cock fight between Raja Chulan and Daeng Rilaka, 89
  networks in the pan-Malay trading diaspora, 32, 87, 186
  and the sultanate of Johor, 88, 155, 217
  trading connections at The Port, 218, 225, 286
Bunma (1744–1803, r. 1782–1803)
  overthrowing and execution of Taksin, 272
  as viceroy (*upparat*), 272

Cambodia
  Cantonese community in, 43
  circuits and provinces. *See* Banteay Meas ("golden citadel"); Bassac Province; Black Water (K: Tuk Khmau V: Cà Mau); Kampot; Longhor (V: Long Hồ); Seashore Province (K: Peam); Steadfast River Circuit (Kramoun Sar), Sacred Pond (K: Preah Trapeang V: Trà Vinh)
Cambodian court. *See also oknha* (highest noble rank of the Cambodian court); viceroy (*oupareach*)
  attention to the maritime zone, 28, 33, 35, 145
  co-kings (*oupayureach*) in the hierarchy of, 36
  Ministry of Foreign Affairs (Kralahom), 35
  Mo Jiu's ties to, 11, 58–60
  Mo Tianci's influence over, 5, 161, 257
  noble ranks and titles issued by, 145
Cambodian court in Longvek
  sacking by Siamese troops (1594), 36
Cambodian court in Oudong – Chey Chettha (1576–1628, r. 1618–1628)
  influence of his wife Ang Chov, 38–39
  Oudong established as the capital, 38
  pursuit of closer ties with Cochinchina, 38–39
Cambodian court in Oudong – Ponhea Chan (1614–1659, r. 1642–1658)
  alienation of Theravada Buddhist clergy, 39
  conversion to Islam, 39
Cambodian court in Oudong – Barom Reachea (1628–1672, r. 1658–1672)
  assumption of the throne, 39
  Xian Biao and his followers invited to Phnom Penh, 44
  Xian Biao's flight from Cambodia, 44
Cambodian court in Oudong – Ang Chee (1652–1677, r. 1673–1676)
  attack on the co-king, Ang Nan, 48
  defeat and death of, 48, **57**
  Mo Jiu allowed to handle "all matters related to trade and merchants," **46**, 48
Cambodian court in Oudong – Ang Nan (1654–1791)
  base in Donay, 45, 50
  Chinese wife of, 50
  as co-king, 45
  Dragon Gate's support of, 53
  Yang Yandi's alliance with, 50–51
Cambodian court in Oudong – Ang Sor (1656–1725)
  bribes sent to his wife by Mo Jiu, 57
  customs stations restored by, 56
  death of, 64

Cambodian court in Oudong – Ang Sor (1656–1725) (cont.)
  judicial reforms enacted by, 56
  reign of, 48, **48**
  Siamese backing of, 49–54
Cambodian court in Oudong – Ang Em (1674–1736)
  ascent to the throne, 56, 62
  death of, 129
  Mo Jiu's support of, **59–60**
  warfare with Ang Tham, 61–63
Cambodian court in Oudong – Ang Tham (1690–1747)
  abdication of his father Ang Sor, 56
  Cochinchinese attack on, 62
  tensions with Ang Em, 56
  warfare with Ang Em, 61–63
Cambodian court in Oudong – Satha (1702–1749)
  ascent to the throne (1722), 63
  flight to Saigon, 129
  Lao rebellion suppressed by, 77
Cambodian court in Oudong – Ang Sngoun (1698–1755, r. 1748–1755)
  ascent to the throne, 134
  conflict with Conchinchinese sparked by abuse of the Khmer (1750), 134–136, 145
  death of, 146
  massacring of the Viet ordered by, 134–135
  refuge sought with Tianci in 1751 and 1754, 136, 141, 146
  Siamese assistance in his fight against Tianci, 135
  Siamese backing his son Ream Reachea, 148
  terms of peace negotiated with the Cochinchinese, 141–142, 146
Cambodian court in Oudong – Preahbat Reameatipadey (1691–1758)
  Ang Sngoun's rule challenged by, 136
  as co-king, 39, 44
  death of, 45, 151
Cambodian court in Oudong – Ang Tan (1740–1777)
  abdication and death of, 265
  Chao Si Sang provided refuge, 239–240
  Cochinchinese demands for territorial rights to secure aid, 148–150
  flight from Oudong to The Port (1757), 146, 148, 187
  Khmer and Austronesian attacks on hinterland Viet settlements supported by, 249–250
  Preah Kse Ek's plot to put him on the throne, 136
  reign of, 147, 151, 190
  Srey Sauryopor's plot to assassinate him, 146
  Taksin's demand that he submit to Siam as a vassal rejected by, 243
  Taksin's forces repulsed by, 246–247
  Taksin's recognition of his rule, 257
  Tianci as his adoptive father, 147, 190, 243
  Tianci replaced with a new viceroy, 247
Cambodian court in Oudong – Ream Reachea (1739–1779)
  Bassac forces led by Mou initially welcomed by, 266
  campaign against, 269, 271
  flight to Ayutthaya, 148
  as king, 265
  power base along the Gulf of Siam, 257
  Taksin's attempt to place him on the throne, 243, 251, 256
  Taksin's onerous requisition for support, 269
Cambodian court in Oudong – Neareay Reachea (1773–1796, r. 1779–1796)
  Oknha Athivongsa Pok as his adoptive father, 268–269, 273
Cambodian court in Oudong – Ang Chan (1791–1835, r. 1806–1835)
  enthronement, 273
  Oknha Athivongsa Pok as his regent, 273
Cambodian Royal Chronicles
  on Ang Sngoun's subduing of Preah Kse Ek and his rebels, 136
  on Banteay Meas and Seashore, 33
  Chen Chong Tok mentioned in, 35
  Preah Sotoat conflated with Tianci in, 145, 189
  tianyun used for years since Buddha's birth in the Vietnamese translation of, 144
Cần Thơ (C: Qinju K: Kampoul Meas)
  allegiance to Cochinchina, 258
  Christians from Cochinchina in, 194
  crops grown on the Mekong floodplain around it, 206
  Franciscan mission under Julián del Pilar, 260
  line of defense against Siamese troops established by Tianci's sons at, 256
  location of, *xvii*, 210
  possibly the same as New Port identified by Dalrymple, 210, 220

Index

refuge given to Tianci's sons, 254
as a term, 21
Cần Thơ – Mo Tianci's regime at, 260
  Eastern Mountain forces support of his fight against the Tây Sơn, 263
  establishment of, 257–258
  fertile lands for rice cultivation exploited at, 260
  Martín Robles's presence in, 257
  as the seat of River Defense Circuit, 192, 261, *262*
  Tây Sơn Huệ's attack forcing Tianci's evacuation, 264
Cham kingdoms
  Cham settlements in The Port, 58, 88, 218
  folk rituals of the Cham, 71, 277
  location of, *xvi*
  on a map presented to the Qianlong Emperor by Mo Tianci, 158, *159*
  networks in the pan-Malay trading diaspora, 32
  Panduranga (1471–1697), 38, 53
  revolt of the Cham in Panduranga in 1746, 133
  southward thrust of the Viet resisted by, 9
Chang'an, 128, 201
Chaozhou
  as Chen Tai's native place, 248
  immigrants from Chaozhou in southeastern Siam, 226
  as Taksin's native place, 226
Chen Ang, 51–53
Chen Ching-ho. *See* Chen Jinghe 陳荊和 (Chen Ching-ho, Chin Keiwa)
Chen clan
  shrine at Tiantou, 75, *76*
Chen Dading (V: Trần Đại Định) (d. 1732)
  as Chen Shangchuan's adopted son, 77
  death of, 77
  Dragon Gate forces led by, 77
  failed suppression of Lao rebellions for Lord Ninh, 77
  genealogy of, 78
Chen Dali (V: Trần Đại Lực) (d. 1770), 78, 167, 232, 244–245
Chen Lian (1741–1782)
  Chen Tai possibly identified with, 251–252
  expedition to chase Tianci dispatched by Taksin, 251, 254
  as governor of Seashore Province, 254
  Phraya Phiphit as his title, 251

Phraya Racha Setthi as his title, 255, 267
Chen Mingxia (V: Trần Minh Hạ), 111, **112**
Chen Ruifeng
  background of, 111
  Ming loyalist messages in his response to "Golden Islet Blocking Waves," **112**
Chen Ruishu (d. 1754), 78–79, 111, 167
Chen Shangchuan (V: Trần Thượng Xuyên, 1626–1715)
  asylum requested from the Nguyễn, 26–27, 64
  base at Mesar, 54–55, 77
  Biên Hòa ceded to the Nguyễn, 54
  Chen Dading adopted by, 77
  Chen Dali identified as his grand nephew, 167, 232
  Chen Ruishu as his clan relative, 78–79, 111, 167
  commemoration in Trịnh Hoài Đức's verses, 279
  death of, 77
  in the Dragon Gate hierarchy, 53–54
  ideal of a restored Ming openly expressed in his poetry, 66, 96
  Jiu allied with, 62–63, 66, 71, 79
  refuge in Biên Hòa sought for his troops, 27, 54
  She Xichun's dedication of a poem to him, 76
  shrine in honor of his ancestors built at Tiantou, 75, *76*
  subordination under Cochinchina, 65
  Tiantou in Wuchuan County as his native village, 54, 111
Chen Tai
  base at White Horse, 248, *249*
  Chen Lian possibly identified with, 251–252
  plot to topple Tianci, 248–249
  Taksin joined at Chanthaburi, 248, 253
Chen Zhikai. *See also* Tan Xiang – "Sending Off Chen Zhikai to Annam"
  contribution to Tianci's poetry anthology on the four seasons of The Port, 119
  Mao Yunyang introduced to poetry society members at Guangzhou, 110, 115
  postscript to the "Ten Verses" anthology, 111, 128
  as She Xichun's associate, 76, 103–104
  "Ten Scenic Views" conceived as an idea with She Xichun, 104
  "Ten Scenic Views" promoted by, 110

Chen Zhikai. (cont.)
  Tianci introduced to poetry society members at Guangzhou, 104, 119
Chin Jinghe 陳荊和 (Chen Ching-ho, Chin Keiwa)
  on Ang Tan's regime, 151
  assertion that The Port was a sovereignty, 12
  on Chen Dali's genealogy, 78
  on the "Musical Ballads," **201**
  on Sun Tianzhen and Sun Tianrui, 112
  on Tianci's contribution of ten poems to the "Ten Verses," **94**
Chin Keiwa. *See* Chen Jinghe 陳荊和 (Chen Ching-ho, Chin Keiwa)
Chin Kong, James, 275
Chinese century
  end of it marked by the tragic outcomes of Mo Tianci and Taksin, 289
  the fortunes of the Mo clan during, 276
  The Port during the heyday of, 3–4, 235, 289
  trade between China and Southeast Asia during, 3–4
Choi Byung Wook, 22
Christianity and Christian missionaries. *See also* Hermosa de Buenaventura, Francisco (1711–1771); Piguel, Guillaume (1722–1771); Pilar, Julián de Nuestra Señora del (1733–1779); Salazar, Pedro (1729–1763)
  alternative hierarchy and avenue for social advancement offered by the Church, 182
  Jean-Baptiste Artaud (d. 1769), 250
  Church of Saint Joseph and Saint Mary established in The Port, 180–182, 184, 198
  José de la Concepción (1687–1761), 180–182, 184
  Juan de Jesús (1732–1778), 264
  missionaries as medical officials in The Port, 182, 211, 260
  Mo clan support of, 15
  Mo Tianci's tolerant attitude toward, 3, 182, 184–185
  persecution by the Martial King, 183, **183**, 185
  Martín Robles de Zugarramurdi (1729–1783), 165, 211, 250, 257
  role of Roman Catholic orders in the recruitment and management of Viet settlers in The Port, 164, 180, 182, 193–195, 200, 277
Clulow, Adam, 16

Cochinchina. *See also* Hội An; Longhor; Nguyễn rulers of Cochinchina
  cosmopolitan and multipolar environment of, 9–11
  demands for territorial rights to secure aid, 148–150
  elements of the Sinosphere and mandala frameworks combined in, 124
  expansion into Champa and the Mekong Delta, 87
  as the realm of the Nguyễn, 24
  as a term, 24
  Tianci's failed attempt to influence the throne of, 3, 236
  VOC factory in, **17**
coins and bullion
  bullion from the New World, 32, 85, 87, 224
  casting of zinc coins in Cochinchina and The Port, 223, 277
  debasement of coinage, 258
  European domination of, 283
  flow of coins, bullion, and drugs through the free ports of Singapore and Hong Kong, 1
  "Great Peace" (*Thái Bình*) on coins cast by Nguyễn lords, 222
  minting and circulation of coins by Portuguese creoles, 90
  official mint at The Port, 16, 222
  "Peace and Law" (*An Pháp*) on imitations of coins cast by the Mạc dynasty, 222
  possible reference to copper in Tan Xiang's "Sending Off Chen Zhikai to Annam," **222**
  silver circulated in The Port, 223–224
Confucianism and Confucian values
  Cochinchina's gradual shift away from a Buddhist worldview towards Confucianism, 11
  Confucian bureaucracy in Tonkin under the Trịnh lords, 9
  Confucian shrine in the center of The Port, 169
  essential elements introduced in the "Musical Ballads," **201**
  the Mo clan's promotion of, 13, 16
  popularization via Vietnamese vernacular versions of Tianci's poetry, 16
  "tremendous virtue" (*shuode*) as reference to a morally upright Confucian, 178
Confucianism and Confucian values – neo-Confucianism

Index   335

decentralized character of Wang
  Yangming's Heart-Mind school,
  93–94, 103, 196
Tianci's integration of Buddhism into his
  framework of, 103
Tianci's promotion of, 3, 14, 16, 93–94,
  97, 103, 116, 121, 278
in Vietnam, 14, 237

Dalrymple, Alexander, 210, 217, 220–221
Deer Cape (C: Luqi K: Phnom Nay V: Mũi
  Nai). *See also* "Ten Scenic Views of Hà
  Tiên" – 9. "Rustic Dwellings at Deer
  Cape"
  Khmer settlements in, 116, 187
  location in the Port's core area, *xviii*,
    108
  Tianci's governance of, 191
Deng Yao (d. 1660)
  base at Dragon Gate, 42
  execution of, 42
  support from the Mo and other gentry, 47
Đỗ Thanh Nhơn (C: Du Qingren, d. 1781)
  arrest and execution of, 271
  campaign against Ream Reachea, 269,
    271
  Eastern Mountain (Đông Sơn) army led
    against the Tây Sơn rebels, 261
  hostilities with Li Cai, 262–263
  offensive against Siam mentioned in a
    secret letter from Saigon, 270–271
  Saigon recaptured from the Tây Sơn,
    268
  Tianci's fight against the Tây Sơn initially
    supported by, 263–264
Donay (V: Đồng Nai). *See also* Biên Hòa;
  Gia Định prefecture
  Ang Nan's base in, 45, 50
  Diamond Temple established by
    Yuanshao in, 72
  location of, xvi–xvii
  settlements under Xian Biao in, 43–44
Donay (V: Đồng Nai) – Mesar (V: Mỹ Tho)
  Chen Shangchuan's base in, 54–55, 77
  location of, *xvii*
  as subsidiary port to Biên Hòa, 55
  Yang Yandi and Huang Jin's base in, 50, 54
Đông Hồ
  as a native to Hà Tiên, 11
  on poetic exchanges sponsored by
    Tianci's literary society, 11, 202
  on Tianci's ambitions to forge a "small,
    independent kingdom," **12**
  on Tianci's contribution of ten poems to
    the "Ten Verses," **94**

Đông Hồ lagoon (C: Donghu 東湖). *See*
  East Lake (C: Donghu V: Đông Hồ)
Dragon Gate (Longmen) Garrison. *See also*
  Deng Yao (d. 1660); Huang Jin (V:
  Hoàng Tiến); Yang Yandi (V: Dương
  Ngạn Địch, d. 1688)
  Ang Nan's revolt against Ang Sor
    supported by, 53
  Chen Shangchuan's position in its
    hierarchy, 53–54
  connections with Jiu, 29, 74
  Frontier Garrison camp at Saigon, 55, 77
  location of, *xvii*, 26
  trade with Cambodia and Batavia, 43
  trading relations with Cochinchina, 49
  Victorious Naval Company led by Chen
    Dali, 167, 232, 244
  the Zheng organization's control of its
    contingent in Taiwan, 43, 50–52
Dutch East India Company (VOC)
  adjudication of the Oeij Tshing and Lauw
    Wo case, 154–155
  ban on tin and pepper on ships headed
    for The Port, 213–214
  "co-colonization" by, 16–17, 41
  control of Batavia, 16, 86
  control of Melaka, 33, 88, 155, 186, 213
  decline of its commercial dominance in
    Southeast Asia, 4, 64–65, 287
  factory in Ayutthaya, 17, 32, 152, 218,
    253
  Governor-General Petrus Albertus van
    der Parra, 153, 155, 253
  massacre of the Chinese population in
    Batavia, 214
  The Port as a petty principality within its
    hegemony, 161
  reliance on Chinese and Austronesian
    traders in Southeast Asia, 17
  Taiwan colonized in 1624, 32
  Taiwan forcibly surrendered in 1662, 42,
    64
  Tokugawa Japan as a trading partner, 16,
    124
  Tonkinese ports blockaded from 1663 to
    1664, 43
  trading posts in Vietnam and Cambodia
    closed by, **17**, 17, 46
  Xian Biao's personal vendetta against, 44
Dutch East India Company (VOC) –
  factory in Guangzhou
  Chanthaburi in a separate category from
    Siam starting from 1764, 231
  port of call known as Tsou geth or Tju-
    hot documented by, 210

336 Index

Dutch East India Company (VOC) –
factory in Guangzhou (cont.)
  trade between Guangzhou and The Port
    documented at, 219–220
Dutton, George E.
  on the Nguyễn southward expansion into
    the Mekong River Delta, 258
  on the Tây Sơn movement, 281

Earthen Mount (C: Tushan K: Phnom Dei
    V: Hòn Đất)
  Ascension of Our Lady on, 194
  location of, *xvii*
  Viet massacred on, 250
East India Company (EIC)
  establishment of colonies in Penang and
    Singapore, 287–288
  factories set up in Guangzhou, 86,
    215
  Mo clan administration of The Port
    compared with, 277–278
  opium traders supported by, 287
  Pigou as director of, 61
East Lake (C: Donghu V: Đông Hồ)
  Hangzhou's West Lake juxtaposed with,
    80
  Jiu's fabricated legend about fairies
    roaming around it, 79–80
  location where the Fortress River
    intersects the Gulf of Siam, *xviii*, 34,
    106
Eoseewong, Nidhi
  on Sino-Viet exiles settled in Thonburi,
    267
  on Taksin's trust in Chaozhouese
    merchants and military men, 245
  on Thongduang and Bunma's plans to
    overthrow Taksin, 272
  on Tianci's contact with the governor of
    Chanthaburi, 231
European maritime power. *See also* Dutch
    East India Company (VOC); East
    India Company (EIC); Portugal and
    the Portuguese; Spain
  the decline of The Port and the
    Mo associated with, 5, 19–20
  emergence of British country traders in
    the Straits in the 1770s, 86, 287
  free trade associated with European
    overseas expansion in the nineteenth
    century, 1, 284
  New World silver sourced through, 32,
    85, 87, 224
  Swedish East India Company, 215,
    224

Fang Qiubai, 120
free trade. *See also* The Port as financial
    center; The Port as a natural resource
    exporter; The Port as a transshipment
    point
  European overseas expansion in the
    nineteenth century associated with, 1,
    284
  Hong Kong and Singapore established as
    free ports, 1, 287–288
Fujian (Minnan). *See also* Zheng
    organization
  Fujianese armed traders, 40
  Fujianese contributors to the "Ten
    Verses" anthology, 102, 111
  Fujianese settlers in Cambodia, 31
  grain shortages and ecological pressures
    in, 16, 84, 86, 207
  Haicheng County merchant scholar Guo
    Jie, 140
  mercantile settlements established by
    Fujianese across maritime East Asia,
    64, 66
  report by Pan Siju, governor of Fujian, to
    the Qing court, 134
  Xie Zhang as a native of, 178
  Zheng organization based in, 41, 45
Funan civilization
  the area of The Port as a core part of, 29
  Water Zhenla as a legacy of, 143,
    143

Gesick, Lorraine, 245, 268
Gia Định prefecture
  location of, *xvii*
  parallel civilian administration at, 55
  Trịnh Hoài Đức's "Ten Scenic Views of
    Gia Định," **279**
Giersch, C. Patterson, 161
Guangdong Province. *See also* Leizhou
    Peninsula; Li Shiyao (d. 1788);
    Tiantou Village, Wuchuan County,
    Guangdong
  Chen Junqing and Liang Shangxuan,
    175–176
  as Chen Shangchuan's home province,
    75
  grain shortages and ecological pressures
    in, 18, 84, 86, 207
  as the native place of contributors to the
    "Ten Verses" anthology, 102, 111
  natives as members of Jiu's mercenary
    force, 67
  works by members of Chen Zhikai's
    poetry society circulated in, 119

Index 337

Zheng organization based in, 41
Guangdong Province – Guangzhou. *See also*
Dutch East India Company (VOC) –
factory in Guangzhou
Chinese migrant-laborers from,
214
EIC factories in, 86, 215
Guangzhou System of trade, 235, 277,
285
selling price of tin at, 216–217
silk, porcelain, and tea sold in, 86

Hà Tiên (The Port)
hinterlands of. (*See* water world or water
frontier – hinterlands of)
incorporation into Vietnam, 12,
274
statue of Mo Jiu, 60
status of garrison (*trấn*) granted by Lord
Minh, 2, 62
submission of its core area to the
suzerainty of Siam, 258
Hà Tiên (The Port) – as a maritime trade
center. *See also* Moat Chrouk (V: Châu
Đốc); Mingbo (V: Minh Bột)
commercial districts; Mo Jiu (V: Mạc
Cửu, 1655–1735) – The Port's rise and
emergence
location of, *xv*, *xvii*, 1, 29
Mo Jiu granted administrative control by
King Ang Sor, 59
Viet settlements clustered around Phnom
Yuon/Hibiscus Mountain, *xviii*, 58,
80, 179
Hà Tiên (The Port) – as a name. *See also*
The Port – as a term
Jiu's use of the name of Hà Tiên
(C: Hexian, River of Fairies), 2, 61,
79–80
labeled as "Ruins" by the French,
81
as Peam ("seashore") in Khmer, 1, 61,
79
as the Vietnamese name for the Port, 2
Hà Tiên thập cảnh khúc vịnh (Musical
Ballads of the Ten Scenes of Hà Tiên)
controversy over its authenticity,
201–202
ongoing circulation of, 203
The Port praised as another Chang'an,
201
Viet population of The Port as its focus,
201
as a Vietnamese vernacular companion
version to the "Ten Verses," **200–201**

Hà Tiên thập cảnh tổng luận (General
Summary of the Ten Views of Hà
Tiên), 163
Hainan Island
location of, *xvi*
as a native place of Chinese creole
migrants, 5, 13, 259
as a point where the maritime routes
diverge, 40
Hangzhou
East Lake (C: Donghu V: Đông Hồ)
juxtaposed with West Lake in, 80
"Ten Scenic Views of West Lake," **105**
"Moon's Reflection on the Pools"
105
Hermosa de Buenaventura, Francisco
(1711–1771)
arrival in Cochinchina, 184
on Christians in Cần Thơ, 194
churches built on Earthen Mount and
Phú Quốc, 194
on Cochinchinese envoys in The Port,
134
on governance of Treang, 191
on the medical practices of
Cochinchinese doctors, 182
hinterlands
area north of Saigon. *See* Donay (V: Đồng
Nai)
of The Port. *See* water world or water
frontier – hinterlands of
Hồ Quý Ly (1336–1407, r. 1400–1401)
"Sacred Origins" (*Thánh Nguyên*) as the
reign name of, 222
Hội An
Chinese products imported through, 89,
212
as a cosmopolitan port, 37
duty imposed on vessels from The Port,
131
Minh Hương community in, 85
Tây Sơn supported by Chinese
merchants in, 259
Holroyd, Ryan, 12
Hong merchants
dependence on Western loans and
advances, 215–216, 283
European traders managed for the Qing
court, 215, 285
junk trade to Southeast Asia, 216, 224,
277
partnerships formed by, 215–216
in The Port and Bassac, 218
Huang Jin (V: Hoàng Tiến)
assassination of Yang Yandi, 52

Huang Jin (V: Hoàng Tiến) (cont.)
  base at Mesar formed with Yang Yandi, 27, 50, 54
  conflict with Yang Yandi, 52, 55
  disappearance of, 53
  as a leading figure in the Dragon Gate, 42, 50
  refuge sought from Lord Hiền, 26–27
Huế. *See also* Nguyễn Lords of southern Vietnam
  location in Vietnam (Annam), xvi
  as the native place of Phan Thiên Quảng (contributor to "Ten Verses"), 112
  as the Nguyễn seat of power, 37, 273
  occupation by Tonkin forces (1774), 259, 274
  Tianci as a vassal of, 125, 158
Huo Ran
  base on Koh Kong, xvi, 227–228
  as a threat to The Port, 228
  Tianci's suppression of, 232, **248**

"Idle Fishing at Sea Perch Creek. *See also* Mo Tianci – "Idle Fishing at Sea Perch Creek" (*Luxi xiandiao*)
Islam and Muslims. *See also* Ponhea Chan (1614–1659, r. 1642–1658)
  of the Cham, Malay, and Javanese, 185–186, 196
  King Ponhea Chan's conversion to, 39
  long-distance maritime trade by Muslim merchants, 86
  Mo clan support of, 15
  mosque in The Port, 3, 185, 225
  participation of Muslims in intrigues and succession struggle, 37

Japan
  Cambodian court supervision of its trade with, 35
  direct ties with Japan banned by the Ming, 31
  intra-Asian trade centered upon Japanese silver and copper during the Ming, 18, 28, 31
  Japanese settlers in Cambodia, 31
  Japanese settlers in the water world, 28, 43, 46
  secondary sources of Japanese products, 218
  trade with the Portuguese at Macao, 32
  trade with the Zheng organization, 41
Japan – Tokugawa period
  copper exports, 90
  forgeries of coins from, 90
  Japanocentric tributary system established by, 124
  quotas imposed on junks in Nagasaki, 86
  restrictions on private trade and withdrawal from sea lanes, 41, 64
  Sinophilia as an intellectual current in, 96
  Tianci's presentation of a turtle to the Tokugawa shogun, 207
  the VOC as a trading partner, 16, 124

Kampong Som (present-day Sihanoukville)
  Cambodian court management of, 33
  location of, xvi, 30
  as one of five provinces given to Tianci by Ang Tan, 190
  Siamese communities in, 191
  villages and communes for the Viet established by Mo Jiu in, 58
Kampot
  Cambodian court management of, 33
  location of, xvii
  as one of five provinces given to Tianci by Ang Tan, 190
  Siamese communities in, 191
  villages and communes for the Viet established by Mo Jiu in, 58
Keith, Charles, 24
Kelley, Liam C.
  on the "Musical Ballads," **201**, 202
  on The Port's incorporation into the Vietnamese state, 12
  on Sinophilia in the poetry of Viet tributary envoys to the Qing, 96
  on Tianci's contribution of ten poems to the "Ten Verses," **94**
  on Tianci's incorporation of Ming loyalist ideals into his poetry, 109
  on the use of the name of Vietnam (Việt Nam), 24
Khin Sok, 265
Kitagawa Takako. *See* Sakurai Yumio and Kitagawa Takako
König, Johann Gerhard (1728–1785)
  on Taksin's brutality and religious fanaticism, 267–268
  on Tianci and Xuân's captivity in Siam, 267
Kramoun Sar. *See* Steadfast River Circuit
Kuhn, Philip, 22

Launay, Adrien, 183
Lê Bá Bình, 137, **137**
Lê dynasty

Index

forgeries of coins from, 90
occupation of territory of Cham
  kingdoms north of Huế to Quy Nhơn,
  37
Tây Sơn defeat of, 272–273
viewed as the sole rulers of Vietnam by
  the Qing, 9, 126
Lê Quý Đôn
  on Tianci, **59**, 274
  on Tianci's naval companies, 166
  on Tianci's poetry anthology on the four
    seasons of The Port, 119
Lefebvre, Urbain, 148–151
Leizhou Peninsula
  ancestral roots of the Mo clan, 2, 13, 23,
    47, 176
  as a base for pirates, 42
  location of, *xvi*, 42
  Mo clan shrine in the village of Dongling,
    47
Levavasseur, Nicolas-Jacques-Gervais
  (1741–1777)
  on Bassac, 149, 195–196, 209–210
  on Mo Tianci's equidistant diplomacy
    (1768), 122, 125, 160
  on prohibitions against the
    Cochinchinese from entering the
    interior of Cambodia, 150
Li Cai
  defection from the Tây Sơn, 261, 281
  Harmonious and Righteous Army (C:
    Heyi V: *Hòa Nghĩa*) commanded by,
    261
  hostilities with Đỗ Thanh Nhơn,
    262–263
  Nguyễn Phúc Dương (the Reformation
    King) protected by, 262
Li Qingxin, 47, 64, 159
Li Shiyao (d. 1788)
  Cai Han as his patrolling admiral,
    243–244, 246, 252, 286
  Chen Junqing and Liang Shangxuan's
    testimony on The Port, 176
  memorial on Chinese migrants in The
    Port, 173
  Mo Wu's testimony, 122, 145
  proclamation drafted to the hypothetical
    ruler of Ayutthaya, 230
  Taksin described as a lowlife from China,
    240
  Tianci's flattering letter to, 241–242
  Xu Quan as his patrolling admiral,
    230–231, 240
  Zheng Rui as his patrolling admiral,
    243–244

Li Tana
  on the casting of zinc coins in
    Cochinchina and The Port, 223, 283
  on Cochinchinese expansion into
    Champa and the Mekong Delta,
    87
  on imitation coins forged in The Port and
    their circulation, 90, 223
  on the role of eclectic faith in unifying
    Conchinchinese governance, 71
  on the shifting and multiple alliances of
    pre-nation states, 161
  on the Southern Advance of the
    Vietnamese, 9, 258
  on the Viet in Cochinchina, 9
Li Tana and Paul Van Dyke
  on Hong merchants, 218
  on The Port as a transshipment hub, 16
  on shipments of tin through The Port,
    216–217
Liang Luan of Shunde
  contribution to the four seasons of The
    Port anthology, 119
  Tianci's hope to remain a sojourner in a
    foreign land disclosed to, 93, 102
Lieberman, Victor, 237
Lin Houqua
  family background of, 153
  Oeij Tshing possibly interrogated by,
    155
  supervision of Chinese merchants and
    sojourners in The Port, 168, 173, 209,
    218
  Tianci's governance of the port facilitated
    by, 153
Lin Weize
  poem on Screen Mountain, 114
  response to "Anchored Fishing Boat at
    Sea Perch Creek," **117**, 118
Longhor (V: Long Hồ) province
  Ang Sngoun's agreement to relinquish
    Cambodia's claim to, 141–142, 146
  counterfeit Cochinchinese coins in,
    223
  location of, *xvii*
  Longhor Camp established at Cái Bè,
    77–78
  Longhor Camp relocated to Vĩnh Long,
    149
  occupation by Cochinchinese forces,
    77–78, 136, 149–150
Lotus Pond (C: Lianchi, V: Ao Sen) open-
  air reservoirs
  Mo Jiu's construction of, 82–83, *177*

340   Index

Lotus Pond (C: Lianchi, V: Ao Sen) open-air reservoirs (cont.)
  surrounding settlement given to Chen Junqing and Liang Shangxuan, 176
Mạc dynasty
  "Peace and Law" (*An Pháp*) on coins imitating, 222
Mạc Triều Đán
  response to Mo Tianci's "Clear Waves on South Bay," 118
  Screen Mountain compared to Mo Tianci himself, 127
Macauley, Melissa
  early modern convergence on both ends of Eurasia asserted by, 18
  on non-statist forms of territoriality, 13, 18
  offshoring viewed as a late nineteenth-century development, 18
  on translocalism, 14
Malay Peninsula
  Chinese migrants in Johor, 214
  cultivation of pepper, 207
  natural resources exported from, 86
  tin exported from, 86, 216
  VOC domination of the spice trade to Europe in, 32
Malay Peninsula – Melaka and the Strait of Melaka
  location of, xv, 1
  Orang Laut active in, 29
  political disorder in Johor, 88, 155
  Portuguese control of, 32, 90
  VOC control of, 33, 88, 155, 186, 213
mandala model of diplomacy
  in Ayutthaya, 124
  elements of the Sinosphere and mandala combined in Cochinchina, 124
  mandalic hierarchy of minor ports and interior hinterlands of The Port, 152
  the Mo clan's flexible exploitation of Sinosphere and mandala frameworks, 125, 152, 161, 277
  Sinosphere conventions contrasted with, 15, 123–124
  skills of the supreme ruler relied on in Siam and Cambodia and island Southeast Asia, 124
Mao Yunyang
  background of, 110
  poem by Chen Zhikai's poetry companions at West Garden dedicated to, 110, 115

Martial King. *See* Nguyễn rulers of Cochinchina – Nguyễn Phúc Khoát
Matsuda, Matt, 13
Melaka. *See* Malay Peninsula – Melaka and the Strait of Melaka
Mesar. *See* Donay (V: Đồng Nai) – Mesar (V: Mỹ Tho)
Mikaelian, Grégory
  Oknha Siv equated with Mo Jiu, 46
  on Khmer identity, 36
Minangkabau of Siak
  cock fight between Raja Chulan and Daeng Rilaka, 89
  networks in the pan-Malay trading diaspora, 32
  rivalry with the sultanate of Johor, 88, 155
  trading connections at The Port, 186, 225, 286
Ming dynasty (1368–1644)
  conquest of Vietnam, 222
  demand for Japanese silver during, 18, 28, 31
  emphasis on coastal defense, 215
  relaxing of its ban on private trade and travel abroad, 31
  Zheng family members as officials during, 41
Ming loyalists and Ming loyalism. *See also* Dragon Gate (Longmen) Garrison; Minh Hương; She Xichun
  arrival in the water world, 28–29, 64
  bases established in the water world, 28–29
  coded messages hidden in "Ten Scenic Views," 109–110, 112
  as the largest and most organized group of Chinese arrivals in Cambodia, 29
  loyalist ideals expressed in Chen Shangchuan's poetry, 66, 96
  as a marker of Chinese ethnicity and generational continuity outside China, 95–96
  Mo Tianci's incorporation of Ming loyalist ideals into his poetry, 109, 139
  as the preeminent mercantile presence on the seas, 65
  Qing efforts to curtail its spread, 84
  role of Chan Buddhism in preserving an overseas Chinese identity for Ming loyalist exiles, 66, 97
  strongmen acting under the banner of, 42
  Tang Yuchong's criticism of in his response to "Clear Waves on South Bay," 114–115

Index   341

Mingbo (V: Minh Bột) commercial districts
  literal meaning as Ming Rising Tide or
    Ming Shoreline, 174
  location east of Suzhou Mountain, *xviii*,
    174
  road between different settlements
    constructed by Tianci, 177
Mingbo Sea Perch Creek Settlement
  (C: Mingbo Luxi suo V: Minh Bột Lư
  Khê Sở)
  location of, *xviii*, 177
  Tianci's establishment of, 176–177
  Viet migrant settlement of, 179
Minh Hương. *See also* Sun Tianzhen; Trịnh
  Hoài Đức
  as a category assigned to Chinese
    refugees in Cochinchina, 10
  communes in Hội An, near Saigon, and
    at Biên Hòa, 84
  status of the Mo clan distinguished from,
    10, 22
Mo clan (V: Mạc). *See also* Vũ Thế Dinh –
  genealogical biography of the Mo clan
  administration of The Port compared
    with the VOC, 13, 277–278
  administration of The Port via
    translocalism, 3, 13–14, 205, 277, 290
  Chen Chong Tok based at The Port as
    prototypes of, 35, 57
  and the "Chinese century" in maritime
    Asia, 276
  Confucian values promoted by, 13,
    16
  contribution to the narrative of the
    Southern Advance, 6–8, 12
  downfall of, 19–20
  flexible exploitation of Sinosphere and
    mandala frameworks by, 277
  fluidity and ambiguity of the world they
    lived and operated in, 25
  Hexian (V: Hà Tiên, "fairy river") as their
    Sinicized name of The Port, 2, 61,
    79–80
  Leizhou Peninsula ancestral roots, 2, 13,
    23, 47, 176
  the Nguyễn's dependence on, 11
  patronage of different religions, 15
  pro-mercantile outlook of Mo leaders,
    17–18
  the Qing court's pragmatic dealings with,
    19, 275
  shrine in Dongling Village, *47*
  terminology related to the Mo and their
    identity, 22–23
  the Medici compared with, 204–205

Water Station (C: Shuichang V: Rạch Ụ)
  dug by, *xviii*, 82, 254
Mo clan – descendants of Mo Jiu and
  Mo Tianci
  as hereditary governors, 290
  restoration of their control of The Port,
    273–275
  the survival of The Port maintained by,
    238
Mo Jinding (V: Mạc Kim Định) (sister of
  Mo Tianci)
  birth of, 59
  Chen Dali as her adopted son, 78–79
  Chen Ruishu as her husband, 79, 167
  described by Julián del Pilar, **184**
  influence of, 165, 183–184, 248
Mo Jiu (V: Mạc Cửu, 1655–1735)
  background of, 2–3, 47
  base in Ream, 58–60, 63
  Buddhist-Daoist synthesis, 14, 66, 71,
    92, 97
  character of his surname changed from 莫
    (Mo) to 鄚 (Mao), 70–71, 102
  Cochinchinese wife of, 10
  death of, 91
  as a hostage in Siam (Ayutthaya), 49, 56
  journey to Phnom Penh at the age of
    sixteen, 47–48
  Oknha Siv (Guangdong shahbandar)
    equated with, 46, 48
  submission to the Nguyễn, 2, 10–11, 63
  Temple of Three Treasures built for his
    mother. *See* Temple of Three
    Treasures (C: *Sanbao* V: *Tam Bảo*)
Mo Jiu (V: Mạc Cửu, 1655–1735) – Bùi Thị
  Lẩm (his Viet wife)
  Biên Hòa as her native place, 59
  birth to a daughter named Mo Jinding (V:
    Mạc Kim Định), 59
  birth to a son known as Tianci, a "gift
    from Heaven," **59**
  Lord Minh's bestowal on her of the royal
    Nguyễn, 68
  role in initiating contacts with
    Cochinchina, 61
Mo Jiu (V: Mạc Cửu, 1655–1735) – The
  Port's rise and emergence
  coincidence with the Chinese century in
    maritime Asia, 276
  development of the sparsely populated
    hinterlands, 58
  Hà Tiên used as the name for The Port,
    61, 79
  legends about fairies fabricated by, 61,
    79–80

Mo Jiu (V: Mạc Cửu, 1655–1735) – The Port's rise and emergence (cont.)
  Lotus Pond open-air reservoirs constructed by, 82–83, *177*
  rearrangement of The Port's layout, 80–82
  power vacuum in the water frontier of mainland Southeast Asia coincident with, 276
  role of Viet, Cham, and Khmer migrants, 88
  status as commander (*tổng binh*) of Hà Tiên granted by Lord Minh, 62
  territory of The Port acquired by, 3
Mo Tianci (V: Mạc Thiên Tứ, d. 1780)
  as Ang Tan's adoptive father, 147, 190, 243
  Ang Tan's disappointment with, 247
  background of, 3
  flattering letter to Li Shiyao, 241–242
  map of the maritime route from Guangdong to Siam presented to Qianlong, 157–159
  memorials to the Qianlong Emperor, *157*, 157–158, 242
  as the overlord of the kingdom of Cambodia, 151
  refuge sought in Siam, 5, 266–267
  regime at Cần Thơ. (*See* Cần Thơ – Mo Tianci's regime at)
  role in potential plot to seize Siam, 269
  suicide of, 5, 238, 270, 275, 279
  ten scenic views from The Port selected by. (*See* "Ten Scenic Views of Hà Tiên")
  tolerant attitudes toward religion, 3, 184–185
  Viet women in the household of, 179
  wife from the Huang clan, 171
  wife, Lady Nguyễn, 125, 130–131, 171, *172*
Mo Tianci – children
  daughter married to Xu Youyong, 167
  daughters carried off by Taksin, 254, 257
Mo Tianci – children – Mo Hao (V: Mạc Tử Hạo), 125, 164, 171
Mo Tianci – children – Mo Huang (V: Mạc Tử Hoàng) (d. 1821), 125, 171
  as commander-in-chief (*chưởng cơ*), 258, 261
  management of The Port's daily administration, 164–165
  oversight of the "Ten Verses 2.0" anthology, 140
  wife, Lady Xu, 173
Mo Tianci – children – Mo Rong (V: Mạc Tử Dung) (d. 1780), 125, 171
  governance of Cần Thơ, 261, *262*
  Taksin's murder of him, 270
Mo Tianci – children – Mo Tang (V: Mạc Tử Thắng) (d. 1780), 125, 171
  as head of the Victorious Naval Regiment, 261
  refuge found at Cần Thơ, 254
Mo Tianci – governance of The Port
  Cambodian title of Preah Sotoat ("Lord of Wealth"), 22, 143–145, 165, 189
  challenges from insurgents, 250
  the Church and Christians utilized by, 182, 203
  cooperation between the Qing and The Port, 241
  dating of his letters to the VOC in the Qing calendar, 153
  decentralized Neo-Confucian values suited to The Port's business of business, 3, 14, 16, 93–94, 97, 103, 121
  equidistant diplomacy of, 123, 125, 159–162, 173, 235
  flexible exploitation of Sinosphere and mandala frameworks by, 125, 152, 161
  ominous portents observed during, **251**
  submission to the Tây Sơn opposed on Confucian grounds, 265
  suppression of Ang Mei Bhen's invasion, 130–131, 133, 137, 166
  translocal society fostered by, 97, 120–121, 203, 278–279
  two forms of domestic administration, 163–164
  Viet civil official described as Tianci's "principal Mandarin," **179–180**
  Viet in military positions in The Port, *179*
Mo Tianci – "Idle Fishing at Sea Perch Creek" (Luxi xiandiao)
  contents and style of, 100
  Daoist theme of seclusion and withdrawal expressed in, 93, 100
  Trịnh Hoài Đức's copying of, 279
  verses painted on the walls of the Mo clan shrine, *101*
Mo Tianci – Pavilion for Summoning Worthies (C: Zhaoying ge V: Chiêu Anh Các). *See also* "Ten Scenic Views of Hà Tiên"

Index   343

Dragon Gate members of, 95
elite Chinese immigrants invited to be
  members, 178
establishment of, 14
four seasons of The Port poetry
  anthology, 119–120, 187–188
growth of its membership after the
  publication of "Ten Verses," 118
influence on southern Vietnamese
  literature, 11
literary compilations that appeared
  throughout Tianci's lengthy career,
  119
strengthened Sinosphere revealed by
  exchanges between members of, 95,
  97, 116–117, 121
Tianci's quest to forge a Confucian
  commonwealth aligned with, 94, 103
Mo Tianci – as viceroy (*oupareach*)
  appointment as, 3, 190–191
  four frontier circuits established next to
    Cochinchina, 192–193, 203
  loss of his status as, 247, 253
  ten percent duty placed on all vessels
    from Cochinchina, 211
Mo Wu (envoy of Mo Tianci)
  testimony to Li Shiyao, 122, 145
Moat Chrouk (V: Châu Đốc)
  as a base for Oknha Reachea Setthi Chov,
    142, 186, 189, 196, 244, 254
  as a Cochinchinese circuit, 150
  defensive fortifications built in, 107
  location of, xvii, 30
  river port of Moat Chrouk, 30, 34,
    150
  Vietnamese adaptation of Châu Đốc, 21
  Vietnamese control of, 274
Mộng Tuyết, 11
"Musical Ballads." See *Hà Tiên thập cảnh
  khúc vịnh* (Musical Ballads of the Ten
  Scenes of Hà Tiên)
Myanmar
  invasion of northern Siam (1774 and
    1775), 268, 271
  invasion of Siam/Ayutthaya (1760s), 4,
    17, 191, 225, 228, 231–232, 238, 246
  Konbaung Dynasty under Hsinbyushin,
    225
  puppet-governor established by
    Hsinbyushin at Thonburi, 231, 239
  Qing campaign against, 230, 242–244,
    246

nativism
  emergence of, 246–247, 272, 280–281

Khmer-based nationalism cultivated by
  Lon Nol, 8
rudimentary nationalism exploited by the
  Tây Sơn movement in Vietnam, 281
Sinophilia compared with, 97
as a threat to the translocal networks in
  The Port, 238, 274, 280
Ngô Thế Lân, 120, 223, 279
Nguyễn Cư Trinh (1716–1767)
  background of, 138
  as controller of camps at Saigon, 137
  criticism of Trương Phúc Loan's policies,
    229
  death of, 229
  memorial to the Martial King advocating
    for Tianci, 142
  military assistance for Tianci approved
    by, 147
  The Port delineated as Cochinchinese
    space and Tianci positioned as a
    temporary caretaker, 138–140
Nguyễn Cư Trinh – contribution to the
  "Ten Verses 2.0" anthology
  response to "Clear Waves on South Bay,"
    139
  response to "Dawn Bell at the Temple of
    Seclusion," **139**
  response to "An Egret Descends from
    Pearl Cliff," **139**
  response to "Verdant Folds of Screen
    Mountain," **139**
  submission to Tianci's transcultural
    mediation signaled by, 140–141
Nguyễn Cửu Vân, 61–62
Nguyễn Dynasty
  founding by Nguyễn Ánh, 24, 273
  old administrative units inherited by,
    174
Nguyễn Dynasty Historiographical Institute
  official biography of Tống Văn Khôi, 229
Nguyễn Dynasty sources
  Chen Shangchuan mentioned in, 53
  establishment of The Port narrated in,
    26–27
  Mo Jiu's escape to Huế not mentioned in,
    62
Nguyễn Hiền Đức, 72
Nguyễn Huệ Chi
  on the "Musical Ballads," **201**
Nguyễn Ngọc Thơ and Nguyễn Thanh
  Phong
  on Tianci's promotion of Confucian
    values, 11, 16, 103, 278
Nguyễn Nhã, 7
Nguyễn rulers of Cochinchina

Nguyễn rulers of Cochinchina (cont.)
  disintegration of the court of, 263
  Cochinchinese troops stationed in The Port by, 68
  Fujianese armed traders relied on by, 40
  "Great Peace" (*Thái Bình*) on coins cast when a new successor assumed the throne, 222
  the Mo clan's mediation relied on, 11
  Mo Jiu's submission to, 2, 10
  noble titles granted to Mo Jiu's subordinate commander, 68
  pro-Qing and pro-ethnic Chinese stance of their outlook and policies, 9, 126
Nguyễn rulers of Cochinchina – Nguyễn Phúc Tần (Lord Hiền, 1620–1687, r. 1648–1687)
  Ponhea Chan captured by his troops, 39
  refuge sought by Yang Yandi and Huang Jin, 26–27
Nguyễn rulers of Cochinchina – Nguyễn Phúc Thái (Lord Nghĩa, 1620–1687, r. 1687–1691)
  Ang Nan supported by, 52–53
Nguyễn rulers of Cochinchina – Nguyễn Phúc Chu (Lord Minh, 1675–1725, r. 1691–1725)
  death of, 77
  Hà Tiên given the status of garrison (*trấn*), 62
  Jiu recognized as a vassal of the independent Hà Tiên Kingdom, 60–62
  the royal Nguyễn bestowed on Jiu's wife, Bùi Thị Lẫm, 68
  Yuanshao appointed as the Buddhist advisor to the court, 71
Nguyễn rulers of Cochinchina – Nguyễn Phúc Thụ (Lord Ninh, 1697–1738, r. 1697–1738)
  consolidation of his power in Saigon, 77
  posthumous honor bequeathed on Mo Jiu, 91
Nguyễn rulers of Cochinchina – Nguyễn Phúc Khoát (1714–1765, r. 1738–1765)
  death of, 229
  as the Martial King (Võ Vương), 131
  persecution of Christians, 183, **183**, 185
  political and social reforms initiated by, 131–132
  Tianci appeased by, 131
  Tianci offered preferential trade policies by, 131
  Tianci's negotiations with, 132–133, 135, 141–142
  violence in Oudong instigated by, 150–151
Nguyễn rulers of Cochinchina – Nguyễn Phúc Thuần (1754–1777, r. 1765–1777)
  ascension as the Stable King (Định Vương), 229
  death of, 264–265
  flight to Saigon, 259
  as king-father (*Thái thượng vương*), 262
  Tianci's abandonment of, 264
Nguyễn rulers of Cochinchina – Nguyễn Phúc Dương (d. 1777)
  ascension as the Reformation King (Tân chính vương), 262
  death of, 264
  as a hostage of Tây Sơn Nhạc, 261
  Li Cai as his patron, 262–263
  Tianci's refusal to assist the forces of, 263
Nguyễn rulers of Cochinchina – Nguyễn Ánh (1762–1820, r. 1801–1820)
  founding of the Nguyễn Dynasty, 24, 273
  Gia Long as his reign name, 273
  Tây Sơn rebels defeated by, 290
non-state space of The Port
  as a cradle of modern Thailand and Vietnam, 290
  Mo Tianci's equidistant diplomacy aligned with, 122, 125, 159, 161–162, 173, 235
  and Mo clan administration of The Port, 3, 13, 277–278
  "soaring dragon" (*longfei*) used by Tianci, *158–159*, 173
  VOC compared with, 13, 277–278
North, Douglass, 235

Oeij Tshing and Lauw Wo
  Cham or Malay members of Lauw Wo's crew, 196
  female crew members on Oeij Tshing's vessel, 197
  Lauw Wo's trade between The Port and Batavia, 173, 233–234
  Oeij's Tshing's trade between Black Water and The Port, 210
  summary of the legal case, 154–155
  translocal justice system showcased in the case of, 154–155, 253
oknha (highest noble rank of the Cambodian court). *See also* Pok, Athivongsa
  Guangdong shahbandar given the rank of *oknha* by King Ang Chee, 46

Index 345

of the head of the Ministry of Foreign Affairs (Kralahom), 35
Oknha Siv equated with Mo Jiu, 46, 48
supervision by the viceroy (*oupareach*), 36, 191
as a title of governors of super-provinces, 34
Orang Laut, 29
piracy and slave trading by, 155–156
Oudong. *See* Cambodian court in Oudong
Outey (1708–1753)
as Ang Tan's biological father, 136
death of, 146
as viceroy, 136

Palembang
Muslim community in, 185
rice shipments from Cambodia and Siam, 207, 213
ships smuggling tin from Bangka to Guangzhou, 216–217
tin exported from, 221, 260
tin mines on the island of Bangka, 212, 216
VOC's tacit sanctioning of trade by, 212–214
Parra, Governor-General Petrus Albertus van der (1714–1775)
adjudication of the Oeij Tshing and Lauw Wo case, 253
Pearl Cliff (C: Jishan K: Phnom Mlou V: Hòn Chông). *See also* "Ten Scenic Views of Hà Tiên" – 6. "An Egret Descends from Pearl Cliff"
location in present-day Kiên Lương, *xviii*, 177
Perdue, Peter, 123
Phạm Nguyễn Du
on Ang Tham's attack on Mo Jiu, 62
on the sparsely populated hinterland of the water world, 58
Phan Huy Lê, 7
Phnom Penh
Cochinchinese migrants settled in villages close to, 38–39, 58
Iberian colony located near, 32
Jiu's journey to Phnom Penh at the age of sixteen, 47–48
Khmer Empire reestablished in the vicinity of, 30–31
location of, *xvi*
shahbandars residing in, 35
VOC factory in, 32
Phraya San (d. 1782)
conversation with his brother Khun Kaew, 237, 272

rebellion in Ayutthaya led by, 272
Phú Quốc (C: Fuguo K: Koh Tral)
fishing in, 30, 206
location of, *xvii*, 30
Tianci's vision for Phú Quốc as a Christian haven, 30
Viet settler population in, 58, 266
Piguel, Guillaume (1722–1771)
on Ang Sngoun's flight to The Port, 136
on Ang Sngoun's massacring of the Viet, 134–135
on Ang Tan's routing of his adversaries, 151
on hostilities between the Cambodians and Cochinchinese during the reign of Ang Sngoun, 136
Pilar, Julián de Nuestra Señora del (1733–1779)
on Ang Tan's support of attacks on hinterland Viet settlements, 250
death of, 264
flight to Cần Thơ, 257
flight from Cần Thơ to Macao, 264
Franciscan mission in Cần Thơ led by, 260
on Mo Huang, 165
Mo Jinding described by, **184**
on Mo Tianci's miraculous recovery from an illness, 184
on Phú Quốc, 195
The Port described as a Livorno of the East by, 204–205
Viet civil official described as Tianci's "principal Mandarin," **179**
pirates and piracy. *See also* Big-bellied Đức (Đức Bụng); Huo Ran; Oeij Tshing and Lauw Wo; Orang Laut
diverse character of groups of, 87
Jiu's efforts to fight piracy and ensure maritime security, 59
Leizhou Peninsula as a base for pirates, 42
maritime infrastructure provided for more elaborate forms of networks and organizations, 40
pirate allies of the Tây Sơn based in Quy Nhơn, 133, 261
political instability in the China Seas related to, 87–88
Qing efforts to fight it, 215
trade disrupted by, 186
the VOC's role in combating it, 161
Po Chung Yam, Ronald, 4, 284–285
Poivre, Pierre (1719–1786)
on Cochinchinese troops stationed in The Port by Nguyễn lords, 68

346   Index

Poivre, Pierre (1719–1786) (cont.)
　on Jiu's trading at Batavia and Manila, 48
　on maritime trade in The Port, 88–89
　on references to Tianci as a king, 156, 159
Pok, Athivongsa
　alliance with the Tây Sơn, 266
　as Ang Chan's regent, 273
　as Neareay Reachea's adoptive father, 268
　nobleman Mou in his service, 266, 269
Pomeranz, Kenneth, 18, 280
The Port as financial center, 205, See also coins and bullion
　capital accumulation from the concentration of merchants, 286
　contribution of Portuguese mestizos to the Mo's financial and monetary expertise, 92, 277
　outflow of specie from Siam, 235
　payments for financial settlements handled in, 224–225
The Port as a natural resource exporter, 1, 16, 88, 203, 205, 210, 225, 276
　bamboo available in, 205–206
　ivory exported from, 88, 206
　rattan as a local product, 206
　rice exports, 207–208, 233–235
The Port as a term. See also Hà Tiên – as a name for Port
　Bamboo City as a nickname for, 2, 204, 206
　Banteay Meas used in some Cambodian sources for, 1–2, 33–34
　Chinese names for, 1
　in European sources, 1–2
　as Gangkou or Gangkou guo, 2, 156
　Kuala (river mouth) as the Malay name for, 2, 152
　Muang Kham ("city of gold") as its Lao name, 2
　Palmeiro or Palmerinha as its Portuguese name, 2
　as Ponteamas or Ponthiamas to Europeans, 1–2
The Port as a transshipment point
　Lin Houqua's role, 153
　location at the intersection of the sea lanes, 1, 16
　offshore Chinese economy serviced by, 4, 18, 205, 219, 235
　and the political and economic climate in maritime East Asia, 126, 205, 216, 225
　role of the Qing maritime ban, 89

Tianci's overseas commercial linkages, 186, 203, 205, 259–260
VOC brutality as a factor, 214
Portugal and the Portuguese
　Coal or Coalha as their term for The Port, 2
　contribution to the Mo's financial and monetary expertise, 92, 277
　control of Melaka, 32, 90
　decline of its maritime trade, 287
　Hà Tiên derived from the Portuguese corruption of the Khmer word for Seashore Province, 61, 79
　minting and circulation of coins by Portuguese creoles, 90
　outpost in Macao, 32, 65, 90
　Palmeiro or Palmerinha as their name for The Port, 2
　retreat to Cambodia following pressure by the VOC, 33
　Southeast Asian trade in ports along the Gulf of Siam, 87
Preah Sotoat ("Lord of Wealth")
　as the Cambodian title of Mo Tianci, 22, 143–145, 165, 189
　sixteenth century individual described in the Cambodian Royal Chronicles, 145, 189

Qing Dynasty (1644–1912). See also Li Shiyao (d. 1788)
　agrarian-centered economy of, 19, 84
　annexation of Taiwan, 50–51, 64
　Chinese naval power in maritime East Asia revived by, 4, 29, 51
　distrust of overseas Chinese immigrants and their descendants, 285
　European traders managed by Hong merchants, 215, 285
　Lê Dynasty viewed as the sole rulers of Vietnam by, 9, 126
　maritime ban established in 1660, 41–42
　maritime ban renewed in 1717, 88–89, 92, 212, 285
　maritime ban repealed in 1684, 83, 92, 276
　the Mo clan's flexible exploitation of Sinosphere and mandala frameworks in their dealings with, 277
　offensive against Myanmar, 230, 242–244, 246
　official encyclopedia of institutions and statecraft. See *Qingchao wenxian tongkao*

Index

political and economic primacy in maritime East Asia of, 96
pragmatism in dealing with the Mo, 19, 275
preservation and perpetuation of a satisfactory status quo as its orientation, 284–285
Rebellion of the Three Feudatories (1674), 44
reformation of the China-centered tributary system to the realities of trade, 4
restricted access for foreign merchants to its shores, 215
Qing Dynasty court – Kangxi Emperor (1654–1722, r. 1761–1722)
  sea ban renewed in 1717, 88, 92, 212, 285
  tightened supervision over the maritime zone, 84
Qing Dynasty court – Yongzheng Emperor (1678–1735, r. 1722–1735)
  death of, 113
  literati relations with the government during his reign, **113**
  maritime ban on trade with Southeast Asia lifted by, **212**
Qing Dynasty court – Qianlong (1711–1799, r. 1736–1799)
  incentive program for grain imports, 207
  literary expression of anti-Qing sentiments punished by, 113
  Taksin not recognized as king until 1777, 285
  Taksin reproached by, 240–241
  Tianci praised by, 241
  Tianci's failed attempt to solicit his help in defeating Taksin, 19, 252, 275, 286–287
  Tianci's letters to the VOC dated as *gengyin* (Kei-ien), Qianlong (Khi-en Lijong), 153
  Tianci's map of the maritime route from Guangdong to Siam presented to, 158, *159*
  Tianci's memorials to, *157*, 157–158, 242
Qingchao wenxian tongkao
  entry on The Port in, 145, 156, 169–171
  as the Qing Dynasty's official encyclopedia of institutions and statecraft, 145
Quy Nhơn
  Lê Dynasty occupation of territory of Cham kingdoms north of Huế, 37

location in south-central Vietnam, *xvi*
Tây Sơn brothers' base in, 259
Ten Stupas Amitabha Temple established by Yuanshao, 71, 200
"wandering people" (*lưu dân*) from, 38–39
the word for sea perch (*vược*) in the central dialect of, 179
Ream
  Jiu's base in, 57–60, 63
  location of, *xvii*
Ream Reachea (1739–1779). *See* Cambodian court in Oudong – Ream Reachea (1739–1779*
Reformation King (Tân chính vương). *See* Nguyễn rulers of Cochinchina – Nguyễn Phúc Dương (d. 1777)
Rosenthal, Jean-Laurent, 19
Rowe, William T., 113
Royal Market (K: Phsar Reachea V: Rạch Giá)
  location of, *xvii*, 30, 192
Rungswadisab, Puangthong, 247

Sacred Pond (K: Preah Trapeang V: Trà Vinh)
  customs from trade in the South China Sea collected in, 34, 56
  honor ranking of nine, 34
  location of, *xvii*, 33
  as a refuge for Ang Tan's relatives, 149
  as a site of contestation among The Port, Cochinchina, Siam, and Cambodia, *148*, 149, 274
Sakurai Yumio
  on Cochinchinese rights over trade and navigation on the main Mekong branch, 150
  on rivalry between Tianci and Taksin, 247, 287
Sakurai Yumio and Kitagawa Takako
  on Chen Tai's conspiracy against Tianci, **248**, 252
  on narratives about Ponteamas (Banteay Meas), 33
  on Tianci's move to Cần Thơ, **260**
  two faces of the port described by, 163–164
Salazar, Pedro (1729–1763)
  arrival in Cochinchina, 184
  imprisonment of, 198
  narrative of his having saved Tianci's life, 184
Salmon, Claudine, 159

Screen Mountain (C: Pingshan V: Bình
San). *See also* "Ten Scenic Views of Hà
Tiên" – 2. "Verdant Folds of Screen
Mountain"
assertions to its Vietnamese identity in
the "Ten Verses," **115–116**
Chen Zilan on, 116–117
compared to Mo Tianci, 127
Hibiscus Temple constructed on,
198–199, *199*, **199**
Lin Weize's poem on, 114
location of, *xviii*, 82
Mo Bang's tomb on, 174–175, *175*, 178
Mo clan tombs located on, 82
Mo Jiu's personal residence on, 82
Mo Jiu's tomb on, 158, *160*
pro-Qing expressions on tombstones on,
178
tombs of core female relatives of the
Mo ruling family, 171–173
tombs of Nguyễn Đình Tú and Nguyễn
Hữu on, 198
Viet women in Mo households indicated
by tombs on, 179
Sea Perch Creek (C: Luxi V: Rạch Vược).
See also Mingbo Sea Perch Creek
Settlement (C: Mingbo Luxi suo V:
Minh Bột Lư Khê Sở); Mo Tianci –
"Idle Fishing at Sea Perch Creek"
(*Luxi xiandiao*); "Ten Scenic Views of
Hà Tiên" – 10. "Anchored Fishing
Boat at Sea Perch Creek"
as the ancestral home of Trương Minh
Đạt, 179
derivation of its vernacular name, 179
location of, *xviii*, 99–100
Ngô Thế Lân's visit to, 120, 223
as Tianci's favorite fishing haunt,
99–100, 165, 176, 179
Seashore Province (K: Peam)
Cambodian court management of, 33
establishment as a province separate from
Banteay Meas, 34, 59, *60*
honor ranking of nine, 34
location of, *xvii*, 33
Moat Chrouk as the seat of, 142
Oknha Reachea Setthi as the governor of,
142, 186, 189, 196, 244
as one of five provinces given to Tianci by
Ang Tan, 190
as originally part of Banteay Meas, 33–34
Seashore Fortress (C: Fangcheng K: Srok
Peam V: Phương Thành) in, *81*, 81
Tianci's military headquarters based in,
145

Sellers, Nicholas
on Hà Tiên under Mo Tianci's
descendants, **275**
on Jiu's construction of two open-air
reservoirs, 83
on Jiu's stay in Ream, **58**
on Jiu's submission to Cochinchina, 10,
67
on Nguyễn Cư Trinh, 138
shahbandar (port master)
as governors of foreign communities in
Cambodia, 35, 40
Oknha Siv (Guangdong shahbandar)
equated with Mo Jiu, 46, 48
Taiwan shahbandar, 46
She Xichun
background of, 75–76
contribution to Tianci's poetry anthology
on the four seasons of The Port,
120
dedication of a poem to Chen
Shangchuan, 76
postscript to the "Ten Verses" anthology,
111
"Ten Scenic Views" conceived as an idea
with Chen Zhikai, 104
Shi Lang (1621–1696), 51–52, 84, 215
Siam. *See also* Ayutthaya Kingdom
(1351–1767)
Chakri Dynasty established in, 272
Myanmar's invasion of northern Siam
(1774 and 1775), 268, 271
Tianci's failed invasion of, 4, 19, 239,
247, 286
Siam – C: Wanfosui T: Bang Pla Soi
Mo Jiu's refuge in Siam identified with, 57
Taksin's base in, 226, 238–239
Vạn Tuế Sơn identified with, 57
Siam – Chanthaburi (C: Jianzhuwen K:
Chan Borei)
immigrants from Chaozhou in, 226
location of, *xvi*
occupation by The Port under Chen
Dali, 244–245
Pulan as the governor of, 231, 239,
256–257
Siam – Thonburi
bronze bell from the Temple of Three
Treasures, *74*, 75, 81
location of, *xvi*
puppet-governor established by
Hsinbyushin at, 231, 239
Tianci and other Sino-Viet exiles settled
by Taksin in, 266–267
Siam – Trat

Index 349

Chen Dali's base in, 232
Chen Tai's flight to, 252
immigrants from China in, 226, *233*
location of, *xvi*
Wat Buppharam in, *233*
Singapore
as a free port, 1, 287–288
Sinosphere
defined, 15
mandala model conventions contrasted with, 14–15, 123–124
Sinophilia of Qing elites, 96
strengthened Sinosphere revealed by exchanges between members of Tianci's literary society, 95, 97, 116–117, 121
slaves and trafficking of humans
causing manpower shortages in Siam, 232
piracy and slave trading by the Orang Laut, 155–156
slaves purchased in Bali, 223
Southeast Asian slave laborers, 18, 207, 214
Sơn Nam, 7
Southern Advance (*Nam tiến*)
as a historical inevitability according to historians in Cold War southern Vietnam, 7
and the Mo's contribution to Vietnam's present-day boundaries, 6–8, 12
Nguyễn Cư Trinh's celebration of, 138
The Port's contribution to the character of southern Vietnam as a distinct space, 280
questioning of its linear progression, 8–9, 258
redefinition under early twentieth-century nationalism, 6–7
validation by Cambodian historiography, 8
viewed as multiethnic project by recent scholars, 7–8
views in the communist north towards, 7
Spain
bullion from the New World traded by, 32, 86–87, 224
funding of the Franciscans in Cần Thơ, 260
Iberian colony near Phnom Penh, 32
Iberians expelled from Japan, 41
spheres of influence in the Indonesian archipelago, 217
Srey Sauryopor (d. 1757)

defeat of, 147
rivalry with Ang Tan, 149
as viceroy, 146
Stable King (Định Vương). *See* Nguyễn rulers of Cochinchina – Nguyễn Phúc Thuần
Steadfast River Circuit (Kramoun Sar)
Cambodian court management of, 33
customs stations restored by Ang Sor at, 56
division between Cochinchina and the suzerainty of Siam running through it, 258
location of, *xvii*, 33, 192
renamed as Steadfast River (C: Jianjiang V: Kiên Giang) Circuit by Mo Tianci, 192
villages and communes for the Viet established by Mo Jiu in, 58
Stone Grotto (C: Shidong V: Thạch Động). *See also* "Ten Scenic Views of Hà Tiên" – 5. "Stone Grotto Swallows Clouds"
location of, *xviii*, 99
Temple of Seclusion located east of, 107
Strait of Melaka. *See* Malay Peninsula – Melaka and the Strait of Melaka
Sun Tianrui of Xiamen
native-place affiliation of, 112
response to "Night Drum of River Wall," **160**
Sun Tianzhen (V: Tôn Thiên Trân)
background of, 111–112, **112**
Screen Mountain described in the "Ten Verses" collection, 116
super-provinces. *See also* Treang
attributes of, 34
Tianci's alliances with governors of, 146, 190
Suzhou Mountain
base of the Java Company located on, 186
location of, *xviii*, 108, 170, 174

Taksin (1734–1782, r. 1767–1782)
access to firearms, 253, 282
alleged conspiracy to topple him and replace him with Tôn Thất Xuân, 268–271, 275
base in Bang Pla Soi, 226, 238–239
biographical information, 226, *227*
brutality and religious fanaticism of, 267–268
claims of accumulated merit and supernatural powers, 245, 268

350   Index

Taksin (1734–1782, r. 1767–1782) (cont.)
  as king of Siam, 5, 240, 290
  massacre of Tianci's family ordered by, 5
  Myanmar forces repulsed by, 228
  nativism and ethnic exclusivity facilitated by his emergence, 246–247
  occupation of The Port (1771), 5, 253–254, 282
  overthrowing of and execution of, 5, 272
  rebellion led by Phraya San, 272
  rebuke by the Qianlong Emperor, 240–241
  repatriation of Chao Chui and Chao Si Sang demanded by, 239
  Tianci's failed attempt to solicit help from the Qing in defeating him, 19, 252, 275, 286–287
Tambiah, S. J., 124
Tan Xiang – "Sending Off Chen Zhikai to Annam"
  City of Bamboo used as a nickname for The Port, 204
  nanjin 南金 used to express "southern talent" or "southern gold," **222**
  a silver market in The Port described in, 204, 223–224
  text, 204
Tang Yuchong
  response to "Anchored Fishing Boat at Sea Perch Creek," 118
  response to "Clear Waves on South Bay," **114–115**
  response to "Golden Islet Blocking Waves," **117**, 128
Tây Sơn brothers
  alliance with Athivongsa Pok, 266
  internal rivalries between Tây Sơn siblings, 273
Tây Sơn brothers – Nguyễn Huệ (1753–1792, r. 1788–1792)
  Cần Thơ attacked forcing Tianci to evacuate, 264
  death of, 273
  Saigon captured by, 263
  Tianci's rejection of his ultimatum to surrender, 265
Tây Sơn brothers – Nguyễn Lữ (d. 1787), 259, 273
Tây Sơn brothers – Nguyễn Nhạc (1743–1793, r. 1778–1788)
  death of, 273
  Nguyễn Phúc Dương held hostage by, 261

  two Cochinchinese princes in Quảng Nam defeated by, 259
Taylor, Keith Weller
  interpretation of Mo Tianci's ambitions based on his poetry, 12
  on Vietnamese terminology referring to the country's northern and southern halves, 25
Taylor, Philip, 185
  on Cham Muslims, 185
  on Chinese-Khmer mestizos, 193
  on royal oversight of The Port during the Angkor period, 30–31
Tây Sơn rebellion
  Hanoi captured by, 272–273
  the Khmer as the victims of, 187, 265
  Li Cai's defection from, 261, 281
  massacre of Saigon's Chinese population, 281
  nativist sentiments associated with, 281
  Nguyễn Ánh's defeat of, 290
  outbreak of, 259
  support of Chinese merchants based at Hội An, 259
Temple of Three Treasures (C: Sanbao V: Tam Bảo)
  bronze bell from, 74, **74**
  Jiu's establishment of, 68, 72
  spirit tablet of Mo Jiu's mother housed at, 68, **69**
  Yellow Dragon as head of, 72, **73**, 197
"Ten Scenic Views of Hà Tiên" (C: *Hexian shijing* V: *Hà Tiên thập cảnh*)
  Chen Zhikai's promotion of, 110
  conceived as an idea by She Xichun and Chen Zhikai, 104
  general summary of, 163
  overview of contributions by Tianci and 31 other poets in 1737, 94
  publication as "Ten Verses". *See* "Ten Verses of Hà Tiên" (C: *Hexian shiyong* V: *Hà Tiên thập vịnh*)
  sun and moon characters used in poems in, 109–110, 112
  travel guide, landscape painting, and poetry combined in, 104–105, 108
  Trịnh Hoài Đức's "Thirty Scenic Views of Gia Định" as an imitation of, 279
"Ten Scenic Views of Hà Tiên" – 1. "Golden Islet Blocking Waves"
  aesthetic qualities and practical value of the Big Golden Islet extolled in, 106
  Chen Ruifeng's response to, 112
  Ming loyalist ideals pitched in, 109–110, 112

Index 351

tribute-bearing ships mentioned in three responses to, 117
Wang Chang's response to, 113
Zhu Pu's response to, 111
"Ten Scenic Views of Hà Tiên" – 2. "Verdant Folds of Screen Mountain"
aesthetic qualities and practical value of Screen Mountain extolled in, 106, 108
Nguyễn Cư Trinh's response to, 139
Wang Chang's response to, 113–114
"Ten Scenic Views of Hà Tiên" – 3. "Dawn Bell at the Temple of Seclusion"
focus on human activity in, 106–107
Nguyễn Cư Trinh's response to, 139
"Ten Scenic Views of Hà Tiên" – 4. "Night Drum of River Wall"
defensive fortifications near the headwaters of Fortress River evoked in, 108
Sun Tianrui's response to, 160
Tianci's ambivalent language of vassalage to a faraway court, 126–127
"Ten Scenic Views of Hà Tiên" – 5. "Stone Grotto Swallows Clouds"
Linglong Mountains outside of Hangzhou associated with, 105
"Ten Scenic Views of Hà Tiên" – 6. "An Egret Descends from Pearl Cliff"
natural beauty celebrated in, 105
Nguyễn Cư Trinh's response to, 139
"Ten Scenic Views of Hà Tiên" – 7. "Moon's Reflection on East Lake"
"Moon's Reflection on the Three Pools" in Hangzhou juxtaposed with, 105
"Ten Scenic Views of Hà Tiên" – 8. "Clear Waves on South Bay"
Mạc Triều Đán's response to, 118
Ming loyalists criticized in Tang Yuchong's response to, 114–115
Nguyễn Cư Trinh's response to, 139–140
Trần Trinh's expression of admiration for the centrality of China, 116
Wang Chang's response to, 114
"Ten Scenic Views of Hà Tiên" – 9. "Rustic Dwellings at Deer Cape"
rustic settings of Deer Cape celebrated in, 187
Trần Trinh's response to, 116
"Ten Scenic Views of Hà Tiên" – 10. "Anchored Fishing Boat at Sea Perch Creek"
Lin Weize's response to, 117
Tang Yuchong's response to, 118

"Ten Verses 2.0" anthology. *See also* Nguyễn Cư Trinh – contribution to the "Ten Verses 2.0" anthology
Mo Huang's oversight of, 140
second round of calls for responses to the original "Ten Scenic Views," **138**
"Ten Verses of Hà Tiên" (C: *Hexian shiyong* V: *Hà Tiên thập vịnh*)
additional contributors after its publication, 118
advertising The Port to a Sinosphere elite audience as its purpose, 121, 201
as the most well-known and best-preserved output of Mo Tianci's literary society, 94
native place affiliations of contributors to, 102, 111
the penetration of Chinese cultural elements in the Sinosphere attested by, 95, 279
pro-Qing contributors to, 96, 121
publication in 1737, 111
ten scenic views described. *See* "Ten Scenic Views of Hà Tiên" (C: *Hexian shijing* V: *Hà Tiên thập cảnh*)
Tianci's preface to, 158
Vietnamese identity of The Port asserted in, 115–116
Thailand. *See also* Ayutthaya Kingdom (1351–1767); Siam
the non-state space of The Port as the cradle of modern Thailand, 290
Thongduang (1737–1809)
ascension as Rama I (r. 1782–1809), 272
overthrowing and execution of Taksin, 272
Tiantou Village, Wuchuan County, Guangdong
Chen clan shrine at, 75, 76
as Chen Shangchuan's native village, 54, 111
Tokugawa. *See* Japan – Tokugawa period
Tôn Thất Xuân (d. 1780)
alleged conspiracy to topple Taksin and replace him, 269–271, 275
escape to Saigon, 259
refuge in Siam, 266–267
Taksin's torturing and murder of, 270
Tống Văn Khôi (1733–1775)
as controller of the five camps in Saigon, 229, 253, 255
depicted as corrupt in Vũ Thế Dinh's biography of the Mo clan, 229
official biography compiled by the Nguyễn Dynasty Historiographical Institute, 229

Tonkin
  agrarian-centered economy of the Chinese state as a model for, 9, 71
  as a center of bureaucracy and Confucian education, 9, 112
  on a map presented to the Qianlong Emperor by Mo Tianci, 158, *159*
  occupation of Huế (1774), 259, 274
  as a term, 24
  VOC blockade of Tonkinese ports from 1663 to 1664, 43
  VOC factory in, **17**
Trần Trinh, 116
translocalism
  of the cosmopolitan and multipolar environment of Cochinchina, 9–11
  cultural homogenization and nativist sentiments in Southeast Asia as a threat to, 237, *274*
  definition of, 13
  the Mo's administration of The Port as a non-state territorial space aligned with, 3, 13–14, 204–205, 277, 290
  nativism as a threat to, 238, 274, 280
  The Port's function as a crossroads, 14, 16, 20, 29, 59, 87, 125, 142, 277
  Tianci's fostering of translocal society, 97, 118, 120–121, 138, 203, 278–279
  Tianci's quest to forge a Confucian commonwealth aligned with, 94, 97, 103, 121
  Tianci's translocal cultural mediation reflected in contributions to the "Ten Verses 2.0" anthology, 140–141
  translocal justice system showcased in the case of Oeij Tshing and Lauw Wo, 154–155, 253
Treang
  dual mode of administration, 191
  location of, *xvii*, 210–211
  as one of five provinces given to Tianci by Ang Tan, 190
  as a super-province, 34, 190
Trịnh Hoài Đức (C: Zheng Huaide) (1765–1825)
  Bình Dương Poetry Club (*thi xã*) founded by, 279
  poetry by, 279
  status as a Minh Hương who served as a Nguyễn Dynasty official, 27
  "Thirty Scenic Views of Gia Định," **150**, 279
  on Tianci's management of The Port, 163
  Tianci's poetry admired by, 279

Trịnh Hoài Đức (C: Zheng Huaide) (1765–1825) – gazetteer
  on additional contributors to "Ten Verses" after its publication, 118
  on Captain Sa, 142–143
  Chen Shangchuan mentioned in, 53
  on the countryside between Steadfast River and Dragon Stream, 195
  on diversity in The Port, 196
  on five provinces given to Tianci by Ang Tan, 190
  on how the Chinese came to the water world, 27
  on the route from Bassac to the Gulf of Siam, 192
  on Sacred Pond as part of Cambodia, 149
  on the Temple of Seclusion, 107
  on Viet contributors to "Ten Verses," **112**
Trịnh Liên Sơn
  background of, 112
  on the Golden Islets in the "Ten Verses," **127–128**
Trịnh lords. *See also* Tonkin
Trocki, Carl A., 3–4, 152
Trương Minh Đạt
  on Chen Dali's genealogy, 78
  farming communities for Viet and Cham migrants identified in Phnom Yuon, 58
  on Hibiscus Temple, **199**
  on Jiu's stay in Ream, **58**
  on Jiu's time in Siam, **57**
  key questions in Hà Tiên's historical past analyzed by, 11
  on the "Musical Ballads," 202
  Zhuang Huiyao's poem interpreted by, 188
Trương Phúc Loan (d. 1776)
  death of, 259
  fiscal policies of, 258, 261
  interventionist approach toward local society and frontier expansion, 229
  Nguyễn Phúc Thuần's displacement of the rightful heir orchestrated by, 229, 259
  Taksin played off against Tianci, 253, 256
  Tống Văn Khôi removed as controller, 255

Van Dyke, Paul, 205, 215–216, 282, *See also* Li Tana and Paul Van Dyke
viceroy (*oupareach*) of the Cambodian court. *See also* Mo Tianci – as viceroy (*oupareach*); Outey (1708–1753)

Index 353

in the Cambodian court hierarchy, 36, 190
Srey Sauryopor (d. 1757) as, 146
Vietnam (Việt Nam). *See also* Cochinchina; Donay (V: Đồng Nai); Nguyễn Dynasty; Nguyễn Lords of southern Vietnam; Quy Nhơn; Tonkin
  Annam (C: Annan V: An Nam) as a name for, 24
  Đại (Great) Việt as a name for, 24
  impact of The Port on southern Vietnam, 279–280
  incorporation of The Port, 5, 12, 274
  neo-Confucianism in, 14, 237, 281
  separation into north and south, 24–25
  unification in 1975, 7
  unification under the Nguyễn Dynasty, 5, 8, **174**, 273, 279
  use of Vietnam as a name, 24
Vietnam (Việt Nam) – Cochinchinese historical novel by Nguyễn Khoa Chiêm, *Việt Nam khai quốc chí truyện* (Chronicle of the founding of Vietnam)
  on asylum requested by Yang Yandi from the Nguyễn, 27, 45
  Chen Shangchuan not mentioned in, 53
  on the Khmer title of Reachea Setthi, 46
  on Yang Yandi's alliance with Ang Nan, 50
Vũ Thế Dinh – genealogical biography of the Mo clan
  on bribes sent to Ang Sor's wife by Mo Jiu, 57
  on the Chen Tai revolt, **248**
  gratitude and remembrance for Tianci as his motivation for writing it, 200
  on King Ang Chee's support of Mo Jiu's trade in The Port, 46
  Tống Văn Khôi's depiction in, 229

Wang Chang
  background of, 111
  response to "Clear Waves on South Bay," **114**
  response to "Golden Islet Blocking Waves," **113**
  response to "Verdant Folds of Screen Mountain," **113–114**
Wang Houlai
  background of, 119
  poem on wintertime for the four seasons of The Port anthology, 119
  Rinan used as figurative term for The Port by, 128
Wang Yuanfei
  on imagined empire, 23, 96

water world or water frontier
  the agrarian-centered interior as a challenge to, 19, 37, 276
  Cambodian court management of, 33, 145
  location of, *xvii*
  Mekong Delta and Gulf of Siam littoral labeled as, 7
  the non-state space of The Port as the cradle of modern Thailand and Vietnam, 290
  trade and access to the South China Sea, 33
  viewed as an empty space in Vietnamese historical studies, 28, 150
water world or water frontier – hinterlands of
  attacks on hinterland Viet settlements in, 249–250
  Cochinchinese migrants in, 38
  Cochinchinese presence encouraged by Lord Hiền, 27
  Jiu's development of, 58
  natural resources exported from, 1, 16, 207–208, 276
  an offshore Chinese economy supplied and maintained by, 18
  Tianci's development of, 203
Wheeler, Charles J.
  on the arrival of Ming loyalists in the water world, 64
  on Chen Shangchuan, 53
  on Dragon Gate as "client military entrepreneurs," **43**
  on Hainan as a point where the maritime routes diverge, 40
  on the Minh Hương in Cochinchina, 10, 183
  on native places tie of Chinese creoles, 22
  on the Qing's annexation of Taiwan, 64
  on the role of religion in sustaining connections with Chinese settlements, 66
  on Zheng and their affiliates' trade with Cochinchina, 49
Wolters, Oliver W., 124
Wong Tze Ken, 87, 132
Wong, John D., 12, 70
Wong, Roy Bin, 18
Wu Zhihan
  response to "Golden Islet Blocking Waves," **117**

Xian Biao
  Cantonese community in Cambodia established by, 44
  fleet brought to Donay, 43–44

Xian Biao (cont.)
  flight from Cambodia, 44
  personal vendetta against the VOC, 44
  role in linking Yang Yandi and Huang Jin to Cambodia, 42, 50
Xie Zhang (d. 1758)
  epitaph on his tombstone, 178
  as a native of Fujian, 178
Xu Xiemin
  on Screen Mountain, 116
Xu Youyong
  Big-bellied Đức and his pirate band captured by, 133, 167
  as circuit governor, 193
  Jiu's commander Xu, Marquis of the Han Sun, as his father, 67–68, 167–168

Yang Yandi (Dương Ngạn Địch) (d. 1688)
  alliance with Ang Nan, 50–51
  assassination of, 52
  asylum requested from the Nguyễn, 26–27, 45, 64
  base at Mesar established with Huang Jin, 27, 50, 54
  conflict with Huang Jin, 52, 55
  in the Dragon Gate hierarchy, 43, 50, 54
  Dragon Gate unit commanded by, 26, 43
Yellow Dragon (C: Huang Long V: Hoàng Long) (d. 1737)
  connections to Ming loyalist networks in Cochinchina, 97
  as head of the Temple of Three Treasures, 72, 197
  message to his believers on a bronze bell, *74*, 74
  White Pagoda constructed in his memory, 197–198
Yincheng (V: Ấn Trừng) as his dharma name, 72, *73*
Yuanshao (V: Nguyên Thiều) (1648–1728)
  Diamond Temple established in Donay, 72
  Ten Stupas Amitabha Temple established by, 72, 200

Zhang Xianying, 178
Zhao Gang, 4, 285
Zheng organization
  anti-Qing resistance of, 29
  control of trade with Japan and Southeast Asia, 41
  demise of, 45, 51, 66
  disagreement amongst its partisans, 50
  Dragon Gate contingent in Taiwan controlled by, 43, 50
  family members as officials in Fujian and Guangdong, 41
  Shi Lang as a former partisan of, 51–52, 84
  Taiwan shahbandar charged with ships and personnel from, 46
  ties with smugglers and pirates in Guangdong, 42
  trading relations with Cochinchina, 49
  Xian Biao and Yang Yandi as part of, 43
Zheng Chenggong (1624–1622), 41–42
Zheng former commanders stripped of their privileges by Kangxi, 84
Zheng Lushe, 50
Zheng Yangwen, 4
Zhu Pu of Guangdong, 111
Zhu Xi (1130–1200), 14
Zhuang Huiyao, 187–188
Zottoli, Brian A., 6

For EU product safety concerns, contact us at Calle de José Abascal, 56–1°,
28003 Madrid, Spain or eugpsr@cambridge.org

www.ingramcontent.com/pod-product-compliance
Lightning Source LLC
LaVergne TN
LVHW011757060526
838200LV00053B/3620